Samuel Richardson's
Clarissa
An Index

Samuel Richardson's
Clarissa
AN INDEX

Analyzing Characters, Subjects,
and Place Names,
with Summaries of Letters Appended

BASED ON THE PENGUIN CLASSICS EDITION, 1985
"a complete text of the first edition"

by
Susan Price Karpuk

AMS PRESS, INC.
New York

Library of Congress Cataloging-in-Publication Data

Karpuk, Susan Price.
  Samuel Richardson's *Clarissa* : An index ; analyzing
characters, subjects, and place names, with summaries of
letters appended : based on the *Penguin Classics edition*,
1985, "a complete text of the first edition" / by Susan
Price Karpuk.
    (AMS Studies in the Eighteenth Century, –
  ISSN 0196-6561; no. 34)
    ISBN 0-404-63534-2 (alk. paper)
    1. Richardson, Samuel, 1689-1761. Clarissa Indexes. 2.
  Epistolary Fiction, English Indexes I. Title. II. Series.
PR3664.C43K37   2000
823' .6—dc21   99-33015
                                                            CIP

All AMS books are printed on acid-free paper that meets the guidelines
for performance and durability of the Committee on Production
Guidelines for Book Longevity of the Council on Library Resources.

AMS Press, Inc.
56 East 13th Street
New York, NY 10003-4686, USA

MANUFACTURED IN THE UNITED STATES OF AMERICA

Acknowledgments

I would like to thank several people who have been especially encouraging and helpful over the several years it took to complete this project. Kathie Coblentz, rare books cataloger, The New York Public Library, gave invaluable help with research. I thank Carolyn McGovern, free lance indexer, and Dr. Clayton M. Shotwell, Department of Fine Arts, Augusta State University, for their useful suggestions on format. Dr. Steven R. Price, Department of English, Louisiana State University, read the text and offered many excellent suggestions. A great deal of encouragement came from Dr. Loftus Jestin, Department of English, Central Connecticut State University. My deepest gratitude goes to my husband, Dr. Paul A. Karpuk, Department of Modern Languages, Central Connecticut State University, who saw the value of this index from the beginning and never failed to be supportive and encouraging.

Contents

Introduction ix

Alphabetical List of Characters, A Complete List, Locating an
    Index for Each 1

Indexes to Characters
    Belford, Mr. John, Lovelace's friend 9
    Harlowe, Mr. Antony, Clarissa's uncle 17
    Harlowe, Miss Arabella, Clarissa's elder sister 19
    Harlowe, Mrs. Charlotte, Clarissa's mamma 21
    Harlowe, Miss Clarissa 24
    Harlowe, Mr. James, Jun., Clarissa's brother 70
    Harlowe, Mr. James, Sen., Clarissa's papa 75
    Harlowe, Mr. John, Clarissa's uncle 77
    Harlowe Family 79
    Hervey, Mrs. Dorothy, Clarissa's aunt 87
    Hickman, Mr. Charles, Anna's suitor 89
    Howe, Miss Anna, Clarissa's friend 93
    Howe, Mrs. Annabella, Anna's mamma 103
    Lord M., Lovelace's uncle 106
    Lovelace, Mr. Robert 116
    Moore, Mrs., Clarissa's landlady at Hampstead 163
    Morden, Colonel William, Clarissa's cousin 164
    Norton, Mrs. Judith, Clarissa's nurse 168
    Sinclair, Mrs., brothelkeeper in London 171
    Smith, Mr. John, shopkeeper in London 177

Subject Index 179

Place Name Index 381

Summaries of Letters, With Letter Numbers for Correlated for
    the Penguin Classics printing of the first edition, 1985,
    S. Richardson's printing of the first edition, 1748, and
    S. Richardson's printing of the third edition, 1751 411

Introduction

Samuel Richardson's *Clarissa*, often called the first English novel, was first published in the course of a year, from December 1747 to December 1748. This epistolary novel, a collection of over 500 letters, appeared in seven volumes. The length of the work makes its great mass of information nearly inaccessible for most students. The access provided by this index is intended to facilitate study and research on *Clarissa* and on the rise of the novel in general.

Like any index, this one is a finding tool. Its most obvious use is to bring together scattered references to a topic. One may want to retrieve a particular reference to cloven foot in regard to Lovelace. The index will retrieve that reference and bring together all other references to cloven foot. It may be useful to compare Richardson's use of the phrase to its occurrences in other literature. Other information on Lovelace's character can be found under related headings, such as Beelzebub, devil, Moloch-deity, Satan, and villain. Headings such as control, generosity, and power give an even fuller description of Lovelace.

Clarissa, on the other hand, is a divine lady. Descriptions and comments scattered throughout the text regarding her character are brought together under the headings angel, divine qualities, example, fall, light, sacrifice, suffering, trials, and virgin. References to her father's house, early on merely social in meaning, take on a very religious meaning toward the end of the novel.

Lovelace's pursuit of Clarissa is a series of contrivances. Under that heading are listed all of his plots and trickery, beginning with the abduction of Clarissa and continuing even beyond her rape and subsequent escape from Lovelace. Several references under hunting and prey, and related entries under animals, suggest by their imagery the nature of his pursuit. Clarissa's various lodgings, removals, and escapes are all brought together under the heading journey. Under that heading one can easily locate her whereabouts at any point in the novel.

Some headings index topics other than characterizations or the main plot of the novel. Interesting and curious information is collected, for example, under the headings cures, drink, food, heraldry, illnesses, and medications, such as ipecacuanha.

Entries under the headings biblical references, classical references, historical references, and literary references form comprehensive lists of titles Richardson mentions in those categories. Quotes from the Bible, references to historical information, classical literature, and mythology are indexed. The entries under literary references form a bibliography of literary works mentioned or quoted by Richardson in *Clarissa*. These references are an indication of his familiarity with the world of letters. The headings for narration, story, and writing locate important statements about a new kind of writing, the novel.

Richardson makes use of theatrical devices such as disguises and eavesdropping. If one wanted to stage *Clarissa*, information under each character about his age, character, costume, hair, jewelry, mannerisms, physical appearance, and spectacles would be useful, as would be descriptions of Clarissa's various lodgings on her journey.

Locators

In this index letter numbers, rather than page numbers, are used as locators. For example, the alphanumeric configuration L24 indicates Letter 24. Since most letters are longer than one page, letter numbers are less specific than page numbers. However, letter numbers allow this index to be used with other printings of *Clarissa*, and, to an extent, with editions other than the Penguin printing of the first edition, which was used to write this index.

Locators may appear consecutively either as L279, L280, L281 or as L279–L281. In the first case, the consecutive locators indicate scattered references in three consecutive letters. In the second case, three consecutive letters are devoted entirely to the topic.

The Notes in the Penguin edition are also indexed. When a reference to *Job* is explained in a note, the locator for the letter number where the reference occurs is followed by a locator for the explanatory note at the end of the volume, for example, L379, L379n1. If the reader is interested in that particular reference to *Job*, he can see directly from the index that there is additional information in the notes.

The Glossary in the Penguin edition is not indexed, although it contains a great deal of information about obsolete vocabulary, Latin phrases, and some book titles. Those titles are indexed in the present index but are not always footnoted in the text of the novel. All entries in the Glossary are, of course, defined but are not located in the text, making it nearly impossible for the user to find where a glossed term appears. Some entries can be searched in the present index, others cannot, as indexing obsolete language was not within the scope of this project.

Indexes to Characters

The main organizing idea in this index is to isolate and index each character separately. Each appearance or mention of a character is noted under that character's name. A thesaurus, or list of headings, accommodates the information collected for each character: his age, correspondence, costume, death, family, friends, illnesses, manners, medications, relations, weapons, will, as well as his biblical, classical, historical, and literary references. The twenty longest character indexes are listed on the Contents page. Indexes for secondary characters are embedded in the longer character indexes and must be located through the Alphabetical List of Characters.

Alphabetical List of Characters and Embedded Indexes

The Alphabetical List of Characters has two kinds of entries. A bolded entry indicates one of the twenty character indexes which can be located directly from the Contents page. Other entries are for secondary characters *indexed under,* or embedded in the index of, a main character, under a heading that suggests the secondary character's relationship to the main character, such as apothecary, constable, family, friend, informant, mantua-maker, relation, servant, suitor, or whore.

The character indexes for Clarissa and Lovelace are the longest. Kit the hostler, however, appears only once in the novel, drinking with the footman at the taphouse at Hampstead, near Mrs. Moore's. His index would have been a single line. For this reason his index was embedded in Mrs. Moore's character index. Kit the hostler is *indexed under* **Moore, Mrs.,** under the heading neighbors. Another example, Mrs. Townsend, known to Anna, is a smuggler, to whom Anna goes for help in rescuing Clarissa. Mrs. Townsend's index appears in Anna's character index under the heading smugglers. She appears in the Alphabetical List of Characters as Townsend, Mrs. *indexed under* **Howe, Miss Anna**, smugglers.

Some of the embedded character indexes are quite long. In Lovelace's character index under the heading friends is an entry for Mr. Thomas Belton. Belton's index is relatively long and could have been a separate character index, but he fit well under the heading friends. Mrs. Moore and Mr. Smith, whose character indexes are relatively short, could have been embedded, but headings such as landladies and shopkeepers did not fit their relationship with Clarissa well, and so their indexes were not embedded. They were stopping points on Clarissa's journey, and, in fact, they appear also under the heading journey in Clarissa's character index.

The Alphabetical List of Characters includes all characters, their aliases, their friends and relations, even those who do not appear in the book but are only remembered by other characters. Those without proper names are not included in the list but are nevertheless indexed. Miss Lardner's footman is not listed in the Alphabetical List of Characters but is indexed under **Harlowe, Miss Clarissa**, friends, Lardner, Miss, her footman.

The Alphabetical List of Characters is a complete list of characters but is not a list of personal names. It does not include Caesar, Dryden, Job, Czar Peter, or Sir Anthony Vandyke. References to these personages appear respectively under the headings classical references, literary references, biblical references, historical references, and art references. For sovereigns of England the Alphabetical List of Characters uses see references to refer the reader from the names of individual sovereigns back to sovereigns, the broader heading. This produces a useful list under the heading sovereigns. Names of all sovereigns of England found in the novel are listed in the Alphabetical List of Characters under that heading.

Clarissa's family, the Harlowe Family, is treated as a separate character even though each family member also has his own character index. The family seems to have a voice of its own. They are of a mind both in loyalty to family and in conflict with Clarissa. Information under the headings businesses, dowries, estates, inheritances, money, and wills shows them to be a very wealthy middle-class family.

Subject Index

The Subject Index is a reorganization of the character indexes. The headings from the twenty long character indexes and all the embedded character indexes were merged, with the characters' names used as subheadings. To find out whether any particular character took ill, one can look in that character's index under illnesses, but in the Subject Index one can look directly under illnesses and find a series of entries describing the illnesses of each character. For example, Mr. Thomas Belton's embedded character index is under friends in the character index for **Lovelace, Mr. Robert**. Belton's illnesses are not indexed with Lovelace's in the character index for **Lovelace, Mr. Robert** under illnesses, but under **Lovelace, Mr. Robert**, friends, Belton, Mr. Thomas, illnesses. In the Subject Index one finds under the heading illnesses successive entries for *Lovelace, Mr. Robert* and *Lovelace, Mr. Robert*, friends, Belton, Mr. Thomas. .

The kind of access afforded by the Subject Index saves looking up the same subject in each character index. Even though everything is duplicated in the Subject Index, that index cannot do what the character indexes do, which is to bring together all information about a single character. Instead, it brings together all information on a single topic.

Place Name Index

A complete list of place names appears as a separate index. It includes gardens, doors, back doors, garden doors, as well as churches, inns, parishes, roads, streets, taverns, and towns. It indexes each occurrence of each place name mentioned in the novel. In and around Harlowe Place it includes plashy lane, the yew hedge, and the haunted coppice. It includes Lovelace's address in Paris, as well as all the stopping points on Clarissa's journey.

Classified Headings

Many headings are classified. They are broader terms under which specific information is indexed. For example, see references direct the user from milk to drink, the broader term, and from wine to drink, and from tea to drink. While the user must search for specific information under the broader heading, drink, the broader heading produces a complete list of beverages. Similar lists appear under books, medications, food, clothing, and weapons. In other cases, such as Moloch-deity, Satan, Beelzebub, and devil, each is a very specific heading linked to the others by see also's.

Order of Entries

The order of entries is more often chronological than alphabetical. Most of the entries are not alphabetizable terms; they are phrases suggesting a context for the heading. Alphabetizing a list of such entries would needlessly scramble them when one prefers to see the progression of an idea or the use of a particular word in order of occurrence throughout the text. Under the heading, marriages, Clarissa's to Lovelace, proposals, are entries that locate Lovelace's proposals. He proposes at times and in ways which make it impossible for Clarissa to accept, as he well knows. Those who argue that Clarissa refused to marry Lovelace will want to see the list of these proposals in order of occurrence. However, lists of animals, books, and personal names of friends, suitors, and relations are usefully alphabetized.

Order of Headings

Some headings are filed logically or chronologically rather than alphabetically. Entries under rape of Clarissa were too voluminous for a single heading, so the heading was divided. The heading rape of Clarissa is preceded by a heading rape of Clarissa, *premeditated*, which is in turn preceded by the heading rape of Clarissa, *foreshadowed*. Some passages could be interpreted to foreshadow the rape; other passages seem to indicate that the rape was premeditated. Since the author's foreshadowings and Lovelace's premeditation must occur before the rape, it is useful to file those headings before the heading rape of Clarissa. Another example, is the heading arrival of Morden, *anticipated* which files before the heading arrival of Morden. Italicized tags are filing elements, but they are italicized to show that they are not filed alphabetically, but in some other way, such as chronologically.

Reference Structure

A "see reference" refers the user from a form of a heading not used to a preferred form, sometimes to more than one preferred form. A "see also reference" gives the user the option of searching for additional information under one or more related headings. Conceptually these two types of references are quite different and are usually formatted differently. However, in this index they appear in the same simple, clear, uniform format as, for example, the see reference, black wax *see* sealings, and the see also reference, wills *see also* bequests. When the user searches the heading black wax, it is clear that no information is displayed under black wax, so he must go to the heading sealings, where there must be some information on black wax. If one searches under the heading wills, it is clear that there is a great deal of information under wills, but that there must be some related information also under bequests. The relationship created by any reference between two or more headings is always defined in this index directly after the filed heading. In other words, see also never appears at the end of a series of entries.

Phrasing and Punctuation

The phrasing of the entries varies. At times it closely follows Richardson's wording, and at other times it is entirely the wording of the indexer.

This index does not in any way edit Richardson's work. His spellings, his use of contractions and italics, and his use of numerals are all retained. Also retained is Richardson's punctuation, such as his frequent dashes and single quotes, the latter to indicate, for example, that Letter 229.2 from 'Clarissa Harlowe' to Miss Howe is a forgery.

Summaries of Letters

The Summaries of Letters serves as a brief outline of the main events. Each summary includes date of writing and names and locations of the correspondents.

The Summaries of Letters also correlates letter numbers for the Penguin printing, 1985, of the first edition; Richardson's first edition, 1747-1748, in seven volumes; and Richardson's third edition, 1751, in eight volumes. These correlated letter numbers allow the present index to serve as an index to Richardson's third edition and at the same time allow Richardson's index to the third edition to be used with either printing of the first edition, the Penguin printing or Richardson's own printing, should the user have that rare book at hand.

To use the present index as an index to the third edition in eight volumes, one will first look up an entry in this index to the Penguin Classics printing of first edition. Then, noting the letter number following that entry, the user will find that letter number in the Summaries of Letters to identify the corresponding letter number in the third edition.

Richardson's Index

A reader once presented Richardson with a list of sentiments in *Clarissa*. Richardson expanded on the idea and added it as an index to the third edition. His eighteenth-century terms and phrases are quite different from the ones used in this twentieth-century index. There is, however, a rough correspondence between his sentiments and what is indexed here under the heading opinions.

Richardson's locators are to volume and page number of the duodecimo edition in eight volumes. When he published his index to *Clarissa* again in *A Collection of the Moral and Instructive Sentiments* in 1755, he added locators for the octavo edition. Richardson's use of volume and page numbers makes it nearly impossible to use his index directly with any printing of the first edition or, indeed, with any printing of the third edition unless the volume and page numbers correspond with his original printing in eight volumes, as they do in the AMS Press facsimile.

To use Richardson's index as an index to the Penguin Classics first edition, the user must look up an entry from Richardson's index in his third edition using his locators to volume and page number. Then, having found the entry in the text, he must note the letter number where that entry occurs, keeping in mind that there may be more than one letter on a page. Having identified the letter in which the entry occurs, he will find that letter number in the Summaries of Letters and note the corresponding letter number for the Penguin printing of the first edition. Of course, the material added in the third edition is not searchable in the present index.

Alphabetical List of Characters, A Complete List, Locating an Index for Each

To locate characters listed in bold, refer to the Indexes to Characters listed on the Contents page.
To locate other characters, refer to the Contents page listing for the character following the
words *indexed under*.

Examples: **Belford, Mr. John**
  Mr. John Belford is listed on the Contents page under his own name. His index
  begins in the section Indexes to Characters on p. 9.
  Alston, Mr. *indexed under* **Morden, Colonel William**, informants
  Mr. Alston is not listed on the Contents page. His index is found in the index for
  Morden, Colonel William, where he is indexed under the heading informants.

Ackland, Mr. *indexed under* **Harlowe Family**, hires
Alexander *see* Wyerley, Mr. Alexander
Allinson *indexed under* **Harlowe Family**, relations
Alston, Mr. *indexed under* **Morden, Colonel William**, informants
Alston, Miss Fanny *indexed under* **Harlowe, Miss Clarissa**, friends
Ambrose, Colonel *indexed under* **Lovelace, Mr. Robert**, friends
Anderson *indexed under* **Lovelace, Mr. Robert**, surgeons
Andrew *indexed under* **Lovelace, Mr. Robert**, servants
Andrew *indexed under* **Smith, Mr. John,** customers
Ann *see* Shelburne, Ann
Anna *see* **Howe, Miss Anna**
Annabella *see* **Howe, Mrs. Annabella**
Anne, Queen *see* Sovereigns
Anthony *see* Holmes, Sir Anthony
Antony *see*
  Harlowe, Mr. Antony
  Tomlinson, Captain Antony
Arabella *see* **Harlowe, Miss Arabella**
Archibald *see* Hutcheson, Archibald
Arnold, Mr. *indexed under* **Harlowe, Miss Clarissa**, correspondence, Harlowe, Miss Clarissa with others
Arthur *see*
  Bedall, Arthur
  Lewin, Dr. Arthur
Atkins, Mrs. Mary *indexed under* **Harlowe, Miss Clarissa**, aliases

Bab (or Barbara) *see* Wallis, Bab
Barker *indexed under* **Smith, Mr. John**, neighbors
Barnes, Betty *indexed under* **Harlowe Family**, servants
Barrow, Colonel *indexed under* **Lovelace, Mr. Robert**, friends
Barton, Johnny *indexed under* **Lovelace, Mr. Robert**, contrivances of Lovelace, specifically, contrivance
  of sparing Rosebud, Rosebud, marriage
Beachcroft, Sir Robert *indexed under* **Norton, Mrs. Judith**, correspondence, Norton, Mrs. Judith
Beaumont, Miss Laetitia *indexed under* **Harlowe, Miss Clarissa**, aliases
Bedall, Arthur *indexed under* **Harlowe, Miss Clarissa**, will, witnesses
Belford, Mr. John
Bella *see* **Harlowe, Miss Arabella**
Belton, Mr. Thomas *indexed under* **Lovelace, Mr. Robert**, friends
Benson, Mrs. *indexed under* **Lord M.**, relations, half-sisters, Sadleir, Lady Sarah, friends
Bess, Queen *see* Sovereigns
Betsey *see* Sadleir, Betsey
Betsy *see* Rosebud
Betterton, Miss *indexed under* **Lovelace, Mr. Robert**, victims

Betty *indexed under* **Lord M.**, housekeepers, Greme, Mrs., relations, Sorlings, Mrs., family
Betty *indexed under* **Lovelace, Mr. Robert**, friends, Belton, Mr. Thomas, servants
    see also
        Barnes, Betty
        Carberry, Betty
        Lawrance, Lady Betty
Bevis, Mrs. *indexed under* **Moore, Mrs.**, relations
Biddulph, Miss Rachel *indexed under* **Harlowe, Miss Clarissa**, friends
Biddulph, Sir Robert *indexed under* **Harlowe, Miss Clarissa**, friends, Biddulph, Miss Rachel, family
Biddy *see*
    D'Ollyffe, Miss Biddy
    Lloyd, Miss Biddy
Biron *see* Byron
Blome, Dr. *indexed under* **Harlowe, Miss Clarissa**, correspondence, Harlowe, Miss Clarissa with others
Blomer *indexed under* **Lovelace, Mr. Robert**, friends, Belton, Mr. Thomas, friends
Brand, Mr. Elias *indexed under* **Harlowe Family**, clergymen
Brookland, Sir Josias *indexed under* **Harlowe, Mrs. Charlotte**, relations
Burton, Hannah *indexed under* **Harlowe, Miss Clarissa**, servants
Byron *indexed under* **Harlowe, Miss Clarissa**, suitors to Harlowe, Miss Clarissa

Campbell, Miss Cartwright *indexed under* **Harlowe, Miss Clarissa**, friends
Campion, Miss *indexed under* **Harlowe, Miss Clarissa**, friends
Carberry, Betty *indexed under* **Sinclair, Mrs.**, whores
Carter, Mrs. *indexed under* **Sinclair, Mrs.**, relations
Cartwright *see* Campbell, Miss Cartwright
Charles *indexed under* **Howe, Miss Anna**, family
    see also
        Hickman, Mr. Charles
        Hickman, Sir Charles
Charles II *see* Sovereigns
Charlotte *see*
    Harlowe, Mrs. Charlotte
    Montague, Miss Charlotte
Clarissa *indexed under* **Howe, Miss Anna**, family
    see also
        Harlowe, Miss Clarissa
Clark, Mrs. Rachel *indexed under* **Harlowe, Miss Clarissa**, aliases
Clements *indexed under* **Lord M.**, servants
Collins, Simon *indexed under*
    Hickman, Mr. Charles, messengers
    Howe, Miss Anna, correspondence, Howe, Miss Anna with Clarissa, conveyed by
Colmar, Sir George *indexed under* **Howe, Miss Anna**, suitors to Howe, Miss Anna
Craggs, Mr. Secretary *indexed under* **Lord M.**, political references

D—r's wife *indexed under* **Lovelace, Mr. Robert**, victims
De la Tour, F. J. *indexed under* **Lovelace, Mr. Robert**, valets
Derham, Counsellor *indexed under* **Harlowe Family**, counsellors
Diggs, Mr. *indexed under* **Harlowe, Mr. James, Jun.**, surgeons
D'Oily, Miss Kitty *indexed under* **Lovelace, Mr. Robert**, friends, Ambrose, Colonel, the ball
D'Oily, Miss Nelly *indexed under* **Harlowe, Mr. James, Jun.**, marriage
Doleman, Mr. Tom *indexed under* **Lovelace, Mr. Robert**, friends
Dolins, Mrs. *indexed under* **Harlowe, Miss Clarissa**, mantua-makers
Dolly *see*
    Hervey, Miss Dolly
    Welby, Dolly

D'Ollyffe, Miss Biddy *indexed under* **Lovelace, Mr. Robert**, friends, Ambrose, Colonel, the ball
Dorcas *see* Wykes, Dorcas
Dormer, Mr. *indexed under* **Hickman, Mr. Charles**, friends
Dorothy *see*
    Hervey, Mrs. Dorothy
      Salcomb, Mrs. Dorothy
Dorrell, Mr. *indexed under* **Belford, Mr. John**, attorneys
Downeton, Sir Harry *indexed under* **Howe, Mrs. Annabella**, friends
Drayton, Lady *indexed under* **Harlowe, Miss Clarissa**, friends
Drayton, Miss *indexed under* **Harlowe, Miss Clarissa**, friends

Edward VI *see* Sovereigns
Elias *see* Brand, Mr. Elias
Elizabeth *see* Swanton, Elizabeth
Elizabeth I *see* Sovereigns
Empson *indexed under* **Lord M.**, servants

Fanny *see* Alston, Miss Fanny
Farley *indexed under* **Belford, Mr. John**, victims
Filmer *indexed under* **Hickman, Mr. Charles**, hires
Finch, Mr. *indexed under* **Lord M.**, goldsmiths
Fortescue, Mrs. *indexed under* **Lord M.**, relations, half-sisters, Lawrance, Lady Betty, friends
Fretchville, Mrs. *indexed under* **Lovelace, Mr. Robert**, contrivances of Lovelace, specifically, contrivance
    of Mrs. Fretchville's house
Fuller *indexed under* **Harlowe Family**, relations
Fynnett, Jenny *indexed under* **Howe, Miss Anna**, relations

Garon, Mr. *indexed under* **Sinclair, Mrs.**, surgeons
George *see* Colmar, Sir George
George II *see* Sovereigns
Goddard, Mr. *indexed under* **Harlowe, Miss Clarissa**, apothecaries
Golding, Johanetta *indexed under* **Lovelace, Mr. Robert**, contrivances of Lovelace, specifically,
    contrivances of the impersonators
Greme, Mrs. *indexed under* **Lord M.**, housekeepers
Grimes *indexed under* **Harlowe, Miss Clarissa**, messengers

H., Mother *see* Mother H.
H., Dr. R. *indexed under* **Harlowe, Miss Clarissa**, physicians
Hal *indexed under* **Lovelace, Mr. Robert**, friends, Belton, Mr. Thomas, family, Thomasine, family
Hale, Dr. *indexed under* **Lovelace, Mr. Robert**, physicians
Hannah *see* Burton, Hannah
Harlowe, Grandfather *indexed under* **Harlowe Family**, relations
Harlowe, Grandmother *indexed under* **Harlowe Family**, relations
Harlowe, Mr. Antony
Harlowe, Miss Arabella
Harlowe, Mrs. Charlotte
Harlowe, Miss Clarissa
Harlowe, Mr. James, Jun.
Harlowe, Mr. James, Sen.
Harlowe, Mr. John
Harlowe Family
Harman, Aunt *indexed under* **Howe, Miss Anna**, relations
Harriot *indexed under* **Harlowe, Miss Clarissa**, friends, Lloyd, Miss Biddy, servants
    see also
        Lucas, Mrs. Harriot

Harry *indexed under* **Belford, Mr. John**, messengers
   see also
        Downeton, Sir Harry
Hartley, Lady *indexed under* **Howe, Miss Anna**, friends
Hartley, Mr. *indexed under* **Harlowe Family**, friends
Hartop, Johnny *indexed under* **Lovelace, Mr. Robert**, rakes
Henry VII *see* Sovereigns
Herbert *indexed under* **Howe, Miss Anna**, relations
Hervey, Uncle *indexed under* **Hervey, Mrs. Dorothy**, family
Hervey, Miss Dolly *indexed under* **Hervey, Mrs. Dorothy**, family
Hervey, Mrs. Dorothy
Hickman, Mr. Charles
Hickman, Sir Charles *indexed under* **Hickman, Mr. Charles**, relations
Hodges, Mrs. Sarah *indexed under* **Harlowe, Mr. John**, housekeepers
Holmes, Sir Anthony *indexed under* **Lovelace, Mr. Robert**, friends
Horton, Mary (Polly) *indexed under* **Sinclair, Mrs.**, whores
Howe, Mr. *indexed under*
   Howe, Miss Anna, family
   Howe, Mrs. Annabella, family
Howe, Miss Anna
Howe, Mrs. Annabella
Hunt, Mr. *indexed under* **Howe, Mrs. Annabella**, friends
Huntingford, Mr. Robert *indexed under* **Lovelace, Mr. Robert**, aliases
Hutcheson, Archibald *indexed under* **Lord M.**, political references

Jack *see* **Belford, Mr. John**
James *see*
   Harlowe, Mr. James, Jun.
   Harlowe, Mr. James, Sen.
   Tourville, Mr. James
James VI of Scotland and I of England *see* Sovereigns
Jenny *see* Fynnett, Jenny
Jenyns, Tony *indexed under* **Belford, Mr. John**, relations
Joel *indexed under* **Lovelace, Mr. Robert**, servants
Johanetta *see* Golding, Johanetta
John *see*
   Belford, Mr. John
   Harlowe, Mr. John
   Loftus, John
   Soberton, Mr. John
   Walton, Mr. John
   Williams, John
Johnny *see*
   Barton, Johnny
   Hartop, Johnny
Jonas *indexed under* **Lord M.**, servants
Jonathan *indexed under* **Belford, Mr. John**, servants
Joseph *indexed under* **Smith, Mr. John**, bodice-makers
   see also
        Leman, Joseph
Josias *see* Brookland, Sir Josias
Judith *see* **Norton, Mrs. Judith**

Katharine *indexed under* **Smith, Mr. John**, servants
Kings of England *see* Sovereigns

Kit the hostler *indexed under* **Moore, Mrs.**, neighbors
Kitty *indexed under* **Howe, Miss Anna**, servants
   see also
       D'Oily, Miss Kitty
Klienfurt, Mr. *indexed under* **Morden, Colonel William**, friends
Knollys, Mrs. *indexed under* **Lord M.**, relations

Laetitia *see* Beaumont, Miss Laetitia
Lardner, Miss *indexed under* **Harlowe, Miss Clarissa**, friends
Larkin, Mrs. *indexed under* **Howe, Mrs. Annabella**, relations
Lawrance, Lady Betty *indexed under* **Lord M.**, relations, half-sisters
Leeson, Mrs. *indexed under* **Lord M.**, relations, half-sisters, Lawrance, Lady Betty, relations
Leman, Joseph *indexed under* **Harlowe Family**, servants
Lewin (or Lewen), Dr. Arthur *indexed under* **Harlowe Family**, clergymen
Lexington, Lord *indexed under* **Lord M.**, friends
Lilburne, Mr. *indexed under* **Lovelace, Mr. Robert**, contrivances of Lovelace, specifically, contrivance of
   Captain Tomlinson and Uncle Harlowe's birthday, Tomlinson, Captain Antony, contrivance
Lloyd, Miss Biddy *indexed under* **Harlowe, Miss Clarissa**, friends
Lockyer, Miss *indexed under* **Lovelace, Mr. Robert**, victims
Loftus, John *indexed under* **Belford, Mr. John**, victims
Lord M.
Lord S. *indexed under* **Lovelace, Mr. Robert**, relations
Lord W. *indexed under* **Lovelace, Mr. Robert**, servants, Summers, Will, relations, Wheatly, Paul
Lorimer, Mrs. *indexed under* **Howe, Mrs. Annabella**, friends
Lovelace, Mr. Robert
Lovell *indexed under* **Harlowe, Mr. James, Jun.**, godmother
Lovick, Mrs. *indexed under* **Smith, Mr. John**, lodgers
Lucas, Mrs. Harriot (or Mrs. Harry Lucas) *indexed under* **Harlowe, Miss Clarissa**, aliases
Lucy *see* Villars, Lucy

M., Lord *see* **Lord M.**
Mabel *indexed under* **Sinclair, Mrs.**, servants
Mallory (or Malory) *indexed under* **Lovelace, Mr. Robert**, friends
Margaret (or Margery) *indexed under* **Moore, Mrs.**, servants
Marplot, Lord *indexed under* **Lord M.**, names
Martha *see* Montague, Miss Patty
Martin, Sarah (Sally) *indexed under* **Sinclair, Mrs.**, whores
Martindale, Dorcas *see* Wykes, Dorcas
Mary *see*
   Atkins, Mrs. Mary
   Horton, Mary (Polly)
McDonald, Patrick *see* Tomlinson, Captain Antony
Melvill, Mr. *indexed under* **Harlowe Family**, clergymen
Mennell, Mr. *see* Newcomb
Metcalf, Tom *indexed under* **Lovelace, Mr. Robert**, friends, Belton, Mr. Thomas, victims
Miles *indexed under* **Lovelace, Mr. Robert**, friends
Montague, Miss Charlotte *indexed under* **Lord M.**, relations, nieces
Montague, Miss Patty *indexed under* **Lord M.**, relations, nieces
Moore, Mrs.
Morden, Robert *indexed under* **Morden, Colonel William**, relations
Morden, Colonel William
Morrison, Susan *indexed under* **Lovelace, Mr. Robert**, contrivances of Lovelace, specifically,
contrivances of the impersonators
Mother H. *indexed under* **Lovelace, Mr. Robert**, dreams, second dream
Mowbray, Mr. Richard *indexed under* **Lovelace, Mr. Robert**, friends

Mullins, Mr. *indexed under* **Harlowe, Miss Clarissa**, suitors to Harlowe, Miss Clarissa

Nancy *see* **Howe, Miss Anna**
Nelly *see* D'Oily, Miss Nelly
Newcomb *indexed under* **Lovelace, Mr. Robert**, friends, Doleman, Mr. Tom, relations
Norton, Mrs. Judith
Norton, Tommy *indexed under* **Norton, Mrs. Judith**, family

Oliver *see* Solmes, Sir Oliver
Osgood, Mr. *indexed under* **Belford, Mr. John**, relations

Parsons, Simon *indexed under* **Lord M.**, servants
Partington, Priscilla *indexed under* **Sinclair, Mrs.**, whores
Partrick, Peter *indexed under* **Sinclair, Mrs.**, servants
Patrick *see* Tomlinson, Captain Antony
Patty (or Patsey) *see* Montague, Miss Patty
Paul *see* Wheatly, Paul
Peggy *see* Margaret
Perkins, Dr. *indexed under* **Lord M.**, physicians
Peter *see* Partrick, Peter
Playford, Miss *indexed under* **Lovelace, Mr. Robert**, friends, Ambrose, Colonel, the ball
Pocock, Mr. *indexed under* **Norton, Mrs. Judith**, correspondence, Norton, Mrs. Judith
Polly *see* Horton, Mary
Priscilla *see* Partington, Priscilla
Pritchard, Mr. *indexed under* **Lord M.**, servants

Queens of England *see* Sovereigns

Rachel *see*
    Biddulph, Miss Rachel
    Clark, Mrs. Rachel
Rawlins, Miss *indexed under* **Moore, Mrs.**, neighbors
Rawlins, Mr. *indexed under* **Moore, Mrs.**, neighbors
Richard *see* Mowbray, Mr. Richard
Robert *indexed under* **Howe, Miss Anna**, servants
    see also
        Beachcroft, Sir Robert
        Biddulph, Sir Robert
        Huntingford, Mr. Robert
        Lovelace, Mr. Robert
Robin *indexed under* **Howe, Miss Anna**, servants, Robert, names
Roger *see* Solmes, Mr. Roger
Rogers *indexed under* **Howe, Miss Anna**, messengers
Rosebud *indexed under* **Lovelace, Mr. Robert**, contrivances of Lovelace, specifically, contrivance of sparing Rosebud
Rowland, Mr. and Mrs. *indexed under* **Harlowe, Miss Clarissa**, constables
Royal Insignificant *see* Sovereigns

S., Dr. *indexed under* **Lord M.**, physicians
S., Lord *see* Lord S.
Sadleir, Betsey *indexed under* **Lord M.**, relations, half-sisters, Sadleir, Lady Sarah, family
Sadleir, Lady Sarah *indexed under* **Lord M.**, relations, half-sisters
Salcomb, Mrs. Dorothy *indexed under* **Harlowe, Miss Clarissa**, aliases
Sally *see* Martin, Sarah
Salter, Colonel *indexed under* **Sinclair, Mrs.**, customers

Sambre, Mrs. *indexed under* **Lovelace, Mr. Robert**, friends, Belton, Mr. Thomas, relations

Sarah *indexed under* **Smith, Mr. John**, servants

    see also

        Hodges, Mrs. Sarah

        Martin, Sarah (Sally)

        Sadleir, Lady Sarah

Shelburne, Ann *indexed under* **Harlowe, Miss Clarissa**, nurses

Shorey *indexed under* **Harlowe, Mrs. Charlotte**, servants

Simon *see*

        Collins, Simon

        Parsons, Simon

Sinclair, Mrs.

Singleton, Captain *indexed under* **Harlowe, Mr. James, Jun.**, friends

Sloane, Captain *indexed under* **Lovelace, Mr. Robert**, friends, Barrow, Colonel, friends

Smith, Mr. John

Smith, Mrs. *indexed under* **Smith, Mr. John**, family

Soberton, Mr. John *indexed under* **Howe, Miss Anna**, aliases

Solcombe, Colonel *indexed under* **Lovelace, Mr. Robert**, friends

Solmes, Sir Oliver *indexed under* **Harlowe, Miss Clarissa**, suitors to Harlowe, Miss Clarissa, Solmes, Mr.
   Roger, relations

Solmes, Mr. Roger *indexed under* **Harlowe, Miss Clarissa**, suitors to Harlowe, Miss Clarissa

Sorlings, Mrs. *indexed under* **Lord M.**, housekeepers, Greme, Mrs., relations

Sovereigns

    Queen Anne *indexed under* **Lovelace, Mr. Robert**, historical references

    Charles II *indexed under*

        Lovelace, Mr. Robert, historical references

        Harlowe, Miss Clarissa, historical references

    Edward VI *indexed under* **Harlowe, Miss Clarissa**, historical references

    Elizabeth I (Queen Bess) *indexed under* **Lovelace, Mr. Robert**, historical references

    George II *indexed under* **Howe, Miss Anna**, political references

    Henry VII *indexed under* **Howe, Miss Anna**, historical references

    James VI of Scotland and I of England (the Royal Insignificant) *indexed under* **Lovelace, Mr. Robert**,
        historical references

Spilsworth *indexed under* **Howe, Miss Anna**, relations

Spurrier, Mr. *indexed under* **Lord M.**, relations, half-sisters, Lawrance, Lady Betty, servants

Stedman *indexed under* **Lord M.**, relations, half-sisters, Lawrance, Lady Betty, solicitors

Summers, Will *indexed under* **Lovelace, Mr. Robert**, servants

Susan *see* Morrison, Susan

Swanton, Elizabeth *indexed under* **Harlowe, Miss Clarissa**, will, witnesses

Symmes, Mr. *indexed under* **Harlowe, Miss Clarissa**, suitors to Harlowe, Miss Clarissa

Symmes, Mr. Edward *indexed under* **Harlowe Family**, neighbors

Thomas *see* Belton, Mr. Thomas

Thomas, Mrs. *indexed under* **Belford, Mr. John**, relations, Jenyns, Tony

Thomasine *indexed under* **Lovelace, Mr. Robert**, friends, Belton, Mr. Thomas, family

Thompson *indexed under* **Howe, Miss Anna**, contrivances of Lovelace, contrivance of Captain Tomlinson
   and Uncle Harlowe's birthday

Tom *indexed under* **Lovelace, Mr. Robert**, friends, Belton, Mr. Thomas, family, Thomasine, family

    see also

        Doleman, Mr. Tom

        Metcalf, Tom

Tomkins *indexed under* **Howe, Miss Anna**, contrivances of Lovelace, contrivance of Captain
   Tomlinson and Uncle Harlowe's birthday

Tomkins *indexed under*
> **Lovelace, Mr. Robert**, surgeons
> **Belford, Mr. John**, friends

Tomlinson, Captain Antony *indexed under* **Lovelace, Mr. Robert**, contrivances of Lovelace, specifically, contrivance of Captain Tomlinson and Uncle Harlowe's birthday

Tommy *see* Norton, Tommy

Tompkins, Mr. *indexed under* **Harlowe, Miss Clarissa**, correspondence, Harlowe, Miss Clarissa with others

Tony *see* **Harlowe, Mr. Antony**

Tourville, Mr. James *indexed under* **Lovelace, Mr. Robert**, friends

Townsend, Mrs. *indexed under* **Howe, Miss Anna**, smugglers

Uncle Harlowe *see* **Harlowe, Mr. John**

Villars, Lucy *indexed under* **Lovelace, Mr. Robert**, victims

W., Lord *see* Lord W.

Wallis, Bab (or Barbara) *indexed under*
> **Belford, Mr. John**, victims
> **Lovelace, Mr. Robert**, contrivances of Lovelace, specifically, contrivances of the impersonators

Walton, Mr. and Mrs. John *indexed under* **Smith, Mr. John**, neighbors

Warneton, Major *indexed under* **Lovelace, Mr. Robert**, friends

Welby, Dolly *indexed under* **Lovelace, Mr. Robert**, curses, Eve's curse

Wheatly, Paul *indexed under* **Lovelace, Mr. Robert**, servants, Summers, Will, relations

Will (or William) *see* Summers, Will

William *see* **Morden, Colonel William**

Williams, Counsellor *indexed under* **Lovelace, Mr. Robert**, counsellors

Williams, Mrs. *indexed under* **Harlowe, Mrs. Charlotte**, housekeepers

Williams, John *indexed under* **Harlowe, Miss Clarissa**, will, witnesses

Wilson, Mr. *indexed under* **Lovelace, Mr. Robert**, friends

Windisgratz, Baron *indexed under* **Lovelace, Mr. Robert**, friends

Wright, Dr. *indexed under* **Lovelace, Mr. Robert**, physicians

Wycherley, William *indexed under* **Lord M.**, friends

Wyerley, Mr. Alexander *indexed under* **Harlowe, Miss Clarissa**, suitors to Harlowe, Miss Clarissa

Wykes, Dorcas *indexed under* **Sinclair, Mrs.**, whores

INDEXES TO CHARACTERS

BELFORD, MR. JOHN, Lovelace's friend

abduction of Clarissa
> one of three or four horsemen galloping with the chariot L98
> with Lovelace at the White Hart Inn L99

accidents
> falling from his horse L261

advocate for Clarissa
> pleading Clarissa's case to Lovelace L143, L189, L222, L268, L332, L334

advocate for Lovelace
> Lovelace asking him to put a favorable face on his actions L261
> mentioned as L370

age
> seven- or eight-and-twenty years, youngest of Lovelace's friends L161

animals see also **prey**
> a bear L105
> his dragon's wings L228
> a dog L259, L264
> falling from his horse L261
> preferring to be a dog, monkey, bear, viper, or toad than a Lovelace L286
> a vulture, boasting gentle usage of its prey, Lovelace as L333
> a cursed toad, Sally as L333
> a post-horse, whom dogs would eat L335
> birds fearing a kite, as we fear people who are ill L364
> mankind in conflict with other animals L364
> rakes and libertines, as a blind mill-horse L366
> a harmless deer, Clarissa as L419
> a bear, Mowbray as L420
> a mongrel, Harry as L420
> a sorrowful monkey L527

arrest of Clarissa
> freeing Clarissa L330, L332, L333, L334

art references
> Swift, Dean, *Lady's Dressing Room*, Mrs. Sinclair's whores compared to L499fn

attorneys
> *Dorrell, Mr.*, Belford visiting, on Belton's account L364, L365

bequests of Belton
> 100 guineas and £20 for a memorial ring L426
> Belford giving his 100-guinea bequest to Belton's sister L426

bequests of Clarissa
> one hundred guineas and twenty guineas for a ring L507

Bible
> understanding as children L364
> admiration for L370

biblical references see also **God, references to**
> *James* 2:19, quoted on devils L222
> raping Clarissa a national sin atoned for by sword, pestilence, or famine L336
> mingled with the dust we sprung from L420

blessings
> blessed by Clarissa L440

books
> to procure for Clarissa's closet L131

caitiff see **devils**

BELFORD, MR. JOHN, Lovelace's friend

character

    description by Clarissa L161

    good-natured L161, L359

    bad enough L189

    his Hottentot heart L191

    a pitiful fellow L276

    a wretched puppet of Lovelace L339

    stiff as Hickman's ruffles L350

    his awkwardness L370

    Mrs. Smith inquiring into his character L379

    dough-baked varlet L395

    well spoken of by Hickman L404

    account of, by Clarissa L458

church

    resolving to attend L499

classical references

    well read in classical authors L161

    Juvenal, quoted L217.3, L217.3n1, L419, L419n2

    Socrates, Clarissa's suffering and death compared L258, L451

    Caesar stabbed by Brutus, Clarissa compared L336

    Democritus and Heraclitus, Lovelace and Belford compared L364, L364n3

    Proteus, Lovelace as L424

clothing see **costume**

codes

    sending Lovelace news of Clarissa's death in a coded message L449

    his hellish Arabick L496

coffins

    seeing Clarissa's L451

collation at Mrs. Sinclair's

    report of L222

contrivances of Lovelace see also **abduction of Clarissa; rape of Clarissa**

    Lovelace revealing himself to Belford in his writing L276

    Belford's knowledge of all Lovelace did L284, L326, L379, L387.1

    will not assist Lovelace in any contrivances L286

    Clarissa realizing that Belford has known all along about Lovelace's actions L339

    asking Lovelace not to molest or visit Clarissa L385, L391, L400, L413

correspondence, Belford, Mr. John with Lovelace

    must return all Lovelace's letters L326

    sending Clarissa extracts of Lovelace's correspondence L388, L395, L396, L415

    Lovelace returning all his correspondence to Belford L423

    wanting his letters returned to give to Anna to vindicate Clarissa's memory L452

    asking Mowbray to return Belford's correspondence with Lovelace L498

correspondence, Harlowe, Miss Clarissa

    one day he will have all Clarissa's letters L391

    sending Anna Clarissa's correspondence L521

correspondence, Howe, Miss Anna with Clarissa, intercepted by Lovelace

    to bring Clarissa's mail to Lovelace L105

    refusing to confiscate Anna's to Clarissa L341

costume

    his old corporal's coat L34

    dressing gaily L161

    removing Clarissa's clothes from Mrs. Sinclair's to Smith's L336

    dressing like a coxcomb L350

    making his ugliness conspicuous by his dress L350

BELFORD, MR. JOHN, Lovelace's friend

costume (cont.)

    should amend his dress after mourning L370

    Beau-Brocade after mourning L527

curses

    cursed by Lovelace L416

death of Harlowe, Miss Clarissa, avenged

    were he Clarissa's brother L258

    wishing to L334

devils

    James 2:19, quoted on L222

    caitiff, Belford as L335, L370, L516

dreams

    after seeing Clarissa's coffin L451

dress see **costume**

education

    well read in classical authors L161

    pride of learning L364

    his knowledge of law L379

estates see also **inheritances**

    paternal estate upwards of £1000 a year L444

executor

    his uncle's executor

        two executorships upon him at present L379

        his affairs in Watford L383

    Clarissa's executor L379, L389, L391, L396, L404, L409, L410, L454, L486.1

        unlocking the drawer holding Clarissa's will and parcel of letters sealed with three black seals L486

        reading Clarissa's will with Morden L486

        Morden giving him proceeds of Grandfather's estate since his death L504

        begins to execute the will now that the funeral is over L505

        James asking him to relinquish executorship L506

        to perform every article within two months time L507

        giving Lovelace a copy of Clarissa's will L527

    Belton's executor L426

    having three executorships L507

    Morden's co-executor, with Hickman L528

    Lovelace's executor L535

expiate

    expiate for thy abominable vileness to her L336

falls

    falling from his horse L261

family see also **relations**

    Montague, Miss Charlotte, wife CONCLUSION

    son CONCLUSION

fortune see **estates**; **inheritances**

friends

    Belton, Mr. Thomas

        caring for Belton L344, L364, L383

        putting Belton's sister into possession of Belton's house L385

        throwing Thomasine and hers out of Belton's house L399

        called to Belton's bedside L419

        caring for Belton's sister L440

    Tomkins, his surgeon-friend L499

friendship

    with Clarissa L284, L339, L343

BELFORD, MR. JOHN, Lovelace's friend

friendship (cont.)

    with Belton L344, L383

    with Morden L487

    with Lovelace L534

gentleman

    gentleman L161

God, references to see also **biblical references**

    that Power L192

    God, the BEING of beings, Supreme Superintendent and Father of all things L293

hatred of Lovelace

    hating Lovelace L349

historical references

    Louis XIV L192, L192n1

    Novogrod and ancient Sarmatia L344, L344n1

    Dr. John Ratcliffe (usually Radcliffe), a physician, quoted L424, L424n1

    Emperor Joseph, Clarissa compared, dying while physicians consult L460

    Francis Chartres, a rapist, Belford compared L513, L513n1

    Bishop Burnet, quoted L533, L533n1 (cf. L157.1n1)

honor

    doubting Lovelace's L286

    Belford having more than some princes L286

    notions of false honor L339

housekeepers

    Lovick, Mrs., housekeeper at Edgware L514, CONCLUSION

hunting see also **prey**

    to hunt Lovelace L333

inheritances see also **estates**

    his uncle's heir L172, L247

    inheriting £5000 cash and £500 a year from his uncle L258

    giving his inheritance all to Lovelace if he will marry Clarissa L258

    his increased fortune L344

    made rich by his uncle's death L425, L444

Jews

    learning Old Testament history from Josephus L364

law

    his knowledge of L379

literary references see also **books**

    Blackwall, Anthony, *The Sacred Classics*, mentioned L364, L364n4

    Congreve, William, *The Mourning Bride*, quoted L365, L365n1

    Dryden, John

        Troilus and Cressida, quoted L364, L364n1

        All for Love, quoted L419, L419n4 (superscript 4 omitted from text)

    Norris, John, *Collection of Miscellanies*, quoted L419, L419n6

    Otway, Thomas, *The History and Fall of Caius Marius*, quoted L336, L336n1

    Pomfret, John, *Prospect of Death*, quoted L419, L419n7

    Rawlins, Thomas, *Tom Essence* L413, L413n3

    Restoration drama, Clarissa's story summed up and compared to examples of L413

    Rowe, Nicholas, *The Fair Penitent*, Clarissa as L413n1 (appearing in Notes as L413n2)

    Shakespeare, William, *Macbeth*, quoted L419, L419n1

    Swift, Jonathan, *Gulliver's Travels*, Yahoos mentioned L499

    untraced quote L424, L424n2

    Virgil, *Aeneid*, harpies mentioned L499, L499n1

lodgings see also **residences**

    near Soho Square with a relation, a lady of virtue and honor L125

BELFORD, MR. JOHN, Lovelace's friend

lodgings (cont.)

with his uncle in Watford L190.1

at Edgware on Sundays L330

lodgings in town L330

lodging with his cousin and her family L440

marriage

no great liking for L143

wishing to marry and reform L344, L531

marriages, Charlotte's to Belford

wanting to marry Miss Charlotte Montague L170, L516

Lovelace suggesting a wife for Belford L527

marrying Miss Charlotte Montague CONCLUSION

marriages, Clarissa's to Lovelace

urging Lovelace to marry Clarissa L110, L143, L258

meals, breakfast

breakfast with Clarissa and Hickman L365, L366

Meditations

Mrs. Lovick giving Clarissa's Meditations to Belford L364

messengers

Harry, messenger L411

a mongrel L420

taking Clarissa's letter to Anna L457, L471

delivering Clarissa's posthumous correspondence L486, L494

reporting the disorder at Harlowe Place on news of Clarissa's death L494

money

offering Clarissa money L339, L349, L350, L444

giving Mrs. Smith twenty guineas for Clarissa's clothes L340, L345

offering to be Clarissa's banker L349

giving his 100-guinea bequest of Belton to Belton's sister L426

sending Tomlinson money L514, L515

restitution to John Loftus and Farley L514

contributing to the Poor's Fund CONCLUSION

mourning

Belford and his servant in mourning L336, L444

amending his dress after mourning L370

Beau-Brocade after mourning L527

music

drum, trumpet, fife, tabret, to express joy L192

names

first called Jack L31

Squire Belford L418

opinions

on friendship

and illness L364

female friendship L366

on keeping L192

on mankind in conflict with other animals L364

on marriage L143, L192

on physicians

their high fees L424

Dr. John Ratcliffe, a physician, quoted L424, L424n1

and Doleman's malady L531

on pride, penitence, virtue and vice as exemplified in Restoration drama L413

on rakes L192, L222, L366

BELFORD, MR. JOHN, Lovelace's friend

opinions (cont.)

    on reform L143

    on religious matters L364

    on Restoration drama L413

    on wit in rakes and libertines L222

    on women

        bad women worse than bad men L333

        female friendship L366

physical appearance

    a bear L105

    making his ugliness conspicuous by his dress L350

    dough-baked varlet L395

    heavier and clumsier than Lovelace L425

    ugly fellow, gaudy and clumsy, tawdry L516

    homely and awkward, boatswain-like air L516, L527

Poor's Fund

    to increase the Poor's Fund L507, CONCLUSION

prey see also **hunting**

    Lovelace, a vulture, boasting gentle usage of its prey L333

rake

    has lain with Bab Wallis L255

    a reformed rake makes the best husband L499

    Francis Chartres, a rapist, Belford compared L513, L513n1

rape of Clarissa, *premeditated*

    his knowledge of L258, L379, L387.1

    his guilt at not acting to protect Clarissa L339

    For *how* wouldst thou have saved her? What methods didst thou *take* to save her? Thou knewest my design

        all along L516

rape of Clarissa

    O thou savage-hearted monster L258

reform

    reform when we can sin no longer L143

    his reformation caused by his uncle's death L347

    resolved to repent and marry L347, L424, L425

    his reformation L364, L395

    his conversion by Clarissa L419, L440

    affected by both Belton and Clarissa L419

    looking to his own reform L498, L514

    his reform doubted by Lovelace L513, L516

    his reform successful L531, CONCLUSION

relations see also **family**

    Jenyns, Tony, cousin L192

        his story L192

        prating against wedlock L192

        his affair with his fencing master's daughter, his good Mrs. Thomas L192

    Osgood, Mr., cousin L105

        a man of reputation L98

        residing near Soho Square, where Clarissa may direct her things sent L98, L102, L105

        a lady of virtue and honor with whom he lodges, near Soho Square L125

        his wife, a pious woman L127

        Aunt Hervey to direct her correspondence to Mr. Osgood L141

        has received correspondence for Clarissa from Arabella L143

    uncle

        attending his dying uncle L172, L190.1, L191

BELFORD, MR. JOHN, Lovelace's friend

relations, uncle (cont.)

        his uncle's heir L172, L247

        his uncle having mortification up to the knee L172

        Lovelace inquiring after Belford's uncle L213, L215

        his uncle bewailing a dissolute life L222

        his death L247

        respecting his uncle L258

        his uncle tortured by his illness L258

        reflecting on his dying uncle L333

residences see also **lodgings**

    of Edgworth [Edgware?] in the County of Middlesex L507

Restoration drama

    comparing Clarissa's story to L413

sayings and proverbs

    The prince on his throne is not safe if a mind so desperate can be found as values not its own life L189

    a drowning man will catch at a straw L419

    a reformed rake makes the best husband L499

servants

    generally

        in mourning L336

        buying snuff L336

        treatment of L420, L423

    Jonathan, mentioned L420

sex

    impossible to think of, in company of Clarissa L446

snuff

    his servant buying L336

story

    protector of Clarissa's memory L389

    Clarissa's, summed up and compared to examples of Restoration drama L413

surgeons

    Tomkins, his surgeon-friend L499

tenant-courtesy

    Lovelace leaving his progeny a worse tenure than L143

transportation

    dismissing his coach and taking a chair back to Rowland's L334

    taking a chair to Smith's L340

    taking a coach to Smith's L445

    taking a chair home from Smith's after seeing Clarissa's coffin L450

travel

    out of town till Monday L391

    to visit Lovelace in Paris L514

victims

    Bab Wallis, or Barbara, has lain with L255

    Farley, restitution L514

    John Loftus, young mistress of, restitution L514

violent behavior

    cutting the throat of Clarissa's destroyer L334

visits

    to Belton L364, L414, L419

    to Clarissa

        on behalf of Lovelace L284, L285

        at Rowland's L334

BELFORD, MR. JOHN, Lovelace's friend

visits, to Clarissa (cont.)

    at Smith's L339, L348, L365, L385, L413, L440, L441, L450, L457

        disapproved by Harlowe Family L431, L459

        causing a scandal L433

        investigated by Mr. Alston L459

  to Dorrell L364, L365

  to Mrs. Sinclair, on her death bed L499

weapons

  sword, pistol, halter, or knife, ending his misery by L333

will

  to make his will L528

writing see also **codes**

  dealing with Lovelace in writing, not in conversation L526

  supposed author of the conclusion CONCLUSION

HARLOWE, MR. ANTONY, Clarissa's uncle

abduction of Clarissa
> all in a rage L100
> renouncing Clarissa L147
> believing Clarissa ruined L183, L184

address to Arabella by Mr. Robert Lovelace
> discussing with Lord M. L2
> introducing Lovelace to the family as suitor to Arabella L2
> his favorable opinion of Lovelace L3, L13
> visited by Lovelace after Arabella's rejection of Lovelace L3
> Arabella mistakenly introduced to Lovelace L31

address to Clarissa by Mr. Roger Solmes
> Clarissa receiving Solmes at Antony's L41.2, L50.1, L51.1, L51.2, L53, L54.1, L55, L61–L63
> interrupting meeting between Clarissa and Solmes L78
> Clarissa no longer to go to Antony's L83

age
> born thirty years before Clarissa L15
> we have lived some of us...thirty or forty years longer than Clarissa L32.4
> youngest of three brothers L197.1

bequests of Clarissa
> family plate L507

biblical references
> *Proverbs* 18:17, quoted L32.4, L32.4n1
> *Ecclesiasticus* 42:9, 10, etc., quoted L406
> *Matthew* 23:24, quoted L32.4, L32.4n3

business
> his East India traffic and successful voyages L4

character
> busy old tarpaulin uncle L31
> sea-prospered gentleman L73
> impetuous in his anger L73
> fusty fellow L100
> odd old ambling soul L111
> his brother Orson L128, L128n1
> thrice cruel, hard-hearted L129, L309
> grey goose L196
> old Triton L197
> old Neptune L197
> his sobriety L197

duel between James and Lovelace
> his poor opinion of Lovelace, following the duel L1

estates
> his very great fortune L182, L183, L197.1

family
> hopes for children L197.1

fearing Lovelace
> double-servanted and double-armed against Lovelace L31

gentleman
> sea-prospered gentleman L73

health
> healthy and sound L197.1

influence on Howe, Mrs. Annabella
> influencing Mrs. Howe against Lovelace after duel L1
> revealing to Mrs. Howe the purpose of an alliance with Solmes L27
> used by Lovelace to influence Mrs. Howe against Clarissa L104, L105, L111, L125, L128

HARLOWE, MR. ANTONY, Clarissa's uncle

inheritances
> regretting Clarissa's L32.4
> family's right to Clarissa's L32.4

literary references
> *Valentine and Orson*, his morals compared to Orson's L128, L128n1

marriage
> bachelor L10, L32.4, L197.1
> his mutual attraction to Mrs. Howe L74
> his intention to marry Mrs. Howe L183, L201
>> formal tender to Mrs. Howe L196
>> his proposals L197, L198
>> will leave her at least ten thousand pounds richer L197.1
>> not wanting Anna to live with them L197.1

meals, dinner
> dining and supping with Papa and James L19

names
> Tony L100

opinions
> on men, their position in the family L32.4
> on parental authority L15, L32.4
> on women L32.4

plate
> bequeathed family plate L507

sayings
> Dunmow flitch L32.4, L32.4n4
> plain Dunstable of the matter L32.4, L32.4n2
> sauce for the goose is sauce for the gander L32.4

servants, treatment of
> see L197.1

tenants
> treatment of L13
> generosity to L15

visits
> to Mrs. Howe L1, L10, L87, L100, L101
> from Lovelace L3

will
> his favoring Clarissa L13
> carrying his great fortune into another family on Clarissa's account L182

HARLOWE, MISS ARABELLA, Clarissa's elder sister

abduction of Clarissa

    renouncing Clarissa L147

accomplishments

    inability for household cares L6

address to Arabella by Mr. Robert Lovelace

    his rejection of her in favor of Clarissa L1

    his three visits to her, as she relates them to Clarissa L2

    lacking peculiarity in his address L2

    her rejection accepted by Lovelace L3

    suspecting Lovelace was not fond of marrying at all L3

    confiding her love for Lovelace in Betty Barnes L15

    her resentment of Lovelace L19

    mistakenly introduced to Lovelace by Antony L31

address to Clarissa by Mr. Roger Solmes

    angry at Clarissa for rejecting Solmes L21

    threats to Clarissa regarding Solmes L29

    confrontation with Clarissa over Solmes L42

    assaulting Clarissa L53

    answering Clarissa's proposals to seek refuge elsewhere L54.1

age

    older than Clarissa L75

    twenty-six years L529

animals

    viper L75

ball, Colonel Ambrose's

    not attending L367

biblical references

    Numbers 17:43–48, Aaron's rod L42

    Matthew 5:15, I hid not my light L42

character

    ill-natured, less sense than ill nature L2, L352

    greedy, plump L10

    self-serving L17

    cruel, hard-hearted L78, L309, L348, L362, L391, L430, L440, L459

    soul of the other sex and the body of ours L78

    malicious and selfish, spiteful L111, L152, L327, L355

    envious, jealous elder sister L145, L152, L189, L223, L261 Paper V, L355

conflict between Harlowe, Miss Arabella and Clarissa see also **sibling rivalry**

    Lovelace's rejection of Arabella in favor of Clarissa L1

    jealous of Clarissa's inheritance L2, L42, L44

    motivations mentioned L27, L115

    taunting Clarissa L75, L433

    taking some of Clarissa's poultry for James to take to Scotland L75

    overheard by Clarissa plotting with James L83

    penetrating Clarissa's proud heart L261 Paper V

    severity with Mrs. Norton, bitter against Miss Howe L308

    indifferent to Clarissa's plight L352

    and James's confederacy to disgrace Clarissa L472

curses

    Clarissa writing Arabella to have Papa's curse revoked L348, L349, L360

    Clarissa asking her to intercede in revoking the part of Papa's curse that relates to the hereafter, as she has already been punished in the here L363

death of Harlowe, Miss Clarissa

    hating James afterwards and regretting her cruel treatment of Clarissa CONCLUSION

HARLOWE, MISS ARABELLA, Clarissa's elder sister

friends

Lloyd, Miss Biddy, a favorite of Arabella L132

gossip

about, that Clarissa has stolen Lovelace from her L1, L2, L3

with Betty and Dolly, causing Clarissa to become desperate L94

gossiping with Miss Lloyd about James's plan to rescue Clarissa L132

harpsichord

playing Clarissa's harpsichord L42

independence

accusing Clarissa of wanting independence L53

manners

ill-mannered L355

marriage

poor prospects L10

match for Solmes L10, L42, L60.2

married, unhappily CONCLUSION

names

Bella L2

Miss Bell L132

A.H. L311

opinions

on daughters L42

on the female sex L53

physical appearance

plump L7, L10

prosecution of Lovelace

favoring L427, L429

reconciliation between Clarissa and the Harlowe Family

Clarissa applying to her for reconciliation L309

Clarissa asking her to intercede for her parents' last blessing L380

Clarissa praying for a kinder heart for Arabella L430

favoring a visit from Mrs. Norton to Clarissa L459

expressing family's desire for reconciliation L484

rescue of Clarissa

gossiping with Miss Lloyd about James's plan to rescue Clarissa L132

revenge

vowing revenge on Clarissa L15

wanting revenge on Lovelace L429

rings

Clarissa to give her the diamond ring L334

sayings

it is good to be related to an estate L13

servants

Barnes, Betty, Arabella's maid L507

Arabella confiding in Betty her love for Lovelace L15

sibling rivalry see also **conflict between Harlowe, Miss Arabella and Clarissa**

overshadowed by Clarissa L10

sisterly feelings lacking L14, L29.3

envious of Clarissa L145, L152, L189, L223, L355

neglected on account of Clarissa's superiority L182

eclipsed by Clarissa L421

visits

from Lovelace L2

HARLOWE, MRS. CHARLOTTE, Clarissa's mamma

abduction of Clarissa
> disagreeing with family's refusal to send Clarissa her things L111
> will send Clarissa her clothes L147

address to Clarissa by Mr. Robert Lovelace
> disapproving of his morals L3

address to Clarissa by Mr. Roger Solmes
> agreeing that Clarissa has been badly treated L6
> promoting Solmes's suit L16, L17, L20, L21
> threatening and intimidating Clarissa into accepting Solmes L18, L20, L21, L41.1
> pleading Clarissa's case, not to marry Solmes L19, L20, L52.1
> accusing Clarissa of preferring Lovelace L20
> yield you must, or be none of our child L20
> not approving the manner in which Solmes's suit was presented to Clarissa L39
> her sympathy for Clarissa L41

authority
> failing to exert her authority to control family dissention L5
> deferring to James on Clarissa's request to attend church L22

banishment of Clarissa
> Clarissa cannot remain at Harlowe Place L54.1

bequests of Clarissa
> whole length picture of Clarissa in the Vandyke taste L507, L510.3
> a piece of needlework L510.3
> book of Meditations L510.3

biblical references
> Clarissa wishing to kiss the hem of Mamma's garment L377

blessings
> Clarissa asking her blessing and forgiveness L393

character
> obedient nature L8
> passive L13, L151, L248, L500
> peace keeper L16
> self-sacrificing L19
> her indolent meekness L27
> unable to show maternal love L181
> her narrowness of mind L183
> will-less L248
> thought hard-hearted and unforgiving on account of Clarissa's errors L307
> conquering by seeming to yield L379
> indulgent and sweet-tempered L409
> her quiet cost her her daughter L500

conflict between Harlowe Family and Clarissa
> blaming James's violence L41

correspondence, Harlowe, Mrs. Charlotte
> her secret correspondence with Clarissa about Lovelace L25.2
> returning Clarissa's letter unopened L59
> her letter to Mrs. Norton not communicated L182

correspondence, Harlowe, Miss Clarissa with Lovelace
> her knowledge of L4, L17, L25.2, L112

death of Harlowe, Mrs. Charlotte
> survived Clarissa by about two and a half years CONCLUSION

death of Harlowe, Miss Clarissa
> hourly fits after receiving news of L494.1
> her quiet cost her her daughter L503
> unable to view the body L503

HARLOWE, MRS. CHARLOTTE, Clarissa's mamma

dowry

her large dowry, compared to Clarissa's L41.1

fearing Lovelace

fearful of Lovelace's vengeful nature following the duel L4, L5

fearing Lovelace's reaction to Solmes's suit L25.2

grieving for Clarissa

her grief over the loss of Clarissa L379

housekeepers

Williams, Mrs., Mamma's former housekeeper L432

visiting Aunt Hervey L432

not allowed to visit Clarissa L432

her kind intentions L433

illnesses

colic L5, L80

hourly fits after hearing of Clarissa's death L494.1

influence in Harlowe Family

lacking influence in the family L27

losing her identity in her family L47

patching up for herself a precarious and sorry quiet L181

cannot help Clarissa as the family is too much against her L182

cannot oppose the rest L376

sympathy for Clarissa

afraid to speak for Clarissa L379, L433

unable to help Clarissa L382

her heart...is in their measures L409

acting contrary to her inclinations L432

would have sympathized with Clarissa L432

will do nothing to help Clarissa without permission of Papa and Uncles Harlowe L459

inheritances

her inheritances increasing Papa's wealth L4

meals, breakfast

going down to breakfast L18

meals, dinner

dinner L17

a short and early dinner L20

money

giving Hannah two guineas on her dismissal L25.2

sending Mrs. Norton five guineas L376

names

Charl. Harlowe L356

opinions

on duty L20

on the male sex and their prerogatives L17

pregnant

hoping Clarissa is not pregnant L376

reconciliation between Clarissa and the Harlowe Family

may urge Uncle Harlowe to join her in favoring Clarissa L174

Mrs. Norton will apply to her on Clarissa's behalf L179

suspecting Clarissa of wanting reconciliation so she can resume her estate L182

relations

daughter of the old viscount L27

Aunt Hervey's sister L433, L500

Brookland, Sir Josias, her uncle L507

HARLOWE, MRS. CHARLOTTE, Clarissa's mamma

sacrifice

mentioned as L47

servants

Shorey

delivering letters and messages between Clarissa and Mamma L16, L18, L22, L25, L41, L80

in whose presence Clarissa must say farewell to Hannah L23

delivering letters between Clarissa and Lovelace L25.2, L26

reporting church scene to Lovelace's discredit L36, L40

sibling rivalry

What a barbarous parent was I, to let two angry children make me forget that I was mother to a third L503

title

daughter of the old viscount L27

born a lady L60.1

visits

to Mrs. Norton, may visit Mrs. Norton to read Clarissa's letter L376

HARLOWE, MISS CLARISSA

abduction of Clarissa

 interviews with Lovelace in the garden L35, L36, L61, L62, L223
 dining in the ivy summer-house, waiting for Lovelace L91, L103
 your Clarissa Harlowe is gone off with a man L92, L127
 I cannot go with you L94
 I will sooner die than go with you L94
 I am resolved not to go with you L94
 Unhand me this moment L94
 her key left inside lock, indicating she left by her own consent L95
 grief stricken at her flight, her regrets L97, L243
 tricked into flight, never intending to go off with Lovelace L98, L101, L181, L253
 writing to Arabella for clothes, books, and money L98, L124
 her letter of countermand disregarded by Lovelace L99
 no one will believe she went unwillingly L100
 fearing to say she was carried off against her will L101, L104, L121
 family will not send her things L111, L112
 her suspicions of Leman's role L113
 April 10, the date she left her father's house, inscribed on her coffin L451

accidents

 bloodying her nose on the edge of the chair L267

accomplishments see also **education**

 harpsichord, music L54, L182, L529
 needlework L79, L147, L182, L529
 drawing L86
 writing, letter writing, her natural talent L86, L486, L529
 her eloquence and oratory L263, L395
 her superior talents L301
 French, Italian, Latin L529

address, forms of

 your servant, to James L75
 your servant, to Captain Tomlinson L243, L245

address to Clarissa by Mr. Robert Lovelace

 gossip that she has stolen Lovelace from Arabella L1, L2, L3
 recovering from his rejection by Arabella, Lovelace turns his attention to Clarissa L3
 supported by Lord M. L3
 his unwanted visits to Clarissa at Anna's L3, L4, L6, L7
 her opinion of Lovelace L40
 Clarissa's favor with Lovelace's relations L40
 resenting his insistence and insolence L64
 lending an ear to Lovelace's address L306

address to Clarissa by Mr. Roger Solmes see also **suitors to Harlowe, Miss Clarissa**, *Solmes, Mr. Roger*

 encouraged by her family
  to thwart Lovelace L6, L7
  Solmes introduced to Clarissa L7
  offer formally made to Clarissa by Aunt Hervey L8
  his offer accepted by the family in her absence L8, L20
 settlements
  mentioned L8, L56, L85, L90.1
  and Clarissa's estate, remaining in the family L13, L17
  terms L16, L17, L32.4, L41.1
  required to sign L20, L52.1, L83, L85
  concluded L39
  jewels for Clarissa L41.1, L90.1
  articles, license, settlements L83, L85

HARLOWE, MISS CLARISSA

address to Clarissa by Mr. Roger Solmes (cont.)

    her rejection of Solmes

        her disgust, rudeness, and firm rejection L7, L8, L16, L21

        her reasons L19, L20, L32.3, L78

        preferring death L36, L39, L45, L90, L94

        refusing to see Solmes L41

        confrontational meeting with Solmes, her objections to him L78

        refusing to sign parchments L83, L144

    family's intimidations

        confined until she agrees to marry Solmes L8, L21, L24.1, L25

        promoted by James and Arabella, taunting and conspiring L13, L53, L75, L83

        family united against her L14

        begging Mamma not to be married to Solmes L16–L20

        begging James to cease his hostile ways L24.2, L25.3

        changing her tactics to prefer Lovelace L29

        begging Uncle John to influence Papa L32.1

        begging Solmes to discontinue his suit L33.1

        offering to give Solmes to Arabella L36, L60.2

        wedding, at Antony's chapel L41.2, L50.1, L51.1, L51.2, L53, L54.1, L55, L61–L63, L83

        offering to seek refuge elsewhere L42, L45, L53.1

        altercation with Arabella L42

        begged by Aunt Hervey to comply L44, L45, L84

        begging parents in a letter to James, as they will receive none from her L51.2

        offering to rid them of Lovelace, if the family will rid her of Solmes L59.2

        Clarissa drawing Betty out on the family's plans L63

        kneeling at Papa's door, James letting her fall in head first L78

        hiding from her family in the garden L80

        believing her family would not follow through on the Solmes plan L94

age see also **birthday**

    James many years older L9

    eighteen years old L52.1, L60, L406

    younger by near a third than James L53.1

    her good fortune for eighteen out of nineteen years L229.1, L362, L376, L458

    under twenty years L234, L349

    born within a few days of Tommy Norton L301

    at eighteen years, enabled by her grandfather to make her will L400

    at eighteen, not having years of discretion L429

    when she is twenty-one the family would send her her estate L429

    Clarissa was twelve when Morden left England seven years ago L442, L474

    year of her birth omitted from the inscription on her coffin L451

    nineteen years old L451, L453, L454, L464, L492

airings and walks

    her morning and evening airings L63, L69, L75

    walking in Mrs. Sorlings's garden with Lovelace L126

    in a coach with Lovelace and the nymphs L210

    walking on Hampstead heath with Lovelace L210, L247, L248

    airing alone with Lovelace, in a chariot L218

    walking in Mrs. Moore's garden with Lovelace L248, L253

    airing with Mrs. Lovick and Mr. and Mrs. Smith in a coach L399

    an airing cancelled L399

    taking an airing L436, L440

aliases see also **correspondence, Harlowe, Miss Clarissa with Anna,** aliases

    Atkins, Mrs. Mary L318

    Beaumont, Miss Laetitia L155, L229, L229.1, L239

HARLOWE, MISS CLARISSA

aliases (cont.)

    Clark, Mrs. Rachel L295, L298

    Lucas, Mrs. Harriot (or Mrs. Harry Lucas) L230, L238, L251

    Salcomb, Mrs. Dorothy L304

    fictitious names no longer needed L338

angel see also **divine qualities; example; fall; light; sacrifice; suffering; trials; virgin**

    Clarissa as L31, L33.3, L34, L94, L97, L99, L110, L120, L138, L153, L157.1, L158, L169, L182, L187, L194, L199, L201, L202, L207, L216, L222, L225, L228, L233, L234, L237, L239, L243, L244, L245, L259, L266, L271, L274, L277, L281, L294, L321, L323, L324, L330, L333, L339, L349, L371, L399, L418, L419, L426, L439, L440, L446, L449, L470, L474, L497, L499, L502, L511, L519, L537

    fallen angel, poor fallen angel L78, L357

    angelic delicacy L124

    trials proving her woman or angel L157.1

    angelic L286

    angel, not a woman L303

    saint and angel L339

    angelic lady L366

    forgiving angel L412

    a companion for angels L441

    angelic sufferer L467

    angelic sister L472

    angel of light L494

animals see also **prey**

    a bird caught in snares L22

    visiting her poultry, forbidden L25, L60, L62, L69, L75, L80, L103

    vile reptile, Solmes as L36

    wild oats, and black oxen L44, L44n1

    bird of Minerva [screech owl], its whooting L54

    Arabella selecting Clarissa's poultry for James to take to Scotland L75

    vultures, hawks, kites, and other villainous birds of prey, parents protecting against L133

    an eel L158.1

    bird dying with grief at being caught, a bird caught L170, L201

    a sweet lamb L172

    lion-hearted lady L201

    a doe from Mother *Damnable*'s park, a deer L228, L419

    dog in the manger L232

    awakened by birds L247

    parable of the lady and the lion L261 Paper III

    canker-worm, moth, caterpillar, Lovelace as L261 Paper VII

    wolf, Lovelace as, and Clarissa the lamb L269

    chicken of a gentleman, Lovelace as, Clarissa a tiger of a lady L276

    prey of a vulture's rapacious talons L333

    crowned serpent, on Clarissa's coffin L451

    a poisonous serpent, Lovelace as L458

    reptile pride of seduction L486.1

apothecaries

    Goddard, Mr. L343

        sent for L333, L336, L338, L340

        calling in Dr. H. L340

        visiting Clarissa L365, L426, L440, L452, L457, L473

        his regimen L366

        bequest of Clarissa, fifteen guineas for a ring L507

arrest of Clarissa

    arrested by two sheriff's officers, with a writ against her L330, L333

HARLOWE, MISS CLARISSA

arrest of Clarissa (cont.)

Lovelace asking Belford to go free her L330

her arrest a mistake L331

as reported by Belford to Lovelace L333

causing her ill health L347, L364, L371

Lovelace innocent of Clarissa's arrest L358, L373

as told to Mrs. Norton L362

arrival of Morden from Florence, *anticipated*

mentioned L25, L36, L52, L57, L62, L69, L73, L76, L81, L85, L101, L129, L137, L138, L145, L185, L199, L200, L319

offering to go to Morden in Florence L42

his arrival meaning Clarissa's independence L53, L152

Clarissa wishing to write to him L86

Lovelace offering to take Clarissa to him L124

his footman, perhaps, appearing at Mrs. Sinclair's L213, L214

art references see also **miniatures**; **pictures**

Highmore, Joseph, his picture of Clarissa in the Vandyke taste L147, L147n1

Vandyke, Sir Anthony L147

authority

Clarissa respecting Papa's L4

banishment

banished from Papa's presence L25.4

turned out of doors L47, L51, L53.1, L59.4

may not remain at Harlowe Place L54.1, L59.3, L78

siblings not sorry to drive her out L69

giving up her keys L78, L91

driven out of paradise, of her home L98, L223

renounced by family, cast from their hearts L147, L307

going abroad rather than returning to Harlowe Place L248

family proposing Clarissa board with Mr. Hartley's friend in Pennsylvania L429

wanting Clarissa to go to some one of the colonies L443

Bath stone

Clarissa compared L245, L245fn

beer see **drink**

bequests of Clarissa see also **executors**; **will**

to her minister, fifteen guineas for a ring L507

to twenty poor people, five pounds L507

to Poor's Fund, proceeds from sale of grandmother's jewels L507

to servants at Harlowe Place, ten pounds each L507

to servants of Mrs. and Miss Howe, thirty guineas L507

to Alston, Miss Fanny, five guineas for a ring L507

to Barnes, Betty, sum of ten pounds L507

to Belford, Mr. John, one hundred guineas and twenty guineas for a ring L507

to Biddulph, Miss Rachel, five guineas for a ring L507

to Burton, Hannah, sum of fifty pounds L507

to Campbell, Miss Cartwright, five guineas for a ring L507

to Goddard, Mr., fifteen guineas for a ring L507

to H., Dr. R., twenty guineas for a ring L507

to Harlowe, Mr. Antony, family plate L507

to Harlowe, Mrs. Charlotte

picture of Clarissa in the Vandyke taste, bequeathed Aunt Hervey, or Mamma L507, L510.3

her book of Meditations, bequeathed Mrs. Norton, Mamma wanting the original L507, L510.3

needlework L510.3

to Harlowe, Mr. James, Sen., real estate L507

HARLOWE, MISS CLARISSA

bequests of Clarissa (cont.)
 to Harlowe, Mr. John, family pictures L507
 to Hervey, Miss Dolly
  watch, equipage, her head-dress, ruffles, gown, and petticoat L507
  twenty-five guineas for a ring L507
  harpsichord, chamber-organ, and music books L507
  her books L507
  Morden presenting her with Clarissa's jewels L520
 to Hervey, Mrs. Dorothy
  picture of Clarissa in the Vandyke taste, unless Mamma wants it L507, L510.3
  fifty guineas for a ring L507
 to Hickman, Mr. Charles
  returning her miniature of Anna to Hickman L476, L507
  fifteen guineas for a ring with Clarissa's hair L507
 to Howe, Miss Anna
  fifteen guineas for a ring with Clarissa's hair L507
  best diamond ring L507
  needlework L507
  her whole length picture L507
  her correspondence, sent by Belford L507, L521
  Clarissa's Memorandum book L510.3
 to Howe, Mrs. Annabella, twenty-five guineas for a ring L507
 to Lewen, Dr. Arthur, or his daughter, twenty guineas for a ring L507
 to Lloyd, Miss Biddy, five guineas for a ring L507
 to Lovelace's family, twenty guineas for enamel rings with Clarissa's hair in crystal L507
 to Lovick, Mrs.
  some books L507
  linen and laces L507
  twenty guineas L507
  copy of her book of Meditations L507
 to Morden, Colonel William
  needlework L507
  rose diamond ring L507
  monies accrued her estate since Grandfather's death L507
  miniature of Clarissa set in gold L507
 to Norton, Mrs. Judith
  thirty guineas, her and her son for mourning L487, L507
  sum of six hundred pounds L507
  clothing L507
  her book of Meditations, Mamma wanting the original L507, L510.3
 to Sarah, Smith's servant, fifteen guineas L507
 to Shelburne, Ann, her nurse, ten guineas L507
 to Smith, Mr., ten guineas L507
 to Smith, Mrs., linen and laces, and 20 guineas L507
Bible
 given Clarissa to read by Mrs. Rowland L333, L334, L336
 doubling down pages at the *Book of Job*, *Ecclesiasticus* L333
biblical references see also **God, references to**
 generally
  I wept L17, L20, L94
  casting the first stone L78
  Old Law, on whose vows shall be binding L88, L89, L89fn
  I have cleared them of blame and taken it upon myself L94
  driven out of paradise L98

HARLOWE, MISS CLARISSA

biblical references, generally (cont.)

>her fall L118, L144, L169, L171, L324, L359, L399, L429
>
>lamb, Clarissa as L172, L515
>
>Lovelace, her Judas protector L227.4
>
>Lovelace holding on to her gown L274
>
>wishing to kiss the hem of Mamma's garment L377
>
>recourse to Scriptures to calm her L399
>
>ascending into Heaven in Lovelace's dream L417
>
>returning to her father's house L421.1, L440, L442, L446, L449, L486, L510.4
>
>Cain's curse, Lovelace having L458, L458n2
>
>Clarissa's death reclaiming Lovelace L467

>Old Testament references
>
>>*Leviticus* 18:21, Moloch-deity L57
>>
>>*Numbers* 30:16, being yet...in her father's house L89
>>
>>*Deuteronomy* 32:35, Vengeance is mine L490, L490n1
>>
>>*2 Samuel* 1:26, quoted on friendship between David and Jonathan L359, L359n1
>>
>>*2 Kings*
>>
>>>9:20, Jehu-driving L53
>>>
>>>23:10, Moloch-deity L57
>>
>>*Job*
>>
>>>her impenetrable afflictions given to her by God L266
>>>
>>>29:2–6, in my father's house L359, L359n1
>>>
>>>30:23, quoted on approaching death L359, L359n2
>>>
>>>some verses forming Clarissa's Meditation L364, L364n2
>>>
>>>reading *Job* L371
>>>
>>>compared to Job L371
>>>
>>>9:20, quoted L379, L379n1
>>>
>>>31:35, 36, 34, adapted L379, L379n2
>>>
>>>6:27, quoted L389, L389n1
>>>
>>>19:2; 6:14, etc., in her Meditation L413
>>>
>>>*Job*, her favorite L416
>>>
>>>iii:17, quoted on Clarissa's coffin L451
>>>
>>>xv:31, 32, 33, quoted L507
>>>
>>>20:5; 18:11, 12, quoted L510.4, L510.4n1
>>
>>*Psalms*
>>
>>>verses from, making up Aug. 21 Meditation L418
>>>
>>>cxvi:7, 8, quoted on Clarissa's coffin L451
>>>
>>>ciii:15, 16, quoted on Clarissa's coffin L451
>>>
>>>119:71, It is good for me that I was afflicted L481, L481n2
>>
>>*Proverbs* 27:5, faithful are the wounds of a friend L309, L309n1
>>
>>*Ecclesiastes* 7:1, quoted L492, L492n1
>>
>>*Ecclesiasticus*
>>
>>>37:13,14, quoted L89
>>>
>>>6:16, quoted L149, L149n1
>>>
>>>41:4, quoted L492, L492n1
>
>New Testament references
>
>>*Romans* 12:19, Vengeance is mine L490, L490n1
>>
>>*I Corinthians* 15:55, Oh death, where is thy sting L481, L481n1
>>
>>*2 Corinthians* 9:7, on the cheerful giver, quoted by Melvill in his eulogy L504

birthday see also **age**

>July 24th L358fn, L361, L364, L378
>
>her last birthday L380

black

>wild oats, and black oxen L44, L44n1

HARLOWE, MISS CLARISSA

black (cont.)

    black as appearances are L308

    a black affair, given Clarissa to make her sleep L346

    Meditation stitched to the bottom of Letter 402 in black silk L402

    who can touch pitch and not be defiled L440

    black clouds of despondency L440

    black cloth covering Clarissa's coffin L451

    with her will a parcel of letters sealed with three black seals L486

    preamble to her will attached on black silk L507

black wax see **sealings**

blessings

    the poor blessing her, praying for her L177, L301

    wanting Papa's blessing L360, L379

    begging a blessing upon both Hickman and Anna L366

    wanting her parents' last blessing L380, L382, L399, L403, L407, L429, L459, L475

    asking Mamma's blessing L391, L393

    blessing Belford L440

    blessing Anna L458, L473.1, L473.2

    being blessed by Dr. H. and the minister L473

    blessing all her family L481

    blessing Morden and Belford L481

blindness

    her sight failing L460

    unable to read Anna's letter L473

    her sight gone L481

blood

    inquisition made for her blood, though she die by her own hand L266

    bloodying her nose on the edge of the chair L267

    Mrs. Howe's reproofs drawing blood L297

    Mrs. Norton's heart bleeding for Clarissa L301

    her bleeding heart L307, L380, L489

books

    Thomas à Kempis, Arabella borrowing from Clarissa L75, L77

    requesting her books after flight, will not be sent L98, L102, L147

    procured for her by Belford, at Mrs. Sinclair's L131, L155

        pieces of devotion L154

        Addison's *Works* L155

        Bishop of Man's *A Sacramental Piece* L155, L155n1

        Mr. Cibber's *The Careless Husband* L155, L155n1

        Dryden's *Miscellanies* L155

        Gauden, Dr., Bishop of Exeter, *A Piece* L155, L155n1

        Inett's *Devotions* L155

        Nelson's *Feasts and Fasts* L155

        Pope's *Works* L155

        Rowe's *Plays* L155

        Shakespeare's *Plays* L155

        Sharp's *Sermons* L155

        South's *Sermons* L155

        Stanhope's *Gospels* L155

        Steele's *Plays* L155

        Swift's *Works* L155

        Tatlers, *Spectators*, and *Guardians* L155

        Telemachus (in French and in English) L155, L155n1

        Tillotson's *Sermons* L155

HARLOWE, MISS CLARISSA

books (cont.)

    sent by Anna

        Norris, John, *Miscellanies* L148

        returning Anna's Norris L149, L150, L156

        Lovelace *out-Norrised* L198, L199, L215

    sent by James

        Drexelius on Eternity L173, L177

        Practice of Piety L173, L177

        Francis Spira L173, L177

    bequeathed Dolly L507

breakfast see **meals, breakfast**

bribes see also **contrivances of Lovelace**, contrivance of the promissory note

    bribing Dorcas with a promissory note L269, L279, L280, L281

burial of Clarissa see also **funeral of Clarissa**; **grave**

    wishing to be buried with her ancestors L486

    in the family vault at Grandfather's feet L486.2

    Lovelace wanting to embalm her L496, L497

    Lovelace wishing to bury her in his family vault between his parents L497

    Lovelace wanting her heart in a golden receptacle L497

    carried down into the burial vault L504

Cain's curse

    Lovelace having L458, L458n2

chair see **transportation**

character

    her prudence L1, L39, L105, L207, L234, L339, L371, L408, L427

    self-examination L19, L82, L94

    prodigy L27

    loyalty to family L31, L44, L59

    witch L42, L215

    description generally L56

    little rogue L99, L106, L439

    steadiness and punctilio L100, L248

    tennis-ball L132

    description by Belford L143, L336, L481

    superior to Lovelace L145, L248, L263

    genteel, open, cheerful, modest, poise, grace, dignity L157.1, L182, L203.2, L216, L222, L225, L229.1, L339, L399, L427

    over-niceness L95, L142, L167, L194, L226, L227.3, L229.1, L233, L245, L248, L268, L323

    description by Anna L177, L529

    description by Mamma L182

    pride and joy of the family L182

    superior to her siblings L182

    Lovelace's fruit L187.1–L187.4

    not a hoyden L201

    charming icicle or frost-piece L219, L220, L371

    Bath stone, Clarissa compared L245, L245fn

    account by Lovelace L252

    compared to Anna L252

    worthy to be Lord M.'s niece L261 Paper VIII

    superior talents L301

    her rank, fortune, talents, and virtue reduced by Lovelace L333

    her piety, dignity, family, fortune, and purity of heart L339

    talent at moving the passions L374, L376, L377, L402, L459

    Uncle Harlowe's doting-piece L420

HARLOWE, MISS CLARISSA

character (cont.)

    account by Morden L442, L519

    triumphant subduer L470

charities see **Poor's Fund**

church

    requesting permission to attend church, refused by James L22, L22.2

    wishing to attend church in London L157, L158.1

    not allowed to attend church without Lovelace L178

    attending church without Lovelace L198, L200

    attending church with Mrs. Moore L248, L251

    dressing as if to go to church L293

    attending church, chapel L320, L399

    attending morning prayers at the Covent Garden church L329, L330, L440

    attending churches near Smith's L368

    going in a chair to prayers at St. Dunstan's L426

    attending devotions L441

    her habit of taking a sedan or chair to morning prayers L444

classical references

    the old Roman and his lentils L20, L20n1

    like another Helen...unable to bear the reflection L40

    Virgil's *Georgic*, translated by Dryden L50, L50.2

    Scipio, wrongly accused L157, L157n1

    Sophocles, *Oedipus*, adapted by Dryden and Lee, quoted L174, L174n1, L261 Paper X, L261 Paper Xn1

    Juvenal, *Satire XV*, translated by Nahum Tate, quoted L217.3, L217.3n1

    Lucretia

        Clarissa as L222, L515

        cost to a Tarquin L261.1, L261n2

    Nemesis, Clarissa as Lovelace's L223

    siren L228

    Caesar

        stabbed by Brutus, Clarissa compared L336

        the die is thrown L362

    more pure than a vestal L346

    Queen of Carthage, Clarissa as L370, L370n1

    her death compared to Socrates' L451

    manes of Clarissa L497, L536

clergymen

    Lovelace will visit Clarissa and bring a parson to marry them L383

    parish minister visiting Clarissa L440, L454, L457, L467, L473

    minister bequeathed fifteen guineas for a ring L507

clothing see **costume**

coffin

    coffin, a flower bed, mentioned by Lovelace L313

    ordering, at the undertaker's in Fleet Street L440

    delivered to Smith's L450

    devices and inscriptions: Here the wicked cease from troubling L450, L451, L500

    expensive L451

    her coffin near the window like a harpsichord L457, L474

    her house, called by Clarissa L457, L474, L486

    filled with flowers and aromatic herbs L487, L495, L501

    taken from the hearse and borne by six neighborhood maidens into the hall L500

    carried from the hall into her parlour L500

    lid unscrewed so family can view the body L501

HARLOWE, MISS CLARISSA

cohabitation

> if she refuse to cohabitate, Lovelace will marry her L194

collation at Mrs. Sinclair's

> a murdered evening L159
>
> reported by Belford L222

conflict between Harlowe Family and Clarissa

> family united against her in the Solmes affair L6, L14
>
> Harlowe Family and motivating forces L8, L13
>
> blaming all on James L9, L112
>
> made an instrument of revenge against Lovelace L13
>
> How impolitic in them all to join two people in one interest whom they wish for ever to keep asunder L14
>
> surely *they* will yield L14
>
> recounting measures taken by family against her L32.3, L112

constables

> constable called as Clarissa shouts from Mrs. Sinclair's window L264
>
> *Rowland, Mr.*, the officer L333
>
>> Mrs. Rowland, his wife L333
>>
>>> offering Clarissa tea, bread, butter L333
>>>
>>> giving Clarissa a Bible to read L333, L334, L336
>>
>> their maid, in whose bed Clarissa lay L333
>>
>> calling an apothecary L333
>>
>> fearing Clarissa will die in his house L333
>>
>> his house described, miserably poor L334, L336
>>
>> Clarissa's gaoler L336

contrivances of Clarissa see also **father's house**

> convincing Lovelace she will return to her father's house L421.1, L440, L442, L446, L449, L486, L510.4
>
> Charlotte Montague recognizing Clarissa's reference to her father's house L439
>
> contriving to be out when Lovelace visits L443

contrivances of Lovelace see also **abduction of Clarissa**; **rape of Clarissa**

> contrivance of sparing Rosebud L34, L35, L70, L71, L72, L73
>
> contrivance of pretending marriage to Clarissa L156, L186, L215, L233, L235, L281
>
> contrivance of the bedfellows L162, L164, L167, L169, L229.1, L248
>
> contrivance of Captain Tomlinson and Uncle Harlowe's birthday L216, L219, L245, L284
>
> contrivances of the impersonators
>
>> Mrs. Bevis impersonating Clarissa to receive hers from Anna L251, L318, L320
>>
>> impersonators of Lady Betty and Charlotte L256, L256.1, L263, L266
>
> contrivance of the promissory note L269, L279, L280, L281
>
> contrivance of the escape L273

cordials see **medications**

corpse

> Clarissa as L333
>
> lovely corpse L486
>
> her corpse put into a hearse L495
>
> face cloth on the corpse L502

correspondence, Harlowe, Miss Clarissa see also **Meditations**; **Memorandum book**; **writing**

> sent to Mrs. Norton, to help tell her story L409, L433
>
> bequeathed Anna L507, L521
>
> posthumous, eleven letters sent after her death, delivered by Belford's Harry L486, L494

correspondence, Harlowe, Miss Clarissa with Anna

> aliases *see also* **aliases**
>
>> Beaumont, Miss Laetitia L155, L229, L229.1, L239
>>
>> Clark, Mrs. Rachel L295
>>
>> Lucas, Mrs. Harriot L230, L238
>>
>> fictitious names no longer needed L338

HARLOWE, MISS CLARISSA

correspondence, Harlowe, Miss Clarissa with Anna (cont.)

 conveyed by

  Hannah L9, L14, L19, L20, L23

  Robert L9, L16, L46, L58, L65, L69, L74, L87

  Joseph Leman L35

  Mrs. Knollys L93, L98, L100

  Mrs. Greme L98

  Mr. Osgood L98, L141

  Mrs. Sorlings L100

  Mr. Hickman L101

  Grimes L119, L120, L127, L233, L238, L238.1

  Mr. Wilson L148, L150, L166, L196

   giving letters directly to Lovelace L217

   forgery of Anna's Letter 229.1, now Letter 238.1, at Wilson's L238.1

  Lovelace L165

  Rogers L251

  Belford L334

  Harry L457, L471

 forbidden

  becoming secret L8, L9

  continuance in doubt L92

  advising Anna to discontinue L101, L146

  interference from Mrs. Howe

   informing Harlowe Family of their secret correspondence L50.1

   Clarissa forbidden further correspondence with Anna L163, L168

   Clarissa's Letter 295 to Anna intercepted by Mrs. Howe L296

   called evil communication by Mrs. Howe L296

  by Lovelace L261, L282

  by Mrs. Sinclair L279

 hidden

  her pockets concealing letters L174.3

  hiding letters in her stays L198

  locking letters in a wainscot box L210

correspondence, Harlowe, Miss Clarissa with Anna, forged by Lovelace

 Letter 229.2 from 'Clarissa,' acknowledging receipt of Letter 229.1 from Anna L229

 Letter 240.1 from 'Clarissa,' acknowledging receipt of Anna's Letter 229.1 rewritten by Lovelace and sent
  as Letter 239.1 to Clarissa L240

correspondence, Harlowe, Miss Clarissa with Anna, intercepted by Lovelace

 Lovelace attempting to seize a letter from Clarissa L175, L176

 Lovelace reading transcripts of Anna's letters (188 and 196) for Clarissa L198, L218

 Wilson giving letters for Clarissa directly to Lovelace L217

 Letter 229.1 for Clarissa delivered by Collins to Wilson's, Wilson giving it directly to Lovelace L229

 Letter 231.2 from Clarissa to Anna, given by Will to Lovelace L231, L231.1

 Will stealing from Grimes Clarissa's to Anna, giving it to Lovelace L233, L235, L238

 Tomlinson returning Letter 229.1 from Anna, stolen and rewritten by Lovelace, to Wilson's L238

 Lovelace trying to intercept Anna's next L239

 Clarissa's to Anna intercepted by Lovelace, substituting Letter 240.1, his forgery L240

 Anna's intercepted by Lovelace L250, L251

 suspecting Lovelace of confiscating Anna's letters L276

 Lovelace intercepting Clarissa's to Anna L284

 Anna's Letter 229.1, Letter 252.1, Letter 275.1 intercepted by Lovelace L310, L311

 Clarissa returning Anna's Letter 239.1, her Letter 229.1 rewritten by Lovelace L311

 Belford refusing to intercept Anna's to Clarissa L341

HARLOWE, MISS CLARISSA

correspondence, Harlowe, Miss Clarissa with Lovelace

    beginning explained, history of, recounted L3, L112

    subverted by Lovelace L3

    her fear of breaking it off L3, L4, L17, L22, L25.1, L26, L36, L57

    encouraged by Mamma L4, L17, L25.2, L112

    forbidden L4, L17, L25.1

    continuance suspected by family L6, L10

    contents recounted to Anna, his letters forwarded to Anna L17, L80

    signed by Lord M. L25.1

    conveyed by Leman L35

    realizing she should not have corresponded with him L94, L98, L101, L110, L121, L306

    Clarissa and Lovelace, a pair of scribbling lovers L105

    her motivation to prevent mischief between her family and Lovelace L229.1

    returning to Lovelace their correspondence L365

correspondence, Harlowe, Miss Clarissa with others

    her letter to Lady Drayton on the consequences of severity in parents L58, L59, L90

    her suspicions of the sudden letters from Lovelace's family L244

    not daring to correspond with her family L304

    with Dr. Blome, Mr. Arnold, Mr. Tompkins, bequeathed Anna L507

costume

    women's fondness for fine clothing L69

    her flowered silver suit L69

    clothing requested after flight L98, L102

    description of her clothing, head-dress, lawns, mob L99

    her dress praised by Lovelace L123

    needing clothing L123, L125

    will be sent to Clarissa by Mamma L147

    receiving her clothes L165, L173, L177

    her pockets concealing letters L174.3

    her elegance in dress L182, L529

    Lovelace offering Clarissa clothes L186

    dressing for the day by breakfast, to keep up forms and distance L194

    having two suits L202

    Lovelace drawing aside the handkerchief to kiss her breast L220

    her night head-dress L225

    escaping from the fire in her under petticoat, bosom half-open, and shoes L225, L230

    escaping from Mrs. Sinclair's in a brown lustring nightgown, a beaver hat, a black riband about her neck, blue knots on her breast, a quilted petticoat of carnation-coloured satin, a rose-diamond ring L228

    little parcel tied up in a handkerchief L228

    threw her handkerchief over her head and neck and sobbed L235

    put a parcel into her pocket L235

    Mrs. Bevis may bring Clarissa's clothes from Mrs. Sinclair's L245

    attending church in her everyday worn clothes L248

    tearing off her head-clothes, ruffle torn L256

    her hood on and a parcel tied in a handkerchief, trying to leave Mrs. Sinclair's L262

    wearing a white damask night-gown, a white handkerchief in hand L263

    will not put off her clothes any more at Mrs. Sinclair's L264, L276

    her apron over her head L264

    disordered head-dress, torn ruffles, after attempted escape L267

    Lovelace holding on to her gown L274

    her rustling silks L281

    key to her chamber door at Mrs. Sinclair's in her pocket L281

    Mrs. Dolins, Clarissa's mantua-maker L293

    giving Mabel her brown lustring gown and quilted coat L293

HARLOWE, MISS CLARISSA

costume (cont.)

gown must be altered for Mabel as sleeves, robings, and facings are above her station L293

Clarissa slipping on Mabel's gown and petticoat over her own white damask, and Mabel's hood, short cloak and ordinary apron to escape Mrs. Sinclair's L293

ruff about her neck, hanging sleeve coat L294

her clothes and the lustring, left at Mrs. Sinclair's, to be put away and sent to Clarissa when her whereabouts is known L294, L307, L330

her dress not appropriate for Leeson's L314

her laces cut to prevent fainting L314, L334

pulling off her head-dress, tearing her ruffles L314

wearing an ordinary gown by way of disguise L320

her face half hid by her mob, careless of her appearance L320

her clothes to be sold by Mrs. Sinclair to pay the debt L333

my father loved to see me fine L333

her valuables and clothes sold to pay debts and burial L334, L340, L345, L347, L364, L365, L426

headdress a little discomposed L334

her white flowing robes L334

having no hoop on L334

her linen white, dressed in white damask L334

her clothes removed from Mrs. Sinclair's and taken to Smith's L336

her fine Brussels lace head L336

richness of her apparel L340

now having her clothes with her L362

ladies imitating her dress, giving fashion to the fashionable L399

in translucent white in Lovelace's dream, her azure robe with stars of embossed silver L417

trunks holding her apparel sealed up till opened as her will directs L460

in a white satin nightgown L471

dressed in virgin white L474

face cloth on the corpse L502

curses

Lovelace's

marriage to Lovelace bringing a curse on her children L359

cursed by Lovelace L395

Papa's

mentioned L146, L147, L152, L172, L173, L189, L191, L201, L216, L225, L226, L230, L235, L261 Paper II, L263, L272, L274, L333, L343, L347, L373, L443

his malediction coming true L243

his heavy curse L261 Paper II

following her into the next world L307

can neither live nor die under Papa's curse L307

wishing for revocation of Papa's malediction L308, L309, L320

taking Papa's imprecation to heart L308

weight of a parent's curse L318

writing to Arabella to ask that Papa's curse be revoked L348, L349, L360

Papa's imprecation weakening Clarissa further L351

asking Arabella to intercede in revoking the part of Papa's curse that relates to the hereafter, as she has already been punished in the here L363

his curse withdrawn L377, L378, L379

curses, Cain's curse

Lovelace having L458, L458n2

death

death, a devil, Clarissa's new lover L346

a journey L333, L349, L441

the end of her painful journey L492

HARLOWE, MISS CLARISSA

death of Harlowe, Miss Clarissa, *foreshadowed*
pleased God to have taken me in my last fever L2
fitter for the next world L10
beware the ides of March L10
dagger to the heart L16
rather die/be buried alive L17
bear...loss of life L20
choosing death rather than Solmes L36, L39, L41, L45, L90, L94
struck dead at the altar L41
fearing if she is turned out she will not see home again L59.4
dreaming she is murdered in a churchyard by Lovelace L84
they would all be glad I were dead—Indeed, I believe it L85
her closet nailed up L147
preferring to be wedded to her shroud rather than any man L149
a bird dying of grief at being caught and caged L170
family will not stir to save her life L183
would prefer death if she knew what Lovelace had in mind L222
Kill me! Kill me! life is a burden L225, L267
Lovelace dreaming he murders her L246
looking forward to death L261 Paper X, L261.1
inquisition will be made for her blood, though she die by her own hand L266
Some of those who will not stir to protect me living, will move heaven and earth to avenge me dead L266
Lovelace: if she die tomorrow...rather die married L268

death of Harlowe, Miss Clarissa, *anticipated* see also **health, declining and ending in death**
heart broken, she will live but a little while L268
wishing to die, I dare die L274, L276, L281
Mrs. Sinclair must let her out or bury her in the garden L293
not expecting to live long, will not recover L293, L333, L359, L395, L399, L418
when I am gone L307
country funeral and coffin, a flower bed, mentioned by Lovelace referring to a virgin L313
oh that I had dropped down dead upon the guilty threshold L314
death withheld from her, let me slide quietly into my grave L314, L315
her last scene, last closing scene, I am quite sick of life L318
will not long be Lovelace's sport or the sport of fortune L333
corpse, Clarissa as L333
starving herself, thoughts of suicide not purposely shortening her own life L333, L359
death to write Anna and ask for money to pay Mrs. Sinclair L333
wishing to die at Rowland's L334
choosing death over Lovelace L339, L359
her refuge must be death, seeking death L349, L358, L359, L371, L399
her disappointment causing her death L370
her death making Lovelace the most miserable man in the world L371
her fault can be expiated only by death L373
wishing to die in peace L386
three to four weeks to live, less than a week, a week, three days, a day or two L389, L426, L440, L461, L462, L467
Lovelace will marry her in the agonies of death L396
her exalted head among the stars L396
tottering on the brink of a grave L409
how this body clings L436
her preparation for death, indulging in thoughts of death L441, L451
date of her death inscribed on her coffin: 10 April L451
her death compared to Socrates' L451
Ann Shelburne, Mrs. Lovick, and Mrs. Smith to care for Clarissa's body after her death L457

HARLOWE, MISS CLARISSA

death of Harlowe, Miss Clarissa, *anticipated* (cont.)

    describing her gradual death, progressive weakness L464

    forebodings of happiness L465

    her death owing to female willfulness, revenge, stronger than desire for life L472

    her last hours compared to Belton's L473

    will not see tomorrow night L473

    will not live till morning L474

    her sight gone L481

    Oh death, where is thy sting L481, L481n1

death of Harlowe, Miss Clarissa

    dead L477

    death scene L481

    time of death, 40 minutes after six o'clock in the afternoon L481, L486.2

    death so lovely L486

    year of her death not given in her will L507, L507fn

    date of death Sept. 7th L511

    compared to that of Belton, Tomlinson, and Mrs. Sinclair L514

death of Harlowe, Miss Clarissa, avenged

    Belford would avenge L258

    Some of those who will not stir to protect me living, will move heaven and earth to avenge me dead L266

    disclaiming vengeance L276

    the law, her resource and refuge L281

    appealing to God to avenge her wrongs L307

    Lovelace to feel the vengeance of her friends L336

    fearing Morden will avenge her L409, L433, L475, L517

    Morden having no title to avenge Clarissa's wrongs L474

    Morden considering vengeance L498

    avenged by Lovelace's conscience L518

    James will avenge Clarissa if Morden does not L519

    finally avenged by Morden L537

death of Harlowe, Miss Clarissa, causes

    that wasting grief will soon put a period to her days L222

    diagnosed with grief L338, L342

    heart-broken L339, L341

    Clarissa a love case L340

    her disorder in her head L340

    her ill health caused by her arrest and her family's implacableness L347, L364

    death from grief L467

despair

    her only fault L342

devils

    her honor inviolate in spite of men and devils L181

diary see **Memorandum book**

dinner see **meals, dinner**

disguises

    asking Anna to procure, to escape Harlowe Place L82

    as Mabel, to escape Mrs. Sinclair's L293, L294

    wearing an ordinary gown by way of disguise L320

divine qualities see also **angel**; **example**; **fall**; **light**; **sacrifice**; **suffering**; **trials**; **virgin**

    divine L31, L110, L201, L216, L286, L333, L348, L419

        divine lady L473, L487, L495

    goddess L31, L99, L105, L157.1, L158.1, L175, L191, L220, L243, L252

    nature to be servant to both Betty and Arabella L53

    her exalted head...among the stars L396

HARLOWE, MISS CLARISSA

divine qualities (cont.)

    beatifical spirit L440

    companionship with saints and angels L440

    as near perfection as any creature can be L459

dowry

    Lovelace's fortune sufficient L88

    Lovelace resigning her fortune, if she die issueless L383

dreams

    murdered in a churchyard by Lovelace L84

    a reverie, a waking dream L243

dress see **costume**

drink see also **food**; **meals**

    surprised by wine L311

    given table-beer, malt liquor L314

    milk was London milk L314

drops see **medications**

drugs see **medications**

duty

    to her grandfather L4

    to Papa L36

    example of failure to do one's duty L112

    dutiful L187, L367

    a breach in her duty L307

eavesdropping

    overhearing her siblings laughing L25, L53

    kneeling at Papa's closed door L78

    hiding from family in garden behind the yew hedge L80

    overhearing her siblings conspiring L83

    overhearing a contrived conversation at Mrs. Sinclair's L195, L196

education see also **accomplishments**

    book-learned and a scribbler L405

entangled

    how am I entangled L14

    more and more entangled L22

    so entangled, as Lovelace has entangled her L189

    so dreadfully entangled L308

escapes see also **contrivances of Lovelace**, contrivance of the escape

    attempted

        desperate to leave Mrs. Sinclair's for Mrs. Leeson's or Hampstead L256

        trying to escape Mrs. Sinclair's, shouting to passers-by L262, L264, L276

        Lovelace stopping her, bruising her hands and arms L266, L267

        Clarissa wishing to return to Mrs. Moore's at Hampstead L277, L278

    successful

        from Harlowe Place L92

        from Mrs. Sinclair's to Hampstead L228, L230

        from Mrs. Sinclair's to Smith's L291, L293

escutcheons

    her hearse not adorned by L500

estates see also **inheritances**; **trustees**

    arrears

        considerable sums accrued since Grandfather's death L202, L487

        Lovelace giving her all arrears in her father's hands for Mrs. Norton L207

        Clarissa to receive L458

        Morden giving to Belford L501

HARLOWE, MISS CLARISSA

estates, arrears (cont.)

        bequeathed Morden L507

     bequeathing, Clarissa's power to bequeath her estate L123, L400

     cause of all her misfortunes L230

     control of, withheld by family

        in Papa's power, her steward L2, L6, L10, L13, L19, L42, L376

        unless she marry Solmes L14, L20, L44

        ought to be in possession of thousands L376

        her fortune and estate withheld by her family L406, L437

        when she is twenty-one, the family would send her her estate L429

     control of, Clarissa resuming

        advised by Anna L15, L27, L49, L52, L100, L183

        litigating with her father may encourage Lovelace L28

        assistance available from Lovelace's family L49

        lacking support within her own family L52, L55

        advised by Lovelace L61, L142

        Morden may support L73

        advised by Dolly L78

        considered by Clarissa L80

        will not demand possession of L142

        asking Lovelace to avoid litigation with Papa L202

        in Lovelace's dream L271

        will not live to take possession of her independence L309

        Morden to put Clarissa into possession of her estate L455, L474

     disposition of, should she marry or die

        in settlements with Solmes, her estate to remain in family L13, L17

        if she should never marry, would go to James L56

        Clarissa's power to bequeath her estate L123, L400

        once married to Lovelace, her estate is his right L164

        inquired into by Lovelace's family in preparation for marriage L325

        not wanting Lovelace to have her estate L379

     forfeiting

        Clarissa offering to forfeit inheritance L42, L60.2

        giving up her estate and Solmes and ridding herself of Lovelace L60

        giving up her grandfather's bequest to appease her brother L174

        sacrifice of her estate not advised by Anna L177

        offers to defer to Papa if he will consider reconciliation L179

     jewels *see also* **jewels**; **rings**

        diamond necklace, solitaire, buckles given her by Sir Josias Brookland, proceeds of sale to estate L507

        her grandmother's, proceeds of sale of, to Poor's Fund, or estate, or Papa L507

     real estate

        after her flight, requesting to retire to L101, L102

        wishing to live upon her estate rather than marry Lovelace L248

        family expecting Clarissa to live at her grandfather's house L459

        bequeathed Papa L507

     value of

        her independent fortune L253

        her fortune the finest in the county L442

eulogy

     at the funeral, by Mr. Melvill L504

     by Anna L529

example see also **angel**; **divine qualities**; **fall**; **light**; **sacrifice**; **suffering**; **trials**; **virgin**

     Clarissa as L1, L39, L75, L110, L116, L120, L177, L246, L253, L260, L372, L456, L459, L508, L519

     a pattern for the rest L37, L296

HARLOWE, MISS CLARISSA

example (cont.)

example of failure to do one's duty L112

and as a warning to others L120, L317, L490

punished for example-sake L301

an exemplary life L308

in imitation of the sublimest exemplar L359

condescentions...for example's sake L467

executors see also **bequests of Clarissa; will**

to be Morden's heir and executrix L459

Belford, Mr. John

asking Belford to be her executor L379, L389, L391, L409

Belford her executor instead of Morden L413

advised by Mrs. Norton to change her executor to Morden L459

no time for joining Morden as co-executor with Belford L475

James asking Belford to relinquish the executorship L506

expiate

her fault expiated only by death L373

eye-beams

darting through Tomlinson L243

fainting see **illnesses**, fainting

fall see also **angel; divine qualities; example; light; sacrifice; suffering; trials; virgin**

Clarissa's mentioned L118, L144, L169, L171, L324, L359, L399, L429

fallen angel L78, L357

Anna's tears embalming a fallen blossom L473.2

family

marriage to Lovelace bringing a curse on her children L359

father's house see also **contrivances of Clarissa; journey, figurative**

only extremity would make her abandon her father's house L57

her decision not to leave her father's house L68

as if I left my father's house L73

the disgrace...of...quitting my father's house L80

quitting her father's house L81

all punctilio is at an end the moment you are out of your father's house L87, L89, L90

Numbers 30:16, being yet...in her father's house L89

oh that I were again in my father's house L94

wishing to be still in her father's house L98

driven out of her father's house L111

leaving her father's house L128

made to fly her father's house Ll42

Job 29:2–6, in my father's house L359, L359n1

April 10, the date she left her father's house, inscribed on her coffin L451

fearing Lovelace

fearing his violent temper L3, L64

I behold him now with fear L98

fearing Lovelace L204

flight see **abduction of Clarissa; escapes; journey**

flowers

her flowered silver suit L69

Clarissa, tender blossom L153

coffin, a flower bed, mentioned by Lovelace in reference to a virgin L313

her hand, the lily not of so beautiful a white L340

white lily inscribed on Clarissa's coffin L451

Anna's tears embalming a fallen blossom L473.2

her hands white as the lily L474

HARLOWE, MISS CLARISSA

flowers (cont.)

    Clarissa, flower of the world L501

food see also **drink**; **meals**

    the old Roman and his lentils L20

    Mrs. Sinclair offering Clarissa chocolate L178

    chicken soup ordered for supper L184

    taking chocolate for breakfast L216

    asks for three or four French rolls with butter and water L228, L228n1

    offered bread and butter and biscakes by Mrs. Moore L232

    bread and water only for dinner L235

    offering to pay for coffee, tea, chocolate, chicken but unable to eat L333

    drinking tea with bread and butter L333

    Dr. H. recommending

        cordials and nourishment L340

        weak jellies and innocent cordials L366

    Mr. Goddard recommending

        for breakfast, water-gruel, or milk pottage, or weak broth L366

        for dinner, dish of tea with milk in the afternoon L366

        for supper, sago L366

forgiveness

    Nothing shall ever make me forgive him...I so much to suffer through him L64

    for her family L307

    wanting Papa's forgiveness L309

    trying to pity Lovelace and forgive him L348, L359

    if Papa forgives her, she can learn to forgive Lovelace L348

    nothing can be more wounding to a spirit...than...forgiveness L360, L508

    her forgiveness of Lovelace L369, L399, L401, L427, L448, L467, L472, L481, L510.4

    writing to Mamma for blessing and forgiveness L391

    hoping for pardon L397

    Lovelace asking her forgiveness L397

    asking Lovelace's family to forgive him L398

    wishing last blessing and forgiveness L399

    forgiveness as consequence of her preparations for death L451

fortune see **estates**; **inheritances**

friends

    Alston, Miss Fanny L507

    Belford, Mr. John, now her warm friend L343

    Biddulph, Miss Rachel

        ball, Colonel Ambrose's, attending L367

        family, Sir Robert Biddulph, her father, where Clarissa met Patty Montague two years ago L233.3

        gossip, hearing from Miss Lardner that Clarissa is at Mrs. Sinclair's, telling Miss Lloyd L229.1

        mentioned L10, L37, L40

        names, called Miss Rachel Biddulph L507

        poetry, hers on the female character L2

        relations, cousin of Miss Lardner L229.1

        visits, to Miss Howe, to inquire about Clarissa L93

    Campbell, Miss Cartwright L507

    Campion, Miss L37, L40

    Drayton, Lady, Clarissa's letter to her on the consequences of severity in parents L58, L59, L90

    Drayton, Miss, Lady Drayton's daughter L58

    H., Dr. R., becoming a friend L441

    Lardner, Miss

        her footman appearing at Mrs. Sinclair's inquiring about Clarissa and Lovelace L213, L214

        a cousin of Miss Biddulph's L229.1

HARLOWE, MISS CLARISSA

friends, *Lardner, Miss* (cont.)

        seeing Clarissa alone at St. James's church and telling Miss Biddulph L229.1

        her servant following Clarissa back to Mrs. Sinclair's from church L229.1

        her information mentioned L316

    Lloyd, Miss Biddy

        ball, Colonel Ambrose's, attending L367

        friends, a favorite of Arabella L132

        gossip

            about Arabella and Lovelace L15

            telling Anna of James's plan to rescue Clarissa L132, L137, L148

            hearing from Miss Biddulph that Clarissa is at Mrs. Sinclair's L229.1

        influence, hers on Clarissa unwanted by the family L9

        mentioned L10, L37, L40, L93

        names, called Miss Biddy Lloyd L507

        servants, *Harriot*, her maid gossiping about Lovelace L15

        visits, to and from Anna L93, L473.1

    Wykes, Dorcas, called a friend, confiding in Dorcas L270, L271

friendship

    with Anna L1, L8, L11, L57, L89, L135, L174, L343, L473.1, L520

        advice to Anna on Hickman L55, L69, L73, L458

        her only friend L146, L295

        saving Anna from marrying a libertine L182, L355

        her love for Anna L343

    Ecclesiasticus 6:16 quoted on L149, L149n1

    Proverbs 27:5 faithful are the wounds of a friend L309, L309n1

    her opinion on ties of friendship L359

funeral of Clarissa see also **burial of Clarissa**; **grave**

    country funeral mentioned by Lovelace L313

    her valuables and clothes to be sold to pay her debts and burial L334

    funeral bell tolling at the parish church as the hearse passes L500

    text for funeral discourse, mentioned L501

    description of L504

    eulogy by Mr. Melvill L504

    eulogy quoting *2 Corinthians* 9:7 L504

    attended by distant relations Fuller and Allinson L504

    attended by Solmes, Mullins, Wyerley L504

gall

    my ink runs nothing but gall L52

    gall in her ink L311

gifts

    diamond necklace, solitaire, and buckles from Sir Josias Brookland L507

    her grandmother's jewels from Grandfather L507, L529

    rose diamond ring from Morden's father L507, L529

God, references to see also **biblical references**

    Providence L51.2, L63, L243, L486.1, L510.4

    my Maker L52, L467

    the Almighty L120, L471, L488, L510.4

    King and Maker of a thousand worlds L157

    Supreme Director L173

    the first gracious Planter L185

    Dispenser of all good L214

    the God within her exalted her L248

    Throne of Mercy L307

    Divine Wisdom L428

HARLOWE, MISS CLARISSA

God, references to (cont.)

>my blessed Redeemer L481
>Divine Grace L488
>HE L489
>Divine mercy L510.4
>God Almighty L518

gold

>some gold which she left behind L152
>pure gold from the assay, Clarissa as L323
>Lovelace wanting her heart in a golden receptacle L497
>miniature of Clarissa set in gold, bequeathed Morden L507

gossip

>that she has stolen Lovelace from Arabella L1, L2, L3
>mentioned L4
>her case widely discussed in public L80
>gossip of her aversion to Solmes L81
>talk of the county L85
>the mouth of common fame L92
>subject of open talk L392

grave see also **burial of Clarissa**; **funeral of Clarissa**

>let me slide quietly into my grave L315
>tottering on the brink of a grave L409
>I hope they bury all their resentments in my grave L465

habits

>seldom eating supper L155
>eating preferences L157
>passing Sundays by herself L200
>writing and reading half the night L224
>beholding the sun-rise L247
>an early riser L365
>daily routine L528, L529

hair see also **bequests of Clarissa**

>her natural ringlets not lately kembed L334
>bequeathing rings with her hair set in crystal L495
>Mrs. Norton cutting off four ringlets of Clarissa's hair L495
>Lovelace wanting a lock of Clarissa's hair L497
>Anna wanting a lock of Clarissa's hair L502

handwriting

>equal and regular hand L239
>her fine handwriting L323
>her charming hand L443

harpsichord

>accomplished at L54
>her coffin near the window like a harpsichord L457
>harpsichord, chamber-organ, and music books bequeathed Dolly L507

hartshorn see **medications**

hatred of Lovelace

>noted L71, L201, L263, L269, L277
>liking Lovelace, and could hate him L145
>despising Lovelace L202, L281

health

>her natural good constitution L320

health, declining and ending in death see also **death of Harlowe, Miss Clarissa,** *anticipated*

>ill from Arabella's letter and Papa's curses L152

HARLOWE, MISS CLARISSA

health, declining and ending in death (cont.)

very ill L201, L202, L243, L270, L313, L318, L327, L329, L333, L334, L336, L338, L339, L340, L342, L343, L346, L357, L372, L379, L391, L413, L435, L439, L440, L444, L458

insensible and stupefied since Tuesday morning L259

heavy torpid pain increasing L314

could not speak though eyelids moved L334

her limbs trembling L336, L471

recovery within her power L366

too ill to go out in a coach, going to water-side for a boat to escape Lovelace L416

shortness of breath L441, L452

two very severe fits L452

confined to her room L454

cannot hold a pen to answer Anna's letter L454

in convulsions L474

hearse

arriving at Harlowe Place at six in the afternoon L500

not adorned by escutcheons L500

heart-broken

or half-heart broken, by her father and Lovelace L370, L375, L376, L418, L426

heiress

Clarissa as L307, L459

heraldry see **escutcheons**; **lozenges**

historical references

Edward VI, and wooing L7, L7n1

Queen of Scots, Clarissa compared L370, L370n3

Duke of Luxemburgh, death bed wishes, Clarissa's compared L486, L486n1

Earl of Shrewsbury, losing his life in an act of vengeance, Morden compared L518, L518n1

Charles II, mentioned L518

Henry IV of France, Clarissa's manner of denying requests compared L529

honor

noted L1, L100

her honor inviolate in spite of men and devils L181

romantic value on her honor L259

Lovelace conspiring against her honor L261 Paper VIII

her honor lost, robbed of her honor L263, L267, L306, L311

defending her honor L281, L294

hour-glass

winged hour-glass on Clarissa's coffin L451

illnesses

fainting

on being commanded to marry Solmes L16

fearing loss of Mamma's love L18

after receiving letter from Arabella L149

after recognizing Lovelace at Mrs. Moore's L233

nearly fainting L313, L314

fainting away at the officer's house L333, L334

low and faint L338, L339

near fainting L426

fainting L440

fever

dangerous fever some time ago L39

violent fever L272

dangerous fever at nine years and at eleven years of age L374

headache L238, L245, L256, L333

HARLOWE, MISS CLARISSA

illnesses (cont.)

    hysterics L333, L399

    small-pox, uncertain whether she ever had L204

    stomach-ache, three hours' violent stomach-ache L276

    weakness of heart L201, L333

illnesses, feigned

    to delay wedding Solmes L73, L83, L85, L90.1

impersonators see **contrivances of Lovelace**, contrivances of the impersonators

independence

    and power conferred by her inheritance L13, L19, L32.3

    Morden's arrival meaning Clarissa's independence L53, L152

    Lord M. making her an independent wife L207

    her independent fortune L253

    will not live to take possession of her independence L309

    I never had any pride in being independent of them L474

inheritances see also **estates; trustees**

    from Grandfather Harlowe

        Anna's Aunt Harman approving L1

        causing sibling jealousy L2, L8, L13

        regretted by Clarissa L2, L6, L8, L17, L42

        Papa's displeasure at L7

        family setting aside his will L7

        may be litigated by James L13

        her independence and power conferred by L13, L19, L32.3

        regretted by Antony L32.4

        family's right to L32.4

        family pictures and family plate L42

        less than half his real estate left to Clarissa L42

        Clarissa not valuing herself upon L135

        wishing to write to Uncle Harlowe about the terms of her inheritance L157

        giving up her grandfather's bequest to appease her brother L174

    from Papa

        inheriting from her father, her uncles, and Morden as well as Grandfather L442

    from her uncles

        intended L13, L75

        no longer favored in Antony's will L182

    from Morden

        intended L455

        Morden's heir and executrix L459

    from Lord M.

        Lord M.'s heir rather than Lovelace, if Lovelace displease him L207

ink

    my ink runs nothing but gall L52

    gall in her ink L311

isinglass

    Grimes's eyes isinglass L238

jellies see **food**

jewels see also **estates,** jewels; **rings**

    her grandmother's jewels L41.1, L45, L202

        wanting new setting L202

        gift from her Grandfather L507

        proceeds of sale, to Poor's Fund, or estate, or Papa L507

        valued and money paid to estate L520

HARLOWE, MISS CLARISSA

jewels (cont.)

    her own jewels L41.1, L202

        not sent in the parcel to Anna before flight L69

        left behind after flight L100

        requested to be sent to her after flight L102

        will not be sent L147, L152

        her rings, her watch, her little money for a coach L314

        a few valuables at her lodgings at Smith's L334

        diamond necklace, solitaire, and buckles given her by Sir Josias Brookland L507

        Anna wanting to purchase Clarissa's jewels L510.3

        valued and given to Dolly L520

    offered by Solmes L41.1, L90.1

    offered by Lovelace L186

        jeweller bringing several sets for her to choose from L207

        Lovelace's mother's jewels may be new set for Clarissa L207

jewels, bequests of see **bequests of Clarissa**

jewels, figurative

    her mind so much a jewel L202

    Clarissa, a jewel, finest jewel, so rich a jewel L258, L321, L399, L501

journey see also **lodgings**

    Harlowe Place L1–L91

        flight, foreshadowed

            suggested L44, L49

            if she left her parents, the world would be against her L56

            only extremity would make her abandon her father's house L57

            fearing if turned out, she will not see home again L59.4

        flight, preparations

            sending parcel of linen and letters to Anna L69

            asking Anna to procure disguise and transportation L82

            writing Lovelace to request assistance in escaping Harlowe Place L83, L86

            only Anna will know her whereabouts L86

        flight, refuge considered

            Lovelace's family L36, L49, L61, L76, L83, L104

            Anna's L52, L53.1, L69, L75, L79, L80, L155

                refused by Mrs. Howe L81

            Grandfather's late house L53.1

            Aunt Hervey's L53.1, L54.1, L145

            Uncle Harlowe's L32.1, L53.1, L54.1

            London L49, L54, L76, L82, L104

            Leghorn L54

            private lodgings near Aunt Lawrance L86, L98

            her estate L101, L102

            Antony's L145

        flight, reconsidered

            finally resolved not to go off with Lovelace L89, L94, L393

            her letter of countermand ignored by Lovelace L99

            her preconcerted escape L103

        flight, Clarissa Harlowe, gone off with a man L92

    St. Albans, at the inn L92–L97

        soon to leave present lodgings L94

        agreeing to an inn near the Lawn L98, L104

        the gentlewoman and her niece who attended Clarissa at the inn at St. Albans L98

        asking family that she be allowed to go to the Grove L102

        not wishing to depend upon Lovelace L102, L152

HARLOWE, MISS CLARISSA

journey, St. Albans, at the inn L92-L97 (cont.)
    wanting Lovelace to leave her L107, L116, L123
  Mrs. Sorlings's dairy farm L98–L148
    accompanied by Mrs. Greme to Mrs. Sorlings's L98
    wishing to stay longer L121
    planning removal to London L126, L135, L137, L153
    considering lodgings in Norfolk Street or Cecil Street L130
    setting out for London L149–L153
  Mrs. Sinclair's, London L154–L227
    would like to go to a neighboring village and await Morden L185
    followed home from church by a footman of Miss Lardner L213, L214
    Clarissa's lodgings known to Misses Lardner, Biddulph, Lloyd, and Howe L229.1
    escape from L228, L230
  Mrs. Moore's, Hampstead L230–L255
    waiting at Hampstead for an answer from Anna L233
    inquiring about the Hampstead coach to Hedon L235
    considering removal from Mrs. Moore's L242
    not wishing to return to Mrs. Sinclair's L245
    returning to Mrs. Sinclair's with Lovelace L312
  Mrs. Sinclair's, London L256–L290
    expecting to return to Mrs. Moore's in Hampstead this night L256
    desperate to leave Mrs. Sinclair's for Mrs. Leeson's or Hampstead L256
    trying to escape Mrs. Sinclair's L262, L264, L266, L267, L276
    wishing to return to Mrs. Moore's at Hampstead L277, L278
    the lady is gone off L291
    details of the escape reported L293
  Mr. and Mrs. Smith's, Covent Garden L291–L330
    describing her lodgings at Smith's L320
    missing from her lodgings L329
  Mr. and Mrs. Rowland's, High Holborn L330–L336
    Clarissa is under arrest L330
    Sally and Polly trying to cajole Clarissa back to Mrs. Sinclair's L333
  Mr. and Mrs. Smith's, Covent Garden L336–L495
    Belford persuading Clarissa to return to Smith's L336
    Anna finding lodgings for Clarissa at a nearby farmhouse, she will not remove L366, L368
    vacating Smith's to avoid Lovelace's visits L418, L426, L440
    body ordered conveyed to Harlowe Place L494.1
  Harlowe Place L500
    the hearse arriving at six in the afternoon L500
journey, figurative see also **father's house**
  to a better world L333
  going on a long journey L343
  death as a journey's end L349
  upon a better preparation than for an earthly husband L362
  returning to her father's house L421.1, L424, L440, L442, L446, L449, L486, L510.4
  death as a journey L441
juleps see **medications**
keyhole
  Lovelace peeking through the keyhole of her door L264
keys
  Lovelace having keys to Harlowe Place L35, L61, L62, L94, L95
  giving up her keys to Harlowe Place L78, L91
  her key left inside the lock, indicating she left by her own consent L95
  Lovelace having no keys to the wainscot box holding her letters L210

HARLOWE, MISS CLARISSA

keys (cont.)

Mrs. Bevis may return Clarissa's keys to Mrs. Sinclair's L245

key to her chamber door at Mrs. Sinclair's in her pocket L281

Clarissa demanding the key to the street door at Mrs. Sinclair's L293

not trusted with keys to her room at Rowland's L333

giving Belford her keys to Smith's L336

giving the keys to her trunks to Mrs. Smith and Mrs. Lovick to inventory them L340

having a key to her own apartment at Smith's L416

giving Belford the keys to the drawer holding her will and papers L460

key to trunks holding her apparel in drawer with her papers and will L460

kisses from Lovelace

kissing her hand L36

first time L103

Lovelace wishing to kiss Clarissa L115

snatching and kissing Clarissa's hand L157

kiss rejected by Clarissa L187

kissed by Lovelace, hands and cheek L194

kissing her hand L199, L211, L215, L216, L248

Lovelace kissing her hand, leaving a red mark L200, L201

Lovelace kissing her unrepulsing hand five times L204

Lovelace wishing for one consenting kiss from Clarissa L205

Lovelace clasping his arms about her, forcing a kiss L215

Lovelace having no title to her lip or cheek L216

Lovelace taking bolder freedoms, kissing her hands, her lips L220

drawing aside the handkerchief and kissing her breast L220

seizing scissors from Clarissa, clasping her to his bosom, kissing her L225

Lovelace snatching her hand and kissing it L276, L277

kisses from Solmes

kissing her hand L78

kneeling

falling on her knees at Papa's door, pressing against it L78

Clarissa wild with apprehensions, begging mercy on her knees before Lovelace L256

on her knees writing to Mamma L391, L399

on her knees writing to Anna L473, L473.2

languages

reading *Telemachus* (in French and in English) L155, L155n1

Italian, French, Latin L529

law

constable called as Clarissa shouts from the window L264

the law her resource and refuge L281

Clarissa arrested, action dismissed L333, L334

light see also **angel**; **divine qualities**; **example**; **fall**; **sacrifice**; **suffering**; **trials**; **virgin**

Clarissa, a shining light L81, L260

flood of brightness L99

flood of brightness...glory...dazzle L136

irradiating every circle she set her foot into L358

appearing in a divine light L397

blazes out with meridian lustre L453

brightest of innocents L456

brightened and purified by her sufferings L459

like the sun L470

among the stars L470

after death, all light and all mind L473.1

her soul now in the regions of light L481

HARLOWE, MISS CLARISSA

light (cont.)
> angel of light L494

literary references see also **books**; **poems**
> Carter, Elizabeth, *Ode to Wisdom*
>> quoted L54, L54n1
>> music APPENDIX (appearing in v.2, Letter IX in editions printed by Richardson)
>
> Cowley, Abraham
>> *Ode to Wit*, quoted L222, L222n1
>> *On the Death of Mrs. Philips*, quoted L222, L222n2
>> *The Mistress*, quoted L261 Paper X, L261 Paper Xn1
>
> Dryden, John
>> *Fables Ancient and Modern*, quoted L21, L21n1
>> *Absalom and Achitophel*, quoted L91, L91n1, L261 Paper X, L261 Paper Xn1
>> *Oedipus*, adapted by Dryden and Lee, quoted L174, L174n1, L261 Paper X, L261 Paper Xn1
>
> Garth, Samuel, *The Dispensary*, quoted L261 Paper X, L261 Paper Xn1
> Howard, John, untraced quote L458, L458n1
> Lee, Nathaniel, *Oedipus*, adapted by Dryden and Lee, quoted L174, L174n1, L261 Paper X, L261 Paper Xn1
> Milton, John, *Paradise Lost*, quoted L161, L161n1
> Otway, Thomas, *Venice Preserved*, quoted L261 Paper X, L261 Paper Xn1
> Rowe, Nicholas, *Ulysses*, quoted L116, L116n3
> Shakespeare, William
>> *A Midsummer Night's Dream*, quoted L98, L98n2
>> *Hamlet*, quoted L261 Paper X, L261 Paper Xn1
>
> Tate, Nahum, his translation of Juvenal's *Satire XV*, quoted L217.3, L217.3n1
> Thomas à Kempis L75, L75n1

livery
> not yet prepared to wear Lovelace's livery L123
> Lovelace offering to wear Clarissa's livery L124
> Lovelace putting on Clarissa's livery and wearing it for life L276

lodgings see also **journey**
> Anna will procure lodgings for Clarissa in a neighboring village L252.1
> at Smith's, described L320, L338, L339
> at Rowland's, described L334, L336
> Anna finding lodgings for Clarissa at a nearby farmhouse, she will not remove L366, L368

love for Lovelace
> lacking L10, L11, L207
> noted L229.1, L241, L511
> admitting her former bias in Lovelace's favor L243
> once could have loved Lovelace L309, L428, L467
> bent upon reclaiming a libertine whom she loved L365

lozenges
> lozenge on the widow's chariot signifying widowhood L273

madness
> wishing to go to Bedlam L261.1
> preferring a private madhouse L261.1
> I began to be mad at Hampstead—so you said L261.1

manes
> of Clarissa L497, L536

mantua-makers
> *Dolins, Mrs.*, Clarissa's mantua-maker L293

marriage
> as duty to protect family honor L7, L8, L16
> order of, among siblings, Clarissa the youngest L9
> preferring a nunnery L13

HARLOWE, MISS CLARISSA

marriage (cont.)

    single life, her choice L25.1, L26, L29.3, L36, L39, L44, L49, L55, L88, L145, L179, L185, L207, L223, L229.1, L253, L359, L438

    why marry when she has power deriving from her own inheritance L32.3

    will never marry any other man than Lovelace L86, L94, L98, L103, L116, L185

    appeasing her brother by promising never to marry L174

    upon a better preparation than for an earthly husband L362

marriages, Clarissa's to Lovelace see also **contrivances of Lovelace**, contrivance of pretending marriage to Clarissa

    generally

        prospects of peerage L13

        advised by Dolly L78

        mentioned by Lovelace L80, L88, L94, L95, L98

        advised by Anna L81, L87, L100, L119, L128, L147, L148, L150, L327, L328

        will marry no other while Lovelace is single and alive L86, L94, L98, L103, L116, L185

        reconciliation and reformation preconditions to marriage L109

        her virtue tested, reward to be marriage L191

        if she refuse to cohabitate, Lovelace will marry her L194

        asking to be free of obligation to Lovelace L201

        her responsibilities and expectations when married to Lovelace L202

        mismatch L202

        renouncing Lovelace forever L244, L266

        not wishing to marry Lovelace L253, L274, L276, L309, L343, L348, L358, L369

        I never, never will be yours L266, L281

        marriage to Lovelace saving her reputation L284

        marriage to Lovelace bringing a curse on her children L359

        asking Anna to send her refusal of Lovelace to the ladies of his family L368

        marrying Lovelace would sanctify his wickedness L386

        her reasons for refusing Lovelace L448

    license

        license in her hands L260

        still in possession of L383

    proposals, Lovelace's

        greeting his proposal with silence as it is too soon and not convincing L107, L108

        why has he not declared himself L120

        Lovelace asking for her hand, unintentionally L137, L138

        rejecting his proposal as she is ill and unprepared L149, L152

        Lovelace proposing, her inclination to accept, if only he would urge her L155

        earlier proposals mentioned L155

        blaming Clarissa that they were not married before coming to town L207, L221

        asking Clarissa to be lawfully his tomorrow L266

        urging Clarissa to meet him at the altar L267

        Lovelace asking Clarissa to make this his happy day L276

    settlements

        proper settlements L164

        Lovelace offering to discuss, she hesitates L185

        her own estate L186

        part of Lovelace's estate in Lancashire L186

        Lord M. giving her £1000 *per annum* L186

        being completed, Lord M. making her independent in his generosity L207

        Lovelace giving her all arrears in her father's hands for Mrs. Norton L207

        drafted and returned to Lovelace L218

        Clarissa receiving £100 *per annum* more than Lovelace's mother L218, L219

HARLOWE, MISS CLARISSA

marriages, Clarissa's to Lovelace (cont.)
> wedding
>> not wanting a public wedding L207
>> Belford wishing to be her father at the altar L258
> wedding gifts
>> from Lord M.: Lancashire seat or the Lawn and a thousand pounds a year, penny rents L206

meals see also **collation at Mrs. Sinclair's**; **drink**; **food**
> family deprived of Clarissa's company at table L91
> Clarissa's eating preferences L157
> will not take meals with Lovelace, eating alone L175, L194
> refusing to eat or drink L228, L261.1, L333
> bread and water at Bedlam L261.1
> accused of starving herself, self-murder L333
> taking water L333
> drinking tea with bread and butter, at Rowland's L333
> offering to pay for coffee, tea, chocolate, chicken but unable to eat L333
> repast with Mrs. Lovick and Mr. and Mrs. Smith L399

meals, breakfast
> breakfast L5, L16
> not appearing at breakfast L18, L22, L23
> Aunt Hervey breakfasting with Clarissa L77
> breakfast ready in the parlour at the inn L98
> will attend Mrs. Sinclair and her nieces at breakfast L155, L157
> refusing breakfast with Lovelace L175, L198, L200, L226
> breakfast with Lovelace L214
> happiest breakfast time since Harlowe Place L216
> taking chocolate for breakfast with Lovelace and Tomlinson L216
> refusing breakfast L333
> inviting Hickman and Belford to breakfast L365
> inviting Belford, Mr. and Mrs. Smith and Mrs. Lovick to breakfast L440

meals, dinner
> attended by Betty at dinner, her poor appetite L63
> a hardship not to dine below, as Dr. Lewin is there L75
> dining in the ivy summer-house, waiting for Lovelace L83, L86, L90, L91, L103
> too busy for Lovelace till dinner was ready L98
> dinner with Lovelace at the inn L98
> preferring to dine alone L157
> all dined together in Mrs. Sinclair's parlour L159
> not wanting to dine with Lovelace, not dining at all L200
> refusing to dine with Lovelace L203, L220, L226, L251
> bread and water only for dinner L235
> dinner ordered for Clarissa at Rowland's L333
> refusing dinner with Sally and Polly L333
> refusing to dine with Mrs. Smith and Belford and Mrs. Lovick L349

meals, supper
> seldom eating supper, declining supper L155
> no admission of Lovelace to supper L175
> chicken soup ordered for supper L184
> supping with Lovelace L194
> Lovelace wishing to sup with Clarissa L199
> expecting to have supper at Mrs. Moore's L256
> the pretend Lady Betty bespeaking supper at nine at Mrs. Moore's L314

meals, tea
> excused from tea L7

meals, tea (cont.)

> sent for to tea L8
> to make tea L16
> excused from afternoon tea L17
> uncles cancelling tea with Clarissa in her apartment L75
> declining tea with Lovelace at Mrs. Sinclair's L155, L199
> meeting Lovelace for tea L201
> a dish of tea at Mrs. Moore's L232
> refusing a dish of tea with Tomlinson L238
> sipping two dishes of tea with Lovelace L253
> will drink a dish of tea with Belford at six to thank him L338

medications see also **potions**

> hartshorn L16, L98, L201, L233, L314, L334, L340
> salts L213, L340
> a line from Anna as a cordial L297
> given juleps by way of cordial L338, L340
> weak jellies and cordials ordered L340, L366, L467
> something given Clarissa to make her sleep L346
> regimen ordered by the doctor L366
> drops prescribed by doctor L426, L474

Meditations

> Meditation, Saturday, July 15, written at Rowland's, extracted from Scriptures L364, L364n2
> Meditation: *Poor mortals the cause of their own misery* L399
> Meditation stitched to the bottom of Letter 402 in black silk L402
> Meditation, a collection of texts from *Job* 19:2; 6:14, etc. L413
> Meditation, Aug. 21: *On being hunted after by the enemy of my soul*, made up of verses from *Psalms* L418
> her book of Meditations L460
>> bequeathed Mrs. Norton, Mamma wanting the original L507, L510.3

Memorandum book

> Clarissa's minutes of all that passed, when she could not correspond with Anna L272
> bequeathed Anna L510.3

memory

> Clarissa's memory cherished by Mrs. Norton L409
> referring to her memory L446
> her memory not honored by Lovelace's death L448
> Belford wanting his letters returned by Lovelace, for Anna, to vindicate Clarissa's memory L452

messengers

> *Grimes*
>> correspondence with Anna conveyed by her old man L119, L120
>> old Grimes, whom Clarissa dispatched with a letter to Anna L235
>> Will looking out for old Grimes with Anna's to Clarissa L237
>> Will has him at the Lower Flask L238
>> in condition of David's sow L238, L238n1
>> losing to Will Anna's letter for Clarissa L238
>> *half seas over*, dropped his hat doffing it L238
>> receiving money for the letter for Clarissa L238
>> his eyes isinglass L238

milk see **drink**

miniatures see also **pictures**

> returning her miniature of Anna to Hickman L476, L507
> miniature of Clarissa set in gold, bequeathed Morden L507

minister see **clergymen**

HARLOWE, MISS CLARISSA

money

> having, not having
>> having seven guineas with L98
>> fifty guineas left behind in her escritoire L98, L100
>> requested after flight, will not be sent to her L98, L102, L147, L152, L173, L177
>> mistrusting Lovelace's economy she would be his steward L202
>> needing but two hundred pounds a year to live on L207
>> Clarissa is poor, moneyless L301, L330
>> having several things of value with her L307
>> her rings, her watch, her little money for a coach L314
>> having but half a guinea and a little silver L333
>> having with her a few valuables L333
>> telling Mrs. Norton she has no occasion for money L382
>> put in great straits to support herself L455
>> not lacking money L458
>> money—a trifle L458
>
> paying, owing
>> providing for Mrs. Norton L39, L45
>> annuity of £50 *per annum* for Mrs. Norton L230
>> Clarissa paying Robert for conveying correspondence L74
>> gift to Hannah L23, L128, L132
>> paying Mrs. Moore half a crown at Hampstead L232
>> giving Mrs. Moore a diamond ring L235
>> paying Grimes for bringing the letter from Anna left at Wilson's L238
>> bilking her lodgings at Mrs. Sinclair's, one hundred and fifty guineas, or pounds, owed L330, L333
>> no money to give Mr. Rowland L333
>> her clothes, sold by Mrs. Sinclair to pay the debt, more sold L333, L426
>> giving Rowland's maid a half-guinea L336
>> selling her diamond ring and clothes to pay for the doctor L340
>> paying the undertaker L451
>
> receiving, refusing
>> refusing a bank note from Lovelace, a bill from Lord M. L98, L157, L158, L205
>> Anna an unlikely source as Antony has made Mrs. Howe watchful L105
>> Anna sending Clarissa fifty guineas in *Norris's Miscellanies* L148
>> refusing Mrs. Norton's offer of money L301, L307
>> Anna wanting to send Clarissa money L317
>> asking Anna for money to pay the one hundred and fifty guineas L333
>> Belford offering Clarissa money L339
>> Belford giving Mrs. Smith twenty guineas for Clarissa's clothes L340
>> refusing Belford's offer of money L349
>> Belford dropping a bank note behind her chair L350
>> refusing money from Hickman L366
>> Mrs. Norton sending Clarissa the five guineas sent to her by Mamma, along with ten guineas belonging to Mrs. Norton L381
>> offer of one hundred guineas *per* quarter from Lovelace's family for life, refused L394, L398
>> Morden bringing Clarissa money L483

motivations

> self-examination of motives L19, L82
> to prevent mischief between Harlowe Family and Lovelace L110
> love for Lovelace L110

murder

> I am afraid there will be murder L30
> dreaming she is murdered in a churchyard by Lovelace L84
> a murdered evening, the collation L159

HARLOWE, MISS CLARISSA

murder (cont.)

    Lovelace dreaming he murdered Clarissa L246

    shouting Murder! out the window at Mrs. Sinclair's L264

    Mrs. Sinclair must let Clarissa out or murder her L293

music

    accomplished at harpsichord, music L54, L182

    harpsichord, chamber-organ, and music books bequeathed Dolly L507

    music for Elizabeth Carter's *Ode to Wisdom* APPENDIX (appearing in v.2, Letter IX in editions printed by
        Richardson)

names

    Miss Cunning-ones L61.1

    Gloriana L105, L167, L209

        as *Gloriana*, Nathaniel Lee's L159, L159n2

    Mrs. Lovelace or Clarissa Lovelace L157, L158.1, L161, L167, L186, L211, L213, L214, L303, L497, L535

    Lovelace's lady L203

    Lady Easy to Lovelace's pleasures L207

    Miss Clary L374, L381, L408, L431, L442

needlework

    wishing to pursue her needleworks L51.2, L52.1

    Clarissa's L79, L147, L182, L529

    bequeathed Mamma, Anna, and Morden L507, L510.3

newspapers

    Tatlers, *Spectators*, and *Guardians*, procured for Clarissa by Belford L155

nurses

    Norton, Mrs., in childhood L31, L301

        cared for these eighteen or nineteen years by Mrs. Norton L376

        prohibited from attending Clarissa L408

    Shelburne, Ann, in her last illness L451

        Clarissa now attended by a nurse L338, L340

        diligent, obliging, silent, and sober L362

        attending Clarissa after her death L457

        Dame Shelburne L460

        bequeathed ten guineas by Clarissa L507

        a widow L507

On being hunted after by the enemy of my soul

    Clarissa's Meditation L418

opinions

    on aging L40, L458

    on death L441, L475

    on duelling L55, L518

    on duty L17, L41.1, L55, L110

        to Papa L7, L8, L9, L78, L123

    on friendship L359

    on generosity L185

    on genius as wit and judgement L310

    on happiness and riches L19

    on innkeepers L98

    on manners L120

    on marriage L32.1

        men and L40

    on men L13, L22, L64, L76, L78, L88

        importance of figure or person L40

        the encroaching sex L85

        and their unpardonable crimes L458

HARLOWE, MISS CLARISSA

opinions (cont.)

on parental authority L110

on people

on perfection in people L19

low people and high L69

on person L187

on religion L261 Paper VII, L293

on riches and happiness L19

on royal title L36

on saints, as preaching and practicing L310

on seduction L486.1

on steadiness of mind L19

on vengeance L518

on wit in ladies and gentlemen L222

on wives, treatment of husbands L435

on women

female character L2, L19, L40

and generosity L5

poems L54

their liveliness and quickness L63

their fondness for fine clothing L69

and courtship L73

writing as proper employment for L529

on writing L135, L529

paintings see **art references**

Papers I–X

delirious writings after being drugged and raped L261

written in her delirium L293

parable of the lady and the lion

see L261 Paper III

paragon

of virtue L110, L243

Clarissa as L453

parchments

refusing to sign L83

parsons see **clergymen**

peculiars

not treating Lovelace with peculiarity L3

called by her grandfather, his own peculiar child L4

obliged to mistrust herself of peculiarity L20

my peculiars, particularly Miss Howe L61

peerage

prospects of, married to Lovelace L13

pencils

writing on the cover...with a pencil L57, L80

red and black pencils used in her drawings L78

physical appearance

her voice all harmony L118

her beauty L187.1–L187.4, L243

fair and slim, tall L251, L529

her snowy hand L263

her natural ringlets not lately kembed L334

her hand, the lily not of so beautiful a white L340

declining looks L348

HARLOWE, MISS CLARISSA

physical appearance (cont.)

> change in her countenance for the worse L365, L385
>
> description by Anna L529

physicians

> *H., Dr. R.*, Clarissa's physician L343
>
>> bequest of Clarissa, twenty guineas for a ring L507
>
>> called for by Mr. Goddard L340
>
>> diagnosis, love case, her disorder in her mind L340
>
>> fees
>
>>> Clarissa having no money to pay L340
>
>>> agreeing to take a fee every other visit L345
>
>>> no longer accepting fees L441
>
>> friends
>
>>> Belford L334, L338
>
>>> Clarissa, becoming a friend of L441
>
>> names, signing his letter R. H. L461
>
>> prognosis, giving Clarissa three to four weeks to live, will not live a week L426, L460, L461
>
>> reconciliation between Clarissa and the Harlowe Family
>
>>> offering to write to the Harlowe Family L349, L441
>
>>> writing to Papa that Clarissa will not live a week L460, L461
>
>> regimen
>
>>> cordials and nourishment L340
>
>>> weak jellies and cordials L366, L467
>
>>> ordering drops L426
>
>>> air L441
>
>> visits
>
>>> to Clarissa L440, L441, L457, L473
>
>>> from Hickman, planned L366

pictures see also **miniatures**

> of Clarissa, in the Vandyke taste, by Joseph Highmore L147, L147n1
>
> family pictures bequeathed Mr. John Harlowe L507

plate

> family plate bequeathed Mr. Antony Harlowe L507

poems

> Miss Biddulph's, on the female character L2
>
> Elizabeth Carter's *Ode to Wisdom*
>
>> quoted L54, L54n1
>
>> music APPENDIX (appearing in v.2, Letter IX in editions printed by Richardson)
>
> Clarissa's, her delirious writings after being drugged and raped L261 Paper X

Poor mortals the cause of their own misery

> Clarissa's Meditation L399

Poor's Fund

> the poor blessing her, praying for her L177, L301
>
> charitable donations L186
>
> her donations one tenth of her income, two hundred pounds a year L202
>
> wishing an annuity of £50 *per annum* for the poor L230
>
> concern for her poor L300
>
> to be administered by Mrs. Norton L507
>
> proceeds of the sale of grandmother's jewels to go to L507
>
> to be increased L507
>
> correspondence between Anna and Belford concerning L528
>
> managed by Mrs. Norton until a week before her death CONCLUSION
>
> cared for by Mrs. Hickman after Mrs. Norton's death CONCLUSION

HARLOWE, MISS CLARISSA

Poor's Fund (cont.)

    contributions to, by Mr. Hickman, Mrs. Howe, and Mr. Belford CONCLUSION

potions

    drug induced delirium L260, L261 Papers I–X, L261.1, L275.1, L314, L320

    potion administered by Mrs. Sinclair L281, L311, L314, L395, L535

poultry see **animals**

power

    why marry when she has power deriving from her own inheritance L32.3

    He may be mean enough, perhaps, if ever I should put it into his power, to avenge himself for the trouble he has had with me—But that...I never shall L69

    I was now in his power L98

    so much in his power as you are L183

    Lovelace's, over Clarissa L243, L287, L308

    Clarissa's, over Lovelace, triumph over Lovelace L282, L395, L453

    she has found her power L287

prayers

    prayer foreshadowing her trials L145

    praying for Lovelace L159

    praying on her knees in her old apartment at Mrs. Sinclair's L256

    Oh save me from myself, and from this man L274

    the poor praying for her L301

    her prayers L333

    her prayer for Lovelace L336, L510.4

    her humble prayer L393

    her prayer to protect James from himself and from Lovelace L407

    her prayer for a kinder heart for Arabella L430

    praying forgiveness for Mr. Brand and his informants L433

    her prayer for Anna's honour and prosperity L436

pregnant

    Lovelace believing Clarissa is pregnant L371, L423

    Mamma hoping Clarissa is not pregnant L376

    Uncle Harlowe wants to know whether she is with child L402

prey

    vultures, hawks, kites, and other villainous birds of prey, parents protecting from L133

    prey of a vulture's rapacious talons L333

pride

    mentioned L82, L115, L253, L364, L529

    now humbled by rape L261 Paper IV

    her proud heart penetrated by Bella L261 Paper V

    her sin L261.1

    pretending to be above L265

    her pride in refusing Lovelace L323

    pride of undeserved treatment L341

    her pride mortified L359

    her disappointment causing her death L370

    a proud heart L399

    her pride in thinking Lovelace has had a loss in Clarissa L428

    reptile pride of seduction L486.1

    punished for her secret pride L492

prisoner

    confined to her apartment at Harlowe Place L24, L24.1, L25, L36, L40, L44, L69

    Lovelace taking Clarissa to such a place as she cannot fly L108

    Will to guard against any attempt by Clarissa to escape L174.3

    a prisoner at Mrs. Sinclair's, not a prisoner L178, L195

HARLOWE, MISS CLARISSA

prisoner (cont.)

> physically detained from going out L201
> a prisoner L263, L266, L274, L278
> asking to be freed L276
> at Rowland's L333
> confined by illness to her room L454

promissory note see also **contrivances of Lovelace**, contrivance of the promissory note

> hers to Dorcas L279

prosecution of Lovelace

> could not bear to appear in a Court of Justice to prosecute L315
> advised by Anna to take legal vengeance L316
> should prosecute Lovelace L317
> not wanting to prosecute L318
> will prosecute, if he threaten Anna or Hickman L320
> not using Lovelace's correspondence with Belford in law L387.1
> Dr. Lewen urging Clarissa to prosecute, as reparation of family dishonor L427
> Counsellor Derham and Mr. Ackland will hear Clarissa's story and begin a process L429
> not favoring legal prosecution L447
> her appearance in court as a condition of reconciliation with the Harlowe Family L456

protection for Clarissa see also **refuge for Clarissa**

> offer of protection from Lady Betty L36
> writing to Lovelace to ask protection of his aunts L83
> considering Lady Betty's protection L120, L123
> Mrs. Townsend offering Clarissa protection L196, L199, L201, L209, L210, L228
> Clarissa not under a legal protection L215
> no protector but Lovelace L225, L256
> Lovelace her Judas protector L227.4
> no hope of protection from Morden L230
> Anna wishing to give Clarissa protection L317
> Anna advises Clarissa to put herself into Lady Betty's protection L327, L328
> no one to protect her from Lovelace L386
> unprotected L419, L437
> Mamma wishing Clarissa to put herself into Morden's protection L459
> her error throwing her out of her father's protection L488

proverbs see **sayings and proverbs**

punishment

> her impenetrable afflictions given to her by God L266
> her punishment is over, Lovelace's is not L266
> her punishment the consequence of her fault L359

rape of Clarissa, *foreshadowed*

> penetrate any depth of Lovelace's character L12
> impenetrable L31
> Rosebud spared L34, L35, L70, L71, L72, L73
> Clarissa penetrating into Lovelace's friends heads, Lovelace entering her heart L159
> lest one be attacked by him when in bed and asleep L177
> the mortal offense L189
> Clarissa called Lucretia L222
> Clarissa wild with apprehensions, begging mercy on her knees before Lovelace L256

rape of Clarissa

> occurring after Letter 256 and before Letter 257 L257
> her proud heart penetrated by Bella L261 Paper V
> marriage not making amends L263
> her impenetrable afflictions given to her by God L266
> Clarissa raped L293

HARLOWE, MISS CLARISSA

rape of Clarissa (cont.)

  reported to Lady Betty L306

  asking Anna and Mrs. Howe to keep it secret L315

  Clarissa as prey of a vulture, its rapacious talons L333

  liberty taken with her when she was asleep L346

  not her fault L379

  Clarissa not knowing the details of how Lovelace brought about her ruin L379

rape of Clarissa, second rape

  saving herself from what she believes would have been a second rape L359

reading

  her deep reading L182

  difficulty reading, her eyes unable L336

reconciliation between Clarissa and Lovelace

  failure to appease Lovelace may cause family to lose James also L243

reconciliation between Clarissa and the Harlowe Family

  offered by Lovelace L61, L88

  no hope L101, L132, L137, L141, L144, L145, L155, L157, L318, L320, L349, L440

  all hopes on Morden L101

  a precondition of marriage to Lovelace L109, L155

  hopes for L112, L120, L121, L123, L124, L132, L135, L141, L149, L151, L179, L187

  attempted through

    Aunt Hervey, writing to Aunt Hervey for her things and reconciliation L116

    Mr. Hickman, to plead with Uncle Harlowe L174, L182, L184, L217.1, L221

    Mrs. Norton, to apply to Mamma for reconciliation L179, L183, L184, L221

      asking Mrs. Norton not to intercede L307, L377, L382

  preferring reconciliation to marriage with Lovelace L179

  importance of L202

  reconciliation a *viaticum* L309

  reconciliation unworthy of her L319

  hard-hearted letter from Arabella L391

  on her knees writing to Mamma L391, L399

  her appearance in court as a condition L456

  family wishing for L483

reform

  believing she could reform Lovelace L294, L306, L359, L365

  hopes for Lovelace's reformation L398

  an instrument of Belford's reform L486.1

  herself a means to reclaim Lovelace L510.4

refuge for Clarissa see also **protection for Clarissa**

  after her flight, requesting to retire to her estate L101

  wishing to live upon her estate rather than marry Lovelace L248

  Anna finding lodgings for Clarissa at a nearby farmhouse, she will not remove L366, L368

  family expecting Clarissa to live at her Grandfather's house L459

relations

  Brookland, Sir Josias, Mamma's uncle L507

  Fuller and *Allinson*, distant relations attending funeral L504

  Morden, Robert, her uncle L507

repentance

  Clarissa's L393

reputation

  concern for L1, L81, L98, L101, L144

  dearer to her than life L102

  grieving for her reputation L107

  reputation destroyed, lost, destroyed by Lovelace L173, L368, L407

HARLOWE, MISS CLARISSA

reputation (cont.)

marriage to Lovelace saving her reputation L284

not patching up her reputation by marrying Lovelace L359

subject of open talk L392

slandered L407, L444

rescue of Clarissa

James's plot

mentioned L132, L137, L140, L142, L145, L155, L157, L158, L158.1, L164

planned with his friend, Singleton, captain of a ship L132

Miss Lloyd telling Anna of James's plan L132, L137, L148

plot may not be abandoned L148, L177

plot abandoned L152

no longer feared by Clarissa L175

Singleton visiting Anna to find Clarissa's whereabouts L175, L177

Singleton sent to find Clarissa's whereabouts L194

Anna's smuggling scheme

Clarissa asking Anna to perfect her scheme L195, L195n1, L200, L230

Mrs. Townsend may give Clarissa protection L196, L199, L201, L209, L210, L228

Mrs. Townsend, her two brothers, and their crews taking Clarissa to Deptford L252.1

revenge

lacking in Clarissa L336

Clarissa's forgiveness and death as L472

Morden: How wounding a thing...is a generous...forgiveness! What revenge can be more effectual and more noble, were revenge intended L508

rings see also **estates**, jewels; **jewels**

her rose-diamond ring, escaping from Mrs. Sinclair's with L228

her rings, sent to her with her clothes L230

giving Mrs. Moore a diamond ring L235

her rings, her watch, her little money for a coach L314

offering her diamond ring to Mr. Rowland for room and board L334

her diamond ring and clothes to pay for the doctor L340

rings, bequests of see **bequests of Clarissa**

ruin

Clarissa's noted L132, L173, L189, L256, L306, L307, L333, L336, L356, L379

Sacraments

receiving the Sacrament L426, L457

receiving Communion L460

sacrifice see also **angel**; **divine qualities**; **example**; **fall**; **suffering**; **trials**; **virgin**

to Solmes L10, L15, L102, L113

to family aggrandizement L17

begging James not to sacrifice her to his projects L25.3, L32.3

Clarissa as L27, L41

struck dead at the altar L41

her noble self-sacrifice L118

sweet lamb, Clarissa L172

the poor sacrifice L314

salts see **medications**

sayings and proverbs

wild oats, and black oxen L44, L44n1

poverty is the mother of health L63

pleasures of the mighty are obtained by the tears of the poor L63

better a bare foot than none at all L63

encouragement and approbation make people show talents they were never suspected to have L63

persecution and discouragement depress *ingenuous* minds, and blunt the edge of lively imaginations L63

HARLOWE, MISS CLARISSA

sayings and proverbs (cont.)

    take a thorn out of my own foot, and to put it into that of my friend L89

    swear and curse like a trooper L98, L98n1

    a jay in the fable L123, L123n1

    can cap sentences with Lord M. L244

    we ought not to do evil that good may come of it L428

    who can touch pitch and not be defiled L440

sealings

    suspecting Lovelace of breaking seals on her correspondence with Anna L155, L156

    Letter 173.1 from Morden sealed in black wax L173

    her correspondence, left for Belford with her will, sealed with black wax L460, L486

sedan see **transportation**

seduction

    Clarissa compared to Rosebud L103

    her fall L118, L144, L169, L171, L324, L359, L399, L429

    she knew Lovelace to be a rake L294

servants

    Burton, Hannah

        attending Clarissa L7, L16, L18

            functioning as Clarissa's ears L13, L14, L16, L19, L21, L22

            loyal to Clarissa L21

            dismissed by Harlowe Family L21, L23, L24.1, L25, L25.2, L84

            Clarissa wishing to recall her L86, L116, L118, L121, L124, L125, L154, L155

            unable to attend Clarissa L127, L129

            soon will be well enough to attend Clarissa L167

            Clarissa wanting her services after marriage to Lovelace L218

            Clarissa wanting her services at Smith's L298

            may go with Clarissa to Pennsylvania, would take Betty instead L429, L430

        bequest of Clarissa, fifty pounds L507

        correspondence, Harlowe, Miss Clarissa with Anna

            conveying Clarissa's secret letters to Anna L9, L14, L19, L20, L23

        illnesses

            violent rheumatic disorder L118, L128

            very ill but not in danger L156

            soon will be well enough to attend Clarissa L167

            Lovelace sending a physician to cause her illness L167

            continuing ill L177, L178, L298, L307

            too ill to stir from her mother's house, St. Albans L298, L299, L301

            if her ill health continue, Mrs. Norton to put her on the Poor's Fund L507

        money

            Clarissa giving her ten guineas upon her dismissal L23

            Mamma giving her two guineas on her departure L25.2

            gifts of from Lovelace, Hickman, Clarissa L130, L132

sibling rivalry

    inheritance causing jealousy L2, L8, L13

    mentioned L10

    superior to her siblings L182

    her siblings to blame for the loss of Clarissa L355

    her grandfather knowing she would be envied L400

silver

    her flowered silver suit L69

    stars of embossed silver L417

    petticoat of flowered silver L507

Singleton plot see **rescue of Clarissa,** James's plot

HARLOWE, MISS CLARISSA

sleep

>sleepless, no rest, trouble sleeping L126, L276, L365
>something given Clarissa to make her sleep L346
>an early riser L365
>to bed early at eight o'clock L399

sleeping arrangements see also **contrivances of Lovelace**, contrivance of the bedfellows

>sharing Mamma's bed for two nights L5
>anticipating a straw bed at Bedlam L261.1
>sleeping in the bed where Rowland's maid lay L333

snuff

>all her oppositions not signifying a pinch of snuff L57
>taking a pinch of Dorcas's snuff L314

stages see **transportation**

starvation see **suicide**

story see also **warning**

>writing a history of her sufferings L57
>to all who will know your story L177, L187
>her story mentioned L306, L379, L448, L502
>her story, when known, will absolve her L307, L380
>telling her story to Mr. and Mrs. Smith, Mrs. Lovick, and Belford L349
>her whole story not yet known to Anna L359
>her tragical story to be published by Anna and Mrs. Howe L372, L459, L515
>her story best recorded in Lovelace's letters L379
>perhaps her story should be forgotten as soon as possible L379
>wishing to leave behind an account to clear up her conduct L387.1
>asking Belford for copies of Lovelace's correspondence to help tell her story L387.1, L391
>no time to write her own story L389
>Clarissa's story summarized by Belford in relation to examples of Restoration drama L413
>Anna collecting Clarissa's letters to tell her story L428
>Counsellor Derham and Mr. Ackland will hear Clarissa's story and begin a process L429
>family not inquiring into the particulars of Clarissa's story L430
>Mrs. Norton wanting to hear Clarissa's story L459
>when James knows her story L490
>her story known by the neighborhood L504
>a compilement to be made of all that relates to L507
>her story not to give Morden cause for vengeance L518

suffering see also **angel**; **divine qualities**; **example**; **fall**; **light**; **sacrifice**; **trials**; **virgin**

>Clarissa's L1, L121, L187, L189, L297, L308
>writing a history of her sufferings L57
>her sufferings her glory L274
>her family knowing not what she has suffered L368
>choosing to be a sufferer rather than an aggressor L451
>brightened and purified by her sufferings L459, L492.2
>her sufferings compared to Lovelace's L463
>angelic sufferer L467
>suffering her injuries herself rather than offering them to others L471
>the right use of her sufferings L490
>her undeserved sufferings L514

suicide

>wishing it were not a sin to put an end to her own life L276
>her penknife held to her bosom threatening to take her own life L281
>accused of starving herself, self-murder L333, L366
>will not shorten her own life L371
>her threat of suicide L395

HARLOWE, MISS CLARISSA

suitors to Harlowe, Miss Clarissa

listed: Wyerly, Biron, Symmes, Solmes, and the laced-hat orator himself L294

Byron

included in list of Clarissa's suitors L15

as Biron L294

Mullins, Mr.

rejected by Clarissa L4, L6

attending Clarissa's funeral L504

Solmes, Mr. Roger, suitor L6, L294 *see also* **address to Clarissa by Mr. Roger Solmes**

animals, vile reptile L36

character

confident and offensive, monster L16, L17

boasting he will marry Clarissa L22, L76

account of, by Anna L27

compared to Lovelace L32.3, L277

illiterate L32.4

his persistence L33.2, L79

his impudent preparations L76

siccofant L90.1

costume

yellow, full-buckled peruke, broad-brimmed beaver L10

white peruke, fine laced shirt and ruffles, coat trimmed with silver, and a waistcoat L78

estates

upstart man, not born to immense riches L13

his fortunes affected by marriage to Clarissa L13, L17, L19

his own family disinherited L16, L27

funeral of Clarissa, attending L504

gossip

sources of information about L27, L56, L57, L58

public talk of Clarissa's aversion to him L81

wishing to pass on information to Clarissa about Lovelace L59.1, L78, L79

would have told Clarissa of Miss Betterton L139

kidnapping, planned by Lovelace L117, L119

kneeling, before Clarissa L78

marriage, unmarried CONCLUSION

names, Squire Solmes L139

opinions, on wives and marriage L56

physical appearance, his ugliness L16, L21

relations

Solmes, Sir Oliver, his father

his yellow, full-buckled peruke, broad-brimmed beaver L10

wretched creature with vast fortunes L17

compared to Roger Solmes L32.4

opinion on women, surly old misogynist L40

sister L32.4

rescue of Clarissa, James's plot, mentioned in L300

servants, treatment of L95

tenants, treatment of L27

vengeance, meditating vengeance on Clarissa L57

visits to Harlowe Place L8, L16, L21, L53, L78, L86

Symmes, Mr., suitor L294

blaming Harlowes' treatment of Lovelace following the duel L1

rejected by Clarissa L4, L6

brother of Mr. Edward Symmes L4

HARLOWE, MISS CLARISSA

suitors to Harlowe, Miss Clarissa, *Symmes, Mr.* (cont.)
>   mentioned L36
> *Wyerley, Mr. Alexander*
>>   address to Clarissa
>>>   rejected by Clarissa L3, L4, L6
>>>>   mentioned L7, L36, L58
>>>   knowing of Clarissa's choice of the single life L26
>>>   suggested as compromise to the Solmes plan L44, L70
>>>   renewing his address to Clarissa L436, L437
>>>   Clarissa cannot love Mr. Wyerley L436
>>>   has always and still loves Clarissa L437
>>>   wishing to marry Clarissa L437
>>   character
>>>   jester upon sacred things L40
>>>   prophaning and ridiculing scripture L78
>>   duel between James and Lovelace, blaming Harlowes' treatment of Lovelace following the duel L1
>>   meals, tea, with Anna and Mrs. Howe L1
>>   names
>>>   included in a list of Clarissa's suitors as Wyerly L294
>>>   signing his letter Alexander Wyerley L437
>>   funeral of Clarissa, attending L504

supper see **meals, supper**

tea see **meals, tea**

theatre
>   attending Otway's *Venice Preserved*, with Lovelace and Miss Horton L194, L194n1, L198, L200

tragedy
>   too late, to remedy the apprehended evil L86

transportation
>   abducted in a chariot and six L94
>   to Mrs. Sorlings's in a chaise L98
>   to London in a chaise L152
>   to church in a chair, a coach L159, L320
>   airing in a chariot with Lovelace L218
>   inquiring about stages and their prices L228
>   taking a coach to Hampstead to escape Mrs. Sinclair's L230, L232
>   paying for vacant seats to Hampstead L232
>   ordering Mabel to get her a coach L293
>   her rings, her watch, her little money for a coach L314
>   writ against her, she is taken away by the sheriff's officers in a chair L333
>   taking a chair back to Smith's L336
>   airing in a coach cancelled L399
>   her habit of taking a sedan or chair to morning prayers L444

travel
>   going abroad rather than returning to Harlowe Place L248
>   Morden wishing to take Clarissa on a tour of France and Italy L459

trials see also **angel**; **divine qualities**; **example**; **fall**; **light**; **sacrifice**; **suffering**; **virgin**
>   before her family L98, L100, L144, L151
>   if she stand her trial, Lovelace will marry her L110, L202
>   Belford cautioning Lovelace against further trials of Clarissa L143, L222
>   trials which will prove her woman or angel L157.1
>   at the height of her trial L244
>   should she fail in the trial L253
>   the hour of her trial L256
>   insensible in her moment of trial, her glory and her pride L279

HARLOWE, MISS CLARISSA

trials (cont.)

        another trial, her last L280

        her trials over if she marry him L287

        her trials make her shine brighter L301

        her talents proportionate to her trials L308

        her trials withstood L319

        her trials, her sufferings L324, L346

        superior to all trials L395

        Lovelace's cruelty, her trial L440

trustees see also **estates**; **inheritances**

        Harlowe, Mr. John

                of Clarissa's estate L27, L55, L214, L406

        Morden, Colonel William

                of Grandfather's will L27, L32.3, L87, L173

                co-trustee with John Harlowe L214

                of Clarissa's estate L248, L253, L455

undertaker

        ordering her coffin at the undertaker's in Fleet Street L440

        paid by Clarissa L451

violent behavior

        taking sharp-pointed scissors against Lovelace L225

        Lovelace trying to raise her, Clarissa wildly slapping his hands L267

virgin see also **angel**; **divine qualities**; **example**; **fall**; **light**; **sacrifice**; **suffering**; **trials**

        virgin saint L224

        fearful virgin, Clarissa L261 Paper VI

        country funeral and coffin, a flower bed, mentioned by Lovelace referring to a virgin L313

        more pure than a vestal L346

        dressed in virgin white L474

virtue

        Clarissa's noted L1, L31, L187.1–L187.4, L222, L225, L266, L248, L259, L301, L316, L339, L427, L437,

            L447, L517

        loving virtue for its own sake L106

        tested by family and found wanting L110

        paragon of L110, L243

        female virtue founded on pride L110

        a cloak L201

        Clarissa virtue itself L287

        unsullied L319

        baffling to Lovelace L349

        admired by Lovelace L358

        a vixen in her virtue L496

        Lovelace's principal intention to try her virtue L517

visits

        to dairy house L2

        to Anna L6

                where she first introduced Lovelace to Anna L252

        to Mrs. Knollys, where Clarissa had once been a guest L26

        to Sir Robert Biddulph, where Clarissa met Patty Montague two years ago L233.3

        from Arabella L2

        from Lovelace

                while at Anna's L7

                Lovelace ambivalent about visiting Clarissa L341, L371, L391, L414

                Clarissa fearing a visit from L440, L446, L467

                not wishing Lovelace to see her after her death L482

HARLOWE, MISS CLARISSA

visits (cont.)

from Uncle Harlowe L75

from Dr. Lewin L75, L77, L82, L83

from the ladies of Lovelace's family

expected L98, L157, L158, L178, L194, L203.1, L233, L242, L245

not expected L244

if she marries Lovelace L339

from Belford

on behalf of Lovelace L284, L285

at Rowland's L334

at Smith's L339, L348, L365, L385, L413, L440, L441, L457

disapproved by Harlowe Family L431, L459

causing a scandal L433

investigated by Mr. Alston L459

from Hickman L360, L365, L444

from the parish minister L440, L454, L457, L467, L473

from Morden L473, L518

from Anna, planned L473.1

warning see also **story**

Clarissa, a warning to others L222, L428, L458

weapons

taking sharp-pointed scissors against Lovelace L225

penknife, threatening to take her own life L281

her penknife, to mend her pen L333

weddings see

marriages, Clarissa's to Lovelace, wedding

address to Clarissa by Mr. Roger Solmes, family's intimidations

weeping

I wept L17, L20, L94

during an interview with Lovelace L201

for Lovelace when he is ill L211

for joy at the prospect of reconciliation L216

at Lovelace's behavior after the fire L227

crying as she escapes Mrs. Sinclair's L228

weeping at Mrs. Moore's L232, L233, L235

weeping as Tomlinson talks of her family and reconciliation L243

weeping after the rape L260

I have wept away all my brains. I can weep no more L261.1

weeping, shouting Murder! Help! out the window of Mrs. Sinclair's L264

eyes red and swollen with weeping L276

weeping, bitterly L333, L349, L426

white

wearing a white damask night-gown, white handkerchief in hand L263

her snowy hand L263

white to come, having seen nothing but black L295

her white flowing robes L334

her linen white L334

dressed in white damask L334

her hand, the lily not of so beautiful a white L340

all in translucent white in Lovelace's dream L417

white lily inscribed on Clarissa's coffin L451

white satin lining Clarissa's coffin L451

in a white satin nightgown L471

dressed in virgin white L474

HARLOWE, MISS CLARISSA

white (cont.)

> her hands white as the lily L474
>
> returning in white paper her miniature of Anna to Hickman L476

widow

> Clarissa as Lovelace's widow L410

will see also **bequests of Clarissa; executors**

> bequeathing her estate, empowered by Grandfather L123, L400
>
> date, second day of September, year not given L507, L507fn
>
> estate sale
>
>> diamond necklace, solitaire, and buckles from Sir Josias Brookland, proceeds of sale to estate L507
>>
>> her grandmother's jewels, proceeds of sale, to Poor's Fund, or estate, or Papa L507
>
> executed
>
>> beginning to execute the will now that the funeral is over L503, L505
>>
>> Morden giving Belford proceeds of Grandfather's estate since his death L504
>>
>> to perform every article within two months time L507
>>
>> Morden assisting Belford in execution L507, L520
>
> executorship disputed
>
>> James not accepting Belford as executor L494.1, L501, L506
>>
>> James will execute the will himself where it is fit or reasonable L494.1
>>
>> Morden intending to enforce Belford's executorship L495
>>
>> Lovelace wanting to execute the will L497
>>
>> James wanting John and Antony Harlowe to execute the will L506
>
> historical references, compared to Louis XIV, whose will was flagrantly broken L508
>
> preamble, attached on black silk L507
>
> reading, Belford and Morden reading her will together L486
>
> text
>
>> completed by Clarissa L454
>>
>> showing her will to Belford and giving him the keys to the drawer L460
>>
>> Belford unlocking drawer holding her will and parcel of letters sealed with three black seals L486
>>
>> full text L507
>>
>> Belford giving Lovelace a copy of Clarissa's will L527
>
> witnesses, John Williams, Arthur Bedall, Elizabeth Swanton L507

wine see **drink**

writ

> writ against her, she is taken away by the sheriff's officers in a chair L333

writing see also **correspondence, Harlowe, Miss Clarissa**

> her love of writing L3, L101, L107, L135, L296
>
> its length L16
>
> her knack of writing, her natural talent L32.4, L33.3, L101, L206, L392, L486, L529
>
> writing a history of my sufferings L57
>
> her anonymous letter to Lady Drayton on severity in parents L58, L59
>
> to be refused pen and ink when she goes to Antony's L63
>
> beginning to hide her writing supplies L78
>
> writing materials taken away L79
>
> leaving harmless pieces of writing for the family to find L90, L91
>
> I know not how to forbear writing....I must write on L135
>
> writing a little book upon the principal acting plays L200
>
> writing continually at Mrs. Moore's L233
>
> resuming her writing after the rape L260
>
> delirious writings L261 Papers I–X
>
> keeps forgetting what she is writing L261.1
>
> asking for pen, ink, and paper when she goes to Bedlam L261.1
>
> penknife, to mend her pen L333
>
> writing materials, paper, pens, ink available at Rowland's L334

HARLOWE, MISS CLARISSA

writing (cont.)

 Mrs. Lovick writing for Clarissa L338
 has been up writing since five L348
 writing is all her diversion L365
 tiring herself writing L372, L405, L457
 book-learned and a scribbler L405
 too ill to read or write L458, L467, L473.2

HARLOWE, MR. JAMES, JUN., Clarissa's brother

abduction of Clarissa
>James's violence precipitating matters L112
>selecting books to send to Clarissa L173

address, forms of
>your servant, to Clarissa L75

address to Arabella by Mr. Robert Lovelace
>unacceptable as a match for Clarissa or Arabella L4

address to Clarissa by Mr. Robert Lovelace
>unacceptable as a match for Clarissa or Arabella L4
>angry about Lovelace's visits to Clarissa at Anna's L7

address to Clarissa by Mr. Roger Solmes
>accusing Clarissa of favoring Lovelace L4, L33.3, L52.1
>using Solmes's suit to thwart Lovelace L8
>threatening Clarissa into marrying Solmes L29
>angry at Mrs. Norton for her failure to persuade Clarissa L39
>threatening to return permanently to Scotland L42.1, L44, L45
>requesting Clarissa to stay at Antony's for a fortnight to receive Solmes L51.1, L52.1
>Clarissa must sign the settlements L52.1
>with Arabella in the garden taunting Clarissa L75
>assaulting Clarissa L78, L79
>keeping everyone inflamed L78
>insulting Aunt Hervey L78
>overheard by Clarissa plotting with Arabella L83

age
>older than Clarissa by many years L9
>a third older than Clarissa L32.4
>Clarissa younger by near a third L53.1

animals
>like a hunted boar L4

authority
>unrestrained by parental authority L5
>wishing Clarissa to accompany him to Scotland and care for his home there L6
>against Clarissa's visit to Anna L6
>authoritarian manner toward Clarissa L6
>usurping parental authority in regard to Clarissa L22, L22.2
>armed with authority of a father L433

books
>sent Clarissa
>>*Drexelius on Eternity* L173, L177
>>*Francis Spira* L173, L177
>>*Practice of Piety* L173, L177

character see also **control**
>violent temper L1, L13, L132, L407, L490
>>compared to Lovelace L3, L4
>dutifulness lacking L5
>haughty, morose L5
>greedy L8, L17
>arrogant L10
>rapacious L13, L223, L233.1
>self-serving, selfish L17, L111, L508
>ambitious L19, L145
>hard-hearted, cruel, malicious L51.2, L78, L111, L129, L145, L339, L437
>villain, half-witted L142
>insolent, ambitious, stupid L327

HARLOWE, MR. JAMES, JUN., Clarissa's brother

character (cont.)

    his family fearing him L437

    a menacer L534

classical references

    Virgil's *Georgic*, translated by Dryden L50.1, L52.1

conflict between Harlowe, James, Jun. and Clarissa see also **sibling rivalry**

    Lovelace his machine, implement L189, L276

    James source of Clarissa's problems L339

    James badly treating Dr. Lewen L408

contrivances of Lovelace see also **abduction of Clarissa**

    contrivance of kidnapping James and Solmes, planned L117, L119

control

    unrestrained by parental authority L5

    uncontrollable L29.1, L145, L233.1

death of Harlowe, Miss Clarissa

    to blame for the family's loss of Clarissa L355, L500

death of Harlowe, Miss Clarissa, avenged

    Clarissa urged to prosecute Lovelace to prevent mischief between James and Lovelace L427

    Clarissa asking James not to avenge her L490

    Lovelace deserving vengeance L494.1

    will avenge Clarissa if Morden does not L519

    Lovelace may answer his challenge L526

    to call Lovelace to account L533

    Belford to inform James of Lovelace's return in March to England L534

duel between James and Lovelace

    reported L1, L2

    wound to James's arm L1, L2, L4

        attended by Mr. Diggs L1

    cause of family dissention L2

    aborted duel preceding main duel L4

    complete report and background L4

    occurring at the home of Mr. Edward Symmes L4

    James as aggressor L4, L42

    destroying possibility of family alliance with Lovelace L13

    motivating revenge on Clarissa L15

    his claim that he was defending Clarissa L42.1

education

    college L53.1, L63

    liberal education L91

    young gentleman of both learning and parts L91

estates see also **inheritances**

    large estates in Scotland L2

    his northern estates L301

friends

    Singleton, Captain see also **rescue of Clarissa**

        his early visits to Harlowe Place L137

        master of a Scots vessel L137

        lives at Leith L137, L140

        his vessel lies at Rotherhithe L155

        sun-burnt sailor L177, L194

        pock-fretten, ill-looking, big-boned, six feet tall, heavy eye, overhanging brow, deck-treading stride, parched lips, brown coat, colored handkerchief, oaken plant in hand, couteau by his side L194

gentleman

    gentleman L91

HARLOWE, MR. JAMES, JUN., Clarissa's brother

godmother

  Lovell, godmother L4

    bequeathing James property in Yorkshire L2

    mentioned in Grandfather's will L4

    inheritance from L13

hanging

  deserving hanging L142

hatred of Lovelace

  grudge begun at college L3, L4

  sharing with Arabella a hatred of L4

  background and summary L13

  rivalry and hatred L91

  allying himself with the Bettertons against Lovelace L127

honor

  lost in the fall of his sister L379

influence in Harlowe Family

  inheritances giving him too much influence L5

  his influence with Papa and Mamma L17

  turning family against Clarissa L24.2, L53.1

  schemes sanctioned by Papa L39

  governing the will of the family L319

  governing Papa L379

informants

  steward (discharged) of Lord M.

    to supply information on Lovelace L4, L12, L14

    his report on Lovelace and his six or seven bad companions L81

inheritances see also **estates**

  his own

    large estates in Scotland L2

    inheritances giving him too much influence L5

    greed resulting from L8

    anticipated, from various relatives L13

    hopes for title based on L13

    from Godmother Lovell L13

      his Yorkshire property L2

      mentioned in Grandfather's will L4

    will not be Morden's heir L508

  Clarissa's, he will litigate to acquire L13

keys

  having keys to Papa's parlour L78

literary references see also **books**

  Dryden, John, translation of Virgil's *Georgic* L50.1

marriage

  match for Anna L5

  his reputation for temper and arrogance go against him L10

  Miss Nelly D'Oily, rejected by James L29.1

  poor prospects L29.3

  will never marry but to qualify for peerage L79

  married, unhappily CONCLUSION

meals, dinner

  dining and supping with Antony and Papa L20

money

  paying off Uncle Hervey's debt L47

HARLOWE, MR. JAMES, JUN., Clarissa's brother

motivations

> mentioned L115

names

> booby-'squire, booby 'squire L31, L127
>
> Jemmy L142

opinions

> on the female sex L8, L78
>> daughters are encumbrances L13
>> wit and L29.2
>> and matrimony L52.1, L78

peerage see also **title**

> hope for peerage, rank, and title L13
>> based on anticipated inheritances L13
>> foolish L36

prayers

> Clarissa's, to protect James from himself and from Lovelace L407

prosecution of Lovelace

> allying himself with Bettertons against Lovelace L127

rape of Clarissa, *foreshadowed*

> his rapacious views, his rapaciousness L13, L223, L223.1
>
> Lovelace disguised as Clarissa's brother L98

reconciliation between Clarissa and the Harlowe Family

> may be obliged to reconcile L216
>
> Clarissa having no hope of through James L309
>
> not allowing while he is away in Scotland L432
>
> family conference on L459
>
> If ever my sister Clary darkens these doors again, I never will L459

rescue of Clarissa see also **friends**, *Singleton, Captain*

> plotting with Singleton to rescue Clarissa L132, L137, L140, L142, L145, L155, L157, L158, L158.1, L164
>
> Singleton conferring with James and Arabella L139
>
> Leman a source of information for Lovelace about the plan L140
>
> may not have abandoned his plot L148, L177, L200
>
> plot abandoned L152, L229.1
>
> plot no longer feared by Clarissa L175
>
> Singleton visiting Anna to locate Clarissa L175, L177
>
> Singleton sent to find Clarissa's whereabouts L194
>
> Singleton attempting to bribe Anna's Kitty L196
>
> Clarissa fearing James may appear at Mrs. Sinclair's door L213, L214
>
> his plot used by Lovelace as an excuse to hide Clarissa L229.1
>
> inquiries from James and Singleton to be guarded against L233
>
> Lovelace claiming James is out looking for Clarissa L245
>
> Clarissa questioning whether James planned a journey with Solmes and Singleton L300
>
> no journey intended with Singleton and Solmes L301

residences

> his house near port of Leith L137

revenge

> on Clarissa L15
>
> plans and vows of, on Lovelace L139, L147

sibling rivalry see also **conflict between Harlowe, Mr. James, Jun. and Clarissa**

> neglected on account of Clarissa's superiority L182
>
> doing more to ruin Clarissa than Lovelace has done L459
>
> and Arabella's confederacy to disgrace Clarissa L472
>
> hating Arabella CONCLUSION
>
> regretting his cruel treatment of Clarissa CONCLUSION

HARLOWE, MR. JAMES, JUN., Clarissa's brother

snuff

> his snuff box L459

surgeons

> *Diggs, Mr.*
>> attending James's arm after the duel L1
>> visiting Anna, who inquires about the duel L1

title see also **peerage**

> hope for peerage, rank, and title L13
>> based on anticipated inheritances L13
>> foolish L36
> will never marry but to qualify for L79

travel

> Scotland, whereabouts at the time of Lovelace's address to Arabella L2, L3
> not intending a journey with Singleton and Solmes L301, L307
> once thought of setting out for his northern estates L301
> sent to Edinburgh by Papa to avoid trouble with Lovelace L378
> in Edinburgh L382, L406
> coming soon from Edinburgh L443
> returned home L455

vengeance

> his causeless vengeance L276

villain

> James as L142

weapons

> his sword L4
> mentioned L142

wills

> Clarissa's
>> not accepting Belford as Clarissa's executor L494.1
>> will execute Clarissa's will himself, where it is fit or reasonable L494.1
>> no need for executor outside the family L501
>> asking Belford to relinquish executorship of Clarissa's will L506
>> wanting John and Antony to execute Clarissa's will L506

writing

> his writing ability L53

HARLOWE, MR. JAMES, SEN., Clarissa's papa

address to Clarissa by Mr. Robert Lovelace

 mild disapproval of L3

 deferring to James on Lovelace's attentions to Clarissa L3, L4

 hinting Lovelace should discontinue his visits L4

 insulting Lovelace L4

 refusing to stop Lovelace's visits L4

 forbidding Clarissa to receive Lovelace while at Anna's L6

address to Clarissa by Mr. Roger Solmes

 intimidating her into accepting Solmes L16, L20

 angry at Mamma for pleading Clarissa's case L19

 sanctioning James's schemes L39

 demanding Clarissa's obedience L41.2

 immoveable on the Solmes plan L78

 ordering Clarissa to be carried to Antony's at once L78

 turning entire matter over to James, Arabella, and Antony L80

authority

 exerting some restraint on James L6

 know that I will be obeyed L8

 threatened by Clarissa's refusal to obey L8, L41.1, L84

 mentioned L18, L36, L39, L84

 wounded L50.1

 turning entire matter over to James, Arabella, and Antony L80

 Clarissa's respect for L94

 sending James to Edinburgh to avoid trouble with Lovelace L378

 governed by James L379, L433

banishment of Clarissa

 banishing Clarissa from his presence L25.4

 ready to turn Clarissa out of doors L51

bequests of Clarissa

 real estate L507

blessings

 Clarissa wanting his blessing L360, L379

business

 his tradesmen in London L126

character

 tyrant, gloomy tyrant L27, L109, L152, L191, L248, L252

 his arbitrariness L36

 immoveable L78

 despotic L248

 much to answer for L316

 implacable L373

 had I never been hard-hearted L503

correspondence, Harlowe, Mr. James, Sen.

 returning Clarissa's letter unopened L59

curses

 on Clarissa L146, L147, L152, L172, L173, L191, L201, L225, L226, L230, L233, L235, L243, L261 Paper II, L263, L273, L274, L318, L343, L347, L348, L373, L443

 his rejection of Clarissa L187

 his curse following Clarissa into the next world L307

 Clarissa hoping for revocation L307, L308, L309, L320, L360

 Clarissa can neither live nor die under it L307

 Clarissa writing to ask Arabella to have it revoked L348, L349

 his curse weakening Clarissa in her already weak condition L351

HARLOWE, MR. JAMES, SEN., Clarissa's papa

curses (cont.)

>Clarissa asking Arabella to intercede in revoking the part of the curse relating to the hereafter, as she has already been punished in the here L363

>withdrawn L377, L378, L379

death of Harlowe, Miss Clarissa

>receiving news of L494.1

>unable to view the body L503

death of Harlowe, Mr. James, Sen.

>survived Clarissa by about three years CONCLUSION

estates

>rich L109

>steward of Clarissa's estate L376

forgiveness

>Clarissa wanting his forgiveness L309

>will never own Clarissa or forgive her L378

grieving for Clarissa

>mentioned L379

illnesses

>gout L4, L5, L8, L20

>gout thrown into his stomach L376, L494.1

inheritances

>his power over Clarissa's L2

>his wealth increased by Mamma's inheritances L4

>will litigate if she marry Lovelace L39

kneeling

>would kneel before Clarissa L144, L145

marriages, Clarissa's to Solmes

>to be next week at Antony's chapel L41.2

meals, dinner

>dining and supping with Antony L20

real estate

>bequeathed Clarissa's real estate L507

HARLOWE, MR. JOHN, Clarissa's uncle

abduction of Clarissa
>> renouncing Clarissa L147

address to Clarissa by Mr. Robert Lovelace
>> approving Lovelace as a match for Clarissa L3
>> ambivalence toward Lovelace L13

address to Clarissa by Mr. Roger Solmes
>> against pushing Clarissa into marrying Solmes L9
>> Clarissa begging his help not to go to Antony's L59.4
>> his angry refusal of Clarissa's proposals L62.1

age
>> will be 74 years on June 29 L272.1

bequests of Clarissa
>> family pictures L507

biblical references
>> soft answers turn away wrath L60.1

birthday
>> June 29th L271, L272.1

bowling
>> a great bowler L214

business
>> his new-found mines L4

character
>> the old gentleman L179
>> Clarissa's second papa L407

contrivances of Lovelace see also **abduction of Clarissa**
>> contrivance of Captain Tomlinson and Uncle Harlowe's birthday
>>> Tomlinson pretends to negotiate a reconciliation through Uncle Harlowe L214, L216, L221
>>> using the green with a gentleman Clarissa did not know L217
>>> to be in Kentish Town June 29th to celebrate his anniversary birthday L271, L272.1
>>> will not be at Kentish Town on Thursday L284
>>> Clarissa questioning truth of Lovelace's claims of a birthday celebration L300, L304
>>> his birthday not kept, not intended to be kept L301, L305, L307
>>> not knowing any Tomlinson L305

correspondence, Harlowe, Miss Clarissa with Lovelace
>> accusing Clarissa of corresponding with Lovelace L32.2

fearing Lovelace
>> double-servanted and double-armed against Lovelace L31

gentleman
>> the old gentleman L179

housekeepers
>> *Hodges, Mrs. Sarah*
>>> suspected of familiarities with his housekeeper L217
>>> Uncle Harlowe's housekeeper and paramour L229.1
>>> Clarissa querying her on Lovelace's contrivance of Uncle Harlowe's birthday L304
>>> called Sarah L305

illnesses
>> his declining health L243

influence in Harlowe Family
>> having great weight in the family L174

names
>> first called Uncle Harlowe L3

paramours
>> *Hodges, Mrs. Sarah*
>>> suspected of familiarities with his housekeeper L217

HARLOWE, MR. JOHN, Clarissa's uncle

paramours, *Hodges, Mrs. Sarah* (cont.)

his housekeeper and paramour L229.1

reconciliation between Clarissa and the Harlowe Family

may be persuaded to go along with Mamma and favor reconciliation L151, L174

Hickman speaking with Uncle Harlowe on Clarissa's behalf L174, L179

Clarissa hoping he will take her part L176

discouraging Hickman's application on Clarissa's behalf L182

sending Mr. Brand to inquire about Clarissa L381

will not have Clarissa be destitute, may allow her some part of her estate L406

would have sympathized with Clarissa L432

after her death, expressing forgiveness, love, and reconciliation L485

refuge for Clarissa

refusing Clarissa's request for refuge L32.2

trustee

trustee of Clarissa's estate L27, L55, L406

co-trustee with Morden L214

visits

to Clarissa, in her confinement L75

from Clarissa, none for ten months L217

will

to favor Clarissa L13, L75

HARLOWE FAMILY

abduction of Clarissa

    supposing Clarissa's flight premeditated L97, L101

    family reaction to Clarissa's flight L100

    raving, implacable L103

    refusing to send Clarissa her things L111

    will not pursue Clarissa L116

    will not have her back L117, L189

    will not stir to save her life L183

    disgraced by Clarissa L392

address to Clarissa by Mr. Roger Solmes

    promotion of Solmes's suit L7, L8, L17, L21

    using Aunt Hervey to make Solmes's formal offer to Clarissa L8

    intimidation and threats to Clarissa L8, L20

    terms of Solmes's suit L16, L17, L39

    Clarissa's confinement L24.1

    using Mrs. Norton to persuade Clarissa L27, L39, L90

    hurrying to execute plan in the face of Clarissa's apparent preference for Lovelace L39

    tumult over Clarissa's refusal to go to Antony's L51

    family assembled in close debate over Clarissa's counter proposals L61

    would have yielded had Clarissa held her ground L144, L151, L317, L432

    glad he was rejected L147

animals

    spider L106

    toads L115

arrival of Morden from Florence, *anticipated*

    his imminent arrival driving the family to hurry Clarissa's marriage to Solmes L53.1

    have written to Morden L61

banishment of Clarissa

    wanting Clarissa to go to one of the plantations L408

    wanting Clarissa to go to Pennsylvania L429

    wanting Clarissa to go to some one of the colonies L443

blessings

    Clarissa wanting their blessing before she dies L382

business

    the plantations L408

character

    Grandfather's opinion L27

    men in straw L106

    tame spirits L106

    malignant hearts, wicked L127

    implacable L128, L319, L347, L348, L358, L364, L372, L385, L399, L413, L418, L439, L456

    hard-hearted L172, L364, L437, L455

    grasping men L233.1

    unforgiving L301

    severe and cruel L405, L446

    hearts of flint L459

church

    attending church L22, L75

    where Lovelace looked challenge at the Harlowe Family L30, L31, L36, L106

    attending church but three times since Clarissa left L301

clergymen

    Brand, Mr. Elias, young Oxford clergyman and scholar L90.1

        character

            to have his fortune made by Uncle Harlowe L90.1

HARLOWE FAMILY

clergymen, *Brand, Mr. Elias*, character (cont.)

        pedant L94, L455

        officious young man, college novice L381, L431, L443, L459

        the young Levite L399, L410, L443

        called Parson Brand, Fire-Brand, incendiary L443, L445, L467

        account of, by Clarissa L446

    classical references

        his knowledge of Latin and Greek L381, L399

        Miserum est aliena vivere quadra L444

        Juvenal, *Satire VIII*, quoted in Latin L444, L444n3

        untraced quote in Latin L444, L444n5

        Horace, *Odes I*, quoted in Latin L444, L444n6

        Ovid, misattributed quote, L444, L444n7

    costume, dressed in a riding-habit L399

    funeral of Clarissa, not chosen to pronounce discourse at Clarissa's interment L501

    informants, the milliner, Mr. Walton L444, L445

    informing on Clarissa

        sent to inquire about Clarissa L361, L381, L399

        not reporting to the Harlowe Family what they do not want to hear L382, L446, L458

        his indifference to Clarissa's poor health L399

        his misrepresentations to the family about Clarissa L408

        creating scandal on account of Belford's visits to Clarissa L431, L433, L455

        his suspicions of Clarissa's attending prayers L444

        his letter of recantation mentioned L460, L464, L466, L467

    literary references

        de Foe, Daniel, *The True-Born Englishman*, quoted L444, L444n2

        Quarles, Francis, *Emblems*, misquoted L444, L444n1

    marriages, Clarissa's to Solmes

        hired to perform wedding L90.1

    names

        as Dr. Brand, minister L90

        signing his letter Elias Brand L444

    sayings, honours change manners L444

    snuff, purchasing Spanish snuff L399

    writing, letter-writing his talent L444

  Lewin, Dr. Arthur

    bequest of Clarissa, twenty guineas for a ring L507

    character

        his wisdom L48

        excellent divine L409

        Clarissa's favorite divine L426

    clergyman, Mr. Brand's learned and worthy principal L381

    conflict between Harlowe Family and Clarissa

        opposed to Clarissa's marriage to Solmes L90, L90.1

        family incurring his displeasure L408

        badly treated by James L409

    death

        dying soon after reading Clarissa's letter L430

        very lately dead L503

    duel between James and Lovelace

        frustrating James's first challenge to Lovelace L4

        distract Lovelace as the latter looks challenge at the Harlowes after church L30, L36

    family

        loving his own child and loving Clarissa L427

HARLOWE FAMILY

clergymen, *Lewin, Dr. Arthur*, family (cont.)

        his daughter L507

        funeral of Clarissa, would have pronounced discourse at L501

        illness, declining health L381, L408, L427

        influence on Clarissa L48

            advising steadiness of mind L19

        marriages, Clarissa's to Solmes

            arbitrator for Clarissa's situation with Solmes L53.1, L54.1

            refusing to marry Clarissa without her consent, opposed to the wedding L90, L90.1

        names

            signing his letter Arthur L427

            as Lewen L408, L409, L427, L501, L503, L507

        prosecution of Lovelace, urging Clarissa to prosecute L427, L429

        reconciliation between Clarissa and the Harlowe Family, offering to mediate L408

        visits

            visiting Clarissa in her confinement L75, L77

            his conversation visits L82

            to visit as preparation for the wedding L83

            will not visit Harlowe Place, badly treated by James L408

    Melvill, Mr.

        Dr. Lewen's assistant L501

        to pronounce discourse at Clarissa's interment L501, L503

        to deliver a brief eulogium L501

        a serious and sensible man L503

        2 Corinthians 9:7, quoted in his eulogy of Clarissa L504

        given a ring by Morden L504

conflict between Harlowe Family and Clarissa

    family united against her in the Solmes affair L6, L14

    Harlowe Family and motivating forces L8, L13

    blaming all on James L9, L112

    made an instrument of revenge against Lovelace L13

    How impolitic in them all to join two people in one interest whom they wish for ever to keep asunder L14

    surely *they* will yield L14

    recounting measures taken by family against her L32.3, L112

conflict between Harlowe Family and Lovelace

    James and Arabella allied against Lovelace L4, L7

    noted L13, L20

    Lovelace an enemy, feared, yet provoked L14

    opinion of Lovelace L40

    their malice and resentment of Lovelace L127

    Lovelace's implacable enemies L158.1

    Lovelace's triumph over them L158.1

    Harlowe Family the aggressors L324

    fearing both Lovelace and James L437

correspondence, Harlowe, Miss Clarissa with Lovelace

    searching Clarissa's room for hidden correspondence L78, L90.1

    removing her writing supplies L78

    suspecting Clarissa of writing letters L90.1

correspondence, Harlowe Family

    having written to Morden L61

    no letter will be received from Clarissa L301, L307

    Miss Howe's angry Letters 351, 353, 355 incensing them L356, L357, L360, L361

    Clarissa's letter to Arabella received in great ferment L374

    receiving Clarissa's posthumous correspondence L494

HARLOWE FAMILY

counsellors

Derham, Counsellor, to attend Clarissa, hear her story, and begin a process L429

death of Harlowe, Miss Clarissa

receiving news of in Morden's letter to James L494

gathered to grieve and await the hearse L500

duel between James and Lovelace

causing contentions L1, L5

ill treatment of Lovelace following duel L4

estates see also **inheritances**

Harlowe Place sprung up from a dunghill within every elderly person's remembrance L34

their *acquired* fortune L109

too rich L455

family alliances

background L13

united against Clarissa L32.2, L50, L60.1

family arguing L78

coldness between Morden and the Harlowe Family L431

Morden's conflict with James about treatment of Clarissa L459

fearing Lovelace

fearing Lovelace L14

fearing both Lovelace and James L437

forgiveness

will forgive Clarissa only at her last extremity L376

unwilling to forgive Clarissa L392

friends

Hartley, Mr., having a widow sister in Pennsylvania with whom Clarissa may board L429

hanging

a man found hanging in the haunted coppice about twenty years ago L35, L86fn

hatred of Lovelace

noted L13, L20

hires

Ackland, Mr., to attend Clarissa to hear her story and begin a process L429

honor

family dishonored by Lovelace L7

Clarissa's duty to protect

by marrying Solmes L7, L8, L16

by prosecuting Lovelace L427

family honor, noted L78

their concern for L221

their young honor supercilious and touchy L221

Mrs. Norton little favoring their honor, in favoring Clarissa L308

illnesses

have been ill L214

not believing that Clarissa is ill L361, L402, L432

inheritances see also **estates**

discussed at length L13

opposed to Clarissa's inheritance, but deferring to Grandfather's wishes L32.4

to be reassessed after her flight L100

marriages, Clarissa's to Lovelace

not believing Lovelace will marry Clarissa L352

marriages, Clarissa's to Solmes

rejoicing at wedding plans for Wednesday L83

believing Clarissa will make herself sick to avoid the wedding L90.1

HARLOWE FAMILY

meals, breakfast
> at breakfast together L22, L501
> breakfast with Morden L502

money
> distressing Clarissa by withholding her money L347, L364, L437
> to allow Clarissa some part of her estate L406

motivations
> greed L8, L10
> family aggrandizement L13, L16, L19
> hatred of Lovelace L13, L20
> inheritances L13
> paternal authority L13
> ambition L19
> questioned by Lovelace L115
> resentments against Clarissa L115

neighbors
> *Symmes, Mr. Edward*
>> duel between James and Lovelace occurring at the home of Mr. Edward Symmes L4
>> brother of the other Symmes L4
>> two miles off from Harlowe Place L4
>> Clarissa inquiring of Mr. Symmes about the duel L4

peerage
> not allied to L79

pictures
> the assembled Harlowes, by Joseph Highmore, book cover of the Penguin edition of *Clarissa* L147n1

plantations
> wanting Clarissa to go to one of the plantations L408

pride
> mentioned L109, L228

prosecution of Lovelace
> will prosecute Lovelace L132
> urging Clarissa to prosecute Lovelace L427
> sending the family's attorneys to take minutes of Clarissa's story L429, L430
> Clarissa's prosecution of Lovelace a precondition to reconciliation L456
> to prosecute Lovelace if Morden die L533

reconciliation between Clarissa and the Harlowe Family
> unreconcilable L320, L443
> Clarissa's prosecution of Lovelace, a precondition L456
> family conference on, with Morden and Mrs. Norton L459
> seeking reconciliation, having received letters from Dr. H., Morden, and Mr. Brand L482

relations
> *Fuller* and *Allinson*, distant relations attending Clarissa's funeral L504
> *Harlowe, Grandfather*
>> bequest to Clarissa
>>> family pictures and plate, and less than half his real estate L42
>>> mentioned L135, L174, L179, L375
>> character
>>> fondness for Clarissa L4, L465
>>> opinion of the Harlowe Family L27
>>> doting, good old man L429
>>> giving gifts to Clarissa L529
>> estate
>>> mentioned L157
>>> less than half the total estate left to Clarissa L42

HARLOWE FAMILY

relations, *Harlowe, Grandfather*, estate (cont.)

    considerable sums arising from his estate since his death L202

    inquired into by Lovelace's family in preparation for marriage L325

    estate he left Clarissa mentioned L375

  trustees

    Morden L27, L32.3, L87, L173

    Uncle Harlowe L27, L55

  will

    Aunt Harman requesting to see L1

    source for family genealogy L4

    flawed, deeds flawed L4, L20, L55

    partial text L4

    mentioning Lovell as James's benefactress L4

    disappointing James L13

    purpose of L27

    giving Clarissa power to bequeath her estate L123, L400

    intending Clarissa to live upon her own estate L248

    Clarissa knowing his will by heart L460

    uncles not following his example with respect to Clarissa L472

Harlowe, Grandmother, her jewels, L41.1, L45, L202, L507, L520

Harlowe, Uncles, position in family and unmarried state L6

religious references

  not Roman Catholic L13

  not Christians, or even pagans with bowels L319

reputation

  their concern L106, L455

revenge

  Solmes as revenge on Lovelace for duel and on Clarissa for her inheritance L36

sealings

  a Harlowe seal L143

servants

Barnes, Betty, Arabella's maid L507

  attending

    Harlowe Family L8

    fainting Clarissa L16

    insolence to Clarissa L23, L53, L57, L63, L78, L117, L175

    attending Clarissa after Hannah's departure L24.1, L25

    carrying threats from Clarissa's siblings L29

    set over Clarissa L32.3, L53, L430

    reporting Solmes's remarks to Clarissa L40

    carrying message to Clarissa to come down and surrender L41

    informing Clarissa of plans to remove her to Antony's L51, L53, L62, L83

    taking letters to Clarissa L59, L61

    message to Clarissa that her proposals are refused L61

    spying on Clarissa L69, L80, L90

    searching Clarissa's closet L69, L91

    letting Clarissa believe Mamma will visit her L77

    Clarissa falling into Papa's room L78

    sent to take Clarissa's pen and ink away L79

    warning Clarissa away from the family in the garden L80

    Clarissa's gaoleress L80, L91

    seeing that Clarissa has been writing L84

    attending Clarissa dining in the ivy summer-house L86, L90, L91

    Clarissa taking her with to Pennsylvania L430

HARLOWE FAMILY

servants, *Barnes, Betty* (cont.)

    bequest of Clarissa, ten pounds L507

    biblical references, *Luke* 15:7, there will be joy in Heaven L90, L90n1

    character

        loyalty to Arabella L23

        her nature L53

        wench L91

        saucy gossip L142

    Coventry Act and Betty L68

    death, pining and consumptive, within a year after Clarissa's CONCLUSION

    gossiping

        with Hannah about Lovelace L14

        source of information for confined Clarissa L21, L63, L78

        with Leman about Lovelace and Rosebud L71, L73

        with Leman about Clarissa's apartment being searched L103

        with Mrs. Norton about Clarissa's letters, Belford's visits L374, L376, L431, L459

    illness L532

    keys

        discovered, key in hand, searching Clarissa's closet L69

        sent to fetch Clarissa's keys L78

    literary references, reading *Mother Goose* and concerning the *Fairies* L63

    low people L73

    marriage

        mate for Leman L95, L140, L175

        Leman's lover L103

        her poor treatment of Leman L532

        unmarried CONCLUSION

    names, Mrs. Betty L25, L53, L61, L63

    punishment, to be punished by Lovelace L117, L175

    reconciliation between Clarissa and the Harlowe Family, changing her note in anticipation L483

    sayings, there's no inconvenience but has its convenience L63

    snuff L63

  Leman, Joseph

    abduction of Clarissa

        causing a commotion, frightening her into flight with Lovelace L94, L113

        seen by family returning from pursuit of Lovelace L100

        reporting to Lovelace the family's reaction to Clarissa's flight L103

    animals, little dog that follows him L113

    biblical references, *Matthew* 16:26, what shall a man get to lose his soul L139, L139n2

    bribes, Lovelace promising him the Blue Beard Inn and Betty for his assistance L113, L140

    common folk, low people L73, L139, L241

    disloyalty

        disloyal L35, L84, L117

        confidant of James L62

        double agent, double agency explained L62, L80, L100, L113, L119

        Lovelace's intelligencer L62, L85

        gossiping with Betty about Lovelace and Rosebud L71, L73

        not entirely loyal to Lovelace L73, L84

        causing family to suspect Clarissa of corresponding with Lovelace L84

        spying on Clarissa for the family L86

        family suspect Lovelace's source of information is Clarissa, when in fact it is Leman L91

        doubted by Clarissa L94

        corrupted by Lovelace L95

        disliking the way Betty treats Clarissa L96

HARLOWE FAMILY

servants, *Leman, Joseph*, disloyalty (cont.)

        vile agent of Lovelace L101, L229.1

        used by Lovelace to influence Antony, who influences Mrs. Howe L104

        informing Lovelace about James's alliance with the Bettertons L127

        informing Lovelace about James's plan to rescue Clarissa L137, L140, L152

        of no more use to Lovelace L175

        Lovelace his cully L189

        could not have revealed to Lovelace Norton's application to Mamma nor Hickman's to Uncle Harlowe L229.1

    keys, having a key to the garden door L35

    marriage

        mate for Betty L95, L113, L175

        Betty's lover L103, L113

    opinions, on matrimony L73

    punishment, Lovelace to punish him L175

    sayings

        plases are no inherittances nowadays L96, L96n1

        to throe my hat at her, or so L96, L96n2

        as if she was among beans L139, L139n1

servants, treatment of

    dismissal of Hannah L23, L25.2

    servants set to watch Clarissa L35, L69

story

    knowing not what Clarissa has suffered L368

    sending the family's attorneys to take minutes of Clarissa's story L430

    not inquiring into the particulars of Clarissa's story L430

title

    peerage, not allied to L79

    beneath Lovelace L109

transportation

    not offering Mrs. Norton the family chariot to visit Clarissa L483

HERVEY, MRS. DOROTHY, Clarissa's aunt

abduction of Clarissa
> not finding Clarissa in the ivy summer-house nor in the cascade L100
> Clarissa writing to ask for her things and some money L116
> renouncing Clarissa L147

address to Arabella by Mr. Robert Lovelace
> cautioning Arabella to be reserved with Lovelace L2

address to Clarissa by Mr. Robert Lovelace
> good match for Clarissa L3
> Lovelace confiding in Aunt Hervey his passion for Clarissa L3
> relating steward's (discharged) report on Lovelace to Clarissa L4
> wanting to send James to Yorkshire till all blows over L6
> cautioning Clarissa about his vengefulness L44
> carrying stories about Lovelace to Clarissa L79

address to Clarissa by Mr. Roger Solmes
> her opposition to Solmes silenced L8, L13, L81
> making the formal offer to Clarissa on behalf of Solmes L8
> advice to Clarissa on Solmes L9, L13
> her support of the Solmes plan L17, L27
> her suggestion that the family reflect on Mrs. Norton's views L39
> suggesting Mr. Wyerley as a compromise L44
> attempting to persuade Clarissa to marry Solmes L44
> her sympathy and kind words to Clarissa L45
> pleading in Clarissa's favor L52.1
> visiting Clarissa, long conversation L77, L83, L85
> censuring James, crying for Clarissa L78
> her opinion of Solmes confided in Dolly L78
> giving Clarissa settlements to sign, the parchments L83
> conversation with Clarissa in the ivy summer-house L91
> claiming Papa would have relented if Clarissa had not L145

bequests of Clarissa
> fifty guineas for a ring L507
> whole length picture of Clarissa in the Vandyke taste, or to Mamma L507, L510.3

character
> example of female passiveness L8, L9, L13

classical references
> Caesar...ides of March L144

conflict between Harlowe, James, Jun. and Clarissa
> There never was so set a malice in man as in your cousin James Harlowe. They will ruin the flower and ornament of their family L78

family see also **relations**
> *Hervey, Uncle,* husband
>> requesting Lovelace to instruct a young man in the grand tour L3
>> Clarissa writing down Lovelace's instructions, beginning their correspondence L3
>> supporting the Solmes plan L17
>> James paying off Uncle Hervey's debt L47
>> would have been sympathetic to Clarissa L432
>> comforting Papa L503
> *Hervey, Miss Dolly,* daughter
>> forbidden to see Clarissa L41
>> her fondness for Clarissa L78, L81, L90.1
>> advising Clarissa to marry Lovelace and resume her estate L78
>> made to request Clarissa's keys L78
>> reporting family opinion to Clarissa L78
>> sent to take Clarissa's writing materials away L79

HERVEY, MRS. DOROTHY, Clarissa's aunt

family, *Hervey, Miss Dolly* (cont.)

slipping Clarissa a secret letter L90

her signature, Dorothy L90

suffering for her attachment to Clarissa L91

her prayers for Clarissa L144

wanting to visit Clarissa L432

her happiness when Clarissa escapes from Harlowe Place L432

Clarissa's cousin L433

bequeathed harpsichord, chamber-organ, music books, head-dress, ruffles, twenty-five guineas for a ring L507

Morden presenting her with Clarissa's jewels L520

fearing Lovelace

cautioning Clarissa about his vengefulness L44

first love

few women...marry their first loves L44

flower

There never was so set a malice in man as in your cousin James Harlowe. They will ruin the flower and ornament of their family L78

gossip

relating the steward's (discharged) report on Lovelace to Clarissa L4

carrying stories about Lovelace to Clarissa L79

influence in Harlowe Family

dare not speak in Clarissa's favor L174, L433

would have sympathized with Clarissa L432

inheritances

confiding in Clarissa her uncles' intentions to favor her in their wills L13

marriage

her own unhappy nuptials L13

murder

fears of L144, L145

names

Dorothy L59.3

opinions

on marriage L13

parents governing in affairs of L39

on obedience L83

on love L83

refuge for Clarissa

her home as L145

relations see also **family**

Harlowe, Mrs. Charlotte, sister, only sister L433, L500, L507

Morden, cousin L503

vengeance

cautioning Clarissa about Lovelace's vengefulness L44

visits

to Mrs. Norton L432

HICKMAN, MR. CHARLES, Anna's suitor

age

> fifteen or twenty years younger than Mrs. Howe L46
> not old enough to need spectacles L346
> his eyes older than the rest of him L346

animals

> an odd dog L236

ball, Colonel Ambrose's

> attending L350, L367

bequests of Clarissa

> ring with Clarissa's hair, miniature of Anna L507

character

> his humility L10
> an unexceptionable man L28
> a puritan L48
> his suspiciously easy grasp of Lovelace's affairs L48
> his horns better hidden than Lovelace's L68
> passive L104, L128
> a fool L117
> good and grave L128, L229
> cringing L128
> Anna's almoner L132
> his generosity L132
> a modest man L134, L136
> prim Gothamite L198
> male-virgin, virtuous, and innocent L236
> a fop, starched as his ruffles L346
> so prim, so affected, so mincing, yet so clouterly in his person L346
> finical and formal but agreeable and sensible L366
> too meek for a man L367
> has not much penetration L404
> a very worthy man, gentle-dispositioned L520

correspondence, Howe, Miss Anna with Clarissa

> hiring Filmer to assist L100
> conveying their secret correspondence L107, L119, L132, L148
> caught by Mrs. Howe passing a letter from Clarissa to Anna L136
> hiring Simon Collins to convey L156, L174.3, L184, L187, L217, L229, L229.1, L316, L318, L327, L328, L338
> believing Anna should continue corresponding with Clarissa L164
> Clarissa suggesting he write for Anna L165
> to whom Clarissa must direct hers for Anna L316

costume

> his long bib and beads L46
> King William cravat L46, L46n1
> his cravat and ruffles L74
> stroking his ruffles, setting his wig, pulling his neckcloth, long enough for a bib L346
> not using spectacles L346
> fribbled with his waistcoat buttons L346

courtship

> suit to Anna L10
> favored by Mrs. Howe L10, L27, L58, L65, L81, L111
> Anna's lukewarm feelings for, her indifferent attitude L55, L58, L151
> appreciated by Clarissa L55, L69, L73
> Anna's poor treatment of L59, L65, L74, L82, L120, L201, L434, L520, L535
> erecting an altar to Anna L128

HICKMAN, MR. CHARLES, Anna's suitor

courtship (cont.)

his whining, creeping, submissive courtship L128

compared to Lovelace's courtship style L128

his treatment of Anna L201

Lovelace claiming Anna hates Hickman and loves Lovelace L236

would fare better with Anna if Mrs. Howe were against him L252

Anna never loving him L341

Lovelace will let him have Anna safe and entire L371

Anna's relations' fondness for Hickman L434

made by Anna to look weak and silly L435

his patience with Anna L458

not appreciated by Anna L458

Clarissa advising him to be patient with Anna L465

history of his courtship with Anna L523

death of Harlowe, Miss Clarissa

receiving news of L494

education

designed for the law, chambers at Lincoln's Inn L196

executors

Morden's co-executor with Belford L528

having a copy of Morden's will L528

family see also **relations**

Charles, son CONCLUSION

Clarissa, daughter CONCLUSION

Howe, Miss Anna, wife CONCLUSION

friends

Dormer, Mr., at whose house Hickman had an interview with Lovelace L341, L510.1

funeral of Clarissa

attending L504

grand tour

must have made the grand tour L198

hires

Filmer

a husbandman in Finch Lane, near Howe residence L100

engaged to receive Anna's secret correspondence from Clarissa L100

informant

finding out opinions of the ladies of Lovelace's family about the state of affairs in the Harlowe Family L26

sounding Lord M. on a subject recommended by Clarissa L27

sent to London by Anna to inquire about Lovelace's life in town L27

results of his investigation reported to Clarissa by Anna L48

inheritances

mother-in-law [stepmother] leaving him jointure of £600 a year, and considerable L459

Jews

miserly citizen L346

law

designed for the law, chambers at Lincoln's Inn L196

mannerisms

stroking his chin, stroking his ruffles, setting his wig, pulling his neckcloth L346

fribbling with his waistcoat buttons L346

manners

his flourishes L119

marriage

match for Clarissa L46

match for Mrs. Howe L46

HICKMAN, MR. CHARLES, Anna's suitor

marriage (cont.)
    if Mrs. Howe marries Antony, Anna will dismiss Hickman L183
marriages, Anna's to Hickman
    anticipated L136
    Anna may marry him soon to provide protection for Clarissa L252.1
    put off because of Clarissa's unhappiness L366
    settlements engrossed L366
    reported CONCLUSION
marriages, Clarissa's to Lovelace
    asking Lovelace his intentions toward Clarissa L346
    believing Lovelace would marry Clarissa L359
meals, breakfast
    breakfasting with Clarissa and Belford L365
messengers
    Collins, Simon
        an honest higgler L156
        going to town Mondays, Wednesdays, and Fridays L156
        delivering Anna's letters to Clarissa L156, L174.3, L184, L187, L316, L318, L327, L328
        found by Lovelace to be a common poacher, deer-stealer, and warren-robber L174.3
        Lovelace will have him robbed L174.3
        Lovelace will confiscate any letters from Anna delivered to Mr. Wilson L217
        delivering Anna's to Wilson's, then directly to Mrs. Sinclair's, and as Clarissa was not there, back to
            Wilson's L229, L229.1
        no longer needed to convey Anna's correspondence L338
miniatures
    Clarissa sending him her miniature of Anna L476, L507
money
    generous gift to Hannah L132
    offering Clarissa money L366
    contributing to the Poor's Fund CONCLUSION
mourning
    new suit of mourning for Clarissa as for a near relation L520
names
    first called Charles L476
physical appearance
    description by Anna L46
    his white hand and fine diamond ring L136
    plump L229
Poor's Fund
    contributing to CONCLUSION
reconciliation between Clarissa and the Harlowe Family
    interposing on Clarissa's behalf with Mrs. Howe L100
    attempting, failing to sway Uncle Harlowe in Clarissa's favor L174, L182, L184
    his application to Uncle Harlowe mentioned L229.1
refuge for Clarissa
    mentioned as L85
    wishing to offer protection of his house L252.1
relations see also **family**
    Hickman, Sir Charles, his father L528
    his elder brother died L196
    his mother-in-law [stepmother] lately dead L459
rings
    his fine diamond ring L136

HICKMAN, MR. CHARLES, Anna's suitor

title

   may one day be a baronet L46

transportation

   offering his chariot and four L252.1

   taking his own chariot to Dormer's L346

travel

   escorting Mrs. Howe and Anna to Mrs. Larkin's L65

   to accompany Anna and Mrs. Howe to the Isle of Wight L342

vengeance

   Lovelace wishing for vengeance on L326

virgin

   male-virgin, virtuous, and innocent L236

visits

   to Lovelace, interview with Lovelace L341, L346, L358, L510.1

   to Clarissa L358, L360, L365, L444

      planned, but being watched by Lovelace L319

   to a neighborhood coffee-house with Belford L366

   to Dr. H. to inquire about Clarissa L366

weeping

   for Clarissa L366

white

   his white hand and fine diamond ring L136

HOWE, MISS ANNA, Clarissa's friend

abduction of Clarissa

will send Clarissa money and clothes L100, L111, L119, L132

accomplishments

harpsichord, singing L128

address, forms of

your servant L12

address to Clarissa by Mr. Roger Solmes

source of information about Solmes L27

advising Clarissa to go to London, hide from Solmes and Lovelace till Morden comes L81

her interference feared by the family L87

advocate for Clarissa

Clarissa's pert advocate L378

aliases

Soberton, Mr. John, to whom Clarissa should address hers, in Finch Lane L100

animals

monkeys, men as L46

basilisk eyes, killing Lovelace at the ball L56, L367

the reptile word, OBEY, in marriage L68

animal hostility, in wolf, lion, lamb, game chicken L136

a vixen L237, L371, L395

a mole L248

vipers, Mrs. Sinclair and her whores as L317

reptiles, men a vile race of L455

hyaena, Lovelace as L456

arrival of Morden from Florence, *anticipated*

advising Clarissa to go to London and hide till Morden come L81

advising Clarissa to write to Morden L148

ball, Colonel Ambrose's

attending L350, L358, L367

interviews with Lovelace L366, L367

bequests of Clarissa

ring with Clarissa's hair L507

Clarissa's whole length picture L507

Clarissa's best diamond ring L507

her needlework L507

Clarissa's correspondence, sent by Belford L507, L521

Clarissa's Memorandum book L510.3

biblical references see also **God, references to**

tell it not in Gath L15

all punctilio is at an end the moment you are out of your father's house L87, L89, L90

Exodus 16:3, your Israelitish hankerings L142, L142n1

as Herod loved his Mariamne L229.1, L229.1n1

black

Rosebud, a plot...to wash a blackamoor white L72

books

Norris, John, *Miscellanies*, sent to Clarissa L148

Clarissa returning Anna's *Norris* L149, L150, L156

Lovelace *out-Norrised* L198, L199, L215

character

her spritely, vivacious nature, fire and spirit, fury L55, L197.2, L252, L347, L435, L502

charming, confoundedly smart and spiritful L104, L117

very saucy girl, saucebox L111, L197

a virago L117, L198, L229, L233, L341

compared to Clarissa L136, L252

HOWE, MISS ANNA, Clarissa's friend

character (cont.)

    plagues the man who puts himself into her power L194, L252

    a devilish rake at heart L198

    had she been a man, would have sworn, cursed, committed rape, and played the devil L236

    account by Lovelace L252

    termagant L252

    her satirical vein L308

    fine, graceful young lady L502

    account by Morden L520

    open, generous, noble L520

classical references

    Hannibal L10, L10n1

    Caesar, and the ides of March, Lovelace compared L10, L12

    Scylla or Charybdis L56

    Narcissuses, men and L58

    the old Greek, quoted on governing L81, L81n1

    Argus-eyed mamma L100

    the old Triton, old Neptune, Antony as L197

    Alexander, compared L252

    love, an *ignis fatuus* L310

clothing see **costume**

conflict between Harlowe Family and Clarissa

    opinion of the Harlowe Family L10

    her raving about them L37, L308

    her resentments on Clarissa's account L309

    blaming James and Arabella for the family's loss of Clarissa L355

    taking liberties with Harlowe Family L376

    not pitying the Harlowe Family L510.3

conflict between Howe Family and Anna

    Anna's relationship with Mrs. Howe L13, L111, L112

    Hickman's suit L46, L48, L55, L58, L68

    Antony's wish to marry Mrs. Howe L183, L197, L197.1

    Anna not loving jangling with Mrs. Howe L358

contrivances of Lovelace see also **abduction of Clarissa**

    contrivance of sparing Rosebud

        inquiring about Lovelace's behavior at the inn L65

        Anna's suspicions of L70, L72

    contrivance of Captain Tomlinson and Uncle Harlowe's birthday

        inquiring about Captain Tomlinson

            finding no such person L229.1

            finding a Thompson, a schoolmaster, of seventy, five miles off from Uncle Harlowe L229.1

            finding a Tomkins, a day-labourer, living four miles off from Uncle Harlowe L229.1

    contrivance of Mrs. Fretchville's house, inquiring about and finding no such person L229.1

correspondence, Harlowe, Miss Clarissa

    collecting Clarissa's letters and papers to tell Clarissa's story L428

    Belford sending to Anna, per Clarissa's will L521

correspondence, Howe, Miss Anna

    with her cousin in the little island L10

    with Arabella

        writing to Arabella to advise of Clarissa's present lodgings and state of health L351

        her angry Letters 351, 353, 355 to Arabella L356, L357, L360, L361, L378

    with Belford L510, L528

correspondence, Howe, Miss Anna with Clarissa

    aliases, Mr. John Soberton, to whom Clarissa should address hers for Anna L100

HOWE, MISS ANNA, Clarissa's friend

correspondence, Howe, Miss Anna with Clarissa (cont.)

    conveyed by

        Robert L9, L16, L46, L58, L65, L69, L81, L87

        Mrs. Knollys L93

        Mr. Charles Hickman L100, L119, L128, L240

        Mr. Wilson

            how he came to be used as a conveyance L148, L150, L229.1

            Anna's letters delivered to Wilson's, given directly to Lovelace L217

            Letter 229.1 from Anna delivered by Wilson directly to Lovelace L229

            Anna afraid to use Wilson's conveyance L261

        Simon Collins

            hers delivered to Wilson's, but as there was a hurry, directly to Mrs. Sinclair's by Collins, but

                again, since Clarissa was out, back to Wilson's L229, L229.1

            assisting Anna in correspondence with Clarissa L316, L318, L327, L328

            no longer needed as a conveyance L338

        Captain Tomlinson

            returning Anna's Letter 229.1 to Wilson's as Letter 239.1 rewritten by Lovelace L238, L239

        Grimes, delivering Anna's Letter 238.1 to Clarissa L238

        Rogers, Anna's tenant's son L319

            delivering Anna's letter for Mrs. Harriot Lucas at Mrs. Moore's L251, L252.1

            cannot be spared to deliver letters L327

            delivering letters for Anna L327, L456

        post, corresponding with Clarissa by L329

        friend of Aunt Harman, delivering Anna's to Clarissa in London L404

    interference from Mrs. Howe

        forbidden L8, L9, L111, L112, L128, L296

        unbeknownst to Mrs. Howe L10

        Harlowe Family informed of by Mrs. Howe L50.1

        Mrs. Howe forbidding Clarissa to correspond with Anna L163, L168

        Mrs. Howe intercepting Letter 295 of Clarissa L296

        called *evil communication* by Mrs. Howe L296, L297

correspondence, Howe, Miss Anna with Clarissa, forged by Lovelace

    Lovelace mastering Anna's handwriting L229

    Letter 239.1 is Anna's double-dated Letter L229.1, rewritten by Lovelace and given as Letter 239.1 to

        Clarissa L229, L238, L239, L310, L316

correspondence, Howe, Miss Anna with Clarissa, intercepted by Lovelace

    Lovelace transcribing Anna's letters (188 and 196) to Clarissa L198, L218

    Anna's Letter 229.1 stolen by Lovelace L229, L238.1, L239, L310

    Will stealing Anna's Letter 238.1, giving it to Lovelace, who reads it and returns it to Grimes L238

    Lovelace trying to intercept Anna's next L239

    hers to Clarissa stolen by Lovelace L250, L251

    her three (229.1, 252.1, 275.1) to Clarissa stolen by Lovelace L275, L310

    Clarissa suspects Lovelace is confiscating Anna's letters L276

    Anna's of June 20th not received by Clarissa L316

    Belford refusing to confiscate Anna's letters to Clarissa L341

costume

    her hoops L74

    her morning sacque L81

    will send Clarissa money and clothes L100, L111, L119, L132

    to buy clothes in London for her approaching nuptials L459

Coventry Act

    and Betty Barnes L68

death of Harlowe, Miss Clarissa, *foreshadowed*

    I am fitter for *this* world than you, you for the *next* than me—that's the difference L10

HOWE, MISS ANNA, Clarissa's friend

death of Harlowe, Miss Clarissa, *foreshadowed* (cont.)
    you are in danger L10
death of Harlowe, Miss Clarissa
    fainting on news of L494
    viewing the corpse at Harlowe Place L501, L502
    wanting a lock of Clarissa's hair L502
devil
    Anna as L127, L239
    a devilish rake at heart L198
    had she been a man, would have sworn, cursed, committed rape, and played the devil L236
dreams
    Lovelace's dream: Anna having a girl by Lovelace, Clarissa a boy by Lovelace, and the two marrying L271
duel between James and Lovelace
    fearing fallout after L1
    visited by Mr. Diggs, she inquires about the duel L1
estates
    advising Clarissa to resume her estate L15, L27, L37, L47, L49, L52, L100, L142, L177, L183
example
    Anna as L38
family see also **relations**
    Anna herself, an only child L197.1
    Charles, son CONCLUSION
    Clarissa, daughter L252.1, CONCLUSION
    Hickman, Mr. Charles, husband CONCLUSION
    Howe, Mr., father
        like her papa L58, L229.1, L358
        mentioned L81, L183, L198
        her poor papa, a violent spirit L100, L197.2
        loving her father L132
        talking as loud as her mamma L150
father's house
    all punctilio is at an end the moment you are out of your father's house L87, L89, L90
fearing Lovelace
    fearing fallout after the duel L1
friends
    Biddulph, Miss Rachel, inquiring about Clarissa L93
    Hartley, Lady, example of a man-woman L132, L133
    Lloyd, Miss Biddy, visits to and from Anna L93, L473.1
friendship
    with Clarissa L1, L8, L11, L87, L135, L146, L183, L229.1, L473, L520
    Clarissa's only friend, her love for Clarissa L295, L329
gall
    dipping her pen in gall L55, L144
God, references to see also **biblical references**
    God Almighty L148
gossip
    her new informant on Lovelace L177
hair
    sweet auburn beauty L252
handwriting
    Lovelace will master Anna's handwriting L229
    showing her natural impatience by its fits and starts L239
    not a bad hand L239

HOWE, MISS ANNA, Clarissa's friend

hanging

custom in the Isle of Man, rape victim choosing rope, sword, or ring L317

harpsichord

accomplished at L128

historical references

Henry VII, the tyrant Tudor, and Elizabeth of the House of York L47

Tom Wharton L48, L48n2

Elizabeth of France...Philip II of Spain L56

illnesses

has she been ill, as Lovelace has said L295, L297

ill, with but a slight cold L310

fainting on news of Clarissa's death L494

influence on Clarissa

Anna's L354

informants

her new informant on Lovelace L177

jewels

Anna wanting to purchase Clarissa's L510.3

journey

Clarissa's preparations

Clarissa should send Anna papers and clothing for safe keeping L68

Anna advising Clarissa to go to London and hide till Morden comes L81

Anna offering to go to London with Clarissa L81

Anna's desire to accompany Clarissa on her flight from Harlowe Place L87

Anna trying to procure vehicle for Clarissa's escape L87

language

he will be *Harlowed off* L100

she had not best *Harlowe* me L100

Antonyed L100

literary references see also **books**

Angelica needing confidants, Violetta, Cleanthe, Clelia, or an old nurse L74

Josephus, *Antiquities of the Jews*, Herod loving his Mariamne L229.1, L229.1n1

Norris, John

quoted L27

his *Miscellanies*, sent to Clarissa, with money L148

Clarissa returning Anna's Norris L149, L150, L156

Lovelace not to be *out-Norrised* L198, L199, L215

Pope, Alexander

perhaps the celebrated bard L47, L47n1

Of the Characters of Women, every woman a rake L115, L115n2, L367, L367n1

Rowe, Nicholas, quoted L119

Steele, Richard, *The Tender Husband*, quoted but not named L132, L132n1

Valentine and Orson L128, L128n1

lodgings

not knowing where Clarissa is lodging L214

now knowing Clarissa's whereabouts L229.1

will procure lodging for Clarissa in a neighboring village L252.1

love for Lovelace

fearing Clarissa may love Lovelace L12, L37

marriage

her aversion to L523

marriages, Anna's to Hickman

marriage postponed because of Clarissa's unhappiness L148, L155, L296, L366

may marry Hickman soon to provide protection for Clarissa L252.1

HOWE, MISS ANNA, Clarissa's friend

marriages, Anna's to Hickman (cont.)

settlements engrossed L366

close to naming a day L434

to buy clothes in London for her approaching nuptials L459

Clarissa requesting in her will that Anna marry Hickman soon L507

Anna not yet fulfilling her part of Clarissa's will L520, L521

married to Hickman CONCLUSION

marriages, Clarissa's to Lovelace

advising Clarissa to marry Lovelace directly L81, L87, L100, L119, L128, L132, L156, L183, L342, L358, L359, L367

advising Clarissa to throw off a little more of the veil L112

cautioning Clarissa against Lovelace L168, L174.3

advising Clarissa to leave Lovelace L177

advising Clarissa to marry the fool L188

advising Clarissa to fly L229.1

approving Clarissa's refusal of Lovelace L372, L379

meals, breakfast

with Mrs. Howe L81

meals, dinner

dining with Lord M.'s nieces L327, L358

meals, tea

with Mr. Wyerley L1

medicines

salts administered L494

a lighted wax-candle with feathers to burn under the nose L494

Memorandum book

receiving Clarissa's Memorandum book from Belford L510.3

messengers

Rogers, Anna's tenant's son L319

delivering Anna's for Mrs. Harriot Lucas at Mrs. Moore's L251, L252.1

eating powdered beef, woundily corned L251

delivering the letter to Clarissa's imposter L275.1

Rogers meeting Clarissa L320, L328, L358

cannot be spared to deliver letters L327

delivering Anna's to Clarissa L456

miniatures

Clarissa sending her miniature of Anna to Hickman L476, L507

money

will send Clarissa money and clothes L100, L111, L119, L132

offering to find Clarissa refuge in London and to send money L142

sending Clarissa fifty guineas in *Norris's Miscellanies* L148

wanting to send Clarissa money L317

mourning

mourning against Clarissa's wishes L523

mourning Clarissa for six months CONCLUSION

music

accomplished at harpsichord, singing L128

names

Nancy L10, L27, L58, L74, L81, L82, L111, L296, L317, L357, L367

Mrs. Charles Hickman CONCLUSION

opinions

on age and wisdom L372

on AUTHORITY L81

on courtship L65, L128

HOWE, MISS ANNA, Clarissa's friend

opinions (cont.)

      on curses, the weight of a parent's curse L148

      on death L65

      on duty L132, L367

      on encroachers L68

      on the female sex L68

            the position of women L47, L128

            that they love to trade in surprises L49

            the Muscovite wife [sequestered] L68

            their passiveness L128

            Lady Hartley, example of a man-woman L132

      on happiness and riches

            you are all too rich to be happy L10

      on husbands and their prerogatives L372

      on love and passion L128

            love an *ignis fatuus* L310

      on the male sex L27, L522

            men as monkeys L46

            men and Narcissuses L58

            husbands and lovers L68

            despising the male sex L132, L456, L510.3

            a vile race of reptiles L455

      on marriage L68

            the reptile word, OBEY, in marriage L68

            as a yoke L128

            on wives and their duties L132

            on men, women, and marriage, her aversion to L523

      on mind and body L132

      on *Ode to Wisdom*, sent by Clarissa L56

      on parents and children L132, L367

            on mothers L100

            on tyrants, parents as L181

      on wills L27

      on writing: speaking is...best: for words leave no traces; they pass as breath; and mingle with air, and may be explained with latitude. But the pen is a witness on record L183

physical appearance

      sweet auburn beauty L252

political references

      George II, robbed of his legal due by contraband traders L196

Poor's Fund

      caring for after Mrs. Norton's death CONCLUSION

prayers

      hers for Clarissa L87, L132, L142, L373

prosecution of Lovelace

      will testify if Clarissa prosecutes L317

protection for Clarissa

      advising Clarissa to seek protection of Lovelace's family L81, L142

      Mrs. Townsend may give Clarissa protection L196

      may marry Hickman soon to provide protection for Clarissa L252.1

      her personal protection for Clarissa L317

punishment

      Lovelace's of Anna L198, L198n1, L207.1 (following), L395

rakes

      Alexander Pope, *Of the Characters of Women*, every woman a rake L115, L115n2, L367, L367n1

HOWE, MISS ANNA, Clarissa's friend

rakes (cont.)

a devilish rake at heart L198

had she been a man, would have sworn, cursed, committed rape, and played the devil L236

rape

had she been a man, would have sworn, cursed, committed rape, and played the devil L236

custom in the Isle of Man, victim choosing rope, sword, or ring L317

rape of Anna, planned

Lovelace's plot upon Anna L207.1 (following), L371

rape of Clarissa, *foreshadowed*

being attacked by him when in bed and asleep L177

reform

believing Clarissa able to reform Lovelace L48

refuge for Clarissa

Lovelace suggesting refuge with Anna L80

refuge not possible with Mrs. Howe L81

offering to find Clarissa refuge in London and to send money L142

her marriage to Hickman providing refuge for Clarissa L155, L252.1, L372

relations see also **family**

Fynnett, Jenny, cousin in the little island L10, L46, L47

Anna's bedfellow L46

Jenny's Grandmother Larkin L47

Harman, Aunt, rich aunt in the Isle of Wight L342

approving Clarissa's inheritance L1

visit from Anna, Mrs. Howe, and Hickman L252, L342, L357, L358, L359, L365, L366, L372, L455

visit to Anna, from Aunt Harman's sister and her lord L342

her friend delivering Anna's to Clarissa in London L404

Spilsworth and *Herbert,* her cousins L456

her family not ancient L238

religious references see also **biblical references**; **God, references to**

Mr. T'Antony, in discussion of figure and pride in men L37

rescue of Clarissa see also **smugglers**

Anna to perfect her smuggling scheme L200, L238.1, L252.1

discovered by Lovelace, no more danger to Lovelace L211, L215, L221, L227

finding Clarissa asylum till Morden comes L248, L319

Mrs. Townsend, her brothers, their crews taking Clarissa to London, then Deptford L252.1, L259, L261

failed, Clarissa having already gone back to Mrs. Sinclair's with Lovelace L316

revenge

to be punished by Lovelace L198, L198n1

Lovelace's revenge upon Anna L209, L229, L252

fearing she is watched by Lovelace L319

her agent watching Lovelace L319

expecting vengeance from Lovelace L326

Lovelace avenging himself on Anna if Clarissa reject him L395

sayings and proverbs

so in for the lamb, in for the sheep L10

to take a thorn out of one's friend's foot, to put it into our own L87

far-fetched and dear-bought L197, L197n1

Lovelace laughing in his sleeve L229.1

sealings

young families loving ostentatious sealings L238

Clarissa's letter of refusal to Lovelace's family sealed with Anna's seal L373

seduction

Lovelace threatening to seduce her L252

HOWE, MISS ANNA, Clarissa's friend

servants

Kitty

source of information about Solmes L27

delivering letters from Clarissa L81

visiting Hannah, requesting her to attend Clarissa L128

Singleton trying to bribe her L196

Robert

animals, his roan Keffel L65

correspondence, Howe, Miss Anna with Clarissa

conveying L9, L16, L46, L47, L58, L81, L87, L132, L148

warned away from the poultry-yard by Leman L74

correspondence, Howe, Mrs. Annabella, with Mr. Hunt, conveying L81

duties

taking Clarissa's parcel and letters to Anna L69

to be sent for Hannah L121

marriage, may buy a ring and marry with money from Clarissa L74

names, called Robin, old Robin L46, L47, L58, L65, L81, L87

sleeping arrangements

Jenny Fynnett, Anna's bedfellow L42

smugglers see also **rescue of Clarissa**

contraband traders robbing George II of his legal due L196

Townsend, Mrs., a contraband trader L196

imports textiles and other curiosities L196

her two brothers, each master of a vessel L196, L252, L252.1

may give Clarissa protection L196

mentioned L199, L201, L209, L210, L228, L248

ready to accommodate Clarissa L229.1, L230

her manlike spirit L252, L252.1

story

Clarissa's

to all who will know your story, you will be an excellent example of watchfulness L177

not knowing all the details of Clarissa's affairs L346, L359, L373

collecting Clarissa's letters and papers to tell Clarissa's story L428

every man...is not a Lovelace...neither is every woman a Clarissa L456

threatening to publish the case L515

suitors to Howe, Miss Anna (other than Mr. Charles Hickman)

Colmar, Sir George

I throbbed no more about him L37

her first passion L151

one of Lovelace's class, once endangered Anna L174.3

Anna saved by Clarissa from marrying a fop and a libertine L182, L355

Anna signed for Sir George Colmar L198

obliged to quit the kingdom L198

Anna would have followed him into exile, but for Clarissa L198

mentioned L252

her first choice of a husband L523

causing her aversion to matrimony L523

Harlowe, Mr. James, Jun., mentioned as L5

transportation

her chariot and four L47

her chariot L87

arriving at Harlowe Place in a chariot to view the body L502

travel

offering to go to London with Clarissa L81

HOWE, MISS ANNA, Clarissa's friend

travel (cont.)

  to Aunt Harman in the Isle of Wight, planned L252, L342

    to set out soon L357, L358, L359, L365, L366, L372

    returned home L455

  would accompany Clarissa abroad L252.1

  abroad when Clarissa escapes Mrs. Sinclair's and writes Letter 295 L296, L297

violent behavior

  snapping her fan in Lovelace's face at the ball L367

virtue

  her virtue noted L435

visits

  to Mrs. Larkin L47, L65

  to Clarissa, planned L456, L459, L473.1

    unable to attend Clarissa because of her mother's illness L455

  to Miss Lloyd L473.1

  from Mr. Diggs, Anna inquiring about the duel L1

  from Mr. Wyerley L1

  from Clarissa L7

  from Lovelace L7, L12, L49

    early social meeting with Lovelace L27

    when Clarissa first introduced Lovelace to Anna L252

  from Jenny Fynnett L46, L47

  from Miss Lloyd inquiring about Clarissa L93

  from Miss Biddulph inquiring about Clarissa L93

  from Captain Singleton L177

  from the Misses Montague L326, L327

  from Aunt Harman's sister and her lord L342

  from Morden, with the ring and other bequest L455, L519, L520

  from Spilsworth and Herbert, her two cousins L456

white

  Rosebud, a plot...to wash a blackamoor white L72

  her mind all robed in spotless white L295

writing

  her talent for scribbling L111

  using crow-quill pens L239.1

HOWE, MRS. ANNABELLA, Anna's mamma

abduction of Clarissa
>   pitying Clarissa and asking Anna to write and comfort her L148

address to Clarissa by Mr. Roger Solmes
>   told of Clarissa's troubles L10
>   praise and sympathy for Clarissa L10, L27, L58
>   engaged by the family against Clarissa L31
>   Solmes plan discussed with her by Antony L32.4
>   believing the Harlowe Family will give up the Solmes plan L56
>   Clarissa should give up her aversion to Solmes L56, L58
>   refusing to get embroiled L81, L86, L89
>   will not provide refuge for Clarissa L81
>   Clarissa's duty to comply L81

age
>   forty years L58

ball, Colonel Ambrose's
>   attending L350, L358, L367

bequests of Clarissa
>   twenty-five guineas for a ring L507

biblical references
>   *I Corinthians* 15:33, on *evil communication* L296, L296n1

character
>   bustling, jealous woman L100
>   Argus-eyed mamma L100
>   good manager L132
>   her face sharpened to an edge L229.1
>   prudent and watchful L354
>   her prudence and good sense L356
>   avaricious L364
>   her character, an account by Morden L520

correspondence, Howe, Miss Anna with Clarissa
>   unaware of their secret correspondence L10, L65
>   discovering it and informing Harlowe Family L50.1
>   forbidding their correspondence L111, L128, L163, L168, L296, L307, L357
>   slapping Anna's hand found writing to Clarissa L132
>   confiscating Clarissa's of June 29th to Anna L310
>   allowing Anna to answer Clarissa's L310
>   prosecuting Lovelace a condition of their continued correspondence L317

death of Harlowe, Miss Clarissa
>   receiving news of L494

duel between James and Lovelace
>   fearing Lovelace's resentments against the Harlowes L1
>   opinion on L27

estates
>   her great estate L197.1

executors
>   Mrs Larkin's executrix L65

family see also **relations**
>   Howe, Mr., her husband L133
>>   Mrs. Howe a widow for ten years L74, L197, L197.2
>>   her father choosing her husband L81
>>   a gentleman L133
>>   talking loud L150
>   Howe, Miss Anna, her only child L197.1

HOWE, MRS. ANNABELLA, Anna's mamma

forgiveness

forgiveness of Clarissa the Harlowes' own decision L357

friends

Downeton, Sir Harry, his information about Solmes L56, L57, L58

Hunt, Mr., with whom she corresponds L81

Lorimer, Mrs., carrying to Antony, Mrs. Howe's response to his proposals L197.2

illnesses

very ill, recovering L455

influence on Mrs. Howe

Antony influencing Mrs. Howe against Lovelace after the duel L1

Antony revealing to Mrs. Howe the purpose of an alliance with Solmes L27

Antony used by Lovelace to set Mrs. Howe against Clarissa L104, L105, L111, L125, L128

marriage

her unhappy marriage L81, L132

husband not her choice, but her father's L81

marriages, Clarissa's to Lovelace

believing Clarissa should marry Lovelace L342, L358

admiring Clarissa's refusal of Lovelace L371

money

contributing to the Poor's Fund CONCLUSION

mourning

in deep mourning for Clarissa L520

names

Queen Annabella Howe L31

Goody Howe L105

opinions

on marriage L58, L132

on parents

duty L10, L27, L65, L357

parental authority L10, L15, L357

parents and children L197.2

disobedience to parents L296

Poor's Fund

contributing to CONCLUSION

proctors

hers intimate with Lovelace's proctor, to whom Lovelace applied for a license L229.1

prosecution of Lovelace

wanting Clarissa to prosecute L317

prosecuting Lovelace a condition of Anna's continued correspondence with Clarissa L317

reconciliation between Clarissa and the Harlowe Family

offering to reconcile Clarissa with her family if she will prosecute Lovelace L317

forgiveness of Clarissa the Harlowes' own decision L357

acquainting the Harlowe Family with the truth about Clarissa's situation L429

refuge for Clarissa

will not provide refuge for Clarissa L81

relations see also **family**

Larkin, Mrs., distant relation L46

long bed-ridden L46, L65

Jenny Fynnett's grandmother L46

her will L46, L65

Mrs. Howe her executrix L65

her death L65

father, chosing a husband for her L81

HOWE, MRS. ANNABELLA, Anna's mamma

suitors to Howe, Mrs. Annabella

Harlowe, Mr. Antony

her mutual attraction L74

Antony wishing to marry her L183, L196, L201

his offer rejected L197

transportation

her chariot, her chaise L80

travel

to the Isle of Wight to visit Aunt Harman L342, L357, L366

visits

to Mrs. Larkin L46, L65

from Antony L10

daily L87

after Clarissa's flight L101

from Sir Harry Downeton L56

his information about Solmes L56, L57, L58

LORD M., Lovelace's uncle

abduction of Clarissa

    his chariot and six used by Lovelace L76, L80

address to Arabella by Mr. Robert Lovelace

    discussing with Antony L2

    proposing a match with Arabella L13

address to Clarissa by Mr. Robert Lovelace

    proposing a match with Clarissa L3

    signing a letter from Lovelace to Clarissa L22, L26

    lending credibility to L25.1

    supporting Lovelace's continuing attempts L26

    to be sounded by Hickman upon a subject recommended by Clarissa L27

age

    not so very old L190

airings

    a little tour for two days L330

apothecaries

    attended by L285

bailiffs see

    servants, steward (discharged)

    servants, *Parsons, Simon*

bequests of Clarissa

    ring with Clarissa's hair L507

biblical references

    I Samuel 25:21, return good for evil L190, L190n1

    Solomon and his proverbs reminding Lovelace of Lord M. L191

black

    his great black mantle covering Lovelace in Lovelace's dream L417

blacks see **funeral of Lord M.**

chaplains

    and Mrs. Sorlings's daughter L118

    Lovelace offering to send for L149, L150

    praying with his chaplain when he has the gout L321

character

    a man of honor L81

    noble podagra-man L170

    the old peer L191, L218, L275, L277, L294, L321, L322, L383

    a sinner L321

    generosity to Clarissa L409

classical references

    Raro antecedentem scelestum deseruit pede poena claudo: where vice goes before, vengeance (sooner or later) will follow L190

    the old Trojan, Lord M. as L191, L321

conflict between Harlowe Family and Lovelace

    mediating conflict L17

conflict between Lord M. and Lovelace

    often falls out with Lovelace L98

    raving against Lovelace L104

    too indulgent with Lovelace L190

    believing Lovelace is up to mischief L218

contrivances of Lovelace see also **abduction of Clarissa; rape of Clarissa**

    contrivance of Captain Tomlinson and Uncle Harlowe's birthday

        Lord M. accused of delaying his answer to Lovelace's invitation L201, L203

        referring to Clarissa as his niece, asking her to defer marriage no longer L206

LORD M., Lovelace's uncle

contrivances of Lovelace, contrivance of Captain Tomlinson and Uncle Harlowe's birthday (cont.)
> gout in his right hand prevents answering invitation L218

correspondence, Harlowe, Miss Clarissa
> Lovelace giving his posthumous letter from Clarissa to Lord M. to read to him L510.3

correspondence, Lord M.
> with Belford L513

correspondence, Lord M., forged by Lovelace
> Letter 233.4 L233, L306

correspondence, Lovelace, Mr. Robert with Clarissa
> letter to Clarissa signed by Lord M. to add credibility to Lovelace's address L22

costume
> his great black mantle covering Lovelace in Lovelace's dream L417

cures
> scarifications L191, L247

death of Lord M.
> wishing to see Lovelace before he dies L278
> Lovelace hoping for an early end L294, L321, L341
> near death L327
> surviving Lovelace by three years CONCLUSION

devils
> having a devil under his roof L349

drink
> lemonade causing gout in his stomach L275

duel between James and Lovelace
> supporting Lovelace L6
> fearing Lovelace for the ill usage received from Harlowes L143

estates
> Clarissa's
>> offering to assist Clarissa in resuming her estate L49
> his own
>> to which Lovelace's mother had better pretensions L88
>> seat in Hertfordshire (the Lawn) L88, L149
>> seat in Lancashire L88
>> seat in Berkshire (M. Hall) L98
>> his three seats L121
>> £8000 a year L275

family see also **relations**
> his deceased wife L206
> his sister Lovelace L324

fearing Lovelace
> fearing Lovelace for the ill usage received from the Harlowes L143

fortune see **estates**

friends
> *Hutcheson, Archibald* L206, L206n4
> *Lexington, Lord* L206
> *Wycherley, William* L190, L190n2

funeral of Lord M.
> Lovelace hiring blacks for the funeral L277

goldsmiths
> *Finch, Mr.*, Lord M.'s goldsmith L510

grave
> mentioned L321

honor
> jealous of the honor of his house L409

LORD M., Lovelace's uncle

housekeepers

Greme, Mrs., housekeeper at Lord M.'s Hertfordshire seat L98

    attending Clarissa

        accompanying Clarissa in the chaise to Mrs. Sorlings's L98

        source of information about Lovelace and his family L98, L183

        attending Clarissa and recommending lodgings L104

        has received no orders for Clarissa's accommodations L233.4

    attending Lord M., reading the Bible to Lord M. L104

    attending Lovelace, in his dangerous fever L410

    character, excellent woman, pious matron, compared to Mrs. Norton L98, L104

    correspondence, Harlowe, Miss Clarissa with Anna, conveying L98

    marriages, Clarissa's to Lovelace, hoping Clarissa will marry Lovelace L120, L128

    relations

        Sorlings, Mrs., sister-in-law, sister of Mrs. Greme L98, L120

            animals, her dunghill cocks, Will compared L238

            attending Clarissa

                requesting Clarissa to defer departure to London L135

                comforting Clarissa after she receives a letter from Arabella L153

            correspondence, Harlowe, Miss Clarissa with Anna, conveying L100

            family

                widow L104, L128, L149, L153

                two grown sons and two younger daughters L98

                Betty, Mrs., her elder daughter L105

                    and Will L118

                    and Lord M.'s chaplain L118

                    attending Clarissa L118, L125, L130

                    to accompany Clarissa to London L130, L149, L152, L154

                    accompanying Clarissa as far as Barnet L155

                    receiving a gift from Lovelace L155

           farm

               living eight miles off from the inn at St. Albans L98

               her dairy works, her farm L105, L117, L130

hunting

    loving hunting L206

illnesses

    gout L104, L121, L187, L190, L203.1, L206, L265, L321

        podagra-man L170

        gout preventing him from visiting Clarissa L194

        gout in his right hand prevents answering invitation L218

        gout in his stomach from drinking lemonade L275

        gout quit the counterscarp of his stomach...storming the citadel of his heart L294

        his just disgouted thumbs L323

        a gouty twinge L323

        his gouty days L341

    his last fit L233.2

    has become very ill L265, L275, L277, L279

    his sufferings, Clarissa's compared L279

    in extremis L281, L282, L284, L285

    given over by his doctors L285

    having no...animal organs to whet out his bodily ones, and to raise his fever above the...helpful one L285

    Lovelace hoping for an early end L294, L321

    Lord M. is better, recovered L294, L323, L371

language see also **sayings and proverbs**

    Lovelace expressing himself in Lord M.'s style L512

LORD M., Lovelace's uncle

language (cont.)

    his phrasing L515

law

    Lovelace argues his defense before Lord M. L515

    peers are judges in the last resort L515

    If by committing an unlawful act, a capital crime is the consequence, you are answerable to both L515

lemonade see **drink**

literary references

    Wycherley, William L190, L190n2

    Harlowes and Lovelace behaving as Orsons L442

manners

    well-mannered peer L203

marriage

    threatening to marry and have children, if Lovelace provoke him L190

    wanting to see his nieces married L190

marriages, Clarissa's to Lovelace

    generally

        using Belford to influence Lovelace to marry Clarissa L110, L143

        hoping Lovelace will marry Clarissa L121, L169, L170, L191

        to be Clarissa's nuptial father L187, L189, L218, L233.2

        offering Lovelace money to marry Clarissa L206

        settlements, agreeing to jointure from Lovelace's own estate L218

        hoping for many boys (no girls) from Clarissa and Lovelace L233.4

        first boy will take Lord M.'s surname by Act of Parliament L233.4

        Clarissa feeling worthy to be his niece L261 Paper VIII

        losing hope for Lovelace if he not marry Clarissa L303

    wedding gifts

        one of his three seats until they are settled L121, L325

        for Clarissa

            £1000 *per annum* to Lovelace's wife L186

            Lancashire seat or the Lawn and a thousand pounds a year, penny rents L206, L207

        for Lovelace

            £1000 *per annum* upon his nuptials L88

            Lancashire or The Lawn to be given to Lovelace upon his nuptials L186

            estates being transferred to Lovelace on his nuptials L203.1

Master of the Buckhounds

    would not have taken a place but Master of the Buckhounds L206

    advising Lovelace not to take a place, not needing it to patch up his broken fortunes L206

meals, breakfast

    breakfasting with his nieces L322

money

    sending a bill to Lovelace enclosed in his letter L205, L206

    offering Lovelace money to marry Clarissa L206

    offering Clarissa 100 guineas *per* quarter for life as reparation L394

names

    first boy will take Lord M.'s surname by Act of Parliament L233.4

    Lord *Marplot* L323

opinions

    on proverbs, the wisdom of nations L190, L191, L198, L205, L206, L215

    on title and legitimate descendants L206

    on women, resenting slights longer than men L233.4

Parliament

    advising Lovelace to get into soon L206, L206n2

    Lovelace's first boy to take Lord M.'s name by Act of Parliament L233.4

LORD M., Lovelace's uncle

Parliament (cont.)

Lord M. and Lovelace having three or four boroughs at their command L254

peers

peers are judges in the last resort L515

physicians

Perkins, Dr., attending Lord M. L282

S., Dr., Lord M.'s servant sent to fetch, and attending L281, L282

attended by three physicians and an apothecary L285

place see **Master of the Buckhounds**

political references

Craggs, Mr. Secretary, mentioned L206, L206n4

Hutcheson, Archibald, quoted L206, L206n4

prayers

praying with his chaplain when he has the gout L321

protection for Clarissa

his protection offered by Lovelace L80

rape of Clarissa

offering Clarissa one hundred guineas *per* quarter for life as reparation L394

reconciliation between Lovelace and the Harlowe Family

Lovelace should reconcile with the Harlowes L206

relations see also **family**

Knollys, Mrs.

character, her excellent character L26

correspondence, Harlowe, Miss Clarissa with Anna

to whom Clarissa should send hers for Anna L93, L98

requested by Mrs. Howe to stop conveying their correspondence L100

relations, kinsman of Lovelace L26

visits, from Clarissa, at whose home Clarissa had once been a guest L26

grandson, bequeathed his Hertfordshire estate CONCLUSION

half-sisters

generally, half-sisters of Lord M. L13

address to Clarissa by Mr. Robert Lovelace, supporting his attempts L26

animals, tabbies, monkies L323

bequests of Clarissa, rings with Clarissa's hair L507

character, excellent character, unblemished honor L26, L81

control, Lovelace not forgiving them for presuming to control him L397

death of Harlowe, Miss Clarissa, indisposed at Clarissa's death L510

family, daughters of an earl, dowagers L36, L323

marriages, Clarissa's to Lovelace

favoring, with gifts L2, L36, L121, L325

losing hope for Lovelace, if he not marry Clarissa L303

relations, Lord M.'s half-sisters, sisters L13, L397

sources of information about Lovelace L12

title

hoping to procure title for Lovelace L13

daughters of an earl, dowagers L36, L323

visits, to Clarissa, looking forward to L282

visits, to Lord M. L323

Lawrance, Lady Betty, half-sister of Lord M. L13

address to Clarissa by Mr. Robert Lovelace

her letter in support and offer of protection L36

character, officious and managing, generous and noble L325

LORD M., Lovelace's uncle

relations, half-sisters, *Lawrance, Lady Betty* (cont.)

 contrivances of Lovelace

  contrivance of the impersonators

   old chancery affair calling her to town L203.1, L233.1, L233.2

   visiting her cousin Leeson L233.2, L256

   impersonated by Barbara Wallis L255

   Clarissa querying her on L302, L303, L313

  contrivance of Captain Tomlinson and Uncle Harlowe's birthday

   her steward telling Lady Betty about Lovelace's marriage L233.1, L233.2

 correspondence, forged, Letter 233.2 forged by Lovelace L233, L272, L303, L306

 estates, Clarissa's, will assist Clarissa in resuming her estate L49

 friends

  Fortescue, Mrs.

   source of information about Lovelace L12, L14, L15

   opinion on the state of affairs in the Harlowe Family L26

   her admiration for Clarissa L27

 heraldry, her arms and crest upon a coach, hers in for repairs L255

 law, her affair in chancery, in a good way L158, L303

 marriages, Clarissa's to Lovelace

  eager to hear of L158, L303

  Lovelace wanting her to assist at Clarissa's nuptials L245

  suspecting Clarissa is not married to Lovelace L303

 names, signing letter Eliz. Lawrance L303

 protection for Clarissa

  her protection considered by Clarissa L120, L200

  Clarissa putting herself into Lady Betty's protection L327, L328

 reconciliation between Clarissa and Lovelace

  Lovelace wanting her to mediate L244

  Clarissa declining her offer L306

 refuge for Clarissa

  her letter to Clarissa supporting Lovelace's suit and offer of protection L36

  Clarissa wishing to lodge near her after her escape L86

  Lovelace offering to take Clarissa to Lady Betty's L98

  Anna encouraging Clarissa to go to Lady Betty's L100

  Harlowe Family expecting Clarissa to go to Lady Betty's L100

  invitation after Clarissa's flight not forthcoming L121, L123

 relations

  Leeson, Mrs., her cousin L233.2

   contrivance of the impersonators L233.2, L256, L302, L313

 servants

  Spurrier, Mr., her steward L302

   telling Lady Betty about Lovelace's marriage L233.1, L233.2

 solicitors, *Stedman*, attending to her Chancery affairs L256

Sadleir, Lady Sarah, half-sister

 airing, a little tour for two days to cure melancholy L332

 character, melancholy, weak-spirited L98, L245, L325

 contrivances of Lovelace

  contrivance of Captain Tomlinson and Uncle Harlowe's birthday

   disobliged with Lovelace for not having heard about the wedding L233.2

 family, *Betsey*, her only child, recently deceased L36, L245, L256, L325, L327

 friends, *Benson, Mrs.*, where Anna and Clarissa met Lady Sarah's Betsey L327

 illnesses, melancholy L98, L332

 marriages, Clarissa's to Lovelace

  worrying over the delays L190

LORD M., Lovelace's uncle

relations, half-sisters, *Sadleir, Lady Sarah*, marriages, Clarissa's to Lovelace (cont.)

      rich presents for L325

   names, spelled Sadlier L190

   relations, Lord M.'s sister, Lady Betty's sister L190, L233.2, L245

  nieces

    generally, nieces of Lord M. L170

      abduction of Clarissa

        to accompany Clarissa on her flight from Harlowe Place L76

        Clarissa requesting their company at her escape L83

        to be with Clarissa in London L85, L142

      animals, grimalkins, apes L323, L410

      ball, Colonel Ambrose's, refusing to accompany Lovelace L350

      bequests of Clarissa, rings with Clarissa's hair L507

      marriages, Lord M. wanting to see his nieces married L190

      meals

        breakfasting with Lord M. L322

        dining with Anna L327, L358

      protection for Clarissa

        requesting Clarissa to put herself into Lady Betty's protection L327

      travel, unlikely to accompany Clarissa abroad to find Morden L124

      visits

        to Clarissa

          anticipated L125, L282

          Clarissa asking Lovelace for their company L231.3

          would attend Clarissa but for Lord M.'s illness L284

        to Anna, dining with Anna L327, L358

        to Lovelace, in his dangerous fever L410

  Montague, Miss Charlotte, niece

    abduction of Clarissa, cold, sore throat make her unable to accompany Clarissa L88

    accomplishments, admirable at her needle L255

    advocate for Lovelace, writing to Clarissa on Lovelace's behalf L383, L384

    biblical references, recognizing Clarissa's reference to her father's house L439

    contrivances of Lovelace

      contrivance of Mrs. Fretchville's house

        visiting Clarissa at L178

        Lovelace writing to her about Mrs. Fretchville's house L203

        will visit Clarissa soon in her new habitation L203.1

      contrivance of the impersonators

        impersonated by Johanetta Golding L255

        Clarissa queries whether Charlotte met Lady Betty at Reading L302

        the pretended Charlotte Montague L313

      contrivance of Captain Tomlinson and Uncle Harlowe's birthday

        Lovelace may write to her about the wedding L187

        Lovelace has told her the delays are on Clarissa's side L190

        Lovelace writing her about Lord M.'s delay in answering the invitation L203

    correspondence, Montague, Miss Charlotte

      her letter giving Clarissa hope L229.1

      with Belford L513

      with Lovelace abroad L534

    correspondence, Montague, Miss Charlotte, Letter 233.3 forged by Lovelace L233, L306

    costume, to supply Clarissa with clothes L123

    estates, family and fortune above Belford L516

    family

      Belford, Mr. John, husband CONCLUSION

LORD M., Lovelace's uncle

relations, nieces, *Montague, Miss Charlotte*, family (cont.)

        son CONCLUSION

        sister of Patty L88

        her family and fortune above Belford L516

    illnesses

        cold and sore throat make her unable to accompany Clarissa L88

        indisposed L121

        ill with stomach disorder L203, L203.1

    marriages, Charlotte's to Belford

        Belford wanting to marry her L170

        wife for Belford L516

        married Belford CONCLUSION

    marriages, Clarissa's to Lovelace

        hopes for speedy nuptials L121

        hoping daily for news of L203.1

        not knowing whether Lovelace is married to Clarissa L303

    reconciliation between Clarissa and Lovelace

        will visit Miss Howe to reconcile them L325, L326

        writing to Clarissa on Lovelace's behalf L383, L384

    visits to Clarissa

        planned L88, L98, L157, L158, L233, L248

        Clarissa wondering whether she intends to visit L243

Montague, Miss Patty, niece

    abduction of Clarissa, will not be asked by Lovelace to visit Clarissa after the escape L88

    character

        her excellent character L26

        low spirited, timorous girl L88

        Lovelace's favorite L332

    family, sister of Charlotte L88

    marriage, to marry a baronet of fortune CONCLUSION

    names

        called Patsey L332

        signing her letter Martha L332

    transportation, sharing Lovelace's phaeton L332

    visits, meeting Clarissa two years ago at Sir Robert Biddulph's L233.3

sayings and proverbs

    generally

        Solomon and his proverbs reminding Lovelace of Lord M. L190, L191

        his wisdom of nations L198, L205, L215, L235

        despised by Lovelace for his proverbs L206

        his fondness for other men's wisdom L206

        his bead-roll of proverbs: black oxen, wild oats, long lanes L233.3

        capping sentences L244

        mentioned L245

    patience is a virtue L105

    slow and sure L105

    eat the calf in the cow's belly L118, L118n1

    love me, and love my dogs L167, L218

    the children of very young and very old men last not long L190

    old men when they marry young women make much of death L190

    Raro antecedentem scelestum deseruit pede poena claudo: where vice goes before, vengeance (sooner
      or later) will follow L190

    a word to the wise is enough L190

    vengeance, though it comes with leaden feet, strikes with iron hands L190

LORD M., Lovelace's uncle

sayings and proverbs (cont.)

Une poignée de bonne vie vaut mieux que plein muy de clergé: a handful of good life is better than a whole bushel of learning L190

when a thing is done, advice comes too late L190

though you have kept company with a wolf, you have not learnt to howl of him L190

I could not cover him with my wings without pecking at him with my bill L190

it is a long lane that has no turning L206

no man is always a fool, everyman sometimes L206

the more noble anyone is, the more humble L206

worth is best known by want L206

God send me a friend that may tell me of my fault: if not, an enemy, and he will L206

all your wild oats will be sown L206

let your actions praise you L206

love honest men, and herd with them, in the House and out of the House L206

keep good men company, and you shall be of the number L206

money makes the mare go L206

he that eats the King's goose shall be choked with his feathers L206

what the right side gives up, the left may be the better for L218

little said is soon amended L233.4

forestall my own market L243

Lovelace adding to Lord M.'s collection of proverbs: Good actions are remembered but for a day: bad ones for many years after the life of the guilty L252

words are wind; but deeds are mind L323

the devil is not quite so black as he is painted L326

protecting one's sister, another man's matter L422

more sacks upon the mill...coals upon the fire L442

one story is good, till another is heard L442

seats see **estates**

servants

steward (discharged)

hired by James to supply information on Lovelace L4, L12, L14

his report on Lovelace L81

Clements, Lord M.'s gentleman L442

Empson, delivering a letter from Charlotte to Lovelace in London L203.1

Jonas, occasionally dispatched to Lovelace L117

Parsons, Simon

steward of Lord M. L265, L323

informing Lovelace of Lord M.'s illness L265, L278, L279

Lord M.'s bailiff L278

making up accounts with Pritchard L323

Pritchard, Mr.

with whom Lord M. consults about transferring estates to Lovelace L203.1

an honest man, in the family for a generation L204

old man, good old servant, diffident and slow L204, L206, L207

knowing the estates and their condition L204

Honest Pritchard L206

has rent rolls for Lord M.'s estates L206

drawing up deeds to assign to Lovelace £1000 *per annum* when Clarissa owns she is married L218

Lovelace meeting him at the King's Arms L218, L220

making up accounts with Simon Parsons L323

altering Lord M.'s will to leave out Lovelace L323

spectacles

his spectacles L323

LORD M., Lovelace's uncle

title

importance of title and legitimate descendants L206

title reversionary L265

titles going with the bulk of his estate L327

transportation

his chariot and six to be used for Clarissa's abduction L76, L80

his chaise taking Clarissa to London L149

will set out in a litter to the wedding L207

sending his chariot and six for Lovelace L278

his chariot and six used by his nieces to visit Anna L327

Lovelace taking Lord M.'s chariot to Colonel Ambrose's ball L350

Lovelace taking his chariot and six to town L416

visits

to Harlowe Place L3

to Clarissa, planned L88, L194, L206, L231.3

to Lovelace at Uxbridge L496, L497

from Lady Betty L233.2

from Morden, to inquire about Lovelace's intentions L431, L442

from Belford, invited to visit M. Hall L525, L527

will

Lovelace is heir presumptive L2, L13, L118

will leave Lovelace more than he could ever wish for L105

will settle all upon Clarissa if Lovelace is not a good husband L206, L233.4

first boy will take Lord M.'s surname by Act of Parliament L233.4

Pritchard altering Lord M.'s will to leave out Lovelace L323

bequeathing his grandson his Hertfordshire estate CONCLUSION

LOVELACE, MR. ROBERT

abduction of Clarissa

    strategy to carry off Clarissa L31

    planning a private interview with Clarissa in the wood-house or garden L35

    having two keys to the garden door L35, L61, L62

    surprising Clarissa in the garden L36, L86

    threatening violence if she refuses to meet him L61

    requesting to meet Clarissa between nine and twelve in the garden L62, L73, L223

    tricking Clarissa into flight from Harlowe Place L94, L101

    throwing down his key to the garden door L94

    if she picks up the key to return to the house, he will accompany her L94

    they struggle L94

    Leman creating a commotion, confusing Clarissa into flight L95

    Leman leaving one key on the inside, to mean that Clarissa left of her own will L95

    not understanding Clarissa's grief, his resentfulness L98, L103, L108, L142

    to set out for Lord M.'s Hertfordshire seat L98

    avoiding her letter of countermand L99

    had once planned to carry her off from the wood-house by surprise L103

    wanting Clarissa to go to London L103, L104, L127

    abduction as reported by Lovelace to Belford L115

    offering Clarissa clothes and money to lay her under obligation L118

    threatening to kidnap Clarissa again if she has outwitted him L439

address, forms of

    your servant, to Anna L12

    your servant, to Clarissa L157

    your servant, to Lord Bishop of London L254

    your servant, to Lady Betty and Lady Sarah L323

    your servant, to Smiths L416

address to Arabella by Mr. Robert Lovelace

    his rejection of Arabella L2, L3

    his introduction to her, a mistake L31

    his morals not an issue at the time L58

address to Clarissa by Mr. Robert Lovelace

    his passion for Clarissa L3, L31

    request to address Clarissa L25.1

    his family's fondness for Clarissa L40, L98

    requesting permission to call on the Harlowes with Lord M. or Aunt Lawrance L62

    Clarissa lending an ear L306

address to Clarissa by Mr. Roger Solmes

    conflict with Solmes L25.2

    Solmes is revenge on Lovelace for duel and on Clarissa for her inheritance L36

    will not allow Clarissa to marry Solmes L49

    wanting to visit Solmes L62

    will rescue her if taken to Antony's L76, L81

    his intimidations put a stop to the plan to take her to Antony's L83, L103

    threats to Solmes L114

age

    younger than Belford's seven- or eight-and-twenty years L161

    Tomlinson twice Lovelace's age, upwards of fifty years L214, L217.1

airings and walks

    walking in Mrs. Sorlings's garden with Clarissa L126

    with Clarissa and the nymphs in a coach, and on Hampstead heath L210

    taking an airing in a chair L211

    taking an airing with Clarissa, the first alone, in a chariot rather than a coach L218

    refused a walk with Clarissa on Hampstead heath L247, L248

LOVELACE, MR. ROBERT

airings and walks (cont.)

    walking in Mrs. Moore's garden with Clarissa L248, L253

    taking an airing L274

aliases

    Huntingford, Robert, Esq., alias L105

        to whom Belford should address his for Lovelace L105

        changing his name without act of Parliament L105

angel

    my black angel plays me booty L152

    the black angels and the white ones L152

    appearing as angel of light, but a black heart L235

    appearing white as an angel L235

animals see also **prey**

    generally

        tormenting animals that he has power over L222

    apes, Montagues as L410

    bear, Lovelace baited as L383

    beasts of prey, rakes as L367

    bee, ranging from flower to flower L153

    birds

        hawk, called a goshawk L70

        strutting cock and his mistress L118

        black swan L123

        an eagle, his eagleship L171, L189

        to kill an innocent chicken L203

        using pigeon and chicken blood to trick Clarissa L209

        his feet and his talons concealed L230

        Mrs. Sorlings's dunghill cocks, Will as L238

        ladies always writing with crow-quills L239

        birds changing mates every Valentine's Day L254

        a kite...chicken L266

        rake, a strutting villain of a bird L268

        chicken of a gentleman, Clarissa a tiger of a lady L276

        shriek-owl, bringing bad news L463

        a thousand vultures...preying upon my heart L511

    canker-worm, caterpillar L261 Paper VII

    dog

        hound, an hungry hound waiting to leap L115

        his dog tricks L190, L203

        dogs, using his power to frighten, as a boy L191

        dog in the manger, Clarissa as L232

        dogs, his servants as L235

        old dog, Hickman as L236

        dog, Tomlinson as L237

        dog, Will as L238

        dog, Belford as L259, L264

        post-horse, whom dogs would eat, Belford as L335

        dogs and dogesses, his family as L395

        gaping puppy, Lovelace yawning as L410, L496

        dog, his messenger as L466

        dog, a foolish duncical dog, a mad dog L470, L480, L515

    dragon

        Belford's dragon's wings L228

        Mrs. Sinclair, the whole brood, dragon and serpents L330

LOVELACE, MR. ROBERT

animals (cont.)

elephant, Lovelace swollen as big as with plotting L131

fish, devil an angler baiting fish L270

fly, buzzing about the bright taper L138

grimalkins, his cousins as L323

hedgehog, Lovelace like an old hedgehog hunted for its grease L480

horse

> reformation his stalking-horse L110
>
> Belford's horse, a vicious toad L261
>
> post-horse, whom dogs would eat, Belford as L335

hyaena L456

lamb

> Rosebud as L34
>
> Clarissa as, and he the wolf L159, L269

lion, struggling like a lion held in toils, claws of a lion L229.1, L416

mole, Anna as L248

monkey L131

> mischievous monkey L100
>
> every little monkey to catechize me L203
>
> monkeys in imitation, men as L216
>
> monkies, his two aunts as L323
>
> crippled monkey, Doleman as L497
>
> sorrowful monkey, Belford as L527

moth, Lovelace as L261 Paper VII

panther, cruel as L143

snake

> his rattle warns of a snake L113
>
> serpent with the dove L234
>
> reptile kneeler L274
>
> conscience writhing around his pericardium like a serpent L276
>
> Mrs. Sinclair, the whole brood, dragon and serpents L330, L396
>
> a poisonous serpent L458
>
> my reptile envy L470

spider

> spider and fly analogy, entangling young girls L106
>
> spider, Clarissa as L256

tabbies, his aunts as L323

tigers

> chicken of a gentleman, Clarissa a tiger of a lady L276
>
> claws of a lion, fangs of a tiger L416

toad

> Dorcas as L211, L261
>
> vicious toad, Belford's horse as L261
>
> Sally as L416

turtle, I never saw the turtles bill afterwards, his attempt upon a bride L219

vixen, Anna as L237

wolf, in sheep's clothing, and Clarissa a lamb L229.1, L269

arrest of Clarissa

a black contrivance L332

Lovelace abusing the messenger who brought him news of L333

Belford stabbing Lovelace in the heart with story of L333

Lovelace innocent, his agent blamed L347, L358, L359, L373

ball, Colonel Ambrose's

attending, his agreeable time at L350, L367, L371

LOVELACE, MR. ROBERT

banishment

banished by Lord M., shunned by his family L394

Barbados see **drink**

Beelzebub see also **devil**; **Moloch-deity**; **Satan**

Lovelace as L164, L198, L207, L227, L256, L260, L271, L523

bequests of Belton

£20 for a ring L426, L440

contributing his to Belton's sister's India Bonds L449

Bible

Lovelace's mother teaching him the Bible L115

reading the Bible, but for *The Proverbs* L191

biblical references

generally

Abraham offering up Isaac L294

Cain's curse, Lovelace having L458, L458n2

David

2 Samuel 12:7, his adultery with Bathsheba L159, L159n1

David and Solomon and polygamy L254

Eve's curse, women made to bear pain L335

Gothamite, Hickman, a prim Gothamite L198

Habakkuk, Lovelace's servant as L466, L466n1

Herod, loving Clarissa as Herod his Mariamne L229.1, L229.1n1, L234

Methusalem, were Lovelace to live so long L453

Pontius Pilate, Tomlinson as L244

Samson and the Philistines L294

Solomon

Clarissa compared L175

Lord M. reminding him of L191

David and Solomon and polygamy L254

hoping for divine pardon through Clarissa L397

touching the hem of Clarissa's garment L418

deceived by Clarissa's reference to her father's house L421.1, L440, L446, L449, L486

Old Testament references

2 Samuel 12:7, David and Bathsheba L159, L159n1

Job

his admiration for L364

Job, Clarissa compared L371

quoted L416

Psalms, singing to himself the dead psalm melody L266, L266n2

Ecclesiasticus 1:9, nothing new under the sun L116, L116n1

Ecclesiasticus 25:19, wickedness of a woman L115

Ecclesiasticus 26:9, 11, on whoredom and manners L255

New Testament references

Matthew 26:42, would not have the cup put from me L110

1 Corinthians 11:9, woman was made for the man, not the man for the woman L110, L110n1

birthdays

knowing all Harlowe birthdays and Mamma and Papa's anniversary L271

black

black swan L123

my black angel plays me booty L152

the black angels and the white ones L152

appearing angel of light, but a black heart L235

imagining an old spectacled parson with a white surplice thrown over a black habit performing the irrevocable ceremony L276

LOVELACE, MR. ROBERT

black (cont.)

    his cause having a black and a white side L323

    the devil not quite so black as he is painted L326

    Lovelace, one of the blackest L329

    a black contrivance, Clarissa's arrest L332

    black blood in his callous heart L333

    the truth making him black L346

    devil is black L395

    Lord M.'s great black mantle covering Lovelace in Lovelace's dream L417

    the black offender L437

    blackest of villains L456

    crimes so black L458

    pailful of black bull's blood taken from Lovelace L496

    black perjuries, black offenses L510.4

blacks see **funeral of Lord M.**

bleeding see **cures**

blood

    using pigeon and chicken blood to trick Clarissa L209

    his blood of as much concern as that of a Neapolitan saint L211

    guilty of bloody murder of Clarissa L246

    were Belford Clarissa's brother, the blood of one of them would be spilled L258

    sooner or later this affair will draw blood L294

    black blood in his callous heart L333

    bloody-minded L416

    his heart bleeding L466

    pailful of black bull's blood taken from Lovelace L496

    poor blood L496

    Morden to have his heart's blood L532

    vomiting blood, duel with Morden L537

Blunt's chariot

    sending for L231, L231n1, L255

bribes

    promising Leman the Blue Beard Inn and Betty for his assistance L113, L140

burgundy see **drink**

burial of Clarissa

    wanting to open and embalm Clarissa L496, L497

    wanting to bury Clarissa in his family vault between his parents L497

    wanting to keep Clarissa's heart in a golden receptacle L497

cabala

    word used by rakes L110

Cain's curse see **curses, Cain's curse**

champagne see **drink**

character see also **control; generosity; power; vanity; violent behavior**

    accounts of

        by Arabella L2

        by steward (discharged) of Lord M. L4

        by James L4

        by Clarissa L11, L30, L40, L55, L73, L217.2

        by himself L12, L31, L34

        by Mrs. Fortescue L12, L14, L15

        by Mrs. Greme L98

        by Anna L142, L367

        by Belford L143

        by Morden L442

LOVELACE, MR. ROBERT

character (cont.)

violent temper, violent spirit L3, L49, L55, L121, L132, L376, L452, L458

trickster, artful and designing, intriguer L10, L34, L99, L101, L145, L229.1

his love-sick soul L34

full of love and revenge, love mixed with revenge and pride, desire for conquest L35, L216, L223

vindictive L40

lacks a heart, cruel L40, L161, L184, L187.1–L187.4, L217.2, L440

arrogant, I am fit to be a prince L101, L423

wicked, savage, evil, cruel, savage seducer, bloody-minded, obdurate, monster L114, L127, L183, L184, L200, L244, L314, L416, L519

bashful, originally L115

no fool, a fool L156, L188, L207

natural dignity, wit and vivacity, smart wit and repartee, man of genius and lively temper, in conversation having no equal L161, L222, L266, L526

a puzzling combination of good and bad L217.2

vile and remorseless L222

finding pleasure in playing the tyrant over what he loves L234

vice itself L261 Paper VIII

brave, generous, frank L261 Paper VIII

not ridiculing things sacred L370

woman-eater L416

a man of defiance L519

church

his confrontation with the Harlowe Family L30, L31, L36, L106

attending church with Clarissa, attendance ensuring reform L159

his dress too gay for church L159

wishing to attend Clarissa to church L200

attending church L323

classical references

Aesop's *Fables* L167, L167n1

Alexander the Great

    Lovelace compared L232

    Anna compared L252

Bamfield, Richard, *Philomel*, Clarissa as L325, L325n1

Boreas, Phoebus, and Thetis, fable of L201

Caesar

    Lovelace compared L12, L261, L512

    and Rubicon L97, L226

    a great rake L110

    compared to Pompey L261

Cassandra L131

Clodius L106, L106n1, L110

dea bona L115

debellare superbos L34

Democratus, Lovelace aping among his friends and Heraclitus to the family L277, L277n1

[Demosthenes] the matrimonial sword hanging over his head by a thread L325

Dii majores L167, L229

Epictetus/Seneca mentioned L453

Erebus, some of our fellow brethren now wandering in L370

Fates

    sparing Clarissa L453

    what they do against him L466

    spinning threads for tragedies for Belford L515

Hannibal, the father of warlike stratagems, Lovelace comparing himself L223

LOVELACE, MR. ROBERT

classical references (cont.)

    hieroglyphics of the marriage license L254

    Heraclitus, Lovelace aping to the family, and Democratus among his friends L277, L277n1

    Hercules-like...in the tortures of Deianira's poisoned shirt L243, L243n1

    Herodotus L191

    Homer L152

    Horace, *Odes*, Book II, translated by Abraham Cowley, quoted L264, L264n1

    Josephus, *Antiquities of the Jews*, quoted L191, L191n2

    Juno L167

    Jupiter

        a rape worthy of L35

        in *Fables of Aesop* L167

        by Jupiter L228, L244, L330, L410, L416, L511, L513, L516

        laughing at the perjuries of lovers L246

    Lucretia-like vengeance unlike Clarissa L263, L263n1

    Lycurgus institutions L254, L254n1

    Mercury, Belford compared L167

    Mulciber L153

    myrmidons, Lovelace's friends as L106

    Niobe L153

    Ovid L103

        Metamorphoses, Philomela, Clarissa as L325, L325n1

    his phaeton, ready to drive, Miss Patsey Montague sharing L322, L332

    Phalaris L252, L252n2

    Philomela, Clarissa as L325, L325n1

        Ovid, *Metamorphoses* L325, L325n1

        Bamfield, Richard, *Philomel* L325, L325n1

    a phoenix of a man L237

    Pompey, Caesar compared L261

    Proteus, Lovelace as L424

    Publius Terentius, quoted L175, L175n1

    the Roman matron and suicide, Clarissa compared L371

    Seneca/Epictetus mentioned L453

    Socrates' wife L115

    Spartans, children of the public L254

    Tarquin

        cost of rape to L261.1, L261n2

        Lovelace comparing himself L371

    Tiresias L115, L115n1

    Virgil's Aeneas, Lovelace comparing himself L370, L370n1, L370n2

clothing see **costume**

cloven foot

    discovering his cloven foot L252.1, L252.1n1

    devil and his cloven feet L326

codes

    Belford sending news of Clarissa's death in a coded message, advising Lovelace to go to Paris L449

    in his cursed algebra L496

    writing in characters to Belford L497

coffin

    may need a coffin or a shroud L410

cohabitation with Clarissa

    planning cohabitation L110

    if she cannot be brought to cohabitation, he will marry her L194

    his darling view, principal view L259

LOVELACE, MR. ROBERT

cohabitation with Clarissa (cont.)

    touching upon L263

    no hope of L264, L281, L289

    will press for L268

collation at Mrs. Sinclair's

    Clarissa to meet his friends L158.1

conflict between Harlowe Family and Lovelace see also **duel between James and Lovelace**

    threats to Harlowe Family L12, L17, L20, L24.1, L26

    enemy of the family L14, L158.1, L202

    looking challenge and defiance at the them after church L30, L31, L36, L106

    despising and manipulating Harlowes and Howes, forcing Clarissa to flee L31, L152

    rivalry and hatred of James L91

    threats to James L114

    hatred of Harlowes L121, L153, L154, L229.1, L294, L324, L376, L512

    machine of James L189

    Clarissa hoping it will subside L202

conflict between Lord M. and Lovelace

    impertinent to Lord M. L190

    despising Lord M. for his proverbs L206

conscience

    troubling him L202, L207, L218, L276, L281, L282, L287, L341, L367, L511, L535

    touched when the French marquis's wife died in childbirth L209

    sobbing to see Clarissa anticipate reconciliation L216

    guilt tormenting him L222

    feeling Clarissa's eye-beams L243

    his conscience *Mennelled* upon him L244

    his vows of revenge forgotten L245

    arguing with his conscience L256

    at times regretting what he has done L259

    I own I have done wrong...to this admirable creature L259

    what...would I have given never to have injured her L263

    shaken by Clarissa's first appearance to him after the rape L263

    conscience writhing around his pericardium like a serpent L276

    temporary remorse L286, L287

    his family believing him penitent L342

    I am sick at my soul L350

    quieting his conscience L370

    stung by his own reflections L383

    tearing his flesh L395

    wrongs fill his mind with anguish and horror L397

    his remorse is enough punishment L413

    his conscience clear L449

    facing his own death with heavy reflection L452

    his heart bleeding L466

    his conscience avenging Clarissa L518

    his opinion on conscience L530

consent

    gloomy that he did not get her consent L261

    she owes me her consent L264

contrivances of Clarissa

    not to be *out-Norrised* by Clarissa and Anna L148, L149, L150, L156, L198, L199, L215

    will not be emulated in contrivance by Clarissa L256

    overmatched by Clarissa L264

    deceived by Clarissa's reference to her father's house L421.1, L440, L446, L449, L486

LOVELACE, MR. ROBERT

contrivances of Lovelace see also **abduction of Clarissa**; **rape of Clarissa**

generally

    a forward contriver, wicked contriver L76, L94

    his conceited contrivances, his fine contrivances L83, L84

    outwitted, he would hang, drown, or shoot himself L117

    so full of his contrivances L155

    I have more contrivances L207

    so many contrivances L209

    his contrivances to keep Clarissa uncertain L209

    delighting in his contrivances L209

    hating himself for his contrivances L216

    a devil in his contrivances L223

    his contrivances explained L223

    reporting his contrivances with stage directions

        contrivance of Tomlinson L214

        reporting his disguise and Clarissa's recapture L232

    promising Tomlinson he will marry Clarissa and give up his contrivances L246

    if he gives up his contrivances, he will be but a common man L264

    confounded number of contrivances to carry his point with Clarissa L267

    entangled in my own inventions L275, L276, L285

    Clarissa querying Anna, Mrs. Howe, and Mrs. Norton on details of contrivances L295, L297, L300

    his family discovering and confronting him L323

    if his contrivances end in wedlock L326

    his cursed inventions his punishment L365

    all my vice is women, and the love of plots and intrigues L370

    I value myself upon my contrivances L439

    his contriving genius L470

    his cursed devices standing in the way of his happiness L535

specifically

    contrivance of sparing Rosebud

        Rosebud

            age, just turned seventeen years L34, L70, L71

            animals

                a lamb L34

                poor quarry L171

            character, modest, simple, uncontending L71, L216

            contrivance

                Lovelace asking Belford to spare Rosebud L34

                Rosebud feared undone L70

                to be fortuned out to a young lover L70

                needing protection of her family L71

                Lovelace giving her to his friend L71

                Clarissa wishing to warn Rosebud L71

                Colonel Barrow's fondness for Rosebud L72

                Lovelace innocent L72

                spared to credit his account with Clarissa L72, L103, L106, L183, L191, L252

                a plot...to wash a blackamoor white L72

                Lovelace's generosity to Rosebud L116, L138, L183, L452

                    explained by the compiler in a footnote L217.2

          family

            father and grandmother L34, L70, L71

            her grandmother asking Lovelace to spare Rosebud L34

            her father proprietor at White Hart Inn L34

LOVELACE, MR. ROBERT

contrivances of Lovelace, specifically, contrivance of sparing Rosebud, Rosebud (cont.)

  marriage

    to Johnny Barton, next week L34, L72, L207

    hundred pounds by Lovelace, matching sum given by the boy's relations L34, L72

    Lovelace begrudging Johnny the maiden L106

  mentioned L35, L159, L171, L198, L207, L496

  money, his friends giving twenty-five guineas to Rosebud's father L72

  name, Betsy L70

  physical appearance, her beauty, pretty rustic L72, L116

contrivance of kidnapping James and Solmes, planned L113, L114, L117, L119

contrivance of pretending marriage to Clarissa

  at Mrs. Sinclair's L154, L156, L186, L215

  at Mrs. Moore's L233, L235, L245

contrivance of Mrs. Fretchville's house L158, L164, L174.1, L175, L178, L183, L185, L194

  her kinsman, Mr. Mennell L174.1

  Miss Martin knowing her very well L194

  wanting to end the affair of Mrs. Fretchville's house L201, L203

  her maid taken with the small-pox and now she herself is ill L201, L203, L218

  Anna's inquiries finding no such person L229.1

  a fiction L252.1

contrivance of the bedfellows L162, L164, L167, L169, L229.1, L248

contrivance of the plot upon Miss Howe *see* **rape of Anna, planned**

contrivance of Lovelace's feigned illness

  taking ipecacuanha to make himself sick L209, L248

contrivance of Captain Tomlinson and Uncle Harlowe's birthday

  Tomlinson, Captain Antony

    age, twice Lovelace's age, upwards of fifty years L214, L217.1

    animals, a dog, puppy, a whore's bird L241, L243, L244

    biblical references, Pontius Pilate like L244

    character

      Clarissa liking him L217.1

      brought to tears by Clarissa's expression of grief L243

      an excellent head L246

    classical references, old Mulciber's, Tomlinson as L244

    conscience, fearing Clarissa's eye-beams L243

    contrivance

      posing as a friend of John Harlowe, at whose request he pretends to mediate a reconciliation L213, L214, L215, L216, L284

      reporting Clarissa's marriage to the Harlowes and Lovelace's relations L233

      correspondence forged by Lovelace L233.1 L233

      telling a Mr. Lilburne of Lovelace's marriage L233.1

      prevailing upon Lovelace to give it up L244

      Clarissa questions Lovelace directly on the truth of this contrivance L266

      Uncle Harlowe's birthday L271, L272.1, L274, L276, L284, L288, L300, L301

      Lovelace will marry Clarissa, before she discover the contrivance L294

      Clarissa questioning this contrivance L302, L303, L304, L305

    costume

      booted and spurred L214

      to get clothes in Monmouth Street L289

      riding dress for first visit to Clarissa L289

      boots not to be over clean, linen rumpled and soily L289

    crimes, forgery, head of a gang of smugglers, criminal L217, L246, L289, L514

    death, in Maidstone Gaol, after receiving Belford's three guineas L514, L515

    death of Harlowe, Miss Clarissa, penitent, acknowledging his guilt in L514, L521

LOVELACE, MR. ROBERT

contrivances of Lovelace, specifically, contrivance of Captain Tomlinson and Uncle Harlowe's birthday,
Tomlinson, Captain Antony (cont.)

    education, expelled from Dublin University L217

    family

        with his wife and five children living on eight hundred pounds a year L216

        daughters as old as Clarissa L243, L289

    imposter, Anna's inquiries about him find no such person L229.1, L281

    mannerisms, pulling down and stroking his ruffles, pulling his wig L237, L244, L289

    meals, taking a dish of tea with the ladies L238

    money

        Lovelace giving him ten guineas L289

        Belford sending him money, three guineas L514, L515

    names

        alias of Patrick McDonald L217

        signing his letter Antony Tomlinson L233.1

    physical appearance L304

    servants, his discarded footman L217

  contrivance of the fire L225, L230

    plot to frighten Clarissa almost naked into his arms L230

    recounted by Lovelace L243

    Clarissa asking Belford for Lovelace's correspondence to clarify this event L387.1

    mentioned L439

  contrivances of the impersonators L251, L255, L256.1, L312–L313

    impersonating Clarissa, Mrs. Bevis receives Clarissa's from Anna L251

    impersonating Lady Betty and Charlotte

        Bab Wallis (or Barbara), a whore, as Lady Betty L255

        Susan Morrison, a tenant-farmer's daughter, Lady Betty's woman L255, L312

        Johanetta Golding, as Charlotte L255

        borrowing jewels and clothes for the impersonators L255

        coaching manners of the impersonators L255

        contrivance recounted by Clarissa L312–L313

  contrivance of the visit to Mrs. Sinclair's by Mrs. Moore, Miss Rawlins, Mrs. Bevis, Belton, Mowbray,
and Tourville, planned

    Lovelace's new intrigue L261, L316

  contrivance of Clarissa's escape into the arms of his accomplice, planned L271

    the widow lady in her chariot waiting for Clarissa at the grocer's shop L273

    Clarissa not fooled L273

  contrivance of the promissory note

    conceived, executed, failed L279, L280, L281

    poor plot, poor contrivance, pride sunk L281, L282, L285

  contrivance of drowning of Thomasine and hers, suggested

    taking Thomasine and hers on a boat trip and drowning them L347

  contrivance of disguising himself as a parson to visit Clarissa, considered L370

control

  unused to control L3

  spoiled L142

  I was never accustomed to check or control L323

  not forgiving his family for presuming to control him L397

  who will control me L497

  I...will not be controlled L497

  why, why did my mother bring me up to bear no control L512

correspondence, Harlowe, Miss Clarissa with Anna, forged by Lovelace

  Letter 229.2 from 'Clarissa,' acknowledging receipt of Letter 229.1 L229

  Letter 240.1 from 'Clarissa,' acknowledging receipt of Anna's Letter 229.1 (now 239.1) L240

LOVELACE, MR. ROBERT

correspondence, Harlowe, Miss Clarissa with Anna, intercepted by Lovelace

attempting to seize a letter from Clarissa L175, L176

Letter 231.2, Clarissa's feint to Anna L231, L231.1

sending Will after Grimes, who has Clarissa's to Anna L233, L235, L238

intercepting correspondence, he keeps seals entire and preserves covers L239

stealing Clarissa's to Anna and substituting Letter 240.1, his forgery L240

watching the post L241

intercepting Clarissa's to Anna L284

correspondence, Howe, Miss Anna with Clarissa, forged by Lovelace

Letter 239.1, which is Anna's Letter 229.1, rewritten by Lovelace L229, L238, L239, L310, L316

rewriting Anna's to Mrs. Harriot Lucas L251

correspondence, Howe, Miss Anna with Clarissa, intercepted by Lovelace

instructing Belford to bring Clarissa's letters to him L105

contriving to steal letters from Simon Collins L174.3

reading transcripts made of Anna's letters (188 and 196) L198, L218

confiscating Anna's delivered by Collins to Wilson's L217

Letter 229.1 from Anna, marking it to show points demanding revenge L229

intercepting Anna's next L238, L239

intercepting and reading Anna's Letter 238.1 to Clarissa L238

Letter 229.1 mistakenly called by Lovelace her double-dated letter L240

Letter 229.1 ends Thursday morn 5 [a.m.]; Lovelace's transcription, Letter 239.1 ends Thursday morn 5th [though Thursday was the 8th] L229.1, L239.1

intercepting Anna's next to Clarissa L245, L248, L250

his crow-quill short-hand notes upon Anna's Letter 252.1 L252

confiscating Anna's last three to Clarissa (229.1, 252.1, 275.1) L275

wishing Belford to intercept Anna's letters to Clarissa L341

correspondence, Lawrance, Lady Betty, forged by Lovelace

Letter 233.2 from 'Lady Elizabeth Lawrance' L233, L272, L303, L306

correspondence, Lord M., forged by Lovelace

Letter 233.4 from 'Lord M.' L233, L306

correspondence, Lovelace, Mr. Robert

his great and secret correspondence L12

his letter case L233

correspondence, Lovelace, Mr. Robert with Belford

wrong to scribble so freely to Belford, but must write on L223

his unreserved communication with Belford L260, L261, L263, L276

asking Belford to return Lovelace's letters L326, L326n1

Clarissa asking Belford for copies of Lovelace's correspondence to tell her story L387.1

asking Belford to burn his, Lovelace's, letters L410, L512

Lovelace returning all his correspondence to Belford L423

correspondence, Lovelace, Mr. Robert with Charlotte

with Charlotte, while travelling L534

correspondence, Lovelace, Mr. Robert with Clarissa

established L3

subverted and used to manipulate Clarissa L3, L10, L17, L26, L36, L55

letter to Clarissa signed by Lord M., adding credibility to Lovelace's address L22

Clarissa and Lovelace a pair of scribbling lovers L105

questioning her motivations for corresponding with him against her family's wishes L110

confesses ignoring her letter of countermand before the abduction L113

writing to Clarissa in the rain in the coppice L223

Clarissa asking Belford to return to Lovelace all their correspondence, his to her and hers to him L365

her posthumous letter to Lovelace, which he gives to Lord M. L510.3

correspondence, Montague, Miss Charlotte, forged by Lovelace

Letter 233.3 from 'Miss Charlotte Montague' L233, L306

LOVELACE, MR. ROBERT
correspondence, Tomlinson, Captain Antony, forged by Lovelace
　　Letters 233.1, 272.1 and 290 from 'Captain Tomlinson' L233, L289
costume
　　his horseman's coat L36, L232
　　a critic of women's dress L99
　　description of Clarissa's clothing L99
　　lace on his hat L99, L232
　　his riding-dress L157
　　too gay for church L159
　　his gorget rumpled L183
　　full dress creates dignity, augments consciousness, and compels distance L194
　　his linen and wig frozen waiting for Clarissa in the coppice L223
　　in his gown and slippers when the fire broke out L225
　　his ruffle L225
　　disguised in a great-coat with a cape buttoned over the lower part of his face L232
　　Will putting in the ties of his wig L232
　　clocked stockings show he is a gentleman L232
　　stirrup-stockings giving his legs a gouty appearance L232
　　using a cane L232, L233
　　his slouched lace hat and wig L233
　　his hat brushed up into the usual smart cock L233
　　pulling his wig L244
　　borrowing clothing, laces, gold tissue for impersonators of Lady Betty and Charlotte L255
　　laced hat orator L294
　　the powder flew from his wig L367
　　so elegant and rich in his dress L367
　　in a broad rose-bound beaver L370, L370n6
　　in his fever, wearing his night-gown over his waistcoat, and his slippers L410
　　John bowed to my fine clothes L416
　　distraught over Clarissa's death, throwing his hat and wig off L480
　　Beau-Brocade, to wear after mourning L527
counsellors
　　Williams, Counsellor
　　　　to draw up settlements conformable to those of Lovelace's mother L207
　　　　drawing up the settlements, nearly finished L216, L229.1
　　　　man of eminence L229.1
courtship
　　a thorny courtship L207
　　his misfortune to have fallen in with Clarissa and hers with him L294
crimes
　　wishing not to be a detested criminal L283
　　unaffected by the sense of his own crimes L339
　　criminal charge L339
　　his crimes L448
　　villainous burglar, felon, thief L453
　　crime upon which he should be arraigned L456
　　crimes so black L458
　　what did I do worth a woman's breaking her heart for L515
　　If by committing an unlawful act, a capital crime is the consequence, you are answerable to both L515
　　Lovelace arguing his defense before Lord M. and his cousins Montague L515
crow-quills see **writing**
cures see also **medications**
　　bleeding, in his dangerous fever L410
　　chicken broth L410

LOVELACE, MR. ROBERT

cures (cont.)

pailful of black bull's blood taken from Lovelace L496

water gruel...soupe-maigre L512

by starving diet, by profuse phlebotomy, by flaying blisters, eyelet-hole-cupping, a dark room L512

treated with gallipots, boluses, and cephalic draughts L512

curses

curse of God, threatened by Lord M. on Lovelace L324

anathematized and cursed by his family L395

cursing Clarissa L395

cursing Mrs. Sinclair's house L395, L416

cursing Sally L416

cursing Belford L416

curses, Cain's curse

Lovelace having Cain's curse L458, L458n2

curses, Eve's curse

women made to bear L335

Dolly Welby describing parturient throes L453

death

death, a devil, Clarissa's new lover L346

not fearing death L422

death not a natural consequence of rape L515

death of Harlowe, Miss Clarissa

Belford sending the news in a coded message, advising him to go to Paris L449, L479

throwing his hat and wig off, sitting grinning like a man in straw L480, L480n2

death of Harlowe, Miss Clarissa, avenged

insolence to avenge Clarissa on Lovelace L535

death of Lord M.

disappointment at Lord M.'s recovery L294, L321, L341

hoping Lord M. would have died by now L321

Lovelace hoping his visit will not extend Lord M.'s life L341

death of Lovelace, Mr. Robert, *foreshadowed*

if Lovelace were to be fairly hanged L132

riddance of him by flight or the gallows L196

dreams of bringing about his own destruction L246

you *shall* be mine, or my life shall be the forfeit L266

singing to himself the thirtieth of January strain and the dead psalm melody L266, L266n2

Belford cutting the throat of Clarissa's destroyer, cutting Lovelace's throat L334, L387

deserving an infamous death L358

Thou (Lovelace) must die, as well as Belton L419

his death not honoring Clarissa's memory L448

facing his own death with heavy reflection L452

death of Lovelace, Mr. Robert

falling in a duel with Morden, dying next day L537

his composure upon his death bed L537

refusing Sacraments in the Catholic way L537

debts

mentioned L3

clear of debt L88

his debts abroad L186

devils see also **Beelzebub**; **Moloch-deity**; **Satan**

Lovelace as L68, L93, L119, L169, L181, L183, L189, L202, L227, L229, L229.1, L233, L235, L252.1, L258, L266, L277, L294, L305

the devil in me L138

acting the part of the grand tempter L157.1

LOVELACE, MR. ROBERT

devils, Lovelace as (cont.)

> devil to rejoice in Clarissa's fall L171
> a devil in his contrivances L223
> discovering his (cloven) foot L252.1, L252.1n1
> the devil himself L316
> a devil, a damned devil L324
> devil and his cloven feet L326
> a true devil L339
> Lord M. having a devil under his roof L349
> the man is a devil—this man is indeed a devil L367
> in whatever shape he chose to appear L370
> calling himself a devil L470

half a score of devils L154
devil take me L167, L395
devil crept out of his heart L199
women as L210
God sends meat, the devil cooks L211
ipecacuanha, a disagreeable medicine that would poison the devil L211
the devil in Milton's *Paradise Lost* L233, L233n1
oh devil of youth, and devil of intrigue L268
devil, an angler baiting fish L270
the devil not quite so black as he is painted L326
Lovelace having a face that would deceive the devil L366
the devil's in Clarissa L395
devil is black L395
the devil always baits with a pretty wench L415
no devil do I fear, but one in your shape L467
the devil and the time of life are against thee L513
the devil knows his own interest L516

disguises

disguised, will meet Clarissa for an interview L61, L62
at the inn as a military man, recently fought a duel in town L70
around Harlowe Place L86
as Clarissa's brother at the inn L98, L103
would change his dress like Clodius to seduce a woman L106, L106n1
offering to accompany Clarissa in disguise L124
disguised in a great-coat as he recaptures Clarissa at Hampstead L232
posing as a lawyer at Mrs. Moore's in Hampstead L233
Waltham disguises L243
his vile disguises L243
will disguise himself as a parson to see Clarissa, a contrivance L370
claiming to be a Justice of the Peace to search Smith's for Clarissa L416

dowry

resigning Clarissa's fortune L383

dreams see also **reveries**; **waking fantasies**

first dream, guilty of murdering Clarissa L246
second dream, Clarissa rescued by a lady, with Dorcas's help; the lady turns into Mother H., and into a young man, Lovelace; that he fathered a boy by Clarissa, a girl by Anna, the two marrying L271
writing a book about dreams, *Lovelace's Reveries* L272
dream, his family all in black interceding for him; Clarissa forgiving him; Morden threatening him; Clarissa ascending into Heaven; and he, covered with Lord M.'s great black mantle, falling through a hole L417
> Lovelace's interpretation L421

dress see **costume**

LOVELACE, MR. ROBERT

drink

>malmsey, Cyprus [wines] as medicine L203, L203n1
>
>directed a bottle of sherry to be added L228
>
>Barbados, having a dram of L255
>
>wine, an opiate L261
>
>a dram or two to the fellows in the mob, when Clarissa shouts for help L264
>
>burgundy and champagne for Morden, Lovelace, and Lord M. L442

duel between James and Lovelace see also **conflict between Harlowe Family and Lovelace**

>mentioned L1, L2, L55
>
>reported, with background L4
>
>aborted L4
>
>visit to Harlowe Place after duel L4
>
>vows revenge for ill treatment following duel with James L4
>
>aftermath, has borne their insults with bitterness L6, L109
>
>summary up to duel L13

duel between Morden and Lovelace

>not going out of his way to avoid Morden L534
>
>answering Morden's gentleman's challenge L534
>
>preparations L536
>
>Lovelace drawing first blood L537
>
>his death next day L537

duels, other

>feigned, at the inn L70
>
>left arm wounded seriously in a duel L116
>
>mentioned L119

eavesdropping

>a thief and an eavesdropper L57
>
>on Clarissa, Mrs. Moore, and Miss Rawlins L235
>
>listeners seldom hear good of themselves L235
>
>on Clarissa and Tomlinson L243, L245

education

>reputation as a student L4, L12
>
>quoting poetry L31
>
>fondness for Latin and English classics L34
>
>liberal education L91
>
>skill in learned and modern languages L161
>
>a man of parts and learning, of talents and learning L173.1, L190
>
>esteemed in Florence and Rome L173.1
>
>a fault in his education, he does good only to atone for bad L217.2
>
>pride of learning L364

elocution

>Lovelace's talent for L206

encroacher

>Lovelace as L69, L85, L94, L98, L101, L116, L155, L173, L220, L229.1
>
>love, an encroacher L220

entangled

>spider and fly analogy, entangling young girls L106
>
>she *must* yield, *entangled as she is* L191
>
>this cursed aversion to wedlock how it has entangled me L227
>
>entangled in his own inventions L275, L276, L285

escutcheons

>blot in my escutcheon L106

LOVELACE, MR. ROBERT

estates

 Clarissa's

  Lovelace agreeing to Clarissa's giving up her estate, if she will be his L36

  her estate not an issue in marriage to Lovelace L88

  Lovelace's right to, married to Clarissa L164, L379

  his lack of interest in L174.3

 Lovelace's

  Arabella's information L2

  report of L4

  two thousand pounds *per annum*, his own estate L88, L186

  unencumbered, no part of ever mortgaged, clear L88, L186, L265

  a thousand pounds *per annum* from Lord M., upon his nuptials L88

  fortune squandered L173.1

  his considerable fortune and alliances L183

  upon his nuptials, receiving Lord M.'s property in Lancashire or the Lawn L186

  his claim to the property in Lancashire better than Lord M.'s L186

  ought to live on two thousand pounds a year L206

  willing to sacrifice his whole estate for Clarissa's favor L207

  estates made over to him on his nuptials L220

  £8000 a year slipping through his fingers L294

euthanasia

 laudanum used in L191

Eve's curse see **curses, Eve's curse**

executors

 asking Belford to be his executor L535

exile

 an exile L35, L119

 his great stake in his country L114

 transported for life L119

 fly his country L132

 may leave this plaguy island and live abroad L233

 will never see England again if Clarissa rejects him L383

 self-imposed exile L395

expiate

 what will expiate for his vileness L336

 loss of life and soul a dreadful expiation L518

 let this expiate L537

eye-strings

 intimidating Clarissa L281

family

 himself an only child L3, L142

 fathering an illegitimate child by Miss Betterton, a son L139, L140

 wanting Clarissa to have his child L371

father's house see also **contrivances of Clarissa**, contrivance of her father's house

 Clarissa's cruel and gloomy father's house L98

 could I once get her out of her father's house L99

fearing Clarissa

 never knowing fear till he met Clarissa and had her in his power L287

fires see also **contrivances of Lovelace,** contrivance of the fire

 wanting to set fire to Mrs. Sinclair's house L396, L511

first blood

 drawing first blood in the duel with Morden L537

first love

 first love jilting him L31, L58, L220

LOVELACE, MR. ROBERT

food see also **drink; meals**

    God sends meat, the devil cooks L211

    taking chocolate for breakfast L216

    not loving kickshaws L233

    apple, oranges, gingerbread, smaller boy running away with L259

    gilt gingerbread at a fair L294

    searching for Clarissa at houses that deal in women's matters, and tea and coffee L294

    taking chicken broth when sick with a fever L410

    water-gruel and soupe-maigre prescribed L512

    starving diet L512

forger

    adroit at manual imitation L218

    mastering Anna's handwriting L229, L316

    his family confronting him for L323

forgiveness

    excluded from Christian forgiveness L373

    asking forgiveness, wishing for forgiveness L397, L399

    hoping for divine pardon through Clarissa L397

    not forgiving his family for presuming to control him L397

    Clarissa hoping his family will forgive him L398

    Clarissa forgiving him L467, L510.4

    Clarissa's forgiveness and death as revenge L472

    rejecting her forgiveness L472

friends

    generally

        in need of reform L34, L81

        meeting at the Cocoa Tree in Pall Mall L48

        his six or seven bad companions L81

        myrmidons L106

        wretches, men of fortune L114

        his gang of fellows L252.1

    Ambrose, Colonel

        the ball

            inviting Lovelace, Mrs. and Miss Howe, Hickman, and Arabella L350

            on the occasion of his wife's birthday and her brother, the governor, receiving good news L358

            an account of L367

            attended by Miss Playford, Miss Biddy D'Ollyffe, and Miss Kitty D'Oily L367

            Miss Kitty D'Oily challenging Lovelace on Clarissa's account L368

        meals, Lovelace breakfasting and dining with the Colonel and his nieces L322

        relations, his nieces, skin deep beauties, fine women L322, L367

        visits, from Lovelace L322

    Barrow, Colonel

        his fondness for Rosebud L72

        friends, *Captain Sloane* L72

    Belton, Mr. Thomas, friend of Lovelace L31

        age, about thirty years L161

        animals, a lion kicked in the jaws by an ass L344

        bequests of Belton

            leaving Belford 100 guineas, which he will give Belton's sister L426

            leaving £20 apiece to Mowbray, Tourville, Lovelace, and Belford for a ring L426

            leaving his sister only £50 L440

        character

            investigated by Hickman L48

            meeting Lovelace at Cocoa Tree in Pall Mall L48

LOVELACE, MR. ROBERT

friends, *Belton, Mr. Thomas,* character (cont.)

    description by Clarissa L161

    drinking hard L161

    his admiration and concern for Clarissa L169

    mischievous spirit L192

  collation at Mrs. Sinclair's, attending L158.1

  contrivances of Lovelace

    taking up quarters for one week at Hampstead in show of support for Lovelace L241

    sent for, as Clarissa is gone off L290

    at Mrs. Sinclair's when Clarissa returns L314

  costume, dressing gaily L161

  death of Belton

    cannot live long L399

    his dying confession, death rattle L424

    reported by Belford to Clarissa L426

    compared to Mrs. Sinclair's L499

  education, university L161

  estates

    his uncle bequeathing him a good estate L161

    his paternal estate in Kent mortgaged and soon to be foreclosed L192

    his broken fortunes, broken spirit, estate in ruin L344, L347

    Belford putting Belton's sister into possession of his house, reinstating Belton to his own house, occupied by Thomasine L344, L364, L385

    fleeced by a woman L347

    Belford consulting his attorney upon Belton's affairs L365

    his house, remains of his fortune saved by Belford L399

  executors, Belford L426

  expiate, may his tortures and repentance expiate L424

  family

    Thomasine, passing as Belton's wife L192

      character

        pretending to dote on him, embezzling his money L192

        a very devil, low-bred L193

        having Belton's house, put out of his house L344, L399

        her infidelity, her suspicious eye L347

        rapacious woman, accursed deceiver, ungrateful L399, L419

      family

        Tom and *Hal,* her sons L192

          supposed by Belton to be his L192, L344

          their father passing as Thomasine's cousin L344

          muscular and big-boned L347

          her cubs L399

        her father, innkeeper at Dorking L192

        her lover, her father's hostler L192

          thrown down the stairs by Belford L399

      funeral of Belton, at Belton's last office, not showing grief L440

      mourning, and widows weeds L399

      physical appearance, not a delicate frame L347

  friends

    Blomer, a physician L424

      earlier known to Belford L424

      his excesses in wine and women L424

      his opinion on the physician's art L424

LOVELACE, MR. ROBERT

friends, *Belton, Mr. Thomas* (cont.)

  funeral of Belton

    not attended by Mowbray or Lovelace L425

    parade hired to mourn him L425

    his funeral, interment, last office L426, L439, L440

  gentleman, came up to town and commenced fine gentleman L161

  historical references, compared to the ancient Sarmatians L344, L344n1

  illnesses

    short consumptive cough, blood L161, L192, L344, L347

    shocking scenes of his illness and agonies L419, L424

    pains in his stomach and head, convulsions L424

  literary references

    admired author, Nick Rowe L413

    his pleasure in poetry, classics, drama L419

  medications, cordial julep, an opiate, sleeping draughts L419

  names, called Thomas, Tommy, Tom L158.1, L419, L439

  opinions, on physicians and surgeons L424

  reform, penitent, regretting his misspent life, can neither repent nor pray, in despair L419

  relations

    Sambre, Mrs., Belton's sister L424

      come to live with him, continuing in Belton's house L419, L440

      bequest of Belton, leaving his sister only £50 L440

      Belford giving her 100 guineas L440, L449

      indigent, her vile husband, her son completing her ruin L440

      Mowbray, Lovelace, Tourville giving her their legacy for India Bonds L449

    nephew, in Antigua, his heir L440

    uncle, bequeathing him a good estate L161

  servants, Betty, maid L419

  story, Belton's story L190.1, L191, L192, L344

  victims, sister of Tom Metcalf, who died protecting her from Belton L419, L422

  visits, from Belford, to Epsom to keep Belton company L364, L414

Colmar, Sir George see **Howe, Miss Anna**, suitors to Howe, Miss Anna

Doleman, Mr. Tom

  animals, crippled monkey L497

  character

    man of fortune and character L126

    former rake L229.1

  contrivances of Lovelace

    to whom Lovelace writes for accommodations for Clarissa L126

    his letter describing Mrs. Sinclair L154

    recommending Mrs. Sinclair's to Lovelace L229.1

    implement of Lovelace L229.1

  family

    married man, married to a woman of family L126, L229.1

  illnesses

    paralytic complaints, palsy L130.1, L229.1, L480, L497

    his empiric and his malady L530, L531

  mentioned L130, L155, L158

  names, as Tom L131

  relations

    Newcomb, his nephew L174.2

      contrivances of Lovelace, contrivance of Mrs. Fretchville's house

        alias Mr. Mennell L174.2

        mischievously used by Lovelace L174.2, L194

LOVELACE, MR. ROBERT

friends, *Doleman, Mr. Tom*, relations, *Newcomb*, contrivances of Lovelace, contrivance of Mrs. Fretchville's house (cont.)

> telling Lovelace of Mrs. Fretchville's small-pox L201
>
> refusing to continue deceiving Clarissa L203
>
> Lovelace's conscience *Mennelled* upon him L244
>
> taking leave of Lovelace L526

his sister L130.1

visits, from Lovelace in Uxbridge L449

Holmes, Sir Anthony, his two nieces attending a party with Misses Martin and Horton L158

Mallory (or Malory), whose proctor helps Lovelace procure a license to marry Clarissa L220, L227

Miles, a caitiff, seducing the farmer's daughter L496

Mowbray, Mr. Richard, friend of Lovelace L31

> age, about thirty-three or thirty-four L161
>
> animals, the bear L420
>
> bequest of Belton
>
>> £20 for a ring L426, L440
>>
>> contributing his to Belton's sister's India bonds L449
>
> character
>
>> investigated by Hickman L48
>>
>> description by Clarissa L161
>>
>> jesting upon sacred things, hating clergy L161
>>
>> admiration and concern for Clarissa L169
>>
>> mischievous spirit, brutal, rough, and untouched L192, L370, L419, L445
>>
>> I ever hated a book L496
>>
>> Kicking...cuffing...orchard-robbing were my early glory L496
>
> collation at Mrs. Sinclair's, attending L158.1
>
> contrivances of Lovelace
>
>> helping Lovelace get the license L227
>>
>> his servant delivering Lovelace's forgery to Hickman L240
>>
>> taking up quarters at Hampstead in show of support for Lovelace L241
>>
>> sent for, as Clarissa is gone off L290
>>
>> present during Lovelace's interview with Morden, offering his sword L442, L445
>
> costume, dressing gaily L161
>
> death of Belton, Mr. Thomas
>
>> uncouth and unreflecting in Belton's dying moments L419
>>
>> comparing Belton's last hours to Clarissa's L473
>
> drink, asking for claret L419
>
> friendship with Belton
>
>> consigning Belton to quarantine L344
>>
>> a bottle-friend, frothy insensibility L419
>
> funeral of Belton, not attending L425
>
> gentleman L161
>
> languages, speaking many languages L161
>
> literary references
>
>> Dryden, John, *Palamon and Arcite*, quoted L496, L496n1
>>
>> Lee, Nathaniel and Dryden, *Oedipus*, quoted L419, L419n5
>
> music, humming a tune L419
>
> names, called Richard L158.1
>
> opinions, on seduction L496
>
> physical appearance
>
>> tall and comely, bold and daring, large and strong L161
>>
>> scar in forehead and right cheek L161
>
> reading, hating reading and books L496
>
> relations, good family L161

LOVELACE, MR. ROBERT

friends, *Mowbray, Mr. Richard* (cont.)

        residence, retired into Yorkshire, his native county CONCLUSION

        servants, treatment of, fearing him L161, L420, L423

        travel, joining Lovelace abroad, setting out with L513, L514, L516, L525, L526

        visits, to M. Hall with Lovelace L341, L421, L425, L511

    Solcombe, Colonel, his two daughters attending a party with Misses Martin and Horton L158

    Tourville, Mr. James

        age, just turned of thirty-one years L161

        bequest of Belton

            £20 for a ring L426, L440

            contributing his to Belton's sister's India Bonds L449

        character

            description by Clarissa L161

            coxcomb, fop, finical, idle flutterer L161, L350, L370, L498

            his admiration and concern for Clarissa L169

            mischievous spirit L192

            satisfied with wit at second-hand L222

        collation at Mrs. Sinclair's, attending L158.1

        contrivances of Lovelace

            taking up quarters at Hampstead in show of support for Lovelace L241

        costume, dressing richly, more tawdry than fine L161

        death of Harlowe, Miss Clarissa

            telling Lovelace that Clarissa is very ill L439

            to go with Mowbray to Lovelace to keep him from harming himself and others L477

            with Lovelace after Clarissa's death L482

        funeral of Belton, present at Belton's last office L440

        gentleman L161

        languages, speaking French and Italian L161

        music, musician, singing Lovelace out of his megrims L161, L421

        names, called James, Jemmy L158.1, L480

        relations, ancient family L161

        residence, retired into Nottinghamshire, his native county CONCLUSION

        travel

            out of town L290

            joining Lovelace abroad, setting out with L513, L514, L516, L525, L526

        visits, to M. Hall with Lovelace L341, L413, L511

    Warneton, Major, Lovelace meeting him at church L323

    Wilson, Mr.

        living in Pall Mall L155

        conveyance for correspondence between Clarissa and Anna L155, L175, L196, L201, L239

        giving Lovelace directly any letters delivered by Collins from Anna L217, L229

        how he came to be used as a conveyance L229.1

    Windisgratz, Baron, with whom Lovelace will reside at the Favorita in Vienna L534.1

friendship

    for Belford L534

funeral of Belton

    Lovelace not attending L425

funeral of Lord M.

    hiring blacks for the funeral L277

Gazette see **newspapers**

generosity

    to servants L11, L13, L15

    to folk at the inn L34, L72, L217.2

    not an ungenerous man L87, L98

LOVELACE, MR. ROBERT

generosity (cont.)

his generosity L140

to tenants L217.2

his generosity owing to pride and vanity rather than philanthropy L217.2

allowing Clarissa to be generous to Mrs. Norton L217.2

gentleman

gentleman L286

his prerogative as a gentleman to affront Joseph and the Smiths L416

gentleman's challenge from Morden L534

gold

not his predominant passion L105

grand tour

Lovelace's advice to the young man taking the grand tour L3

hair

wanting a lock of Clarissa's L497, L498

hanging

outwitted, he would hang, drown, or shoot himself L117

hanged L132

riddance of him by flight or the gallows L196

rake's neck in danger from the hangman L261

indemnity for a rapist, to fly or be hanged L293

meriting the gallows L452

hatred of Clarissa

I hate her L198

hating name of Harlowe L198

regrets having known Clarissa L264

hatred of Lovelace

as hateful to Clarissa as the vile Solmes L277

Belford hating Lovelace L349

hating himself L350

heir

Lovelace heir presumptive of Lord M. L2, L13, L118, L265

heraldry see also **lozenge**

description of arms on the marriage license L254

Lady Betty's arms and crest upon a coach, hers in for repairs L255

historical references

Antonio Perez L127

Don John of Austria L171

Charles XII of Sweden L198

Czar Peter

and the Muscovites L198

Cossacks at Pultowa L416, L416n3

Grand Signor L198, L198n3

Eastern monarchs sequester themselves to excite adoration L220

Queen Bess

would agree with his opinion on rape L223

Elizabeth I, comparing himself L370, L370n3

would have warred with the Great Turk, the Persian, the Mogul, Eastern monarchs L232

Sixtus the Vth, as the half-dead Montaldo, Lovelace compared L233

South Sea stock, subscriptions leading to ruin in 1720 L241

Catalans holding up their English treaty, Clarissa and her license compared L260, L260n1

Queen Anne

the late Queen Anne, a good woman, always fond of prerogative L265

Lovelace comparing himself L265

LOVELACE, MR. ROBERT

historical references (cont.)

singing to himself the thirtieth of January strain and the dead psalm melody L266, L266n2

James VI of Scotland and I of England (the Royal Insignificant), his book, *Demonology* L272, L272n1

Charles II, his death anticipated, as Lovelace anticipates Lord M.'s L294

Italian eunuchs L321, L321n1

true father of a certain monarque (his identity kept secret by murder) L326, L326n1

Martin Luther, Belford compared L370

Charles V, Luther appearing before L370

Queen of Scots, Clarissa compared L370, L370n3

Harry IVth L371

Madam Maintenon and Lewis XIV of France L422, L422n1 (note omitted from text)

Dame Elizabeth Carteret, her monument in Westminster Abbey, Belford compared L449, L449n1, L453

Francis Chartres, rapist, Belford compared L513, L513n1

Christian princes, Lovelace comparing his crime to theirs L515

honor

of unblemished honor, honor noted L81, L153, L222, L225, L333

his family's honor L222

conspiring against Clarissa's honor L261 Paper VIII

Harlowe Family dishonored by Lovelace L267

little regard for the honor of his family L286

Belford doubting his honor L286

dishonoring his family by marrying a person whom he has so treated L323

hunting see also **prey**; **sport**

has hunted in the forest at Windsor L116

caught in his own snares L138

an artful fowler L152

drawing sprindges about Clarissa L152

foxhunter in pursuit of vermin not fit for food L170

hunting Clarissa L230, L386, L418, L456, L467

Lovelace like an old hedgehog, hunted for its grease L480

husband

wanting to act as Clarissa's husband after her death L497

illnesses

from waiting for Clarissa in the rain in the garden for the interview L62, L73, L223

egregiously cropsick L410

dangerously ill with a violent fever, almost well L411, L412, L414

Tourville singing Lovelace out of his megrims L421

in a fever, recovering from his grief over Clarissa L511, L512

illnesses, feigned

broken vessel caused by taking a few grains of ipecacuanha, vomiting blood L209, L210, L212

gout, ague, limping, using a cane L232, L233

impersonators see **contrivances of Lovelace,** contrivances of the impersonators

impostors see

contrivances of Lovelace, contrivance of Captain Tomlinson and Uncle Harlowe's birthday

contrivances of Lovelace, contrivance of Mrs. Fretchville's house, her kinsman, Mr. Mennell

informants

Leman, Joseph

double agent, double agency explained L35, L62, L80, L100, L113, L119

Lovelace's intelligencer L62, L85

gossiping with Betty about Lovelace and Rosebud L71, L73

not entirely loyal to Lovelace L73, L84

causing family to suspect Clarissa of corresponding with Lovelace L84

spying on Clarissa for the family L86

family suspect Lovelace's source of information is Clarissa, when in fact it is Leman L91

LOVELACE, MR. ROBERT

informants, *Leman, Joseph* (cont.)
>> doubted by Clarissa L94
>> corrupted by Lovelace L95
>> vile agent of Lovelace L101, L229.1
>> used by Lovelace to influence Antony, who influences Mrs. Howe L104
>> informing Lovelace about James's alliance with Bettertons L127
>> informing Lovelace about James's plan to rescue Clarissa L137, L140, L152

inheritances see also **estates**
> heir presumptive to Lord M.'s estate L2, L13, L118
> expecting a large estate from Lord M. L105
> willing to lay obligation of one half of his estate upon Clarissa L105
> if not a good husband, Lord M. will leave all to Clarissa and none to Lovelace L206
> would like £8000 a year and the title reversionary L265
> trouble with some of his relations anticipated after Lord M.'s death L285
> titles going with the bulk of Lord M.'s estate L327

interviews
> early meeting with Anna mentioned L27
> with Hickman L346
> with Anna L366, L367
> with Clarissa planned L371

jesting
> on jesting, in poor men L140
> all that has passed between Lovelace and Clarissa, a jest L453

jewels see also **rings**
> borrowing jewels, ear-rings, solitaire for the impersonators of Lady Betty and Charlotte L255

Jews
> synagogue lattices promoting piety L106
> Josephus, *Antiquities of the Jews*, quoted L191, L191n2
> women have no souls, or so he believes as a Jew L219, L219n2
> and Lovelace's description of death L346

keyhole
> looking through the keyhole of Clarissa's door L264

keys
> having two keys to the garden door at Harlowe Place L35, L61, L62, L94, L95
> key used to lock up the prude while Lovelace seduced the French marquis's wife L209
> has not keys to the wainscot box where Clarissa has moved her letters L210
> Clarissa keeping her chamber keys in her pocket, foiling second rape L281

kidnapping see **contrivances of Lovelace**, contrivance of kidnapping James and Solmes, planned

kisses
> for Clarissa
>> kissing her hand L36, L94
>> the first time L103
>> wishing to kiss Clarissa L115
>> giving Clarissa a fervent kiss L175
>> attempting to kiss Clarissa L187
>> kissing Clarissa's hand, cheek L194
>> kissing her hand L199, L211, L215, L216, L248
>> kissing Clarissa's hand, leaving a red mark L200, L201
>> kissing her unrepulsing hand five times L204
>> wishing for one consenting kiss from Clarissa L205
>> clasping his arms about Clarissa and forcing a kiss L215
>> kissing her hands, his cheek on her shoulder, arm around her waist, kisses her lips L220
>> drawing aside the handkerchief and kissing her breast L220
>> seizes scissors from Clarissa, clasps her to his bosom, kissing her L225

LOVELACE, MR. ROBERT

kisses, for Clarissa (cont.)
>> snatching Clarissa's hand, kisses it L276, L277
> for Mrs. Sorlings's younger daughter L105

kneeling
> kneeling as he writes in the coppice to Clarissa L64.1
> kneeling before Clarissa L94, L98, L201
> upon his knees L137, L138
> reptile kneeler L274
> kneeling L281

language see also **sayings and proverbs**; **women's language**
> cabala, word used by rakes L110
> using out-of-the-way words and phrases L117
> expletives
>> by Jupiter L228, L244, L330, L410, L416, L511, L513, L516
>> Io Triumphe! Io Clarissa, sing L231
> *in coelo salus—*or *quies* L294
> prating L323
> I was *Belforded* all over L416
> in Lord M.'s style L512, L515

languages
> skill in learned and modern languages, speaking many languages L161

law
> narrate...in the Scottish phrase L322, L322n1
> peers are judges in the last resort L515
> if by committing an unlawful act, a capital crime is the consequence, you are answerable to both L515
> believing his crime was common theft L515
> commission...quorum L516, L516n1

libertine
> free liver L118, L217.2
> Lovelace as L144, L173.1, L177, L182, L222, L229.1, L316, L342, L346, L366, L367, L379
> libertine whom Clarissa loved and wished to reclaim L365
> rake and libertine L402

lies
> never lied to a man nor said truth to a woman L513

liquor see **drink**

literary references
> Addison, Joseph
>> *Remarks on Several Parts of Italy*, quoted L350, L350n1
>> Steele's Prologue to Addison's *Cato*, quoted L370, L370n8
>> *The Campaign*, quoted L463, L463n1
> *Aesop's Fables*, quoted L371, L371n2
> Aesop's traveller, Belford compared L472
> Ariosto, *Orlando Furioso* L110, L110fn, L267, L267n1, L512, L512n1
> Baxter, Richard, *Baxter's History of Spirits and Apparitions* L272, L272n1
> Boileau-Despréaux, Nicholas, *Le Lutrin* L171, L171n1
> Burnet, Gilbert, quoted but not named L157.1, L157.1n1
> Butler, Samuel
>> quoted but not named L110, L110n1
>> *Hudibras*, quoted L231, L231n2
> Cibber, Colley, *The Careless Husband*, Clarissa as *Lady Easy* to Lovelace's pleasures L207
> Congreve, William
>> quoted L157, L157n3
>> *The Mourning Bride* L365, L365n1, L370, L370n4

LOVELACE, MR. ROBERT

literary references (cont.)

Cowley, Abraham
  quoted L31, L31n6
  Destiny, quoted L202, L202n1
  translation of Horace, *Odes*, Book II, quoted L264, L264n1
Cromwell, Oliver, quoted L99
Dryden, John
  quoted L31, L31n3, L31n5, L35, L35n1, L154, L154n2
  Aureng-Zebe, quoted L169, L169n1, L191, L191n1
  Don Sebastian, quoted L159, L159n3, L530, L530n3
  rearrangement of Shakespeare's *Troilus and Cressida*, quoted L235, L235n1
  Alexander's Feast, mentioned, not quoted L370, L370n7
  Conquest of Granada, quoted L530, L530n2
Glanville, Joseph, *Glanville of Witches* L272, L272n1
Greene, Robert, *History of Dorastus and Faunia,* Mrs. Sinclair's cook-maid reading L225, L225n1
Horace, *Odes*, quoted in Latin L530, L530n1
Howard, Robert, quoted L31, L31n1
James VI of Scotland and I of England, *Demonology* L272, L272n1
Kennet, White, *History of England from...Charles I to...William II* L294, L294n2
Lee, Nathaniel
  Death of Alexander the Great, quoted L97, L97n1
  Gloriana, Clarissa as L159, L159n2
  his left-handed gods at work L194
  Caesar Borgia, quoted L228, L228n3
  Mithridates, quoted L417, L417n2, L497, L497n1
  mentioned, on dying L422
Mandeville, Bernard, private vices are public benefits L246, L246n1
Milton, John, *Paradise Lost*, the devil in L233, L233n1
Montaigne, *Essays* L193, L193n1
More, Chancellor, Lovelace compared L346, L346n3
Otway, Thomas
  History and Fall of Caius Marius, quoted L31, L31n2
  Venice Preserved L194, L194n1
  Orphan, mentioned L442, L442n1
Pope, Alexander, *Of the Characters of Women*, quoted L115, L115n2
Prior, Matt
  Erle Robert's Mice, quoted L259, L259n2
  Alma, quoted L346, L346n2
  The Ladle, quoted L453, L453n1
Rochester, Earl of, *Valentinian. A Tragedy as 'tis altered by the late Earl of Rochester,* quoted L228, L228n2
Rowe, Nicholas
  Ambitious Stepmother, quoted L154, L154n1
  Tamerlane, quoted L159, L159n4, L511, L511n2
  quoted L227
  learning Spanish L229, L229n2
  The Fair Penitent, quoted L371, L371n1
  mentioned L415
Royal Insignificant, *Demonology* L272, L272n1
Shakespeare, William
  Othello, quoted L31, L31n4
  The Tempest, quoted L31, L31n7
  Macbeth, quoted L175, L175n2
  Troilus and Cressida
    quoted L209, L209n1

LOVELACE, MR. ROBERT

literary references, Shakespeare, William, *Troilus and Cressida* (cont.)

   rearrangement by Dryden, quoted L235, L235n1

  Julius Caesar, quoted L221, L221n1

  much ado about nothing L227

  a line! a line! a kingdom for a line L330

  Measure for Measure, quoted L371, L371n3

  Hamlet, quoted L396, L396n1

 Steele, Richard

  Prologue to Addison's *Cato*, quoted L370, L370n8

  The Tender Husband, mentioned L516, L516n2

 Swift, Jonathan

  Tale of a Tub

   quoted L103, L103n1, L218, L218n1

   a tub to the whale L323

   Digressions in Praise of Digressions, mentioned, not quoted L346, L346n1

   mentioned L370

  Gulliver's Travels, quoted L439

 Taylor, Jeremy, *Taylor's Holy Living and Dying* L313, L313n1

 untraced L174.3, L174.3n1, L225, L225n2, L416, L416n1, L463, L463n2, L511, L511n1, L535, L535n1

 Valentinian. A Tragedy as 'tis altered by the late Earl of Rochester, quoted L228, L228n2

 Waller, Edmund, *Of Love*, quoted L207, L207n1

 Whitefield, George, an enthusiast, quoted L370, L370n5

livery

 Clarissa not prepared to wear Lovelace's livery yet L123

 offering to wear Clarissa's livery L124

 Will wearing Lovelace's livery L231.1

 Will in a new livery L416

 Lovelace putting on Clarissa's livery and wearing it for life L276

lodgings

 putting up at the inn in the village of Neale L63

 taking all vacant apartments at Mrs. Sinclair's L154

 lodging, boarding at Mrs. Moore's, engaging all her rooms for one month L233, L241

 Clarissa's objections forcing him to lodge about twelve doors off from Mrs. Moore's L239

 returning to his lodgings at Mrs. Sinclair's L416

 offering to lodge at Smith's at ten guineas a day, till Clarissa returns L416

 returning to M. Hall L421, L424

love

 love, an encroacher L220

love for Clarissa

 confiding in Aunt Hervey his passion for Clarissa L3

 in love with Clarissa L31

 his passion for Clarissa, second to revenge L137, L143

 noted L137, L187.1–L187.4, L194, L229.1, L282, L281, L287, L303, L350, L395, L470

 revering Clarissa L187.1–L187.4

 his love for, now more intellectual than personal L453

Lovelace's Reveries

 book about dreams, planned by Lovelace L272

lozenge see also **heraldry**

 on the widow lady's chariot signifying widowhood L273

manners

 not so polite as she would expect L101

 his flourishes L107

 careless manners L121

 his unpoliteness L127, L204

LOVELACE, MR. ROBERT

manners (cont.)

    polite L123, L128

    self-pluming air L187

    keeping eyes within bounds L210

    rough-mannered disgrace of his birth L243

    coaching impersonators of Lady Betty and Charlotte L255

    Susan Morrison, her hands before her L255

    uncivil gentleman L416

marriage see also **opinions**, on marriage

    family wishing him to marry L98

    I cannot...cannot marry L202

    will not marry because it is for life, will never marry L254, L527

    Lovelace's marriage ruining Mrs. Sinclair's house L336

marriages, Clarissa's to Lovelace

    generally

        suggested by Lovelace to Clarissa L80, L88, L94, L95, L98

        promise you will never marry any other man while I am living and single L98

        doubting his intentions toward Clarissa L99

        not marrying Clarissa till he is sure of her L103

        his family knowing of his intentions toward Clarissa L104

        proposing speedy solemnization L107

        declining two considerable families for Clarissa L109

        never marrying anyone but Clarissa L109, L350

        why has he not declared himself L120

        family favoring alliance with Clarissa, urging him to marry Clarissa L128, L324, L327

        blaming Clarissa that they are not married L140

        better that they do not marry L153

        again mentioning their wedding, searching for a house L158

        writing to Lord M. about terms and requesting him to be Clarissa's nuptial father L187

        will marry Clarissa after he gratifies his pride, ambition, and revenge L187.1–L187.4

        delaying marriage and accusing Clarissa of delaying L188

        Let me perish, if I marry a woman who has given her...friend reason to say she despises me L199

        I should be a fool to proceed as I do and mean matrimony L199

        ambivalent about marrying Clarissa L201, L227, L268, L279

        blaming Clarissa that they were not married before coming to town L221

        this project is not to end in matrimony surely L224

        his strange suspensions of marriage L229.1

        if ever he marries, it will be Clarissa L259

        can want of a church ceremony make such a difference L264

        now there is but one man in the world whom she can have—and that is me L268

        putting on her livery and wearing it for life L276

        resolved to marry Clarissa L278, L281, L285, L286, L289, L350, L383, L396, L423

        Clarissa should marry him to save her reputation and that of her family L284

        to marry Clarissa Thursday before his contrivances are found out L287, L288, L294

        claiming to be married to Clarissa L308

        dishonoring his family by marrying a person whom he has so treated L323

        the matrimonial sword hanging over his head by a thread L325

        giving his aunts his word that he will marry Clarissa L341

        agreeing to marry Clarissa upon her terms L346

        she shall die a Lovelace L383

        swearing he will marry her L383

        will bring a parson to marry them L383

        rejection making him desperate L383, L387, L397

        will marry her even in the agonies of death L396

LOVELACE, MR. ROBERT

marriages, Clarissa's to Lovelace, generally (cont.)

wanting to act as Clarissa's husband L497

license

getting a license at Doctors' Commons L219, L227.5

difficulty in getting a license L219, L223

proctor of his friend Mallory helping Lovelace procure license L220, L227

near arranged, applied for L226, L229.1

will get license tomorrow L245, L253

description of arms on the license, its hieroglyphics L254

having the license L266

Clarissa still in possession of the license L383

proposals

Clarissa greeting his with silence as it is too soon and not convincing L107, L108

asking for her hand, unintentionally L137, L138

proposing marriage before they go to London L149, L152

again proposing marriage L155

earlier marriage proposals mentioned L155

hoping Clarissa will name the happy day L157

regretting her refusal of his earlier proposal before coming to Mrs. Sinclair's L207

blaming Clarissa that they were not married before coming to town L221

asking Clarissa to be lawfully his tomorrow L266

urging Clarissa to meet him at the altar L267, L282, L283

make this my happy day L276

proposing instant marriage L278

offering to let Clarissa decide his fate, church or the gallows L332.2

asking Clarissa to marry him L397

settlements

not talking of settlements or license L183

offering to discuss settlements with Clarissa L185

his proposals regarding Clarissa's estate, as well as his own and his inheritance L186, L253

being completed L207

similar to those for his mother L207, L216, L218, L229.1

settlements to be ready in one week L215

drafted and ready for Lovelace, nearly ready to sign L218, L226

Lord M. agreeing to jointure from Lovelace's own estate L218

if Lovelace can have Clarissa, the devil take everything else L218

draft of settlements sent to Tomlinson by Lovelace L220

Pritchard ready with his indentures tripartite L226

wedding, after the wedding they will retire to the Lawn L207

wedding gifts

Lord M. to give Lovelace a thousand pounds *per annum* on his nuptials L88

Lord M. will give large estate to Lovelace L105

Lord M. will give Lovelace his estate in Lancashire or The Lawn upon his nuptials L186

consulting with Pritchard about estates transferred to Lovelace upon his nuptials L203.1

estates made over to him upon his nuptials L220

meals, breakfast

denied breakfast with Clarissa L198

breakfast with Clarissa L214

taking chocolate for breakfast with Clarissa and Tomlinson L216

invited to breakfast and dinner with Colonel Ambrose and his nieces L322

not breakfasting, not dining with his family, on hearing of Clarissa's arrest L332

meals, dinner

dining out L194

not admitted to dine with Clarissa and so not dining at all L200

LOVELACE, MR. ROBERT

meals, dinner (cont.)

 dinner at Mrs. Moore's L233, L235

meals, supper

 supping with Clarissa L194

 wishing to sup with Clarissa L199, L200

meals, tea

 tea with Clarissa L200, L201

medications see also **cures**

 ipecacuanha

  taking a few grains to make himself vomit blood L209, L248, L272

  a disagreeable medicine that would poison the devil L211

 laudanum

  in euthanasia L191

  and the wet cloth L294, L294n1, L323, L323n1

 malmsey, Cyprus [wines] as L203, L203n1

 opiates

  allowing Mrs. Sinclair to administer something to make Clarissa insensible to rape L260

  fearing the quantity may dampen her intellect L260

  prescribed by physicians L261

  wine an opiate, intoxicating viands, somnivolences L261

 styptic

  Eaton's styptic, a balsamic medicine to cure the effects of ipecacuanha L209

  taking styptic administered by Clarissa L211

Moloch-deity see also **Beelzebub**; **devil**; **Satan**

 Lovelace as L57

money

 a hundred pounds to Rosebud L34, L72

 twenty-five guineas to Rosebud's father L72

 offering Clarissa a £100 bank note L98

 gold not his predominant passion L105

 five guineas to Hannah L130, L132

 to Mrs. Sorlings's elder daughter L155

 offering Clarissa a bank note L157

 despising money, valuing not money, not a money lover L190, L217.2, L258

 offering Clarissa the bill he received from Lord M. L205

 Lord M. offering Lovelace money to marry Clarissa L206

 returning the bill to Lord M., as it is not needed L207

 a guinea to Mrs. Moore L233

 offering Mrs. Moore a £30 bank note L233

 to Mrs. Bevis L239

 giving Margaret one guinea for bringing Anna's for Mrs. Harriot Lucas L251

 offering the messenger one half guinea for the letter L251

 ten guineas to M'Donald L289

 offering to lodge at Smith's at ten guineas a day L416

 half a crown to Joseph L416

 giving his servant five guineas for good news about Clarissa L470

 offering Dr. H. a thousand guineas if he recover Clarissa L470

mourning

 wearing mourning for Clarissa L496

murder

 Harlowe Family will prosecute for L132

 committing L171

 no assassin, no night-murderer L196

 dreaming of murdering Clarissa L246

LOVELACE, MR. ROBERT

murder (cont.)

    Belford looking guilty of L277

    drawn in to commit a murder L323

music

    singing to himself the thirtieth of January strain and the dead psalm melody L266, L266n2

    Lovelace humming tunes L416

    women's grief like notes of well-tuned viol L416

    Tourville singing Lovelace out of his megrims L421

names

    changing his name without Act of Parliament, by Act of Parliament L105, L271, L327

    Bob, Bobby L222, L294, L323, L333, L411, L442, L496

    the V. L316

newspapers

    will advertise in the *Gazette*, the newspapers, for Clarissa, an eloped wife L228, L326

nurses

    Greme, Mrs., attending him in his fever L410

opiates see **medications**

opinions

    on bashfulness L115

    on churches, some for men and some for women L106

    on conscience L530

    on courtship L3

    on euthanasia L191

    on fallen women L157.1, L171, L205

        more girls ruined...prepared for ruin, by their own sex...than directly by...men L252

    on the female sex L31, L58, L99, L115, L117, L175, L223

        their gossip L15

        their sweet cowardice, confoundedly sly sex L103

        how greedily they swallow praise L105

        his universal adoration of the sex L106

        not yet found virtue to withstand his test, now believes there are truly virtuous girls L110, L225

        must be dealt with doubly L127

        their cruelty L127

        his contempt for L173.1

        meek, patient, and resigned, inappropriate to be in a passion L202

        loving rakes, smart fellows, preferring libertines to novices L207, L236

        women are devils L210

        women have no souls L219, L219n2

        women are plotters L228, L235

        women creating storms L242

        and friendship L252

        their imbecility L267

        a bad woman more terrible to her sex than a bad man L276

        all women are cowards at bottom L289

        the curse of Eve, made to bear pain L335

        revenge, obstinacy in L346, L371

        as unforgiving L410

        his hatred of all women L449

        he, the plague of a sex that has been my plague L512

        never lied to a man nor said truth to a woman L513

        his mean opinion of, from early manhood L535

    on friendship L252

    on hard-heartedness L187.1–L187.4

    on honor and death L371

LOVELACE, MR. ROBERT

opinions (cont.)

on human nature L127

on innkeepers L98

on jesting, in poor men L140

on love L326

his hatred and contempt for L31

the woman who resents not initiatory freedoms is lost. For love is an encroacher L220

on the lower classes L214

on the male sex L34

perfidy of L191

men, monkeys in imitation L216

the nobler sex L252

never lied to a man nor said truth to a woman L513

on marriage L117, L152, L153

regretting ridiculing, ridiculing L75, L143

marriage-hater, antipathy, aversion, disrelish L79, L110, L190, L223, L227, L229.1, L246, L346, L376, L421

favoring annual marriages and marrying thirty-one times L254

imagining an old spectacled parson with a white surplice thrown over a black habit performing the irrevocable ceremony L276

his prejudice to the state of shackles L279

foolish ceremony L287

on medicine L191, L203, L211

on parenting L115, L234

on physicians L203, L209, L211, L212

on polygamy, David and Solomon L254

on rakes L115, L191

on rape L254

Queen Bess, would agree with his opinion on rape L223

none ever committed without a yielding reluctance L223

on seduction L294

on servants, characteristics of good servants L423

on smuggling, a national evil L289

on trade, the dignity of in this mercantile nation L416

on tragedy and comedy L194

on virtue

his love of, platitudes L36

not yet found virtue to withstand his test L110

more important in women than in men L110

female virtue founded in pride L110

on wives L153

keeper of a man's honor L110

Parliament

changing his name without act of, changing names by act of L105, L271, L327

advised by Lord M. to get into soon L206, L206n2

his gift for elocution L206

neither a courtier nor a malcontent be L206, L206n3

first boy to take Lord M.'s name by Act of Parliament L233.4

Lord M. and Lovelace have three or four boroughs at their command L254

annual Parliaments L254, L254n2

peculiars

another of his peculiars L40

their own peculiar talents L202

I know thou likest this lively *present-tense* manner, as it is one of my peculiars L256

LOVELACE, MR. ROBERT

peerage see also **title**

    hopes for L13

peers

    judges in the last resort L515

pencil

    Clarissa, a glory to the pencil L138

    giving Dorcas a pocket book and a silver pencil L174.3

phaeton

    his phaeton ready to drive L322

    Miss Patsey Montague sharing his phaeton L332

physical appearance

    a handsome fellow L294, L516

    one of the handsomest men in England L346

    advantages in his person, air, intellect, and a face that would deceive the devil L366

physicians

    sending a physician to Hannah with medicine to make her weaker L167

    Hale, Dr., treating Lovelace L512

    Wright, Dr., attending Lovelace in his dangerous fever L410

platonic love

    and Clarissa L194

poems

    his poetry L116

    Lovelace's verses to his Stella L153

power

    female sex, whose infidelity I vow to revenge upon as many as shall come into my power L31

    and is she not in my power L99

    every time I attend her...she is less in my power—I more in hers L99

    dogs, using his power to frighten, as a boy L191

    tormenting animals that he has power over L222

    tyrant over what he loves L234

    Lovelace's over Clarissa L98, L183, L243, L287, L308

    Clarissa's over Lovelace L282, L395, L453

    never knowing fear till he met Clarissa and had her in his power L287

prayers

    Clarissa's for Lovelace L336, L510.4

    parson of the parish praying for him in his fever L410

    praying for Clarissa L472

pregnant

    believing Clarissa pregnant L371, L423

prey see also **hunting**

    Lovelace's L127, L170

    birds, women as quarry compared L170

    his quarry, wrens and sparrows L70

    Sally and Polly his prey L157.1

    lion...sheep, women compared, as his prey, his noble quarry L171

    wrens, phil-tits, wagtails not noble quarry L171, L189

    quitting too-easy prey to reptile rakes L239

    beasts of prey, rakes as L367

    a thousand vultures...preying upon my heart L511

pride

    Lovelace's noted L112, L117, L123, L173, L189, L217.2, L227, L229.1, L253

    his pride sunk at failure of his contrivance of the promissory note L285

    his pride mortified L395

LOVELACE, MR. ROBERT

prosecution of Lovelace
> Harlowe Family prosecuting for murder L132
> Lovelace should be prosecuted L317

protection for Clarissa see also **refuge for Clarissa**
> false offers of from Lovelace
>> with Lord M., the Lawn, M. Hall, Berkshire L22, L104, L116
>> with Lady Betty L36, L49, L98, L116, L123, L233, L243
>> in London L49, L76, L98, L104, L116
>> with his family L61, L80, L85, L98, L104
>> at her own house L80, L85
>> at Anna's L85, L124
>> believing Mrs. Howe should have taken Clarissa in L98
>> private lodgings L98
>> in Windsor L116
>> Morden in Florence L124
>> Mr. Doleman L126
> Clarissa's only protector, Judas protector L225, L227.4, L256

proverbs see **sayings and proverbs**

punishment
> to whom should he be accountable for the harm he does women L219
> hymeneal torch and a white sheet L221, L221n2
> deserving broken bones L252, L252.1
> Clarissa's punishment is over, Lovelace's is not L266
> defying Clarissa's right to vengeance through the law or through Morden L274
> indemnity for a rapist, to fly or be hanged L293
> his punishment just beginning L293, L330
> his condemnation L293
> cat-o'-nine-tails L294
> offers to let Clarissa decide his fate, church or the gallows L332.2
> raping Clarissa a national sin atoned for by sword, pestilence, or famine L336
> his punishment, justice of his country and vengeance of her friends L336
> what will expiate for his vileness L336
> his cursed inventions his punishment L365
> punishment by God L373
> his remorse is punishment enough L413
> answerable with his life for his crime L429
> meriting the gallows L452

The Quarrelsome Lovers
> a comedy planned by Lovelace L175, L216

rakes
> universal lover, his popularity with ladies L31
> whoremonger L32.4
> comparing Clarissa to Rosebud L103
> prince and leader of such a confraternity L104
> reflecting upon his reputation as a rake L104, L105
> mad fellows as are above all law L106
> Caesar as L110
> accustomed to triumph over other women L110
> every woman as L115
> Lovelace as L127, L173.1, L190, L246, L252, L294, L316, L366, L402, L406
> General Robert Lovelace, the general of his fellow rakes, head of a gang of wretches L158.1, L171, L177, L209, L223, L252.1, L370
> his opinion that the female sex love rakes L207
> twenty times the pains to be rogues, than to be honest L215

LOVELACE, MR. ROBERT

rakes (cont.)

Johnny Hartop, the punster, example of the wit of rakes L222

though a rake, not a rake's friend L223

a notorious woman-eater L223

a smart fellow and a rake L236

quitting too-easy prey to reptile rakes L239

rake's neck in danger from the hangman L261

a rake's a rake L279

and his confraternity L293

rakes as beasts of prey L367

rake's creed

mentioned L110, L116

Lord Shaftsbury's test L116, L116n2

libertine's creed, once subdued, always subdued L110, L198, L209, L256, L264, L274, L294

but oh, Jack, she never was subdued L274

in part L219

rape

a rape worthy of Jupiter L35

none intended in the affair with Miss Betterton L140

Francis Chartres, rapist, Belford compared L513, L513n1

death not a natural consequence of L515

rape of Anna, planned

regretting he cannot also have Anna L104

account of a scheme to be revenged on Miss Howe L207.1 (following)

I will have Miss Howe if I cannot have her more exalted friend L229

as to the comparison between the two ladies, I will expatiate more...when I have had them both L252

as she sets out on her journey to the Isle of Wight L371

Lovelace will let Hickman have Anna safe and entire L371

rape of Clarissa, *foreshadowed*

Lovelace's penetration L2, L10

Rosebud spared L34, L35, L70, L71, L72, L73

a rape worthy of Jupiter L35

tempted to carry Clarissa off L35

his quarry, wrens and sparrows L70

threats to Clarissa, should he doubt her love L97

penetration L99

Harlowe Family will prosecute him for L132

lest one be attacked by him when in bed and asleep L177

nearly making a violent attempt upon Clarissa L187.1–L187.4

his midnight attempt on Clarissa after the fire L227

his eyes endeavouring to penetrate her soul L248

rape of Clarissa, *premeditated*

such triumph over the whole sex, if I can subdue this lady L103

the lady must fall L115

I might have had her before now, if I would L157.1

the house to be taken in three weeks...three days...three hours L159

I must make all service before I pull off the mask. This was my motive for bringing her hither L191

will not take her by force L198

her trial to be at midnight, surprise and terror necessary L199

so near to execution of my plot L224

this project is not to end in matrimony surely L224

his purpose to wake Clarissa in terrors L225

ashamed before the women below as he has failed with Clarissa L225, L226

carrying Clarissa back to Mrs. Sinclair's or consummating his marriage at Mrs. Moore's L242

LOVELACE, MR. ROBERT

rape of Clarissa, *premeditated* (cont.)
    subduing Clarissa by violence if necessary L244
    her very fall will be her glory...my shame...my destruction L246
    will either marry Clarissa or rape her L247
    comparison between the two ladies, I will expatiate more...when I have had them both L252
    the hour of her trial...so long premeditated L256
    would have avoided force L256

rape of Clarissa
    occurring after Letter 256 and before Letter 257 L257
    Lovelace allowing Mrs. Sinclair to administer something to Clarissa to make her insensible L260
    some little art has been made use of L260, L266
    Clarissa's insensibility robbing Lovelace of his pleasure L260
    gloomy that he did not get her consent L261
    Lovelace feeling triumphant L262
    stung by Clarissa's rejection L264
    wishing to make amends L266
    his actions by Clarissa of a capital nature L315
    raping Clarissa a national sin atoned for by sword, pestilence, or famine L336
    admits to Hickman that he took liberty with Clarissa when she was asleep L346
    I acknowledge...that I have basely injured her L346
    not understanding why Clarissa does not keep her secret L371
    Lovelace destroyer of Clarissa's honor L407

rape of Clarissa, second rape
    planned L281
    second attempt mentioned L386

reading
    Latin and English classics L34
    judging women by what they read L154
    Poor mortals the cause of their own misery, Clarissa's Meditation L410

reconciliation between Clarissa and the Harlowe Family
    fearing Clarissa will throw herself on her own relations L235
    believing there is reconciliation between Clarissa and her family L439

reconciliation between Lovelace and the Harlowe Family
    promising reconciliation L61, L88
    dreading reconciliation L105
    to pave the way for L107
    precondition for marriage to Clarissa L109
    his contempt for reconciliation with the Harlowes L109
    not reconciling with a family he despises L214, L215
    willing to reconcile, disclaiming interest in Harlowe estates L216
    wishing for reconciliation L220

reform
    mentioned L34, L99, L104, L118, L120, L124, L161
    friends in need of reform L34, L81
    not reformed enough for a husband L105
    precondition for marriage to Clarissa L109
    reformation his stalking-horse L110
    to be undertaken by Clarissa L116
    ensured by marriage to Clarissa L158
    reformed by Clarissa L294, L306
    Clarissa once thought she could reclaim him L359
    libertine whom Clarissa loved and wished to reclaim L365
    promising penance, reformation L397
    Clarissa hoping for his reformation L398

LOVELACE, MR. ROBERT

reform (cont.)

> Clarissa cautioning him to reform L510.4
>
> the devil and the time of life are against thee L513
>
> will reform upon his return to England L527

refuge for Clarissa see also **protection for Clarissa**

> depriving Clarissa of all other refuge to make her dependent on him L201

relations

> generally, trouble with anticipated after Lord M.'s death L285
>
> *Knollys, Mrs.*
>> kinsman of Lovelace L26
>>
>> her excellent character L26
>>
>> at whose home Clarissa had once been a guest L26
>>
>> to whom Clarissa should send letters addressed to Anna L93
>>
>> to whom a man takes Clarissa's for Anna L98
>>
>> Mrs. Howe requesting that she stop conveying correspondence for Anna and Clarissa L100
>
> *Lord S.*
>> the great Lord S., who prepared settlements for Lovelace's mother L218
>
> son
>> child surviving the affair with Miss Betterton, a son L139, L140
>>
>> wishing for a boy by Clarissa, as revenge on the Harlowes L268
>
> mother
>> had better pretensions to estate now held by Lord M. L88
>>
>> teaching him the Bible L115
>>
>> spoiled by his mother L190
>>
>> his mother's jewels may be new set for Clarissa L207
>>
>> settlements drawn up for Clarissa conformable to those of his own mother L207, L218
>>
>> settlements for Lovelace's mother prepared by the great Lord S. L218
>>
>> deserved a better son L267
>>
>> this favorite boy of hers L324
>>
>> why, why did my mother bring me up to bear no control L512
>
> parents, encouraging qualities in children that made them, grown, the plague of their hearts L234

religious references see also **biblical references**

> Oliver Cromwell, quoted L99
>
> cabala, word used by rakes L110
>
> dean and chapter L131, L131n1
>
> his blood of as much concern as that of a Neapolitan saint L211
>
> his jesuitical qualifyings L286
>
> Hickman, as if telling his beads L346
>
> Martin Luther, Belford compared L370
>
> refusing ghostly attendance and the Sacraments in the Catholic way L537

repentance

> wishing to atone for his injuries to Clarissa L397
>
> repenting L470, L472

reputation

> concern for, hypocritical L106
>
> not valuing his reputation L114

rescue of Clarissa

> Lovelace's threats
>> will rescue her if taken to Antony's L76, L81
>>
>> his intimidations put a stop to the plan to take her to Antony's L83
>
> James's rescue plot
>> mentioned L132, L137, L140, L142, L145, L155, L157, L158, L158.1, L164
>>
>> an excuse to keep Clarissa under close watch L137, L158, L215, L221, L229.1
>>
>> Singleton conferring with James and Arabella L139

LOVELACE, MR. ROBERT

rescue of Clarissa, James's rescue plot (cont.)

        Leman as a source of information for Lovelace about the plan L140

        may or may not have abandoned the plan L148, L177, L200

        plot abandoned L152

        plot no longer feared by Clarissa L175

        Singleton sent to find Clarissa's whereabouts L194

    Anna's smuggling scheme

        mentioned L199, L201, L209, L210, L228

        Lovelace's plot upon Anna in revenge L207.1

        discovered by Lovelace, no more danger to Lovelace L211

        feared by Lovelace L215, L227

        provided against by Lovelace's contrivance of Captain Tomlinson L217, L221

revenge

    generally

        harboring resentments L1

        his love of, his predominant passion L31, L35, L40, L143, L189, L198, L215, 217.2, L234, L235

        revenge...keep thy throne in my heart L243

        his vows of revenge forgotten L245

        the rage of love, the rage of revenge is upon me L256

    on Anna and Clarissa, on Anna L127, L201, L223, L229, L395

    on Betty Barnes L113, L117

    on Clarissa

        for her loyalty to her family and not to him L31, L44, L187.1–L187.4

        for waiting for Clarissa in the rain in the garden L62, L73, L223

        for her dislike of him and his friends and Miss Partington L167

        for running away L228

        renewed L239

        for slighted love L276

    on James

        vows of, after duel L4

        if I have not his sister, I will have him L31

    on the Harlowe Family

        vows revenge for ill treatment following duel with James L4

        his triumph over them L158.1

        revenge against the Harlowes L206

        I have not done with the Harlowes yet. They were the aggressors L324

    on Joseph Leman L117

    on Miss Rawlins L239

    on Mrs. Sinclair, for Clarissa's rejection, setting fire to that den of serpents L396

    on women

        whose infidelity I have vowed to revenge upon as many as shall come into my power L31

        for his first love, who jilted him L31, L58

reveries see also **dreams**; **waking fantasies**

    producing sleep and then a dream L271

    Lovelace's Reveries, a book about dreams, planned by Lovelace L272

rings see also **jewels**

    his diamond ring, turning it around L233, L237

rings, bequests of see **bequests of Belton**

Sacraments

    refusal of Sacraments in the Catholic way L537

sacrifice

    as sacrifice L64.1, L121

Satan see also **Beelzebub**; **devil**; **Moloch deity**

    spreading his snares L106

LOVELACE, MR. ROBERT

Satan (cont.)

the tempter L110

Lovelace, Satan himself L261.1

sold himself to Satan L261.1

Satan, having such faithful instruments L270

an instrument of Satan L510.4

Old Satan, Belford in his clutches L513

sayings and proverbs see also **language**

always be careful of back doors L117

credulity is the God of Love's prime minister L117

eat the calf in the cow's belly L118, L118n1

black angel plays me booty L152

love me, and love my dogs L167

so long a harvest of so little corn L198

all your wild oats will be sown L206

about marriage: caught up in his own gin L207

once subdued, always subdued L209, L256, L264, L274, L294

once any other man's, and I know it, and never more mine L209

God sends meat, the devil cooks L211

listeners seldom hear good of themselves L235

calling Mrs. Bevis hail fellow well met L238

calling Will *half seas over* L238

I'll get her for thee with a *wet finger* L239

might be routed horse and foot L239

forestall my own market L243

Clarissa has mended her markets L245

Bernard Mandeville's rule: Private vices are public benefits L246, L246n1

no rest to the wicked L246

quoting the honest corregidor: Good actions are remembered but for a day: bad ones for many years after
the life of the guilty L252

a pope: having caught the fish, laying aside the net L252

Honest Hickman may now sleep in a whole skin L252

his plot thickens L255

no difference between the skull of King Philip and that of another man L259, L259n1

how one crime, as the good folks say, brings on another L266

it costs a man ten times more pains to be wicked, than it would cost him to be good L267

a wife at any time L268

hatred appeased is love begun L270

he who kills a man has all that man's sins to answer for, as well as his own, because he gave him not time to
repent L326

for the blood of me L346

the eye is the casement at which the heart looks out L347

quoting Clarissa: it is not lawful to do evil that good might come of it L443

a reformed rake makes the best husband L499

in Lord M.'s style: wits may not be sent a wool-gathering L512

in Lord M.'s style: thou dost work it going L515

sealings

young families loving ostentatious sealings L238

intercepting correspondence, he keeps seals entire and preserves covers L239

seduction

generally

triumph in subduing L34

seducer L94, L98, L121, L198, L222

would change his dress like Clodius to seduce a woman L106, L106n1

LOVELACE, MR. ROBERT

seduction, generally (cont.)

    triumph over the female sex L119, L388

    delighting in seduction L193

  of Clarissa

    desire to triumph over Clarissa L103

    strategy L157.1

    his motive for bringing Clarissa to Mrs. Sinclair's L191

    seduce her and take care of her out of wedlock L223

    techniques to overcome: intimidation, love, see-saw, surprise L223

    not possible while she is in her senses L263

  of Mrs. Bevis, considered L248

  of Anna rather than Clarissa L252

  of Colonel Ambrose's nieces L322

  of his cousins Montague L322

servants

 Andrew

    new servant, watching Clarissa L235, L237, L253

    attending Lovelace L241

 Joel

    with Lovelace L449

    delivering letters between Belford and Lovelace L475, L482

    Lovelace may pistol him if he brings bad news L475

 Summers, Will, Lovelace's servant for upwards of seven years L235

    animals

      like one of widow Sorlings's dunghill cocks L238

      a dog L480

    black, in a black wig watching Mrs. Moore's, Smith's to find Clarissa L231.1, L416

    character

      clever fellow, could do anything but write and spell L117

      faithful honest dog L480

    contrivances of Lovelace

      supposed by Harlowes to be Leman's source of information about Lovelace L103

      Lovelace offering to leave his servant with Clarissa L117, L157

      to be on guard against any attempt Clarissa may make to escape L174.3

      called Peter to say Clarissa was going out to church alone L198

      directed to get a chair for Clarissa L201

      Clarissa sending him to Wilson's with hers for Anna, but he gives it to Lovelace L228

      spying on Clarissa L230, L248

      taking Clarissa's feint for Anna to Wilson's, and another to Lovelace L230, L231.1

      his account of Clarissa's flight from Mrs. Sinclair's and his finding her L230

      disguised in another coat and a black wig, to spy on Clarissa at Mrs. Moore's L231.1

      stealing Clarissa's and Anna's letters from Grimes L233, L235, L237, L238

      sleeping at Mrs. Moore's to keep an eye on Clarissa L239, L241, L242, L253

      Lovelace sending him for a coach for Clarissa to return to Hampstead L256

      an errand to Hampstead L261

      keeping Clarissa under close watch L273, L281

      threatening to hang or drown himself L290

      to be taken dead out of some horse-pond L292

      allowing Clarissa to slip out in Mabel's clothing L293

      setting the sheriff's officers after Clarissa L333

      knowing location of Clarissa's lodgings at Smith's L334

      disguised in a black wig lurking about Smith's to find Clarissa L416

      watching for Clarissa at Smith's L416, L418, L421, L425

      dispatched by Lovelace to Belford L439

LOVELACE, MR. ROBERT

servants, *Summers, Will,* contrivances of Lovelace (cont.)

      delivering correspondence between Belford and Lovelace L463, L477

  death, his untimely death.CONCLUSION

  disguises, in a black wig watching Moore's, Smith's to find Clarissa L231.1, L416

  livery, wearing Lovelace's livery L231.1, L416

  money, has saved £150 L241

  names, called Will Summers, William L174.3, L201

  physical appearance, missing some foreteeth on account of Lovelace L233, L333, L416, L420

  relations

      Wheatly, Paul, his cousin L175

          Lord W.'s necessary man L175

          Singleton's mate L175

  sweethearts

      Mrs. Sorlings's daughter L118

      Mrs. Moore's maid L238, L241

      his sweetheart posting a letter for Clarissa to Anna L240

      Margaret L251

  weapons

      a gardener, carrying a pruning knife L416

      his pistol snatched by Lovelace L443

      taking Lovelace's pistols away to prevent mischief L480

servants, treatment of

  animals, calling his servants his dogs L235

  contempt for L241, L512

  corrupting

      Joseph Leman and Betty Barnes

          his knowledge of all that passes at Harlowe Place, unexplained L26, L61

          mentioned L35, L62, L73, L98, L140

          Lovelace caring for Leman L95

          using Leman to influence Antony and Antony Mrs. Howe L104

          punishing him, and Betty Barnes L117, L175

          feeding Harlowes information through Leman L140

          bribing Leman with the Blue Boar Inn and Betty to assist James in Clarissa's rescue L140

          no more use for L175

          Lovelace, cully of Leman L189

      servants of other families L62

  management of

      generosity noted L11, L13, L15

      both loved and feared L98

      rough treatment of L420

      the art of governing L423

      his capacity for managing L445

  mischievous use of L11

      sending a physician to Hannah with medicine to make her weaker L167

      threatening to kill his messenger bringing bad news L472, L475

sex

  no sex in ethereals L219, L219n2

  preferring plot to enjoyment of a woman L271

sexual language

  her throbbing partners L99

  suckling Clarissa's breasts L220, L220n1

  calling Hickman a male-virgin L236

  I'll get her for thee with a wet finger L239

  all the gentle and ungentle pressures of the lover's warfare L271

LOVELACE, MR. ROBERT

sexual language (cont.)

> I hung over her throbbing bosom L277

Lord Shaftsbury's test

> mentioned L116, L116n2

shroud

> may need a coffin or a shroud L410

silver

> wanting to purchase for Clarissa a short cloak trimmed with silver L98
>
> giving Dorcas a silver pencil L174.3

sleep

> sleepless after the rape L264
>
> sleepless, as he will have to go to M. Hall L281

snuff

> taking rapee from Smith's L416
>
> serving customers at Smith's Scots snuff and Portugal snuff L416

sport see also **hunting**

> has hunted in the forest at Windsor L116
>
> his game at racquet L128
>
> the hunt L170
>
> can swim like a fish L347
>
> Clarissa will not long be Lovelace's sport or the sport of fortune L333
>
> swordsmanship a sport he loves L535

suffering

> comparing his to Clarissa's L335, L463
>
> suffering L511

suicide

> thoughts of L511

surgeons

> Anderson and Tomkins, hired by Lovelace to embalm Clarissa L497
>
> suggested by De la Tour for the duel L536
>
> attending Lovelace after the duel, Morden giving a purse of gold to L537

swordsmanship

> a sport he loves L535

tenant-courtesy

> tenant-courtesy, a vile tenure L118

tenants

> never rack-renting old tenants L13
>
> kindness to his tenants L13, L116, L183

theatre

> attending Otway's *Venice Preserved*, with Clarissa and Miss Horton L194, L194n1, L200
>
> stage directions, used in his letters L214, L232
>
> dialogue format, used in his letters L235, L243

title see also **peerage**

> entitled to wear swords L26
>
> Harlowe Family beneath him, their *acquired* fortune L79, L109, L421
>
> giving himself airs on account of his family L79
>
> esquire, respectable though overused L104
>
> captain, usual travelling addition L105
>
> pride of ancestry L143, L308
>
> not using his family name to further his designs L191
>
> noble descent L196, L327
>
> may come in for the title when Lord M. is dead and gone L206
>
> no title to Clarissa's lip or cheek L216
>
> continuing liberties with Clarissa, as he feels entitled L219

LOVELACE, MR. ROBERT

title (cont.)

    earl, looking forward to being Right Honorable Robert, Earl Lovelace L254

    hoping for on Lord M.'s death, his title reversionary L265

    title to eternal infamy and disgrace L285

    titles going with the bulk of Lord M.'s estate L327

transportation

    using Lord M.'s chariot and six to take Clarissa from Harlowe Place L76, L80, L85, L98

    chaise and pair from Lord M.'s Hertfordshire seat L98

    chariot and six with horsemen L144

    taking a chair to the Park L209, L212

    sending for a Blunt's chariot L231, L231n1, L255

    his chariot L232, L233

    Lady Betty's arms and crest upon a coach, hers in for repairs L255

    a set will be ready to carry Lovelace L284

    flying coaches and flying horses at a county fair L294

    his phaeton ready to drive, Miss Patsey Montague sharing L322, L332

    attending a ball at Colonel Ambrose's in Lord M.'s chariot L350

    taking Lord M.'s chariot and six to London to visit Clarissa L416

    taking a chair to Smith's L416

transportation (sentence) see **exile**

travel

    abroad after the affair with Miss Betterton L139

    to France and Italy to forget about Clarissa, if she reject him L341

    preparing to go abroad L394

    will go abroad L480

    Belford asking Lord M. to urge Lovelace to go abroad L509

    preparing for a foreign tour L510

    planning to leave the kingdom L511, L513, L516

    departed from England L524

    to London, then Dover to embark L525, L526

    De la Tour, travelling valet engaged by Lovelace L530

    returning to England in March L534

    travelling to Munich with French valet and English footman L535.2

trial

    Lovelace's confrontation with his family over Clarissa's letter to Lady Betty L323–L325, L339

trials

    if I doubt her love, I can put her to trials as mortifying to her niceness, as glorious to my pride L97

    not yet found virtue to withstand his test L110

    will marry Clarissa if she stand her trial L110, L152, L191

    inclined to spare her all further trial L138

    bringing virtue to a trial L191

    resolved to continue Clarissa's trials, then marry her L202

    trials his pretense L222

    her trials continue L223

    she resists his trial of the fire L225

    would put an end to her trials L227

    mentioned L244, L253

    the hour of her trial...so long premeditated L256

    another trial for Clarissa, if she refuse to forgive him L280

Valentine's Day

    birds changing mates every Valentine's Day L254

valets

    De la Tour, F. J., travelling valet L530

        not speaking English L535

LOVELACE, MR. ROBERT

valets, *De la Tour, F. J.* (cont.)

        will write to Belford if anything happen to Lovelace L535

        suggesting a surgeon for the duel L536

        dispatching a packet of Lovelace's papers after the duel L537

vanity

    Clarissa curing him of L117, L161, L236, L322

    so light, so vain, so various L125

vengeance

    vengeful nature, vengeance uppermost L44, L216

    vengeance on the Harlowe Family L169

    Lovelace an instrument, implement of James's vengeance L191, L276

    vengeance justified L252

    defying Clarissa's right to vengeance through the law or Morden L274

    his punishment, justice of his country and vengeance of her friends L336

victims (other than Clarissa)

    generally, Lovelace making them laugh and cry at once L370

    Miss Betterton

        of Nottingham L127

        her family's resentment L127

        dying in childbirth, 18 months ago L139, L140

        child surviving L139

        rape victim of Lovelace L139

        loving Lovelace L140

        mentioned L177, L198

    Polly Horton L157.1, L198, L226, L277

    Sally Martin L157.1, L198, L209, L226, L227

    D—r's wife L157.1

    Miss Lockyer L177, L198

    the French marquis's wife L209

    his attempt on a bride L219

    Lucy Villars L252

    the pretty gipsy L252

villains

    his plotting villain of a heart L153

    mentioned as L154, L188, L207, L225, L227, L229, L229.1, L238, L252.1, L256, L260, L274, L276, L281, L314, L367, L402, L429, L470, L510.3

    called the V. L316

    blackest of L456

    execrable villain L497

violent behavior

    generally

        abusing the messenger who brought him news of Clarissa's arrest L333

        threatening to cut the throat of anyone happy while he is dejected L463

        threatening to kill his messenger bringing bad news L472

    toward Joseph Leman, threatening to cut off his ear L113

    toward Clarissa

        dragging Clarissa, sword in hand L94

        trying to seize Clarissa's letter L175

        nearly making a violent attempt upon Clarissa L187.1–L187.4

        seizing, grasping, snatching Clarissa's hands in anger L199, L281, L314

        very angry at Clarissa, ugly in his violent outburst L200

        wrapping his arms around her knees L201

        physically detaining her from going abroad L201

        continuing liberties with Clarissa, as he feels entitled L219

LOVELACE, MR. ROBERT

violent behavior, toward Clarissa (cont.)

> his midnight attempt on Clarissa after the fire L227
> stopping her way as she tries to leave the room L243
> stopping her attempt to leave Mrs. Sinclair's, folding his arms about her L256
> clasping his arms about, stops her leaving Mrs. Sinclair's, carries her upstairs L264
> stopping her leaving, bruising her hands and arms L266
> stopping Clarissa escaping L267, L277
> wishing he had given Clarissa cause to hate him L395

toward Belford

> will cut Belford's throat to prevent telling tales L326
> killing Belford L516

toward Anna, refusing to let go Anna's hand L367

toward Mrs. Howe, refusing to let go Mrs. Howe's hand L367

toward Joseph, threatening to remove Joseph's teeth with Will's pruning knife L416

toward Joel, may pistol Joel if he brings bad news L475

virtue

> his principal intention to try Clarissa's virtue L517

visits

to Anna Howe L7, L12, L49

> early social meeting L27
> mentioned L173
> where Clarissa first introduced him to Anna L252
> wishing to visit L346

to Lord M.

> who is very ill L275
> must go to M. Hall, to Berkshire L277
> Lord M. wishing to see Lovelace before Lord M. dies L278

to Colonel Ambrose *see also* **ball, Colonel Ambrose's**

> breakfast and dinner with the Colonel and his nieces L322

to Clarissa

> Belford assuring Clarissa that Lovelace will not visit her at Smith's L337
> agreeing not to visit Clarissa L341
> determined to visit Clarissa L370, L371
> will visit Clarissa in a few days with a parson to marry them L383
> Belford asking Lovelace not to visit Clarissa L391, L400, L413
> will try to visit Clarissa L395
> will visit Clarissa L410, L414
> still trying to visit Clarissa at Smith's L421
> expecting to visit Clarissa at Harlowe Place L439
> will not further molest Clarissa L449, L452
> may visit Clarissa L453
> Clarissa specifying in her will that she does not wish Lovelace to see her dead L482

to Doleman, in Uxbridge L449

to Hickman, interview at Dormer's, mentioned L346, L358, L510.1

to Smith's, in search of Clarissa L416, L418

to Belford, in London L525

from Lord M. L497

from the Montagues, while he is ill with a fever L410

from Morden, at M. Hall L426, L442, L445, L446

waking fantasies see also **dreams**; **reveries**

> guilty of murdering Clarissa L246
> as Clarissa's hour of trial nears L256

weapons

> his sword L4

LOVELACE, MR. ROBERT

weapons (cont.)

entitled to wear swords L26

offering Clarissa his unsheathed sword L94

swords, pistols, guns, blunderbusses L95

fire and faggot...dagger L127

the pommel of his sword L233

his sword drawn, threatening Dorcas L281

the matrimonial sword hanging over his head by a thread L325

sword, pistol, halter, or knife, Lovelace ending his misery by L333

snatching Will's pistol L443

his pistol, too ready a mischief L463, L466

may pistol Joel if he returns too slowly with Belford's letter L475

Will taking Lovelace's pistols away to prevent mischief L480

white

the black angels and the white ones L152

appearing white as an angel L235

imagining an old spectacled parson with a white surplice thrown over a black habit performing the irrevocable ceremony L276

his cause having a black and a white side L323

wife see also **contrivances of Lovelace**, contrivance of pretending marriage to Clarissa

Clarissa's reference to a first wife and a second wife for Lovelace L187

will advertise in the *Gazette* for his eloped wife L228

will

wanting to execute Clarissa's will L497

wanting to see a copy of Clarissa's will L526

receiving a copy of Clarissa's will from Belford L527

wine see **drink**

women's language

women's words: figaries, tostications, marry come up L242

expressing himself in women's dialect L323

broken heart being women's language L341

writing see also **codes**

his knack of writing L3

his love of writing L12

Lovelace and Clarissa, a pair of scribbling lovers L105

his poetry L116

writing a comedy, *The Quarrelsome Lovers* L175, L216

stage directions, used in his letters L214, L232

wrong to scribble so freely to Belford, but must write on L223

I love to write to the moment L224

dialogue format L235, L243

ladies always writing with crow-quills L239

writing in his vellum-leaved book L243

though this was written afterwards, yet...I write it as it was spoken, and happened; as if I had retired to put down every sentence as spoken. I know thou likest this lively *present-tense* manner, as it is one of my peculiars L256

I must write on. Nothing else can divert me L264

familiar writing is but talking L268

writing a book about dreams, *Lovelace's Reveries* L272, L273

compelled to write L281

MOORE, MRS., Clarissa's landlady at Hampstead

church
    accompanying Clarissa L251
family
    the widow Moore L232
keys
    may return Clarissa's to Mrs. Sinclair's L245
lodgings
    letting to Clarissa L230–L255
    letting to Lovelace L233–L239
names
    goody Moore L232, L235
    our mother, compared to Mrs. Sinclair L237
neighbors
    Kit the hostler, who drank with the footman at the taphouse L232
    Rawlins, Miss
        caring for fainting Clarissa L223
        prim L233
        mumbling a paternoster L237
        her snuff-box L237
        not inclined to do Lovelace favors L239
        unconvinced by Lovelace L241
        dissuading Clarissa from removing from Mrs. Moore's L242
        too inquisitive to be confided in L244
        secret-keeper-general L248
        a Pandora's box L248
        Clarissa informing her of her story L318
    Rawlins, Mr.
        showing concern for Clarissa L233
        saying his sister *lives* at Mrs. Moore's L241
relations
    Bevis, Mrs., her niece L236
        conspiring with Lovelace
            offering to contrive a midnight visit for Lovelace to see Clarissa L239
            inclined to do Lovelace favors L239
            to be given a gift by Lovelace L239
            convinced by Lovelace L241
        costume, may bring Clarissa's clothes from Mrs. Sinclair's L245
        family, a young widow L236, L237
        impersonating Clarissa to receive a letter from Anna L251, L318, L320
        informing Will of Clarissa's movements L253
        keys, may take Clarissa's keys to return to Mrs. Sinclair's L245
        literary references, Butler, Samuel, *Hudibras*, quoted L237, L237n1
        mannerisms, making faces L243
        manners, hail fellow well met with Mrs. Moore's servants L238
        meals, dining with Lovelace and others at Mrs. Moore's L236
        physical appearance, brown and plump L251
        visits, to Lovelace in his new lodgings L239, L242, L251
religious references
    a print of St. Cecilia hung over the closet door L233
servants
    Margaret, maid-servant L237
        called Peggy, Margery L251
        Will's sweetheart L251
        Lovelace giving her a guinea L251

MORDEN, COLONEL WILLIAM, Clarissa's cousin

advocate for Clarissa
>zealous on Clarissa's behalf L432
>Clarissa's dear blessed friend L443

arrival from Florence
>has arrived in Canterbury, where he is attending to concerns L408, L409, L413

bequests of Clarissa
>proceeds of Clarissa's estate since Grandfather's death L507
>miniature of Clarissa L507

black wax see **sealings**

burial of Clarissa
>bespeaking his own place in the vault next to Clarissa's L504
>accompanying the coffin into the vault to see it laid at Grandfather's feet L504

character
>a man of honor and bravery L415
>slender notion of women's virtue L456
>skilful swordsman L533
>cool and sedate L533
>a man of principle L533

classical references
>Juvenal, *Satire XIII*, quoted in Latin L503, L503n1

conflict between Harlowe Family and Clarissa
>coldness between Morden and the Harlowe Family L431
>conflict with James about treatment of Clarissa L459

correspondence, Morden, Colonel William
>Harlowe Family have written to Morden L61
>Clarissa wishing to write to him L86
>Anna advising Clarissa to write to Morden L148
>his letter to Clarissa forwarded by family L173.1
>advising Clarissa about Lovelace's character L173.1, L263
>Anna reading his letter to Clarissa L177
>with Belford, continuing CONCLUSION

costume
>putting letters in his pocket-book L443

death of Harlowe, Miss Clarissa
>attending Clarissa's hearse to Harlowe Place L487, L495, L500
>taking a ringlet of Clarissa's hair for a locket L495

death of Harlowe, Miss Clarissa, avenged
>may avenge Clarissa L274, L456, L498, L517, L519
>will see justice done Clarissa's person L319, L427
>Clarissa fearing Morden will try to avenge her L409
>Lovelace dreaming he is threatened by Morden L417, L421
>Clarissa urged to prosecute to prevent mischief between Morden and Lovelace L427
>cutting the throat of any young fellow who made free with any sister of his L442
>having no title to avenge Clarissa L474
>Clarissa avenged L537

duel between Morden and Lovelace
>Lovelace may answer his challenge L526
>Lovelace not going out of his way to avoid Morden L534
>calling Lovelace to account L535
>accepting Lovelace's offer to accept a challenge L535.1
>his meeting with Lovelace to prepare L536
>his weapon of choice, a single rapier L536
>Lovelace fatally wounded L537

MORDEN, COLONEL WILLIAM, Clarissa's cousin

estates see also **trustees**

    Clarissa's

        assisting Clarissa in resuming her estate L36

        helping Clarissa pursue life on her own estate without litigation L248

        to put Clarissa into possession of her estate L253, L455

        will see justice done Clarissa's estate L319

    Morden's

        his own ample fortune L455

        residing upon his paternal estate in Kent L526

executors

    Belford's, Morden L528

    Clarissa's

        Morden considered L413, L459

        reading Clarissa's will with Belford L486

        intending to enforce Belford's executorship L495

        assisting Belford in executing Clarissa's will L507, L520

    Morden's

        Clarissa intended to be his heir and executrix L459

forgiveness

    How wounding a thing...is a generous...forgiveness! What revenge can be more effectual and more noble,

        were revenge intended L508

fortune see **estates**

friends

    Klienfurt, Mr., in Munich, where Lovelace can direct correspondence for Morden L535.1

friendship

    with Belford L487

funeral of Clarissa

    attending L504

gentleman

    gentleman's challenge to Lovelace L534

gold

    giving a purse of gold to the surgeons who attend Lovelace after the duel L537

historical references

    Louis XIV, his will flagrantly broken, Clarissa compared L508

influence in Harlowe Family

    lacking influence to bring about reconciliation L455

    cannot prevail against James L459

informants

    Alston, Mr., gentleman farmer

        old farmer-looking man, sent to ask about Clarissa's health L426

        honest, serious man sent to inquire about Clarissa's condition L455

        his inquiries about Clarissa L459

literary references

    inflaming novels and idle romances read by women L442

lodgings

    with Antony while in England, and refusing to continue L459

marriages, Clarissa's to Lovelace

    encouraging Clarissa to accept Lovelace's offer L447

    believing marriage would effect reconciliation L447

money

    taking money to Clarissa L483

    giving a purse of gold to the surgeons who attend Lovelace after the duel L537

names

    Wm. Morden L173.1

MORDEN, COLONEL WILLIAM, Clarissa's cousin

opinions

on rakes and free-livers L173.1, L217.2, L263

on inflaming novels and idle romances, read by women L442

on forgiveness and revenge L508

on friendship and women L520

prayers

for Clarissa's recovery when she had the fever at ages nine and eleven L377

protection for Clarissa

his protection preferable to Lovelace's L88

Clarissa having no hope of, from Morden L230

Morden, as protection for Clarissa L252.1

rakes

free-livers are remorseless L217.2

Lovelace believing Morden to be a rake L415

reconciliation between Clarissa and the Harlowe Family

believing Clarissa's marriage to Lovelace would effect reconciliation L447

trying to effect reconciliation L454, L460

attending Harlowe Family meeting about reconciliation L459

relations

Morden, Robert, father

Clarissa's uncle L507

giving gifts to Clarissa L529

living chiefly abroad L529

his high opinion of Clarissa's needlework L529

cousins

Aunt Hervey L503

John and Antony Harlowe L504

residences

will reside upon his paternal estate in Kent L526

finally settled in Florence CONCLUSION

revenge

How wounding a thing...is a generous...forgiveness! What revenge can be more effectual and more noble, were revenge intended L508

rings

giving Mr. Melvill a ring L504

sealings

his Letter 173.1 to Clarissa sealed in black wax L173

story

not yet acquainted with Clarissa's L448

title

having no title to avenge Clarissa's wrongs L474

travel

wishing to take Clarissa on a tour of France and Italy L459

setting out for Italy L526

will settle his affairs in Florence L526

trustee

of Grandfather Harlowe's will L27, L32.3, L87, L173

co-trustee with John Harlowe L214

of Clarissa's estate L27, L32.3, L87, L173, L248, L253, L455

valets

Morden's, attending the duel L536

visits

to Lovelace L426, L433, L439, L440, L441

interview with Lovelace at M. Hall L442, L445, L447

MORDEN, COLONEL WILLIAM, Clarissa's cousin

visits (cont.)

    to Lord M., to inquire about Lovelace's intentions L431, L439, L440

    to Clarissa L441, L473, L474, L518

    to Miss Howe, with Clarissa's bequest L455, L519, L520

weapons

    skilful swordsman L533

    rapier, weapon of choice for duel with Lovelace L536

will

    leaving to Clarissa, if he die unmarried without children, as her grandfather did L443

    leaving his ample fortune to Clarissa L455

    Clarissa his heir and executrix L459

    James will not be his heir L508

    Belford, along with Hickman, to be his executor L528

    giving Belford his will, copy to Hickman, copy to banker L528

NORTON, MRS. JUDITH, Clarissa's nurse

abduction of Clarissa

Lovelace offering to send for Mrs. Norton L125, L127, L128

ashamed of Clarissa L147

address to Clarissa by Mr. Roger Solmes

opposing plan for Clarissa to marry Solmes L8

reportedly favoring Solmes L27

visiting Clarissa on behalf of the family, urging Clarissa to comply L39, L90

family refusing to hear her point of view L39

tendering Solmes's settlements for Clarissa to sign L144

bequests of Clarissa

thirty guineas, her and her son for mourning L487, L507

sum of six hundred pounds L507

Clarissa's clothing L507

biblical references

I wept L459

King Hezekiah, his days lengthened, Clarissa compared L459, L459n1

character

prudent, wise, pious L15, L47, L56, L82, L88, L125

Mrs. Lovick compared L338

conflict between Harlowe Family and Clarissa

Clarissa will not put her in opposition to Harlowe Family L125

under the direction of the Harlowe Family L189

family prohibiting Mrs. Norton from attending Clarissa L408

correspondence, Harlowe, Miss Clarissa

Clarissa sending Mrs. Norton a packet of letters L409, L433

correspondence, Norton, Mrs. Judith

with Clarissa forbidden L8, L13

hers to Clarissa delivered by servant of Sir Robert Beachcroft L361

hers to Clarissa delivered by Mr. Pocock L459

cures

a vein breathed L487

death of Harlowe, Miss Clarissa

finding Clarissa dead L487

cutting off four ringlets of Clarissa's hair L495

accompanying the hearse to Harlowe Place L500, L503

death of Norton, Mrs. Judith

will not live long L520

family

Tommy, son L127, L301

giving her son money to start a business L207

Clarissa calling him her foster brother L300, L307, L362

born within a few days of Clarissa L301

born after his father's death L301

Mrs. Norton nursing both her son and Clarissa L301

good to Mrs. Norton L301

illnesses

a feverish disorder, violent fever L301, L307, L308

at death's door L361

recovering L374, L377, L381, L382

a fine youth L494

happily settled CONCLUSION

husband, her very unkind husband, his death L301

parents, their deaths L301

NORTON, MRS. JUDITH, Clarissa's nurse

family (cont.)

    father

        her reverend father's wisdom L69, L82

        a clergyman L301

        sayings, the satirist has a natural spleen to gratify L308

        a sound divine and a fine scholar L381

housekeeper

    at the Grove L520

illnesses

    has been extremely ill L361

    health improved L374, L377

    recovered L381, L382

    on seeing Clarissa dead, they were forced to breathe a vein L487

    too ill to continue in company with the hearse on the way to Harlowe Place L500

    will not live long L520

marriages, Clarissa's to Lovelace

    encouraging Clarissa to marry Lovelace L408

marriages, Clarissa's to Solmes

    to attend wedding L41.2, L83, L85

money

    lacking money to back up her point of view L13

    Clarissa's wish to provide for Mrs. Norton L39, L45, L207

    Lovelace allowing Clarissa to give her all arrears in her father's hands L207

    may give her son money to begin a business L207

    wishing to give Clarissa money L301

    her humble fortunes L307

    Clarissa refusing her offer of money L307

    Mamma sending her five guineas L376

    sending Clarissa the five guineas from Mamma and ten of her own L381

mourning

    thirty guineas bequeathed her and her son for mourning L487, L507

names

    Goody Norton L39, L459

    worthy Mamma Norton L52.1, L409

    first called Judith L179

    Clarissa calling her her own mamma L307

nurse

    raising Clarissa, from her cradle L20, L31, L182, L301, L362

    assisting Clarissa in her anonymous letter to Lady Drayton L59

    her fondness for Clarissa L88, L308

    uncertain as to whether Clarissa had had small-pox L204

    attending Clarissa in her last illness

        Clarissa wishing to live with her upon Clarissa's estate L248, L253

        Lovelace dreaming she lives with Clarissa L271

        attending Clarissa as soon as Tommy's indisposition permits L301, L361

        wishing to attend Clarissa L301, L381, L408

        Clarissa asking her not to come, will need her later L307, L382

        Harlowe Family prohibiting Mrs. Norton from attending Clarissa L408

opinions

    on life's momentary joys and troubles L408

Poor's Fund

    Mrs. Norton to administer after Clarissa's death L507

    administering until a week before her own death CONCLUSION

NORTON, MRS. JUDITH, Clarissa's nurse

prayers

    her prayer for Clarissa L408, L459

reconciliation between Clarissa and the Harlowe Family

    to apply to Mamma for reconciliation on Clarissa's behalf L179, L184, L229.1

    Anna trying to influence her for reconciliation L183

    acquainting the Harlowe Family with the truth about Clarissa's situation L429

refuge for Clarissa

    Lovelace offering refuge with Mrs. Norton L80

residences

    at the Grove L520

    living the rest of her life at the Grove CONCLUSION

story

    Mrs. Norton's L301

    Clarissa's

        family not inquiring into through Mrs. Norton L430

        Clarissa sending Mrs. Norton a packet of letters L433

        Mrs. Norton wanting to hear Clarissa's L459

transportation

    taking a chariot to Harlowe Place L459

    not offered the Harlowe Family chariot to visit Clarissa L483

    visiting Clarissa in a chaise and pair L483

visits

    to Clarissa

        visits with Clarissa forbidden L8, L13

        urging her on family's behalf to wed Solmes L39, L90

        Clarissa asking her not to come L382

        wanting to visit Clarissa L459

        planned L483

        finding Clarissa dead L487

    to Harlowe Place for family conference L459

    from Mamma, planned, to read Clarissa's letter L376

    from Aunt Hervey L432

SINCLAIR, MRS., brothelkeeper in London

animals

    vipers, serpents L317, L330, L396

arrack punch see **drink**

arrest of Clarissa

    her false arrest of Clarissa for board and room owed L330–L333, L339, L535

    action dismissed L334

business

    Dover Street, not Dover Street L130.1, L229.1

    a back house within a front one and looking to a garden rather than a street L137

    her home and dress carry marks of good circumstances L155

    Mother *Damnable*'s park L228

    two houses, one reputable appearance and one not L229.1

    genteel wicked house L229.1

    her house very handsome L233

    iron rails before the windows L264

    a brothel L266

    her concern for the reputation of her house L281

    her parlour in the back-house L293

    her house ruined if Lovelace and his friends get married L336

    Lovelace wanting to burn down her house L396, L511

character

    her respectfulness studied L155

    sly and leering L157

    pretending to weep for her husband still L157

    her puritanical behavior before Clarissa L158.1

    hypocritical L169, L222

    Hottentot L175

    assuming violent airs and terrifying Clarissa L256

    feared by Clarissa L261.1

    blustering with her worse than mannish airs L261.1

classical references

    cursed Circes L294

customers

    Salter, Colonel, Mrs. Sinclair drinking arrack punch bought by L493

death of Harlowe, Miss Clarissa

    acknowledging her guilt in Clarissa's death L521, L535

death of Sinclair, Mrs.

    howling at the prospect of death L499

    died Thursday, Sept. 21 L499

    her death reported to Lovelace by Belford L514

devils

    Mrs. Sinclair as L228, L330

    her hellborn nymphs L511

drink

    drinking arrack punch, bought by Colonel Salter L493

family

    of Highland extraction L131

    widow, gentlewoman L154, L155, L158.1, L233, L256, L261.1

    a woman of family L277

    husband

        an officer of the guards, Colonel Sinclair, a Scot L130.1, L131, L233

        gentleman L155

        lieutenant-colonel L158.1

        man of honor L261.1

SINCLAIR, MRS., brothelkeeper in London

food

      ordering chicken for supper L184

illnesses

      broken leg, mortifying L493

      dying of a broken leg L499

keys

      key to be kept in the door L293

literary references

      preferring comedy to tragedy L194

names

      Magdalen L158.1

      the mother L158.1, L228, L233, L237, L264, L333, L396

      her maiden name Sinclair L158.1

      her right name not Sinclair L159, L229.1

      Sinclair, as thou callest her L169

      the mother and sisterhood L228, L277, L279, L281

opinions

      on women L294

physical appearance

      features broad and full blown L131

      masculine appearance L154, L256

      an odd winking eye L155

      her horse mouth L158.1

      her fat arms L158.1, L256

      described L256

potions

      administered to Clarissa to make her insensible L260, L261, L281

      their damned potions L395

      Mrs. Sinclair's invention and mixture given to Clarissa L535

rape of Clarissa, *premeditated*

      urging Lovelace on L198, L218

rape of Clarissa

      should be prosecuted for L317

relations

      Carter, Mrs., her sister, keeping a bagnio near Bloomsbury L499

      Horton, Polly and *Sally Martin,* her nieces L131, L155

servants

      Mabel, the waiting-maid L291

            poor, silly Mabel, awkward and bent-shouldered L211, L294

            stopping Clarissa's attempt to escape L264

            attending Clarissa L282, L333

            a run away, her mother living in Chick Lane, West Smithfield L290

            ordering a coach for Clarissa L293

            fetching the mantua-maker's journeywoman L293

            Clarissa changing clothes with Mabel to escape L293

            accused and threatened for allowing Clarissa to escape L293

            Mabel's clothes thrown into the passage this morning L293

      Partrick, Peter, house servant, footman L198, L264

            called Petur Partrick L231.1

            sent by Will with a letter for Lovelace to say where Will found Clarissa L231.1, L232

            Peter was paid five shillings L231.1

            stopping Clarissa's attempt to escape L264

      cook-maid

            reading Robert Greene, *History of Dorastus and Faunia* L225, L225n1

SINCLAIR, MRS., brothelkeeper in London

servants, cook-maid (cont.)

        setting fire to the curtains L225

surgeons

    Garon, Mr. L499

visits

    from Belford, on her death bed L499

whores

    generally

        airing, with Clarissa and Lovelace L210

        animals, vipers, serpents L317, L330

        character

            brought up too high for their fortunes L157.1

            jealous, proud, vain L157.1

            compared L158

            young persons of good sense L159

            sensualists L169

            Hottentots L175

            seeking Clarissa's advice L194

            full of cruelty and enterprise L277

            sorceresses L416

            hellborn nymphs L511

        collation, attending or not attending L158

        contrivances of Lovelace

            contrivance of the promissory note

                their role L281

                ridiculing Lovelace for his failed contrivance L281

        correspondence, Harlowe, Miss Clarissa with Anna, intercepted by Lovelace

            helping Dorcas transcribe Clarissa's letters for Lovelace to read L174.3, L198

            confiscating any letters to or from Clarissa L279

        costume

            trying to steal some of Clarissa's clothes L336

            their dress and makeup the next morning, described L499

        escape of Clarissa

            fearing Lovelace, blubbering L228, L292

            stopping her attempt L264

         rape of Clarissa, *premeditated*

            urging Lovelace to make a daytime attempt upon Clarissa L218

            advising Lovelace to try terror rather than love L264

        rape of Clarissa

            should be prosecuted for L317

        reading, readers L154

        victims of Lovelace, mentioned as L157.1, L198

    Carberry, Betty

        veteran, breaking news to Lovelace that Clarissa is gone L228

    Horton, Mary (Polly)

        character

            taking a liking to Clarissa L158

             gentler temper and manners than Miss Martin L158

            her insolence to Clarissa L416

        death, by a violent cold CONCLUSION

        death of Sinclair, Mrs. L499

        duties, comforting Clarissa, attending her L201, L293

        education, well educated L277

SINCLAIR, MRS., brothelkeeper in London

whores, *Horton, Mary (Polly)* (cont.)
    escape of Clarissa
        stopping Clarissa from leaving L276
        trying to cajole Clarissa back to Mrs. Sinclair's L333
    names, called Polly L154
    reading, has read L277
    relations, niece of Mrs. Sinclair L155
    theatre, accompanying Clarissa and Lovelace L200
    victim of Lovelace L157.1, L198, L226, L277
  Martin, Sarah (Sally)
    angel L157.1
    animals, a toad L333, L416
    arrest of Clarissa, discovering Clarissa's whereabouts and having her arrested L330
    biblical references
        Prior, Matt, *Poems on Several Occasions*, on doubling down places of the Bible L333, L333n1
        Bible, *Book of Job, Ecclesiasticus,* Apocrypha, remarking over L333
    character
        thinking herself as well descended and educated as Clarissa L333
        her insolence to Clarissa L416
    contrivances of Lovelace
        contrivance of Mrs. Fretchville's house
            known to Mrs. Fretchville L194
    costume
        hoping Lovelace will give her Clarissa's clothes L333
        trying to steal Clarissa's fine Brussels lace head, searching for the ruffles L336
    death, died of a fever and surfeit CONCLUSION
    death of Harlowe, Miss Clarissa, visiting Smith's to find Belford and finding Clarissa dead L493
    devils, a devil L157.1, L209, L333
    education, well educated L277
    escape of Clarissa
        leaving after Clarissa's escape, escaping to her relations L293
        trying to cajole Clarissa back to Mrs. Sinclair's L333
    literary references
        Shakespeare misquoted L157, L157n2
        preferring comedy to tragedy L194
        Prior, Matt, *Poems on Several Occasions*, on doubling down places of the Bible L333, L333n1
    marriage, expecting Lovelace to marry her L333
    marriages, Sally's to the woollen-draper
        her humble servant a woollen-draper of great reputation L159
        near marriage with a tradesman in the Strand L163
        quarreling with her woollen-draper L194
    medicine, taking salts L493
    names, called Sally L154
    opinions, on vows L157
    reading, has read L277
    relations, niece of Mrs. Sinclair L155, L333
    sayings, Clarissa not to quarrel with her bread and butter L228
    victims of Lovelace, Lovelace as Sally's first lover L209, L226
    visits
        to Smith's to find Belford and finding Clarissa dead L493
        to Belford to take him to visit Mrs. Sinclair L499
  Partington, Priscilla
    character
        spinster L158.1

SINCLAIR, MRS., brothelkeeper in London

whores, *Partington, Priscilla*, character (cont.)

        modest, genteel girl, specious, flippant L158.1, L169, L222

        disliked by Clarissa L167

      collation, attending L158, L161

      contrivances of Lovelace

        contrivance of the bedfellows

            wishing to be Clarissa's bedfellow L162

            rejected by Clarissa L164, L169

            sharing a press-bed with Dorcas L167

            Lovelace attempting to fasten her upon Clarissa L229.1

      names, called Priscilla L158.1

      relations, her guardian, Mrs. Sinclair L158

Wykes, Dorcas

      accomplishments, her skill in the needle L155

      animals, toad L228, L261, L281

      bribes, Clarissa offering her twenty pounds a year and a diamond ring to help her escape L269

      character

        honest, neat in person and dress...not vulgar L154, L155

        Clarissa's dislike of her L154

        discrete, loyal, genteel, obliging, sly eye, well-bred, well-spoken L155

        compassionate temper L269

      contrivances of Lovelace

        contrivance of Clarissa's escape

            assisting Clarissa's escape in Lovelace's contrivance L272

            recognizing the lozenge on the widow lady's chariot L273

        contrivance of the fire, crying Fire! Fire!, petticoats in hand L225

      correspondence, Harlowe, Miss Clarissa with Anna, intercepted by Lovelace

        searching Clarissa's clothing for letters L174.3

        helping Lovelace come by Clarissa's letters L175

        searching Clarissa's room while she is at the theatre with Lovelace L194

        searching Clarissa's chamber for letters L198

        transcribing Clarissa's letters for Lovelace L198, L202, L210

        noting that Clarissa has moved her letters L210

        trying to open the wainscot box where Clarissa keeps her letters L218

        transcribing Clarissa's fragments and letters for Lovelace to send Belford L261

      costume, dangling in her own garters from her bed's tester L292

      death, untimely CONCLUSION

      death of Sinclair, Mrs. L499

      duties

        attending Clarissa L154, L155, L175

        carrying messages between Clarissa and Lovelace L157, L184, L185, L186, L198, L200, L226

        having key to Clarissa's clothing chest L174.3

        using her key to search Clarissa's chamber for letters L198

        preparing tea, offering Clarissa food and drink L201, L261.1

        the upper servant, greeting the footman who appears at Mrs. Sinclair's door L213

        watching Clarissa L262

      education, illiterate wench L154

      escape of Clarissa

        to be watchful of any attempt to escape L174.3

        her opinion that Clarissa should be allowed to go L267

        Clarissa offering her twenty pounds a year and a diamond ring to help her escape L269

        trying to cajole Clarissa back to Mrs. Sinclair's L333

        first to discover Clarissa at Smith's L334

      fearing Lovelace, hiding from Lovelace's rage after Clarissa escapes Mrs. Sinclair's L228

SINCLAIR, MRS., brothelkeeper in London

whores, *Wykes, Dorcas* (cont.)

        friendship with Clarissa

                Clarissa trying to befriend Dorcas L177, L268, L270, L271, L275

                sympathetic to Clarissa L264

                seeming to come into favor with Clarissa L267

        keys

                having keys to Clarissa's clothing chest L174.3

                using her key to search Clarissa's chamber for letters L198

        loyal to Lovelace L273

        lozenges, recognizing the lozenge on the widow lady's chariot L273

        names, Dorcas Martindale L269, L270

        reading, illiterate wench, can neither write, nor read writing L154, L155

        relations, Mrs. Sinclair's niece L154, L273

        sleeping arrangements

                Lovelace hoping Clarissa will accept her as a bedfellow L154

                in a press-bed with Miss Partington L162, L167

SMITH, MR. JOHN, shopkeeper in London

bequests of Clarissa

    ten guineas L507

bodice-makers

    Joseph, a bodice-maker L416

        lion's-face grinning fellow, broad black teeth, bushy hair L416

        Lovelace threatening him L416

        Lovelace giving him half a crown L416

business

    his glove shop, hosier in King Street L295, L320, L351

    dealer, trader in stockings, ribands, snuff, and perfumes L320

    selling powder, wash-balls, snuff, gloves, and stockings L416

    selling rapee, Scots snuff, and Portugal snuff L416

character

    honest, humane, industrious L307, L320

costume

    his glove shop L295, L320, L351

    dealer, trader in gloves, stockings, ribands L320, L416

    bowing to Lovelace's fine clothes L416

customers

    the genteel lady and *Andrew*, her footman, Lovelace and L416

family

    Smith, Mrs., his wife

        shopkeeper L320

        matron-like woman, plain hearted and prudent L320

        helping Belford remove Clarissa's clothes from Mrs. Sinclair's L336

        not knowing whether Clarissa is married L336

        attending Clarissa L348, L349

        inviting Clarissa and Belford to dine with her on her wedding day L349

        her compassion L349

        childless L416

        bequest of Clarissa, linen and laces, twenty guineas L507

lodgers

    Lovick, Mrs.

        age, turned of fifty L514

        attending Clarissa

            her voluntary attendance on Clarissa L338, L348, L349

            writing letters for Clarissa L338, L473.2

            giving Clarissa's Meditation to Belford L364

            inquiring into Belford's general character L379

            interview with Lovelace, telling him Clarissa went out to avoid him L418

            Clarissa visiting Mrs. Lovick's friend in town L426

            reading Anna's to Clarissa L473

        bequest of Clarissa

            some books L507

            Clarissa's linen and laces L507

            twenty guineas L507

            copy of Clarissa's book of Meditations L507

        character

            of great merit L307, L320

            respected, pious, prudent L320

            compared to Mrs. Norton L338

            her love for Clarissa, her compassion L338, L349

        costume, selling Clarissa's clothes L345, L365, L426

        death of Harlowe, Miss Clarissa, caring for Clarissa's body after her death L457

SMITH, MR. JOHN, shopkeeper in London

lodgers, *Lovick, Mrs.* (cont.)

        family, widow of low fortunes L307, L320

        housekeeper, hired by Belford at Edgware L514, CONCLUSION

        lodgings, over Clarissa L338

        meals, breakfasting with Clarissa L440

lodgings

    letting to Mrs. Lovick L307–L514

    letting to Clarissa L336–L495

meals

    breakfasting with Clarissa L440

names

    called John, familiarly by his wife L416

    called Father and Mother Smith, contemptuously by Lovelace L416

neighbors

    Barker

        cousin of the Waltons L445

        informant of Brand's L445

        a mantua-maker L445

        lodging with the Waltons L445

    Walton, Mr. and Mrs. John

        cousins of Barker L445

        their milliners shop over-against Smith's L445

        he, a petty officer in the excise L445

        informants of Mr. Brand L445

        John Walton, friend of Mr. Brand, receiving a letter of recantation L467

servants

    Katharine, maid

        attending Clarissa L336

        Clarissa not remembering her name L336

    Sarah, maid-servant

        bequest of Clarissa, five guineas L507

snuff

    dealer, trader in Scots snuff and Portugal snuff L320, L416

visits

    from Belford L334

    from Lovelace L416

A

abduction of Clarissa

Belford, Mr. John
    one of three of four horsemen galloping with the chariot L98
    with Lovelace at the White Hart Inn L99

Harlowe, Mr. Antony
    all in a rage L100
    renouncing Clarissa L147
    believing Clarissa ruined L183, L184

Harlowe, Miss Arabella
    renouncing Clarissa L147

Harlowe, Mrs. Charlotte
    disagreeing with the family's refusal to send Clarissa her things L111
    will send Clarissa her clothes L147

Harlowe, Miss Clarissa
    interviews with Lovelace in the garden L35, L36, L61, L62, L223
    dining in the ivy summer-house, waiting for Lovelace L91, L103
    your Clarissa Harlowe is gone off with a man L92, L127
    I cannot go with you L94
    I will sooner die than go with you L94
    I am resolved not to go with you L94
    Unhand me this moment L94
    her key left inside lock, indicating she left by her own consent L95
    grief-stricken at her flight, her regrets L97, L243
    tricked into flight, never intending to go off with Lovelace L98, L101, L181, L253
    writing to Arabella for clothes, books, and money L98, L124
    her letter of countermand disregarded by Lovelace L99
    no one will believe she went unwillingly L100
    fearing to say she was carried off against her will L101, L104, L121
    family not sending her things L111, L112
    her suspicions of Leman's role L113
    April 10, the date she left her father's house, inscribed on her coffin L451

Harlowe, Mr. James, Jun.
    James's violence precipitating matters L112
    selecting books to send Clarissa L173

Harlowe, Mr. John
    renouncing Clarissa L147

Harlowe Family
    supposing Clarissa's flight premeditated L97, L101
    family reaction to Clarissa's flight L100
    raving, implacable L103, L121
    refusing to send Clarissa her things L111
    will not pursue Clarissa L116
    will not have her back L117, L189
    will not stir to save her life L183
    disgraced by Clarissa L392

Harlowe Family, servants, Leman, Joseph
    causing a commotion, frightening her into flight L94, L113
    seen by family returning from pursuit of Lovelace L100
    reporting to Lovelace the family's reaction L103

abduction of Clarissa (cont.)

Hervey, Mrs. Dorothy

    not finding Clarissa in the ivy summer-house nor in the cascade L100

    Clarissa writing to ask for her things and money L116

    renouncing Clarissa L147

Hervey, Mrs. Dorothy, family, Hervey, Miss Dolly

    her happiness when Clarissa escaped from Harlowe Place L432

Howe, Miss Anna

    will send Clarissa money and clothes L100, L111, L119, L132

Howe, Mrs. Annabella

    pitying Clarissa and asking Anna to write and comfort her L148

Lord M.

    his chariot and six used by Lovelace L76, L80

Lord M., relations, nieces

    to accompany Clarissa on her flight from Harlowe Place L76

    Clarissa requesting their company at her escape L83

    to be with Clarissa in London L85, L142

Lord M., relations, nieces, Montague, Miss Charlotte

    cold and sore throat make her unable to accompany Clarissa L88

Lord M., relations, nieces, Montague, Miss Patty

    will not be asked by Lovelace to visit Clarissa after the escape L88

Lovelace, Mr. Robert

    strategy to carry off Clarissa L31

    planning a private interview with Clarissa in the wood-house or garden L35

    having two keys to the garden door L35, L61, L62

    surprising Clarissa in the garden L36, L86

    threatening violence if she refuses to meet him L61

    requesting to meet her between nine and twelve in the garden L62, L73, L223

    tricking Clarissa into flight from Harlowe Place L94, L101

    throwing down his key to the garden door L94

    if she picks up the key to return to the house, he will accompany her L94

    they struggle L94

    Leman creating a commotion, confusing Clarissa into flight L95

    Leman leaving one key on the inside, to mean that she left of her own will L95

    not understanding Clarissa's grief, his resentfulness L98, L103, L108, L142

    to set out for Lord M.'s Hertfordshire seat L98

    avoiding Clarissa's letter of countermand L99

    had once planned to carry her off from the wood-house by surprise L103

    wanting Clarissa to go to London L103, L104, L127

    abduction as reported by Lovelace to Belford L115

    offering Clarissa clothes and money to lay her under obligation L118

    threatening to kidnap Clarissa again if she has outwitted him L439

Norton, Mrs. Judith

    Lovelace offering to send for Mrs. Norton L125, L127, L128

    ashamed of Clarissa L147

accidents

Belford, Mr. John

    falling from his horse L261

Harlowe, Miss Clarissa

    bloodying her nose on the edge of the chair L267

accomplishments see also **education**

Harlowe, Miss Arabella

    inability for household cares L6

accomplishments (cont.)
Harlowe, Miss Clarissa
    harpsichord, music L54, L182, L529
    needlework L79, L147, L182, L529
    drawing L86
    writing, letter writing, her natural talent L86, L486, L529
    her eloquence and oratory L263, L395
    her superior talents L301
    French, Italian, Latin L529
Howe, Miss Anna
    harpsichord, singing L128
Lord M., relations, nieces, Montague, Miss Charlotte
    admirable at her needle L255
Sinclair, Mrs., whores, Wykes, Dorcas
    needlework L155

address, forms of
Harlowe, Miss Clarissa
    your servant, to James L75
    your servant, to Captain Tomlinson L243, L245
Harlowe, Mr. James, Jun.
    your servant, to Clarissa L75
Howe, Miss Anna
    your servant L12
Lovelace, Mr. Robert
    your servant, to Anna L12
    your servant, to Clarissa L157
    your servant, to Lord Bishop of London L254
    your servant, to Lady Betty and Lady Sarah L323
    your servant, to Smiths L416

address to Arabella by Mr. Robert Lovelace
Harlowe, Mr. Antony
    discussing with Lord M. L2
    introducing Lovelace to the family as suitor to Arabella L2
    his favorable opinion of Lovelace L3, L13
    visited by Lovelace after Arabella's rejection of Lovelace L3
    Arabella mistakenly introduced to Lovelace L31
Harlowe, Miss Arabella
    his rejection of her in favor of Clarissa L1
    his three visits to her, as she relates them to Clarissa L2
    lacking peculiarity in his address L2
    her rejection accepted by Lovelace L3
    suspecting Lovelace was not fond of marrying at all L3
    confiding her love for Lovelace in Betty Barnes L15
    her resentment of Lovelace L19
    mistakenly introduced to Lovelace by Antony L31
Harlowe, Mr. James, Jun.
    unacceptable as a match for Clarissa or Arabella L4
Hervey, Mrs. Dorothy
    cautioning Arabella to be reserved with Lovelace L2
Lord M.
    discussing with Antony L2
    proposing a match with Arabella L13

address to Arabella by Mr. Robert Lovelace (cont.)

Lovelace, Mr. Robert

> his rejection of Arabella L2, L3
> his introduction to her, a mistake L31
> his morals not an issue at the time L58

address to Clarissa by Mr. Robert Lovelace

Harlowe, Mrs. Charlotte

> disapproving of his morals L3

Harlowe, Miss Clarissa

> gossip that she has stolen Lovelace from Arabella L1, L2, L3
> recovering from his rejection by Arabella, Lovelace turns his attention to Clarissa L3
> supported by Lord M. L3
> his unwanted visits to Clarissa at Anna's L3, L4, L6, L7
> her opinion of Lovelace L40
> Clarissa's favor with Lovelace's relations L40
> resenting his insistence and insolence L64
> lending an ear to Lovelace's address L306

Harlowe, Mr. James, Jun.

> unacceptable as a match for Clarissa or Arabella L4
> angry about Lovelace's visits to Clarissa at Anna's L7

Harlowe, Mr. James, Sen.

> mild disapproval of L3
> deferring to James on Lovelace's attentions to Clarissa L3, L4
> hinting Lovelace should discontinue his visits L4
> insulting Lovelace L4
> refusing to stop Lovelace's visits L4
> forbidding Clarissa to receive Lovelace while at Anna's L6

Harlowe, Mr. John

> approving Lovelace as a match for Clarissa L3
> ambivalence toward Lovelace L13

Hervey, Mrs. Dorothy

> good match for Clarissa L3
> Lovelace confiding in Aunt Hervey his passion for Clarissa L3
> relating steward's (discharged) report on Lovelace to Clarissa L4
> wanting to send James to Yorkshire till all blows over L6
> cautioning Clarissa about his vengefulness L44
> carrying stories about Lovelace to Clarissa L79

Lord M.

> proposing match with Clarissa L3
> signing a letter from Lovelace to Clarissa L22, L26
> lending credibility to L25.1
> supporting Lovelace's continuing attempts L26
> to be sounded by Hickman upon a subject recommended by Clarissa L27

Lord M., relations, half-sisters

> supporting his attempts L26

Lord M., relations, half-sisters, Lawrance, Lady Betty

> her letter in support and offer of protection L36

Lovelace, Mr. Robert

> his passion for Clarissa L3, L31
> request to address Clarissa L25.1
> his family's fondness for Clarissa L40, L98
> requesting permission to call on the Harlowes with Lord M. or Aunt Lawrance L62
> Clarissa lending an ear L306

address to Clarissa by Mr. Roger Solmes see also **suitors to Harlowe, Miss Clarissa**, *Harlowe, Miss Clarissa*,
Solmes, Mr. Roger

Harlowe, Mr. Antony
Clarissa receiving Solmes at Antony's L41.2, L50.1, L51.1, L51.2, L53, L54.1, L55, L61–L63
interrupting meeting between Clarissa and Solmes L78
Clarissa no longer to go to Antony's L83

Harlowe, Miss Arabella
angry at Clarissa for rejecting Solmes L21
threats to Clarissa regarding Solmes L29
confrontation with Clarissa over Solmes L42
assaulting Clarissa L53
answering Clarissa's proposals to seek refuge elsewhere L54.1

Harlowe, Mrs. Charlotte
agreeing that Clarissa has been badly treated L6
promoting Solmes's suit L16, L17, L20, L21
threats and intimidations of Clarissa into accepting Solmes L18, L20, L21, L41.1
pleading Clarissa's case, not to marry Solmes L19, L20, L52.1
accusing Clarissa of preferring Lovelace L20
yield you must, or be none of our child L20
not approving the manner in which Solmes's suit was presented to Clarissa L39
her sympathy for Clarissa L41

Harlowe, Miss Clarissa
encouraged by family
to thwart Lovelace L6, L7
Solmes introduced to Clarissa L7
offer formally made to Clarissa by Aunt Hervey L8
his offer accepted by the family in her absence L8, L20
settlements
mentioned L8, L56, L85, L90.1
and Clarissa's estate, remaining in the family L13, L17
terms L16, L17, L32.4, L41.1
required to sign L20, L52.1, L83, L85
concluded L39
jewels for Clarissa L41.1, L90.1
articles, license, settlements L83, L85
her rejection of Solmes
her disgust, rudeness, and firm rejection L7, L8, L16, L21
her reasons L19, L20, L32.3, L78
preferring death L36, L39, L45, L90, L94
refusing to see Solmes L41
confrontational meeting with Solmes, her objections to him L78
refusing to sign parchments L83, L144
family's intimidations
confined until she agrees to marry Solmes L8, L21, L24.1, L25
promoted by James and Arabella, taunting and conspiring L13, L53, L75, L83
family united against her L14
begging Mamma not to be married to Solmes L16–L20
begging James to cease his hostile ways L24.2, L25.3
changing her tactics to prefer Lovelace L29
begging Uncle John to influence Papa L32.1
begging Solmes to discontinue his suit L33.1
offering to give Solmes to Arabella L36, L60.2
wedding, at Antony's chapel L41.2, L50.1, L51.1, L51.2, L53, L54.1, L55, L61–L63, L83
offering to seek refuge elsewhere L42, L45, L53.1
altercation with Arabella L42

address to Clarissa by Mr. Roger Solmes, *Harlowe, Miss Clarissa*, family's intimidations (cont.)

        begged by Aunt Hervey to comply L44, L45, L84

        begging parents in a letter to James, as they will receive none from her L51.2

        offering to rid them of Lovelace, if the family will rid her of Solmes L59.2

        Clarissa drawing Betty out on the family's plans L63

        kneeling at Papa's door, James letting her fall in head first L78

        hiding from her family in the garden L80

        believing her family would not follow through on the Solmes plan L94

Harlowe, Mr. James, Jun.

        accusing Clarissa of favoring Lovelace L4, L33.3, L52.1

        using Solmes's suit to thwart Lovelace L8

        threatening Clarissa into marrying Solmes L29

        angry at Mrs. Norton for her failure to persuade Clarissa L39

        threatening to return permanently to Scotland L42.1, L44, L45

        requesting Clarissa to stay at Antony's for a fortnight to receive Solmes L51.1, L52.1

        Clarissa must sign the settlements L52.1

        with Arabella in the garden taunting Clarissa L75

        assaulting Clarissa L78, L79

        keeping everyone inflamed L78

        insulting Aunt Hervey L78

        overheard by Clarissa plotting with Arabella L83

Harlowe, Mr. James, Sen.

        intimidating her into accepting Solmes L16, L20

        angry at Mamma for pleading Clarissa's case L19

        sanctioning James's schemes L39

        demanding Clarissa's obedience L41.2

        immoveable on the Solmes plan L78

        ordering Clarissa to be carried to Antony's at once L78

        turning entire matter over to James, Arabella, and Antony L80

Harlowe, Mr. John

        against pushing Clarissa into marrying Solmes L9

        Clarissa begging his help not to go to Antony's L59.4

        angry refusal of Clarissa's proposals L62.1

Harlowe Family

        promotion of Solmes's suit L7, L8, L17, L21

        using Aunt Hervey to make Solmes's formal offer to Clarissa L8

        intimidation and threats to Clarissa L8, L20

        terms of Solmes's suit L16, L17, L39

        Clarissa's confinement L24.1

        using Mrs. Norton to persuade Clarissa L27, L39, L90

        hurrying to execute plan in the face of Clarissa's apparent preference for Lovelace L39

        tumult over Clarissa's refusal to go to Antony's L51

        family assembled in close debate over Clarissa's counter proposals L61

        would have yielded had Clarissa held her ground L144, L151, L317, L432

Hervey, Mrs. Dorothy

        her opposition to Solmes silenced L8, L13, L81

        making formal offer to Clarissa on behalf of Solmes L8

        advice to Clarissa on Solmes L9, L13

        her support of the Solmes plan L17, L27

        her suggestion that the family reflect on Mrs. Norton's views L39

        suggesting Mr. Wyerley as a compromise L44

        attempting to persuade Clarissa to marry Solmes L44

        her sympathy and kind words to Clarissa L45

        pleading in Clarissa's favor L52.1

        visiting Clarissa, long conversation L77, L83, L85

address to Clarissa by Mr. Roger Solmes, *Hervey, Mrs. Dorothy* (cont.)
  censuring James, crying for Clarissa L78
  her opinion of Solmes confided in Dolly L78
  giving Clarissa settlements to sign, the parchments L83
  conversation with Clarissa in the ivy summer-house L91
  claiming Papa would have relented if Clarissa had not L145
Howe, Miss Anna
  source of information about Solmes L27
  advising Clarissa to go to London, hide from Solmes and Lovelace till Morden comes L81
  her interference in wedding plans, feared by family L87
Howe, Mrs. Annabella
  told of Clarissa's troubles L10
  praise and sympathy for Clarissa L10, L27, L58
  engaged by the family against Clarissa L31
  Solmes plan discussed with her by Antony L32.4
  believing Harlowe Family will give up the Solmes plan L56
  Clarissa should give up her aversion to Solmes L56, L58
  refusing to get embroiled L81, L86, L89
  will not provide refuge for Clarissa L81
  Clarissa's duty to comply L81
Lovelace, Mr. Robert
  conflict with Solmes L25.2
  Solmes is revenge on Lovelace for duel and on Clarissa for her independence L36
  will not allow Clarissa to marry Solmes L49
  wanting to visit Solmes L62
  will rescue her if taken to Antony's L76, L81
  his intimidations put a stop to the plan to take her to Antony's L83, L103
  threats to Solmes L114
Norton, Mrs. Judith
  opposing plan for Clarissa to marry Solmes L8
  reportedly favoring Solmes L27
  visiting Clarissa on behalf of family, urging Clarissa to comply L39, L90
  family refusing to hear her point of view L39
  tendering Solmes's settlements for Clarissa to sign L144

advocate for Clarissa
Belford, Mr. John
  pleading Clarissa's case to Lovelace L143, L189, L222, L268, L332, L334
Howe, Miss Anna
  Clarissa's pert advocate L378
Morden, Colonel William
  zealous on Clarissa's behalf L432

advocate for Lovelace
Belford, Mr. John
  Lovelace asking him to put a favorable face on his actions L261
  mentioned as L370
Lord M., relations, nieces, Montague, Miss Charlotte
  writing to Clarissa on Lovelace's behalf L383, L384

ages see also **birthdays**
Belford, Mr. John
  seven- or eight-and-twenty years, youngest of Lovelace's friends L161
Harlowe, Mr. Antony
  thirty years older than Clarissa L15

ages, *Harlowe, Mr. Antony* (cont.)

we have lived some of us...thirty or forty years longer than Clarissa L32.4

youngest of three brothers L197.1

Harlowe, Miss Arabella

older than Clarissa L75

twenty-six L529

Harlowe, Miss Clarissa

James many years older L9

eighteen years old L52.1, L60, L406

younger by near a third than James L53.1

her good fortune for eighteen out of nineteen years L229.1, L362, L376, L458

under twenty years L234, L349

born within few days of Tommy Norton L301

at eighteen years, enabled by her grandfather to make her will L400

at eighteen not having years of discretion L429

when she is twenty-one, the family would send her her estate L429

Clarissa was twelve when Morden left England seven years ago L442, L474

year of her birth omitted from the inscription on her coffin L451

nineteen years old L451, L453, L454, L464, L492

Harlowe, Mr. James, Jun.

older than Clarissa by many years L9

a third older than Clarissa L32.4

Clarissa younger by near a third than James L53.1

Harlowe, Mr. John

will be seventy-four years on June 29 L272.1

Hickman, Mr. Charles

fifteen or twenty years younger than Mrs. Howe L46

not old enough to need spectacles L346

his eyes older than the rest of him L346

Howe, Mrs. Annabella

forty years L58

Lord M.

not so very old L190

Lovelace, Mr. Robert

younger than Belford's seven- or eight-and-twenty years L161

Lovelace, Mr. Robert, contrivances of Lovelace, specifically, contrivance of sparing Rosebud, Rosebud

just turned seventeen years L34, L70, L71

Lovelace, Mr. Robert, contrivances of Lovelace, specifically, contrivance of Captain Tomlinson and Uncle Harlowe's birthday, Tomlinson, Captain Antony

twice Lovelace's age, upwards of fifty years L214, L271.1

Lovelace, Mr. Robert, friends, Belton, Mr. Thomas

about thirty years L161

Lovelace, Mr. Robert, friends, Mowbray, Mr. Richard

about thirty-three or thirty-four years L161

Lovelace, Mr. Robert, friends, Tourville, Mr. James

just turned thirty-one years L161

Norton, Mrs. Judith, family, Tommy

born within a few days of Clarissa L301

Smith, Mr. John, lodgers, Lovick, Mrs.

turned of fifty L514

airings and walks

Harlowe, Miss Clarissa

her morning and evening airings L63, L69, L74

walking in Mrs. Sorlings's garden with Lovelace L126

airings and walks, *Harlowe, Miss Clarissa* (cont.)

    in a coach with Lovelace and the nymphs L210

    walking on Hampstead heath with Lovelace L210, L247, L248

    airing alone with Lovelace, in a chariot L218

    walking in Mrs. Moore's garden with Lovelace L248, L253

    airing with Mrs. Lovick and Mr. and Mrs. Smith in a coach L399

    an airing cancelled L399

    taking an airing L436, L440

Lord M.

    a little tour for two days L330

Lord M., relations, half-sisters, Sadleir, Lady Sarah

    a little tour for two days to cure melancholy L332

Lovelace, Mr. Robert

    walking in Mrs. Sorlings's garden with Clarissa L126

    with Clarissa and the nymphs in a coach, and on Hampstead heath L210

    taking an airing in a chair L211

    taking an airing with Clarissa, the first alone, in a chariot rather than a coach L218

    refused a walk with Clarissa on Hampstead heath L247, L248

    walking in Mrs. Moore's garden with Clarissa L248, L253

    taking an airing L274

Sinclair, Mrs., whores

    airing with Clarissa and Lovelace L210

aliases

Harlowe, Miss Clarissa see also **correspondence, Harlowe, Miss Clarissa with Anna**, *Harlowe, Miss Clarissa*, aliases

    Atkins, Mrs. Mary L318

    Beaumont, Miss Laetitia L155, L229, L229.1, L239

    Clark, Mrs. Rachel L295, L298

    Lucas, Mrs. Harriot (or Mrs. Harry Lucas) L230, L238, L251

    Salcomb, Mrs. Dorothy L304

    fictitious names no longer needed L338

Howe, Miss Anna

    Soberton, Mr. John, to whom Clarissa should address hers, in Finch Lane L100

Lovelace, Mr. Robert

    Huntingford, Robert, Esq.

        to whom Belford should address his for Lovelace L105

        changing his name without Act of Parliament L105

Lovelace, Mr. Robert, contrivances of Lovelace, specifically, contrivance of Captain Tomlinson and Uncle Harlowe's birthday, Tomlinson, Captain Antony

    Tomlinson, Captain Antony, alias of Patrick McDonald L217

Lovelace, Mr. Robert, contrivances of Lovelace, specifically, contrivance of Mrs. Fretchville's house

    Mennell, Mr., alias of Newcomb L174.2

angel

Harlowe, Miss Clarissa see also **divine qualities**; **example**; **fall**; **light**; **sacrifice**; **suffering**; **trials**; **virgin**

    Clarissa as L31, L33.3, L34, L94, L97, L99, L110, L120, L138, L153, L157.1, L158, L169, L182, L187, L194, L199, L201, L202, L207, L216, L222, L225, L228, L233, L234, L237, L239, L243, L244, L245, L259, L266, L271, L274, L277, L281, L294, L321, L323, L324, L330, L333, L339, L349, L371, L399, L418, L419, L426, L439, L440, L446, L449, L470, L474, L497, L499, L502, L511, L519, L537

    fallen angel, poor fallen angel L78, L357

    angelic delicacy L124

    trials proving her woman or angel L157.1

    angelic L286

    angel, not a woman L303

angel, *Harlowe, Miss Clarissa* (cont.)
    saint and angel L339
    angelic lady L366
    forgiving angel L412
    a companion for angels L441
    angelic sufferer L467
    angelic sister L472
    angel of light L494
Lovelace, Mr. Robert
    my black angel plays me booty L152
    the black angels and the white ones L152
    appearing as angel of light, but a black heart L235
    appearing white as an angel L235
Sinclair, Mrs., whores, Martin, Sarah (Sally)
    an angel L157.1

animals see also **prey**
Belford, Mr. John
    a bear L105
    his dragon's wings L228
    a dog L259, L264
    falling from his horse L261
    preferring to be a dog, monkey, bear, viper, or a toad than a Lovelace L286
    a vulture, boasting gentle usage of its prey, Lovelace as L333
    a cursed toad, Sally as L333
    a post-horse, whom dogs would eat L335
    birds fearing a kite, as we fear people who are ill L364
    mankind in conflict with other animals L364
    rakes and libertines, as a blind mill-horse L366
    a harmless deer, Clarissa as L419
    a mongrel, Harry as L420
    a bear, Mowbray as L420
    a sorrowful monkey L527
Belford, Mr. John, messengers, Harry
    a mongrel L420
Harlowe, Miss Arabella
    viper L75
Harlowe, Miss Clarissa
    a bird caught in snares L22
    visiting her poultry, forbidden L25, L60, L62, L69, L75, L80, L103
    vile reptile, Solmes as L36
    wild oats, and black oxen L44, L44n1
    bird of Minerva [screech owl], its whooting L54
    Arabella selecting Clarissa's poultry for James to take to Scotland L75
    vultures, hawks, kites, and other villainous birds of prey, parents protecting from L133
    an eel L158.1
    bird dying with grief at being caught, a bird caught L170, L201
    a sweet lamb L172
    lion-hearted lady L201
    a doe from Mother *Damnable*'s park, a deer L228, L419
    dog in a manger L232
    awakened by birds L247
    parable of the lady and the lion L261 Paper III
    canker-worm, moth, caterpillar, Lovelace as L261 Paper VII
    wolf, Lovelace as, and Clarissa the lamb L269

animals, *Harlowe, Miss Clarissa* (cont.)
    chicken of a gentleman, Lovelace as, Clarissa a tiger of a lady L276
    prey of a vulture's rapacious talons L333
    crowned serpent, on Clarissa's coffin L451
    a poisonous serpent, Lovelace as L458
    reptile pride of seduction L486.1
Harlowe, Miss Clarissa, suitors to Harlowe, Miss Clarissa, Solmes, Mr. Roger
    vile reptile L36
Harlowe, James, Jun.
    like a hunted boar L4
Harlowe Family
    spider L106
    toads L115
Harlowe Family, servants, Leman, Joseph
    little dog that follows him L113
Hickman, Mr. Charles
    an odd dog L236
Howe, Miss Anna
    monkeys, men as L46
    basilisk eyes, killing Lovelace at the ball L56, L367
    the reptile word, obey, in marriage L68
    animal hostility, in wolf, lion, lamb, game chicken L136
    a vixen L237, L371, L395
    a mole L248
    vipers, Mrs. Sinclair and her whores as L317
    reptiles, men a vile race of L455
    hyaena, Lovelace as L456
Howe, Miss Anna, servants, Robert
    his roan, Keffel L65
Lord M., housekeepers, Greme, Mrs., relations, Sorlings, Mrs.
    her dunghill cocks, Will compared L238
Lord M., relations, half-sisters
    tabbies, monkies L323
Lord M., relations, nieces
    grimalkins, apes L323, L410
Lovelace, Mr. Robert
    generally
        tormenting animals that he has power over L222
    apes, Montagues as L410
    bear, Lovelace baited as L383
    beasts of prey, rakes as L367
    bee, ranging from flower to flower L153
    birds
        hawk, called a goshawk L70
        strutting cock and his mistress L118
        black swan L123
        an eagle, his eagleship L171, L189
        to kill an innocent chicken L203
        using pigeon and chicken blood to trick Clarissa L209
        his feet and his talons concealed L230
        Mrs. Sorlings's dunghill cocks, Will as L238
        ladies always writing with crow-quills L239
        birds changing mates every Valentine's Day L254
        a kite...chicken L266
        rake, a strutting villain of a bird L268

animals, *Lovelace, Mr. Robert*, birds (cont.)

> chicken of a gentleman, Clarissa a tiger of a lady L276
> shriek-owl, bringing bad news L463
> a thousand vultures...preying upon my heart L511

canker-worm, caterpillar L261 Paper VII

dogs

> hound, an hungry hound waiting to leap L115
> his dog tricks L190, L203
> dogs, using his power to frighten, as a boy L191
> dog in the manger, Clarissa as L232
> dogs, his servants as L235
> odd dog, Hickman as L236
> dog, Tomlinson as L237
> dog, Will as L238
> dog, Belford as L259, L264
> post-horse, whom dogs would eat, Belford as L335
> dogs and dogesses, his family as L395
> gaping puppy, Lovelace yawning as L410, L496
> dog, his messenger as L466
> dog, a foolish duncical dog, a mad dog L470, L480, L515

dragon

> Belford's dragon wings L228
> Mrs. Sinclair, the whole brood, dragon and serpents L330

elephant, Lovelace swollen as big with plotting L131

fish, devil an angler baiting fish L270

fly, buzzing about the bright taper L138

grimalkins, his cousins as L323

hedgehog, Lovelace like an old hedgehog hunted for its grease L480

horse

> reformation his stalking-horse L110
> Belford's horse, a vicious toad L261
> post-horse, whom dogs would eat, Belford as L335

hyaena L456

lamb

> Rosebud as L34
> Clarissa as, and he the wolf L159, L269

lion, struggling like a lion held in toils, claws of a lion L229.1, L416

mole, Anna as L248

monkey L131

> mischievous monkey L100
> every little monkey to catechize me L203
> monkeys in imitation, men as L216
> monkies, his two aunts as L323
> crippled monkey, Doleman as L497
> sorrowful monkey, Belford as L527

moth, Lovelace as L261 Paper VII

panther, cruel as L143

snake

> his rattle warns of a snake L113
> serpent with the dove L234
> reptile kneeler L274
> conscience writhing around his pericardium like a serpent L276
> Mrs. Sinclair, the whole brood, dragon and serpents L330, L396
> a poisonous serpent L458
> my reptile envy L470

animals, *Lovelace, Mr. Robert* (cont.)

> spider
>> spider and fly analogy, entangling young girls L106
>> spider, Clarissa as L256
>
> tabbies, his aunts as L323
> tiger
>> chicken of gentleman, Clarissa a tiger of a lady L276
>> claws of a lion, fangs of a tiger L416
>
> toad
>> Dorcas as L211, L261
>> vicious toad, Belford's horse as L261
>> Sally as L416
>
> turtle, I never saw the turtle's bill afterwards, his attempt upon a bride L219
> vixen, Anna as L237
> wolf, in sheep's clothing, and Clarissa a lamb L229.1, L269

Lovelace, Mr. Robert, contrivances of Lovelace, specifically, contrivance of Captain Tomlinson and Uncle Harlowe's birthday, Tomlinson, Captain Antony

> a dog L241
> puppy L243
> a whore's bird L244

Lovelace, Mr. Robert, friends, Belton, Mr. Thomas

> a lion kicked in the jaws by an ass L344

Lovelace, Mr. Robert, friends, Doleman, Mr. Tom

> crippled monkey L497

Lovelace, Mr. Robert, friends, Mowbray, Mr. Richard

> the bear L420

Lovelace, Mr. Robert, servants, Summers, Will

> like one of Mrs. Sorlings's dunghill cocks L238
> a dog L480

Sinclair, Mrs.

> and hers, vipers, serpents L317, L330, L396

Sinclair, Mrs., whores, Martin, Sarah (Sally)

> a toad L333, L416

Sinclair, Mrs., whores, Wykes, Dorcas

> a toad L228, L261, L281

apothecaries

Harlowe, Miss Clarissa

> Goddard, Mr., Clarissa's apothecary L343
>> sent for L333, L336, L338, L340
>> calling in Dr. H. L340
>> visiting Clarissa L365, L426, L440, L452, L457, L473
>> his regimen L366
>> bequest of Clarissa, fifteen guineas for a ring L507

Harlowe, Miss Clarissa, constables, Rowland, Mr.

> calling an apothecary L333

Lord M.

> attended by L285

arrack punch see **drink**, *Sinclair, Mrs.*

arrest of Clarissa

Belford, Mr. John

> freeing Clarissa L330, L332, L333, L334

arrest of Clarissa (cont.)

Harlowe, Miss Clarissa

>arrested by two sheriff's officers, with a writ against her L330, L333
>Lovelace asking Belford to go free her L330
>her arrest a mistake L331
>as reported by Belford to Lovelace L333
>causing her ill health L347, L364, L371
>Lovelace innocent of Clarissa's arrest L358, L373
>as told to Mrs. Norton L362

Lovelace, Mr. Robert

>a black contrivance L332
>Lovelace abusing the messenger who brought him the news of L333
>Belford stabbing Lovelace in the heart with the story of L333
>Lovelace innocent, his agent blamed L347, L358, L359, L373

Sinclair, Mrs.

>her false arrest of Clarissa for board and room owed L330–L333, L339, L535
>action dismissed L334

Sinclair, Mrs., whores, Martin, Sarah (Sally)

>finding Clarissa and having her arrested L330

arrival of Morden from Florence, *anticipated*

Harlowe, Miss Clarissa

>mentioned L25, L36, L52, L57, L62, L69, L73, L76, L81, L85, L101, L129, L137, L138, L145, L185, L199, L200, L319
>Clarissa offering to go to Morden in Florence L42
>his arrival meaning Clarissa's independence L53, L152
>Clarissa wishing to write to him L86
>Lovelace offering to take Clarissa to him L124
>his footman, perhaps, appearing at Mrs. Sinclair's L213, L214

Harlowe Family

>his imminent arrival driving the family to hurry Clarissa's marriage to Solmes L53.1
>have written to Morden L61

Howe, Miss Anna

>advising Clarissa to go to London and hide till Morden comes L81
>advising Clarissa to write to Morden L148

arrival of Morden from Florence

Morden, Colonel William

>has arrived in Canterbury, where he is attending to concerns L408, L409, L413

art references see also **miniatures**; **pictures**

Belford, Mr. John

>Swift, Dean, *Lady's Dressing Room*, Mrs. Sinclair's whores compared L499fn

Harlowe, Miss Clarissa

>Highmore, Joseph, his whole-length picture of Clarissa in the Vandyke taste L147, L147n1
>Vandyke, Sir Anthony L147

Harlowe Family

>the Harlowes, by Joseph Highmore, book cover of the Penguin Classics edition of *Clarissa* L147n1

attorneys

Belford, Mr. John

>Dorrell, Mr., visiting, on Belton's account L364, L365

authority
Harlowe, Mrs. Charlotte
    failing to exert her authority to control family dissention L5
    deferring to James on Clarissa's request to attend church L22
Harlowe, Miss Clarissa
    respecting Papa's L4
Harlowe, Mr. James, Jun.
    unrestrained by parental authority L5
    wishing Clarissa to accompany him to Scotland and care for his home there L6
    against Clarissa's visit to Anna L6
    authoritarian manner toward Clarissa L6
    usurping parental authority in regard to Clarissa L22, L22.2
    armed with authority of a father L433
Harlowe, Mr. James, Sen.
    exerting some restraint on James L6
    know that I will be obeyed L8
    threatened by Clarissa's refusal to obey L8, L41.1, L84
    mentioned L18, L36, L39, L84
    wounded L50.1
    turning entire matter over to James, Arabella, and Antony L80
    Clarissa's respect for L94
    sending James to Edinburgh to avoid trouble with Lovelace L378
    governed by James L379, L433

avenging Clarissa's death see **death of Harlowe, Miss Clarissa, avenged**

B

bailiffs see
    servants, *Lord M.,* steward (discharged)
    servants, *Lord M.,* Parsons, Simon

ball, Colonel Ambrose's
Harlowe, Miss Arabella
    not attending L367
Harlowe, Miss Clarissa, friends, Biddulph, Miss Rachel
    attending L367
Harlowe, Miss Clarissa, friends, Lloyd, Miss Biddy
    attending L367
Hickman, Mr. Charles
    attending L350, L367
Howe, Miss Anna
    attending L350, L358, L367
    interviews with Lovelace L366, L367
Howe, Mrs. Annabella
    attending L350, L358, L367
Lord M., relations, nieces
    refusing to accompany Lovelace L350
Lovelace, Mr. Robert
    attending, his agreeable time at L350, L367, L371

banishment
Harlowe, Mrs. Charlotte
> Clarissa cannot remain at Harlowe Place L54.1

Harlowe, Miss Clarissa
> banished from Papa's presence L25.4
> turned out of doors L47, L51, L53.1, L59.4
> may not remain at Harlowe Place L54.1, L59.3, L78
> siblings not sorry to drive her out L69
> giving up her keys L78, L91
> driven out of paradise, of her home L98, L223
> renounced by family, cast from their hearts L147, L307
> going abroad rather than returning to Harlowe Place L248
> family proposing that Clarissa board with Mr. Hartley's friend in Pennsylvania L429

Harlowe, Mr. James, Sen.
> banishing Clarissa from his presence L25.4
> ready to turn Clarissa out of doors L51

Harlowe Family
> wanting Clarissa to go to one of the plantations L408
> wanting Clarissa to go to Pennsylvania L429
> wanting Clarissa to go to some one of the colonies L443

Lovelace, Mr. Robert
> banished by Lord M., shunned by his family L394

Barbados see **drink**, *Lovelace, Mr. Robert*

basilisk
Howe, Miss Anna
> basilisk eyes, killing Lovelace at the ball L56, L367

Bath stone
Harlowe, Miss Clarissa
> Clarissa compared L245, L245fn

beds see **sleeping arrangements**

Beelzebub see also **devil**; **Moloch-deity**; **Satan**
Lovelace, Mr. Robert
> Lovelace as L164, L198, L207, L227, L256, L260, L271, L523

beer see **drink**, *Harlowe, Miss Clarissa*

bequests of Belton see also **executors**
Belford, Mr. John
> 100 guineas and £20 for a ring L426
> Belford giving his 100 guinea bequest to Belton's sister L426

Lovelace, Mr. Robert
> £20 for a ring L426, L440
> contributing his to Belton's sister's India Bonds L449

Lovelace, Mr. Robert, friends, Belton, Mr. Thomas
> 100 guineas to Belford L426
> £20 apiece to Mowbray, Tourville, Lovelace, Belford for rings L426, L440
> leaving his sister only £50 L440

Lovelace, Mr. Robert, friends, Mowbray, Mr. Richard
> £20 for a ring L426, L440
> contributing his to Belton's sister's India Bonds L449

bequests of Belton (cont.)

Lovelace, Mr. Robert, friends, Tourville, Mr. James

  £20 for a ring L426, L440

  contributing his to Belton's sister's India Bonds L449

bequests of Clarissa see also **executors**; **wills**

Harlowe, Miss Clarissa

  to her minister, fifteen guineas for a ring L507

  to twenty poor people, five pounds L507

  to Poor's Fund, proceeds from sale of Grandmother's jewels L507

  to servants at Harlowe Place, ten pounds each L507

  to servants of Mrs. and Miss Howe, thirty guineas L507

  to Alston, Miss Fanny, five guineas for a ring L507

  to Barnes, Betty, sum of ten pounds L507

  to Belford, Mr. John, one hundred guineas and twenty guineas for a ring L507

  to Biddulph, Miss Rachel, five guineas for a ring L507

  to Burton, Hannah, sum of fifty pounds L507

  to Campbell, Miss Cartwright, five guineas for a ring L507

  to Goddard, Mr., her apothecary, fifteen guineas for a ring L507

  to H., Dr. R., twenty guineas for a ring L507

  to Harlowe, Mr. Antony, old family plate L507

  to Harlowe, Mrs. Charlotte

    whole length picture of Clarissa in the Vandyke taste, to Aunt Hervey, or Mamma L507, L510.3

    needlework L510.3

    book of Meditations, bequeathed Mrs. Norton, Mamma wanting the original L507, L510.3

  to Harlowe, Mr. James, Sen., real estate L507

  to Harlowe, Mr. John, family pictures L507

  to Hervey, Miss Dolly

    watch, equipage, head-dress, ruffles, gown, and petticoat L507

    twenty-five guineas for a ring L507

    harpsichord, chamber-organ, and music books L507

    her books L507

    Morden presenting her with Clarissa's jewels L520

  to Hervey, Mrs. Dorothy

    fifty guineas for a ring L507

    whole length picture of Clarissa in the Vandyke taste, or to Mamma L507, L510.3

  to Hickman, Mr. Charles

    returning to Hickman her miniature of Anna L476, L507

    fifteen guineas for a ring with Clarissa's hair L507

  to Howe, Miss Anna

    fifteen guineas for a ring with Clarissa's hair L507

    her whole length picture L507

    her best diamond ring L507

    needlework L507

    her correspondence, sent by Belford L507, L521

    Clarissa's Memorandum book L510.3

  to Howe, Mrs. Annabella, twenty-five guineas for a ring L507

  to Lewen, Dr., or his daughter, twenty guineas for a ring L507

  to Lloyd, Miss Biddy, five guineas for a ring L507

  to Lovelace's family, enamel rings with Clarissa's hair in crystal L507

  to Lovick, Mrs.

    some books L507

    linen and laces L507

    twenty guineas L507

    copy of her book of Meditations L507

bequests of Clarissa, *Harlowe, Miss Clarissa* (cont.)
    to Morden, Colonel William
        needlework L507
        miniature of Clarissa set in gold L507
        proceeds of her estate since Grandfather's death L507
        rose diamond ring L507
    to Norton, Mrs. Judith
        thirty guineas, her and her son for mourning L487, L507
        sum of six hundred pounds, her clothing L507
        her book of Meditations, Mamma wanting the original L507, L510.3
    to Sarah, Mr. Smith's servant, five guineas L507
    to Shelburne, Ann, her nurse, ten guineas L507
    to Smith, Mr. John, ten guineas L507
    to Smith, Mrs., linen and laces, twenty guineas L507

bequests of Grandfather Harlowe see also **inheritances**, *Harlowe, Miss Clarissa*, from Grandfather Harlowe
Harlowe Family, relations, Harlowe, Grandfather
    family pictures and family plate to Clarissa L42
    less than half his real estate left to Clarissa L42
    Clarissa not valuing herself upon L135
    giving up her grandfather's bequest to appease her brother L174

bequests of Mrs. Larkin
Howe, Mrs. Annabella
    rings and mourning for Anna and Mrs. Howe L65
    Jenny Fynnett well provided for L65

bequests of Lord M.
Lord M.
    bequeathing his grandson his Hertfordshire estate CONCLUSION

bequests of Lovell
Harlowe, Mr. James, Jun.
    Lovell, godmother L4
        James's Yorkshire property, mentioned in Grandfather's will L2, L4
        James's inheritance from L13

Bible
Belford, Mr. John
    understanding as children L364
    admiration for L370
Harlowe, Miss Clarissa
    given Clarissa to read by Mrs. Rowland L333, L334, L336
    doubling down pages at the *Book of Job, Ecclesiasticus* L333
Lord M., housekeeper, Greme, Mrs.
    reading the Bible to Lord M. L104
Lovelace, Mr. Robert
    Lovelace's mother teaching him the Bible L115
    reading the Bible, but for *The Proverbs* L191

biblical references see also **God, references to**
Belford, Mr. John
    James 2:19, quoted on devils L222
    raping Clarissa a national sin atoned for by sword, pestilence, or famine L336
    mingled with the dust we sprung from L420

biblical references (cont.)

Harlowe, Mr. Antony

 Proverbs 18:17, quoted L32.4, L32.4n1

 Ecclesiasticus 42:9, 10, etc., quoted L406

 Matthew 23:24, quoted L32.4, L32.4n3

Harlowe, Miss Arabella

 Numbers 17:43–48, Aaron's rod L42

 Matthew 5:15, I hid not my light L42

Harlowe, Mrs. Charlotte

 Clarissa wishing to kiss the hem of Mamma's garment L377

Harlowe, Miss Clarissa

 general

  I wept L17, L20, L94

  casting the first stone L78

  Old Law, on whose vows shall be binding L88, L89

  I have cleared them of blame, and taken it upon myself L94

  driven out of paradise L98

  Clarissa's fall L118, L144, L169, L171, L324, L359, L399, L429

  lamb, Clarissa as L172, L515

  Lovelace her Judas protector L227.4

  Lovelace holding on to her gown L274

  wishing to kiss the hem of Mamma's garment L377

  recourse to Scriptures to calm her L399

  ascending into Heaven in Lovelace's dream L417

  returning to her father's house L421.1, L440, L442, L446, L449, L486, L510.4

  Cain's curse, Lovelace having L458, L458n2

  Clarissa's death reclaiming Lovelace L467

 Old Testament references

  Leviticus 18:21, Moloch-deity L57

  Numbers 30:16, being yet...in her father's house L89

  Deuteronomy 32:35, Vengeance is mine L490, L490n1

  2 Samuel 1:26, quoted on friendship between David and Jonathan L359, L359n1

  2 Kings

   9:20, Jehu-driving L53

   23:10, Moloch-deity L57

  Job

   her impenetrable afflictions given to her by God L266

   29:2–6, in my father's house L359, L359n1

   30:23, quoted on approaching death L359, L359n2

   some verses forming Clarissa's Meditation L364, L364n2

   reading *Job* L371

   Job, Clarissa compared L371

   9:20, quoted L379, L379n1

   31:35, 36, 34, adapted L379, L379n2

   6:27, quoted L389, L389n1

   19:2; 6:14, etc., in her Meditation L413

   Job, her favorite L416

   iii:17, quoted on her coffin L451

   xv:31, 32, 33, quoted L507

   20:5; 18:11, 12, quoted L510.4, L510.4n1

  Psalms

   verses from, making up Aug. 21 Meditation L418

   cxvi:7, 8, quoted on her coffin L451

   ciii:15,16, quoted on her coffin L451

   119:71, It is good for me that I was afflicted L481, L481n2

biblical references, *Harlowe, Miss Clarissa*, Old Testament references (cont.)

    Proverbs 27:5, faithful are the wounds of a friend L309, L309n1

    Ecclesiastes 7:1, quoted L492, L492n1

    Ecclesiasticus

        37:13, 14, quoted L89

        6:16, quoted L149, L149n1

        41:4, quoted L492, L492n1

  New Testament references

    Romans 12:19, Vengeance is mine L490, L490n1

    I Corinthians 15:55, Oh death, where is thy sting L481, L482n1

    2 Corinthians 9:7, on the cheerful giver, quoted by Melvill in his eulogy L504

Harlowe, Mr. John

  soft answers turn away wrath L60.1

Harlowe Family, clergymen, Melvill, Mr.

  2 Corinthians 9:7, quoted in his eulogy of Clarissa L504

Harlowe Family, servants, Barnes, Betty

  Luke 15:7, there will be joy in Heaven L90, L90n1

Harlowe Family, servants, Leman, Joseph

  Matthew 16:26, what shall a man get to lose his soul L139, L139n2

Howe, Miss Anna

  tell it not in Gath L15

  all punctilio is at an end the moment you are out of your father's house L87, L89, L90

  Exodus 16:3, your Israelitish hankerings L142, L142n1

  as Herod loved his Mariamne L229.1, L229.1n1

Howe, Mrs. Annabella

  I Corinthians 15:33, on *evil communication* L296, L296n1

Lord M.

  I Samuel 25:21, return good for evil L190, L190n1

  Solomon and his proverbs reminding Lovelace of Lord M. L191

Lord M., relations, nieces, Montague, Miss Charlotte

  recognizing Clarissa's reference to her father's house L439

Lovelace, Mr. Robert

  generally

    Abraham offering up Isaac L294

    Cain's curse, Lovelace having L458, L458n2

    David

        2 Samuel 12:7, his adultery with Bathsheba L159, L159n1

        David and Solòmon and polygamy L254

    Eve's curse, women made to bear pain L335

    Gothamite, Hickman, a prim Gothamite L198

    Habakkuk, Lovelace's servant as L466, L466n1

    Herod, loving Clarissa as Herod his Mariamne L229.1, L229.1n1, L234

    Methusalem, were Lovelace to live so long L453

    Pontius Pilate, Tomlinson as L244

    Samson and the Philistines L294

    Solomon

        Clarissa as L175

        Lord M. reminding him of L191

        David and Solomon and polygamy L254

    hoping for Divine pardon through Clarissa L397

    touching the hem of Clarissa's garment L418

    deceived by Clarissa's reference to her father's house L446

    Clarissa writing Lovelace from her father's house L486

  Old Testament references

    2 Samuel 12:7, David and Bathsheba L159, L159n1

biblical references, *Lovelace, Mr. Robert*, Old Testament references (cont.)

Job

his admiration for L364

Job, Clarissa compared L371

quoted L416

Psalms, singing to himself the dead psalm melody L266, L266n2

Ecclesiasticus

1:9, nothing new under the sun L116, L116n1

25:19, wickedness of a woman L115

26:9, 11, on whoredom and manners L255

New Testament references

Matthew 26:42, would not have the cup put from me L110

1 Corinthians 11:9, woman was made for the man, not the man for the woman L110, L110n1

Lovelace, Mr. Robert, contrivances of Lovelace, specifically, contrivance of Captain Tomlinson and Uncle

Harlowe's birthday, Tomlinson, Captain Antony

Pontius Pilate, Tomlinson as L244

Norton, Mrs. Judith

I wept L459

King Hezekiah, his days lengthened, Clarissa compared L459, L459n1

Sinclair, Mrs., whores, Martin, Sarah (Sally)

Bible, *Book of Job*, *Ecclesiasticus*, Apocrypha, remarking over L333

Prior, Matt, *Poems on Several Occasions*, on doubling down the useful places of the Bible L333, L333n1

birthdays see also **ages**

Harlowe, Miss Clarissa

July 24th L358fn, L361, L364, L378

her last birthday L380

Harlowe, Mr. John

June 29th L271, L272.1

Lovelace, Mr. Robert

knowing all the Harlowe birthdays and Mamma and Papa's anniversary L271

black

Harlowe, Miss Clarissa

wild oats, and black oxen L44, L44n1

black as appearances are L308

a black affair, given Clarissa to make her sleep L346

her Meditation stitched to the bottom of Letter 402 in black silk L402

who can touch pitch and not be defiled L440

black clouds of despondency L440

black cloth covering Clarissa's coffin L451

with her will a parcel of letters sealed with three black seals L486

preamble to her will attached on black silk L507

Howe, Miss Anna

Rosebud, a plot...to wash a blackamoor white L72

Lord M.

his great black mantle covering Lovelace in Lovelace's dream L417

Lovelace, Mr. Robert

black swan L123

my black angel plays me booty L152

the black angels and the white ones L152

appearing angel of light, but a black heart L235

old spectacled parson with a white surplice thrown over a black habit performing the ceremony L276

his cause having a black and a white side L323

the devil not quite so black as he is painted L326

black, *Lovelace, Mr. Robert* (cont.)

    Lovelace, one of the blackest L329

    a black contrivance, Clarissa's arrest L332

    black blood in his callous heart L333

    the truth making him black L346

    devil is black L395

    Lord M.'s great black mantle covering Lovelace in Lovelace's dream L417

    the black offender L437

    blackest of villains L456

    crimes so black L458

    pailful of black bull's blood taken from Lovelace L496

    black perjuries, black offenses L510.4

Lovelace, Mr. Robert, servants, Summers, Will

    in a black wig watching for Clarissa at Moore's, Smith's L231.1, L416

black wax see **sealings**, *Harlowe, Miss Clarissa*

blacks see **funeral of Lord M.**

bleeding see **cures**

blessings

Harlowe, Miss Clarissa

    the poor blessing her, praying for her L177, L301

    wanting Papa's blessing L360, L379

    begging a blessing upon both Hickman and Anna L366

    wanting her parents' last blessing L380, L382, L399, L403, L407, L429, L459, L475

    asking Mamma's blessing L391, L393

    blessing Belford L440

    blessing Anna L458, L473.1, L473.2

    blessed by Dr. H. and the minister L473

    blessing all her family L481

    blessing Morden and Belford L481

blindness

Harlowe, Miss Clarissa

    her sight failing L460

    unable to read Anna's letter L473

    her sight gone L481

blood

Harlowe, Miss Clarissa

    an inquisition made for her blood, though she die by her own hand L266

    bloodying her nose on the edge of the chair L267

    Mrs. Howe's reproofs drawing blood L297

    Mrs. Norton's heart bleeding for Clarissa L301

    her bleeding heart L307, L380, L489

Lovelace, Mr. Robert

    using pigeon and chicken blood to trick Clarissa L209

    his blood of as much concern as that of a Neapolitan saint L211

    guilty of bloody murder of Clarissa L246

    were Belford Clarissa's brother, the blood of one of them would be spilled L258

    sooner or later this affair will draw blood L294

    black blood in his callous heart L333

    bloody-minded L416

blood, *Lovelace, Mr. Robert* (cont.)
 his heart bleeding L466
 pailful of black bull's blood taken from Lovelace L496
 poor blood L496
 Morden to have his heart's blood L532
 vomiting blood, duel with Morden L537

Blunt's chariot
Lovelace, Mr. Robert
 sending for L231, L231n1, L255

bodice-makers
Smith, Mr. John
 Joseph, bodice-maker L416
  lion's-face grinning fellow, broad black teeth, bushy hair L416
  Lovelace threatening him L416
  Lovelace giving him half a crown L416

bonds see **India Bonds**

books
Harlowe, Miss Clarissa
 Thomas à Kempis, Arabella borrowing from Clarissa L75, L77
 books requested after flight, will not be sent L98, L102, L147
 procured for her by Belford, at Mrs. Sinclair's L131, L155
  pieces of devotion L154
  Addison's *Works* L155
  Bishop of Man's *A Sacramental Piece* L155, L155n1
  Mr. Cibber's *The Careless Husband* L155, L155n1
  Dryden's *Miscellanies* L155
  Gauden, Dr., Bishop of Exeter, *A Piece* L155, L155n1
  Inett's *Devotions* L155
  Nelson's *Feasts and Fasts* L155
  Pope's *Works* L155
  Rowe's *Plays* L155
  Shakespeare's *Plays* L155
  Sharp's *Sermons* L155
  South's *Sermons* L155
  Stanhope's *Gospels* L155
  Steele's *Plays* L155
  Swift's *Works* L155
  Tatlers, Spectators, and *Guardians* L155
  Telemachus (in French and in English) L155, L155n1
  Tillotson's *Sermons* L155
 sent by Anna
  Norris, John, *Miscellanies* L148
  returning Anna's Norris L149, L150, L156
  Lovelace *out-Norrised* L198, L199, L215
 sent by James
  Drexelius on Eternity L173, L177
  Francis Spira L173, L177
  Practice of Piety L173, L177
 bequeathed Dolly L507

bowling
Harlowe, Mr. John
    a great bowler L214

breakfast see **meals, breakfast**

bribes
Harlowe, Miss Clarissa
    bribing Dorcas with a promissory note for twenty pounds and a diamond ring L269, L279, L280, L281
Howe, Miss Anna, servants, Kitty
    Singleton bribing her for information about Clarissa L196
Lovelace, Mr. Robert
    promising Leman the Blue Beard Inn and Betty for his assistance L113, L140

burgundy see **drink**, *Lovelace, Mr. Robert*

burial of Clarissa see also **funeral of Clarissa**; **grave**
Harlowe, Miss Clarissa
    wishing to be buried with her ancestors L486
    in the family vault at Grandfather's feet L486.2
    carried down into the burial vault L504
Lovelace, Mr. Robert
    wanting to open and embalm Clarissa L496, L497
    wanting to bury Clarissa in his family vault between his parents L497
    wanting to keep Clarissa's heart in a golden receptacle L497
Morden, Colonel William
    bespeaking his own place in the vault next to Clarissa's L504
    accompanying the coffin into the vault to see it laid at Grandfather's feet L504

businesses
Harlowe, Mr. Antony
    his East India traffic and successful voyages L4
Harlowe, Mr. James, Sen.
    his tradesmen in London L126
Harlowe, Mr. John
    his new-found mines L4
Harlowe Family
    the plantations L408
Howe, Miss Anna, smugglers, Townsend, Mrs.
    importing textiles and other curiosities L196
Lovelace, Mr. Robert, contrivances of Lovelace, contrivance of sparing Rosebud, Rosebud, family
    her father proprietor at the White Hart Inn L34
Lovelace, Mr. Robert, friends, Belton, Mr. Thomas, family, Thomasine, family
    her father, innkeeper at Dorking L192
Lovelace, Mr. Robert, friends, Belton, Mr. Thomas, relations, Sambre, Mrs.
    Belford, Mowbray, Lovelace, Tourville giving her their legacy for India Bonds L449
Norton, Mrs. Judith
    giving her son money to start a business L207
Sinclair, Mrs.
    Dover Street, not Dover Street L130.1, L229.1
    a back house within a front one and looking to a garden rather than a street L137
    her home and dress carrying marks of good circumstances L155
    Mother *Damnable*'s park L228
    two houses, one reputable appearance and one not L229.1
    genteel wicked house L229.1

businesses, *Sinclair, Mrs.* (cont.)
> her house very handsome L233
> iron rails before the windows L264
> a brothel L266
> her concern for the reputation of her house L281
> her parlour in the back-house L293
> her house ruined if Lovelace and his friends get married L336
> Lovelace wanting to burn down her house L396, L511

Sinclair, Mrs., relations, Carter, Mrs.
> keeping a bagnio near Bloomsbury L499

Smith, Mr. John
> his glove shop, hosier in King Street L295, L320, L351
> dealer, trader in stockings, ribands, snuff, and perfumes L320
> selling powder, wash-balls, snuff, gloves, and stockings L416
> selling rapee, Scots snuff, and Portugal snuff L416

C

cabala
Lovelace, Mr. Robert
> word used by rakes L110

Cain's curse
Lovelace, Mr. Robert
> Lovelace having L458, L458n2

caitiff see
> **devils**, *Belford, Mr. John*
> **devils**, *Lovelace, Mr. Robert*, friends, Miles

chair see **transportation**

chaise see **transportation**

champagne see **drink**, *Lovelace, Mr. Robert*

chaplains see also **clergymen**
Lord M.
> and Mrs. Sorlings's daughter L118
> Lovelace offering to send for L149, L150
> praying with his chaplain when he has the gout L321

character
Belford, Mr. John
> description by Clarissa L161
> good natured L161, L359
> bad enough L189
> a pitiful fellow L276
> a wretched puppet of Lovelace L339
> stiff as Hickman's ruffles L350
> his awkwardness L370
> Mrs. Smith inquiring into his character L379

character, *Belford, Mr. John* (cont.)

    dough-baked varlet L395

    well spoken of by Hickman L404

    account of, by Clarissa L458

Harlowe, Mr. Antony

    busy old tarpaulin uncle L31

    sea-prospered gentleman L73

    impetuous in his anger L73

    fusty fellow L100

    odd old ambling soul L111

    his brother Orson L128, L128n1

    thrice cruel, hard-hearted L129, L309

    grey goose L196

    old Triton L197

    old Neptune L197

    his sobriety L197

Harlowe, Miss Arabella

    ill-natured, less sense than ill nature L2, L352

    greedy, plump L10

    self-serving L17

    cruel, hard-hearted L78, L309, L348, L362, L391, L430, L440, L459

    soul of the other sex and the body of ours L78

    malicious and selfish, spiteful L111, L152, L327, L355

    envious, jealous elder sister L145, L152, L189, L223, L261 Paper V, L355

    ill-mannered L355

Harlowe, Mrs. Charlotte

    obedient nature L8

    passive L13, L151, L248, L500

    peace keeper L16

    self-sacrificing L19

    her indolent meekness L27

    unable to show maternal love L181

    her narrowness of mind L183

    will-less L248

    thought hard-hearted and unforgiving on account of Clarissa's errors L307

    conquering by seeming to yield L379

    indulgent and sweet-tempered L409

    her quiet cost her her daughter L500

Harlowe, Miss Clarissa

    her prudence L1, L39, L105, L207, L234, L339, L371, L408, L427

    self-examination L19, L82, L94

    prodigy L27

    loyalty to family L31, L44, L59

    witch L42, L215

    described generally L56

    little rogue L99, L106, L439

    steadiness and punctilio L100, L248

    tennis-ball L132

    description by Belford L143, L336, L481

    superior to Lovelace L145, L248, L263

    genteel, open, cheerful, modest, poise, grace, dignity L157.1, L182, L203.2, L216, L222, L225, L229.1, L339, L399, L427

    over-niceness L95, L142, L167, L194, L226, L227.3, L229.1, L233, L245, L248, L268, L323

    description by Anna L177, L529

    description by Mamma L182

character, *Harlowe, Miss Clarissa* (cont.)
    pride and joy of the family L182
    superior to her siblings L182
    Lovelace's fruit L187.1–L187.4
    not a hoyden L201
    charming icicle or frost-piece L219, L220, L371
    Bath stone, Clarissa compared L245, L245fn
    description by Lovelace L252
    compared to Anna L252
    worthy to be Lord M.'s niece L261 Paper VIII
    her rank, fortune, talents, and virtue reduced by Lovelace L333
    her piety, dignity, family, fortune, and purity of heart L339
    talent at moving the passions L374, L376, L377, L402, L459
    Uncle Harlowe's doting-piece L420
    description by Morden L442, L519
    triumphant subduer L470
Harlowe, Miss Clarissa, suitors to Harlowe, Miss Clarissa, Solmes, Mr. Roger
    confident and offensive, monster L16, L17
    boasting he will marry Clarissa L22, L76
    account of, by Anna L27
    compared to Lovelace L32.3, L277
    illiterate L32.4
    his persistence L33.2, L79
    his impudent preparations L76
    siccofant L90.1
Harlowe, Miss Clarissa, suitors to Harlowe, Miss Clarissa, Wyerley, Mr. Alexander
    jester upon sacred things L40, L78
Harlowe, Mr. James, Jun. see also **control**
    violent temper L1, L13, L132, L407, L490
    compared to Lovelace L3, L4
    dutifulness lacking L5
    haughty, morose L5
    greedy L8, L17
    arrogant L10
    rapacious L13, L223, L233.1
    self-serving, selfish L17, L111, L508
    ambitious L19, L145
    hard-hearted, cruel, malicious L51.2, L78, L111, L129, L145, L339, L437
    villain, half-witted L412
    insolent, ambitious, stupid L327
    his family fearing him L437
    a menacer L534
Harlowe, Mr. James, Sen.
    tyrant, gloomy tyrant L27, L109, L152, L191, L248, L252
    his arbitrariness L36
    immoveable L78
    despotic L248
    much to answer for L316
    implacable L373
    had I never been hard-hearted L503
Harlowe, Mr. John
    the old gentleman L179
    Clarissa's second papa L407
Harlowe Family
    Grandfather's opinion L27

character, *Harlowe Family* (cont.)
 men in straw L106
 tame spirits L106
 malignant hearts, wicked L127
 implacable L128, L319, L347, L348, L358, L364, L372, L385, L399, L413, L418, L439, L456
 hard-hearted L172, L364, L437, L455
 grasping men L233.1
 unforgiving L301
 severe and cruel L446
 hearts of flint L459
Harlowe Family, clergymen, Brand, Mr. Elias
 pedant L94, L455
 officious L381, L431, L443, L459
 his character, by Clarissa L446
Harlowe Family, clergymen, Lewin, Dr. Arthur
 his wisdom, excellent divine L48, L409, L426
Harlowe Family, relations, Harlowe, Grandfather
 doting good old man L429
Harlowe Family, servants, Barnes, Betty
 her nature L53
 wench L91
 vixen L95
 saucy gossip L142
Hervey, Mrs. Dorothy
 female passiveness, an example L8, L9, L13
Hickman, Mr. Charles
 his humility L10
 an unexceptionable man L28
 a puritan L48
 his suspiciously easy grasp of Lovelace's affairs L48
 his horns better hidden than Lovelace's L68
 passive L104, L128
 a fool L117
 good and grave L128, L229
 cringing L128
 Anna's almoner L132
 his generosity L132
 a modest man L134, L136
 prim Gothamite L198
 male-virgin, virtuous and innocent L236
 a fop, starched as his ruffles L346
 so prim, so affected, so mincing, yet so clouterly in his person L346
 finical and formal but agreeable and sensible L366
 too meek for a man L367
 has not much penetration L404
 a very worthy man, gentle-dispositioned L520
Hickman, Mr. Charles, messengers, Collins, Simon
 common poacher, deer-stealer, and warren-robber L174.3
Howe, Miss Anna
 her spritely, vivacious nature, fire and spirit, fury L55, L197.2, L252, L347, L435, L502
 charming, confoundedly smart and spiritful L104, L117
 very saucy girl, saucebox L111, L197
 a virago L117, L198, L229, L233, L341
 compared to Clarissa L136, L252
 plagues the man who puts himself into her power L194, L252

character, *Howe, Miss Anna* (cont.)

 a devilish rake at heart L198

 had she been a man, would have sworn, cursed, committed rape, and played the devil L236

 account by Lovelace L252

 termagant L252

 her satirical vein L308

 fine, graceful young lady L502

 account by Morden L520

 open, generous, noble L520

Howe, Miss Anna, suitors to Howe, Miss Anna, Colmar, Sir George

 a fop and a libertine L182, L355

Howe, Mrs. Annabella

 bustling, jealous woman L100

 Argus-eyed mamma L100

 good manager L132

 her face sharpened to an edge L229.1

 prudent and watchful L354

 her prudence and good sense L356

 avaricious L364

 her character, an account by Morden L520

Lord M.

 a man of honor L81

 noble podagra-man L170

 the old peer L191, L218, L275, L277, L294, L321, L322, L383

 a sinner L218

 generosity to Clarissa L409

Lord M., housekeepers, Greme, Mrs.

 excellent woman, pious matron L98, L104

Lord M., relations, Knollys, Mrs.

 her excellent character L26

Lord M., relations, half-sisters

 excellent character, unblemished honor L26, L81

Lord M., relations, half-sisters, Lawrance, Lady Betty

 officious and managing, generous and noble L325

Lord M., relations, half-sisters, Sadleir, Lady Sarah

 melancholy, weak-spirited L98, L245, L325

Lord M., relations, nieces, Montague, Miss Patty

 her excellent character L26

 low spirited, timorous girl L88

 Lovelace's favorite L332

Lovelace, Mr. Robert see also **control**; **generosity**; **power**; **vanity**; **violent behavior**

 accounts of

  by Arabella L2

  by steward (discharged) of Lord M. L4

  by James L4

  by Clarissa L11, L30, L40, L55, L73, L217.2

  by Lovelace L12, L31, L34

  by Mrs. Fortescue L12, L14, L15

  by Mrs. Greme L98

  by Anna L142, L367

  by Belford L143

  by Morden L442

 violent temper, violent spirit L3, L49, L55, L121, L132, L376, L452, L458

 trickster, artful and designing, intriguer L10, L34, L99, L101, L145, L229.1

 his love-sick soul L34

character, *Lovelace, Mr. Robert* (cont.)

 full of love and revenge, love mixed with revenge and pride, desire for conquest L35, L216, L223

 vindictive L40

 lacking a heart, cruel L40, L161, L184, L187.1–L187.4, L217.2, L440

 arrogant, I am fit to be a prince L101, L423

 wicked, savage, evil, cruel, savage seducer, bloody-minded, obdurate, monster L114, L127, L183, L184, L200, L244, L314, L416, L519

 bashful, originally L115

 no fool, a fool L156, L188, L207

 natural dignity, wit and vivacity, smart wit and repartee, man of genius, lively temper, in conversation has no equal L161, L222, L266, L526

 a puzzling combination of good and bad L217.2

 vile and remorseless L222

 finding pleasure in playing the tyrant over what he loves L234

 vice itself L261 Paper VIII

 brave, generous, frank L261 Paper VIII

 not ridiculing things sacred L370

 woman-eater L416

 a man of defiance L519

Lovelace, Mr. Robert, friends, Belton, Mr. Thomas

 drinking hard L161

 mischievous spirit L192

Lovelace, Mr. Robert, friends, Belton, Mr. Thomas, family, Thomasine

 pretending to dote on Belton, embezzling his money L192

 her infidelity, accursed deceiver, ungrateful L347, L419

Lovelace, Mr. Robert, friends, Doleman, Mr. Tom

 man of fortune and character, former rake L126, L229.1

Lovelace, Mr. Robert, friends, Mowbray, Mr. Richard

 investigated by Hickman L48

 jesting upon sacred things, hating clergy L161

 admiration and concern for Clarissa L169

 mischievous, brutal, rough, and untouched L192, L370, L419, L445

 I ever hated a book. Kicking...cuffing...orchard-robbing were my early glory L496

Lovelace, Mr. Robert, friends, Tourville, Mr. James

 coxcomb, fop, finical, idle flutterer L161, L350, L370, L498

 admiration and concern for Clarissa L169

 mischievous spirit L192

 satisfied with wit at second-hand L222

Lovelace, Mr. Robert, servants, Summers, Will

 clever fellow, could do anything but write and spell L117

 faithful honest dog L480

Morden, Colonel William

 man of honor and bravery L415

 slender notion of women's virtue L456

 skilful swordsman L533

 cool and sedate L533

 man of principle L533

Norton, Mrs. Judith

 prudent, wise, pious L15, L47, L56, L82, L88, L125

 Mrs. Lovick compared L338

Norton, Mrs. Judith, family, Tommy

 a fine youth L494

Norton, Mrs. Judith, family, father

 his wisdom, a sound divine and fine scholar L69, L82, L381

character (*cont.*)

Sinclair, Mrs.
    her respectfulness studied L155
    sly and leering L157
    pretending to weep for her husband still L157
    her puritanical behavior before Clarissa L158.1
    hypocritical L169, L222
    Hottentot L175
    assuming violent airs and terrifying Clarissa L256
    feared by Clarissa L261.1
    blustering with her worse than mannish airs L261.1
Sinclair, Mrs., whores, Horton, Mary (Polly)
    gentler temper and manners than Miss Martin L158
Sinclair, Mrs., whores, Martin, Sarah (Sally)
    thinking herself as well descended and educated as Clarissa L333
    her insolence to Clarissa L416
Sinclair, Mrs., whores, Partington, Priscilla
    modest, genteel girl, specious, flippant L158.1, L169, L222
    disliked by Clarissa L167
Sinclair, Mrs., whores, Wykes, Dorcas
    honest, illiterate wench, neat in person and dress, not vulgar L154
    Clarissa's dislike of her L154
    discrete, loyal, genteel, obliging, sly eye, well-bred, well-spoken L155
    compassionate temper L269
Smith, Mr. John
    honest, humane, industrious L307, L320
Smith, Mr. John, lodgers, Lovick, Mrs.
    respected, pious, prudent L320

chariot see **transportation**

charities see **Poor's Fund**

church

Belford, Mr. John
    resolving to attend L499
Harlowe, Miss Clarissa
    requesting permission to attend church, refused by James L22, L22.2
    wishing to attend church in London L157, L158.1
    not allowed to attend church without Lovelace L178
    attending church without Lovelace L198, L200
    attending church with Mrs. Moore L248, L251
    dressing as if to go to church L293
    attending church, chapel L320, L399
    attending morning prayers at the Covent Garden church L329, L330, L440
    attending churches near Smith's L368
    going in a chair to prayers at St. Dunstan's L426
    attending devotions L441
    her habit of taking a sedan or chair to morning prayers L444
Harlowe Family
    attending church L22, L75
    where Lovelace looked challenge at the Harlowe Family L30, L31, L36, L106
    attending church but three times since Clarissa left L301
Lovelace, Mr. Robert
    his confrontation with the Harlowe Family L30, L31, L36, L106

church, *Lovelace, Mr. Robert* (cont.)
>   attending church with Clarissa, attendance ensuring reform L159
>   his dress too gay for church L159
>   wishing to attend Clarissa to church L200
>   attending church L323

Moore, Mrs.
>   accompanying Clarissa L251

claret see **drink**, *Lovelace, Mr. Robert*, friends, Mowbray, Mr. Richard

classical references

Belford, Mr. John
>   well read in classical authors L161
>   Juvenal, quoted L217.3, L217.3n1, L419, L419n2
>   Socrates, Clarissa's suffering and death compared L258, L451
>   Caesar stabbed by Brutus, Clarissa compared L336
>   Democritus and Heraclitus, Lovelace and Belford compared L364, L364n3
>   Proteus, Lovelace as L424

Harlowe, Miss Clarissa
>   the old Roman and his lentils L20, L20n1
>   like another Helen...unable to bear the reflection L40
>   Virgil's *Georgic*, translated by Dryden L50, L50.2
>   Scipio, wrongly accused L157, L157n1
>   Sophocles, *Oedipus*, adapted by Dryden and Lee, quoted L174, L174n1, L261 Paper X, L261 Paper Xn1
>   Juvenal, *Satire XV*, translated by Nahum Tate, quoted L217.3, L217.3n1
>   Lucretia
>>   Clarissa as L222, L515
>>   cost to a Tarquin L261.1, L261n2
>   Nemesis, Clarissa as Lovelace's L223
>   siren L228
>   Caesar
>>   stabbed by Brutus, Clarissa compared L336
>>   the die is thrown L362
>   more pure than a vestal L346
>   Queen of Carthage, Clarissa as L370, L370n1
>   her death compared to Socrates' L451
>   manes of Clarissa L497, L536

Harlowe, Mr. James, Jun.
>   Virgil's *Georgic*, translated by Dryden L50.1, L52.1

Harlowe Family, clergymen, Brand, Mr. Elias
>   his knowledge of Latin and Greek L381, L399
>   Miserum est aliena vivere quadra L444
>   Juvenal, *Satire VIII*, quoted in Latin L444, L444n3
>   untraced quote L444, L444n5
>   Horace, *Odes I*, quoted in Latin L444, L444n6
>   Ovid, misattributed quote, L444, L444n7

Hervey, Mrs. Dorothy
>   Caesar...ides of March L144

Howe, Miss Anna
>   Hannibal L10, L10n1
>   Caesar, the ides of March, Lovelace compared L10, L12
>   Scylla or Charybdis L56
>   Narcissuses, men and L58
>   the old Greek, quoted on governing L81, L81n1
>   Argus-eyed mamma L100

classical references, *Howe, Miss Anna* (cont.)

 the old Triton, old Neptune, Antony as L197

 Alexander, compared L252

 love, an *ignis fatuus* L310

Lord M.

 Raro antecedentem scelestum deseruit pede poena claudo: where vice goes before, vengeance (sooner or later) will follow L190

 the old Trojan, Lord M. as L191, L321

Lovelace, Mr. Robert

 Aesop's *Fables* L167, L167n1

 Alexander the Great

  Lovelace comparing himself L232

  comparing Anna L252

 Bamfield, Richard, *Philomel*, Clarissa as L325, L325n1

 Boreas, Phoebus, and Thetis, fable L201

 Caesar

  Lovelace comparing himself L12, L261, L512

  and Rubicon L97, L226

  a great rake L110

  compared to Pompey L261

 Cassandra L131

 Clodius L106, L106n1, L110

 dea bona L115

 debellare superbos L34

 Democritus, Lovelace aping among his friends, and Heraclitus to the family L277, L277n1

 [Demosthenes] the matrimonial sword hanging over his head by a thread L325

 Dii majores L167, L229

 Epictetus/Seneca, mentioned L453

 Erebus, some of our fellow brethren now wandering in L370

 Fates

  sparing Clarissa L453

  what they do against him L466

  spinning threads for tragedies for Belford L515

 Hannibal, the father of warlike stratagems, Lovelace comparing himself L223

 hieroglyphics of the marriage license L254

 Heraclitus, Lovelace aping to the family, and Democritus among his friends L277, L277n1

 Hercules-like...in the tortures of Deianira's poisoned shirt L243, L243n1

 Herodotus L191

 Homer L152

 Horace, *Odes*, Book II, translated by Abraham Cowley, quoted L264, L264n1

 Josephus, *Antiquities of the Jews*, quoted L191, L191n2

 Juno L167

 Jupiter

  a rape worthy of L35

  in *Fables of Aesop* L167

  by Jupiter L228, L244, L330, L410, L416, L511, L513, L516

  laughing at the perjuries of lovers L246

 Lucretia-like vengeance unlike Clarissa L263, L263n1

 Lycurgus institutions L254, L254n1

 Mercury, Belford compared L167

 Mulciber L153

 myrmidons, Lovelace's friends as L106

 Niobe L153

 Ovid L103

  Metamorphoses, Philomela, Clarissa as L325, L325n1

classical references, *Lovelace, Mr. Robert* (cont.)

    his phaeton, ready to drive, Miss Patsey Montague sharing L322, L332

    Phalaris L252, L252n2

    Philomela, Clarissa as L325, L325n1

        Ovid, *Metamorphoses* L325, L325n1

        Bamfield, Richard, *Philomel* L325, L325n1

    a phoenix of a man L237

    Pompey, compared to Caesar L261

    Proteus, Lovelace as L424

    Publius Terentius, quoted L175, L175n1

    the Roman matron and suicide, Clarissa compared L371

    Seneca/Epictetus, mentioned L453

    Socrates' wife L115

    Spartans, children of the public L254

    Tarquin

        cost of rape to L261.1, L261n2

        Lovelace comparing himself L371

    Tiresias L115, L115n1

    Virgil's Aeneas, comparing himself L370, L370n1, L370n2

Lovelace, Mr. Robert, contrivances of Lovelace, specifically, contrivance of Captain Tomlinson and Uncle Harlowe's birthday, Tomlinson, Captain Antony

    old Mulciber's, Tomlinson as L244

Moore, Mrs., neighbors, Rawlins, Miss

    a Pandora's box L248

Morden, Colonel William

    Juvenal, *Satire XIII*, quoted in Latin L503, L503n1

Sinclair, Mrs.

    cursed Circes L294

clergymen see also **chaplains**

Harlowe, Miss Clarissa

    Lovelace will visit Clarissa and bring a parson to marry them L383

    parish minister visiting Clarissa L440, L454, L457, L467, L473

    bequeathing her minister fifteen guineas for a ring L507

Harlowe Family

    Brand, Mr. Elias, young Oxford clergyman and scholar L90.1

        character

            to have his fortune made by Uncle Harlowe L90.1

            pedant L94, L455

            officious young man, college novice L381, L431, L443, L459

            the young Levite L399, L410, L443

            called Parson Brand, Fire-Brand, incendiary L443, L445, L467

            account of, by Clarissa L446

        classical references

            knowledge of Latin and Greek L381, L399

            Miserum est aliena vivere quadra L444

            Juvenal, *Satire VIII*, quoted in Latin L444, L444n3

            untraced quote L444, L444n5

            Horace, *Odes I*, quoted in Latin L444, L444n6

            Ovid, misattributed quote, L444, L444n7

        costume, dressed in a riding-habit L399

        funeral of Clarissa, not chosen to pronounce discourse at Clarissa's interment L501

        informant, the milliner, Mr. Walton L444, L445

        informing on Clarissa

            sent to inquire about Clarissa L361, L381, L399

clergymen, *Harlowe Family*, Brand, Mr. Elias, informing on Clarissa (cont.)

    not reporting to the Harlowe Family what they do not want to hear L382, L446, L458

    his indifference to Clarissa's poor health L399

    his misrepresentations to the family about Clarissa L408

    creating scandal on account of Belford's visits to Clarissa L431, L433, L455

    his suspicions of Clarissa's attending prayers L444

    his letter of recantation mentioned L460, L464, L466, L467

  literary references

    de Foe, Daniel, *The True-Born Englishman*, quoted L444, L444n2

    Quarles, Francis, *Emblems*, misquoted L444, L444n1

  marriages, Clarissa's to Solmes, hired to perform wedding L90.1

  names

    as Dr. Brand, minister L90

    signing his name Elias Brand L444

  sayings, honours change manners L444

  snuff, purchasing Spanish snuff L399

  writing, his talent, letter-writing L444

Lewin, Dr. Arthur, excellent divine, Clarissa's favorite divine L409, L426

  bequest of Clarissa, twenty guineas for a ring L507

  character, his wisdom L48

  clergyman, Mr. Brand's learned and worthy principal L381

  conflict with Harlowe Family

    opposed to the wedding L90.1

    badly treated by James L408

    family incurring his displeasure L409

  death, dying soon after reading Clarissa's letter, very lately dead L430, L503

  duel between James and Lovelace

    frustrating James's first challenge to Lovelace L4

    distracting Lovelace as Lovelace looks challenge at the Harlowes after church L30, L36

  family

    loving his own child and loving Clarissa L427

    his daughter L507

  funeral of Clarissa, would have pronounced discourse at L501

  illnesses, declining health L381, L408, L427

  influence on Clarissa L48

    advising steadiness of mind L19

  marriages, Clarissa's to Solmes

    arbitrator for Clarissa's situation with Solmes L53.1, L54.1

    refusing to marry Clarissa without her consent L90, L90.1

    opposed to the wedding L90.1

  names

    as Lewen L408, L409, L427, L501, L503, L507

    signing his letter Arthur L427

  prosecution of Lovelace, urging Clarissa to prosecute L427, L429

  reconciliation between Clarissa and the Harlowe Family, offering to mediate L408

  visits

    visiting Clarissa in her confinement L75, L77

    his conversation visits L82

    to visit as preparation for the wedding L83

    will not visit Harlowe Place, badly treated by James L408

Melvill, Mr., Dr. Lewen's assistant L501

  to pronounce discourse at Clarissa's interment L501, L503

  to deliver a brief eulogium L501, L504

  a serious and sensible man L503

  2 Corinthians 9:7, quoted in his eulogy of Clarissa L504

clergymen, *Harlowe Family*, Melvill, Mr. (cont.)
    given a ring by Morden L504
Norton, Mrs. Judith, family
    her father, a clergyman L301

clothing see **costume**

cloven foot
Lovelace, Mr. Robert
    discovering his cloven foot L252.1, L252.1n1
    devil and his cloven feet L326

codes
Belford, Mr. John
    sending Lovelace news of Clarissa's death in a coded message, advising him to go to Paris L449
    his hellish Arabick L496
Lovelace, Mr. Robert
    in Lovelace's cursed algebra L496
    writing in characters to Belford L497

coffins
Belford, Mr. John
    seeing Clarissa's L451
Harlowe, Miss Clarissa
    coffin, a flower bed, mentioned by Lovelace L313
    ordering, at the undertaker's in Fleet Street L440
    delivered to Smith's L450
    devices and inscriptions L450, L451
        Here the wicked cease from troubling L500
    expensive L451
    her coffin near the window like a harpsichord L457, L474
    her house, called by Clarissa L457, L474, L486
    filled with flowers and aromatic herbs L487, L495, L501
    taken from the hearse and borne by six neighborhood maidens into the hall L500
    carried from the hall into her parlour L500
    lid unscrewed so family can view the body L501
Lovelace, Mr. Robert
    may need a coffin or a shroud L410

cohabitation
Lovelace, Mr. Robert
    planning cohabitation with Clarissa L110
    if she cannot be brought to cohabitation, he will marry her L194
    his darling view, principal view L259
    touching upon L263
    no hope of L264, L281, L289
    will press for L268

collation at Mrs. Sinclair's
Belford, Mr. John
    report of L222
Harlowe, Miss Clarissa
    a murdered evening L159
Lovelace, Mr. Robert
    Clarissa to meet his friends L158.1

collation at Mrs. Sinclair's (cont.)

Lovelace, Mr. Robert, friends, Belton, Mr. Thomas
  attending L158.1
Lovelace, Mr. Robert, friends, Mowbray, Mr. Richard
  attending L158.1
Lovelace, Mr. Robert, friends, Tourville, Mr. James
  attending L158.1
Sinclair, Mrs., whores
  attending or not attending L158
Sinclair, Mrs., whores, Partington, Priscilla
  attending L158, L161

comedy

Lovelace, Mr. Robert
  The Quarrelsome Lovers, a comedy planned by Lovelace L175, L216
  his trial, ending with the word comedy L323–L325
Sinclair, Mrs.
  preferring comedy to tragedy L194

common folk

Harlowe Family, servants, Barnes, Betty
  low people L73
Harlowe Family, servants, Leman, Joseph
  low people L73
  common folk L139, L241
Lovelace, Mr. Robert, friends, Belton, Mr. Thomas, family, Thomasine
  low-bred L193

conflict between Harlowe, Miss Arabella and Clarissa see also **sibling rivalry**

Harlowe, Miss Arabella
  Lovelace's rejection of Arabella in favor of Clarissa L1
  jealous of Clarissa's inheritance L2, L42, L44
  motivations mentioned L27, L115
  taunting Clarissa L75, L433
  taking some of Clarissa's poultry for James to take to Scotland L75
  overheard by Clarissa plotting with James L83
  penetrating Clarissa's proud heart L261 Paper V
  severity with Mrs. Norton L308
  bitter against Miss Howe L308
  indifferent to Clarissa's plight L352
  and James's confederacy to disgrace Clarissa L472
  hating James afterwards CONCLUSION
  regretting her cruel treatment of Clarissa CONCLUSION

conflict between Harlowe, Mr. James, Jun. and Clarissa see also **sibling rivalry**

Harlowe, Mr. James, Jun.
  Lovelace his machine, implement L189, L276
  James as the source of Clarissa's problems L339
  James badly treating Dr. Lewen L408
Hervey, Mrs. Dorothy
  There never was so set a malice in man as in your cousin James Harlowe. They will ruin the flower and
   ornament of their family L78

conflict between Harlowe Family and Clarissa

Harlowe, Mrs. Charlotte

    blaming James's violence L41

Harlowe, Miss Clarissa

    family united against her in the Solmes affair L6, L14

    Harlowe Family and motivating forces L8, L13

    blaming all on James L9, L112

    made an instrument of revenge against Lovelace L13

    How impolitic in them all to join two people in one interest whom they wish for ever to keep asunder L14

    surely *they* will yield L14

    recounting measures taken by the family against her L32.3, L112

Harlowe Family, clergymen, Lewin, Dr. Arthur

    opposing Clarissa's marriage to Solmes L90, L90.1

    badly treated by James L408, L409

Howe, Miss Anna

    opinion of the Harlowe Family L10

    raving about them L37, L308

    her resentments on Clarissa's account L309

    blaming James and Arabella for the family's loss of Clarissa L355

    taking liberties with the Harlowe Family L376

    not pitying the Harlowe Family L510.3

Morden, Colonel William

    coldness between Morden and the Harlowe Family L431

    conflict with James about treatment of Clarissa L459

Norton, Mrs. Judith

    Clarissa will not put her in opposition to the Harlowe Family L125

    under the direction of the Harlowe Family L189

    family prohibiting Mrs. Norton from attending Clarissa L408

conflict between Harlowe Family and Lovelace see also **duel between James and Lovelace**

Harlowe Family

    James and Arabella allied against Lovelace L4, L7

    noted L13, L20

    Lovelace, an enemy, feared, yet provoked L14

    opinion of Lovelace L40

    malice and resentment of Lovelace L127

    Lovelace's implacable enemies L158.1

    Lovelace's triumph over them L158.1

    Harlowe Family the aggressors L324

    fearing both Lovelace and James L437

Lord M.

    mediating conflict L17

Lovelace, Mr. Robert

    threats to the Harlowe Family L12, L17, L20, L24.1, L26

    enemy of the family L14, L158.1, L202

    looking challenge and defiance at them after church L30, L31, L36, L106

    despising and manipulating Harlowes and Howes, forcing Clarissa to flee L31, L152

    rivalry and hatred of James L91

    threats to James L114

    hatred of the Harlowes L121, L153, L154, L229.1, L294, L324, L376, L512

    machine of James L189

    Clarissa hoping it will subside L202

conflict between Howe Family and Anna

Howe, Miss Anna

    Anna's relationship with Mrs. Howe L13, L111, L112

    Hickman's suit L46, L48, L55, L58, L68

    Antony's wish to marry Mrs. Howe L183, L197, L197.1

    Anna not loving jangling with Mrs. Howe L358

conflict between Lord M. and Lovelace

Lord M.

    often falls out with Lovelace L98

    raving against Lovelace L104

    too indulgent with Lovelace L190

    believing Lovelace is up to mischief L218

Lovelace, Mr. Robert

    impertinent to Lord M. L190

    despising Lord M. for his proverbs L206

conscience

Lovelace, Mr. Robert

    troubling him L202, L207, L218, L276, L281, L282, L287, L341, L367, L511, L535

    touched when the French marquis's wife died in childbirth L209

    sobbing to see Clarissa anticipate reconciliation L216

    guilt tormenting him L222

    feeling Clarissa's eye-beams L243

    his conscience *Mennelled* upon him L244

    his vows of revenge forgotten L245

    arguing with his conscience L256

    at times regretting what he has done L259

    I own I have done wrong...to this admirable creature L259

    what...would I have given never to have injured her L263

    shaken by Clarissa's first appearance to him after the rape L263

    conscience writhing around his pericardium like a serpent L276

    temporary remorse L286, L287

    his family believing him penitent L342

    I am sick at my soul L350

    quieting his conscience L370

    stung by his own reflections L383

    tearing his flesh L395

    wrongs fill his mind with anguish and horror L397

    his remorse is enough punishment L413

    his conscience clear L449

    facing his own death with heavy reflection L452

    his heart bleeding L466

    his conscience avenging Clarissa L518

    his opinion on conscience L530

consent

Lovelace, Mr. Robert

    she owes me her consent L264

constables

Harlowe, Miss Clarissa

    constable called as Clarissa shouts from Mrs. Sinclair's window L264

constables, *Harlowe, Miss Clarissa* (cont.)
    Rowland, Mr., the officer L333
        Mrs. Rowland, wife L333
            offering Clarissa tea, bread, butter L333
            giving Clarissa a Bible to read L333, L334, L336
        their maid, in whose bed Clarissa lay L333
        calling an apothecary L333
        fearing Clarissa will die in his house L333
        his house described, miserably poor L334, L336
        Clarissa's gaoler L336

contrivances of Clarissa see also **father's house**
Harlowe, Miss Clarissa
    ambiguous meaning of her father's house L421.1, L440, L442, L446, L449, L486, L510.4
    contriving to be out when Lovelace visits Smith's L443
Lord M., relations, nieces, Montague, Miss Charlotte
    recognizing Clarissa's reference to her father's house L439
Lovelace, Mr. Robert
    not to be *out-Norrised* by Clarissa and Anna L148, L149, L150, L156, L198, L199, L215
    will not be emulated in contrivance by Clarissa L256
    overmatched by Clarissa L264
    deceived by her reference to her father's house L421.1, L440, L442, L446, L449, L486, L510.4

contrivances of Lovelace see also **abduction of Clarissa**; **rape of Clarissa**
Belford, Mr. John
    Lovelace revealing himself to Belford in his writing L276
    Belford's knowledge of all Lovelace did L284, L326, L379, L387.1
    will not assist Lovelace in any contrivances L286
    Clarissa realizing that Belford has known all along about Lovelace's actions L339
    asking Lovelace not to further molest or visit Clarissa L385, L391, L400, L413
Harlowe, Miss Clarissa
    contrivance of Rosebud spared L34, L35, L70, L71, L72, L73
    contrivance of pretending marriage to Clarissa L156, L186, L215, L233, L235, L281
    contrivance of the bedfellows L162, L164, L167, L169, L229.1, L248
    contrivance of Captain Tomlinson and Uncle Harlowe's birthday L216, L219, L245, L284
    contrivances of the impersonators L256, L256.1, L263, L266
    contrivance of the promissory note L269, L279, L280, L281
    contrivance of the escape L273
Harlowe, Mr. James, Jun.
    contrivance of kidnapping James and Solmes, planned L117, L119
Harlowe, Mr. John
    contrivance of Captain Tomlinson and Uncle Harlowe's birthday
        Tomlinson pretends to negotiate a reconciliation through Uncle Harlowe L214, L216, L221
        using the green with a gentleman Clarissa did not know L217
        to be in Kentish Town June 29th to celebrate his anniversary birthday L271, L272.1
        will not be in Kentish Town on Thursday L284
        Clarissa questioning truth of Lovelace's claims of a birthday celebration L300, L304
        his birthday not kept, not intended to be kept L301, L305, L307
        not knowing any Tomlinson L305
Howe, Miss Anna
    contrivance of sparing Rosebud
        inquiring about Lovelace's behavior at the inn L65
        Anna's suspicions of L70, L72

contrivances of Lovelace, *Howe, Miss Anna* (cont.)
> contrivance of Captain Tomlinson and Uncle Harlowe's birthday
>> inquiring about Tomlinson
>>> finding no such person L229.1
>>> finding a Thompson, a poor schoolmaster, of seventy, five miles from Uncle Harlowe L229.1
>>> finding a Tomkins, a day-labourer, living four miles off from Uncle Harlowe L229.1
> contrivance of Mrs. Fretchville's house, inquiring about, finding no such person L229.1

Lord M.
> contrivance of Captain Tomlinson and Uncle Harlowe's birthday
>> Lord M. accused of delaying his answer to Lovelace's invitation L201, L203
>> referring to Clarissa as his niece, asking her to defer marriage no longer L206
>> gout in his right hand prevents answering Lovelace's invitation L218

Lord M., relations, half-sisters, Lawrance, Lady Betty
> contrivance of the impersonators
>> old chancery affair calling her to town L203.1, L233.1, L233.2
>> visiting her cousin Leeson L233.2, L256
>> impersonated by Barbara Wallis L255
>> Clarissa querying her on L302, L303, L313
> contrivance of Captain Tomlinson and Uncle Harlowe's birthday
>> her steward telling Lady Betty of Lovelace's marriage L233.1, L233.2

Lord M., relations, half-sisters, Sadleir, Lady Sarah
> contrivance of Captain Tomlinson and Uncle Harlowe's birthday
>> disobliged with Lovelace not having heard directly of the wedding L233.2

Lord M., relations, nieces, Montague, Miss Charlotte
> contrivance of Mrs. Fretchville's house
>> visiting Clarissa at L178
>> Lovelace writing to her about Mrs. Fretchville's house L203
>> will visit Clarissa soon in her new habitation L203.1
> contrivance of the impersonators
>> impersonated by Johanetta Golding L255
>> Clarissa queries whether Charlotte met Lady Betty at Reading L302
>> the pretended Charlotte Montague L313
> contrivance of Captain Tomlinson and Uncle Harlowe's birthday
>> Lovelace may write to her about the wedding L187
>> Lovelace has told her that the delays are on Clarissa's side L190
>> Lovelace writing her about Lord M.'s delay in answering the invitation L203

Lovelace, Mr. Robert
> generally
>> a forward contriver, wicked contriver L76, L94
>> his conceited contrivances, his fine contrivances L83, L84
>> outwitted, he would hang, drown, or shoot himself L117
>> so full of his contrivances L155
>> I have more contrivances L207
>> so many contrivances L209
>> his contrivances to keep Clarissa uncertain L209
>> delighting in his contrivances L209
>> reporting his contrivances with stage directions L214, L232
>> hating himself for his contrivances L216
>> a devil in his contrivances L223
>> his contrivances explained L223
>> promising Tomlinson he will marry Clarissa and give up his contrivances L246
>> if he give up his contrivances, he will be but a common man L264
>> confounded number of contrivances to carry his point with Clarissa L267
>> entangled in my own contrivances L275, L276, L285
>> Clarissa querying Anna, Mrs. Howe, and Mrs. Norton on details of L295, L297, L300

contrivances of Lovelace, *Lovelace, Mr. Robert*, generally (cont.)

> his family discovering and confronting him L323
>
> if his contrivances end in wedlock L326
>
> his cursed inventions his punishment L365
>
> all my vice is women, and the love of plots and intrigues L370
>
> I value myself upon my contrivances L439
>
> his contriving genius L470
>
> his cursed devices standing in the way of his happiness L535

> specifically

>> contrivance of sparing Rosebud

>>> Rosebud

>>>> age, just turned seventeen years L34, L70, L71
>>>>
>>>> animals, poor quarry L171
>>>>
>>>> character, modest, simple, uncontending L71, L216
>>>>
>>>> contrivance

>>>>> Lovelace asking Belford to spare Rosebud L34
>>>>>
>>>>> Rosebud feared undone L70
>>>>>
>>>>> to be fortuned out to a young lover L70
>>>>>
>>>>> needing protection of her family L71
>>>>>
>>>>> Lovelace giving her to his friend L71
>>>>>
>>>>> Clarissa wishing to warn Rosebud L71
>>>>>
>>>>> Colonel Barrow's fondness for Rosebud L72
>>>>>
>>>>> Lovelace innocent L72
>>>>>
>>>>> Rosebud spared to credit his account with Clarissa L72, L103, L106, L159, L183, L191, L252
>>>>>
>>>>> a plot...to wash a blackamoor white L72
>>>>>
>>>>> Lovelace's generosity to Rosebud L116, L138, L183, L452

>>>>>> explained by the compiler in a footnote L217.2

>>>> family

>>>>> father and grandmother L34, L70, L71
>>>>>
>>>>> her grandmother asking Lovelace to spare Rosebud L34
>>>>>
>>>>> her father proprietor at the White Hart Inn L34

>>>> marriage

>>>>> to Johnny Barton, next week L34, L72, L207
>>>>>
>>>>> given a hundred pounds by Lovelace, matching sum from his aunt L34, L72
>>>>>
>>>>> Lovelace begrudging Johnny the maiden L106

>>>> mentioned L35, L159, L171, L198, L207, L496
>>>>
>>>> money, his friends giving Rosebud's father twenty-five guineas L72
>>>>
>>>> names, Betsy L70
>>>>
>>>> physical appearance, her beauty, pretty rustic L72, L116

>> contrivance of kidnapping James and Solmes, planned L113, L114, L117, L119

>> contrivance of pretending marriage to Clarissa

>>> at Mrs. Sinclair's L154, L156, L186, L215
>>>
>>> at Mrs. Moore's L233, L235, L245

>> contrivance of Mrs. Fretchville's house L158, L164, L174.1, L175, L178, L183, L185, L194

>>> Mr. Mennell, her kinsman L174.1
>>>
>>> Miss Martin knowing her very well L194
>>>
>>> wanting to end the affair of Mrs. Fretchville's house L201, L203
>>>
>>> her maid taken with the small-pox and now she herself is ill L201, L203, L218
>>>
>>> Anna's inquiries finding no such person L229.1
>>>
>>> a fiction L252.1

>> contrivance of the bedfellows L162, L164, L167, L169, L229.1, L248

>> contrivance of the plot upon Miss Howe *see also* **rape of Anna, planned**

>>> not carried out L207.1 (following)

contrivances of Lovelace, *Lovelace, Mr. Robert*, specifically (cont.)

contrivance of Lovelace's feigned illness
    taking ipecacuanha to make himself sick L209, L248
contrivance of Captain Tomlinson and Uncle Harlowe's birthday
    Tomlinson, Captain Antony
        age, twice Lovelace's age, upwards of fifty years L214, L217.1
        alias of Patrick McDonald L217
        animals, a dog, puppy, a whore's bird L241, L243, L244
        biblical references, Pontius Pilate like L244
        character
            Clarissa liking him L217.1
            brought to tears by Clarissa's expression of grief L243
            an excellent head L246
        classical references, old Mulciber's L244
        conscience, fearing Clarissa's eye-beams L243
        contrivance
            posing as a friend of John Harlowe, at whose request he tries to mediate a
                reconciliation L213, L214, L215, L216, L284
            reporting Clarissa's marriage to the Harlowes and Lovelace's relations L233
            correspondence, Letter 233.1 forged by Lovelace L233
            telling a Mr. Lilburne of Lovelace's marriage L233.1
            prevailing upon Lovelace to give it up L244
            Clarissa questions Lovelace directly on truth of this contrivance L266
            Uncle Harlowe's birthday L271, L272.1, L274, L276, L284, L288, L300, L301
            Lovelace to marry Clarissa before she discover the contrivance L294
            Clarissa questioning this contrivance L302, L303, L304, L305
        costume
            booted and spurred L214
            to get clothes in Monmouth Street L289
            riding dress for first visit to Clarissa L289
            boots not to be over clean, linen rumpled and soily L289
        crimes, forgery, head of a gang of smugglers, criminal L217, L246, L289, L514
        death, in Maidstone Gaol, after receiving Belford's three guineas L514, L515
        death of Harlowe, Miss Clarissa, penitent, acknowledging his guilt in L514, L521
        education, expelled from Dublin University L217
        family
            with his wife and five children, living on eight hundred pounds a year L216
            daughters as old as Clarissa L243, L289
        imposter, Anna's inquiries about him find no such person L229.1, L281
        mannerisms, pulling down, stroking his ruffles, pulling his wig L237, L244, L289
        meals, taking a dish of tea with the ladies L238
        money
            Lovelace giving him ten guineas L289
            Belford sending him three guineas L514, L515
        names
            Tomlinson, an alias of Patrick McDonald L217
            signing his letter Antony Tomlinson L233.1
        physical appearance L304
        servants, his discarded footman L217
contrivance of the fire L225, L230
    plot to frighten Clarissa almost naked into his arms L230
    recounted by Lovelace L243
    Clarissa asking Belford for Lovelace's letters to clarify this event L387.1
    mentioned L439

contrivances of Lovelace, *Lovelace, Mr. Robert*, specifically (cont.)
    contrivances of the impersonators L251, L255, L256.1, L312–L313
        impersonating Clarissa, Mrs. Bevis receives Clarissa's from Anna L251, L318, L320
        impersonating Lady Betty and Charlotte
            Barbara Wallis, a whore, as Lady Betty L255
            Susan Morrison, a tenant-farmer's daughter, Lady Betty's woman L255, L312
            Johanetta Golding, as Charlotte L255
            Lovelace borrowing jewels and clothes for the impersonators L255
            Lovelace coaching manners of the impersonators L255
            contrivance recounted by Clarissa L312–L313
    contrivance of the visit to Mrs. Sinclair's by Mrs. Moore, Miss Rawlins, Mrs. Bevis, Belton, Mowbray
      and Tourville, planned
        Lovelace's new intrigue L261, L316
    contrivance of the escape L271
        widow lady in her chariot waiting for Clarissa at the grocer's L273
        Clarissa not fooled L273
    contrivance of the promissory note
        conceived, executed, failed L279, L280, L281
        poor plot, poor contrivance, pride sunk L281, L282, L285
    contrivance of drowning Thomasine and hers, suggested
        taking Thomasine and hers on a boat trip and drowning them L347
    contrivance of disguising himself as a parson to visit Clarissa, considered L370
Lovelace, Mr. Robert, friends, Belton, Mr. Thomas
    to take up quarters for a week at Hampstead, show of support for Lovelace L241
    sent for, as Clarissa is gone off L290
    at Mrs. Sinclair's when Clarissa returns L314
Lovelace, Mr. Robert, friends, Doleman, Mr. Tom
    to whom Lovelace writes for accommodations for Clarissa L126
    his letter describing Mrs. Sinclair L154
    recommending Mrs. Sinclair's to Lovelace L229.1
    implement of Lovelace L229.1
Lovelace, Mr. Robert, friends, Doleman, Mr. Tom, relations, Newcomb
    contrivance of Mrs. Fretchville's house
        alias Mr. Mennell L174.2
        mischievously used by Lovelace L174.2, L194
        telling Lovelace of Mrs. Fretchville's small-pox L201
        refusing to continue deceiving Clarissa L203
        Lovelace's conscience *Mennelled* upon him L244
        taking leave of Lovelace L526
Lovelace, Mr. Robert, friends, Mowbray, Mr. Richard
    helping Lovelace get the marriage license L227
    his servant delivering Lovelace's forgery to Hickman L240
    taking up quarters at Hampstead in show of support for Lovelace L241
    sent for, as Clarissa is gone off L290
    present during Lovelace's interview with Morden, offering his sword L442, L445
Lovelace, Mr. Robert, friends, Tourville, Mr. James
    taking up quarters at Hampstead in show of support for Lovelace L241
Lovelace, Mr. Robert, servants, Summers, Will
    supposed by Harlowes to be Leman's source of information about Lovelace L103
    Lovelace offering to leave his servant with Clarissa L117, L157
    to be on guard against any attempt Clarissa may make to escape L174.3
    calling Peter to say Clarissa was going out to church alone L198
    directed to get a chair for Clarissa L201
    Clarissa sending him with hers for Anna to Wilson's, but Will gives it directly to Lovelace L228
    spying on Clarissa L230, L248

contrivances of Lovelace, *Lovelace, Mr. Robert*, servants, Summers, Will (cont.)

    taking a letter, a feint, for Anna from Clarissa to Wilson's and another to Lovelace L230, L231.1

    his account of Clarissa's flight from Mrs. Sinclair's and his finding her L230

    stealing Clarissa's and Anna's letters from Grimes L233, L235, L237, L238

    sleeping at Mrs. Moore's to keep an eye on Clarissa L239, L241, L242, L253

    Lovelace sending him for a coach for Clarissa to return to Hampstead L256

    keeping Clarissa under close watch L273, L281

    threatening to hang or drown himself L290

    to be taken dead out of some horse-pond L292

    allowing Clarissa to slip out in Mabel's clothing L293

    setting the sheriff's officers after Clarissa L333

    knowing location of Clarissa's lodgings at Smith's L334

    watching for Clarissa at Smith's L416, L418, L421, L425

    dispatched by Lovelace to Belford L439

Sinclair, Mrs., whores

    contrivance of the promissory note

        their role L281

        ridiculing Lovelace for his failed contrivance L281

Sinclair, Mrs., whores, Martin, Sarah (Sally)

    contrivance of Mrs. Fretchville's house

        known to Mrs. Fretchville L194

Sinclair, Mrs., whores, Partington, Priscilla

    contrivance of the bedfellows

        wishing to be Clarissa's bedfellow L162

        rejected by Clarissa L164, L169

        sharing a press-bed with Dorcas L167

        Lovelace attempting to fasten her upon Clarissa L229.1

Sinclair, Mrs., whores, Wykes, Dorcas

    contrivance of the fire

        crying Fire! Fire!, petticoats in hand L225

    contrivance of the escape

        assisting Lovelace in L272

        recognizing the lozenge on the widow lady's chariot L273

control

Harlowe, Mr. James, Jun.

    unrestrained by parental authority L5

    uncontrollable L29.1, L145, L233.1

Lovelace, Mr. Robert

    unused to control L3

    spoiled L142

    I was never accustomed to check or control L323

    not forgiving his family for presuming to control him L397

    who will control me L497

    I...will not be controlled L497

    why, why did my mother bring me up to bear no control L512

cordials see **medications**

corpse

Harlowe, Miss Clarissa

    Clarissa as L333

    lovely corpse L486

    her corpse put into a hearse L495

    face cloth on the corpse L502

correspondence, Belford, Mr. John with Lovelace
Belford, Mr. John
    must return all Lovelace's letters L326
    sending Clarissa extracts of Lovelace's correspondence L388, L395, L396, L415
    Lovelace returning all his correspondence to Belford L423
    wanting his letters returned to give to Anna to vindicate Clarissa's memory L452
    asking Mowbray to return Belford's correspondence with Lovelace L498

correspondence, Harlowe, Mrs. Charlotte
Harlowe, Mrs. Charlotte
    her secret correspondence with Clarissa about Lovelace L25.2
    returning Clarissa's letter unopened L59
    her letter to Mrs. Norton not communicated L182

correspondence, Harlowe, Miss Clarissa
Belford, Mr. John
    one day he will have all Clarissa's letters L391
    sending Clarissa's correspondence to Anna L521
Belford, Mr. John, messengers, Harry
    delivering Clarissa's posthumous correspondence L486, L494
Harlowe, Miss Clarissa
    sent to Mrs. Norton, to help tell her story L409, L433
    bequeathed Anna L507, L521
    posthumous, eleven letters sent after her death L486, L494
Howe, Miss Anna
    collecting Clarissa's letters and papers to tell Clarissa's story L428
    Belford sending to Anna, as Clarissa's will requests L521
Lord M.
    Lovelace giving his posthumous letter from Clarissa to Lord M. to read to him L510.3
Norton, Mrs. Judith
    Clarissa sending Mrs. Norton a packet of letters L409, L433

correspondence, Harlowe, Miss Clarissa with Anna
Harlowe, Miss Clarissa
    aliases *see also* **aliases**, *Harlowe, Miss Clarissa*
        Beaumont, Miss Laetitia L155, L229, L229.1, L239
        Clark, Mrs. Rachel L295
        Lucas, Mrs. Harriot L230, L238
        no longer needed L338
    conveyed by
        Hannah L9, L14, L19, L20, L23
        Robert L9, L16, L46, L58, L65, L69, L74, L87
        Joseph Leman L35
        Mrs. Knollys L93, L98, L100
        Mrs. Greme L98
        Mr. Osgood L98, L141
        Mrs. Sorlings L100
        Mr. Charles Hickman L101
        Grimes L119, L120, L127, L233, L238, L238.1
        Mr. Wilson L148, L150, L166, L196
            giving letters directly to Lovelace L217
            forgery of Anna's Letter 229.1, now Letter 238.1, at Wilson's L238.1
        Mr. Robert Lovelace L165
        Rogers L251
        Mr. John Belford L334

correspondence, Harlowe, Miss Clarissa with Anna, *Harlowe, Miss Clarissa*, conveyed by (cont.)

        Harry L457, L471

    forbidden

        becoming secret L8, L9

        continuance in doubt L92

        advising Anna to discontinue L101, L146

        interference from Mrs. Howe

            informing Harlowe Family of their secret correspondence L50.1

            Clarissa forbidden further correspondence with Anna L163, L168

            Clarissa's Letter 295 to Anna intercepted by Mrs. Howe L296

            called *evil communication* by Mrs. Howe L296

        by Lovelace L261, L282

        by Mrs. Sinclair L279

    hidden

        her pockets concealing letters L174.3

        hiding letters in her stays L198

        locking letters in a wainscot box L210

correspondence, Harlowe, Miss Clarissa with Anna, forged by Lovelace

Lovelace, Mr. Robert

    Letter 229.2 from 'Clarissa,' acknowledging receipt of Letter 229.1 from Anna L229

    Letter 240.1 from 'Clarissa,' acknowledging receipt of Letter 229.1, rewritten by Lovelace and sent as Letter 239.1 to Clarissa L240

correspondence, Harlowe, Miss Clarissa with Anna, intercepted by Lovelace

Harlowe, Miss Clarissa

    Lovelace attempting to seize a letter from Clarissa L175, L176

    Lovelace reading transcripts of Anna's Letters 188 and 196 for Clarissa L198, L218

    Wilson giving letters for Clarissa directly to Lovelace L217

    Letter 229.1 for Clarissa delivered by Collins to Wilson's, Wilson giving it directly to Lovelace L229

    Letter 231.2 from Clarissa to Anna, given by Will to Lovelace L231, L231.1

    Will stealing from Grimes Clarissa's to Anna, giving it to Lovelace L233, L235, L238

    Tomlinson returning Letter 229.1 from Anna, stolen and rewritten by Lovelace, to Wilson's L238

    Lovelace trying to intercept Anna's next L239

    Clarissa's to Anna intercepted by Lovelace, substituting Letter 240.1, his forgery L240

    Anna's intercepted by Lovelace L250, L251

    suspecting Lovelace of confiscating Anna's letters L276

    Lovelace intercepting Clarissa's to Anna L284

    Anna's Letter 229.1, Letter 252.1, Letter 275.1 intercepted by Lovelace L310, L311

    Clarissa returning Anna's Letter 239.1, her Letter 229.1 rewritten by Lovelace L311

    Belford refusing to intercept Anna's to Clarissa L341

Lovelace, Mr. Robert

    attempting to seize a letter from Clarissa L175, L176

    Letter 231.2, Clarissa's feint to Anna L231, L231.1

    sending Will after Grimes, who has Clarissa's to Anna L233, L235, L238

    intercepting correspondence, he keeps seals entire and preserves covers L239

    stealing Clarissa's to Anna and substituting Letter 240.1, his forgery L240

    watching the post L241

    intercepting Clarissa's to Anna L284

Sinclair, Mrs., whores

    helping Dorcas transcribe Clarissa's letters for Lovelace to read L174.3, L198

    confiscating any letters to or from Clarissa L279

Sinclair, Mrs., whores, Wykes, Dorcas

    searching Clarissa's clothing for letters L174.3

    helping Lovelace come by Clarissa's letters L175

correspondence, Harlowe, Miss Clarissa with Anna, intercepted by Lovelace, *Sinclair, Mrs.*, whores, Wykes, Dorcas (cont.)

    searching Clarissa's room while she is at the theatre with Lovelace L194

    searching Clarissa's chamber for letters L198

    transcribing Clarissa's letters for Lovelace L198, L202, L210

    noting Clarissa has moved her letters L210

    trying to open the wainscot box where Clarissa keeps her letters L218

    transcribing Clarissa's fragments and letters for Lovelace to send Belford L261

correspondence, Harlowe, Miss Clarissa with Lovelace

Harlowe, Mrs. Charlotte

    her knowledge of L4, L17, L25.2, L112

Harlowe, Miss Clarissa

    beginning explained, history of, recounted L3, L112

    subverted by Lovelace L3

    her fear of breaking it off L3, L4, L17, L22, L25.1, L26, L36, L57

    encouraged by Mamma L4, L17, L25.2, L112

    forbidden L4, L17, L25.1

    continuance suspected by family L6, L10

    contents recounted to Anna, his letters forwarded to Anna L17, L80

    signed by Lord M. L25.1

    conveyed by Leman L35

    realizing she should not have corresponded with him L94, L98, L101, L110, L121, L306

    Clarissa and Lovelace a pair of scribbling lovers L105

    her motivation to prevent mischief between her family and Lovelace L229.1

    returning to Lovelace their correspondence L365

Harlowe, Mr. John

    accusing Clarissa of corresponding with Lovelace L32.2

Harlowe Family

    searching Clarissa's room for hidden correspondence L78, L90.1

    removing her writing supplies L78

    suspecting Clarissa of writing letters L90.1

Hervey, Mrs. Dorothy, family, Uncle Hervey

    its beginning explained L3

correspondence, Harlowe, Miss Clarissa with others

Harlowe, Miss Clarissa

    her letter to Lady Drayton on the consequences of severity in parents L58, L59, L90

    her suspicions of the sudden letters from Lovelace's family L244

    not daring to correspond with her family L304

    with Dr. Blome, Mr. Arnold, Mr. Tompkins, bequeathed Anna L507

correspondence, Harlowe, Mr. James, Sen.

Harlowe, Mr. James, Sen.

    returning Clarissa's unopened L59

correspondence, Harlowe Family

Harlowe Family

    having written to Morden L61

    no letter will be received from Clarissa L301, L307

    Miss Howe's angry Letters 351, 353, 355 incensing them L356, L357, L360, L361

    Clarissa's letter to Arabella received in great ferment L374

    receiving Clarissa's posthumous correspondence L494

correspondence, Howe, Miss Anna

Howe, Miss Anna

> with her cousin in the little island L10
>
> with Arabella
>
>> writing to Arabella to advise of Clarissa's present lodgings and state of health L351
>>
>> her angry Letters 351, 353, 355 to Arabella L356, L357, L360, L361, L378
>
> with Belford L510, L528

correspondence, Howe, Miss Anna with Clarissa

Hickman, Mr. Charles

> hiring Filmer to assist L100
>
> conveying their secret correspondence L107, L119, L132, L148
>
> caught by Mrs. Howe passing a letter from Clarissa to Anna L136
>
> Simon Collins conveying L156, L174.3, L184, L187, L217, L229, L229.1, L316, L318, L327, L328, L338
>
> believing Anna should continue corresponding with Clarissa L164
>
> Clarissa suggesting he write for Anna L165
>
> to whom Clarissa must direct hers for Anna L316

Howe, Miss Anna

> aliases, Mr. John Soberton, to whom Clarissa may address hers in Finch Lane L100
>
> conveyed by
>
>> Robert L9, L16, L46, L47, L58, L65, L69, L81, L87, L132, L148
>>
>> Mrs. Knollys L93
>>
>> Mr. Charles Hickman L100, L119, L128, L240
>>
>> Mr. Wilson
>>
>>> how he came to be used as a conveyance L148, L150, L229.1
>>>
>>> Anna's letters delivered to Wilson's, given directly to Lovelace L217
>>>
>>> Letter 229.1 from Anna delivered by Wilson to Lovelace L229
>>>
>>> Anna afraid to use Wilson's conveyance L261
>>
>> Simon Collins
>>
>>> hers delivered to Wilson's, but as there was a hurry, directly to Mrs. Sinclair's by Collins, but again, since Clarissa was out, back to Wilson's L229, L229.1
>>>
>>> assisting Anna in correspondence with Clarissa L316, L318, L327, L328
>>>
>>> no longer needed as a conveyance L338
>>
>> Captain Tomlinson
>>
>>> returning Anna's Letter 229.1 to Wilson's as Letter 239.1 rewritten by Lovelace L238, L239
>>
>> Grimes, delivering Anna's Letter 238.1 to Clarissa L238
>>
>> Rogers, Anna's tenant's son L319
>>
>>> delivering Anna's letter for Mrs. Harriot Lucas at Mrs. Moore's L251, L252.1
>>>
>>> cannot be spared to deliver letters L327
>>>
>>> delivering letters for Anna L327, L456
>>
>> post, corresponding with Clarissa by L329
>>
>> friend of Aunt Harman, delivering Anna's to Clarissa in London L404

Howe, Mrs. Annabella

> unaware of their secret correspondence L10, L65
>
> discovering it and informing the Harlowe Family L50.1
>
> forbidding their correspondence L8, L9, L111, L112, L128, L163, L168, L296, L307, L357
>
> slapping Anna's hand found writing to Clarissa L132
>
> Clarissa's Letter 295 intercepted by Mrs. Howe L296
>
> called *evil communication* by Mrs. Howe L296, L297
>
> confiscating Clarissa's of June 29th to Anna L310
>
> allowing Anna to answer Clarissa's L310
>
> prosecuting Lovelace a condition of their continued correspondence L317

correspondence, Howe, Miss Anna with Clarissa, forged by Lovelace
Lovelace, Mr. Robert
>   Lovelace mastering Anna's handwriting L229
>   Letter 239.1, Anna's double-dated Letter 229.1 rewritten by Lovelace L229, L238, L239, L310, L316
>   rewriting Anna's for Mrs. Harriot Lucas L251

correspondence, Howe, Miss Anna with Clarissa, intercepted by Lovelace
Belford, Mr. John
>   to bring Clarissa's mail to Lovelace L105
>   refusing to confiscate Anna's letters to Clarissa L341
Howe, Miss Anna
>   Lovelace transcribing Anna's Letters 188 and 196 to Clarissa L198, L218
>   Anna's Letter 229.1 stolen by Lovelace L229, L238.1, L239, L310
>   Will stealing Anna's Letter 238.1, giving it to Lovelace who reads it and returns it to Grimes L238
>   Lovelace trying to intercept Anna's next L239
>   hers to Clarissa stolen by Lovelace L250, L251
>   her three Letters 229.1, 252.1, 275.1 to Clarissa stolen by Lovelace L275, L310
>   Clarissa suspects Lovelace of confiscating Anna's letters L276
>   Anna's of June 20th not received by Clarissa L316
>   Belford refusing to confiscate Anna's to Clarissa L341
Lovelace, Mr. Robert
>   instructing Belford to bring Clarissa's letters to him L105
>   contriving to steal it from Simon Collins L174.3
>   reading transcripts made of Anna's Letters 188 and 196 L198, L218
>   confiscating Anna's delivered by Collins to Wilson's L217
>   Letter 229.1 from Anna, marking it to show points demanding revenge L229
>   intercepting Anna's next L238, L239
>   intercepting and reading Anna's Letter 238.1 to Clarissa L238
>   Letter 229.1 mistakenly called by Lovelace her double-dated letter L240
>>   Letter 229.1 ends Thursday morn 5 [a.m.]; Lovelace's transcription, Letter 239.1, ends Thursday morn 5th [though Thursday was the 8th] L229.1, L239.1
>   intercepting Anna's next to Clarissa L245, L248, L250
>   his crow-quill short-hand notes upon Anna's Letter 252.1 L252
>   confiscating Anna's last three to Clarissa (229.1, 252.1, 275.1) L275
>   wishing Belford to intercept Anna's letters to Clarissa L341

correspondence, Lawrance, Lady Betty, forged by Lovelace
Lovelace, Mr. Robert
>   Letter 233.2 from 'Lady Elizabeth Lawrance' L233, L272, L303, L306

correspondence, Lord M.
Lord M.
>   letter to Clarissa signed by Lord M. lending credibility to Lovelace's address L22
>   with Belford L513

correspondence, Lord M., forged by Lovelace
Lovelace, Mr. Robert
>   Letter 233.4 from Lord M. L233, L306

correspondence, Lovelace, Mr. Robert
Lord M.
>   Lovelace giving Clarissa's posthumous letter to Lord M. to read to him L510.3
Lovelace, Mr. Robert
>   his great and secret correspondence L12
>   his letter case L233

correspondence, Lovelace, Mr. Robert with Belford
Lovelace, Mr. Robert
    wrong to scribble so freely to Belford, but must write on L223
    his unreserved communication with Belford L260, L261, L263, L276
    asking Belford to return Lovelace's letters L326, L326n1
    Clarissa asking Belford for copies of Lovelace's correspondence to tell her story L387.1
    asking Belford to burn his, Lovelace's, letters L410, L512
    Lovelace returning all his correspondence to Belford L423

correspondence, Lovelace, Mr. Robert with Charlotte
Lovelace, Mr. Robert
    while travelling L534

correspondence, Lovelace, Mr. Robert with Clarissa
Lord M.
    letter to Clarissa signed by Lord M., lending credibility to Lovelace's address L22
Lovelace, Mr. Robert
    established L3
    subverted and used to manipulate Clarissa L3, L10, L17, L26, L36, L55
    letter to Clarissa signed by Lord M., lending credibility to Lovelace's address L22
    Clarissa and Lovelace a pair of scribbling lovers L105
    questioning her motivations for corresponding with him against her family's wishes L110
    confesses ignoring her letter of countermand before abduction L113
    writing to Clarissa in the rain in the coppice L223
    Clarissa asking Belford to return to Lovelace all their correspondence, his to her and hers to him L365
    her posthumous letter to Lovelace, which he gives to Lord M. to read to him L510.3

correspondence, Montague, Miss Charlotte
Lord M., relations, nieces, Miss Charlotte Montague
    her letter giving Clarissa hope L229.1
    with Belford L513
    with Lovelace abroad L534

correspondence, Montague, Miss Charlotte, forged by Lovelace
Lovelace, Mr. Robert
    Letter 233.3 from 'Miss Charlotte Montague' L233, L306

correspondence, Morden, Colonel William
Morden, Colonel William
    Harlowe Family have written to Morden L61
    Clarissa wishing to write to him L86
    Anna advising Clarissa to write to Morden L148
    his letter to Clarissa forwarded by family L173.1
    advising and warning Clarissa about Lovelace's character L173.1, L263
    Anna reading his to Clarissa L177
    with Belford, continuing CONCLUSION

correspondence, Norton, Mrs. Judith
Norton, Mrs. Judith
    with Clarissa forbidden L8, L13
    hers to Clarissa delivered by servant of Sir Robert Beachcroft L361
    hers to Clarissa delivered by Mr. Pocock L459

correspondence, Tomlinson, Captain Antony, forged by Lovelace
Lovelace, Mr. Robert
      Letters 233.1, 272.1 and 290 from 'Captain Tomlinson' L233, L289

costume
Belford, Mr. John
      his old corporal's coat L34
      dressing gaily L161
      removing Clarissa's clothes from Mrs. Sinclair's to Smith's L336
      dressing like a coxcomb L350
      making his ugliness conspicuous by his dress L350
      amending his dress after mourning L370
      Beau-Brocade after mourning L527
Harlowe, Miss Clarissa
      her flowered silver suit L69
      women's fondness for fine clothing L69
      clothing requested after flight L98, L102
      description of her clothing, head-dress, lawns, mob L99
      her dress praised by Lovelace L123
      needing clothing L123, L125
      will be sent to Clarissa by Mamma L147
      receiving her clothes L165, L173, L177
      her pockets concealing letters L174.3
      her elegance in dress L182, L529
      Lovelace offering Clarissa clothes L186
      dressing for the day by breakfast, to keep up forms and distance L194
      having two suits L202
      Lovelace drawing aside the handkerchief to kiss her breast L220
      her night head-dress L225
      escaping from the fire in her under petticoat, bosom half open, and shoes L225, L230
      escaping from Mrs. Sinclair's in a brown lustring nightgown, a beaver hat, a black riband about her neck,
        blue knots on her breast, a quilted petticoat of carnation-coloured satin, a rose-diamond ring L228
      little parcel tied up in a handkerchief L228
      threw her handkerchief over her head and neck and sobbed L235
      put a parcel into her pocket L235
      Mrs. Bevis may bring Clarissa's clothes from Mrs. Sinclair's L245
      attending church in her everyday worn clothes L248
      tearing off her head-clothes, ruffle torn L256
      her hood on and a parcel tied in a handkerchief, trying to leave Mrs. Sinclair's L262
      wearing a white damask night-gown, a white handkerchief in hand L263
      will not put off her clothes any more at Mrs. Sinclair's L264, L276
      her apron over her head L264
      disordered head-dress, torn ruffles, after attempted escape L267
      Lovelace holding on to her gown L274
      her rustling silks L281
      key to her chamber door at Mrs. Sinclair's in her pocket L281
      Mrs. Dollins, Clarissa's mantua-maker L293
      giving Mabel her brown lustring gown and quilted coat L293
      gown must be altered for Mabel as sleeves, robings, and facings are above her station L293
      Clarissa slipping on Mabel's gown and petticoat over her own white damask, and Mabel's hood, short cloak
        and ordinary apron to escape Mrs. Sinclair's L293
      ruff about her neck, hanging sleeve coat L294
      her clothes and the lustring, left at Mrs. Sinclair's, to be put away and sent to Clarissa when her whereabouts
        is known L294, L307, L330
      her dress not appropriate for Leeson's L314

costume, *Harlowe, Miss Clarissa* (cont.)
    her laces cut to prevent fainting L314, L334
    pulling off her head-dress, tearing her ruffles L314
    wearing an ordinary gown by way of disguise L320
    her face half hid by her mob, careless of her appearance L320
    her clothes to be sold by Mrs. Sinclair to pay the debt L333
    my father loved to see me fine L333
    valuables, clothes sold to pay debts and burial L334, L340, L345, L347, L364, L365, L426
    headdress a little discomposed L334
    her white flowing robes L334
    having no hoop on L334
    her linen white, dressed in white damask L334
    her clothes removed from Mrs. Sinclair's and taken to Smith's L336
    her fine Brussels lace head L336
    richness of her apparel L340
    now having her clothes with her L362
    ladies imitating her dress, giving fashion to the fashionable L399
    in translucent white in Lovelace's dream, her azure robe with stars of embossed silver L417
    trunks holding her apparel sealed up till opened as her will directs L460
    in a white satin nightgown L471
    dressed in virgin white L474
    face cloth on the corpse L502
Harlowe, Miss Clarissa, suitors to Harlowe, Miss Clarissa, Solmes, Mr. Roger
    yellow, full-buckled peruke, broad brimmed beaver L10
    white peruke, fine laced shirt and ruffles, coat trimmed with silver, and a waistcoat L78
Harlowe, Mr. James, Jun., friends, Singleton, Captain
    brown coat, colored handkerchief L194
Harlowe Family, clergymen, Brand, Mr. Elias
    in a riding-habit L399
Hickman, Mr. Charles
    his long bib and beads L46
    King William cravat L46, L46n1
    his cravat and ruffles L74
    stroking his ruffles, setting his wig, pulling his neckcloth, long enough for a bib L346
    not using spectacles L346
    fribbled with his waistcoat buttons L346
Howe, Miss Anna
    her hoops L74
    her morning sacque L81
    will send Clarissa money and clothes L100, L111, L119, L132
    to buy clothes in London for her approaching nuptials L459
Lord M.
    his great black mantle covering Lovelace in Lovelace's dream L417
Lord M., relations, nieces, Montague, Miss Charlotte
    to supply Clarissa with clothes L123
Lovelace, Mr. Robert
    his horseman's coat L36, L232
    a critic of women's dress L99
    description of Clarissa's clothing L99
    lace on his hat L99, L232
    his riding-dress L157
    too gay for church L159
    his gorget rumpled L183
    full dress creating dignity, augmenting consciousness, and compelling distance L194
    his linen and wig frozen waiting for Clarissa in the coppice L223

costume, *Lovelace, Mr. Robert* (cont.)

    in his gown and slippers when the fire broke out L225

    his ruffle L225

    disguised in a great-coat and a cape buttoned over the lower part of his face L232

    Will putting in the ties of his wig L232

    clocked stockings showing he is a gentleman L232

    stirrup-stockings giving his legs a gouty appearance L232

    using a cane L232, L233

    his slouched lace hat and wig L233

    his hat brushed up into the usual smart cock L233

    pulling his wig L244

    borrowing clothing, laces, gold tissue for impersonators of Lady Betty and Charlotte L255

    laced hat orator L294

    the powder flew from his wig L367

    so elegant and rich in his dress L367

    in a broad rose-bound beaver L370, L370n6

    in his fever, wearing his night-gown over his waistcoat, and his slippers L410

    John bowed to my fine clothes L416

    distraught over Clarissa's death, throwing his hat and wig off L480

    Beau-Brocade, to wear after mourning L527

Lovelace, Mr. Robert, contrivances of Lovelace, specifically, contrivance of Captain Tomlinson and Uncle Harlowe's birthday, Tomlinson, Captain Antony

    booted and spurred L214

    to get clothes in Monmouth Street L289

    riding dress for first visit to Clarissa L289

    boots not to be over clean, linen rumpled and soily L289

Lovelace, Mr. Robert, friends, Belton, Mr. Thomas

    dressing gaily L161

Lovelace, Mr. Robert, friends, Mowbray, Mr. Richard

    dressing gaily L161

Lovelace, Mr. Robert, friends, Tourville, Mr. James

    dressing richly, more tawdry than fine L161

Moore, Mrs.

    or Mrs. Bevis may bring Clarissa's clothes from Mrs. Sinclair's L245

Morden, Colonel William

    putting letters in his pocket-book L443

Sinclair, Mrs., servants, Mabel

    Clarissa escaping disguised in Mabel's clothes L293

Sinclair, Mrs., whores

    trying to steal some of Clarissa's clothes L336

    their dress and makeup the next morning, described L499

Sinclair, Mrs., whores, Martin, Sarah (Sally)

    hoping Lovelace will give her Clarissa's clothes L333

    trying to steal Clarissa's fine Brussels lace head L336

    searching for the ruffles belonging to Clarissa's fine Brussels lace head L336

Sinclair, Mrs., whores, Wykes, Dorcas

    dangling in her own garters from her bed's tester L292

Smith, Mr. John

    his glove shop L295, L320, L351

    dealer, trader in gloves, stockings, ribands L320, L416

    Mrs. Smith helping Belford remove Clarissa's clothes from Mrs. Sinclair's L336

    bowing to Lovelace's fine clothes L416

Smith, Mr. John, bodice-makers, Joseph

    a bodice-maker L416

costume (cont.)

Smith, Mr. John, lodgers, Lovick, Mrs.

> selling Clarissa's clothes L345, L365, L426

Smith, Mr. John, neighbors, Barker

> a mantua-maker L445

costume, bequests of see **bequests of Clarissa**

counsellors

Harlowe Family

> Derham, Counsellor, to attend Clarissa, hear her story, and begin a process L429

Lovelace, Mr. Robert

> Williams, Counsellor

>> to draw up settlements conformable to those of Lovelace's mother L207

>> drawing up the settlements, nearly finished L216, L229.1

>> man of eminence L229.1

courtship

Hickman, Mr. Charles

> suit to Anna L10

> favored by Mrs. Howe L10, L27, L58, L65, L81, L111

> Anna's lukewarm feelings for, her indifferent attitude L55, L58, L151

> appreciated by Clarissa L55, L69, L73

> Anna's poor treatment of L59, L65, L74, L82, L120, L201, L434, L520, L535

> erecting an altar to Anna L128

> his whining, creeping, submissive courtship L128

> compared to Lovelace's courtship style L128

> his treatment of Anna L201

> Lovelace claiming Anna hates Hickman and loves Lovelace L236

> would fare better with Anna if Mrs. Howe were against him L252

> Anna never loving him L341

> Lovelace will let him have Anna safe and entire L371

> Anna's relations' fondness for Hickman L434

> made by Anna to look weak and silly L435

> his patience with Anna L458

> not appreciated by Anna L458

> Clarissa advising him to be patient with Anna L465

> history of his courtship with Anna L523

Lovelace, Mr. Robert

> a thorny courtship L207

> his misfortune to have fallen in with Clarissa and hers with him L294

couteau

Harlowe, Mr. James, Jun., friends, Singleton, Captain

> couteau by his side L194

Coventry Act

Howe, Miss Anna

> and Betty Barnes L68

crimes see also **forgers; smugglers**

Lovelace, Mr. Robert

> wishing not to be a detested criminal L283

> unaffected by the sense of his own crimes L339

> criminal charge L339

crimes, *Lovelace, Mr. Robert* (cont.)

> his crimes L448
>
> villainous burglar, felon, thief L453
>
> crime upon which he should be arraigned L456
>
> crimes so black L458
>
> what did I do worth a woman's breaking her heart for L515
>
> If by committing an unlawful act, a capital crime is the consequence, you are answerable to both L515
>
> Lovelace arguing his defense before Lord M. and his cousins Montague L515

cures see also **medications**

Lord M.

> scarifications L191, L247

Lovelace, Mr. Robert

> bleeding, in his dangerous fever L410
>
> chicken broth L410
>
> pailful of black bull's blood taken from Lovelace L496
>
> water-gruel and soupe-maigre L512
>
> by starving diet, by profuse phlebotomy, by flaying blisters, eyelet-hole-cupping, a dark room L512
>
> gallipots, boluses, and cephalic draughts L512

Norton, Mrs. Judith

> a vein breathed L487

curses

Belford, Mr. John

> cursed by Lovelace L416

Harlowe, Miss Arabella

> Clarissa writing Arabella to have Papa's curse revoked L348, L349, L360, L363

Harlowe, Miss Clarissa

> Papa's
>
>> mentioned L146, L147, L152, L172, L173, L189, L191, L201, L216, L225, L226, L230, L235, L261 Paper II, L263, L272, L274, L333, L343, L347, L373, L443
>>
>> his malediction coming true L243
>>
>> his heavy curse L261 Paper II
>>
>> following her into the next world L307
>>
>> can neither live nor die under Papa's curse L307
>>
>> wishing for revocation of Papa's malediction L308, L309, L320
>>
>> taking Papa's imprecation to heart L308
>>
>> weight of a parent's curse L318
>>
>> writing to Arabella to ask that Papa's curse by revoked L348, L349, L360
>>
>> Papa's imprecation weakening Clarissa further L351
>>
>> asking Arabella to intercede in revoking the part of Papa's curse that relates to the hereafter, as she has already been punished in the here L363
>>
>> his curse withdrawn L377, L378, L379
>
> Lovelace's
>
>> marriage to Lovelace bringing a curse on her children L359
>>
>> cursed by Lovelace L395
>>
>> Lovelace having Cain's curse L458, L458n2

Harlowe, Mr. James, Sen.

> his on Clarissa L146, L147, L152, L172, L173, L191, L201, L225, L226, L230, L233, L235, L243, L261 Paper II, L263, L273, L274, L318, L343, L347, L348, L373, L443
>
> his rejection of Clarissa L187
>
> his curse following Clarissa into the next world L307
>
> Clarissa hoping for revocation L307, L308, L309, L320, L360
>
> Clarissa can neither live nor die under Papa's curse L307
>
> Clarissa writing to ask Arabella to have Papa's curse revoked L348, L349

curses, *Harlowe, Mr. James, Sen.* (cont.)
>curse weakening Clarissa in her already weak condition L351
>Clarissa asking Arabella to intercede in revoking the part of the curse relating to the hereafter, as she has already been punished in the here L363
>Papa's curse withdrawn L377, L378, L379

Lovelace, Mr. Robert
>curses of God, threatened by Lord M. L324
>Eve's curse, women made to bear pain L335
>anathematized and cursed by his family L395
>cursing Clarissa L395
>cursing Mrs. Sinclair's house L395, L416
>cursing Sally L416
>cursing Belford L416
>Lovelace having Cain's curse L458, L458n2

curses, Cain's curse
Lovelace, Mr. Robert
>Lovelace having L458, L458n2

curses, Eve's curse
Lovelace, Mr. Robert
>women made to bear L335
>Dolly Welby describing parturient throes L453

customers
Sinclair, Mrs
>Colonel Salter, Mrs. Sinclair drinking arrack punch bought by L493
Smith, Mr. John
>the genteel lady and Andrew, her footman, Lovelace and L416

Cyprus (wine)
Lovelace, Mr. Robert
>as medication L203, L203n1

D

death
Harlowe, Miss Clarissa
>a journey L333, L349, L441
>the end of her painful journey L492
Lovelace, Mr. Robert
>death, a devil, Clarissa's new lover L346
>not fearing death L422
>death not a natural consequence of rape L515

death of Barnes, Betty
Harlowe Family, servants, Barnes, Betty
>pining and consumptive death within a year after Clarissa's CONCLUSION

death of Belford, Mr. John's uncle
Belford, Mr. John, relations, uncle
>his death L247

death of Belton, Mr. Thomas

Lovelace, Mr. Robert, friends, Belton, Mr. Thomas
    cannot live long L399
    his dying confession, death rattle L424
    reported by Belford to Clarissa L426
    compared to Mrs. Sinclair's L499
Lovelace, Mr. Robert, friends, Mowbray, Mr. Richard
    uncouth and unreflecting in Belton's dying moments L419
    comparing Belton's last hours to Clarissa's L473

death of Harlowe, Mrs. Charlotte

Harlowe, Mrs. Charlotte
    survived Clarissa by about two and a half years CONCLUSION

death of Harlowe, Miss Clarissa, *foreshadowed*

Harlowe, Miss Clarissa
    pleased God to have taken me in my last fever L2
    fitter for the next world L10
    beware the ides of March L10
    dagger to the heart L16
    rather die, be buried alive L17
    bear...loss of life L20
    choosing death rather than Solmes L36, L39, L41, L45, L90, L94
    struck dead at the altar L41
    fearing if turned out she will not see home again L59.4
    dreaming she is murdered in a churchyard by Lovelace L84
    they would all be glad I were dead—Indeed, I believe it L85
    her closet nailed up L147
    preferring to be wedded to her shroud rather than any man L149
    a bird dying of grief at being caught and caged L170
    family will not stir to save her life L183
    would prefer death if she know what Lovelace had in mind L222
    Kill me! Kill me! life is a burden, begging Lovelace to kill her L225, L267
    Lovelace dreaming he murders her L246
    looking forward to death L261 Paper X, L261.1
    inquisition will be made for her blood, though she die by her own hand L266
    Some of those who will not stir to protect me living, will move heaven and earth to avenge me dead L266
    Lovelace: if she die tomorrow...rather die married L268
Howe, Miss Anna
    I am fitter for *this* world than you, you for the *next* than me—that's the difference L10
    you are in danger L10

death of Harlowe, Miss Clarissa, *anticipated* see also **health, declining and ending in death**
Harlowe, Miss Clarissa
    heart broken, she will live but a little while L268
    wishing to die, I dare die L274, L276, L281
    Mrs. Sinclair must let her out or bury her in the garden L293
    not expecting to live long, will not recover L293, L333, L359, L395, L399, L418
    when I am gone L307
    country funeral and coffin, a flower bed, mentioned by Lovelace referring to a virgin L313
    oh that I had dropped down dead upon the guilty threshold L314
    death withheld from her, let me slide quietly into my grave L314, L315
    her last scene, last closing scene, I am quite sick of life L318
    will not long be Lovelace's sport or the sport of fortune L333
    corpse, Clarissa as L333

death of Harlowe, Miss Clarissa, *anticipated*, *Harlowe, Miss Clarissa* (cont.)

    starving herself, thoughts of suicide not purposely shortening her own life L333, L359

    death to write Anna and ask for money to pay Mrs. Sinclair L333

    wishing to die at Rowland's L334

    choosing death over Lovelace L339, L359

    her refuge must be death, seeking death L349, L358, L359, L371, L399

    her disappointment causing her death L370

    her death making Lovelace the most miserable man in the world L371

    her fault can be expiated only by death L373

    wishing to die in peace L386, L426

    three to four weeks to live, less than a week, a week, three days, a day or two L389, L426, L440, L461, L462, L467

    Lovelace will marry her in the agonies of death L396

    her exalted head among the stars L396

    tottering on the brink of a grave L409

    how this body clings L436

    her preparation for death, indulging in thoughts of death L441, L451

    date of her death inscribed on her coffin, 10 April L451

    her death compared to Socrates' L451

    describing her gradual death, progressive weakness L464

    forebodings of happiness L465

    her death owing to female willfulness, revenge, stronger than desire for life L472

    her last hours compared to Belton's L473

    will not see tomorrow night L473

    will not live till morning L474

    her sight gone L481

    Oh death, where is thy sting L481, L481n1

death of Harlowe, Miss Clarissa

Belford, Mr. John, messengers, Harry

    reporting disorder at Harlowe Place after news of Clarissa's death L494

Harlowe, Miss Arabella

    hating James afterwards and regretting her cruel treatment of Clarissa CONCLUSION

Harlowe, Mrs. Charlotte

    hourly fits after receiving news of L494.1

    her quiet cost her her daughter L503

    unable to view the body L503

Harlowe, Miss Clarissa

    dead L477

    death scene L481

    time of death, 40 minutes after six o'clock in the afternoon L481, L486.2

    death so lovely L486

    year of her death not given in her will L507, L507fn

    date of death Sept. 7th L511

    compared to that of Belton, Tomlinson, and Mrs. Sinclair L514

Harlowe, Miss Clarissa, nurses, Shelburne, Ann

    attending Clarissa after her death L457

Harlowe, Mr. James, Jun.

    to blame for the family's loss of Clarissa L355, L500

Harlowe, Mr. James, Sen.

    receiving news of L494.1

    unable to view the body L503

Harlowe Family

    receiving news of by Morden's letter to James L494

    gathered to grieve and await the hearse L500

death of Harlowe, Miss Clarissa (cont.)

Hickman, Mr. Charles
    receiving news of L494
Howe, Miss Anna
    fainting on news of L494
    viewing the corpse at Harlowe Place L501, L502
    wanting a lock of Clarissa's hair L502
Howe, Mrs. Annabella
    receiving news of L494
Lord M., relations, half-sisters
    indisposed at Clarissa's death L510
Lovelace, Mr. Robert
    Belford sending the news in a coded message, advising him to go to Paris L449, L479
    throwing his hat and wig off, sitting grinning like a man in straw L480, L480n2
Lovelace, Mr. Robert, contrivances of Lovelace, specifically, contrivance of Captain Tomlinson and Uncle
  Harlowe's birthday, Tomlinson, Captain Antony
    penitent, acknowledging his guilt L514, L521
Lovelace, Mr. Robert, friends, Tourville, Mr. James
    telling Lovelace that Clarissa is very ill L439
    going with Mowbray to Lovelace to keep him from harming himself on hearing of Clarissa's death L477
    with Lovelace after Clarissa's death L482
Morden, Colonel William
    attending Clarissa's hearse to Harlowe Place L487, L495, L500
    taking a ringlet of Clarissa's hair for a locket L495
Norton, Mrs. Judith
    finding Clarissa dead L487
    taking four ringlets of Clarissa's hair L495
    accompanying the hearse to Harlowe Place L500, L503
Sinclair, Mrs.
    acknowledging her guilt in Clarissa's death L521, L535
Sinclair, Mrs., whores, Martin, Sarah (Sally)
    visiting Smith's to find Belford and finding Clarissa dead L493
Smith, Mr. John, lodgers, Lovick, Mrs.
    caring for Clarissa's body after her death L457

death of Harlowe, Miss Clarissa, avenged see also **duel between Morden and Lovelace**
Belford, Mr. John
    were he Clarissa's brother L258
    wishing to L334
Harlowe, Miss Clarissa
    Belford would avenge L258
    Some of those who will not stir to protect me living, will move heaven and earth to avenge me dead L266
    disclaiming vengeance L276
    the law, her resource and refuge L281
    appealing to God to avenge her wrongs L307
    Lovelace to feel the vengeance of her friends L336
    fearing Morden will avenge her L409, L433, L475, L517
    Morden considering vengeance L498
    avenged by Lovelace's conscience L518
    James will avenge Clarissa if Morden does not L519
    finally avenged by Morden L537
Harlowe, Mr. James, Jun.
    Clarissa urged to prosecute Lovelace to prevent mischief between James and Lovelace L427
    Clarissa asking James not to avenge her L490
    Lovelace deserving vengeance L494.1

death of Harlowe, Miss Clarissa, avenged, *Harlowe, Mr. James, Jun.* (cont.)
>will avenge Clarissa if Morden does not L519
>Lovelace may answer James's challenge L526
>to call Lovelace to account L533
>Belford to inform James of Lovelace's return in March to England L534

Lovelace, Mr. Robert
>insolence to avenge Clarissa on Lovelace L535

Morden, Colonel William
>may avenge Clarissa L274, L456, L498, L517, L519
>will see justice done Clarissa's person L319, L427
>Clarissa fearing Morden will try to avenge her L409
>Lovelace dreaming he is threatened by Morden L417, L421
>Clarissa urged to prosecute to prevent mischief between Morden and Lovelace L427
>cutting the throat of any young fellow who made free with any sister of his L442
>having no title to avenge Clarissa L474
>will not pursue vengeance L528
>his threats of vengeance reported by Leman to Lovelace L532
>Clarissa avenged L537

death of Harlowe, Miss Clarissa, causes
Harlowe, Miss Clarissa
>that wasting grief will soon put a period to her days L222
>diagnosed with grief L338, L342
>heart-broken L339, L341
>Clarissa a love case, her disorder in her head L340
>her ill health caused by her arrest and her family's implacableness L347, L364
>death from grief L467

death of Harlowe, Mr. James, Sen.
Harlowe, Mr. James, Sen.
>survived Clarissa by about three years CONCLUSION

death of Hickman, Mr. Charles's relations
Hickman, Mr. Charles, relations
>his elder brother died L196
>his mother-in-law [stepmother] lately dead L459

death of Horton, Mary
Sinclair, Mrs., whores, Horton, Mary (Polly)
>died by a violent cold CONCLUSION

death of Howe, Mrs. Annabella's relations
Howe, Mrs. Annabella, relations, Larkin, Mrs.
>died L65

death of Lewin, Dr. Arthur
Harlowe Family, clergymen, Lewin, Dr. Arthur
>dying soon after reading Clarissa's letter L430
>his death L503

death of Lord M.
Lord M.
>wishing to see Lovelace before he dies L278
>near death L327
>surviving Lovelace by three years CONCLUSION

death of Lord M. (cont.)

Lovelace, Mr. Robert

> his disappointment at Lord M.'s recovery L294, L321, L341
> hoping Lord M. would have died by now L321
> Lovelace hoping his visit will not extend Lord M.'s life L341

death of Lovelace, Mr. Robert, *foreshadowed*

Lovelace, Mr. Robert

> if Lovelace were to be fairly hanged L132
> riddance of him by flight or the gallows L196
> dreaming of bringing about his own destruction L246
> you shall be mine, or my life shall be the forfeit L266
> singing to himself the thirtieth of January strain and the dead psalm melody L266, L266n2
> Belford cutting the throat of Clarissa's destroyer, cutting Lovelace's throat L334, L387
> deserving an infamous death L358
> thou [Lovelace] must die, as well as Belton L419
> his death not honoring Clarissa's memory L448
> facing his own death with heavy reflection L452

death of Lovelace, Mr. Robert

Lovelace, Mr. Robert

> falling in a duel with Morden, dying next day L537
> his composure upon his death bed L537
> refusing Sacraments in the Catholic way L537

death of Martin, Sarah

Sinclair, Mrs., whores, Martin, Sarah (Sally)

> died of a fever and surfeit CONCLUSION

death of Norton, Mrs. Judith

Norton, Mrs. Judith

> will not live long L520

death of Norton, Mrs. Judith's husband

Norton, Mrs. Judith, family, husband

> his death L301

death of Norton, Mrs. Judith's parents

Norton, Mrs. Judith, family, parents

> their deaths L301

death of Sinclair, Mrs.

Sinclair, Mrs.

> howling at the prospect of death L499
> died Thursday Sept. 21 L499
> her death reported to Lovelace by Belford L514

death of Summers, Will

Lovelace, Mr. Robert, servants, Summers, Will

> untimely death CONCLUSION

death of Tomlinson, Captain Antony

Lovelace, Mr. Robert, contrivances of Lovelace, specifically, contrivance of Captain Tomlinson and Uncle Harlowe's birthday, Tomlinson, Captain Antony

> death in Maidstone Gaol L514, L515

death of Wykes, Dorcas

Sinclair, Mrs., whores, Wykes, Dorcas
    untimely death CONCLUSION

debts

Harlowe, Mr. James, Jun.
    paying off Uncle Hervey's debt L47
Lovelace, Mr. Robert
    mentioned L3
    clear of debt L88
    his debts abroad L186

despair

Harlowe, Miss Clarissa
    her only fault L342

devils see also **Beelzebub; Moloch-deity; Satan**

Belford, Mr. John
    James 2:19, quoted on L222
    caitiff, Belford as L335, L370, L516
Harlowe, Miss Clarissa
    her honor inviolate in spite of men and devils L181
Howe, Miss Anna
    Anna as L127, L239
    a devilish rake at heart L198
    had she been a man, would have sworn, cursed, committed rape, and played the devil L236
Lord M.
    having a devil under his roof L349
Lovelace, Mr. Robert
    Lovelace as L68, L93, L119, L169, L181, L183, L189, L202, L227, L229, L229.1, L233, L235, L252.1,
    L258, L266, L277, L294, L305
        the devil in me L138
        acting the part of the grand tempter L157.1
        devil to rejoice in Clarissa's fall L171
        a devil in his contrivances L223
        discovering his [cloven] foot L252.1, L252.1n1
        the devil himself L316
        a devil, a damned devil L324
        devil and his cloven feet L326
        a true devil L339
        Lord M. having a devil under his roof L349
        the man is a devil—this man is indeed a devil L367
        in whatever shape he chose to appear L370
        calling himself a devil L470
    half a score of devils L154
    devil take me L167, L395
    devil crept out of his heart L199
    women as L210
    God sends meat, the devil cooks L211
    ipecacuanha, a disagreeable medicine that would poison the devil L211
    the devil in Milton's *Paradise Lost* L233, L233n1
    oh devil of youth, and devil of intrigue L268
    devil, an angler baiting fish L270
    the devil not quite so black as he is painted L326
    Lovelace having a face that would deceive the devil L366

devils, *Lovelace, Mr. Robert* (cont.)
    the devil's in Clarissa L395
    devil is black L395
    the devil always baits with a pretty wench L415
    no devil do I fear, but one in your shape L467
    the devil and the time of life are against thee L513
    the devil knows his own interest L516
Lovelace, Mr. Robert, friends, Belton, Mr. Thomas, family, Thomasine
    a very devil L193
Lovelace, Mr. Robert, friends, Miles
    a caitiff, seducing the farmer's daughter L496
Sinclair, Mrs.
    a devil L228, L330
    her hellborn nymphs L511
Sinclair, Mrs., whores, Martin, Sarah (Sally)
    a devil L157.1, L209, L333

dialogue format see also **narration**; **stage directions**
Howe, Miss Anna
    reporting a scene in L197
Lovelace, Mr. Robert
    reporting scenes in L235, L243, L251, L442

diary see **Memorandum book**

dinner see **meals, dinner**

disguises
Harlowe, Miss Clarissa
    asking Anna to procure, to escape Harlowe Place L82
    as Mabel, to escape Mrs. Sinclair's L293, L294
    wearing an ordinary gown by way of disguise L320
Lovelace, Mr. Robert
    disguised, will meet Clarissa for an interview L61, L62
    at the inn as a military man, recently fought a duel in town L70
    around Harlowe Place L86
    as Clarissa's brother at the inn L98, L103
    would change his dress like Clodius to seduce a woman L106, L106n1
    offering to accompany Clarissa in disguise L124
    disguised in a great-coat as he recaptures Clarissa at Hampstead L232
    posing as a lawyer at Mrs. Moore's in Hampstead L233
    Waltham disguises L243
    his vile disguises L243
    will disguise himself as a parson to see Clarissa, a contrivance L370
    claiming to be a Justice of the Peace to search Smith's for Clarissa L416
Lovelace, Mr. Robert, servants, Summers, Will
    in a black wig watching for Clarissa at Moore's, Smith's L231.1, L416

divine qualities see also **angel**; **example**; **fall**; **light**; **sacrifice**; **suffering**; **trials**; **virgin**
Harlowe, Miss Clarissa
    divine L31, L110, L201, L216, L286, L333, L348, L419
        divine lady L473, L487, L495
    goddess L31, L99, L105, L157.1, L158.1, L175, L191, L220, L243, L252
    nature to be servant to both Betty and Arabella L53
    her exalted head...among the stars L396

divine qualities, *Harlowe, Miss Clarissa* (cont.)

    beatifical spirit L440

    companionship with saints and angels L440

    as near perfection an any creature can be L459

dowries

Harlowe, Mrs. Charlotte

    her large dowry, compared to Clarissa's L41.1

Harlowe, Miss Clarissa

    Lovelace's fortune sufficient L88

    Lovelace resigning her fortune, if she die issueless L383

dreams

Belford, Mr. John

    after seeing Clarissa's coffin L451

Harlowe, Miss Clarissa

    murdered in a churchyard by Lovelace L84

    a reverie, a waking dream L243

Lovelace, Mr. Robert

    first dream, guilty of murdering Clarissa L246

    second dream, Clarissa rescued by a lady, with Dorcas's help; the lady turns into Mother H., and into a young man, Lovelace; and that he fathered a boy by Clarissa, a girl by Anna, the two marrying L271

    writing a book about dreams, *Lovelace's Reveries* L272

    dream, his family all in black intercede for him; Clarissa forgives him; Morden threatens him; Clarissa ascends into Heaven; and he, covered with Lord M.'s great black mantle, falls through a hole L417

        Lovelace's interpretation L421

drink see also **food**; **meals**

Harlowe, Miss Clarissa

    surprised by wine L311

    given table-beer, malt liquor L314

    the milk was London milk L314

Lord M.

    lemonade causing gout in his stomach L275

Lovelace, Mr. Robert

    malmsey, Cyprus [wines] as medicine L203, L203n1

    directing a bottle of sherry to be added L228

    Barbados, having a dram of L255

    wine, an opiate L261

    a dram or two to the fellows in the mob, when Clarissa shouts for help L264

    burgundy and champagne for Morden, Lovelace and Lord M. L442

Lovelace, Mr. Robert, friends, Mowbray, Mr. Richard

    asking for claret L419

Sinclair, Mrs.

    drinking arrack punch, bought by Colonel Salter L493

Sinclair, Mrs., whores, Wykes, Dorcas

    preparing tea, offering Clarissa food and drink L201, L261.1

drops see **medications**

drugs see **medications**

duel between James and Lovelace

Harlowe, Mr. Antony

    his poor opinion of Lovelace, following the duel L1

duel between James and Lovelace (cont.)

Harlowe, Mrs. Charlotte

> fearful of Lovelace's vengeful nature following L4, L5

Harlowe, Mr. James, Jun.

> reported L1, L2
>
> wound to James's arm L1, L2, L4
>
> cause of family dissention L2
>
> aborted duel preceding main duel L4
>
> complete report and background L4
>
> occurring at Mr. Edward Symmes's home L4
>
> James as aggressor L4, L42
>
> destroying possibility of an alliance with Lovelace L13
>
> motivating revenge on Clarissa L15
>
> his claim that he was defending Clarissa L42.1

Harlowe Family

> causing contentions L1, L5
>
> ill treatment of Lovelace following duel L4

Howe, Miss Anna

> fearing fallout after L1
>
> visited by Mr. Diggs, she inquires about the duel L1

Howe, Mrs. Annabella

> fearing Lovelace's resentments against the Harlowes L1
>
> opinion on L27

Lord M.

> supporting Lovelace L6
>
> fearing Lovelace for the ill usage received from Harlowes L143

Lovelace, Mr. Robert

> mentioned L1, L2, L55
>
> reported, with background L4
>
> aborted L4
>
> visit to Harlowe Place after the duel L4
>
> vowing revenge for ill treatment following L4
>
> aftermath, has borne their insults with bitterness L6, L109
>
> summary up to duel L13

duel between Morden and Lovelace see also **death of Harlowe, Miss Clarissa, avenged**

Lovelace, Mr. Robert

> not going out of his way to avoid Morden L534
>
> answering Morden's gentleman's challenge L534
>
> preparations L536
>
> Lovelace drawing first blood L537
>
> his death next day L537

Morden, Colonel William

> Lovelace may answer his challenge L526
>
> calling Lovelace to account L535
>
> accepting Lovelace's offer to accept a challenge L535.1
>
> his meeting with Lovelace to prepare L536
>
> his weapon of choice, a single rapier L536
>
> fatally wounding Lovelace L537

duels, other

Lovelace, Mr. Robert

> feigned, at the inn L70
>
> left arm wounded seriously in a duel L116
>
> mentioned L119

duty

Harlowe, Miss Clarissa

      to her grandfather L4

      to Papa L36

      example of failure to do one's duty L112

      dutiful L187, L367

      a breach of her duty L307

E

Eaton's styptic

Lovelace, Mr. Robert

      a balsamic medicine to cure effects of ipecacuanha L209, L211

eavesdropping

Harlowe, Miss Clarissa

      overhearing her siblings laughing L25, L53

      kneeling at Papa's closed door L78

      hiding from the family in the garden behind the yew hedge L80

      overhearing her siblings conspiring L83

      overhearing a contrived conversation at Mrs. Sinclair's L195, L196

Lovelace, Mr. Robert

      a thief and an eavesdropper L57

      on Clarissa, Mrs. Moore and Miss Rawlins L235

      listeners seldom hear good of themselves L235

      on Clarissa and Tomlinson L243, L245

education see also **accomplishments**

Belford, Mr. John

      well read in classical authors L161

      pride of learning L364

      his knowledge of law L379

Harlowe, Miss Clarissa

      book-learned and a scribbler L405

Harlowe, Mr. James, Jun.

      college L53.1, L63

      liberal education L91

      young gentleman of both learning and parts L91

Hickman, Mr. Charles

      designed for the law, chambers in Lincoln's Inn L196

Lovelace, Mr. Robert

      reputation as a student L4, L12

      quoting poetry L31

      fondness for Latin and English classics L34

      liberal education L91

      skill in learned and modern languages L161

      a man of parts and learning, of talents and learning L173.1, L190

      esteemed in Florence and Rome L173.1

      a fault in his education, he does good only to atone for bad L217.2

      pride of learning L364

education (cont.)

Lovelace, Mr. Robert, contrivances of Lovelace, specifically, contrivance of Captain Tomlinson and Uncle
    Harlowe's birthday, Tomlinson, Captain Antony
        expelled from Dublin University L217

Lovelace, Mr. Robert, friends, Belton, Mr. Thomas
        university L161

Lovelace, Mr. Robert, servants, Summers, Will
        could do anything but write and spell L117

Sinclair, Mrs., whores, Horton, Mary (Polly)
        well educated, has read L277

Sinclair, Mrs., whores, Martin, Sarah (Sally)
        well educated, has read L277
        thinking herself as well descended and educated as Clarissa L333

Sinclair, Mrs., whores, Wykes, Dorcas
        illiterate wench L154

elocution

Lovelace, Mr. Robert
        Lovelace's talent for L206

encroacher

Lovelace, Mr. Robert
        Lovelace as L69, L85, L94, L98, L101, L116, L155, L173, L220, L229.1
        love, an encroacher L220

entangled

Harlowe, Miss Clarissa
        how am I entangled L14
        more and more entangled L22
        so entangled, as Lovelace has entangled her L189
        so dreadfully entangled L308

Lovelace, Mr. Robert
        spider and fly analogy, entangling young girls L106
        she must yield, entangled as she is L191
        this cursed aversion to wedlock how it has entangled me L227
        entangled in his own inventions L275, L276, L285

escapes see also **contrivances of Lovelace**, *Lovelace, Mr. Robert*, specifically, contrivance of the escape

Harlowe, Miss Clarissa
        attempted
            desperate to leave Mrs. Sinclair's for Mrs. Leeson's or Hampstead L256
            trying to escape Mrs. Sinclair's, shouting to passers-by L262, L264, L276
            Lovelace stopping her, bruising her hands and arms L266, L267
            Clarissa wishing to return to Mrs. Moore's at Hampstead L277, L278
        successful
            from Harlowe Place L92
            from Mrs. Sinclair's to Hampstead L228, L230
            from Mrs. Sinclair's to Smith's L291, L293

escutcheons

Harlowe, Miss Clarissa
        her hearse not adorned by L500

Lovelace, Mr. Robert
        blot in my escutcheon L106

estates see also **inheritances**; **trustees**
Belford, Mr. John
    paternal estate upwards of £1000 a year L444
Harlowe, Mr. Antony
    his very great fortune L182, L183, L197.1
Harlowe, Miss Clarissa
    arrears
        considerable sums accrued since Grandfather's death L202, L487
        Lovelace giving her all arrears in her father's hands for Mrs. Norton L207
        Clarissa to receive L458
        Morden giving to Belford L501
        bequeathed Morden L507
    bequeathing, her power to bequeath her estate L123, L400
    cause of all her misfortunes L230
    control of, withheld by family
        in Papa's power, her steward L2, L6, L10, L13, L19, L42, L376
        unless she marry Solmes L14, L20, L44
        ought to be in possession of thousands L376
        her fortune and estate withheld by her family L406, L437
        when she is twenty-one, the family would send her her estate L429
    control of, Clarissa resuming
        advised by Anna L15, L27, L49, L52, L100, L183
        litigating with her father may encourage Lovelace L28
        assistance available from Lovelace's family L49
        lacking support within her own family L52, L55
        advised by Lovelace L61, L142
        Morden may support L73
        advised by Dolly L78
        considered by Clarissa L80
        will not demand possession of L142
        asking Lovelace to avoid litigation with Papa L202
        in Lovelace's dream L271
        will not live to take possession of her independence L309
        Morden to put Clarissa into possession of her estate L455, L474
    disposition of, should she marry or die
        in settlements with Solmes, her estate to remain in family L13, L17
        if she should never marry, would go to James L56
        Clarissa's power to bequeath her estate L123, L400
        once married to Lovelace, her estate is his right L164
        inquired into by Lovelace's family in preparation for marriage L325
        not wanting Lovelace to have her estate L379
    forfeiting
        Clarissa offering to forfeit her inheritance L42, L60.2
        giving up her estate and Solmes and ridding herself of Lovelace L60
        giving up her grandfather's bequest to appease her brother L174
        sacrifice of her estate not advised by Anna L177
        offering to defer to Papa if he will consider reconciliation L179
    jewels *see also* **jewels**; **rings**
        diamond necklace, solitaire, buckles from Sir Josias Brookland, proceeds of sale to estate L507
        her grandmother's jewels, proceeds of sale, to Poor's Fund, or estate, or Papa L507
    real estate
        after her flight, requesting to retire to L101, L102
        wishing to live upon her estate rather than marry Lovelace L248
        family expecting Clarissa to live at her grandfather's house L459
        bequeathed Papa L507

estates, *Harlowe, Miss Clarissa* (cont.)
    value of
        her independent fortune L253
        her fortune the finest in the county L442
Harlowe, Miss Clarissa, suitors to Harlowe, Miss Clarissa, Solmes, Mr. Roger
    upstart man, not born to immense riches L13
    his fortunes affected by marriage to Clarissa L13, L17, L19, L27
    disinheriting his own family L16, L27
Harlowe, Mr. James, Jun.
    large estates in Scotland L2
    his northern estates L301
Harlowe, Mr. James, Sen
    rich L109
    steward of Clarissa's estate L376
Harlowe, Mr. John
    trustee of Clarissa's estate L27, L55, L214, L406
Harlowe Family
    Harlowe Place sprung up from a dunghill within every elderly person's memory L34
    their *acquired* fortune L109
    too rich L455
Harlowe Family, relations, Harlowe, Grandfather
    mentioned L157
    less than half the total left to Clarissa L42
    considerable sums arising from his estate since his death L202
    inquired into by Lovelace's family in preparation for marriage L325
    estate he left to Clarissa mentioned L375
Howe, Miss Anna
    advising Clarissa to resume her estate L15, L27, L37, L47, L49, L52, L100, L142, L177, L183
Howe, Mrs. Annabella
    her great estate L197.1
Lord M.
    to which Lovelace's mother had better pretensions L88
    seat in Hertfordshire, the Lawn L88, L149
    seat in Lancashire L88
    seat in Berkshire, M. Hall L98
    his three seats L121
    £8000 a year L275
Lord M., relations, half-sisters, Lawrance, Lady Betty
    will assist Clarissa in resuming hers L49
Lord M., relations, nieces, Montague, Miss Charlotte
    her family and fortune above Belford L516
Lovelace, Mr. Robert
    Clarissa's
        Lovelace agreeing to Clarissa's giving up her estate, if she will be his L36
        her estate not an issue in marriage to Lovelace L88
        Lovelace's right to, married to Clarissa L164, L379
        his lack of interest in L174.3
    Lovelace's
        Arabella's information L2
        report of L4
        two thousand pounds *per annum*, his own estate L88, L186
        unencumbered, no part of ever mortgaged, clear L88, L186, L265
        one thousand pounds *per annum* from Lord M., upon his nuptials L88
        fortune squandered L173.1
        his considerable fortune and alliances L183

estates, *Lovelace, Mr. Robert*, Lovelace's (cont.)
    upon his nuptials, receiving Lord M.'s property in Lancashire or the Lawn L186
    his claim to property in Lancashire better than Lord M.'s L186
    ought to live on two thousand pounds a year L206
    willing to sacrifice his whole estate for Clarissa's favor L207
    estates made over to him on his nuptials L220
    £8000 a year slipping through his fingers L294
Lovelace, Mr. Robert, friends, Belton, Mr. Thomas
  his paternal estate in Kent mortgaged and soon to be foreclosed L192
  broken fortunes, in ruin L344, L347
  fleeced by a woman L347
  house and remains of his fortune saved by Belford L399
  Belford putting Belton's sister into possession of Belton's house, reinstating Belton to his own house,
    occupied by Thomasine L344, L385
  Belford consulting his attorney upon Belton's affairs L365
Morden, Colonel William
  Clarissa's estate
    trustee for Clarissa's estate L27, L32.3, L87, L173, L248, L253, L455
    assisting Clarissa in resuming her estate L36
    helping Clarissa pursue life on her own estate without litigation L248
    to put Clarissa into possession of her estate L253, L455
    will see justice done Clarissa's estate L319
  Morden's estate
    his own ample fortune L455
    residing upon his paternal estate in Kent L526

eulogy for Clarissa
Harlowe, Miss Clarissa
  delivered by Mr. Melvill L501, L504
  by Anna L529
Harlowe Family, clergymen, Brand, Mr. Elias
  not delivering L501

euthanasia
Lovelace, Mr. Robert
  laudanum used in L191

example see also **angel; divine qualities; fall; light; sacrifice; suffering; trials; virgin**
Harlowe, Miss Clarissa
  noted as L1, L39, L75, L110, L116, L120, L177, L246, L253, L260, L372, L456, L459, L508, L519
  a pattern for the rest L37, L296
  example of failure to do one's duty L112
  a warning to others L120, L317, L490
  punished for example-sake L301
  an exemplary life L308
  in imitation of the sublimest exemplar L359
  condescentions...or example's sake L467
Howe, Miss Anna
  Anna as L38

executors see also **bequests of...; wills**
Belford, Mr. John
  his uncle's executor
    two executorships upon him at present L379
    his affairs in Watford L383

executors, *Belford, Mr. John* (cont.)

    Clarissa's executor L379, L389, L391, L396, L404, L409, L410, L454, L486.1

        unlocking the drawer holding Clarissa's will and parcel of letters sealed with three black seals L486

        reading Clarissa's will with Morden L486

        Morden giving him proceeds of Grandfather's estate since his death L504

        beginning to execute the will now that the funeral is over L505

        to perform every article within two months time L507

        giving Lovelace a copy of Clarissa's will L527

    Belton's executor L426

    having three executorships L507

    Morden's co-executor with Hickman L528

    Lovelace's executor L535

Harlowe, Miss Clarissa

    asking Belford to be her executor L379, L389, L391, L409

    Belford her executor instead of Morden L413

    advised by Mrs. Norton to change her executor to Morden L459

    Morden's intended heir and executrix L459

    no time for joining Morden as co-executor L475

Hickman, Mr. Charles

    Morden's co-executor with Belford L528

    having a copy of Morden's will L528

Howe, Mrs. Annabella, relations, Larkin, Mrs.

    Mrs. Howe her executrix L65

Lovelace, Mr. Robert

    asking Belford to be his executor L535

Lovelace, Mr. Robert, friends, Belton, Mr. Thomas

    Belford, his executor L426

Morden, Colonel William

    Belford's executor L528

    Clarissa's

        considered as L413, L459

        no time for joining Morden as co-executor L475

        reading Clarissa's will with Belford L486

        intending to enforce Belford's executorship L495

        assisting Belford in executing Clarissa's will L507, L520

    Morden's, Clarissa to be Morden's heir and executrix L459

exile

Howe, Miss Anna, suitors to Howe, Miss Anna, Colmar, Sir George

    obliged to quit the kingdom L198

    Anna following him into exile, but for Clarissa L198

Lovelace, Mr. Robert

    his great stake in his country L114

    an exile, transported for life L35, L119

    fly his country L132

    may leave this plaguy island and live abroad L233

    will never see England again if Clarissa reject him L383

    self-imposed exile L395

expiate

Belford, Mr. John

    expiate for thy abominable vileness to her L336

Harlowe, Miss Clarissa

    her fault expiated only by death L373

expiate (cont.)

Lovelace, Mr. Robert
>what will expiate for his vileness L336
>loss of life and soul a dreadful expiation L518
>let this expiate L537

Lovelace, Mr. Robert, friends, Belton, Mr. Thomas
>may his tortures and repentance expiate L424

eye-beams

Harlowe, Miss Clarissa
>darting through Tomlinson L243

eye-strings

Lovelace, Mr. Robert
>intimidating Clarissa L281

F

fainting see **illnesses**

fall

Belford, Mr. John
>falling from his horse L261

Harlowe, Miss Clarissa see also **angel**; **divine qualities**; **example**; **light**; **sacrifice**; **suffering**; **trials**; **virgin**
>her fall L118, L144, L169, L171, L324, L359, L399, L429
>her fall will be her glory L246
>fallen angel L78, L357
>Anna's tears embalming a fallen blossom L473.2

family see also **relations**

Belford, Mr. John
>Montague, Miss Charlotte, wife CONCLUSION
>son CONCLUSION

Harlowe, Mr. Antony
>hopes for children L197.1

Harlowe, Miss Clarissa
>marriage to Lovelace bringing a curse on her children L359

Harlowe Family, clergymen, Lewin, Dr. Arthur
>daughter L427, L507

Hervey, Mrs. Dorothy
>Uncle Hervey, husband
>>requesting Lovelace to instruct a young man in the grand tour L3
>>Clarissa writing down Lovelace's instructions, beginning their correspondence L3
>>supporting the Solmes plan L17
>>James paying off Uncle Hervey's debt L47
>>would have been sympathetic to Clarissa L432
>>comforting Papa L503
>Hervey, Miss Dolly, daughter
>>forbidden to see Clarissa L41
>>her fondness for Clarissa L78, L81, L90.1
>>advising Clarissa to marry Lovelace and resume her estate L78
>>made to request Clarissa's keys L78

family, *Hervey, Mrs. Dorothy*, Hervey, Miss Dolly (cont.)

        reporting family opinion to Clarissa L78

        sent to take Clarissa's writing materials away L79

        slipping Clarissa a secret letter L90

        her signature: Dorothy L90

        suffering for her attachment to Clarissa L91

        wanting to visit Clarissa L432

        her happiness when Clarissa escaped from Harlowe Place L432

        Clarissa's cousin L433

        bequeathed harpsichord, chamber-organ, music books, head-dress, ruffles, twenty-five guineas for a
           ring L507

        Morden presenting her with Clarissa's jewels L520

Hickman, Mr. Charles

    Charles, son CONCLUSION

    Clarissa, daughter CONCLUSION

    Howe, Miss Anna, wife CONCLUSION

Howe, Miss Anna

    Charles, son CONCLUSION

    Clarissa, daughter L252.1, CONCLUSION

    Hickman, Mr. Charles, husband CONCLUSION

    Howe, Mr., her papa

        like her papa L58, L229.1, L358

        mentioned L81, L183, L198

        her poor papa, a violent spirit L100, L197.2

        loving her father L132

        a gentleman L133

        talking as loud as her mamma L150

Howe, Mrs. Annabella

    Howe, Mr., her husband L133

        Mrs. Howe a widow for ten years L74, L197, L197.2

        her father choosing her husband L81

        a gentleman L133

        talking loud L150

    Howe, Miss Anna, her only child L197.1

Lord M.

    his deceased wife L206

    his sister Lovelace L324

Lord M., housekeepers, Greme, Mrs., relations, Sorlings, Mrs.

    widow L104, L128, L149, L153

    two grown sons and two younger daughters L98

    Betty, Mrs., her elder daughter L105

        and Will L118

        and Lord M.'s chaplain L118

        attending Clarissa L118, L125, L130

        to accompany Clarissa to London L130, L149, L152, L154

        accompanying Clarissa as far as Barnet L155

        receiving a gift from Lovelace L155

Lord M., relations, half-sisters

    daughters of an earl, dowagers L36, L323

Lord M., relations, half-sisters, Sadleir, Lady Sarah

    Betsey, her only child, recently deceased L36, L245, L256, L325, L327

Lord M., relations, nieces, Montague, Miss Charlotte

    Belford, Mr. John, husband CONCLUSION

    a son CONCLUSION

    sister of Patty L88

family, *Lord M.*, relations, nieces, Montague, Miss Charlotte (cont.)
  her family and fortune above Belford L516
Lord M., relations, nieces, Montague, Miss Patty
  sister of Charlotte L88
Lovelace, Mr. Robert
  an only child L3, L142
  fathering an illegitimate child by Miss Betterton, a son L139, L140
  wanting Clarissa to have his child L371
Lovelace, Mr. Robert, contrivances of Lovelace, specifically, contrivance of sparing Rosebud, Rosebud
  father and grandmother L34, L70, L71
  father proprietor at the White Hart Inn L34
Lovelace, Mr. Robert, contrivances of Lovelace, specifically, contrivance of Captain Tomlinson and Uncle
  Harlowe's birthday, Tomlinson, Captain Antony
  with his wife and five children living on £800 a year L216
  daughters as old as Clarissa L243, L289
Lovelace, Mr. Robert, friends, Belton, Mr. Thomas
  Thomasine, passing as Belton's wife L192
    character
      pretending to dote on him, embezzling his money L192
      a very devil, low-bred L193
      having Belton's house, put out of his house L344, L399
      her infidelity, suspicious eye L347
      rapacious woman, accursed deceiver, ungrateful L419
    family
      Tom and Hal, sons L192
        supposed by Belton to be his L192
        their father passing as Thomasine's cousin L344
        muscular and big-boned L347
        her cubs L399
      father, innkeeper at Dorking L192
      lover, her father's hostler L192
        thrown down the stairs by Belford L399
    funeral of Belton, not showing grief L440
    mourning, and widow's weeds L399
    physical appearance, not a delicate frame L347
Lovelace, Mr. Robert, friends, Doleman, Mr. Tom
  married man, married to a woman of family L126, L229.1
Moore, Mrs.
  the widow Moore L232
Norton, Mrs. Judith
  Tommy, her son L127, L301
    giving her son money to start a business L207
    Clarissa calling him her foster brother L300, L307, L362
    born within a few days of Clarissa L301
    born after his father's death L301
    nursing both her son and Clarissa L301
    good to Mrs. Norton L301
    illnesses
      a feverish disorder, violent fever L301, L307, L308
      at death's door L361
      recovering L374, L377, L381, L382
    a fine youth L494
    happily settled CONCLUSION
  husband, her very unkind husband, his death L301
  parents, their deaths L301

family, *Norton, Mrs. Judith* (cont.)
>father
>>her reverend father's wisdom L69, L82
>>a clergyman L301
>>sayings, the satirist has a natural spleen to gratify L308
>>a sound divine and a fine scholar L381

Sinclair, Mrs.
>of Highland extraction L131
>widow, gentlewoman L154, L155, L158.1, L233, L256, L261.1
>a woman of family L277
>husband
>>an officer of the guards, Colonel Sinclair, a Scot L130.1, L131, L233
>>gentleman L155
>>lieutenant-colonel L158.1
>>man of honor L261.1

Smith, Mr. John
>Smith, Mrs., his wife
>>shopkeeper L320
>>matron-like woman, plain-hearted and prudent L320
>>helping Belford remove Clarissa's clothes from Mrs. Sinclair's L336
>>not knowing whether Clarissa is married L336
>>attending Clarissa L348, L349
>>inviting Clarissa and Belford to dine with her on her wedding day L349
>>her compassion L349
>>childless L416
>>bequest of Clarissa, linen and laces, twenty guineas L507

family alliances
Harlowe Family
>background L13
>family arguing L78
>coldness between Morden and Harlowe Family L431
>Morden's conflict with James about treatment of Clarissa L459

father's house see also **contrivances of Clarissa**
Harlowe, Miss Clarissa
>only extremity would make her abandon her father's house L57
>her decision not to leave her father's house L68
>as if I left my father's house L73
>the disgrace...of...quitting my father's house L80
>quitting her father's house L81
>all punctilio is at an end the moment you are out of your father's house L87, L89, L90
>*Numbers* 30:16, being yet...in her father's house L89
>oh that I were again in my father's house L94
>wishing to be still in her father's house L98
>driven out of her father's house L111
>leaving her father's house L128
>made to fly her father's house L142
>*Job* 29:2–6, in my father's house L359, L359n1
>April 10, the date she left her father's house, inscribed on her coffin L451

Howe, Miss Anna
>all punctilio is at an end the moment you are out of your father's house L87, L89, L90

Lovelace, Mr. Robert
>her cruel and gloomy father's house L98
>could I once get her out of her father's house L99

fearing Clarissa
Lovelace, Mr. Robert
> never knowing fear till he met Clarissa and had her in his power L287

fearing Lovelace
Harlowe, Mr. Antony
> double-servanted and double-armed against Lovelace L31
Harlowe, Mrs. Charlotte
> fearful of Lovelace's vengeful nature following the duel L4, L5
> fearing Lovelace's reaction to Solmes's suit L25.2
Harlowe, Miss Clarissa
> fearing his violent temper L3, L64
> I behold him now with fear L98
> fearing Lovelace L204
Harlowe, Mr. John
> double-servanted and double-armed against Lovelace L31
Harlowe Family
> fearing Lovelace L14
> fearing both Lovelace and James L437
Hervey, Mrs. Dorothy
> cautioning Clarissa about his vengefulness L44
Howe, Miss Anna
> fearing fallout after the duel L1
Lord M.
> fearing Lovelace for the ill usage received from the Harlowes after the duel L143
Sinclair, Mrs., whores
> hiding from Lovelace's rage after Clarissa escapes Mrs. Sinclair's, blubbering L228, L292
Smith, Mr. John, bodice-makers, Joseph
> threatened by Lovelace L416

fires see also **contrivances of Lovelace**, *Lovelace, Mr. Robert*, specifically, contrivance of the fire
Lovelace, Mr. Robert
> wanting to set fire to Mrs. Sinclair's house L396, L511
Sinclair, Mrs., servants, cook-maid
> setting fire to the curtains L225

first blood
Lovelace, Mr. Robert
> drawing first blood in the duel with Morden L537

first love
Hervey, Mrs. Dorothy
> few women...marry their first loves L44
Howe, Miss Anna
> Sir George Colmar, her first passion L151
Lovelace, Mr. Robert
> first love jilting him L31, L58, L220

flight see **abduction of Clarissa**; **escapes**; **journey**

flowers
Harlowe, Miss Clarissa
> her flowered silver suit L69
> Clarissa, tender blossom L153
> coffin, a flower bed, mentioned by Lovelace in reference to a virgin L313

flowers, *Harlowe, Miss Clarissa* (cont.)
>   her hand, the lily not of so beautiful a white L340
>   white lily inscribed on Clarissa's coffin L451
>   Anna's tears embalming a fallen blossom L473.2
>   her hands white as the lily L474
>   Clarissa, flower of the world L501
Hervey, Mrs. Dorothy
>   There never was so set a malice in man as in your cousin James Harlowe. They will ruin the flower and
>   ornament of their family L78
Lovelace, Mr. Robert
>   Lovelace, a bee ranging from flower to flower L153

food see also **drink**; **meals**
Harlowe, Miss Clarissa
>   the old Roman and his lentils L20
>   Mrs. Sinclair offering Clarissa chocolate L178
>   chicken soup ordered for supper L184
>   taking chocolate for breakfast L216
>   asking for three or four French rolls with butter and water L228, L228n1
>   offered bread and butter and biscakes by Mrs. Moore L232
>   bread and water only for dinner L235
>   offering to pay for coffee, tea, chocolate, chicken but unable to eat L333
>   drinking tea with bread and butter L333
>   Dr. H. recommending
>   cordials and nourishment L340
>   weak jellies and innocent cordials L366
>   Mr. Goddard recommending
>   for breakfast, water-gruel, or milk pottage, or weak broth L366
>   for dinner, dish of tea with milk in the afternoon L366
>   for supper, sago L366
Harlowe, Miss Clarissa, constables, Rowland, Mr., wife, Rowland, Mrs.
>   offering Clarissa tea, bread, butter L333
Howe, Miss Anna, messengers, Rogers
>   eating powdered beef, woundily corned L251
Lovelace, Mr. Robert
>   God sends meat, the devil cooks L211
>   taking chocolate for breakfast L216
>   not loving kickshaws L233
>   apple, oranges, gingerbread, smaller boy running away with L259
>   gilt gingerbread at a fair L294
>   searching for Clarissa at houses that deal in women's matters, and tea and coffee L294
>   taking chicken broth when sick with a fever L410
>   water-gruel and soupe-maigre prescribed L512
>   starving diet L512
Sinclair, Mrs.
>   ordering chicken for supper L184
Sinclair, Mrs., whores, Wykes, Dorcas
>   preparing tea, offering Clarissa food and drink L201, L261.1

forgeries see

> **correspondence, Harlowe, Miss Clarissa with Anna, forged by Lovelace**
> **correspondence, Howe, Miss Anna with Clarissa, forged by Lovelace**
> **correspondence, Lawrance, Lady Betty, forged by Lovelace**
> **correspondence, Lord M., forged by Lovelace**
> **correspondence, Montague, Miss Charlotte, forged by Lovelace**
> **correspondence, Tomlinson, Captain Antony, forged by Lovelace**

forgers

Lovelace, Mr. Robert
>   adroit at manual imitation L218
>   mastering Anna's handwriting L229, L316
>   his family confronting him for L323

Lovelace, Mr. Robert, contrivances of Lovelace, specifically, contrivance of Captain Tomlinson and Uncle
  Harlowe's birthday, Tomlinson, Captain Antony
>   a forger L217

forgiveness

Harlowe, Miss Clarissa
>   nothing shall ever make me forgive him...I so much to suffer through him L64
>   for her family L307
>   wanting Papa's forgiveness L309
>   trying to pity Lovelace and forgive him L348, L359
>   if Papa forgives her, she can learn to forgive Lovelace L348
>   nothing can be more wounding to a spirit...than...forgiveness L360, L508
>   her forgiveness of Lovelace L369, L399, L401, L427, L448, L467, L472, L481, L510.4
>   writing to Mamma for blessing and forgiveness L391
>   hoping for pardon L397
>   Lovelace asking her forgiveness L397
>   asking Lovelace's family to forgive him L398
>   wishing last blessing and forgiveness L399
>   forgiveness as consequence of her preparations for death L451
Harlowe, Mr. James, Sen.
>   Clarissa wanting his forgiveness L309
>   will never own Clarissa or forgive her L378
Harlowe Family
>   will forgive Clarissa only at her last extremity L376
>   unwilling to forgive Clarissa L392
Howe, Mrs. Annabella
>   forgiveness of Clarissa the Harlowes' own decision L357
Lovelace, Mr. Robert
>   excluded from Christian forgiveness L373
>   asking forgiveness, wishing for forgiveness L397, L399
>   hoping for divine pardon through Clarissa L397
>   not forgiving his family for presuming to control him L397
>   Clarissa hoping his family will forgive him L398
>   Clarissa forgiving him L467, L510.4
>   Clarissa's forgiveness and death as revenge L472
>   rejecting her forgiveness L472
Morden, Colonel William
>   How wounding a thing...is a generous...forgiveness! What revenge can be more effectual and more noble,
>   were revenge intended L508

fortunes see **estates**; **inheritances**; **trustees**

friends

Belford, Mr. John

    Belton, Mr. Thomas

        caring for Belton L344, L364, L383

        putting Belton's sister into possession of Belton's house L385

        throwing Thomasine and hers out of Belton's house L399

        called to Belton's bedside L419

        caring for Belton's sister L440

    Tomkins, his surgeon-friend L499

Harlowe, Miss Arabella

    Lloyd, Miss Biddy, a favorite of Arabella L132

Harlowe, Miss Clarissa

    Alston, Miss Fanny L507

    Belford, Mr. John, now her warm friend L343

    Biddulph, Miss Rachel

        ball, Colonel Ambrose's, attending L367

        family, Sir Robert Biddulph, her father, where Clarissa met Patty Montague two years ago L233.3

        gossip, hearing from Miss Lardner that Clarissa is at Mrs. Sinclair's, then telling Miss Lloyd L229.1

        mentioned L10, L37, L40, L93

        names, called Miss Rachel Biddulph L507

        poems, hers on the female character L2

        relations, cousin of Miss Lardner L229.1

        visits, to Miss Howe, to inquire about Clarissa L93

    Campbell, Miss Cartwright L507

    Campion, Miss L37, L40

    Drayton, Lady, Clarissa's letter to her on the consequences of severity in parents L58, L59, L90

    Drayton, Miss, Lady Drayton's daughter L58

    H., Dr. R., becoming a friend L441

    Lardner, Miss

        her footman appearing at Mrs. Sinclair's to inquire about Clarissa and Lovelace L213, L214

        her servant following Clarissa back to Mrs. Sinclair's from church L229.1

        a cousin of Miss Biddulph's L229.1

        seeing Clarissa alone at St. James's church and telling Miss Biddulph L229.1

        her information mentioned L316

    Lloyd, Miss Biddy

        ball, Colonel Ambrose's, attending L367

        friends, a favorite of Arabella L132

        gossip

            about Arabella and Lovelace L15

            telling Anna of James's plan to rescue Clarissa L132, L137, L148

            hearing from Miss Biddulph that Clarissa is at Mrs. Sinclair's L229.1

        influence, hers on Clarissa unwanted by the family L9

        mentioned L10, L37, L40, L93

        names, called Miss Biddy Lloyd L507

        servants, Harriot, her maid, gossiping about Lovelace L15

        visits, to and from Anna L93, L473.1

    Wykes, Dorcas

        called a friend L270

        confiding in Dorcas L271

Harlowe, Mr. James, Jun.

    Singleton, Captain *see also* **rescue of Clarissa,** *Harlowe, Mr. James, Jun.*

        master of a Scots vessel L137

        lives at Leith L137, L140

        his vessel lies at Rotherhithe L155

        sun-burnt sailor L177, L194

friends, *Harlowe, Mr. James, Jun.*, Singleton, Captain (cont.)

    pock-fretten, ill-looking, big-boned, six feet tall, heavy eye, overhanging brow, deck-treading stride, parched lips, brown coat, colored handkerchief, oaken plant in hand, couteau by his side L194

Harlowe Family

    Hartley, Mr., having a widow sister in Pennsylvania with whom Clarissa may board L429

Hickman, Mr. Charles

    Dormer, Mr., at whose house Hickman had an interview with Lovelace L341, L510.1

Howe, Miss Anna

    Biddulph, Miss Rachel, inquiring about Clarissa L93

    Hartley, Lady, example of a man-woman L132, L133

    Lloyd, Miss Biddy, inquiring about Clarissa L93

Howe, Mrs. Annabella

    Downeton, Sir Harry, his information about Solmes L56, L57, L58

    Hunt, Mr., with whom she corresponds L81

    Lorimer, Mrs., carrying to Antony Mrs. Howe's answer to his proposals L197.2

Lord M.

    Hutcheson, Archibald L206, L206n4

    Lexington, Lord L206

    Wycherley, William L190, L190n2

Lord M., relations, half-sisters, Lawrance, Lady Betty

    Fortescue, Mrs.

        source of information about Lovelace L12, L14, L15

        opinion on the state of affairs in the Harlowe Family L26

        her admiration for Clarissa L27

Lord M., relations, half-sisters, Sadleir, Lady Sarah

    Benson, Mrs., where Anna and Clarissa met Lady Sarah's Betsey L327

Lovelace, Mr. Robert

    generally

        in need of reform L34, L81

        meeting at the Cocoa Tree in Pall Mall L48

        six or seven bad companions L81

        as myrmidons L106

        wretches, men of fortune L114

        his gang of fellows L252.1

    Ambrose, Colonel

        the ball

            inviting Lovelace, Mrs. and Miss Howe, Hickman, and Arabella L350

            on the occasion of his wife's birthday and marriage, Mrs. Ambrose's brother, the governor, having received good news L358

            an account of the ball L367

            attended by Miss Playford, Miss Biddy D'Ollyffe, and Miss Kitty D'Oily L367

            Miss D'Oily challenging Lovelace on Clarissa's account L368

        meals, Lovelace breakfasting and dining with the Colonel and his nieces L322

        relations, his nieces, skin deep beauties, fine women L322, L367

        visits, from Lovelace L322

    Barrow, Colonel

        his fondness for Rosebud L72

        friends, Captain Sloane L72

    Belton, Mr. Thomas, friend of Lovelace L31

        age, about thirty years L161

        animals, a lion kicked in the jaws by an ass L344

        bequests of Belton

            leaving Belford 100 guineas, which Belford gives to Belton's sister L426

            leaving Mowbray, Tourville, Lovelace, and Belford £20 apiece for rings L426

            leaving his sister only £50 L440

friends, *Lovelace, Mr. Robert*, Belton, Mr. Thomas (cont.)

 character
  investigated by Hickman L48
  meeting Lovelace at Cocoa Tree in Pall Mall L48
  description by Clarissa L161
  drinking hard L161
  his admiration and concern for Clarissa L169
  mischievous spirit L192
 collation at Mrs. Sinclair's, attending L158.1
 contrivances of Lovelace
  taking up quarters for a week at Hampstead in show of support for Lovelace L241
  sent for, as Clarissa is gone off L290
  at Mrs. Sinclair's when Clarissa returns L314
 costume, dressing gaily L161
 death of Belton
  cannot live long L399
  his dying confession, death rattle L424
  reported by Belford to Clarissa L426
  compared to Mrs. Sinclair's L499
 education, university L161
 estates
  his uncle bequeathing him a good estate L161
  his paternal estate in Kent mortgaged and soon to be foreclosed L194
  his broken fortunes, broken spirit, estate in ruin L344, L347
  Belford putting Belton's sister into possession of his house, reinstating Belton to his own house,
   occupied by Thomasine L344, L364, L385
  fleeced by a woman L347
  his house, remains of his fortune, saved by Belford L399
 executors, Belford L426
 expiate, may his tortures and repentence expiate L424
 family
  Thomasine, passing as Belton's wife L192
   character
    pretending to dote on him, embezzling his money L192
    a very devil, low-bred L193
    having Belton's house, put out of his house L344, L399
    her infidelity, her suspicious eye L347
    ràpacious woman, accursed deceiver, ungrateful L399, L419
   family
    Tom and Hal, her sons L192
     supposed by Belton to be his L192, L344
     their father passing as Thomasine's cousin L344
     muscular and big-boned L347
     her cubs L399
    father, innkeeper at Dorking L192
    lover, her father's hostler L192
     thrown down the stairs by Belford L399
   funeral of Belton, at Belton's last office, not showing grief L440
   mourning, and widow's weeds L399
   physical appearance, not a delicate frame L347
  uncle, bequeathing him a good estate L161
 friends
  Blomer, a physician L424
   earlier known to Belford L424
   his excesses in women and wine L424

friends, *Lovelace, Mr. Robert*, Belton, Mr. Thomas, friends, Blomer (cont.)
>>>his opinion of his profession L424
>>funeral of Belton
>>>not attended by Mowbray or Lovelace L425
>>>parade hired to mourn him L425
>>>funeral, interment, last office L426, L439, L440
>>gentleman, came up to town and commenced fine gentleman L161
>>historical references, compared to the ancient Sarmatians L344, L344n1
>>illnesses
>>>short consumptive cough, blood L161, L192, L344, L347
>>>shocking scenes of illness and agonies L419, L424
>>>pains in stomach and head, convulsions L424
>>literary references
>>>admired author, Nick Rowe L413
>>>his pleasure in poetry, classics, drama L419
>>medications, cordial julep, opiate, sleeping draughts L419
>>names, Thomas, Tommy, Tom L158.1, L419, L439
>>opinions, on physicians and surgeons L424
>>reform
>>>penitent, regretting his misspent life L419
>>>can neither repent nor pray, his heart hardened, in despair L419
>>relations
>>>Sambre, Mrs., his sister L424
>>>>come to live with him, continuing in Belton's house L419, L440
>>>>Belton leaving her only £50 L440
>>>>Belford giving her 100 guineas L440, L449
>>>>indigent, her vile husband, her son completing her ruin L440
>>>>Mowbray, Lovelace, Tourville giving her their legacy for India Bonds L449
>>>nephew, in Antigua, his heir L440
>>servants, Betty, maid L419
>>story, Belton's story L190.1, L191, L192, L344
>>victims, sister of Tom Metcalf, who died protecting his sister from Belton L419, L422
>>visits, from Belford, will go to Epsom to keep Belton company L364, L414
Colmar, Sir George *see* **suitors to Howe, Miss Anna**
Doleman, Mr. Tom
>animals, crippled monkey L497
>character
>>man of fortune and character L126
>>former rake L229.1
>contrivances of Lovelace
>>to whom Lovelace writes for accommodations for Clarissa L126
>>his letter describing Mrs. Sinclair L154
>>recommending Mrs. Sinclair's to Lovelace L229.1
>>implement of Lovelace L229.1
>family, married man, married to a woman of family L126, L229.1
>illnesses
>>paralytic complaints, palsy L130.1, L229.1, L480, L497
>>his empiric and his malady L530, L531
>mentioned L130, L155, L158
>names, Tom L131
>relations
>>Newcomb, his nephew, alias Mr. Mennell L174.2
>>>contrivances of Lovelace
>>>>contrivance of Mrs. Fretchville's house
>>>>>mischievously used by Lovelace L174.2, L194

friends, *Lovelace, Mr. Robert*, Doleman, Mr. Tom, relations, Newcomb, contrivances of Lovelace, contrivance of Mrs. Fretchville's house (cont.)

telling Lovelace of Mrs. Fretchville's small-pox L201

refusing to continue deceiving Clarissa L203

Lovelace's conscience *Mennelled* upon him L244

taking leave of Lovelace L526

visits, from Lovelace in Uxbridge L449

sister L130.1

Holmes, Sir Anthony, his two nieces attending a party with Misses Martin and Horton L158

Mallory, or Malory, whose proctor helps Lovelace procure a license to marry Clarissa L220, L227

Miles, a caitiff, seducing the farmer's daughter L496

Mowbray, Mr. Richard, friend of Lovelace L31

> age, thirty-three or thirty-four years L161
> animals, bear L420
> bequests of Belton
> > £20 for a ring L426, L440
> > contributing his to Belton's sister's India Bonds L449
>
> character
> > investigated by Hickman L48
> > description by Clarissa L161
> > jesting upon sacred things, hating clergy L161
> > admiration and concern for Clarissa L169
> > mischievous, brutal, rough, and untouched L192, L370, L419, L445
> > I ever hated a book. Kicking...cuffing...orchard-robbing were my early glory L496
>
> collation at Mrs. Sinclair's, attending L158.1
> contrivances of Lovelace
> > helping Lovelace get the marriage license L227
> > his servant delivering Lovelace's forged letter to Hickman L240
> > taking up quarters at Hampstead in show of support for Lovelace L241
> > sent for, as Clarissa is gone off L290
> > present during Lovelace's interview with Morden, offering his sword L442, L445
>
> costume, dressing gaily L161
> death of Belton
> > uncouth and unreflecting in Belton's dying moments L419
> > comparing Belton's last hours to Clarissa's L473
>
> drink, asking for claret L419
> friendship with Belton
> > consigning Belton to quarantine L344
> > a bottle-friend, frothy insensibility L419
>
> funeral of Belton, not attending L425
> gentleman L161
> languages, speaking many languages L161
> literary references
> > Dryden, John, *Palamon and Arcite*, quoted L496, L496n1
> > Lee, Nathaniel and Dryden, *Oedipus*, quoted L419, L419n5
> > hating reading and books L496
>
> music, humming a tune L419
> names, called Richard L158.1
> opinions, on seduction L496
> physical appearance
> > tall and comely, bold and daring, large and strong L161
> > scars in forehead and right cheek L161
>
> relations, good family L161
> residence, retired into Yorkshire, his native county CONCLUSION
> servants, treatment of, fearing him L161, L420, L423

friends, *Lovelace, Mr. Robert*, Mowbray, Mr. Richard (cont.)

    travel, joining Lovelace abroad, setting out with L513, L514, L516, L525, L526

    visits, to M. Hall L341, L421, L425, L511

Solcombe, Colonel, his daughters attending a party with Misses Martin and Horton L158

Tourville, Mr. James

    age, just turned of thirty-one L161

    bequests of Belton

        £20 for a ring L426, L440

        contributing his to Belton's sister's India Bonds L449

    character

        description by Clarissa L161

        coxcomb, fop, finical, idle flutterer L161, L350, L370, L498

        admiration and concern for Clarissa L169

        mischievous spirit L192

        satisfied with wit at second-hand L222

    collation at Mrs. Sinclair's, attending L158.1

    contrivances of Lovelace

        taking up quarters at Hampstead in show of support for Lovelace L241

    death of Harlowe, Miss Clarissa

        telling Lovelace that Clarissa is very ill L439

        to go with Mowbray to Lovelace to keep him from harming himself or others on receiving

           news of Clarissa's death L477

        with Lovelace after Clarissa's death L482

    costume, dressing richly, more tawdry than fine L161

    funeral of Belton, present at Belton's last office L440

    gentleman L161

    languages, speaking French and Italian L161

    music

        musician L161

        singing Lovelace out of his megrims L421

    names, James, Jemmy L158.1, L480

    relations, ancient family L161

    residence, retired into Nottinghamshire, his native county CONCLUSION

    travel

        out of town L290

        joining Lovelace abroad, setting out with L513, L514, L516, L525, L526

    visits, to M. Hall with Lovelace L341, L413, L511

Warneton, Major, Lovelace meeting him at church L323

Wilson, Mr.

    living in Pall Mall L155

    conveyance for correspondence for Clarissa and Anna L155, L175, L196, L201, L239

    giving Anna's for Clarissa directly to Lovelace L217, L229

    how he came to be used as a conveyance L229.1

Windisgratz, Baron, with whom Lovelace will reside at the Favorita, in Vienna L534.1

Lovelace, Mr. Robert, friends, Barrow, Colonel

Sloane, Captain L72

Lovelace, Mr. Robert, friends, Belton, Mr. Thomas

Blomer, a physician L424

    earlier known to Belford L424

    his excesses in women and wine L424

    his opinion of his profession L424

Morden, Colonel William

Klienfurt, Mr., in Munich, where Lovelace can direct correspondence for Morden L535.1

friendship

Belford, Mr. John
    with Belton L344, L383
    with Clarissa L284, L339, L343
    with Lovelace L534
    with Morden L487

Harlowe, Miss Clarissa
    with Anna L1, L8, L11, L57, L89, L135, L174, L343, L473.1, L520
        advice to Anna on Hickman L55, L69, L73, L458
        her only friend L146, L295
        her love for Anna L343
        saving Anna from marrying a libertine L182, L355
    Ecclesiasticus 6:16, quoted on L149, L149n1
    Proverbs 27:5, faithful are the wounds of a friend L309, L309n1
    her opinion on ties of friendship L359

Howe, Miss Anna
    with Clarissa L1, L8, L11, L87, L135, L146, L183, L229.1, L473, L520
    Clarissa's only friend, her love for Clarissa L295, L329

Lovelace, Mr. Robert
    friendship with Belton L534

Lovelace, Mr. Robert, friends, Mowbray, Mr. Richard
    consigning Belton to quarantine L344
    a bottle-friend to Belton, frothy insensibility L419

Morden, Colonel William
    with Belford L487

Sinclair, Mrs., whores, Wykes, Dorcas
    Clarissa trying to befriend Dorcas L177, L268, L270, L271, L275
    sympathetic to Clarissa L264
    seeming to come into favor with Clarissa L267

funeral of Belton

Lovelace, Mr. Robert
    not attending L425

Lovelace, Mr. Robert, friends, Belton, Mr. Thomas
    parade hired to mourn him L425
    arranged, his interment, last office L426, L439, L440

Lovelace, Mr. Robert, friends, Belton, Mr. Thomas, family, Thomasine
    at Belton's last office, not showing grief L440

Lovelace, Mr. Robert, friends, Mowbray, Mr. Richard
    not attending L425

Lovelace, Mr. Robert, friends, Tourville, Mr. James
    present at Belton's last office L440

funeral of Clarissa see also **burial of Clarissa**

Harlowe, Miss Clarissa
    country funeral mentioned by Lovelace L313
    her valuables and clothes to be sold to pay her debts and burial L334
    funeral bell tolling at the parish church as the hearse passes L500
    text for funeral discourse, mentioned L501
    description of L504
    eulogy by Mr. Melvill, quoting *2 Corinthians* 9:7 L504
    attended by distant relations Fuller and Allinson L504
    attended by Solmes, Mullins, Wyerley L504

Harlowe Family, clergymen, Brand, Mr. Elias
    not chosen to pronounce discourse L501

funeral of Clarissa (cont.)
Harlowe Family, clergymen, Lewin, Dr. Arthur
  would have pronounced discourse at her interment L501
Harlowe Family, clergymen, Melvill, Mr.
  delivering a brief eulogium L501
Hickman, Mr. Charles
  attending L504
Morden, Colonel William
  attending L504

funeral of Lord M.
Lovelace, Mr. Robert
  hiring blacks for the funeral L277

G

gall
Harlowe, Miss Clarissa
  my ink runs nothing but gall L52
  in her ink L311
Howe, Miss Anna
  dipping her pen in gall L55, L134

Gazette see **newspapers**

genealogy
Harlowe Family, relations, Harlowe, Grandfather
  his will as a source L4

generosity
Lovelace, Mr. Robert
  to servants L11, L13, L15
  to the folk at the inn L34, L72, L217.2
  not an ungenerous man, his generosity L87, L98, L140
  to tenants L217.2
  his generosity owing to pride and vanity rather than philanthropy L217.2
  allowing Clarissa to be generous to Mrs. Norton L217.2

gentleman
Belford, Mr. John
  gentleman L161
Harlowe, Mr. Antony
  sea-prospered gentleman L73
Harlowe, Mr. James, Jun.
  gentleman L91
Harlowe, Mr. John
  the old gentleman L179
Howe, Mrs. Annabella, family, Howe, Mr.
  a gentleman L133
Lord M., servants, Clements
  Clements, Lord M.'s gentleman L442

gentleman (cont.)

Lovelace, Mr. Robert

gentleman L286

his prerogative as a gentleman to affront Joseph and the Smiths L416

gentleman's challenge from Morden L534

Lovelace, Mr. Robert, friends, Belton, Mr. Thomas

came up to town and commenced fine gentleman L161

Lovelace, Mr. Robert, friends, Mowbray, Mr. Richard

gentleman L161

Lovelace, Mr. Robert, friends, Tourville, Mr. James

gentleman L161

Morden, Colonel William

gentleman's challenge L534

Sinclair, Mrs., husband

gentleman L155

gifts

Harlowe, Miss Clarissa

diamond necklace, solitaire, and buckles from Sir Josias Brookland L507

rose diamond ring from Morden's father L507, L529

her grandmother's jewels from her grandfather L507, L529

God, references to see also **biblical references**

Belford, Mr. John

that Power L192

God, the BEING of beings, Supreme Superintendent and Father of all things L293

Harlowe, Miss Clarissa

Providence L51.2, L63, L243, L486.1, L510.4

my Maker L52, L467

the Almighty L120, L471, L488, L510.4

King and Maker of a thousand worlds L157

Supreme Director L173

the first gracious Planter L185

Dispenser of all good L214

the God within her exalted her L248

Throne of Mercy L307

Divine Wisdom L428

my blessed Redeemer L481

Divine Grace L488

HE L489

Divine mercy L510.4

God Almighty L518

Howe, Miss Anna

God Almighty L148

godmother

Harlowe, Mr. James, Jun.

Lovell, godmother L4

his Yorkshire property L2

mentioned in Grandfather's will L4

inheritance from L13

gold

Harlowe, Miss Clarissa

some gold which she left behind L152

gold, *Harlowe, Miss Clarissa* (cont.)

    pure gold from the assay, Clarissa as L323

    Lovelace wanting her heart in a golden receptacle L497

    miniature of Clarissa set in gold bequeathed Morden L507

Lovelace, Mr. Robert

    not his predominant passion L105

Morden, Colonel William

    miniature of Clarissa set in gold bequeathed Morden L507

    giving a purse of gold to the surgeons attending Lovelace after the duel L537

goldsmiths

Lord M.

    Finch, Mr., Lord M.'s goldsmith L510

gossip

Harlowe, Miss Arabella

    that Clarissa has stolen Lovelace from her L1, L2, L3

    with Betty and Dolly, causing Clarissa to become desperate L94

    gossiping with Miss Lloyd about James's plan to rescue Clarissa L132

Harlowe, Miss Clarissa

    mentioned L4

    her case widely discussed in public L80

    gossip of her aversion to Solmes L81

    talk of the county L85

    the mouth of common fame L92

    subject of open talk L392

Harlowe, Miss Clarissa, friends, Biddulph, Miss Rachel

    hearing from Miss Lardner that Clarissa is at Mrs. Sinclair's, then telling Miss Lloyd L229.1

Harlowe, Miss Clarissa, friends, Lardner, Miss

    seeing Clarissa alone at St. James's church, then telling Miss Biddulph L229.1

Harlowe, Miss Clarissa, friends, Lloyd, Miss Biddy

    gossiping about Arabella and Lovelace L15

    Harriot, her maid, gossiping about Lovelace L15

    telling Anna of James's plan to rescue Clarissa L132, L137, L148

    hearing from Miss Biddulph that Clarissa is at Mrs. Sinclair's L229.1

Harlowe, Miss Clarissa, suitors to Harlowe, Miss Clarissa, Solmes, Mr. Roger

    sources of information about L27, L56, L57, L58

    public talk of Clarissa's aversion to him L81

    wishing to pass on information to Clarissa about Lovelace L59.1, L78, L79

    would have told Clarissa of Miss Betterton L139

Harlowe Family, servants, Barnes, Betty

    with Hannah about Lovelace L14

    source of information for confined Clarissa L21, L63, L78

    with Leman about Lovelace and Rosebud L71, L73

    with Leman about Clarissa's apartment being searched L103

    with Mrs. Norton about Clarissa's letters, Belford's visits L374, L376, L431, L459

Hervey, Mrs. Dorothy

    relating steward's (discharged) report on Lovelace to Clarissa L4

    carrying stories about Lovelace to Clarissa L79

Howe, Miss Anna

    her new informant on Lovelace L177

Howe, Miss Anna, servants, Kitty

    source of information about Solmes L27

Gothamite
Hickman, Mr. Charles
  prim Gothamite L198

gout see
  illnesses, *Harlowe, Mr. James, Sen.*
  illnesses, *Lord M.*

grand tour
Hervey, Mrs. Dorothy, family, Hervey, Uncle
  requesting Lovelace to instruct a young man in the grand tour L3
Hickman, Mr. Charles
  must have made the grand tour L198
Lovelace, Mr. Robert
  his advice to the young man taking the grand tour L3

grave
Harlowe, Miss Clarissa
  let me slide quietly into my grave L315
  tottering on the brink of a grave L409
  I hope they bury all their resentments in my grave L465
Lord M.
  mentioned L321

grieving for Clarissa
Harlowe, Mrs. Charlotte
  her grief over the loss of Clarissa L379
Harlowe, Mr. James, Sen.
  his grief L379

Guardian see **newspapers**

H

habits
Harlowe, Miss Clarissa
  seldom eating supper L155
  eating preferences L157
  passing Sundays by herself L200
  writing and reading half the night L224
  beholding the sun-rise L247
  an early riser L365
  her daily routine L528, L529

hair see also **bequests of Clarissa**
Harlowe, Miss Clarissa
  her natural ringlets not lately kembed L334
  bequeathing rings with her hair set in crystal L495, L507
Howe, Miss Anna
  wanting a lock of Clarissa's hair L502
Lovelace, Mr. Robert
  wanting a lock of Clarissa's hair L497, L498

hair (cont.)
Norton, Mrs. Judith
      cutting off four ringlets of Clarissa's hair L495

handwriting
Harlowe, Miss Clarissa
      equal and regular hand L239
      her fine handwriting L323
      her charming hand L443
Howe, Miss Anna
      Lovelace will master Anna's handwriting L229
      showing her natural impatience by its fits and starts L239
      not a bad hand L239

hanging
Harlowe, Mr. James, Jun.
      deserving hanging L142
Harlowe Family
      a man found hanging in the haunted coppice about twenty years ago L35, L86fn
Howe, Miss Anna
      custom in the Isle of Man, rape victim choosing rope, sword, or ring L317
Lovelace, Mr. Robert
      outwitted, he would hang, drown, or shoot himself L117
      if Lovelace were to be fairly hanged L132
      deserving hanging L142
      riddance of him by flight or the gallows L196
      rake's neck in danger from the hangman L261
      indemnity for a rapist, to fly or be hanged L293
      meriting the gallows L452

harpsichord
Harlowe, Miss Arabella
      playing Clarissa's harpsichord L42
Harlowe, Miss Clarissa
      accomplished at L54
      her coffin near the window like a harpsichord L457
      harpsichord, chamber-organ, and music books bequeathed Dolly L507
Hervey, Mrs. Dorothy, family, Hervey, Miss Dolly
      bequeathed Clarissa's harpsichord L507
Howe, Miss Anna
      accomplished at L128

hartshorn see **medications**

hatred of Clarissa
Lovelace, Mr. Robert
      I hate her L198
      hating the name of Harlowe L198
      regretting having known Clarissa L264

hatred of Lovelace
Belford, Mr. John
      noted L349
Harlowe, Miss Clarissa
      noted L71, L201, L263, L269, L277

hatred of Lovelace, *Harlowe, Miss Clarissa* (cont.)
    liking Lovelace, and could hate him L145
    despising Lovelace L202, L281
Harlowe, Mr. James, Jun.
    grudge begun at college L3, L4
    sharing with Arabella a hatred of L4
    background and summary L13
    rivalry and hatred of L91
    allying himself with the Bettertons against Lovelace L127
Harlowe Family
    noted L13, L20
Lovelace, Mr. Robert
    hating himself L350

health
Harlowe, Mr. Antony
    healthy and sound L197.1
Harlowe, Miss Clarissa
    her natural good constitution L320

health, declining and ending in death see also **death of Harlowe, Miss Clarissa**, *anticipated*
Harlowe, Miss Clarissa
    ill from Arabella's letter and Papa's curses L152
    very ill L201, L202, L243, L270, L313, L318, L327, L329, L333, L334, L336, L338, L339, L340, L342,
      L343, L346, L357, L372, L379, L391, L413, L435, L439, L440, L444, L458
    insensible and stupefied since Tuesday morning L259
    heavy torpid pain increasing L314
    could not speak, though eyelids moved L334
    her limbs trembling L336, L471
    recovery within her power L366
    too ill to go out in a coach, going to water-side for a boat to escape Lovelace L416
    shortness of breath L441, L452
    two very severe fits L452
    confined to her room L454
    cannot hold a pen to answer Anna's letter L454
    in convulsions L474

hearse
Harlowe, Miss Clarissa
    arriving at Harlowe Place at six in the afternoon, not adorned by escutcheons L500

heart-broken
Harlowe, Miss Clarissa
    or half heart-broken, by her father and Lovelace L370, L375, L376, L418, L426

heirs
Belford, Mr. John
    his uncle's heir L172, L247
Harlowe, Miss Clarissa
    Clarissa as L307, L459
Lovelace, Mr. Robert
    heir presumptive of Lord M.'s estate L2, L13, L118, L265
Lovelace, Mr. Robert, friends, Belton, Mr. Thomas
    his heir, a nephew in Antigua L440

heraldry see also **escutcheons**; **lozenges**
Lovelace, Mr. Robert

  description of arms on the marriage license L254
  Lady Betty's arms and crest upon a coach, hers in for repairs L255

Highmore, Joseph

  his whole-length picture of Clarissa in the Vandyke taste L147, L147n1
  his picture of the assembled Harlowes, book cover of the Penguin Classics edition of *Clarissa* L147n1

hires
Harlowe Family

  Ackland, Mr., attending Clarissa to hear her story and begin a process L429
Hickman, Mr. Charles

  Filmer

    a husbandman in Finch Lane, near the Howe residence L100
    engaged to receive Anna's secret correspondence from Clarissa L100

historical references
Belford, Mr. John

  Louis XIV L192, L192n1
  Novogrod and ancient Sarmatia L344, L344n1
  Dr. John Ratcliffe (usually Radcliffe), a physician, quoted L424, L424n1
  Emperor Joseph, Clarissa compared, dying while physicians consult L460
  Francis Chartres, a rapist, Belford compared L513, L513n1
  Bishop Burnet, quoted L533, L533n1 (cf. L157.1n1)
Harlowe, Miss Clarissa

  Edward the Sixth, and wooing L7, L7n1
  Queen of Scots, Clarissa compared L370, L370n3
  Duke of Luxemburgh, death bed wishes, Clarissa's compared L486, L486n1
  Earl of Shrewsbury, losing his life in an act of vengeance, Morden compared L518, L518n1
  Charles II, mentioned L518
  Henry IV of France, Clarissa's manner of denying requests compared L529
Howe, Miss Anna

  Henry VII, the tyrant Tudor, and Elizabeth of the House of York L47
  Tom Wharton L48, L48n2
  Elizabeth of France...Philip II of Spain L56
Lovelace, Mr. Robert

  Antonio Perez L127
  Don John of Austria L171
  Charles XII of Sweden L198
  Czar Peter

    and the Muscovites L198
    Cossacks at Pultowa L416, L416n3
  Grand Signor L198, L198n3
  Eastern monarchs sequestering themselves to excite adoration L220
  Queen Bess

    would agree with his opinion on rape L223
    Queen Elizabeth I, Lovelace comparing himself L370, L370n3
  would have warred with the Great Turk, the Persian, the Mogul, Eastern monarchs L232
  Sixtus the Vth, as the half-dead Montaldo, Lovelace compared L233
  South Sea stock, subscriptions leading to ruin 1720 L241
  Catalans holding up their English treaty, Clarissa and her license compared L260, L260n1
  Queen Anne

    the late Queen Anne, a good woman, always fond of prerogative L265
    Lovelace comparing himself L265

historical references, *Lovelace, Mr. Robert* (cont.)

    singing to himself the thirtieth of January strain and the dead psalm melody L266, L266n2

    James VI of Scotland and I of England (the Royal Insignificant), his book, *Demonology* L272, L272n1

    Charles II, his death anticipated, as Lovelace anticipates Lord M.'s L294

    Italian eunuchs L321, L321n1

    true father of a certain monarque, his identity kept secret by murder L326, L326n1

    Martin Luther, Belford compared L370

    Charles V, Luther appearing before L370

    Queen of Scots, Clarissa compared L370, L370n3

    Harry IVth L371

    Madam Maintenon and Lewis XIV of France L422, L422n1

    Dame Elizabeth Carteret, monument in Westminster Abbey, Belford compared L449, L449n1, L453

    Francis Chartres, rapist, Belford compared L513, L513n1

    Christian princes, Lovelace comparing his crime to theirs L515

Lovelace, Mr. Robert, friends, Belton, Mr. Thomas

    compared to the ancient Sarmatians L344, L344n1

Morden, Colonel William

    Louis XIV, his will flagrantly broken, Clarissa compared L508

honor

Belford, Mr. John

    doubting Lovelace's L286

    Belford having more than some princes L286

    notions of false honor L339

Harlowe, Miss Clarissa

    noted L1, L100

    her honor inviolate in spite of men and devils L181

    romantic value on her honor L259

    Lovelace conspiring against her honor L261 Paper VIII

    her honor lost, robbed of her honor L263, L267, L306, L311

    defending her honor L281, L294

Harlowe, Mr. James, Jun.

    lost in the fall of his sister L379

Harlowe Family

    dishonored by Lovelace L7

    Clarissa's duty to protect

        by marrying Solmes L7, L8, L16

        by prosecuting Lovelace L427

    family honor, noted L78

    their concern for L221

    their young honor supercilious and touchy L221

    Mrs. Norton little favoring their honor, in favoring Clarissa L308

Lord M.

    jealous of the honor of his house L409

Lovelace, Mr. Robert

    of unblemished honor, his honor noted L81, L153, L222, L225, L333

    his family's honor L222

    conspiring against Clarissa's honor L261 Paper VIII

    Harlowe Family dishonored by Lovelace L267

    little regard for honor of his family L286

    Belford doubting his honor L286

    dishonoring his family by marrying a person whom he has so treated L323

hostlers

Lovelace, Mr. Robert, friends, Belton, Mr. Thomas, family, Thomasine, family
 her lover, her father's hostler L192
Moore, Mrs.
 Kit the hostler, who drank with the footman at the taphouse L232

Hottentots

Belford, Mr. John
 his Hottentot heart L191
Sinclair, Mrs., whores
 as Hottentots L175

hour-glass

Harlowe, Miss Clarissa
 winged hour-glass on her coffin L451

housekeepers

Belford, Mr. John
 Lovick, Mrs., his housekeeper at Edgware L514, CONCLUSION
Harlowe, Mrs. Charlotte
 Williams, Mrs., Mamma's former housekeeper L432
  visiting Aunt Hervey L432
  not allowed to visit Clarissa L432
  her kind intentions L433
Harlowe, Mr. John
 Hodges, Mrs. Sarah, housekeeper and paramour L229.1
  suspected of familiarities with his housekeeper L217
  Clarissa querying her on Lovelace's contrivance of Uncle Harlowe's birthday L304
  called Sarah L305
Lord M.
 Greme, Mrs., housekeeper at Lord M.'s Hertfordshire seat L98
  attending Clarissa
   accompanying Clarissa in the chaise to Mrs. Sorlings's L98
   source of information about Lovelace and his family L98, L183
   attending Clarissa and recommending lodgings L104
   has received no orders for Clarissa's accommodations L233.4
  attending Lord M., reading the Bible to Lord M. L104
  attending Lovelace, in his dangerous fever L410
  character, excellent woman, pious matron, compared to Mrs. Norton L98, L104
  correspondence, Harlowe, Miss Clarissa with Anna, assisting in L98
  marriages, Clarissa's to Lovelace, hoping Clarissa will marry Lovelace L120, L128
  relations
   Sorlings, Mrs., sister-in-law, sister of Mrs. Greme L98, L120
    animals, her dunghill cocks, Will compared L238
    attending Clarissa
     requesting Clarissa to defer departure to London L135
     comforting Clarissa after she receives a letter from Arabella L153
    correspondence, Harlowe, Miss Clarissa with Anna, assisting in L100
    family
     widow L104, L128, L149, L153
     two grown sons and two younger daughters L98
     Betty, Mrs., her elder daughter L105
      and Will L118
      and Lord M.'s chaplain L118
      attending Clarissa L118, L125, L130

housekeepers, *Lord M.*, Greme, Mrs., relations, Sorlings, Mrs., family, Betty, Mrs. (cont.)
>> to accompany Clarissa to London L130, L149, L152, L154
>> accompanying Clarissa as far as Barnet L155
>> receiving a gift from Lovelace L155
> farm
>> eight miles off from the inn at St. Albans L98
>> her dairy works, her farm L105, L117, L130

Norton, Mrs. Judith
> housekeeper at the Grove L520

hunting see also **prey**; **sport**
Belford, Mr. John
> to hunt Lovelace L333
Harlowe, Miss Clarissa
> *On being hunted after by the enemy of my soul*, her Meditation L418
Harlowe, Mr. James., Jun.
> like a hunted boar L4
Lord M.
> loving hunting L206
Lovelace, Mr. Robert
> has hunted in the forest at Windsor L116
> caught in his own snares L138
> an artful fowler L152
> drawing sprindges about Clarissa L152
> foxhunter in pursuit of vermin not fit for food L170
> hunting Clarissa L230, L386, L418, L456, L467
> Lovelace like an old hedgehog hunted for its grease L480

husband
Lovelace, Mr. Robert
> wanting to act as Clarissa's husband after her death L497

husbandman
Hickman, Mr. Charles, hires, Filmer
> husbandman L100

I

ignis fatuus
Harlowe, Miss Clarissa
> misled by L173
Howe, Miss Anna
> love an *ignis fatuus* L310

illnesses
Belford, Mr. John, relations, uncle
> mortification up to the knee L172
Harlowe, Mrs. Charlotte
> colic L5, L80
> hourly fits after hearing of Clarissa's death L494.1

illnesses (cont.)

Harlowe, Miss Clarissa

fainting

on being commanded to marry Solmes L16

fearing loss of Mamma's love L18

after receiving a letter from Arabella L149

after recognizing Lovelace at Mrs. Moore's L233

nearly fainting L313, L314

fainting away at the officer's house L333, L334

low and faint L338, L339

near fainting L426

fainting L440

fever

dangerous fever some time ago L39

violent fever L272

dangerous fever at nine years and at eleven years of age L374

headache L238, L245, L256, L333

hysterics L333, L399

small-pox, uncertain whether she ever had L204

stomach-ache, three hours' violent stomach-ache L276

weakness of heart L201, L333

Harlowe, Mr. James, Sen.

gout L4, L5, L8, L20

gout thrown into his stomach L376, L494.1

Harlowe, Mr. John

his declining health L243

Harlowe Family

have been ill L214

not believing that Clarissa is ill L361, L402, L432

Harlowe Family, servants, Barnes, Betty

ill L532

Howe, Miss Anna

has she been ill, as Lovelace has said L295, L297

ill, with but a slight cold L310

fainting on news of Clarissa's death L494

Howe, Mrs. Annabella

very ill, recovering L455

Howe, Mrs. Annabella, relations, Larkin, Mrs.

long bed-ridden L46, L65

Lord M.

gout L104, L121, L187, L190, L203.1, L206, L265, L321

podagra-man L170

gout preventing him from visiting Clarissa L194

gout in his right hand prevents answering invitation L218

gout in his stomach from drinking lemonade L275

gout quit the counterscarp of his stomach, just as it had collected all of its strength in order to storm the citadel of his heart L294

his just disgouted thumbs L323

a gouty twinge L323

his gouty days L341

his last fit L233.2

has become very ill L265, L275, L277, L279

Clarissa's sufferings compared to Lord M.'s L279

in extremis L281, L282, L284, L285

given over by his doctors L285

illnesses, *Lord M.* (cont.)

he has no sharp or acute animal organs to whet out his bodily ones, and to raise his fever above the
symptomatic helpful one L285

Lord M. better, recovered L294, L323, L371

Lord M., relations, half-sisters, Sadleir, Lady Sarah

melancholy L98, L332

Lord M., relations, nieces, Montague, Miss Charlotte

cold and sore throat make her unable to accompany Clarissa L88

indisposed L121

ill with stomach disorder L203, L203.1

Lovelace, Mr. Robert

from waiting for Clarissa in the rain in the garden L62, L73, L223

egregiously cropsick L410

dangerously ill with a violent fever, almost well L411, L412, L414

Tourville singing Lovelace out of his megrims L421

in a fever, recovering from his grief over Clarissa L511, L512

Lovelace, Mr. Robert, friends, Belton, Mr. Thomas

consumptive cough, blood L161, L192, L344, L347

shocking scenes of illness and agonies L419, L424

pains in his stomach and head, convulsions L424

Lovelace, Mr. Robert, friends, Doleman, Mr. Tom

paralytic complaints, palsy L130.1, L229.1, L480, L497

his empiric and his malady L530, L531

Norton, Mrs. Judith

has been extremely ill L361

health improved L374, L377

recovered L381, L382

on seeing Clarissa dead, they were forced to breathe a vein L487

too ill to accompany the hearse to Harlowe Place L500

will not live long L520

Norton, Mrs. Judith, family, Tommy

a feverish disorder, violent fever L301, L307, L308

at death's door L361

recovering L374, L377, L381, L382

Sinclair, Mrs.

broken leg, mortifying L493

dying of a broken leg L499

Sinclair, Mrs., whores, Horton, Mary (Polly)

dying of a violent cold CONCLUSION

illnesses, feigned

Harlowe, Miss Clarissa

to delay wedding Solmes L73, L83, L85, L90.1

Lovelace, Mr. Robert

stomach disorder, broken vessel caused by ipecacuanha, vomiting blood L209, L210, L212

gout, ague, limping, using a cane L232, L233

impersonators see **contrivances of Lovelace**, *Lovelace, Mr. Robert*, specifically, contrivances of the impersonators

impostors see

contrivances of Lovelace, *Lovelace, Mr. Robert*, specifically, contrivance of Captain Tomlinson and
Uncle Harlowe's birthday, Tomlinson, Captain Antony, imposter

contrivances of Lovelace, *Lovelace, Mr. Robert*, specifically, contrivance of Mrs. Fretchville's house

independence

Harlowe, Miss Arabella
      accusing Clarissa of wanting independence L53
Harlowe, Miss Clarissa
      and power conferred by her inheritance L13, L19, L32.3
      Morden's arrival meaning Clarissa's independence L53, L152
      Lord M. making her an independent wife L207
      her independent fortune L253
      will not live to take possession of her independence L309
      I never had any pride in being independent of them L474

India Bonds

Lovelace, Mr. Robert, friends, Belton, Mr. Thomas, relations, Sambre, Mrs.
      Mowbray, Tourville, Lovelace giving her their legacy for India Bonds L449

influence in Harlowe Family

Harlowe, Mrs. Charlotte
      lacking influence in the family L27
      losing her identity in her family L47
      patching up for herself a precarious and sorry quiet L181
      cannot help Clarissa as the family is too much against her L182
      cannot oppose the rest L376
      sympathy for Clarissa
            afraid to speak for Clarissa L379, L433
            unable to help Clarissa L382
            her heart...is in their measures L409
            acting contrary to her inclinations L432
            would have sympathized with Clarissa L432
            will do nothing to help Clarissa without permission of Papa and Uncles Harlowe L459
Harlowe, Mr. James, Jun.
      inheritances giving him too much influence L5
      influence with Papa and Mamma L17
      turning family against Clarissa L24.2, L53.1
      schemes sanctioned by Papa L39
      governing the will of the family L319
      governing Papa L379
Harlowe, Mr. John
      having great weight in the family L174
Hervey, Mrs. Dorothy
      dare not speak in Clarissa's favor L174, L433
      would have sympathized with Clarissa L432
Morden, Colonel William
      lacking influence to bring about reconciliation L455
      cannot prevail against James L459
Norton, Mrs. Judith
      lacking money to back up her point of view L13

influence on Clarissa

Harlowe Family, clergymen, Lewin, Dr. Arthur
      influence noted L48
Howe, Miss Anna
      Anna's L354

influence on Howe, Mrs. Annabella

Harlowe, Mr. Antony

 influencing Mrs. Howe against Lovelace after the duel L1

 revealing to Mrs. Howe the purpose of an alliance with Solmes L27

 used by Lovelace to influence Mrs. Howe against Clarissa L104, L105, L111, L125, L128

informants

Harlowe, Miss Clarissa, friends, Lardner, Miss

 her footman appearing at Mrs. Sinclair's inquiring about Clarissa and Lovelace L213, L214

 her servant following Clarissa back to Mrs. Sinclair's from church L229.1

Harlowe, Mr. James, Jun.

 steward (discharged) of Lord M.

  hired to supply information on Lovelace L4, L12, L14

  his report on Lovelace and his six or seven bad companions L81

Harlowe Family, clergymen, Brand, Mr. Elias

 his informants, the milliner L444, L445

 informing on Clarissa

  sent to inquire about Clarissa L361, L381, L399

  not reporting to the Harlowe Family what they do not want to hear L382, L446, L458

  his indifference to Clarissa's poor health L399

  his misrepresentations to the family about Clarissa L408

  creating scandal on account of Belford's visits to Clarissa L431, L433, L455

  his suspicions of Clarissa's attending prayers L444

  his letter of recantation mentioned L460, L464, L466, L467

Hervey, Mrs. Dorothy

 relating steward's (discharged) report on Lovelace to Clarissa L4

Hickman, Mr. Charles

 to find out opinions of the ladies of Lovelace's family about the state of affairs in the Harlowe Family L26

 sounding Lord M. on a subject recommended by Clarissa L27

 sent to London by Anna to inquire about Lovelace's life in town L27

 results of his investigation reported to Clarissa by Anna L48

Howe, Miss Anna

 her new informant on Lovelace L177

Lord M., servants, steward (discharged)

 hired by James to supply information on Lovelace L4, L12, L14

 his report on Lovelace L81

Lovelace, Mr. Robert

 Leman, Joseph

  double agent, double agency explained L35, L62, L80, L100, L113, L119

  Lovelace's intelligencer L62, L85

  gossiping with Betty about Lovelace and Rosebud L71, L73

  not entirely loyal to Lovelace L73, L84

  causing family to suspect Clarissa of corresponding with Lovelace L84

  spying on Clarissa for the family L86

  family suspect Lovelace's source of information is Clarissa, when in fact it is Leman L91

  doubted by Clarissa L94

  corrupted by Lovelace L95

  vile agent of Lovelace L101, L229.1

  used by Lovelace to influence Antony, who influences Mrs. Howe L104

  informing Lovelace about James's alliance with the Bettertons L127

  informing Lovelace about James's plan to rescue Clarissa L137, L140, L152

Moore, Mrs., relations, Bevis, Mrs.

 informing Will of Clarissa's movements L253

informants (cont.)

Morden, Colonel William

    Alston, Mr., gentleman farmer

        old farmer-looking man, sent to ask about Clarissa's health L426

        honest, serious man sent by Morden to inquire about Clarissa's condition L455

        his inquiries about Clarissa L459

Smith, Mr. John, neighbors, Barker

    informants of Brand's L444, L445

Smith, Mr. John, neighbors, Walton, Mr. and Mrs. John

    informant of Brand's L444, L445

inheritances see also **bequests of...; wills**

Belford, Mr. John

    his uncle's heir L172, L247

    inheriting £5000 cash and £500 a year from his uncle L258

    giving his inheritance all to Lovelace if he will marry Clarissa L258

    his increased fortune L344

    made rich by his uncle's death L425, L444

Harlowe, Mrs. Charlotte

    her inheritances increasing Papa's wealth L4

Harlowe, Miss Clarissa

    from Grandfather Harlowe

        Anna's Aunt Harman approving L1

        causing sibling jealousy L2, L8, L13

        regretted by Clarissa L2, L6, L8, L17, L42

        Papa's displeasure at L7

        family setting aside his will L7

        may be litigated by James L13

        her independence and power conferred by L13, L19, L32.3

        regretted by Antony L32.4

        family's right to L32.4

        family pictures and family plate L42

        less than half his real estate left to Clarissa L42

        Clarissa not valuing herself upon L135

        wishing to write to Uncle Harlowe about the terms of her inheritance L157

        giving up her grandfather's bequest to appease her brother L174

    from Papa

        inheriting from her father, her uncles, and Morden as well as from Grandfather L442

    from Uncles Harlowe

        intended L13, L75

        no longer favored in Antony's will L182

    from Morden

        intended L455

        Morden's heir and executrix L459

    from Lord M.

        Lord M.'s heir rather than Lovelace, if Lovelace displease him L207

Harlowe, Mr. Antony

    Clarissa's inheritance

        regretted by Antony L32.4

        family's right to L32.4

Harlowe, Mr. James, Jun.

    his own inheritance

        large estates in Scotland L2

        inheritances giving him too much influence L5

        greed resulting from L8

inheritances, *Harlowe, Mr. James, Jun.*, his own inheritance (cont.)
>> anticipated, from various relatives L13
>> hopes for title based on L13
>> from Godmother Lovell L13
>>> his Yorkshire property L2
>>> mentioned in Grandfather's will L4
>> will not be Morden's heir L408
> Clarissa's inheritance, he will litigate to acquire L13

Harlowe, Mr. James, Sen.
> Mamma's inheritances increasing his wealth L4
> his power over Clarissa's inheritance L2
> will litigate if she marries Lovelace L39

Harlowe Family
> discussed at length L13
> opposed to Clarissa's inheritance, but deferring to Grandfather's wishes L32.4
> to be reassessed after her flight L100

Hervey, Mrs. Dorothy
> confiding in Clarissa her uncles' intentions to favor her in their wills L13

Hickman, Mr. Charles
> mother-in-law [stepmother] leaving him a jointure of £600 a year, and considerable L459

Howe, Miss Anna, relations, Harman, Aunt
> approving Clarissa's inheritance L1

Lovelace, Mr. Robert
> heir presumptive to Lord M.'s estate L2, L13, L118
> expecting a large estate from Lord M. L105
> willing to lay obligation of one half of his estate upon Clarissa L105
> if not a good husband, Lord M. will leave all to Clarissa and none to Lovelace L206
> would like £8000 a year and the title reversionary L265
> trouble with some of his relations anticipated after Lord M.'s death L285
> titles going with the bulk of Lord M.'s estate L327

ink
Harlowe, Miss Clarissa
> my ink runs nothing but gall L52
> gall in her ink L311

Howe, Miss Anna
> dipping her pen in gall L55

interviews
Lovelace, Mr. Robert
> early meeting with Anna mentioned L27
> with Hickman L346
> with Anna L366, L367
> with Clarissa planned L371

ipecacuanha
Lovelace, Mr. Robert
> taking a few grains to make himself vomit blood L209, L211, L272

isinglass
Harlowe, Miss Clarissa, servants, Grimes
> his eyes as L238

J

jellies see **medications**, *Harlowe, Miss Clarissa*

jesting
Harlowe, Miss Clarissa, suitors to Harlowe, Miss Clarissa, Wyerley, Mr. Alexander
      jester upon sacred things L40, L78
Lovelace, Mr. Robert
      on jesting, in poor men L140
      all that has passed between Lovelace and Clarissa, a jest L453
Lovelace, Mr. Robert, friends, Mowbray, Mr. Richard
      jesting upon sacred things L161

jewels see also **estates,** *Harlowe, Miss Clarissa*, jewels; **rings**
Harlowe, Miss Clarissa
      her grandmother's jewels L41.1, L45, L202
            wanting new setting L202
            proceeds of sale, to Poor's Fund, or estate, or Papa L507
            a gift from her Grandfather L507
            valued and money paid to estate L520
      her own jewels L41.1, L202
            not sent in the parcel to Anna before flight L69
            left behind after flight L100
            requested to be sent to her after flight L102
            will not be sent L147, L152
            her rings, her watch, her little money for a coach L314
            a few valuables at her lodgings at Smith's L334
            diamond necklace, solitaire, and buckles given her by Sir Josias Brookland L507
                  proceeds of sale of to estate L507
            Anna wanting to purchase Clarissa's jewels L510.3
            valued and given to Dolly L520
      offered by Solmes L41.1, L90.1
      offered by Lovelace L186
            jeweller bringing several sets for her to choose from L207
            Lovelace's mother's jewels may be new set for Clarissa L207
Hervey, Mrs. Dorothy, family, Hervey, Miss Dolly
      Morden presenting her with Clarissa's jewels L520
Howe, Miss Anna
      Anna wanting to purchase Clarissa's jewels L510.3
Lovelace, Mr. Robert
      borrowing jewels, ear-rings, solitaire for impersonators of Lady Betty and Charlotte L255

jewels, figurative
Harlowe, Miss Clarissa
      her mind so much a jewel L202
      Clarissa a jewel, finest jewel, so rich a jewel L258, L321, L399, L501

Jews
Belford, Mr. John
      learning Old Testament history from Josephus L364
Hickman, Mr. Charles
      miserly citizen L346

Jews (cont.)

Lovelace, Mr. Robert

    synagogue lattices promoting piety L106

    Josephus, *Antiquities of the Jews*, quoted L191, L191n2

    women have no souls, or so he believes as a Jew L219, L219n2

    and Lovelace's description of death L346

journey see also **lodgings**

Harlowe, Miss Clarissa

  Harlowe Place L1–L91

    flight, foreshadowed

      suggested L44, L49

      if she left her parents, the world would be against her L56

      only extremity would make her abandon her father's house L57

      fearing if turned out, she will not see home again L59.4

    flight, preparations

      sending parcel of linen and letters to Anna L69

      asking Anna to procure disguise and transportation L82

      writing to Lovelace to request assistance in escaping Harlowe Place L83, L86

      only Anna will know her whereabouts L86

    flight, refuge considered

      Lovelace's family L36, L49, L61, L76, L83, L104

      Anna's L52, L53.1, L69, L75, L79, L80, L155

        refused by Mrs. Howe L81

      Grandfather's late house L53.1

      Aunt Hervey's L53.1, L54.1, L145

      Uncle Harlowe's L32.1, L53.1, L54.1

      London L49, L54, L76, L82, L104

      Leghorn L54

      private lodgings near Aunt Lawrance L86, L98

      her estate L101, L102

      Antony's L145

    flight, reconsidered

      finally resolved not to go off with Lovelace L89, L94, L393

      her letter of countermand ignored by Lovelace L99

      her preconcerted escape L103

    flight, Clarissa Harlowe, gone off with a man L92

  St. Albans, at the inn L92–L97

    soon to leave present lodgings L94

    the gentlewoman and her niece attending Clarissa at the inn L98

    agreeing to an inn near the Lawn L98, L104

    asking family that she be allowed to go to the Grove L102

    not wishing to depend upon Lovelace L102, L152

    wanting Lovelace to leave her L107, L116, L123

  Mrs. Sorlings's dairy farm L98–L148

    accompanied by Mrs. Greme to Mrs. Sorlings's L98

    wishing to stay longer L121

    planning removal to London L126, L135, L137, L153

    considering lodgings in Norfolk Street or Cecil Street L130

    setting out for London L149–L153

  Mrs. Sinclair's, London L154–L227

    would like to go to a neighboring village and await Morden L185

    followed home from church by a footman of Miss Lardner L213, L214

    Clarissa's lodgings known to Misses Lardner, Biddulph, Lloyd, and Howe L229.1

    escape from L228, L230

journey, *Harlowe, Miss Clarissa* (cont.)
> Mrs. Moore's, Hampstead L230–L255
>> waiting at Hampstead for an answer from Anna L233
>> inquiring about the Hampstead coach to Hedon L235
>> considering removal from Mrs. Moore's L242
>> not wishing to return to Mrs. Sinclair's L245
>> tricked into returning to Mrs. Sinclair's with Lovelace L312
>
> Mrs. Sinclair's, London L256–L290
>> expecting to return to Mrs. Moore's at Hampstead this night L256
>> desperate to leave for Mrs. Leeson's or Hampstead L256
>> trying to escape L262, L264, L266, L267, L276
>> wishing to return to Mrs. Moore's at Hampstead L277, L278
>> the lady is gone off L291
>> details of her escape reported L293
>
> Mr. and Mrs. Smith's, Covent Garden L291–L330
>> missing from her lodgings L329
>
> Mr. and Mrs. Rowland's, High Holborn L330–L336
>> Clarissa under arrest L330
>> Sally and Polly trying to cajole Clarissa back to Mrs. Sinclair's L333
>
> Mr. and Mrs. Smith's, Covent Garden L336–L495
>> Belford persuading Clarissa to return to Smith's L336
>> her lodgings at Smith's described, her happiness there L338, L339
>> Anna finds lodgings for Clarissa at a nearby farmhouse, she will not remove L366, L368
>> vacating Smith's to avoid Lovelace's visits L418, L426, L440
>> her body ordered conveyed to Harlowe Place L494.1
>
> Harlowe Place L500
>> the hearse arriving at six in the afternoon L500

journey, figurative see also **father's house**
Harlowe, Miss Clarissa
> to a better world L333
> going on a long journey L343
> death as a journey's end L349
> upon a better preparation than for an earthly husband L362
> returning to her father's house L421.1, L424, L440, L442, L446, L449, L486, L510.4
> death as a journey L441

juleps see **medications**

K

keyhole
Lovelace, Mr. Robert
> looking through the keyhole of Clarissa's door L264

keys
Harlowe, Miss Clarissa
> Lovelace having keys to Harlowe Place L35, L61, L62, L94, L95
> giving up her keys to Harlowe Place L78, L91
> her key left inside lock, indicating she left by her own consent L95
> Lovelace having no keys to the wainscot box holding her letters L210
> Mrs. Bevis may return Clarissa's keys to Mrs. Sinclair's L245

keys, *Harlowe, Miss Clarissa* (cont.)

    key to her chamber door at Mrs. Sinclair's in her pocket L281

    Clarissa demanding a key to the street door at Mrs. Sinclair's L293

    not trusted with keys to her room at Rowland's L333

    giving Belford her keys to Smith's L336

    giving the keys to her trunks to Mrs. Smith and Mrs. Lovick to inventory them L340

    having a key to her own apartment at Smith's L416

    giving Belford the keys to the drawer holding her will and papers L460

    the key to trunks holding her apparel in the drawer with her papers and will L460

Harlowe, Mr. James, Jun.

    having keys to Papa's parlour L78

Harlowe Family, servants, Barnes, Betty

    discovered, key in hand, searching Clarissa's closet L69

    sent to fetch keys from Clarissa L78

Harlowe Family, servants, Leman, Joseph

    having a key to the garden door L35

Hervey, Mrs. Dorothy, family, Hervey, Miss Dolly

    made to request Clarissa's keys L78

Lovelace, Mr. Robert

    having two keys to the garden door at Harlowe Place L35, L61, L62, L94, L95

    key used to lock up the prude while Lovelace seduced the French marquis's wife L209

    not having the keys to the wainscot box where Clarissa has moved her letters L210

    Clarissa keeping her chamber keys in her pocket, foiling a second rape L281

Moore, Mrs.

    or Mrs. Bevis, may return Clarissa's to Mrs. Sinclair L245

Sinclair, Mrs.

    keys to be kept at the door L293

Sinclair, Mrs., whores, Wykes, Dorcas

    having keys to Clarissa's clothing chest L174.3

    using her key to search Clarissa's chamber for letters L198

kidnapping see **contrivances of Lovelace**, *Lovelace, Mr. Robert*, specifically, contrivance of kidnapping James and Solmes, planned

kings see

    historical references

    political references, *Howe, Miss Anna*

kisses

Harlowe, Miss Clarissa, suitors to Harlowe, Miss Clarissa, Solmes, Mr. Roger

    kissing Clarissa's hand L78

Lovelace, Mr. Robert

    for Clarissa

        kissing her hand L36, L94

        first time L103

        wishing to kiss Clarissa L115

        snatching and kissing Clarissa's hand L157

        giving Clarissa a fervent kiss L175

        attempting to kiss Clarissa L187

        kissing Clarissa's hand, cheek L194

        kissing her hand L199, L211, L215, L216, L248

        kissing Clarissa's hand, leaving a red mark L200, L201

        kissing her unrepulsing hand five times L204

        wishing for one consenting kiss from Clarissa L205

        clasping his arms about Clarissa and forcing a kiss L215

kisses, *Lovelace, Mr. Robert*, for Clarissa (cont.)
  kissing her hands, his cheek on her shoulder, arm around her waist, kissing her lips L220
  drawing aside the handkerchief and kissing her breast L220
  seizing scissors from Clarissa, clasping her to his bosom, kissing her L225
  snatching Clarissa's hand, kissing it L276, L277
    for Mrs. Sorlings's younger daughter L105

kneeling
Harlowe, Miss Clarissa
  falling on her knees at Papa's door, pressing against it L78
  Clarissa wild with apprehensions, begging mercy on her knees before Lovelace L256
  on her knees writing to Mamma L391, L399
  on her knees writing to Anna L473, L473.2
Harlowe, Miss Clarissa, suitors to Harlowe, Miss Clarissa, Solmes, Mr. Roger
  kneeling before Clarissa L78
Harlowe, Mr. James, Sen.
  would kneel before Clarissa L144, L145
Lovelace, Mr. Robert
  kneeling as he writes in the coppice to Clarissa L64.1
  kneeling before Clarissa L94, L98, L201
  upon his knees L137, L138
  reptile kneeler L274
  kneeling L281

L

language see also **sayings and proverbs**; **women's language**
Belford, Mr. John, relations, Jenyns, Tony
  prating against wedlock L192
Howe, Miss Anna
  he will be *Harlowed off* L100
  she had not best *Harlowe* me L100
  Antonyed L100
Lord M.
  Lovelace expressing himself in Lord M.'s style L512
  his phrasing, typified L515
Lovelace, Mr. Robert
  cabala, word used by rakes L110
  using out-of-the-way words and phrases L117
  expletives
    by Jupiter L228, L244, L330, L410, L416, L511, L513, L516
    Io Triumphe! Io Clarissa, sing L231
  in coelo salus—or *quies* L294
  prating L323
  I was *Belforded* all over L416
  in Lord M.'s style L512, L515

languages
Harlowe, Miss Clarissa
  reading *Telemachus* in French L155, L155n1
  Italian, French, Latin L529

languages (cont.)
Lovelace, Mr. Robert
      skill in learned and modern languages, speaking many languages L161
Lovelace, Mr. Robert, friends, Mowbray, Mr. Richard
      speaking many languages L161
Lovelace, Mr. Robert, friends, Tourville, Mr. James
      speaking French and Italian L161

law
Belford, Mr. John
      his knowledge of L379
Harlowe, Miss Clarissa
      constable called as Clarissa shouts from the window L264
      the law her resource and refuge L281
      Clarissa arrested, action dismissed L333, L334
Hickman, Mr. Charles
      designed for the law, chambers at Lincoln's Inn L196
Lord M.
      Lovelace argues his defense before Lord M. L515
      peers are judges in the last resort L515
      If by committing an unlawful act, a capital crime is the consequence, you are answerable to both L515
Lord M., relations, half-sisters, Lawrance, Lady Betty
      her affair in chancery, in a good way L158, L303
Lovelace, Mr. Robert
      narrate...the Scottish phrase L322, L322n1
      believing his crime was common theft L515
      commission...quorum L516, L516n1

lemonade see **drink**, *Lord M.*

Levite
Harlowe Family, clergymen, Brand, Mr. Elias
      the young Levite L399, L410, L443

libertine
Howe, Miss Anna, suitors to Howe, Miss Anna, Colmar, Sir George
      a fop and a libertine L182, L355
Lovelace, Mr. Robert
      free liver L118, L217.2
      Lovelace as L144, L173.1, L177, L182, L222, L229.1, L316, L342, L346, L366, L367, L379
      libertine whom Clarissa loved and wished to reclaim L365
      rake and libertine L402

lies
Lovelace, Mr. Robert
      never lied to a man nor said truth to a woman L513

light see also **angel**; **divine qualities**; **example**; **fall**; **sacrifice**; **suffering**; **trials**; **virgin**
Harlowe, Miss Clarissa
      shining light L81, L260
      flood of brightness L99
      flood of brightness...glory...dazzle L136
      irradiating every circle she set her foot into L358
      appearing in a divine light L397
      blazes out with meridian lustre L453

light, *Harlowe, Miss Clarissa* (cont.)
    brightest of innocents L456
    brightened and purified by her sufferings L459
    like the sun L470
    among the stars L470
    after death, all light and all mind L473.1
    her soul now in the regions of light L481
    angel of light L494

liquor see **drink**, *Lovelace, Mr. Robert*

literary references see also **books**; **poems**
Belford, Mr. John
    Blackwall, Anthony, *The Sacred Classics*, mentioned L364, L364n4
    Congreve, William, *The Mourning Bride*, quoted L365, L365n1
    Dryden, John
        Troilus and Cressida, quoted L364, L364n1
        All for Love, quoted L419, L419n4 (superscript 4 omitted from text)
    Norris, John, *Collection of Miscellanies*, quoted L419, L419n6
    Otway, Thomas, *The History and Fall of Caius Marius*, quoted L336, L336n1
    Pomfret, John, *Prospect of Death*, quoted L419, L419n7
    Rawlins, Thomas, *Tom Essence* L413, L413n3
    Restoration drama, Clarissa's story summed up and compared L413
    Rowe, Nicholas, *The Fair Penitent*, Clarissa as L413n1 (appearing in Notes as L413n2)
    Shakespeare, William, *Macbeth*, quoted L419, L419n1
    Swift, Jonathan, *Gulliver's Travels*, Yahoos mentioned L499
    untraced quote L424, L424n2
    Virgil, *Aeneid*, Harpies mentioned L499, L499n1
Harlowe, Mr. Antony
    Valentine and Orson, his morals compared to Orson's L128, L128n1
Harlowe, Miss Clarissa
    Carter, Elizabeth, *Ode to Wisdom*
        text L54, L54n1
        music APPENDIX (appearing in v.2, Letter IX in editions printed by Richardson)
    Cowley, Abraham
        Ode to Wit, quoted L222, L222n1
        On the Death of Mrs. Philips, quoted L222, L222n2
        The Mistress, quoted L261 Paper X, L261 Paper Xn1
    Dryden, John
        Fables Ancient and Modern, quoted L21, L21n1
        Absalom and Achitophel, quoted L91, L91n1, L261 Paper X, L261 Paper Xn1
        Oedipus, adapted by Dryden and Lee, quoted L174, L174n1, L261 Paper X, L261 Paper Xn1
    Garth, Samuel, *The Dispensary*, quoted L261 Paper X, L261 Paper Xn1
    Howard, John, untraced quote L458, L458n1
    Lee, Nathaniel, *Oedipus*, adapted by Dryden and Lee, quoted L174, L174n1, L261 Paper X, L261 Paper Xn1
    Milton, John, *Paradise Lost*, quoted L161, L161n1
    Otway, Thomas, *Venice Preserved*, quoted L261 Paper X, L261 Paper Xn1
    Rowe, Nicholas, *Ulysses*, quoted L116, L116n3
    Shakespeare, William
        A Midsummer Night's Dream, quoted L98, L98n2
        Hamlet, quoted L261 Paper X, L261 Paper Xn1
    Tate, Nahum, his translation of Juvenal's *Satire XV*, quoted L217.3, L217.3n1
    Thomas à Kempis L75, L75n1
Harlowe, Mr. James, Jun.
    Dryden, John, translation of Virgil's *Georgic* L50.1

literary references (cont.)

Harlowe Family, clergymen, Brand, Mr. Elias
  de Foe, Daniel, *The True-Born Englishman*, quoted L444, L444n2
  Quarles, Francis, *Emblems*, misquoted L444, L444n1
  untraced quote L444, L444n5
Harlowe Family, servants, Barnes, Betty
  reading *Mother Goose* and concerning the *Fairies* L63
Howe, Miss Anna
  Angelica needing confidants, Violetta, Cleanthe, Clelia, or an old nurse L74
  Josephus, *Antiquities of the Jews*, Herod loving his Mariamne L229.1, L229.1n1
  Norris, John
    quoted L27
    his *Miscellanies*, sent to Clarissa, with money L148
    Clarissa returning Anna's Norris L149, L150, L156
    Lovelace not to be *out-Norrised* L198, L199, L215
  Pope, Alexander
    perhaps the celebrated bard L47, L47n1
    Of the Characters of Women, every woman a rake L115, L115n2, L367, L367n1
  Rowe, Nicholas, quoted L119
  Steele, Richard, *The Tender Husband*, quoted but not named L132, L132n1
  Valentine and Orson L128, L128n1
Lord M.
  Wycherley, William, mentioned L190, L190n2
  Harlowes and Lovelace behaving as Orsons L442
Lovelace, Mr. Robert
  Addison, Joseph
    Remarks on Several Parts of Italy, quoted L350, L350n1
    Steele's Prologue to Addison's *Cato*, quoted L370, L370n8
    The Campaign, quoted L463, L463n1
  Aesop's Fables, quoted L371, L371n2
  Aesop's traveller, Belford compared L472
  Ariosto, *Orlando Furioso* L110, L110fn, L267, L267n1, L512, L512n1
  Baxter, Richard, *Baxter's History of Spirits and Apparitions* L272, L272n1
  Boileau-Despréaux, Nicholas, *Le Lutrin* L171, L171n1
  Burnet, Gilbert, quoted but not named L157.1, L157.1n1
  Butler, Samuel
    quoted but not named L110, L110n1
    Hudibras, quoted L231, L231n2
  Cibber, Colley, *The Careless Husband*, Clarissa as *Lady Easy* to Lovelace's pleasures L207
  Congreve, William
    quoted L157, L157n3
    The Mourning Bride L365, L365n1, L370, L370n4
  Cowley, Abraham
    quoted L31, L31n6
    Destiny, quoted L202, L202n1
    translation of Horace, *Odes*, Book II, quoted L264, L264n1
  Cromwell, Oliver, quoted L99
  Dryden, John
    quoted L31, L31n3, L31n5, L35, L35n1, L154, L154n2
    Aureng-Zebe, quoted L169, L169n1, L191n1
    Don Sebastian, quoted L159, L159n3, L530, L530n3
    rearrangement of Shakespeare's *Troilus and Cressida*, quoted L235, L235n1
    Alexander's Feast, mentioned, not quoted L370, L370n7
    Conquest of Granada, quoted L530, L530n2
  Glanville, Joseph, *Glanville of Witches* L272, L272n1

literary references, *Lovelace, Mr. Robert* (cont.)

    Greene, Robert, *History of Dorastus and Faunia,* Mrs. Sinclair's cook-maid reading L225, L225n1

    Horace, *Odes,* quoted in Latin L530, L530n1

    Howard, Robert, quoted L31, L31n1

    James VI of Scotland and I of England, *Demonology* L272, L272n1

    Kennet, White, *History of England from...Charles I to...William II* L294, L294n2

    Lee, Nathaniel

        Death of Alexander the Great, quoted L97, L97n1

        Gloriana, Clarissa as L159, L159n2

        his left-handed gods at work L194

        Caesar Borgia, quoted L228, L228n3

        Mithridates, quoted L417, L417n2, L497, L497n1

        mentioned, on dying L422

    Mandeville, Bernard, private vices are public benefits L246, L246n1

    Milton, John, *Paradise Lost,* the devil in L233, L233n1

    Montaigne, *Essays* L193, L193n1

    More, Chancellor, Lovelace comparing himself L346, L346n3

    Otway, Thomas

        History and Fall of Caius Marius, quoted L31, L31n2

        Venice Preserved L194, L194n1

        Orphan, mentioned L442, L442n1

    Pope, Alexander, *Of the Characters of Women,* quoted L115, L115n2

    Prior, Matt

        Erle Robert's Mice, quoted L259, L259n2

        Alma, quoted L346, L346n2

        The Ladle, quoted L453, L453n1

    Rochester, Earl of, *Valentinian. A Tragedy, as 'tis altered by the late Earl of Rochester,* quoted L228, L228n2

    Rowe, Nicholas

        Ambitious Stepmother, quoted L154, L154n4

        Tamerlane, quoted L159, L159n4, L511, L511n2

        quoted L227

        learning Spanish L229, L229n2

        The Fair Penitent, quoted L371, L371n1

        mentioned L415

    Royal Insignificant, *Demonology* L272, L272n1

    Shakespeare, William

        Othello, quoted L31, L31n4

        The Tempest, quoted L31, L31n7

        Macbeth, quoted L175, L175n2

        Troilus and Cressida

            quoted L209, L209n1

            rearrangement of, by Dryden, quoted L235, L235n1

        Julius Caesar, quoted L221, L221n1

        much ado about nothing L227

        a line! a line! a kingdom for a line L330

        Measure for Measure, quoted L371, L371n3

        Hamlet, quoted L396, L396n1

    Steele, Richard

        Prologue to Addison's *Cato,* quoted L370, L370n8

        The Tender Husband, mentioned L516, L516n2

    Swift, Jonathan

        Tale of a Tub

            quoted L103, L103n1, L218, L218n1

            a tub to the whale L323

literary references, *Lovelace, Mr. Robert*, Swift, Jonathan, *Tale of a Tub* (cont.)

      Digressions in Praise of Digressions, mentioned, not quoted L346, L346n1

      mentioned L370

    Gulliver's Travels, quoted L439

  Taylor, Jeremy, *Taylor's Holy Living and Dying* L313, L313n1

  untraced quotes L174.3, L174.3n1, L225, L225n2, L416, L416n1, L463, L463n2, L511, L511n1, L535, L535n1

  Valentinian. A Tragedy, as 'tis altered by the late Earl of Rochester, quoted L228, L228n2

  Waller, Edmund, *Of Love*, quoted L207, L207n1

  Whitefield, George, an enthusiast, quoted L370, L370n5

Lovelace, Mr. Robert, friends, Belton, Mr. Thomas

  admired author, Nick Rowe L413

  his pleasure in poetry, classics, drama L419

Lovelace, Mr. Robert, friends, Mowbray, Mr. Richard

  Lee, Nathaniel and John Dryden, *Oedipus*, quoted L419, L419n5

  hating reading and books L496

  Dryden, John, *Palamon and Arcite*, quoted L496, L496n1

Moore, Mrs., relations, Bevis, Mrs

  Butler, Samuel, *Hudibras*, quoted L237, L237n1

Morden, Colonel William

  inflaming novels and idle romances read by women L442

Sinclair, Mrs.

  preferring comedy to tragedy L194

Sinclair, Mrs., servants, cook-maid

  Greene, Robert, *History of Dorastus and Faunia*, reading L225, L225n1

Sinclair, Mrs., whores, Martin, Sarah (Sally)

  Shakespeare misquoted L157, L157n2

  Prior, Matt, *Poems on Several Occasions*, doubling down the useful places of the Bible L333, L333n1

litter see **transportation**, *Lord M.*

livery

Harlowe, Miss Clarissa

  not yet prepared to wear Lovelace's livery L123

Harlowe, Miss Clarissa, friends, Lardner, Miss

  servant, footman in blue livery inquiring after Clarissa and Lovelace at Mrs. Sinclair's L213

Lovelace, Mr. Robert

  offering to wear Clarissa's livery L124

  Lovelace putting on Clarissa's livery and wearing it for life L276

Lovelace, Mr. Robert, servants, Summers, Will

  wearing Lovelace's livery L231.1, L416

lodgers

Smith, Mr. John

  Lovick, Mrs.

    age, turned of fifty L514

    attending Clarissa

      her voluntary attendance on Clarissa L338, L348, L349

      writing a letter for Clarissa L338, L473.2

      giving Clarissa's Meditation to Belford L364

      inquiring into Belford's general character L379

      interview with Lovelace, telling him Clarissa went out to avoid him L418

      Clarissa visiting Mrs. Lovick's friend in town L426

      caring for Clarissa's body after her death L457

      reading Anna's letter to Clarissa L473

lodgers, *Smith, Mr. John*, Lovick, Mrs. (cont.)
       bequest of Clarissa, linen and laces, and some books L507
       character
             of great merit L307, L320
             respected, pious, prudent L320
             compared to Mrs. Norton L338
             her love for Clarissa, her compassion L338, L349
       costume, selling Clarissa's clothes L345, L365, L426
       family, widow of low fortunes L307, L320
       housekeeper, hired by Belford at Edgware L514, CONCLUSION
       lodgings, over Clarissa L338
       meals, breakfasting with Clarissa L440
Smith, Mr. John, neighbors, Barker
       lodging with the Waltons L445

lodgings see also **journey**; **residences**
Belford, Mr. John
       near Soho Square with a relation, a lady of virtue and honor L125
       with his uncle in Watford L190.1
       at Edgware on Sundays L330
       lodgings in town L330
       lodgings with his cousin and her family L440
Harlowe, Miss Clarissa
       Anna will procure lodgings for Clarissa in a neighboring village L252.1
       at Smith's, described L320, L338, L339
       at Rowland's, described L334, L336
       Anna finding lodgings for Clarissa at a nearby farmhouse, she will not remove L366, L368
Howe, Miss Anna
       not knowing where Clarissa is lodging L214
       now knowing Clarissa's whereabouts L229.1
       will procure lodgings for Clarissa in a neighboring village L252.1
Lovelace, Mr. Robert
       putting up at the inn in the village of Neale L63
       taking all vacant apartments at Mrs. Sinclair's L154
       lodging, boarding at Mrs. Moore's, engaging all her rooms for one month L233, L241
       Clarissa's objections forcing him to lodge about twelve doors off from Mrs. Moore's L239
       returning to his lodgings at Mrs. Sinclair's L416
       offering to lodge at Smith's, till Clarissa returns, at ten guineas a day L416
       returning to M. Hall L421, L424
Moore, Mrs.
       letting to Clarissa L230–L255
       letting to Lovelace L233–L239
Morden, Colonel William
       with Antony while in England, and refusing to continue L459
Smith, Mr. John
       letting to Mrs. Lovick L307–L514
       letting to Clarissa L336–L495

love
Lovelace, Mr. Robert
       love, an encroacher L220

love for Clarissa
Lovelace, Mr. Robert
       confiding in Aunt Hervey his passion for Clarissa L3

love for Clarissa, *Lovelace, Mr. Robert* (cont.)
>in love with Clarissa L13
>his passion for Clarissa, second to revenge L137, L143
>noted L137, L187.1–L187.4, L194, L229.1, L281, L282, L287, L303, L350, L395, L470
>revering Clarissa L187.1–L187.4
>his love for, now more intellectual than personal L453

love for Lovelace
Harlowe, Miss Clarissa
>love for, lacking L10, L11, L207
>noted L229.1, L241, L511
>admitting her former bias in Lovelace's favor L243
>once could have loved Lovelace L309, L428, L467
>bent upon reclaiming a libertine whom she loved L365
Howe, Miss Anna
>fearing Clarissa may love Lovelace L12, L37
Lovelace, Mr. Robert
>doubting Clarissa's love L171, L209

Lovelace's Reveries
Lovelace, Mr. Robert
>book about dreams, planned by Lovelace L272

lozenges
Harlowe, Miss Clarissa
>lozenge on the widow's chariot signifying widowhood L273
Sinclair, Mrs., whores, Wykes, Dorcas
>recognizing the lozenge on the widow lady's chariot L273

M

madness
Harlowe, Miss Clarissa
>wishing to go to Bedlam L261.1
>preferring a private madhouse L261.1
>I began to be mad at Hampstead—so you said L261.1

malmsey
Lovelace, Mr. Robert
>as medication L203, L203n1

manes
Harlowe, Miss Clarissa
>of Clarissa L497, L536

mannerisms
Hickman, Mr. Charles
>stroking his chin, stroking his ruffles, setting his wig, pulling his neckcloth L346
>fribbling with his waitcoat buttons L346
Lovelace, Mr. Robert, contrivances of Lovelace, specifically, contrivance of Captain Tomlinson and Uncle Harlowe's birthday, Tomlinson, Captain Antony
>pulling down and stroking his ruffles, pulling his wig L237, L244, L289

mannerisms (cont.)
Moore, Mrs., relations, Bevis, Mrs.
    making faces L243

manners
Harlowe, Miss Arabella
    ill-mannered L355
Hickman, Mr. Charles
    his flourishes L119
Lord M.
    well-mannered peer L203
Lovelace, Mr. Robert
    not so polite as she would expect L101
    his flourishes L107
    careless manners L121
    polite L123, L128
    his unpoliteness L127, L204
    self-pluming air L187
    keeping eyes within bounds L210
    rough-mannered disgrace of his birth L243
    coaching impersonators of Lady Betty and Charlotte L255
    Susan Morrison, her hands before her L255
    uncivil gentleman L416
Moore, Mrs., relations, Bevis, Mrs.
    hail fellow well met with Mrs. Moore's servants L238

mantua-makers
Harlowe, Miss Clarissa
    Dolins, Mrs., Clarissa's mantua-maker L293
Smith, Mr. John, neighbors, Barker
    a mantua-maker L445

marriage see also **opinions...**on marriage
Belford, Mr. John
    no great liking for L143
    wanting to marry and reform L344, L531
Harlowe, Mr. Antony
    bachelor L10, L32.4, L197.1
    his mutual attraction to Mrs. Howe L74
    his intention to marry Mrs. Howe L183, L201
        formal tender to Mrs. Howe L196
        his proposals L197, L198
        will leave her £10,000 richer L197.1
        not wanting Anna to live with them L197.1
Harlowe, Miss Arabella
    poor prospects L10
    match for Solmes L10, L42, L60.2
    married, unhappily CONCLUSION
Harlowe, Miss Clarissa
    as duty to protect family honor L7, L8, L16
    order of among siblings, Clarissa the youngest L9
    preferring a nunnery L13
    single life, her choice L25.1, L26, L29.3, L36, L39, L44, L49, L55, L88, L145, L179, L185, L207, L223, L229.1, L253, L359, L438
    why marry when she has power deriving from her own inheritance L32.3

marriage, *Harlowe, Miss Clarissa* (cont.)
      will never marry any other man than Lovelace L86, L94, L98, L103, L116, L185
      appeasing her brother by promising never to marry L174
      upon a better preparation than for an earthly husband L362
Harlowe, Miss Clarissa, suitors to Harlowe, Miss Clarissa, Solmes, Mr. Roger
      unmarried CONCLUSION
Harlowe, Mr. James, Jun.
      match for Anna L5
      his reputation for temper and arrogance go against him L10
      Miss Nelly D'Oily, rejected by James L29.1
      poor prospects L29.3
      will never marry but to qualify for peerage L79
      married, unhappily CONCLUSION
Harlowe Family, servants, Barnes, Betty
      mate for Leman L95, L140, L175
      unmarried CONCLUSION
Harlowe Family, servants, Leman, Joseph
      mate for Betty L95, L113, L175
      Betty's lover L103, L113
Hervey, Mrs. Dorothy
      her own unhappy nuptials L13
Hickman, Mr. Charles
      match for Clarissa L46
      match for Mrs. Howe L46
      if Mrs. Howe marries Antony, Anna will dismiss Hickman L183
Howe, Miss Anna
      her aversion to L523
Howe, Miss Anna, servants, Robert
      may buy a ring and marry with money from Clarissa L74
Howe, Mrs. Annabella
      widow, for ten years L74, L197, L197.2
      her unhappy marriage L81, L132
      husband not her choice, but her father's L371
Lord M.
      threatening to marry and have children, if Lovelace provoke him L190
      wanting to see his nieces married L190
Lord M., relations, nieces, Montague, Miss Patty
      to marry a baronet of fortune CONCLUSION
Lovelace, Mr. Robert
      family wishing him to marry L98
      I cannot...cannot marry L202
      will not marry because it is for life, will never marry L254, L527
      Lovelace's marriage ruining Mrs. Sinclair's house L336
Lovelace, Mr. Robert, contrivances of Lovelace, contrivance of sparing Rosebud, Rosebud
      to wed next week L34, L72, L106, L207
Sinclair, Mrs., whores, Martin, Sarah (Sally)
      her humble servant a woollen-draper of great reputation L159
      near marriage with a tradesman in the Strand L163
      quarreling with her woollen draper L194
      expecting Lovelace to marry her L333
Sinclair, Mrs., whores, Partington, Priscilla
      a spinster L158.1

marriages, Anna's to Hickman
Hickman, Mr. Charles
      anticipated L136
      Anna may marry him soon to provide protection for Clarissa L252.1
      put off because of Clarissa's unhappiness L366
      settlements engrossed L366
      reported CONCLUSION
Howe, Miss Anna
      marriage postponed because of Clarissa's unhappiness L148, L155, L296, L366
      may marry Hickman soon to provide protection for Clarissa L252.1
      settlements engrossed L366
      close to naming a day L434
      to buy clothes in London for her approaching nuptials L459
      Clarissa requesting in her will that Anna marry Hickman soon L507
      Anna not yet fulfilling her part of Clarissa's will L520, L521
      married to Hickman CONCLUSION

marriages, Charlotte's to Belford
Belford, Mr. John
      wanting to marry Charlotte Montague L170, L516
      Lovelace suggesting a wife for Belford L527
      marrying Charlotte Montague CONCLUSION

marriages, Clarissa's to Lovelace see also **contrivances of Lovelace**, *Lovelace, Mr. Robert*, specifically,
    contrivance of pretending marriage to Clarissa
Belford, Mr. John
      urging Lovelace to marry Clarissa L110, L143, L258
Harlowe, Miss Clarissa
    generally
        prospects of peerage L13
        advised by Dolly L78
        mentioned by Lovelace L80, L88, L94, L95, L98
        advised by Anna L81, L87, L100, L119, L128, L147, L148, L150, L327, L328
        will marry no other while Lovelace is single and alive L86, L94, L98, L103, L116, L185
        reconciliation and reformation preconditions to marriage L109
        her virtue tested, reward to be marriage L191
        if she refuse to cohabitate, Lovelace will marry her L194
        asking to be free of obligation to Lovelace L201
        her responsibilities and expectations when married to Lovelace L202
        mismatch L202
        renouncing Lovelace forever L244, L266
        not wishing to marry Lovelace L253, L274, L276, L309, L343, L348, L358, L369
        I never, never will be yours L266, L281
        marriage to Lovelace saving her reputation L284
        marriage to Lovelace bringing a curse on her children L359
        asking Anna to send her refusal of Lovelace to the ladies of his family L368
        marrying Lovelace would sanctify his wickedness L386
        her reasons for refusing Lovelace L448
    license
        license in her hands L260
        still in possession of L383
    proposals, Lovelace's
        greeting his proposal with silence, as it is too soon and not convincing L107, L108
        why has he not declared himself L120
        Lovelace asking for her hand, unintentionally L137, L138

marriages, Clarissa's to Lovelace, *Harlowe, Miss Clarissa*, proposals, Lovelace's (cont.)

      rejecting his proposal, as she is ill and unprepared L149, L152

      Lovelace proposing, her inclination to accept, if only he would urge her L155

      earlier proposals mentioned L155

      blaming Clarissa that they were not married before coming to town L207, L221

      asking Clarissa to be lawfully his tomorrow L266

      urging Clarissa to meet him at the altar L267

      Lovelace asking Clarissa to make this his happy day L276

    settlements

      proper settlements L164

      Lovelace offering to discuss, she hesitates L185

      her own estate L186

      part of Lovelace's estate in Lancashire L186

      Lord M. giving her £1000 *per annum* L186

      being completed, Lord M. making her independent in his generosity L207

      Lovelace giving her all arrears in her father's hands for Mrs. Norton L207

      drafted and returned to Lovelace L218

      Clarissa receiving £100 *per annum* more than Lovelace's mother L218, L219

    wedding

      not wanting a public wedding L207

      Belford wishing to be her father at the altar L258

    wedding gifts

      from Lord M., one of his three seats, until they are settled L121, L325

      from Lord M. for Clarissa

        £1000 *per annum* to Lovelace's wife L186

        Lancashire seat or the Lawn and a thousand pounds a year, penny rents L206, L207

Harlowe Family

    not believing Lovelace will marry Clarissa L352

Hickman, Mr. Charles

    asking Lovelace his intentions toward Clarissa L346

    believing Lovelace would marry Clarissa L359

Howe, Miss Anna

    advising Clarissa to marry Lovelace directly L81, L87, L100, L119, L128, L132, L156, L183, L342, L358, L359, L367

    advising Clarissa to throw off a little more of the veil L112

    cautioning Clarissa against Lovelace L168, L174.3

    advising Clarissa to leave Lovelace L177

    advising Clarissa to marry the fool L188

    advising Clarissa to fly L229.1

    approving Clarissa's refusal of Lovelace L372, L379

Howe, Mrs. Annabella

    believing Clarissa should marry Lovelace L342, L358

    admiring Clarissa's refusal of Lovelace L371

Lord M.

    generally

      using Belford to influence Lovelace to marry Clarissa L110, L143

      hoping Lovelace will marry Clarissa L121, L169, L170, L191

      to be Clarissa's nuptial father L187, L189, L218, L233.2

      offering Lovelace money to marry Clarissa L206

      settlements, agreeing to jointure from Lovelace's own estate L218

      hoping for many boys (no girls) from Clarissa and Lovelace L233.4

      first boy will take Lord M.'s surname by Act of Parliament L233.4

      Clarissa feeling worthy to be Lord M.'s niece L261 Paper VIII

      losing hope for Lovelace if he not marry Clarissa L303

marriages, Clarissa's to Lovelace, *Lord M.* (cont.)
    wedding gifts
        one of his three seats, until they are settled L121, L325
        for Clarissa
            £1000 *per annum* to Lovelace's wife L186
            Lancashire seat or the Lawn and a thousand pounds a year, penny rents L206, L207
        for Lovelace
            a thousand pounds *per annum* upon his nuptials L88
            estate in Lancashire or the Lawn upon his nuptials L186
            estates being transferred to Lovelace upon his nuptials L203.1
Lord M., housekeepers, Greme, Mrs.
    hoping Clarissa will marry Lovelace L120, L128
Lord M., relations, half-sisters
    favoring, with gifts L2, L36, L121, L325
    losing hope for Lovelace if he not marry Clarissa L303
Lord M., relations, half-sisters, Lawrance, Lady Betty
    eager to hear of L158, L303
    Lovelace wanting her to assist at Clarissa's nuptials L245
    suspecting Clarissa is not married to Lovelace L303
Lord M., relations, nieces, Montague, Miss Charlotte
    hoping for speedy nuptials L121
    hoping daily for news of L203.1
    not knowing whether Lovelace is married to Clarissa L303
Lovelace, Mr. Robert
    generally
        suggested by Lovelace to Clarissa L80, L88, L94, L95, L98
        promise you will never marry any other man while I am living and single L98
        doubting his intentions toward Clarissa L99
        not marrying Clarissa till he is sure of her L103
        his family knowing of his intentions toward Clarissa L104
        proposing speedy solemnization L107
        declining two considerable families for Clarissa L109
        never marrying anyone but Clarissa L109, L350
        why has he not declared himself L120
        family favoring alliance with Clarissa, urging him to marry Clarissa L128, L324, L327
        blaming Clarissa that they are not married L140
        better that they do not marry L153
        again mentioning their wedding, searching for a house L158
        writing to Lord M. about terms and requesting him to be Clarissa's nuptial father L187
        will marry Clarissa after he gratifies his pride, ambition, and revenge L187.1–L187.4
        delaying marriage and accusing Clarissa of delaying L188
        let me perish, if I marry a woman who has given her friend reason to say she despises me L199
        I should be a fool to proceed as I do and mean matrimony L199
        ambivalent about marrying Clarissa L201, L227, L268, L279
        blaming Clarissa that they were not married before coming to town L221
        this project is not to end in matrimony surely L224
        his strange suspensions of marriage L229.1
        if ever he marries, it will be Clarissa L259
        can want of a church ceremony make such a difference L264
        now there is but one man in the world whom she can have—and that is me L268
        putting on her livery and wearing it for life L276
        resolved upon marrying L278, L281, L285, L286, L289, L350, L383, L396, L423
        Clarissa should marry him to save her reputation and that of her family L284
        to marry Clarissa Thursday before his contrivances are found out L287, L288, L294
        claiming to be married to Clarissa L308

marriages, Clarissa's to Lovelace, *Lovelace, Mr. Robert*, generally (cont.)

      dishonoring his family by marrying a person whom he has so treated L323

      the matrimonial sword hanging over his head by a thread L325

      giving his aunts his word that he will marry Clarissa L341

      agreeing to marry Clarissa upon her terms L346

      swearing he will marry her L383

      will bring a parson to marry them L383

      she shall die a Lovelace L383

      rejection making him desperate L383, L387, L397

      will marry her in the agonies of death L396

      wanting to act as Clarissa's husband L497

    license

      getting a license at Doctors' Commons L219, L227.5

      difficulty in getting a license L219, L223

      proctor of his friend Mallory and Mowbray helping Lovelace to procure L220, L227

      near arranged, applied for L226, L229.1

      will get license tomorrow L245, L253

      description of arms on the license, its hieroglyphics L254

      having the license L266

      Clarissa still in possession of the license L383

    proposals

      Clarissa greeting his with silence as it is too soon and not convincing L107, L108

      asking for her hand, unintentionally L137, L138

      proposing marriage before they go to London L149, L152

      again proposing marriage L155

      earlier marriage proposals mentioned L155

      hoping Clarissa will name the happy day L157

      regretting her refusal of his earlier proposal before coming to Mrs. Sinclair's L207

      blaming Clarissa that they were not married before coming to town L221

      asking Clarissa to be lawfully his tomorrow L266

      urging Clarissa to meet him at the altar L267, L282, L283

      make this my happy day L276

      proposing instant marriage L278

      offering to let Clarissa decide his fate, church or the gallows L332.2

      asking Clarissa to marry him L397

    settlements

      not talking of settlements or license L183

      offering to discuss settlements with Clarissa L185

      his proposals regarding Clarissa's estate, as well as Lovelace's own estate and inheritance L186, L253

      being completed L207

      similar to those for his mother L207, L216, L218, L229.1

      settlements to be ready in one week L215

      drafted and ready for Lovelace, nearly ready to sign L218, L226

      Lord M. agreeing to jointure from Lovelace's own estate L218

      if Lovelace can have Clarissa, the devil take everything else L218

      draft of settlements sent to Tomlinson by Lovelace L220

      Pritchard ready with his indentures tripartite L226

   wedding, after the wedding they will retire to the Lawn L207

   wedding gifts

      Lord M. giving Lovelace a thousand pounds *per annum* upon his nuptials L88

      Lord M. giving large estate to Lovelace L105

      Lord M. giving Lovelace his estate in Lancashire or in Hertfordshire upon his nuptials L186

      consulting with Pritchard about estates transferred to Lovelace upon his nuptials L203.1

      estates made over to him on his nuptials L220

marriages, Clarissa's to Lovelace (cont.)
Morden, Colonel William
      encouraging Clarissa to accept Lovelace's offer L447
      believing marriage would effect reconciliation L447
Norton, Mrs.
      encouraging Clarissa to marry Lovelace L408

marriages, Clarissa's to Solmes see also **address to Clarissa by Mr. Roger Solmes**
Harlowe, Mr. James, Sen.
      wedding to be next week at Antony's chapel L41.2
Harlowe Family
      rejoicing at wedding plans for Wednesday L83
      believing Clarissa will make herself sick to avoid the wedding L90.1
Harlowe Family, servants, Barnes, Betty
      Luke 15:7, there will be joy in Heaven L90, L90n1
Norton, Mrs. Judith
      will attend the wedding L41.2, L83, L85

Master of the Buckhounds
Lord M.
      would not have taken a place but Master of the Buckhounds L206
      advising Lovelace not to take a place, not needing it to patch up his broken fortunes L206

meals see also **collation at Mrs. Sinclair's; drink; food**
Harlowe, Miss Clarissa
      family deprived of Clarissa's company at table L91
      Clarissa's eating preferences L157
      will not take meals with Lovelace, eating alone L175, L194
      refusing to eat or drink L228, L261.1, L333
      bread and water at Bedlam L261.1
      accused of starving herself, self-murder L333
      taking water L333
      drinking tea with bread and butter, at Rowland's L333
      offering to pay for coffee, tea, chocolate, chicken but unable to eat L333
      repast with Mrs. Lovick and Mr. and Mrs. Smith L399

meals, breakfast
Belford, Mr. John
      breakfast with Clarissa and Hickman L365, L366
Harlowe, Mrs. Charlotte
      going down to breakfast L18
Harlowe, Miss Clarissa
      breakfast L5, L16
      not appearing at breakfast L18, L22, L23
      Aunt Hervey breakfasting with Clarissa L77
      breakfast ready in the parlour at the inn L98
      will attend Mrs. Sinclair and her nieces at breakfast L155, L157
      refusing breakfast with Lovelace L175, L198, L200, L226
      breakfast with Lovelace L214
      happiest breakfast time since Harlowe Place L216
      taking chocolate for breakfast with Lovelace and Tomlinson L216
      refusing breakfast L333
      inviting Hickman and Belford to breakfast L365
      inviting Belford, Mrs. Smith, and Mrs. Lovick to breakfast L440

meals, breakfast (cont.)

Harlowe Family
      at breakfast together L22, L501
      breakfast with Morden L502
Hickman, Mr. Charles
      breakfasting with Clarissa and Belford L365
Howe, Miss Anna
      breakfast with Mrs. Howe L81
Lord M.
      breakfasting with his nieces L322
Lovelace, Mr. Robert
      denied breakfasting with Clarissa L198
      breakfast with Clarissa L214
      taking chocolate for breakfast with Clarissa and Tomlinson L216
      invited to breakfast and dinner with Colonel Ambrose and his nieces L322
      not breakfasting, not dining with his family, on hearing of Clarissa's arrest L332
Smith, Mr. John, family, Smith, Mrs.
      and Mrs. Lovick breakfasting with Clarissa L440

meals, dinner

Harlowe, Mr. Antony
      dining and supping with Papa and James L19, L20
Harlowe, Mrs. Charlotte
      dining, a short and early dinner L17, L20
Harlowe, Miss Clarissa
      attended by Betty at dinner, her poor appetite L63
      a hardship not to dine below, as Dr. Lewin is there L75
      dining in the ivy summer-house, waiting for Lovelace L83, L86, L90, L91, L103
      too busy for Lovelace till dinner was ready, at the inn L98
      preferring to dine alone L157
      all dining together in Mrs. Sinclair's parlour L159
      not wanting to dine with Lovelace, not dining at all L200
      refusing to dine with Lovelace L203, L220, L226, L251
      bread and water only for dinner L235
      dinner ordered for Clarissa at Rowland's L333
      refusing dinner with Sally and Polly L333
      refusing to dine with Mrs. Smith, Belford, and Mrs. Lovick L349
Howe, Miss Anna
      dining with Lord M.'s nieces L327, L358
Lovelace, Mr. Robert
      dining out L194
      not admitted to dine with Clarissa and so not dining at all L200
      dinner at Mrs. Moore's L233, L235
Moore, Mrs., relations, Bevis, Mrs.
      dining with Lovelace and others at Mrs. Moore's L236
Smith, Mr. John, family, Smith, Mrs.
      inviting Clarissa and Belford to dine with her on her wedding day L349

meals, supper

Harlowe, Miss Clarissa
      seldom eating supper, declining supper L155
      no admission of Lovelace to supper L175
      chicken soup ordered for supper L184
      supping with Lovelace L194
      Lovelace wishing to sup with Clarissa L199

meals, supper, *Harlowe, Miss Clarissa* (cont.)
    expecting to have supper at Mrs. Moore's L256
    the pretend Lady Betty bespeaking supper at nine at Mrs. Moore's L314
Lovelace, Mr. Robert
    supping with Clarissa L194
    wishing to sup with Clarissa L199, L200

meals, tea
Harlowe, Miss Clarissa
    excused from tea L7
    sent for to tea L8
    to make tea L16
    excused from afternoon tea L17
    uncles cancelling tea with Clarissa in her apartment L75
    declining tea with Lovelace at Mrs. Sinclair's L155, L199
    meeting Lovelace for tea L201
    a dish of tea at Mrs. Moore's L232
    refusing a dish of tea with Tomlinson L238
    sipping two dishes of tea with Lovelace L253
    will drink a dish of tea with Belford at six to thank him L338
Howe, Miss Anna
    tea with Mr. Wyerley L1
Lovelace, Mr. Robert
    tea with Clarissa L200, L201

medications see also **cures**; **potions**
Harlowe, Miss Clarissa
    hartshorn L16, L98, L201, L233, L314, L334, L340
    salts L213, L340
    a line from Anna as a cordial L297
    given juleps by way of cordial L338, L340
    weak jellies and cordials ordered L340, L366, L467
    something given Clarissa to make her sleep L346
    regimen ordered by the doctor L366
    drops prescribed by her doctor L426, L474
Howe, Miss Anna
    salts administered L494
    a lighted wax-candle with feathers to burn under the nose L494
Lovelace, Mr. Robert
    ipecacuanha
        taking a few grains to make himself vomit blood L209, L248, L272
        a disagreeable medicine that would poison the devil L211
    laudanum
        in euthanasia L191
        and the wet cloth L294, L294n1, L323, L323n1
    malmsey, Cyprus [wines] as L203, L203n1
    opiates
        allowing Mrs. Sinclair to administer something making Clarissa insensible to rape L260
        fearing the quantity may dampen her intellect L260
        prescribed by physicians L261
        wine, intoxicating viands, somnivolences, as L261
    styptic
        Eaton's styptic, a balsamic medicine to cure the effects of ipecacuanha L209
        taking styptic administered by Clarissa L211

medications (cont.)

Lovelace, Mr. Robert, friends, Belton, Mr. Thomas
   cordial julep, opiate, sleeping draughts L419
Sinclair, Mrs., whores, Martin, Sarah (Sally)
   taking salts L493

Meditations

Belford, Mr. John
   Mrs. Lovick giving Clarissa's Meditations to Belford L364
Harlowe, Miss Clarissa
   Meditation, Saturday, July 15, written at Rowland's, extracted from Scriptures L364, L364n2
   Meditation, *Poor mortals the cause of their own misery* L399
   Meditation stitched to the bottom of Letter 402 in black silk L402
   Meditation, a collection of texts from *Job* 19:2; 6:14, etc. L413
   Meditation, Aug. 21: *On being hunted after by the enemy of my soul*, made up of verses from *Psalms* L418
   her book of Meditations L460
     bequeathed Mrs. Norton, Mamma wanting the original L507, L510.3
Smith, Mr. John, lodgers, Lovick, Mrs.
   giving Clarissa's Meditations to Belford L364

Memorandum book

Harlowe, Miss Clarissa
   Clarissa's minutes of all that passed when she could not correspond with Anna L272
   bequeathed Anna L510.3
Howe, Miss Anna
   receiving Clarissa's Memorandum book from Belford L510.3

memory

Harlowe, Miss Clarissa
   Clarissa's memory cherished by Mrs. Norton L409
   referring to her memory L446
   her memory not honored by Lovelace's death L448
   Belford wanting his letters returned by Lovelace, for Anna, to vindicate Clarissa's memory L452

messengers

Belford, Mr. John
   Harry, messenger L411
     a mongrel L420
     taking Clarissa's letter to Anna L457, L471
     delivering Clarissa's posthumous correspondence L486, L494
     reporting the disorder at Harlowe Place on news of Clarissa's death L494
Harlowe, Miss Clarissa
   Grimes
     correspondence with Anna conveyed by her old man L119, L120
     old Grimes, whom Clarissa dispatched with a letter to Anna L235
     Will looking out for old Grimes with Anna's to Clarissa L237
     Will has him at the Lower Flask L238
     in condition of David's sow L238, L238n1
     losing to Will Anna's for Clarissa L238
     half seas over, dropped his hat doffing it L238
     receiving money for the letter for Clarissa L238
     his eyes isinglass L238
Hickman, Mr. Charles
   Collins, Simon, an honest higgler L156
     going to town Mondays, Wednesdays, and Fridays L156

messengers, *Hickman, Mr. Charles*, Collins, Simon (cont.)
    delivering Anna's letters to Clarissa L156, L174.3, L184, L187, L316, L318, L327, L328
    found by Lovelace to be a common poacher, deer-stealer, and warren-robber L174.3
    Lovelace will have him robbed L174.3
    Lovelace will confiscate any letters from Anna delivered to Mr. Wilson L217
    delivering Anna's to Wilson's, then directly to Mrs. Sinclair's, and as Clarissa was not there, back to Wilson's L229, L229.1
    no longer needed to convey Anna's correspondence L338
Howe, Miss Anna
    Rogers, her tenant's son L319
        delivering Anna's for Mrs. Harriot Lucas at Mrs. Moore's L251, L252.1
        eating powdered beef, woundily corned L251
        delivering the letter to Clarissa's impersonator L275.1
        Rogers meeting Clarissa L320, L328, L358
        cannot be spared to deliver letters L327
        delivering Anna's letter to Clarissa L456

milk see **drink**

milliners
Smith, Mr. John, neighbors, Walton, Mr. and Mrs. John
    their milliner's shop L445

miniatures see also **pictures**
Harlowe, Miss Clarissa
    returning her miniature of Anna to Hickman L476, L507
    miniature of Clarissa set in gold, bequeathed Morden L507

ministers see **clergymen**

Moloch-deity see also **Beelzebub**; **devil**; **Satan**
Lovelace, Mr. Robert
    Lovelace as L57

money
Belford, Mr. John
    offering Clarissa money L339, L349, L350, L444
    giving Mrs. Smith twenty guineas for Clarissa's clothes L340, L345
    offering to be Clarissa's banker L349
    giving his 100-guinea bequest from Belton to Belton's sister L426
    sending Tomlinson money L514, L515
    restitution to John Loftus and Farley L514
    contributing to the Poor's Fund CONCLUSION
Harlowe, Mrs. Charlotte
    giving Hannah two guineas on her dismissal L25.2
    sending Mrs. Norton five guineas L376
Harlowe, Miss Clarissa
    having, not having
        having seven guineas with L98
        fifty guineas left behind in her escritoire L98, L100
        requested after flight, will not be sent to her L98, L102, L147, L152, L173, L177
        mistrusting Lovelace's economy, she would be his steward L202
        needing but two hundred pounds a year to live on L207
        Clarissa is poor, moneyless L301, L330
        having several things of value with her L307

money, *Harlowe, Miss Clarissa*, having, not having (cont.)

    her rings, her watch, her little money for a coach L314

    having but half a guinea and a little silver L333

    having with her a few valuables L333

    telling Mrs. Norton she has no occasion for money L382

    put in great straits to support herself L455

    not lacking money L458

    money—a trifle L458

  paying, owing

    providing for Mrs. Norton L39, L45

    annuity for Mrs. Norton of £50 *per annum* L230

    Clarissa paying Robert for conveying correspondence L74

    gift to Hannah L23, L128, L132

    paying Mrs. Moore half a crown at Hampstead L232

    giving Mrs. Moore a diamond ring L235

    paying Grimes for bringing the letter from Anna left at Wilson's L238

    bilking her lodgings at Mrs. Sinclair's, £150, or guineas, owed L330, L333

    no money to give Mr. Rowland L333

    her clothes, sold by Mrs. Sinclair to pay the debt, more sold L333, L426

    giving Rowland's maid a half-guinea L336

    selling her diamond ring and clothes to pay for the doctor L340

    paying the undertaker L451

  receiving, refusing

    refusing bank note from Lovelace, a bill from Lord M. L98, L157, L158, L205

    Anna an unlikely source as Antony has made Mrs. Howe watchful L105

    Anna sending Clarissa money in *Norris's Miscellanies* L148

    refusing Mrs. Norton's offer of money L301, L307

    Anna wanting to send Clarissa money L317

    asking Anna for money to pay one hundred and fifty guineas, or pounds L333

    Belford offering Clarissa money L339

    Belford giving Mrs. Smith twenty guineas for Clarissa's clothes L340

    refusing Belford's offer of money L349

    Belford dropping a bank note behind her chair L350

    refusing money from Hickman L366

    Mrs. Norton sending Clarissa the five guineas, sent to her by Mamma, along with ten guineas belonging to Mrs. Norton L381

    offer of one hundred guineas *per* quarter from Lovelace's family for life, refused L394, L398

    Morden bringing Clarissa money L384

Harlowe, Mr. James, Jun.

  paying off Uncle Hervey's debt L47

Harlowe Family

  distressing Clarissa by withholding her money L347, L364, L437

  to allow Clarissa some part of her estate L406

Hickman, Mr. Charles

  generous gift to Hannah L132

  contributing to the Poor's Fund CONCLUSION

Howe, Miss Anna

  will send Clarissa money and clothes L100, L111, L119, L132

  offering to find Clarissa refuge in London and to send money L142

  sending Clarissa fifty guineas in *Norris's Miscellanies* L148

  wanting to send Clarissa money L317

Howe, Mrs. Annabella

  contributing to the Poor's Fund CONCLUSION

Lord M.

  sending a bill to Lovelace enclosed in his letter L205, L206

money, *Lord M.* (cont.)

 offering Lovelace money to marry Clarissa L206

 offering Clarissa one hundred guineas *per* quarter for life as reparation L394

Lovelace, Mr. Robert

 a hundred pounds to Rosebud L34, L72

 twenty-five guineas to Rosebud's father L72

 offering Clarissa a £100 bank note L98

 gold not his predominant passion L105

 five guineas to Hannah L130, L132

 gift to Mrs. Sorlings's elder daughter L155

 offering Clarissa a bank note L157

 despising money, valuing not money L190, L217.2

 offering Clarissa the bill he received from Lord M. L205

 Lord M. offering Lovelace money to marry Clarissa L206

 returning the bill to Lord M., as it is not needed L207

 a guinea to Mrs. Moore L233

 offering Mrs. Moore a thirty-pound bank note L233

 a gift to Mrs. Bevis L239

 giving Margaret one guinea for bringing Anna's for Mrs. Harriot Lucas L251

 offering the messenger one half guinea for the letter L251

 not a money lover L258

 ten guineas to M'Donald L289

 half a crown to Joseph L416

 offering to lodge at Smith's, till Clarissa returns, at ten guineas a day L416

 giving his servant five guineas for good news about Clarissa L470

 offering Dr. H. a thousand guineas if he recovers Clarissa L470

Lovelace, Mr. Robert, contrivances of Lovelace, specifically, contrivance of sparing Rosebud, Rosebud

 Lovelace giving a hundred pounds L34, L72

 his friends giving Rosebud's father twenty-five guineas L72

Lovelace, Mr. Robert, contrivances of Lovelace, specifically, contrivance of Captain Tomlinson and Uncle Harlowe's birthday, Tomlinson, Captain Antony

 Lovelace giving him ten guineas L289

 Belford sending him money, three guineas L514, L515

Lovelace, Mr. Robert, friends, Belton, Mr. Thomas, relations, Sambre, Mrs.

 indigent L440

 Mowbray, Lovelace, Tourville giving her their legacy for India Bonds L449

Lovelace, Mr. Robert, servants, Summers, Will

 saving £150 L241

Moore, Mrs., servants, Margaret

 Lovelace giving her a guinea L251

Morden, Colonel William

 taking money to Clarissa L483

 giving a purse of gold to the surgeons who attend Lovelace after the duel L537

Norton, Mrs. Judith

 lacking money to back up her point of view L13

 Clarissa's wish to provide for Mrs. Norton L39, L45, L207

 Lovelace allowing Clarissa to give her all arrears in her father's hands L207

 may give her son money to begin a business L207

 wishing to give Clarissa money L301

 her humble fortunes L307

 Clarissa refusing her offer of money L307

 Mamma sending her five guineas L376

 sending Clarissa the five guineas from Mamma and ten of her own L381

Sinclair, Mrs., servants, Partrick, Peter

 paid five shillings for delivering a letter to Lovelace L231.1

money (cont.)

Smith, Mr. John, employees, Joseph
    Lovelace giving him half a crown L416

motivations

Harlowe, Miss Clarissa
    self-examination of motives L19, L82
    to prevent mischief between Harlowe Family and Lovelace L110
    love for Lovelace L110
Harlowe, Mr. James, Jun.
    mentioned L115
Harlowe Family
    greed L8, L10
    family aggrandizement L13, L16, L19
    hatred of Lovelace L13, L20
    inheritances L13
    paternal authority L13
    ambition L19
    questioned by Lovelace L115
    resentments against Clarissa L115

mourning

Belford, Mr. John
    Belford and his servant in mourning L336, L444
    amending his dress after mourning L370
    Beau-Brocade after mourning L527
Hickman, Mr. Charles
    new suit of mourning for Clarissa as for a near relation L520
Howe, Miss Anna
    mourning, against Clarissa's wishes L523
    mourning Clarissa for six months CONCLUSION
Howe, Mrs. Annabella
    in deep mourning for Clarissa L520
Howe, Mrs. Annabella, relations, Larkin, Mrs.
    bequeathing mourning for Anna and Mrs. Howe L65
Lovelace, Mr. Robert
    wearing mourning for Clarissa L496
Lovelace, Mr. Robert, friends, Belton, Mr. Thomas, family, Thomasine
    and widow's weeds L399
Norton, Mrs. Judith
    thirty guineas bequeathed her and her son for mourning L487

Mulciber

Lovelace, Mr. Robert, contrivances of Lovelace, specifically, contrivance of Captain Tomlinson and Uncle
    Harlowe's birthday, Tomlinson, Captain Antony
        old Mulciber's, Tomlinson as L244

murder

Harlowe, Miss Clarissa
    I am afraid there will be murder L30
    dreaming she is murdered in a churchyard by Lovelace L84
    a murdered evening, the collation L159
    Lovelace dreaming he murdered Clarissa L246
    shouting Murder! out the window at Mrs. Sinclair's L264
    Mrs. Sinclair must let Clarissa out or murder her L293

murder (cont.)

Hervey, Mrs. Dorothy

    fears of L144, L145

Lovelace, Mr. Robert

    Harlowe Family will prosecute for L132

    committing L171

    no assassin, no night-murderer L196

    dreaming of murdering Clarissa L246

    Belford looking guilty of L277

    drawn in to commit a murder L323

Muscovite wife [sequestered]

Howe, Miss Anna

    opinion on L68

music

Belford, Mr. John

    drum, trumpet, fife, tabret, expressing joy L192

Harlowe, Miss Clarissa

    accomplished at harpsichord, music L54, L182

    harpsichord, chamber-organ, and music books bequeathed Dolly L507

    Elizabeth Carter's *Ode to Wisdom* L54, APPENDIX (music appearing in v.2, Letter IX in editions printed by Richardson)

Hervey, Mrs. Dorothy, family, Hervey, Miss Dolly

    bequeathed harpsichord, chamber-organ, music books L507

Howe, Miss Anna

    accomplished at harpsichord, singing L128

Lovelace, Mr. Robert

    singing to himself the thirtieth of January strain and the dead psalm melody L266, L266n2

    Lovelace humming tunes L416

    women's grief like notes of a well-tuned viol L416

    Tourville singing Lovelace out of his megrims L421

Lovelace, Mr. Robert, friends, Mowbray, Mr. Richard

    humming a tune L419

Lovelace, Mr. Robert, friends, Tourville, Mr. James

    musician, singing Lovelace out of his megrims L161, L421

N

names

Belford, Mr. John

    first called Jack L31

    Squire Belford L418

Harlowe, Mr. Antony

    Tony L100

Harlowe, Miss Arabella

    Bella L2

    Miss Bell L132

    A.H. L311

Harlowe, Mrs. Charlotte

    Charl. Harlowe L356

names (cont.)

Harlowe, Miss Clarissa
    Miss Cunning-ones L61.1
    Gloriana L105, L167, L209
        as Gloriana, Nathaniel Lee's L159, L159n2
    Mrs. Lovelace or Clarissa Lovelace L157, L158.1, L161, L167, L186, L211, L213, L214, L303, L497, L535
    Lovelace's lady L203
    Lady Easy to Lovelace's pleasures L207
    Miss Clary L374, L381, L408, L431, L442
Harlowe, Miss Clarissa, suitors to Harlowe, Miss Clarissa, Solmes, Mr. Roger
    Squire Solmes L139
Harlowe, Miss Clarissa, suitors to Harlowe, Miss Clarissa, Wyerley, Mr. Alexander
    included in a list of Clarissa's suitors as Wyerly L294
    signing his letter Alexander Wyerley L437
Harlowe, Mr. James, Jun.
    booby-'squire, booby 'squire L31, L127
    Jemmy L142
Harlowe, Mr. John
    first called Uncle Harlowe L3
Harlowe Family, clergymen, Brand, Mr. Elias
    as Dr. Brand, minister L90
    signing his letter Elias Brand L444
Harlowe Family, clergymen, Lewin, Dr. Arthur
    signing his letter Arthur L427
    as Lewen L408, L409, L427, L501, L503, L507
Harlowe Family, servants, Barnes, Betty
    Mrs. Betty L25, L53, L61, L63
Hervey, Mrs. Dorothy
    Dorothy L59.3
Hervey, Mrs. Dorothy, family, Hervey, Miss Dolly
    signature, Dorothy L90
Hickman, Mr. Charles
    first called Charles L476
Howe, Miss Anna
    Nancy L10, L27, L58, L74, L81, L82, L111, L296, L317, L357, L367
Howe, Miss Anna, family, daughter
    named Clarissa L252.1, CONCLUSION
Howe, Miss Anna, servants, Robert
    Robin, old Robin L46, L47, L58, L65, L81, L87
Howe, Mrs. Annabella
    Queen Annabella Howe L31
    Goody Howe L105
Lord M.
    first boy will take Lord M.'s surname by Act of Parliament L233.4
    Lord *Marplot* L323
Lord M., relations, half-sisters, Lawrance, Lady Betty
    signature, Eliz. Lawrance L303
Lord M., relations, half-sisters, Sadleir, Lady Sarah
    spelled Sadlier L190
Lord M., relations, nieces, Montague, Miss Patty
    called Patsey L332
    signing her letter Martha L332
Lovelace, Mr. Robert
    changing his name without, or by, Act of Parliament L105, L271, L327
    Bob, Bobby L222, L294, L323, L333, L411, L442, L496

names, *Lovelace, Mr. Robert* (cont.)
> the V. L316

Lovelace, Mr. Robert, contrivances of Lovelace, specifically, contrivance of sparing Rosebud, Rosebud
> Rosebud's name is Betsy L70

Lovelace, Mr. Robert, contrivances of Lovelace, specifically, contrivance of Captain Tomlinson and Uncle
Harlowe's birthday, Tomlinson, Captain Antony
> alias of Patrick McDonald L217
> Anna's inquiries about him find no such person L229.1
> signing his letter Antony Tomlinson (a forgery) L233.1
> imposter L281

Lovelace, Mr. Robert, friends, Belton, Mr. Thomas
> Thomas, Tommy, Tom L158.1, L419, L439

Lovelace, Mr. Robert, friends, Doleman, Mr. Tom
> Tom L131

Lovelace, Mr. Robert, friends, Mowbray, Mr. Richard
> Richard L158.1

Lovelace, Mr. Robert, friends, Tourville, Mr. James
> James, Jemmy L158.1, L480

Lovelace, Mr. Robert, servants, Summers, Will
> Will Summers, William L174.3, L201

Moore, Mrs.
> Goody Moore L232, L235
> our mother, compared to Mrs. Sinclair L237

Morden, Colonel William
> Wm. Morden L173.1

Norton, Mrs. Judith
> Goody Norton L39, L459
> worthy Mamma Norton L52.1, L409
> first called Judith L179
> Clarissa calling her her own mamma L307

Sinclair, Mrs.
> Magdalen L158.1
> the mother L158.1, L228, L233, L237, L264, L333, L396
> her maiden name Sinclair L158.1
> her right name not Sinclair L159, L229.1
> Sinclair, as thou callest her L169
> the mother and sisterhood L228, L277, L279, L281

Sinclair, Mrs., whores, Horton, Mary
> called Polly L154

Sinclair, Mrs., whores, Martin, Sarah
> called Sally L154

Sinclair, Mrs., whores, Partington, Priscilla
> called Priscilla L158.1

Sinclair, Mrs., whores, Wykes, Dorcas
> called Dorcas Martindale L269, L270

Smith, Mr. John
> called John, familiarly by his wife L416
> Father and Mother Smith, contemptuously by Lovelace L416

narration see also **dialogue format**; **omniscient footnotes**; **stage directions**
Lovelace, Mr. Robert
> I love to write to the moment L224
> though this was written afterwards, yet...I write it as it was spoken, and happened; as if I had retired to put down every sentence as spoken. I know thou likest this lively *present-tense* manner, as it is one of my peculiars L256

needlework

Harlowe, Miss Clarissa
>> wishing to pursue her needleworks L51.2, L52.1
>> Clarissa's L79, L147, L182, L529
>> bequeathed Mamma, Anna, and Morden L507, L510.3

Lord M., relations, nieces, Montague, Miss Charlotte
>> admirable at her needle L255

Morden, Colonel William, family, Morden, Robert
>> his high opinion of Clarissa's needlework L529

Sinclair, Mrs., whores, Wykes, Dorcas
>> her skill in the needle L155

neighbors

Harlowe Family
>> Symmes, Mr. Edward
>>> duel between James and Lovelace occurring at the home of Mr. Edward Symmes L4
>>> brother of the other Symmes L4
>>> two miles off from Harlowe Place L4
>>> Clarissa inquiring of Mr. Symmes about the duel L4

Moore, Mrs.
>> Kit the hostler, who drank with the footman at the taphouse L232
>> Rawlins, Miss
>>> caring for fainting Clarissa L223
>>> prim L233
>>> mumbling a paternoster L237
>>> her snuff-box L237
>>> not inclined to do Lovelace favors L239
>>> unconvinced by Lovelace L241
>>> dissuading Clarissa from removing from Mrs. Moore's L242
>>> too inquisitive to be confided in L244
>>> secret-keeper-general L248
>>> a Pandora's box L248
>>> Clarissa informing her of her story L318
>> Rawlins, Mr.
>>> showing concern for Clarissa L233
>>> his sister *living* at Mrs. Moore's L241

Smith, Mr. John
>> Barker, cousin of the Waltons L445
>>> informant of Mr. Brand L445
>>> a mantua-maker L445
>>> lodging with the Waltons L445
>> Walton, Mr. and Mrs. John, cousins of Barker L445
>>> their milliner's shop over-against Smith's L445
>>> he, a petty officer in the excise L445
>>> informants of Mr. Brand L445
>>> receiving Mr. Brand's letter of recantation L467

newspapers

Harlowe, Miss Clarissa
>> reading *Tatlers*, *Spectators*, and *Guardians* L155

Lovelace, Mr. Robert
>> will advertise in the *Gazette*, the newspapers, for his eloped wife L228, L326

nurses

Harlowe, Miss Clarissa

Norton, Mrs., in childhood L31, L301

cared for these eighteen or nineteen years by Mrs. Norton L376

prohibited from attending Clarissa L408

Shelburne, Ann, in her last illness L451

Clarissa now attended by a nurse L338, L340

diligent, obliging, silent, and sober L362

attending Clarissa after her death L457

called Dame Shelburne, a widow L460, L507

bequest of Clarissa, ten guineas L507

Lovelace, Mr. Robert

Greme, Mrs., attending him in his fever L410

Norton, Mrs. Judith

raising Clarissa, from her cradle L20, L31, L182, L301, L362

assisting Clarissa in her anonymous letter to Lady Drayton L59

her fondness for Clarissa L88, L308

uncertain as to whether Clarissa had had small-pox L204

attending Clarissa in her last illness

Clarissa wishing to live with her upon Clarissa's estate L248, L253

Lovelace dreaming she lives with Clarissa L271

attending Clarissa as soon as Tommy's indisposition permits L301, L361

wishing to attend Clarissa L301, L381, L408

Clarissa asking her not to come, will need her later L307, L382

Harlowe Family prohibiting Mrs. Norton from attending Clarissa L408

O

omniscient footnotes see also **narration**

see L86, L89, L103, L110, L115, L117, L118, L127, L131, L138, L139, L140, L148, L150, L151, L154, L157.1, L158.1, L160, L173, L174, L174.1–L174.3, L176, L183, L187.1–L187.4, L195, L199, L200, L203.2, L204, L207.1, L217.1–L217.3, L228, L229.1, L246, L272, L273, L276, L301, L315, L316, L317, L358, L362, L373, L385, L400, L413, L436, L492.1, L492.2, L496, L499, L503.1, L505, L509, L510, L510.1, L510.3, L528

On being hunted after by the enemy of my soul

Harlowe, Miss Clarissa

her Meditation L418

opiates see **medications**

opinions

Belford, Mr. John

on friendship

and illness L364

female friendship L366

on keeping L192

on mankind in conflict with other animals L364

on marriage L143, L192

on physicians

their high fees L424

Ratcliffe, Dr. John, a physician, quoted L424, L424n1

opinions, *Belford, Mr. John*, on physicians (cont.)
   and Doleman's malady L531
  on pride, penitence, virtue, and vice as exemplified in Restoration drama L413
  on rakes L192, L222, L336
  on reform L143
  on religious matters L364
  on Restoration drama L413
  on wit in rakes and libertines L222
  on women
    bad women worse than bad men L333
    female friendship L366
Belford, Mr. John, relations, Jenyns, Tony
  on marriage, prating against wedlock L192
Harlowe, Mr. Antony
  on men, their position in the family L32.4
  on parental authority L15, L32.4
  on women L32.4
Harlowe, Miss Arabella
  on daughters L42
  on the female sex L53
Harlowe, Mrs. Charlotte
  on duty L20
  on the male sex and their prerogatives L17
Harlowe, Miss Clarissa
  on aging L40, L458
  on death L441, L475
  on duelling L55, L518
  on duty L17, L41.1, L55, L110
    to Papa L7, L8, L9, L78, L123
  on friendship L359
  on generosity L185
  on genius as wit and judgement L310
  on happiness and riches L19
  on innkeepers L98
  on manners L120
  on marriage L32.1
    men and L40
  on men L13, L22, L64, L76, L78, L88
    importance of figure or person L40
    the encroaching sex L85
    and their unpardonable crimes L458
  on parental authority L110
  on people
    on perfection in people L19
    low people and high L69
  on person L187
  on religion L261 Paper VII, L293
  on riches and happiness L19
  on royal title L36
  on saints, as preaching and practicing L310
  on seduction L486.1
  on steadiness of mind L19
  on vengeance L518
  on wit in ladies and gentlemen L222
  on wives, treatment of husbands L435

opinions, *Harlowe, Miss Clarissa* (cont.)
    on women
        female character L2, L19, L40
        and generosity L5
        poems L54
        their liveliness and quickness L63
        and courtship L73
        writing as proper employment for L529
    on writing L135, L529
Harlowe, Miss Clarissa, suitors to Harlowe, Miss Clarissa, Solmes, Mr. Roger
    on wives and marriage L56
Harlowe, Mr. James, Jun.
    on the female sex L8, L78
        daughters are encumbrances L13
        wit and L29.2
        and matrimony L52.1, L78
Harlowe Family, servants, Leman, Joseph
    on matrimony L73
Hervey, Mrs. Dorothy
    on marriage L13
        on parents governing in affairs of L39
    on obedience L83
    on love L83
Howe, Miss Anna
    on age and wisdom L372
    on authority L81
    on courtship L65, L128
    on curses, the weight on a parent's curse L148
    on death L65
    on duty L132, L367
    on encroachers L68
    on the female sex L68
        the position of women L47, L128
        that they love to trade in surprises L49
        the Muscovite wife [sequestered] L68
        their passiveness L128
        Lady Hartley, example of a man-woman L132
    on happiness and riches
        you are all too rich to be happy L10
    on husbands and their prerogatives L372
    on love and passion L128
        love an *ignis fatuus* L310
    on the male sex L27, L522
        men as monkeys L46
        men and Narcissuses L58
        husbands and lovers L68
        despising the male sex L132, L456, L510.3
        a vile race of reptiles L455
    on marriage L68
        the reptile word, obey, in marriage L68
        as a yoke L128
        on wives and their duties L132
        on men, women, and marriage, her aversion to L523
    on mind and body L132
    on *Ode to Wisdom*, sent by Clarissa L56

opinions, *Howe, Miss Anna* (cont.)
  on parents and children L132, L367
    on mothers L100
    on parents as tyrants L181
  on wills L27
  on writing: speaking is...best: for words leave no traces; they pass as breath; and mingle with air, and may
    be explained with latitude. But the pen is a witness on record L183
Howe, Mrs. Annabella
  on marriage L58, L132
  on parents
    duty L10, L27, L65, L357
    parental authority L10, L15, L357
    parents and children L197.2
    disobedience to parents L296
Lord M.
  on proverbs, the wisdom of nations L190, L191, L198, L205, L206
  on title and legitimate descendants L206
  on women, resenting slights longer than men L233.4
Lovelace, Mr. Robert
  on bashfulness L115
  on churches, some for men, some for women L106
  on conscience L530
  on courtship L3
  on euthanasia L191
  on fallen women L157.1, L171, L205
    more girls ruined...prepared for ruin, by their own sex...than directly by...men L252
  on the female sex L31, L58, L99, L115, L117, L175, L223
    their gossip L15
    their sweet cowardice, confoundedly sly sex L103
    how greedily they swallow praise L105
    his universal adoration of the sex L106
    not yet found virtue to withstand his test, now believing there are truly virtuous girls L110, L225
    must be dealt with doubly L127
    their cruelty L127
    his contempt for L173.1
    meek, patient, and resigned, inappropriate to be in a passion L202
    loving rakes, smart fellows, preferring libertines to novices L207, L236
    women are devils L210
    having no souls L219, L219n2
    women are plotters L228, L235
    creating storms L242
    and friendship L252
    their imbecility L267
    a bad woman more terrible to her sex than a bad man L276
    all women are cowards at bottom L289
    the curse of Eve, made to bear pain L335
    revenge, obstinacy in L346, L371
    unforgiving L410
    his hatred of all women L449
    he, the plague of a sex that has been my plague L512
    never lied to a man nor said truth to a woman L513
    his mean opinion of from early manhood L535
  on friendship L252
  on hard-heartedness L187.1–L187.4
  on honor and death L371

opinions, *Lovelace, Mr. Robert* (cont.)

    on human nature L127

    on innkeepers L98

    on jesting, in poor men L140

    on love L326

        his hatred and contempt for L31

        the woman who resents not initiatory freedoms must be lost. For love is an encroacher L220

    on the lower classes L214

    on the male sex L34

        perfidy of L191

        men, monkeys in imitation L216

        the nobler sex L252

        never lied to a man nor said truth to a woman L513

    on marriage

        regretting ridiculing, ridiculing L75, L143

        marriage-hater, antipathy, aversion, disrelish L79, L110, L190, L223, L227, L246, L346, L376, L421

        favoring annual marriages and marrying thirty-one times L254

        imagining an old spectacled parson with a white surplice thrown over a black habit performing the
           irrevocable ceremony L276

        his prejudice to the state of shackles L279

        foolish ceremony L287

    on medicine L191, L203, L211

    on parenting L115, L234

    on physicians L203, L209, L211, L212

    on polygamy, David and Solomon L254

    on rakes L115, L191

    on rape L254

        Queen Bess would agree with his opinion on rape L223

        none ever committed without yielding reluctance L223

    on seduction L294

    on servants, characteristics of good servants L423

    on smuggling, a national evil L289

    on trade, the dignity of in this mercantile nation L416

    on tragedy and comedy L194

    on virtue

        his love of it, platitudes L36

        not yet finding to withstand his test, now believing there are virtuous girls L110, L225

        more important in women than in men L110

        female virtue founded in pride L110

    on wives L153

        keeper of a man's honor L110

Lovelace, Mr. Robert, friends, Belton, Mr. Thomas

    on physicians and surgeons L424

Lovelace, Mr. Robert, friends, Belton, Mr. Thomas, friends, Blomer

    on physicians L424

Lovelace, Mr. Robert, friends, Mowbray, Mr. Richard

    on seduction L496

Morden, Colonel William

    on rakes and free-livers L173.1, L217.2, L263

    on inflaming novels and idle romances read by women L442

    on forgiveness and revenge L508

    on friendship and women L520

Norton, Mrs. Judith

    on life's momentary joys and troubles L408

opinions (cont.)
Sinclair, Mrs.
      on women L294
Sinclair, Mrs., whores, Martin, Sarah (Sally)
      on vows L157

Orsons
Howe, Miss Anna
      Antony Harlowe, his brother Orson L128, L128n1
Lord M.
      Harlowes and Lovelace behaving as Orsons L442

P

paintings see **art references**; **Highmore, Joseph**; **miniatures**; **pictures**

Papers I–X
Harlowe, Miss Clarissa
      delirious writings after being drugged and raped L261, L293

parable of the lady and the lion
Harlowe, Miss Clarissa
      see L261 Paper III

paragon
Harlowe, Miss Clarissa
      of virtue L110, L243
      Clarissa as L453

paramours
Harlowe, Mr. John
      Hodges, Mrs. Sarah
            suspected of familiarities with his housekeeper, and paramour L217, L229.1

parchments
Harlowe, Miss Clarissa
      refusing to sign L83

Parliament
Howe, Miss Anna
      Coventry Act and Betty Barnes L68
Lovelace, Mr. Robert
      changing his name without Act of, changing names by Act of L105, L271, L327
      advised by Lord M. to get into soon L206, L206n2
      his gift for elocution L206
      neither a courtier nor a malcontent be L206, L206n3
      first boy will take Lord M.'s name by Act of Parliament L233.4
      Lord M. and Lovelace have three or four boroughs at their command L254
      annual Parliaments L254, L254n2

parsons see **clergymen**

peculiars

Harlowe, Miss Arabella
  Lovelace's address lacking peculiarity L2
Harlowe, Miss Clarissa
  not treating Lovelace with peculiarity L3
  called by her grandfather, his own peculiar child L4
  obliged to mistrust herself of peculiarity L20
  my peculiars, particularly Miss Howe L61
Lovelace, Mr. Robert
  another of his peculiars L40
  their own peculiar talents L202
  I know thou likest this lively *present-tense* manner, as it is one of my peculiars L256

peerage see also **title**

Harlowe, Miss Clarissa
  prospects of, married to Lovelace L13
Harlowe, Mr. James, Jun.
  hope for peerage, rank, and title L13
      based on anticipated inheritances L13
      foolish L36
Harlowe Family
  not allied to L79
Lovelace, Mr. Robert
  hopes for L13

peers

Lord M.
  peers are judges in the last resort L515

pencils

Harlowe, Miss Clarissa
  writing on the cover...with a pencil L57, L80
  her red and black pencils she uses in her drawings L78
Lovelace, Mr. Robert
  Clarissa, a glory to the pencil L138
  giving Dorcas a pocket book and a silver pencil L174.3

Penguin Classics edition of *Clarissa* (1985)
book cover, the assembled Harlowes, by Joseph Highmore L147n1
printing mistakes
  p. 883, *l.* 1, text omitted: the relict of a L256
  p. 883, *l.* 1, appearing at top left corner: L259] L256
  p. 885, heading, [Loo] appearing at left running head L258
  p. 1226, quote from Dryden lacking note number 4 L419

penknives see **weapons**

penny rents

Lord M.
  giving Clarissa a thousand pounds a year, penny rents L206, L207

phaeton

Lovelace, Mr. Robert
  his ready to drive L322
  Miss Patsey Montague sharing his L332

physical appearance

Belford, Mr. John

    a bear L105

    making his ugliness conspicuous by his dress L350

    dough-baked varlet L395

    heavier and clumsier than Lovelace L425

    ugly fellow, gaudy and clumsy, tawdry L516

    homely and awkward, boatswain-like air L516, L527

Harlowe, Miss Arabella

    plump L7, L10

Harlowe, Miss Clarissa

    her voice all harmony L118

    her beauty L187.1–L187.4, L243

    fair and slim, tall L251, L529

    her snowy hand L263

    her natural ringlets not lately kembed L334

    her hand, the lily not of so beautiful a white L340

    declining looks L348

    change in her countenance for the worse L365, L385

    description by Anna L529

Harlowe, Miss Clarissa, suitors to Harlowe, Miss Clarissa, Solmes, Mr. Roger

    his ugliness L16, L21

Harlowe, Mr. James, Jun., friends, Singleton, Captain

    sun-burnt sailor L177, L194

    pock-fretten sailor, ill-looking, big-boned, six feet tall, heavy eye, overhanging brow, deck-treading stride, parched lips L194

Hickman, Mr. Charles

    description by Anna L46

    his white hand and fine diamond ring L136

    plump L229

Howe, Miss Anna

    sweet auburn beauty L252

Lovelace, Mr. Robert

    a handsome fellow L294, L516

    one of the handsomest men in England L346

    advantages in his person, air, intellect and a face that would deceive the devil L366

Lovelace, Mr. Robert, contrivances of Lovelace, specifically, contrivance of sparing Rosebud, Rosebud

    her beauty, pretty rustic L72, L116

Lovelace, Mr. Robert, contrivances of Lovelace, specifically, contrivance of Captain Tomlinson and Uncle Harlowe's birthday, Tomlinson, Captain Antony

    appearance described L304

Lovelace, Mr. Robert, friends, Belton, Mr. Thomas, family, Thomasine

    not a delicate frame L347

Lovelace, Mr. Robert, friends, Belton, Mr. Thomas, family, Thomasine, family, Hal and Tom

    muscular and big-boned L347

Lovelace, Mr. Robert, friends, Mowbray, Mr. Richard

    tall and comely, bold and daring, large and strong L161

    scar in forehead and right cheek L161

Lovelace, Mr. Robert, servants, Summers, Will

    missing some foreteeth on account of Lovelace L233, L333, L416, L420

Moore, Mrs., relations, Bevis, Mrs.

    brown and plump L251

Sinclair, Mrs.

    features broad and full blown L131

    masculine appearance L154, L256

physical appearance, *Sinclair, Mrs.* (cont.)
> an odd winking eye L155
> her horse mouth L158.1
> her fat arms L158.1, L256
> appearance described L256

Sinclair, Mrs., servants, Mabel
> awkward and bent-shouldered L211, L294

Smith, Mr. John, employees, Joseph
> lion's-grinning fellow, broad black teeth, bushy hair L416

physicians

Harlowe, Miss Clarissa

> H., Dr. R., Clarissa's physician L343
>> bequest of Clarissa, twenty guineas for a ring L507
>> called for by Mr. Goddard L340
>> diagnosis, love case, her disorder in her mind L340
>> fees
>>> Clarissa having no money to pay L340
>>> agreeing to take a fee every other visit L345
>>> no longer accepting fees L441
>> friends
>>> Belford L334, L338
>>> Clarissa, becoming a friend L441
>> names, signing his letter R. H. L461
>> prognosis
>>> giving Clarissa three to four weeks to live, less than a week L426, L460, L461
>> reconciliation between Clarissa and the Harlowe Family
>>> offering to write Harlowe Family L349, L441
>>> writing to Papa that Clarissa will not live a week L460, L461
>> regimen
>>> cordials and nourishment L340
>>> weak jellies and cordials L366, L467
>>> ordering drops L426
>>> air L441
>> visits
>>> to Clarissa L440, L441, L457, L473
>>> from Hickman, planned L366

Lord M.
> Perkins, Dr., attending Lord M. L282
> S., Dr., attending Lord M. L281, L282
> attended by three physicians and an apothecary L285

Lovelace, Mr. Robert
> sending a physician to Hannah with medicine to make her weaker L167
> Hale, Dr., treating Lovelace L512
> Wright, Dr., attending Lovelace in his dangerous fever L410

Lovelace, Mr. Robert, friends, Belton, Mr. Thomas, friends, Blomer
> physician L424
> earlier known to Belford L424
> his excesses in women and wine L424
> his opinion of his profession L424

pictures see also **miniatures**

Harlowe, Miss Clarissa
> of Clarissa, in the Vandyke taste, by Joseph Highmore L147, L147n1
> family pictures bequeathed Mr. John Harlowe L507

pictures (cont.)
Harlowe Family
> the assembled Harlowes, by Joseph Highmore, book cover of the Penguin edition of *Clarissa* L147n1

Harlowe Family, relations, Harlowe, Grandfather, bequest to Clarissa
> family pictures L42

Moore, Mrs.
> a print of St. Cecilia hung over the closet door L233

place see **Master of the Buckhounds**

plantations
Harlowe Family
> wanting Clarissa to go to one of the plantations L408

plate
Harlowe, Mr. Antony
> bequeathed family plate L507

platonic love
Lovelace, Mr. Robert
> and Clarissa L194

poems
Harlowe, Miss Clarissa
> Carter, Elizabeth, *Ode to Wisdom*
>> text L54, L54n1
>> music APPENDIX (appearing in v.2, Letter IX in editions printed by Richardson)
> Clarissa's, her delirious writings after being drugged and raped L261 Paper X

Harlowe, Miss Clarissa, friends, Biddulph, Miss Rachel
> her poem on the female character L2

Lovelace, Mr. Robert
> his poetry L116
> Lovelace's verses to his Stella L153

political references
Howe, Miss Anna
> George II, robbed of his legal due by contraband traders L196

Lord M.
> Craggs, Mr. Secretary, mentioned L206, L206n4
> Hutcheson, Archibald, quoted L206, L206n4

Poor mortals the cause of their own misery
Harlowe, Miss Clarissa
> Clarissa's Meditation L399

Poor's Fund
Belford, Mr. John
> to increase the Poor's Fund L507, CONCLUSION

Harlowe, Miss Clarissa
> the poor blessing her, praying for her L177, L301
> charitable donations L186
> her donations one tenth of her income, two hundred pounds a year L202
> wishing an annuity of fifty pounds *per annum* for the poor L230
> concern for her poor L300
> to be administered by Mrs. Norton after Clarissa's death L507

Poor's Fund, *Harlowe, Miss Clarissa* (cont.)

  proceeds of the sale of her grandmother's jewels to go to L507
  to be increased L507
  correspondence between Anna and Belford concerning L528
  managed by Mrs. Norton until a week before her death CONCLUSION
  cared for by Mrs. Hickman after Mrs. Norton's death CONCLUSION
  contributions, by Mr. Hickman, Mrs. Howe, and Mr. Belford CONCLUSION

potions

Harlowe, Miss Clarissa

  drug induced delirium L260, L261 Papers I–X, L261.1, L275.1, L314, L320
  potion given by Mrs. Sinclair L281, L311, L314, L395, L535

Sinclair, Mrs.

  administering to Clarissa to make her insensible L260, L261, L281
  their damned potions L395
  given Clarissa, Mrs. Sinclair's invention and mixture L535

poultry see **animals**, *Harlowe, Miss Clarissa*

power

Harlowe, Miss Clarissa

  why marry when she has power deriving from her own inheritance L32.3
  he may be mean enough, perhaps, if ever I should put it into his power, to avenge himself for the trouble he
   has had with me—But that...I never shall L69
  I was now in his power L98
  so much in his power as you are L183
  Lovelace's over Clarissa L243, L287, L308
  Clarissa's over Lovelace, triumph over Lovelace L282, L395, L453
  she has found her power L287

Lovelace, Mr. Robert

  female sex, whose infidelity I have vowed to revenge upon as many as shall come into my power L31
  and is she not in my power L99
  every time I attend her...she is less in my power—I more in hers L99
  dogs, using his power to frighten, as a boy L191
  tormenting animals that he has power over L222
  tyrant over what he loves L234
  Lovelace's over Clarissa L98, L183, L243, L287, L308
  Clarissa's over Lovelace L282, L395, L453
  never knowing fear till he met Clarissa and had her in his power L287

prayers

Harlowe, Miss Clarissa

  prayer foreshadowing her trials L145
  praying for Lovelace L159
  praying on her knees in her old apartment at Mrs. Sinclair's L256
  oh save me from myself, and from this man L274
  the poor praying for her L301
  her prayers L333
  her prayer for Lovelace L336, L510.4
  her humble prayer L393
  her prayer to protect James from himself and from Lovelace L407
  her prayer for a kinder heart for Arabella L430
  praying forgiveness for Mr. Brand and his informants L433
  her prayer for Anna's honour and prosperity L436

prayers (cont.)

Harlowe, Mr. James, Jun.
> Clarissa's to protect James from himself and from Lovelace L407

Hervey, Mrs. Dorothy, family, Hervey, Miss Dolly
> hers for Clarissa L144

Howe, Miss Anna
> hers for Clarissa L87, L132, L142, L373

Lord M.
> praying with his chaplain when he has the gout L321

Lovelace, Mr. Robert
> Clarissa's for Lovelace L336, L510.4
>
> parson of the parish praying for him in his fever L410
>
> praying for Clarissa L472

Morden, Colonel William
> for Clarissa's recovery when she had the fever at ages nine and eleven L377

Norton, Mrs. Judith
> her prayer for Clarissa L408, L459

pregnant

Harlowe, Mrs. Charlotte
> hoping Clarissa is not pregnant L376

Harlowe, Mr. John
> Uncle Harlowe wanting to know whether she is with child L402

Lovelace, Mr. Robert
> believing Clarissa pregnant L371, L423

press-beds see **contrivances of Lovelace**, *Lovelace, Mr. Robert*, specifically, contrivance of the bedfellows

prey see also **hunting**

Belford, Mr. John
> Lovelace, a vulture, boasting gentle usage of its prey L333

Harlowe, Miss Clarissa
> vultures, hawks, kites, and other villainous birds of prey, parents protecting from L133
>
> prey of a vulture's rapacious talons L333

Lovelace, Mr. Robert
> his quarry, wrens and sparrows L70
>
> Lovelace's L127, L170
>
> Sally and Polly his prey L157.1
>
> birds compared to women as quarry L170
>
> lion...sheep, women compared, his noble quarry L171
>
> wrens, phil-tits, wagtails not noble quarry L171, L189
>
> quitting too-easy prey to reptile rakes L239
>
> beasts of prey, rakes as L367
>
> a thousand vultures...preying upon my heart L511

Lovelace, Mr. Robert, contrivances of Lovelace, specifically, contrivance of sparing Rosebud, Rosebud
> poor quarry L171

pride

Harlowe, Miss Clarissa
> mentioned L82, L115, L253, L364, L529
>
> now humbled by rape L261 Paper IV
>
> her proud heart penetrated by Bella L261 Paper V
>
> her sin L261.1
>
> pretending to be above L265
>
> her pride in refusing Lovelace L323

pride, *Harlowe, Miss Clarissa* (cont.)
    pride of undeserved treatment L341
    her pride mortified L359
    her disappointment causing her death L370
    a proud heart L399
    her pride in thinking Lovelace has had a loss in Clarissa L428
    reptile pride of seduction L486.1
    punished for her secret pride L492
Harlowe Family
    theirs noted L109, L228
Lovelace, Mr. Robert
    his noted L112, L117, L123, L173, L189, L217.2, L227, L229.1, L253
    his pride sunk at failure of his contrivance of the promissory note L285
    his pride mortified L395

prisoner
Harlowe, Miss Clarissa
    confined to her apartment at Harlowe Place L24, L24.1, L25, L36, L40, L44, L69
    Lovelace taking Clarissa to such a place as she cannot fly L108
    Will to guard against any attempt by Clarissa to escape L174.3
    a prisoner at Mrs. Sinclair's, not a prisoner L178, L195
    physically detained from going out L201
    a prisoner L263, L266, L274, L278
    asking to be freed L276
    at Rowland's L333
    confined by illness to her room L454
Harlowe, Miss Clarissa, constables, Rowland, Mr.
    Clarissa's gaoler L336

proctor
Howe, Mrs. Annabella
    hers intimate with Lovelace's, to whom Lovelace applied for a license L229.1

promissory note see also **contrivances of Lovelace**, *Lovelace, Mr. Robert*, specifically, contrivance of the
  promissory note
Harlowe, Miss Clarissa
    Clarissa's to Dorcas L269, L279, L280, L281

prosecution of Lovelace
Harlowe, Miss Arabella
    favoring L427, L429
Harlowe, Miss Clarissa
    could not bear to appear in a Court of Justice to prosecute L315
    advised by Anna to take legal vengeance L316
    should prosecute Lovelace L317
    not wanting to prosecute L318
    will prosecute, if he threaten Anna or Hickman L320
    not using Lovelace's correspondence with Belford in law L387.1
    Dr. Lewen urging Clarissa to prosecute, as reparation of family dishonor L427
    Counsellor Derham and Mr. Ackland will hear Clarissa's story and begin a process L429
    not favoring legal prosecution L447
    her appearance in court as a condition of reconciliation with Harlowe Family L456
Harlowe, Mr. James, Jun.
    allying himself with the Bettertons against Lovelace L127

prosecution of Lovelace (cont.)

Harlowe Family

    will prosecute for murder L132

    urging Clarissa to prosecute L427

    sending the family's attorneys to take minutes of Clarissa's story L429, L430

    Clarissa's prosecution of, a precondition to reconciliation L456

    to prosecute Lovelace if Morden die L533

Harlowe Family, clergymen, Lewin, Dr. Arthur

    urging Clarissa to prosecute L427, L429

Harlowe Family, counsellors, Derham, Counsellor

    to attend Clarissa, hear her story, and begin a process L429, L430

Howe, Miss Anna

    will testify if Clarissa prosecute L317

Howe, Mrs. Annabella

    wanting Clarissa to prosecute L317

    a condition of Anna's continued correspondence with Clarissa L317

Lovelace, Mr. Robert

    Harlowe Family prosecuting for murder L132

    Lovelace should be prosecuted L317

protection for Clarissa see also **refuge for Clarissa**

Harlowe, Miss Clarissa

    offer of protection from Lady Betty L36

    writing to Lovelace to ask protection of his aunts L83

    considering Lady Betty's protection L120, L123

    Mrs. Townsend offering Clarissa protection L196, L199, L201, L209, L210, L228

    Clarissa not under a legal protection L215

    no protector but Lovelace L225, L256

    Lovelace her Judas protector L227.4

    no hope of protection from Morden L230

    Anna wishing to give Clarissa protection L317

    Anna advising Clarissa to put herself into Lady Betty's protection L327, L328

    no one to protect her from Lovelace L386

    unprotected L419, L437

    Mamma wishing Clarissa to put herself into Morden's protection L459

    her error throwing her out of her father's protection L488

Howe, Miss Anna

    advising Clarissa to seek protection of Lovelace's family L81, L142

    may marry Hickman soon to provide protection for Clarissa L252.1

    her personal protection for Clarissa L317

Howe, Miss Anna, smugglers, Townsend, Mrs.

    may give Clarissa protection L196, L229.1, L230

Lord M.

    his protection offered by Lovelace L80

Lord M., relations, half-sisters, Lawrance, Lady Betty

    her protection considered by Clarissa L120, L200

    Clarissa putting herself into Lady Betty's protection L327, L328

Lord M., relations, nieces

    requesting Clarissa to put herself into Lady Betty's protection L327

Lovelace, Mr. Robert

    false offers of from Lovelace

        with Lord M., the Lawn, M. Hall, Berkshire L22, L104, L116

        with Lady Betty L36, L49, L98, L116, L123, L233, L243

        in London L49, L76, L98, L104, L116

        with his family L61, L80, L85, L98, L104

protection of Clarissa, *Lovelace, Mr. Robert*, false offers of from Lovelace (cont.)

        at her own house L80, L85

        at Anna's L85, L124

        believing Mrs. Howe should have taken Clarissa in L98

        private lodgings L98

        in Windsor L116

        Morden in Florence L124

        Mr. Doleman L126

    Clarissa's only protector L225, L256

    her Judas protector L227.4

Morden, Colonel William

    his protection preferable to Lovelace's L88

    Clarissa having no hope of, from Morden L230

    as protection for Clarissa L252.1

proverbs see **sayings and proverbs**

punishment

Harlowe, Miss Clarissa

    her impenetrable afflictions given to her by God L266

    her punishment is over, Lovelace's is not L266

    her punishment the consequence of her fault L359

Harlowe Family, servants, Barnes, Betty

    to be punished by Lovelace L117, L175

Harlowe Family, servants, Leman, Joseph

    to be punished by Lovelace L175

Howe, Miss Anna

    to be punished by Lovelace L198, L198n1, L207.1 (following), L395

Lovelace, Mr. Robert

    to whom should he be accountable for the harm he does women L219

    hymeneal torch and a white sheet L221, L221n2

    deserving broken bones L252, L252.1

    Clarissa's punishment is over, Lovelace's is not L266

    defying Clarissa's right to vengeance through the law or through Morden L274

    indemnity for a rapist, to fly or be hanged L293

    his punishment just beginning L293, L330

    his condemnation L293

    cat-o'-nine-tails L294

    offering to let Clarissa decide his fate, church or the gallows L332.2

    raping Clarissa a national sin atoned for by sword, pestilence, or famine L336

    his punishment, justice of his country and vengeance of her friends L336

    what will expiate for his vileness L336

    his cursed inventions his punishment L365

    punishment by God L373

    his remorse is punishment enough L413

    answerable with his life for his crime L429

    meriting the gallows L452

Q

The Quarrelsome Lovers
Lovelace, Mr., Robert
      a comedy planned by Lovelace L175, L216

R

rakes
Belford, Mr. John
      has lain with Bab Wallis L255
      a reformed rake makes the best husband L499
      Chartres, Francis, a rapist, Belford compared L513, L513n1
Howe, Miss Anna
      Alexander Pope, *Of the Characters of Women*, every woman a rake L115, L115n2, L367, L367n1
      a devilish rake at heart L198
      had she been a man, would have sworn, cursed, committed rape, and played the devil L236
Lovelace, Mr. Robert
      universal lover, his popularity with the ladies L31
      whoremonger L32.4
      comparing Clarissa to Rosebud L103
      prince and leader of such a confraternity L104
      reflecting upon his reputation as a rake L104, L105
      mad fellows as are above all law L106
      Caesar as L110
      accustomed to triumph over other women L110
      every woman as L115
      Lovelace as L127, L173.1, L190, L246, L252, L294, L316, L366, L402, L406
      General Robert Lovelace, general of his fellow rakes, head of a gang of wretches L158.1, L171, L177, L209, L223, L252.1, L293, L370
      his opinion that the female sex love rakes L207
      twenty times the pains to be rogues than to be honest L215
      Johnny Hartop, the punster, example of the wit of rakes L222
      though a rake, not a rake's friend L223
      a notorious woman-eater L223
      a smart fellow and a rake L236
      quitting too-easy prey to reptile rakes L239
      rake's neck in danger from the hangman L261
      a rake's a rake L279
      rakes as beasts of prey L367
Lovelace, Mr. Robert, friends, Doleman, Mr. Tom
      former rake L229.1
Morden, Colonel William
      free-livers are remorseless L217.2
      Lovelace believing Morden to be a rake L415

rake's creed
Lovelace, Mr. Robert
      mentioned L110, L116
      Lord Shaftsbury's test L116, L116n2
      libertine's creed, once subdued, always subdued L110, L198, L209, L256, L264, L274, L294

rake's creed, *Lovelace, Mr. Robert* (cont.)
>   but oh, Jack, she never was subdued L274
>   in part L219

rape
Howe, Miss Anna
>   had she been a man, would have sworn, cursed, committed rape, and played the devil L236
>   custom in the Isle of Man, victim choosing rope, sword, or ring L317
Lovelace, Mr. Robert
>   a rape worthy of Jupiter L35
>   none intended in the affair with Miss Betterton L140
>   Chartres, Francis, rapist, Belford compared L513, L513n1
>   death not a natural consequence of L515
Lovelace, Mr. Robert, friends, Belton, Mr. Thomas, family, Thomasine
>   rapacious woman L399

rape of Anna, planned
Howe, Miss Anna
>   Lovelace's plot upon Anna L207.1 (following), L371
Lovelace, Mr. Robert
>   regretting he cannot also have Anna L104
>   account of a scheme to be revenged on Miss Howe L207.1 (following)
>   I will have Miss Howe, if I cannot have her more exalted friend L229
>   as to the comparison between the two ladies, I will expatiate more...when I have had them both L252
>   as she sets out on her journey to the Isle of Wight L371
>   Lovelace will let Hickman have Anna safe and entire L371

rape of Clarissa, *foreshadowed*
Harlowe, Miss Clarissa
>   penetrate any depth of Lovelace's character L12
>   impenetrable L31
>   Rosebud spared L34, L35, L70, L71, L72, L73
>   Clarissa penetrating into Lovelace's friends' heads, Lovelace entering her heart L159
>   lest one be attacked by him when in bed and asleep L177
>   the mortal offense L189
>   Clarissa called Lucretia L222
>   Clarissa wild with apprehensions, begging mercy on her knees before Lovelace L256
Harlowe, Mr. James, Jun.
>   his rapacious views, his rapaciousness L13, L223, L223.1
>   Lovelace disguised as Clarissa's brother L98
Howe, Miss Anna
>   lest one be attacked by him when in bed and asleep L177
Lovelace, Mr. Robert
>   Lovelace's penetration L2, L10
>   Rosebud spared L34, L35, L70, L71, L72, L73
>   a rape worthy of Jupiter L35
>   tempted to carry Clarissa off L35
>   his quarry, wrens and sparrows L70
>   threats to Clarissa, should he doubt her love L97
>   penetration L99
>   Harlowe Family will prosecute him for L132
>   lest one be attacked by him when in bed and asleep L177
>   his eyes endeavouring to penetrate her soul L248

rape of Clarissa, *premeditated*

Belford, Mr. John

> his knowledge of L258, L379, L387.1
>
> his guilt at not acting to protect Clarissa L339
>
> For *how* wouldst thou have saved her? What methods didst thou *take* to save her? Thou knewest my design all along L516

Lovelace, Mr. Robert

> such triumph over the whole sex, if I can subdue this lady L103
>
> the lady must fall L115
>
> I might have had her before now, if I would L157.1
>
> the house to be taken in three weeks...three days...three hours L159
>
> nearly making a violent attempt upon Clarissa L187.1–L187.4
>
> I must make all service before I pull off the mask. This was my motive for bringing her hither L191
>
> will not take her by force L198
>
> her trial to be at midnight, surprise and terror necessary L199
>
> urged by Mrs. Sinclair and her nymphs to make a daytime attempt L218
>
> so near to execution of my plot L224
>
> this project is not to end in matrimony surely L224
>
> his purpose to wake Clarissa in terrors L225
>
> ashamed before the women below as he has failed with Clarissa L225, L226
>
> his midnight attempt on Clarissa after the fire L227
>
> carrying Clarissa back to Mrs. Sinclair's, or consummating his marriage at Mrs. Moore's L242
>
> subduing Clarissa by violence if necessary L244
>
> her very fall will be her glory...my destruction L246
>
> will either marry Clarissa or rape her L247
>
> as to the comparison between the two ladies, I will expatiate more...when I have had them both L252
>
> the hour of her trial...so long premeditated L256
>
> would have avoided force L256

Sinclair, Mrs.

> urging Lovelace on L198, L218

Sinclair, Mrs., whores

> urging Lovelace to make a daytime attempt upon Clarissa L218
>
> advising Lovelace to try terror rather than love L264

rape of Clarissa

Belford, Mr. John

> O thou savage-hearted monster L258

Harlowe, Miss Clarissa

> occurring after Letter 256 and before Letter 257 L257
>
> her proud heart penetrated by Bella L261 Paper V
>
> marriage not making amends L263
>
> her impenetrable afflictions given to her by God L266
>
> Clarissa raped L293
>
> reported to Lady Betty L306
>
> asking Anna and Mrs. Howe to keep it secret L315
>
> Clarissa as prey of a vulture, its rapacious talons L333
>
> liberty taken with her when she was asleep L346
>
> not her fault L379
>
> Clarissa not knowing the details of how Lovelace brought about her ruin L379

Lord M.

> offering Clarissa one hundred guineas *per* quarter for life as reparation L394

Lovelace, Mr. Robert

> occurring after Letter 256 and before Letter 257 L257
>
> Lovelace allowing Mrs. Sinclair to administer something to Clarissa to make her insensible L260
>
> some little art has been made use of L260, L266

rape of Clarissa, *Lovelace, Mr. Robert* (cont.)
> Clarissa's insensibility robbing Lovelace of his pleasure L260
> gloomy that he did not get her consent L261
> feeling triumphant L262
> stung by Clarissa's rejection L264
> wishing to make amends L266
> his actions of a capital nature L315
> raping Clarissa a national sin atoned for by sword, pestilence, or famine L336
> admitting to Hickman that he took liberty with Clarissa when she was asleep L346
> I acknowledge...that I have basely injured her L346
> not understanding why Clarissa does not keep her secret L371
> destroyer of Clarissa's honor L407

Sinclair, Mrs.
> Mrs. Sinclair and her whores should be prosecuted for L317

rape of Clarissa, second rape
Harlowe, Miss Clarissa
> saving herself from what she believes would have been a second rape L359
Lovelace, Mr. Robert
> planned L281
> second attempt mentioned L386

reading
Harlowe, Miss Clarissa
> her deep reading L182
> difficulty reading, her eyes unable L336
Lovelace, Mr. Robert
> Latin and English classics L34
> judging women by what they read L154
> Clarissa's Meditation, *Poor mortals the cause of their own misery* L410
Lovelace, Mr. Robert, friends, Mowbray, Mr. Richard
> I ever hated a book L496
Morden, Colonel William
> inflaming novels and idle romances, read by women L442
Sinclair, Mrs., whores, generally
> readers L154
Sinclair, Mrs., whores, Horton, Mary (Polly)
> well educated, has read L277
Sinclair, Mrs., whores, Martin, Sarah (Sally)
> well educated, has read L277
Sinclair, *Mrs.*, whores, Wykes, Dorcas
> illiterate wench, can neither write, nor read writing L154, L155

real estate
Harlowe, Mr. James, Sen.
> bequeathed Clarissa's real estate L507

reconciliation between Clarissa and Lovelace
Harlowe, Miss Clarissa
> failure to appease Lovelace may cause family to lose James also L243
Lord M., relations, half-sisters, Lawrance, Lady Betty
> Lovelace wanting her to mediate L244
> Clarissa declining her offer L306
Lord M., relations, nieces, Montague, Miss Charlotte
> will visit Miss Howe to reconcile them L325, L326

reconciliation between Clarissa and Lovelace, *Lord M.* (cont.)
    writing to Clarissa on Lovelace's behalf L383, L384

reconciliation between Clarissa and the Harlowe Family see also **contrivances of Lovelace,** *Lovelace, Mr.*
Robert, contrivance of Captain Tomlinson and Uncle Harlowe's birthday
Harlowe, Miss Arabella
    Clarissa applying to her for reconciliation L309
    Clarissa asking her to intercede for her parents' last blessing L380
    Clarissa praying for a kinder heart for Arabella L430
    favoring a visit from Mrs. Norton to Clarissa L459
    expressing the family's desire for reconciliation L484
Harlowe, Mrs. Charlotte
    may urge Uncle Harlowe to join her in favoring Clarissa L174
    Mrs. Norton applying to her on Clarissa's behalf L179
    suspecting Clarissa of wanting reconciliation so she can resume her estate L182
Harlowe, Miss Clarissa
    offered by Lovelace L61, L88
    no hope L101, L132, L137, L141, L144, L145, L155, L157, L318, L320, L349, L440
    all hopes on Morden L101
    a precondition of marriage to Lovelace L109, L155
    hopes for L112, L120, L121, L123, L124, L132, L135, L141, L149, L151, L179, L187
    attempted through
        Aunt Hervey, writing to Aunt Hervey for her things and reconciliation L116
        Mr. Hickman, to plead with Uncle Harlowe L174, L182, L184, L217.1, L221
        Mrs. Norton, to apply to Mamma for reconciliation L179, L183, L184, L221
            asking Mrs. Norton not to intercede L307, L377, L382
    preferring reconciliation to marriage to Lovelace L179
    importance of L202
    reconciliation a *viaticum* L309
    reconciliation unworthy of her L319
    hard-hearted letter from Arabella L391
    on her knees writing to Mamma L391, L399
    her appearance in court as a condition of reconciliation with the Harlowe Family L456
    family wishing for L483
Harlowe, Mr. James, Jun.
    may be obliged to reconcile L216
    Clarissa having no hope of through James L309
    not allowing while he is away in Scotland L432
    family conference on L459
    If ever my sister Clary darkens these doors again, I never will L459
Harlowe, Mr. John
    may be persuaded to go along with Mamma, favoring reconciliation L151, L174
    Hickman speaking with Uncle Harlowe on Clarissa's behalf L174, L179
    Clarissa hoping he will take her part L176
    discouraging Hickman's application on Clarissa's behalf L182
    sending Mr. Brand to inquire about Clarissa L381
    will not have Clarissa be destitute, may allow her some part of her estate L406
    would have sympathized with Clarissa L432
    after her death, expressing forgiveness, love, and reconciliation L485
Harlowe Family
    unreconcilable L320, L443
    Clarissa's prosecution of Lovelace, a precondition L456
    family conference on, with Morden and Mrs. Norton L459
    seeking reconciliation, having received letters from Dr. H., Morden, and Mr. Brand L482

reconciliation between Clarissa and the Harlowe Family (cont.)

Harlowe Family, clergymen, Lewin, Dr. Arthur
  offering to mediate L408

Hickman, Mr. Charles
  interposing on Clarissa's behalf with Mrs. Howe L100
  attempting, failing to sway Uncle Harlowe in Clarissa's favor L174, L182, L184
  his application to Uncle Harlowe mentioned L229.1

Howe, Mrs. Annabella
  offering to reconcile Clarissa with her family if she will prosecute Lovelace L317
  forgiveness of Clarissa, the Harlowes' own decision L357
  acquainting the Harlowe Family with the truth about Clarissa's situation L429

Lovelace, Mr. Robert
  fearing Clarissa will throw herself on her own relations L235
  believing there is reconciliation between Clarissa and her family L439

Morden, Colonel William
  believing Clarissa's marriage to Lovelace would effect reconciliation L447
  trying to effect reconciliation L454, L460
  attending family meeting about reconciliation L459

Norton, Mrs. Judith
  to apply to Mamma for reconciliation on Clarissa's behalf L179, L184, L229.1
  Anna trying to influence her for reconciliation L183
  acquainting the Harlowe Family with the truth about Clarissa's situation L429

reconciliation between Lovelace and the Harlowe Family

Lord M.
  Lovelace should reconcile with the Harlowes L206

Lovelace, Mr. Robert
  promising reconciliation L61, L88
  dreading reconciliation L105
  to pave the way for L107
  precondition for marriage to Clarissa L109
  his contempt for reconciliation L109
  not reconciling with a family he despises L214, L215
  willing to reconcile, disclaiming interest in Harlowe estates L216
  wishing for reconciliation L220

reform

Belford, Mr. John
  reform when we can sin no longer L143
  his reformation caused by his uncle's death L347
  resolved to repent and marry L347, L424, L425
  his reformation L364, L395
  his conversion by Clarissa L419, L440
  affected by both Belton and Clarissa L419
  looking to his own reform L498, L514
  his reform doubted by Lovelace L513, L516
  his reform successful L531, CONCLUSION

Belford, Mr. John, relations, Jenyns, Tony
  unreformed, his story L192

Belford, Mr. John, relations, uncle
  bewailing a dissolute life L222

Harlowe, Miss Clarissa
  believing she could reform Lovelace L294, L306, L359, L365
  hopes for Lovelace's reformation L398
  an instrument of Belford's reform L486.1

reform, *Harlowe, Miss Clarissa* (cont.)
>>herself a means to reclaim Lovelace L510.4
Howe, Miss Anna
>>believing Clarissa able to reform Lovelace L48
Lovelace, Mr. Robert
>>mentioned L34, L99, L104, L118, L120, L124, L161
>>friends in need of reform L34, L81
>>not reformed enough for a husband L105
>>precondition for marriage to Clarissa L109
>>reformation his stalking-horse L110
>>to be undertaken by Clarissa L116
>>ensured by marriage to Clarissa L158
>>reformed by Clarissa L294, L306
>>Clarissa once thought she could reclaim him L359
>>libertine whom Clarissa loved and wished to reclaim L365
>>promising penance, reformation 397
>>Clarissa hoping for his reformation L398
>>Clarissa cautioning him to reform L510.4
>>the devil and the time of life are against thee L513
>>will reform upon his return to England L527
Lovelace, Mr. Robert, friends, Belton, Mr. Thomas
>>penitent, regretting his misspent life L419
>>can neither repent nor pray, his heart hardened, in despair L419

refuge for Clarissa see also **protection for Clarissa**
Harlowe, Miss Clarissa
>>offering to seek refuge elsewhere L42, L45, L53.1
>>after her flight, requesting to retire to her estate L101
>>wishing to live upon her estate rather than marry Lovelace L248
>>Anna finding lodgings for Clarissa at a nearby farmhouse, she will not remove L366, L368
>>family expecting Clarissa to live at her Grandfather's house L459
Harlowe, Mr. John
>>refusing Clarissa's request for L32.2
Hervey, Mrs. Dorothy
>>her home as L145
Hickman, Mr. Charles
>>mentioned as L85
>>wishing to offer protection of his house L252.1
Howe, Miss Anna
>>Lovelace suggesting refuge with Anna L80
>>refuge not possible with Mrs. Howe L81
>>offering to find Clarissa refuge in London and to send money L142
>>her marriage to Hickman providing refuge for Clarissa L155, L252.1, L372
Howe, Mrs. Annabella
>>will not provide L81
Lord M., relations, half-sisters, Lawrance, Lady Betty
>>her letter offering protection L36
>>Clarissa wishing to lodge near her after her escape L86
>>Lovelace offering to take Clarissa to Lady Betty's L98
>>Anna encouraging Clarissa to go to Lady Betty's L100
>>Harlowe Family expecting Clarissa to go to Lady Betty's L100
>>invitation after Clarissa's flight not forthcoming L121, L123
Lovelace, Mr. Robert
>>depriving Clarissa of all other refuge to make her dependent on him L201

refuge for Clarissa (cont.)
Norton, Mrs. Judith
        Lovelace offering Clarissa refuge with Mrs. Norton L80

relations see also **family**
Belford, Mr. John
        Jenyns, Tony, cousin L192
                his story L192
                prating against wedlock L192
                his affair with his fencing master's daughter, his good Mrs. Thomas L192
        Osgood, Mr., cousin L105
                a man of reputation L98
                resides near Soho Square, where Clarissa may direct her things sent L98, L102, L105
                a lady of virtue and honor with whom he lodges, near Soho Square L125
                his wife, a pious woman L127
                Aunt Hervey to direct her correspondence to Mr. Osgood L141
                has received correspondence for Clarissa from Arabella L143
        uncle
                attending his dying uncle L172, L191, L190.1
                his uncle's heir L172, L247
                his uncle having mortification up to the knee L172
                Lovelace inquiring after Belford's uncle L213, L215
                bewailing a dissolute life L222
                his death L247
                respecting his uncle L258
                his uncle tortured in his illness L258
                reflecting on his dying uncle L333
Harlowe, Mrs. Charlotte
        daughter of the old Viscount L27
        Aunt Hervey's sister L433, L500
        Brookland, Sir Josias, her uncle L507
Harlowe, Miss Clarissa
        Brookland, Sir Josias, Mamma's uncle L507
        Fuller and Allinson, distant relations attending her funeral L504
        Morden, Robert, her uncle L507
Harlowe, Miss Clarissa, friends, Biddulph, Miss Rachel
        cousin of Miss Lardner L229.1
Harlowe, Miss Clarissa, suitors to Harlowe, Miss Clarissa, Solmes, Mr. Roger
        Sir Oliver, his father
                yellow, full-buckled peruke, broad-brimmed beaver, Sir Oliver's L10
                wretched creature with vast fortunes L17
                compared to Roger Solmes L32.4
                surly old misogynist, opinion on women L40
        sister L32.4
Harlowe, Miss Clarissa, suitors to Harlowe, Miss Clarissa, Symmes, Mr.
        Symmes, Mr. Edward, his brother L4
Harlowe Family
        Fuller and Allinson, distant relations attending Clarissa's funeral L504
        Harlowe, Grandfather
                bequest to Clarissa
                        family pictures and plate, and less than half his real estate L42
                        mentioned L135, L174, L179, L375
                character
                        fondness for Clarissa L4, L465
                        opinion of the Harlowe Family L27

relations, *Harlowe Family*, Harlowe, Grandfather, character (cont.)
doting, good old man L429
giving gifts to Clarissa L529
estate
mentioned L157
less than half his total estate left to Clarissa L42
considerable sums arising from his estate since his death L202
inquired into by Lovelace's family in preparation for marriage L325
estate he left Clarissa mentioned L375
trustees
Morden L27, L32.3, L87, L173
Uncle Harlowe L27, L55
will
Aunt Harman requesting to see L1
source for family genealogy L4
flawed L4, L20, L55
partial text L4
mentioning Lovell as James's benefactress L4
disappointing James L13
purpose of L27
deeds flawed L55
giving Clarissa power to bequeath her estate L123, L400
intending Clarissa should live upon her own estate L248
Clarissa knowing his will by heart L460
uncles not following his example with respect to Clarissa L472
Harlowe, Grandmother, her jewels L41.1, L45, L202, L507, L520
Harlowe, Uncles, position in family and unmarried state L6
Harlowe Family, neighbors, Symmes, Mr. Edward
brother of the other Symmes L4
Hervey, Mrs. Dorothy
Harlowe, Mrs. Charlotte, sister, only sister L433, L500, L507
Morden, cousin L503
Hickman, Mr. Charles
Hickman, Sir Charles, his father L528
his elder brother died L196
his mother-in-law [stepmother] lately dead L459
Howe, Miss Anna
Fynnett, Jenny, cousin in the little island L10, L46, L47
Anna's bedfellow L46
Jenny's Grandmother Larkin L47
Harman, Aunt, rich aunt in the Isle of Wight L342
approving Clarissa's inheritance L1
visit, from Anna, Mrs. Howe, and Hickman L252, L342, L357, L358, L359, L365, L366, L372, L455
visit, to Anna from Aunt Harman's sister and her lord L342
her friend delivering Anna's to Clarissa in London L404
Spilsworth and Herbert, her cousins L456
her family not ancient L238
Howe, Mrs. Annabella
Larkin, Mrs., distant relation L46
long bed-ridden L46
Jenny Fynnett's grandmother L46
her will L46
her death L65
father, choosing a husband for her L81

relations (cont.)
Lord M.
 Knollys, Mrs.
  character, her excellent character L26
  correspondence, Harlowe, Miss Clarissa with Anna
   to whom Clarissa should send hers for Anna L93, L98
   requested by Mrs. Howe to stop assisting their correspondence L100
  relations, kinsman of Lovelace L26
  visits, at whose home Clarissa had once been a guest L26
 grandson, bequeathed his Hertfordshire estate CONCLUSION
 half-sisters
  generally, Lord M.'s half-sisters L13
   address to Clarissa by Mr. Robert Lovelace, supporting his attempts L26
   animals, tabbies, monkies L323
   bequests of Clarissa, rings with Clarissa's hair L507
   character, excellent character, unblemished honor L26, L81
   control, Lovelace not forgiving them for presuming to control him L397
   death of Clarissa, indisposed at Clarissa's death L510
   family, daughters of an earl, dowagers L36, L323
   marriages, Clarissa's to Lovelace, favoring, with gifts L2, L36, L121, L325
   relations, half-sisters of Lord M., his sisters L13, L397
   source of information about Lovelace L12
   title
    hoping to procure title for Lovelace L13
    daughters of an earl L36
    dowagers L323
   visits to Clarissa, looking forward to L282
   visits to Lord M. L323
  Lawrance, Lady Betty, half-sister of Lord M. L13
   address to Clarissa by Mr. Robert Lovelace
    her letter in support and offer of protection L36
   character, officious and managing, generous and noble L325
   contrivances of Lovelace
    contrivance of Mrs. Fretchville's house
     would have visited Clarissa by now L178
    contrivance of the impersonators
     old chancery affair calls her to town L203.1, L233.1, L233.2
     visiting her cousin Leeson L233.2, L256
     impersonated by Barbara Wallis L255
     Clarissa querying her on L302
     not in town for six months L303
     the pretended Lady Betty L313
    contrivance of Captain Tomlinson and Uncle Harlowe's birthday
     her steward, Spurrier, telling her of Lovelace's marriage L233.1, L233.2
   correspondence, Lawrance, Lady Betty, Letter 233.2 forged by Lovelace L303, L306
   estates, will assist Clarissa in resuming her estate L49
   friends
    Fortescue, Mrs.
     source of information about Lovelace L12, L14, L15
     opinion on the state of affairs in the Harlowe Family L26
     her admiration for Clarissa L27
   heraldry, her arms and crest upon a coach, hers in for repairs L255
   law, her affair in chancery in a good way L158, L303
   marriages, Clarissa's to Lovelace
    eager to hear of Lovelace's marriage to Clarissa L158, L303

relations, *Lord M.*, half-sisters, Lawrance, Lady Betty, marriages, Clarissa's to Lovelace (cont.)
    Lovelace wanting her to assist at Clarissa's nuptials L245
    losing hope for Lovelace, if he not marry Clarissa L303
  names, signing letter Eliz. Lawrance L303
  protection for Clarissa
    considered by Clarissa L120, L200
    Clarissa putting herself into Lady Betty's protection L327, L328
  reconciliation between Clarissa and Lovelace
    Lovelace wanting her to mediate L244
    Clarissa declining her offer L306
  refuge for Clarissa
    her letter to Clarissa supporting Lovelace's suit and offer of protection L36
    Clarissa wishing to lodge near her after her escape L86
    Lovelace offering to take Clarissa to Lady Betty's L98
    Anna encouraging Clarissa to go to Lady Betty's L100
    Harlowe Family expecting Clarissa to go to Lady Betty's L100
    invitation after Clarissa's flight not forthcoming L121, L123
  relations, Leeson, Mrs., her cousin L233.2
    contrivance of the impersonators L233.2, L256, L302, L313
  servants, Spurrier, Mr., her steward L302
    telling Lady Betty about Lovelace's marriage L233.1, L233.2
  solicitors, Stedman, attending to her chancery affairs L256
 Sadleir, Lady Sarah, half-sister of Lord M. L13
  airing, a little tour for two days to cure melancholy L332
  character, melancholy, weak-spirited L98, L245, L325
  contrivances of Lovelace, contrivance Captain Tomlinson and Uncle Harlowe's birthday
    disobliged with Lovelace, not having heard directly L233.2
  family, Betsey, daughter, only child recently deceased L36, L245, L256, L325, L327
  friends, Mrs. Benson, where Anna and Clarissa met Lady Sarah's Betsey L327
  illnesses, melancholy L98, L332
  marriages, Clarissa's to Lovelace
    losing hope for Lovelace if he not marry Clarissa L303
    wedding
      worrying over the delays L190
      rich presents for L325
  names, spelled Sadlier L190
  relations, Lord M.'s sister, Lady Betty's sister L190, L233.2, L245
nieces
 generally, nieces of Lord M. L170
  abduction of Clarissa
    to accompany Clarissa on her flight from Harlowe Place L76
    Clarissa requesting their company at her escape L83
    to be with Clarissa in London L85, L142
  animals, grimalkins, apes L323, L410
  ball, Colonel Ambrose's, refusing to accompany Lovelace L350
  bequests of Clarissa, rings with Clarissa's hair L507
  marriage, Lord M. wanting to see his nieces married L190
  meals
    breakfasting with Lord M. L322
    dining with Anna L327, L358
  protection for Clarissa, requesting she put herself into Lady Betty's protection L327
  travel, unlikely to accompany Clarissa abroad to find Morden L124
  visits
    to Clarissa, anticipated L125, L282
    Clarissa asking Lovelace for their company L231.3

relations, *Lord M.*, nieces, generally, visits (cont.)

    would attend Clarissa but for Lord M.'s illness L284

    to Anna, dining with Anna L327, L358

    to Lovelace in his dangerous fever L410

  Montague, Miss Charlotte, niece of Lord M. L170

    abduction of Clarissa, cold and sore throat make her unable to accompany Clarissa L88

    accomplishments, admirable at her needle L255

    advocate for Lovelace, writing to Clarissa on Lovelace's behalf L383, L384

    biblical references, recognizing Clarissa's reference to her father's house L439

    contrivances of Lovelace

      contrivance of Mrs. Fretchville's house

        to visit Clarissa at L178

        Lovelace writing to her about Mrs. Fretchville's house L203

        will visit Clarissa soon in her new habitation L203.1

      contrivance of the impersonators

        impersonated by Johanetta Golding L255

        Clarissa querying whether Charlotte met Lady Betty at Reading L302

        the pretended Charlotte Montague L313

      contrivance of Captain Tomlinson and Uncle Harlowe's birthday

        Lovelace may write to her about the wedding L187

        Lovelace telling her the delays are on Clarissa's side L190

        Lovelace writing her about Lord M.'s delay in answering the invitation L203

    correspondence, Montague, Miss Charlotte

      her letter giving Clarissa hope L229.1

      with Belford L513

      with Lovelace abroad L534

    correspondence, Montague, Miss Charlotte, Letter 233.3 forged by Lovelace L233, L306

    costume, to supply Clarissa with clothes L123

    estates, her family and fortune above Belford L516

    family

      Belford, Mr. John, husband CONCLUSION

      son CONCLUSION

      her family and fortune above Belford L516

      sister of Patty L88

    illnesses

      cold and sore throat make her unable to accompany Clarissa L88

      indisposed L121

      ill with stomach disorder L203, L203.1

    marriages, Charlotte's to Belford

      Belford wanting to marry her L170

      wife for Belford L516

      married Belford CONCLUSION

    marriages, Clarissa's to Lovelace

      hoping for speedy nuptials L121

      hoping daily for news of L203.1

      not knowing whether Lovelace is married to Clarissa L303

    reconciliation between Clarissa and Lovelace

      will visit Miss Howe to reconcile them L325, L326

      writing to Clarissa on Lovelace's behalf L383, L384

    visits to Clarissa

      planned L88, L98, L157, L158, L233, L248

      Clarissa wondering whether she intends to visit L243

  Montague, Miss Patty, niece of Lord M. L170

    abduction of Clarissa, will not be asked by Lovelace to visit Clarissa after L88

relations, *Lord M.*, nieces, Montague, Miss Patty (cont.)

        character

            her excellent character L26

            low spirited, timorous girl L88

            Lovelace's favorite L332

        family, sister of Charlotte L88

        marriage, to marry a baronet of fortune CONCLUSION

        names, called Patsey, signing her letter Martha L332

        transportation, sharing Lovelace's phaeton L332

        visits, meeting Clarissa two years ago at Sir Robert Biddulph's L233.3

Lord M., housekeepers, Greme, Mrs.

    Sorlings, Mrs., sister-in-law, sister of Mrs. Greme L98, L120

        animals, her dunghill cocks, Will compared L238

        attending Clarissa

            assisting in secret correspondence, Clarissa's with Anna L100

            requesting Clarissa to defer departure to London L135

            comforting Clarissa after she receives a letter from Arabella L153

        family

            widow L104, L128, L149, L153

            two grown sons and two younger daughters L98

            Betty, Mrs., her elder daughter L105

                and Will L118

                and Lord M.'s chaplain L118

                attending Clarissa L118, L125, L130

                to accompany Clarissa to London L130, L149, L152, L154

                accompanying Clarissa as far as Barnet L155

                receiving a gift from Lovelace L155

      farm

            eight miles off from the inn at St. Albans L98

            her dairy works, her farm L105, L117, L130

Lord M., relations, Knollys, Mrs.

    kinsman of Lovelace L26

Lord M., relations, half-sisters, Lawrance, Lady Betty

    Leeson, her cousin L233.2

        contrivances of Lovelace, contrivance of the impersonators L233.2, L256, L302, L313

Lord M., relations, half-sisters, Sadleir, Lady Sarah

    Lord M.'s sister, Lady Betty's sister L190, L223.2, L245

Lovelace, Mr. Robert

    generally, trouble with anticipated after Lord M.'s death L285

    Knollys, Mrs.

        kinsman of Lovelace L26

        her excellent character, at whose home Clarissa has once been a guest L26

        to whom Clarissa should send hers addressed to Anna L93

        to whom a man takes Clarissa's for Anna L98

        Mrs. Howe requesting she stop conveying correspondence for Clarissa and Anna L100

    Lord S.

        the great Lord S., who prepared settlements for Lovelace's mother L218

    son

        child surviving the affair with Miss Betterton L139

        wishing for a boy by Clarissa, as revenge on the Harlowes L268

    parents, encouraging qualities in children that made them, grown, the plague of their hearts L234

    mother

        had better pretensions to the estate now held by Lord M. L88

        teaching him the Bible L115

        spoiled by his mother L190

relations, *Lovelace, Mr. Robert*, mother (cont.)

        his mother's jewels may be new set for Clarissa L207

        settlements drawn up for Clarissa conformable to those of his own mother L207, L218

        settlements for Lovelace's mother prepared by the great Lord S. L218

        deserved a better son L267

        why, why did my mother bring me up to bear no control L512

Lovelace, Mr. Robert, friends, Belton, Mr. Thomas

    Sambre, Mrs., his sister L424

        come to live with him, continuing in his house L419, L440

        Belton leaving her only £50 L440

        Belford giving her 100 guineas L440, L449

        indigent, her vile husband, her son completing her ruin L440

        Mowbray, Tourville, Lovelace giving their legacy to her for India Bonds L449

    nephew, in Antigua, his heir L440

    uncle, bequeathing him a good estate L161

Lovelace, Mr. Robert, friends, Doleman, Mr. Tom

    Newcomb, his nephew L174.2

        contrivances of Lovelace

            contrivance of Mrs. Fretchville's house

                alias Mr. Mennell, mischievously used by Lovelace L174.2, L194

                telling Lovelace of Mrs. Fretchville's small-pox L201

                refusing to continue deceiving Clarissa L203

                Lovelace's conscience Mennelled upon him L244

                taking leave of Lovelace L526

    his sister L130.1

Lovelace, Mr. Robert, friends, Tourville, Mr. James

    ancient family L161

Lovelace, Mr. Robert, servants, Summers, Will

    Wheatly, Paul, his cousin

        Lord W.'s necessary man, Singleton's mate L175

Moore, Mrs.

    Bevis, Mrs., Mrs. Moore's niece L236

        conspiring with Lovelace

            offering to contrive a midnight visit for Lovelace to see Clarissa L239

            inclined to do Lovelace favors L239

            to be given a gift by Lovelace L239

            convinced by Lovelace L241

        costume, may bring Clarissa's clothes from Mrs. Sinclair's L245

        family, a young widow L236, L237

        impersonating Clarissa to receive a letter from Anna L251, L318, L320

        informing Will of Clarissa's movements L253

        keys, may take Clarissa's keys to return to Mrs. Sinclair's L245

        literary references, Butler, Samuel, *Hudibras*, quoting L237, L237n1

        mannerisms, making faces L243

        manners, *hail fellow well met* with Mrs. Moore's servants L238

        meals, dining with Lovelace and others at Mrs. Moore's L236

        physical appearance, brown and plump L251

        visits, to Lovelace in his new lodgings L239, L242, L251

Morden, Colonel William

    Morden, Robert, his father

        Clarissa's uncle L507

        giving gifts to Clarissa L529

        living chiefly abroad L529

        his high opinion of Clarissa's needlework L529

relations, *Morden, Colonel William* (cont.)
    cousins
        Aunt Hervey L503
        John and Antony Harlowe L504
Sinclair, Mrs.
    Polly and Sally, her nieces L131, L155
    Mrs. Carter, her sister, keeping a bagnio near Bloomsbury L499
Sinclair, Mrs., whores, Horton, Mary (Polly)
    niece of Mrs. Sinclair L155
Sinclair, Mrs., whores, Martin, Sarah (Sally)
    niece of Mrs. Sinclair L155, L333
Sinclair, Mrs., whores, Partington, Priscilla
    her guardian, Mrs. Sinclair L158
Sinclair, Mrs., whores, Wykes, Dorcas
    niece of Mrs. Sinclair L154, L273
Smith, Mr. John, neighbors, Walton, Mr. and Mrs. John
    their cousin Barker L445

religious references see also **biblical references**; **God, references to**
Harlowe Family
    not Roman Catholic L13
    not Christians, or even pagans with bowels L319
Howe, Miss Anna
    Mr. T'Antony, in discussion of figure and pride in men L37
Lovelace, Mr. Robert
    Oliver Cromwell, quoted L99
    cabala, word used by rakes L110
    dean and chapter L131, L131n1
    Lovelace's blood of as much concern as that of a Neapolitan saint L211
    his Jesuitical qualifyings L286
    Hickman, as if telling his beads L346
    Martin Luther, Belford compared L370
    refusing ghostly attendance and the Sacraments in the Catholic way L537
Moore, Mrs.
    a print of St. Cecilia hung over the closet door L233
Moore, Mrs., neighbors, Rawlins, Miss
    mumbling a paternoster L237

repentance
Harlowe, Miss Clarissa
    Clarissa's L393
Lovelace, Mr. Robert
    wishing to atone for his injuries to Clarissa L397
    repenting L470, L472

reputation
Harlowe, Miss Clarissa
    concern for L1, L81, L98, L101, L144
    dearer to her than life L102
    grieving for her reputation L107
    reputation destroyed, lost, destroyed by Lovelace L173, L368, L407
    marriage to Lovelace saving her reputation L284
    not patching up her reputation marrying Lovelace L359
    subject of open talk L392
    slandered L407, L444

reputation (cont.)

Harlowe Family
> their concern L106, L455

Lovelace, Mr. Robert
> concern for, hypocritical L106
> not valuing his reputation L114

rescue of Clarissa

Harlowe, Miss Arabella
> gossiping with Miss Lloyd about James's plan to rescue Clarissa L132

Harlowe, Miss Clarissa
> James's rescue plot
>> mentioned L132, L137, L140, L142, L145, L155, L157, L158.1, L164
>> planned with his friend, Singleton, captain of a ship L132
>> Miss Lloyd telling Anna of James's plan L132, L137, L148
>> plot may not be abandoned L148, L177
>> plot abandoned L152
>> no longer feared by Clarissa L175
>> Singleton visiting Anna to learn Clarissa's whereabouts L175, L177
>> Singleton sent to find Clarissa's whereabouts L194
> Anna's smuggling scheme
>> Clarissa asking Anna to perfect her scheme L195, L195n1, L200, L230
>> Mrs. Townsend may give Clarissa protection L196, L199, L201, L209, L210, L228
>> Mrs. Townsend, her two brothers, and their crews taking Clarissa to Deptford L252.1

Harlowe, Miss Clarissa, suitors to Harlowe, Miss Clarissa, Solmes, Mr. Roger
> Clarissa questioning whether James planned a journey with Solmes and Singleton L300

Harlowe, Mr. James, Jun. see also **friends**, *Harlowe, James, Jun.*, Singleton, Captain
> plotting with Singleton to rescue Clarissa L132, L137, L140, L142, L145, L155, L157, L158, L158.1, L164
> Singleton conferring with James and Arabella L139
> Leman a source of information for Lovelace about the plan L140
> may not have abandoned his plot L148, L177, L200
> plot abandoned L152, L229.1
> plot no longer feared by Clarissa L175
> Singleton visiting Anna to locate Clarissa L175, L177
> Singleton sent to find Clarissa's whereabouts L194
> Singleton attempting to bribe Anna's Kitty L196
> Clarissa fearing James may appear at Mrs. Sinclair's door L213, L214
> his plot used by Lovelace as an excuse to hide Clarissa L229.1
> inquiries from James and Singleton to be guarded against L233
> Lovelace claiming James is out looking for Clarissa L245
> Clarissa questioning whether James planned a journey with Solmes and Singleton L300
> no journey intended with Singleton and Solmes L301

Howe, Miss Anna see also **smugglers**, *Howe, Miss Anna*, Townsend, Mrs.
> Anna to perfect her smuggling scheme L200, L238.1, L252.1
> discovered by Lovelace, no more danger to Lovelace L211, L215, L221, L227
> finding Clarissa asylum till Morden come L248, L319
> Mrs. Townsend, her brothers, and their crews to take Clarissa to Deptford L252.1, L259, L261
> failed, Clarissa having already gone back to Mrs. Sinclair's with Lovelace L316

Lovelace, Mr. Robert
> Lovelace's threats
>> will rescue Clarissa if taken to Antony's L76, L81
>> his intimidations putting a stop to the plan to take her to Antony's L83
> James's rescue plot
>> mentioned L132, L137, L140, L142, L145, L155, L157, L158, L158.1, L164
>> used as an excuse to keep Clarissa under close watch L137, L158, L215, L221, L229.1

rescue of Clarissa, *Lovelace, Mr. Robert*, James's rescue plot (cont.)

        Singleton conferring with James and Arabella L139

        Leman as a source of information for Lovelace about the plan L140

        may or may not have abandoned the plan L148, L177, L200

        plot abandoned L152

        plot no longer feared by Clarissa L175

        Singleton sent to find Clarissa's whereabouts L194

    Anna's smuggling scheme

        mentioned L199, L201, L209, L210, L228

        Lovelace's plot upon Anna in revenge L207.1 (following)

        discovered by Lovelace, no more danger to Lovelace L211

        feared by Lovelace L215, L227

        provided against by Lovelace's contrivance of Captain Tomlinson L217, L221

residences see also **lodgings**

Belford, Mr. John

    of Edgworth [Edgware?] in the County of Middlesex L507

Harlowe, Mr. James, Jun.

    his house near port of Leith L137

Harlowe, Mr. James, Jun., friends, Singleton, Captain

    lives at Leith L137, L140

Lovelace, Mr. Robert, friends, Mowbray, Mr. Richard

    retired into Yorkshire, his native county CONCLUSION

Lovelace, Mr. Robert, friends, Tourville, Mr. James

    retired into Nottinghamshire, his native county CONCLUSION

Morden, Colonel William

    will reside upon his paternal estate in Kent L526

    finally settled in Florence CONCLUSION

Norton, Mrs. Judith

    housekeeper at the Grove, living the rest of her life at the Grove L520, CONCLUSION

Restoration drama

Belford, Mr. John

    comparing Clarissa's story to L413

revenge

Harlowe, Miss Arabella

    vowing revenge on Clarissa L15

    wanting revenge on Lovelace L429

Harlowe, Miss Clarissa

    lacking in Clarissa L336

    Clarissa's forgiveness and death as L472

    How wounding a thing...is a generous...forgiveness! What revenge can be more effectual and more noble,
        were revenge intended L508

Harlowe, Mr. James, Jun.

    on Clarissa L15

    plans and vows of, on Lovelace L139, L147

Harlowe Family

    Solmes as revenge on Lovelace for duel and on Clarissa for her inheritance L36

Howe, Miss Anna

    to be punished by Lovelace L198, L198n1

    Lovelace's revenge upon Anna L209, L229, L252

    fearing she is watched by Lovelace L319

    her agent watching Lovelace L319

    expecting vengeance from Lovelace L326

revenge, *Howe, Miss Anna* (cont.)

    Lovelace avenging himself on Anna if Clarissa reject him L395

Lovelace, Mr. Robert

    generally

        harboring resentments L1

        his love of, his predominant passion L31, L35, L40, L143, L189, L198, L215, L217.2, L234, L235

        revenge...keep thy throne in my heart L243

        his vows of revenge forgotten L245

        the rage of love, the rage of revenge is upon me L256

    on Anna and Clarissa, on Anna L127, L201, L223, L229, L395

    on Betty Barnes L113, L117

    on Clarissa

        for her loyalty to her family and not to him L31, L44, L187.1–L187.4

        for waiting for Clarissa in the rain in the garden L62, L73, L223

        for her dislike of him and his friends and Miss Partington L167

        for running away L228

        renewed L239

        for slighted love L276

    on the Harlowe Family

        vows of revenge for ill treatment following duel with James L4

        his triumph over them L158.1

        revenge against the Harlowes L206

        I have not done with the Harlowes yet. They were the aggressors L324

    on James

        if I have not his *sister*, I will have *him* L31

        vows of, after the duel L4

    on Leman L117

    on Miss Rawlins L239

    on Mrs. Sinclair, for Clarissa's rejection, setting fire to that den of serpents L396

    on women

        whose infidelity I have vowed to revenge upon as many as shall come into my power L31

        for his first love, who jilted him L31, L58

Morden, Colonel William

    How wounding a thing...is a generous...forgiveness! What revenge can be more effectual and more noble, were revenge intended L508

reveries see also **dreams**; **waking fantasies**

Lovelace, Mr. Robert

    producing sleep and then a dream L271

    Lovelace's Reveries, book about dreams, planned by Lovelace L272

rings see also **estates**, *Harlowe, Miss Clarissa*, jewels; **jewels**

Harlowe, Miss Arabella

    Clarissa to give her the diamond ring L334

Harlowe, Miss Clarissa

    her rose-diamond ring, escaping from Mrs. Sinclair's with L228

    her rings sent her with her clothes L230

    giving Mrs. Moore a diamond ring L235

    her rings, her watch, her little money for a coach L314

    offering her diamond ring to Mr. Rowland for room and board L334

    her diamond ring and clothes to pay for the doctor L340

Hickman, Mr. Charles

    his fine diamond ring L136

Howe, Miss Anna, servants, Robert

    may buy a ring and marry with money from Clarissa L74

rings (cont.)
Lovelace, Mr. Robert
      his diamond ring, turning it around L233, L237
Morden, Colonel William
      giving Mr. Melvill a ring L504
Sinclair, Mrs., whores, Wykes, Dorcas
      offered a diamond ring by Clarissa for her help in escaping Mrs. Sinclair's L269

rings, bequests of see **bequests of Belton**; **bequests of Clarissa**; **bequests of Larkin, Mrs.**

ruin
Harlowe, Miss Clarissa
      Clarissa's noted L132, L173, L189, L256, L306, L307, L333, L336, L356, L379

S

Sacraments
Harlowe, Miss Clarissa
      receiving the Sacrament L426, L457
      receiving Communion L460
Lovelace, Mr. Robert
      his refusal of Sacraments in the Catholic way L537

sacrifice see also **angel**; **divine qualities**; **example**; **fall**; **light**; **suffering**; **trials**; **virgin**
Harlowe, Mrs. Charlotte
      mentioned as L47
Harlowe, Miss Clarissa
      to Solmes L10, L15, L102, L113
      to family aggrandizement L17
      begging James not to sacrifice her to his projects L25.3, L32.3
      Clarissa as L27, L41
      struck dead at the altar L41
      her noble self-sacrifice L118
      sweet lamb, Clarissa L172
      the poor sacrifice L314
Lovelace, Mr. Robert
      Lovelace as L64.1, L121

St. Antony
Howe, Miss Anna
      Mr. T'Antony, in discussion of figure and pride in men L37

St. Cecilia
Moore, Mrs.
      a print of St. Cecilia hung over the closet door L233

St. Januarius
Lovelace, Mr. Robert
      Lovelace's blood of as much concern as that of a Neapolitan saint L211

salts see **medications**

Satan see also **Beelzebub**; **devil**; **Moloch deity**

Lovelace, Mr. Robert

    spreading his snares L106

    the tempter L110

    Lovelace, Satan himself L261.1

    sold himself to Satan L261.1

    Satan, having such faithful instruments L270

    an instrument of Satan L510.4

    Old Satan, Belford in his clutches L513

sayings and proverbs see also **language**

Belford, Mr. John

    the prince on his throne is not safe if a mind so desperate can be found as values not its own life L189

    a drowning man will catch at a straw L419

    a reformed rake makes the best husband L499

Harlowe, Mr. Antony

    Dunmow flitch L32.4, L32.4n4

    plain Dunstable of the matter L32.4, L32.4n2

    sauce for the goose is sauce for the gander L32.4

Harlowe, Miss Arabella

    it is good to be related to an estate L13

Harlowe, Miss Clarissa

    wild oats, and black oxen L44, L44n1

    poverty is the mother of health L63

    pleasures of the mighty are obtained by the tears of the poor L63

    better a bare foot than none at all L63

    encouragement and approbation make people show talents they were never suspected to have L63

    persecution and discouragement depress *ingenuous* minds, and blunt the edge of lively imaginations L63

    take a thorn out of my own foot, and put it into that of my friend L89

    swear and curse like a trooper L98, L98n1

    a jay in the fable L123, L123n1

    can cap sentences with Lord M. L244

    we ought not to do evil that good may come of it L428

    who can touch pitch and not be defiled L440

Harlowe Family, servants, Leman, Joseph

    plases are no inherittanses nowadays L96, L96n1

    to throe my hat at her, or so L96, L96n2

    as if she was among beans L139, L139n1

Howe, Miss Anna

    to in for the lamb, in for the sheep L10

    to take a thorn out of one's friend's foot, to put it into our own L87

    far fetched and dear-bought L197, L197n1

    Lovelace laughing in his sleeve L229.1

Lord M.

    generally

        his wisdom of nations L190, L191, L198, L205, L215, L235

        Solomon and his proverbs reminding Lovelace of Lord M. L191

        despised by Lovelace for his proverbs L206

        his fondness for other men's wisdom L206

        his bead-roll of proverbs: black oxen, wild oats, long lanes L233.3

        capping sentences L244

        his sayings mentioned L245

    patience is a virtue L105

    slow and sure L105

    eat the calf in the cow's belly L118, L118n1

sayings and proverbs, *Lord M.* (cont.)

love me, and love my dogs L167, L218

the children of very young and very old men last not long L190

old men when they marry young women make much of death L190

Raro antecedentem scelestum deseruit pede poena claudo: where vice goes before, vengeance (sooner or later) will follow L190

a word to the wise is enough L190

vengeance, though it comes with leaden feet, strikes with iron hands L190

Une poignée de bonne vie vaut mieux que plein muy de clergé (A handful of good life is better than a whole bushel of learning) L190

when a thing is done, advice comes too late L190

though you have kept company with a wolf, you have not learnt to howl of him L190

I could not cover him with my wings without pecking at him with my bill L190

it is a long lane that has no turning L206

no man is always a fool, everyman sometimes L206

the more noble anyone is, the more humble L206

worth is best known by want L206

God send me a friend that may tell me of my fault: if not, an enemy, and he will L206

all your wild oats will be sown L206

let your actions praise you L206

love honest men, and herd with them, in the House and out of the House L206

keep good men company, and you shall be of the number L206

money makes the mare go L206

he that eats the King's goose shall be choked with his feathers L206

what the right side gives up, the left may be the better for L218

little said is soon amended L233.4

forestall my own market L243

Lovelace adding to Lord M.'s collection of proverbs: Good actions are remembered but for a day: bad ones for many years after the life of the guilty L252

words are wind; but deeds are mind L323

the devil is not quite so black as he is painted L326

protecting one's sister, another man's matter L422

more sacks upon the mill...coals upon the fire L442

one story is good, till another is heard L442

Lovelace, Mr. Robert

always be careful of back doors L117

credulity is the God of Love's prime minister L117

eat the calf in the cow's belly L118, L118n1

black angel plays me booty L152

love me, and love my dogs L167

so long a harvest of so little corn L198

all his wild oats will be sown L206

about marriage: caught up in his own gin L207

once subdued, always subdued L209, L256, L264, L274, L294

once any other man's, and I know it, and never more mine L209

God sends meat, the devil cooks L211

listeners seldom hear good of themselves L235

calling Mrs. Bevis *hail fellow well met* L238

calling Will *half seas over* L238

about Miss Rawlins to Belford: I'll get her for thee with a wet finger L239

might be routed horse and foot L239

forestall my own market L243

Clarissa has mended her markets L245

Bernard Mandeville's rule: Private vices are public benefits L246, L246n1

no rest to the wicked L246

sayings and proverbs, *Lovelace, Mr. Robert* (cont.)

 quoting the honest corregidor: Good actions are remembered but for a day: bad ones for many years after the life of the guilty L252

 a pope: having caught the fish, laying aside the net L252, L252fn

 Honest Hickman may now sleep with a whole skin L252

 his plot thickens L255

 no difference between the skull of King Philip and that of another man L259, L259n1

 how one crime, as the good folks say, brings on another L266

 it costs a man ten times more pains to be wicked, than it would cost him to be good L267

 a wife at any time L268

 hatred appeased is love begun L270

 he who kills a man has all that man's sins to answer for, as well as his own, because he gave him not time to repent L326

 for the blood of me L346

 the eye is the casement at which the heart looks out L347

 quoting Clarissa: it is not lawful to do evil that good might come of it L443

 a reformed rake makes the best husband L499

 in Lord M.'s style: wits may not be sent a wool-gathering L512

 in Lord M.'s style: thou dost work it going L515

Norton, Mrs. Judith, family, father

 the satirist has a natural spleen to gratify L308

Sinclair, Mrs., whores, Martin, Sarah (Sally)

 Clarissa not to quarrel with her bread and butter L228

sealings

Harlowe, Miss Clarissa

 suspecting Lovelace of breaking seals on her correspondence with Anna L155, L156

 Letter 173.1 from Morden sealed in black wax L173

 her correspondence left for Belford with her will sealed with black wax L460, L486

Harlowe Family

 a Harlowe seal L143

Howe, Miss Anna

 young families loving ostentatious sealings L238

 Clarissa's letter of refusal to Lovelace's family sealed with Anna's seal L373

Lovelace, Mr. Robert

 intercepting correspondence, he keeps seals entire and preserves covers L239

 young families loving ostentatious sealings L238

seats see **estates**, *Lord M.*

sedan see **transportation**, *Harlowe, Miss Clarissa*

seduction

Harlowe, Miss Clarissa

 Clarissa compared to Rosebud L103

 her fall L118, L144, L169, L171, L324, L359, L399, L429

 she knew Lovelace to be a rake L294

Howe, Miss Anna

 Lovelace threatening to seduce her L252

Lovelace, Mr. Robert

 generally

  triumph in subduing L34

  seducer L94, L98, L121, L198, L222

  would change his dress like Clodius...to seduce a woman L106, L106n1

  triumph over the female sex L119, L388

seduction, *Lovelace, Mr. Robert*, generally (cont.)

        delighting in seduction L193

    of Clarissa

        desire to triumph over Clarissa L103

        strategy L157.1

        his motive for bringing Clarissa to Mrs. Sinclair's L191

        seduce her and take care of her out of wedlock L223

        techniques to overcome: intimidation, love, see-saw, surprise L223

        not possible while she is in her senses L263

    of Mrs. Bevis, considered L248

    of Anna, rather than Clarissa L252

    of Colonel Ambrose's nieces L322

    of his cousins Montague L322

Lovelace, Mr. Robert, friends, Miles

    seducing the farmer's daughter L496

servants

Belford, Mr. John

    generally

        in mourning L336

        buying snuff L336

    Jonathan, mentioned L420

Harlowe, Miss Arabella

    Barnes, Betty, Arabella's maid L507

    Arabella confiding her love for Lovelace in Betty L15

Harlowe, Mrs. Charlotte

    Shorey

        delivering letters and messages between Clarissa and Mamma L16, L18, L22, L25, L41, L80

        in whose presence Clarissa must say farewell to Hannah L23

        delivering letters between Clarissa and Lovelace L25.2, L26

        reporting the church scene to Lovelace's discredit L36, L40

Harlowe, Miss Clarissa

    Burton, Hannah

        attending Clarissa L7, L16, L18

            functioning as Clarissa's ears L13, L14, L16, L19, L21, L22

            loyal to Clarissa L21

            dismissed by Harlowe Family L21, L23, L24.1, L25, L25.2, L84

            Clarissa wishing to recall her L86, L116, L118, L121, L124, L125, L154, L155

            unable to attend Clarissa L127, L129

            soon will be well enough to attend Clarissa L167

            Clarissa wanting her services after marriage to Lovelace L218

            Clarissa wanting her services at Mr. Smith's L298

            may go with Clarissa to Pennsylvania, would take Betty instead L429, L430

        bequest of Clarissa, fifty pounds L507

        correspondence, Harlowe, Miss Clarissa with Anna

            conveying Clarissa's secret letters to Anna L9, L14, L19, L20, L23

        illnesses

            violent rheumatic disorder L118, L128

            very ill but not in danger L156

            soon will be well enough to attend Clarissa L167

            Lovelace sending a physician to cause her illness L167

            continuing to be ill L177, L178, L298, L307

            too ill to stir from her mother's house, St. Albans L298, L299, L301

            if her ill health continue, Mrs. Norton to put her on the Poor's Fund L507

servants, *Harlowe, Miss Clarissa*, Burton, Hannah (cont.)

money

    ten guineas from Clarissa, upon her dismissal L23

    two guineas from Mamma, upon her dismissal L25.2

    gifts of, from Lovelace, Hickman, Clarissa L130, L132

Harlowe Family

Barnes, Betty, Arabella's maid L507

    attending

        Harlowe Family L8

        fainting Clarissa L16

        her insolence to Clarissa L23, L53, L57, L63, L78, L117, L175

        attending Clarissa after Hannah's departure L24.1, L25

        carrying threats from Clarissa's siblings L29

        set over Clarissa L32.3, L53, L430

        reporting Solmes's remarks to Clarissa L40

        carrying a message to Clarissa to come down and surrender L41

        informing Clarissa on plans to remove her to Antony's L51, L53, L62, L83

        taking letters to Clarissa L59, L61

        message to Clarissa that her proposals are refused L61

        spying on Clarissa, searching her closet L69, L80, L90, L91

        letting Clarissa believe Mamma will visit her L77

        Clarissa falling into Papa's room L78

        sent to take Clarissa's pen and ink away L79

        warning Clarissa away from the family in the garden L80

        Clarissa's gaoleress L80, L91

        seeing that Clarissa has been writing L84

        attending Clarissa dining in the ivy summer-house L86, L90, L91

        Clarissa taking her with to Pennsylvania L430

    bequest of Clarissa, ten pounds L507

    biblical references, *Luke* 15:7, there will be joy in Heaven L90, L90n1

    character

        loyalty to Arabella L23

        her nature L53

        wench L91

        saucy gossip L142

    Coventry Act and L68

    death, pining and consumptive, within a year after Clarissa's CONCLUSION

    gossiping

        with Hannah about Lovelace L14

        source of information for confined Clarissa L21, L63, L78

        with Leman about Lovelace and Rosebud L71, L73

        with Leman about Clarissa's apartment being searched L103

        with Mrs. Norton about Clarissa's letters, Belford's visits L374, L376, L431, L459

    illness L532

    keys

        discovered, key in hand, searching Clarissa's closet L69

        sent to fetch Clarissa's keys L78

    literary references, reading *Mother Goose* and concerning the *Fairies* L63

    low people L73

    marriage

        mate for Leman L95, L140, L175

        Leman's lover L103

        her poor treatment of Leman L532

        unmarried CONCLUSION

    names, Mrs. Betty L25, L53, L61, L63

servants, *Harlowe Family*, Barnes, Betty (cont.)

        punishment, to be punished by Lovelace L117, L175

        reconciliation between Clarissa and the Harlowe Family

                changing her note, anticipating reconciliation L483

        sayings, there's no inconvenience but has its convenience L63

        snuff L63

    Leman, Joseph

        abduction of Clarissa

                causing a commotion, frightening her into flight with Lovelace L94, L113

                seen by family returning from pursuit of Lovelace L100

                reporting to Lovelace the family's reaction to Clarissa's flight L103

        animals, little dog that follows him L113

        biblical references, *Matthew* 16:26, what shall a man get to lose his soul L139, L139n2

        bribes, Lovelace promising him the Blue Beard Inn and Betty for his assistance L113, L140

        common folk, low people L73, L139, L241

        disloyalty

                disloyal L35, L84, L117

                confidant of James L62

                double agent, double agency explained L62, L80, L100, L113, L119

                Lovelace's intelligencer L62, L85

                gossiping with Betty about Lovelace and Rosebud L71, L73

                not entirely loyal to Lovelace L73, L84

                causing family to suspect Clarissa of corresponding with Lovelace L84

                spying on Clarissa for the family L86

                family suspect Lovelace's source of information is Clarissa, when in fact it is Leman L91

                doubted by Clarissa L94

                corrupted by Lovelace L95

                disliking the way Betty treats Clarissa L96

                vile agent of Lovelace L101, L229.1

                used by Lovelace to influence Antony, who influences Mrs. Howe L104

                informing Lovelace about James's alliance with Bettertons L127

                informing Lovelace about James's plan to rescue Clarissa L137, L140, L152

                of no more use to Lovelace L175

                Lovelace his cully L189

                could not have revealed to Lovelace Mrs. Norton's application to Mamma nor Hickman's to

                   Uncle Harlowe L229.1

      keys, having a key to the garden door L35

      marriage

              mate for Betty L95, L113, L175

              Betty's lover L103, L113

      opinions, on matrimony L73

      punishment, Lovelace to punish him L175

      sayings

              plases are no inherittances nowadays L96, L96n1

              to throe my hat at her, or so L96, L96n2

              as if she was among beans L139, L139n1

Howe, Miss Anna

    Kitty

        source of information about Solmes L27

        delivering letters from Clarissa L81

        visiting Hannah, requesting her to attend Clarissa L128

        Singleton trying to bribe her L196

    Robert

        animals, his roan, Keffel L65

servants, *Howe, Miss Anna*, Robert (cont.)
    correspondence, Howe, Miss Anna with Clarissa
        conveying L9, L16, L46, L47, L58, L65, L69, L81, L87, L132, L148
        warned away from the poultry-yard by Leman L74
    correspondence, Howe, Mrs. Annabella with Mr. Hunt, Robert conveying L81
    duties
        taking Clarissa's parcel and letters to Anna L69
        to be sent for Hannah L121
    marriage, may buy a ring and marry with money from Clarissa L74
    names, called Robin, old Robin L46, L47, L58, L65, L81, L87
Lord M.
    steward (discharged)
        hired by James to supply information on Lovelace L4, L12, L14
        his report on Lovelace L81
    Clements, Lord M.'s gentleman L442
    Empson, delivering a letter from Charlotte to Lovelace in London L203.1
    Jonas, occasionally dispatched to Lovelace L117
    Parsons, Simon
        steward of Lord M. L265, L323
        informing Lovelace of Lord M.'s illness L265, L278, L279
        Lord M.'s bailiff L278
        making up accounts with Pritchard L323
    Pritchard
        with whom Lord M. consults about transferring estates to Lovelace L203.1
        an honest man, in the family for a generation L204
        old man, good old servant, diffident and slow L204, L206, L207
        knowing the estates and their condition L204
        Honest Pritchard L206
        has rent rolls for Lord M.'s estates L206
        drawing up deeds assigning Lovelace £1000 *per annum*, when Clarissa owns she is married L218
        Lovelace meeting him at the King's Arms L218, L220
        making up accounts with Simon Parsons L323
        altering Lord M.'s will to leave out Lovelace L323
Lord M., relations, half-sisters, Lawrance, Lady Betty
    Spurrier, Mr., her steward L302
        telling Lady Betty about Lovelace's marriage L233.1, L233.2
Lovelace, Mr. Robert
    Andrew
        new servant, watching Clarissa L235, L237, L253
        attending Lovelace L241
    Joel
        with Lovelace L449
        delivering letters between Belford and Lovelace L475, L482
        Lovelace may pistol him if he brings bad news L475
    Summers, Will, Lovelace's servant for upwards of seven years L235
        animals
            like one of Widow Sorlings's dunghill cocks L238
            a dog L480
        black, in a black wig watching Mrs. Moore's, Smith's for Clarissa L231.1, L416
        character
            clever fellow, could do anything but write and spell L117
            faithful honest dog L480
        contrivances of Lovelace
            supposed by Harlowes to be Leman's source of information about Lovelace L103
            Lovelace offering to leave his servant with Clarissa L117, L157

servants, *Lovelace, Mr. Robert*, Summers, Will, contrivances of Lovelace (cont.)

      to be on guard against any attempt Clarissa may make to escape L174.3

      calling Peter to say Clarissa was going out to church alone L198

      directed to get a chair for Clarissa L201

      Clarissa sending him with hers for Anna to Wilson's, but he gives it directly to Lovelace L228

      spying on Clarissa L230, L248

      taking Clarissa's feint for Anna to Wilson's, and another to Lovelace L230, L231.1

      his account of Clarissa's flight from Mrs. Sinclair's and his finding her L230

      stealing Clarissa's and Anna's letters from Grimes L233, L235, L237, L238

      sleeping at Mrs. Moore's to keep an eye on Clarissa L239, L241, L242, L253

      Lovelace sending him for a coach for Clarissa to return to Hampstead L256

      an errand to Hampstead L261

      keeping Clarissa under close watch L273, L281

      threatening to hang or drown himself L290

      to be taken dead out of some horse-pond L292

      allowing Clarissa to slip out in Mabel's clothing L293

      setting the sheriff's officers after Clarissa L333

      knowing location of Clarissa's lodgings at Smith's L334

      watching for Clarissa at Smith's L416, L418, L421, L425

      dispatched by Lovelace to Belford L439

      delivering correspondence between Belford and Lovelace L463, L477

    death, untimely CONCLUSION

    disguises, in a black wig watching Mrs. Moore's, Smith's for Clarissa L231.1, L416

    livery, wearing Lovelace's livery L231.1, L416

    money, saving £150 L241

    names, Will Summers, William L174.3, L201

    physical appearance, missing some foreteeth on account of Lovelace L233, L333, L416, L420

    relations

      Wheatly, Paul, his cousin L175

        Lord W.'s necessary man L175

        Singleton's mate L175

    sweethearts

      Mrs. Sorlings's daughter L118

      Mrs. Moore's maid, Margaret L238, L241, L251

      his sweetheart posting Clarissa's to Anna L240

    weapons

      a gardener, carrying a pruning knife L416

      his pistol snatched by Lovelace L443

      taking Lovelace's pistols away to prevent mischief L480

Lovelace, Mr. Robert, contrivances of Lovelace, specifically, contrivance of Captain Tomlinson and Uncle

  Harlowe's birthday, Tomlinson, Captain Antony

    his discarded footman L217

Lovelace, Mr. Robert, friends, Belton, Mr. Thomas

    Betty, his maid L419

Moore, Mrs.

    Margaret, maid-servant L237

      called Peggy, Margery L251

      Will's sweetheart L251

      Lovelace giving her a guinea L251

Sinclair, Mrs.

    Mabel, the waiting-maid L291

      poor, silly Mabel, awkward and bent-shouldered L211, L294

      stopping Clarissa's attempt to escape L264

      attending Clarissa L282, L333

      a run away, her mother living in Chick Lane, West Smithfield L291

servants, *Sinclair, Mrs.*, Mabel (cont.)

   ordering a coach for Clarissa L293

   fetching the mantua-maker's journeywoman L293

   Clarissa escaping disguised in Mabel's clothes L293

   accused and threatened for allowing Clarissa to escape L293

   Mabel's clothes thrown into the passage this morning L293

  Partrick, Peter, house servant, footman L198, L264

   as Petur Partrick L231.1

   sent by Will with a letter for Lovelace to say where Will found Clarissa L231.1, L232

   Peter was paid five shillings L231.1

   stopping Clarissa's attempt to escape L264

  cook-maid

   reading Robert Greene, *History of Dorastus and Faunia* L225, L225n1

   setting fire to the curtains L225

Sinclair, Mrs., whores, Wykes, Dorcas

  the upper servant, greeting the footman who appears at Mrs. Sinclair's door L213

Smith, Mr. John

  Katharine, maid

   attending Clarissa L336

   Clarissa forgetting her name L336

  Sarah, maid-servant

   bequest of Clarissa, five guineas L507

servants, treatment of

Belford, Mr. John

  his kindness L420, L423

Harlowe, Mr. Antony

  his servants often deserving his anger L197.1

Harlowe, Miss Clarissa, suitors to Harlowe, Miss Clarissa, Solmes, Mr. Roger

  his vile stinginess L95

Harlowe Family

  dismissal of Hannah L23, L25.2

  servants set to watch Clarissa L35, L69

Lovelace, Mr. Robert

  animals, calling his servants his dogs L235

  contempt for L241, L512

  corrupting

   Joseph Leman and Betty Barnes

    his knowledge of all that passes in Harlowe Place, unexplained L26, L61

    mentioned L35, L62, L73, L98, L140

    Lovelace caring for Leman L95

    using Leman to influence Antony and Antony, Mrs. Howe L104

    punishing them L117, L175

    feeding Harlowes information through Leman L140

    bribing Leman with the Blue Boar Inn and Betty to assist James in Clarissa's rescue L140

    no more use for L175

    Lovelace, cully of Leman L189

   servants of other families L62

  management of

   generosity noted L11, L13, L15

   both loved and feared L98

   rough treatment of L420

   the art of governing L423

   his capacity for managing L445

  mischievous use of L11

servants, treatment of, *Lovelace, Mr. Robert* (cont.)
> sending a physician to Hannah with medicine to make her weaker L167
> threatening to kill his messenger bringing bad news L472, L475

Lovelace, Mr. Robert, friends, Mowbray, Mr. Richard
> fearing him L161, L420, L423

sex
Belford, Mr. John
> impossible to think of, in conversation with Clarissa L446

Lovelace, Mr. Robert
> no sex in ethereals L219, L219n2
> preferring plot to enjoyment of a woman L271

sexual language
Lovelace, Mr. Robert
> her throbbing partners L99
> suckling Clarissa's breasts L220, L220n1
> calling Hickman a male-virgin L236
> I'll get her for thee with a wet finger L239
> all the gentle and ungentle pressures of the lover's warfare L271
> I hung over her throbbing bosom L277

Lord Shaftsbury's test
Lovelace, Mr. Robert
> mentioned L116, L116n2

shopkeepers
Smith, Mr. John
> his glove shop, hosier in King Street L295, L320, L351

Smith, Mr. John, neighbors, Walton, Mr. and Mrs. John
> their milliner's shop over-against Smith's L445

shroud
Lovelace, Mr. Robert
> may need a coffin or a shroud L410

sibling rivalry see also **conflict between Harlowe, Miss Arabella and Clarissa; conflict between Harlowe, Mr. James, Jun. and Clarissa**
Harlowe, Miss Arabella
> overshadowed by Clarissa L10
> sisterly feelings lacking L14, L29.3
> envious of Clarissa L145, L152, L189, L223, L355
> neglected on account of Clarissa's superiority L182
> eclipsed by Clarissa L421

Harlowe, Mrs. Charlotte
> What a barbarous parent was I, to let two angry children make me forget that I was mother to a third L503

Harlowe, Miss Clarissa
> inheritance causing jealousy L2, L8, L13
> mentioned L10
> superior to her siblings L182
> her siblings to blame for the loss of Clarissa L355
> her grandfather knowing she would be envied L400

Harlowe, Mr. James, Jun.
> neglected on account of Clarissa's superiority L182
> doing more to ruin Clarissa than Lovelace has done L459

sibling rivalry, *Harlowe, Mr. James, Jun.* (cont.)
> and Arabella's confederacy to disgrace Clarissa L472
> hating Arabella CONCLUSION
> regretting his cruel treatment of Clarissa CONCLUSION

silver
Harlowe, Miss Clarissa
> her flowered silver suit L69
> her azure robe with stars of embossed silver L417
> petticoat of flowered silver L507
Harlowe, Miss Clarissa, suitors to Harlowe, Miss Clarissa, Solmes, Mr. Roger
> coat trimmed with silver L78
Lovelace, Mr. Robert
> wanting to purchase for Clarissa a short cloak trimmed with silver L98
> giving Dorcas a silver pencil L174.3

Singleton plot see **rescue of Clarissa**, *Harlowe, Mr. James, Jun.*

sleep
Harlowe, Miss Clarissa
> sleepless, no rest, trouble sleeping L126, L276, L365
> something given Clarissa to make her sleep L346
> an early riser L365
> to bed early at 8 o'clock L399
Lovelace, Mr. Robert
> sleepless after the rape L264
> sleepless, as he will have to go to M. Hall L281

sleeping arrangements see also **contrivances of Lovelace**, *Lovelace, Mr. Robert*, specifically, contrivance of the
> bedfellows
Harlowe, Miss Clarissa
> sharing Mamma's bed for two nights L5
> anticipating a straw bed at Bedlam L261.1
> sleeping in the bed where Rowland's maid lay L333
Howe, Miss Anna
> Jenny Fynnett, Anna's bedfellow L46
Sinclair, Mrs., whores, Wykes, Dorcas
> Lovelace hoping Clarissa will accept her as a bedfellow L154

smugglers
Howe, Miss Anna
> George II robbed of his legal due by contraband traders L196
> Townsend, Mrs. *see also* **rescue of Clarissa**, *Howe, Miss Anna*
>> a contraband trader L196
>> importing textiles and other curiosities L196
>> her two brothers, each master of a vessel L196, L252, L252.1
>> may give Clarissa protection L196
>> mentioned L199, L201, L209, L210, L228, L248
>> ready to accommodate Clarissa L229.1, L230
>> her manlike spirit L252, L252.1
Lovelace, Mr. Robert, contrivances of Lovelace, specifically, contrivance of Captain Tomlinson and Uncle
> Harlowe's birthday, Tomlinson, Captain Antony
>> head of a gang of smugglers L289, L514

snuff

Belford, Mr. John, servants
      buying snuff L336
Harlowe, Miss Clarissa
      all her oppositions not signifying a pinch of snuff L57
      taking a pinch of Dorcas's snuff L314
Harlowe, Mr. James, Jun.
      his snuff-box L459
Harlowe Family, clergymen, Brand, Mr. Elias
      buying Spanish snuff L399
Harlowe Family, servants, Barnes, Betty
      taking snuff L63
Lovelace, Mr. Robert
      taking rapee from Smith's L416
      serving customers at Smith's Scots snuff and Portugal snuff L416
Moore, Mrs., neighbors, Rawlins, Miss
      her snuff-box L237
Smith, Mr. John
      dealer, trader in Scots snuff and Portugal snuff L320, L416

solicitors

Lord M., relations, half-sisters, Lawrance, Lady Betty
      Stedman, attending to her Chancery affairs L256

sovereigns see
      historical references
      political references, *Howe, Miss Anna*

spectacles

Hickman, Mr. Charles
      not old enough to need L346
Lord M.
      his mentioned L323

Spectator see **newspapers**

sport see also **hunting**

Lovelace, Mr. Robert
      has hunted in the forest at Windsor L116
      his game at racquet L128
      the hunt L170
      Clarissa, will not long be Lovelace's sport or the sport of fortune L333
      can swim like a fish L347
      swordsmanship a sport he loves L535

stage directions

Lovelace, Mr. Robert
      reporting scenes in L214, L232, L323–L325

stages see **transportation**, *Harlowe, Miss Clarissa*

story

Belford, Mr. John
      protector of Clarissa's memory L389
      Clarissa's, summed up and compared to examples of Restoration drama L413

story (cont.)

Belford, Mr. John, relations, Jenyns, Tony
      Tony Jenyns's story L192

Harlowe, Miss Clarissa see also **warning**
      writing a history of her sufferings L57
      to all who will know your story L177, L187
      her story mentioned L306, L379, L448, L502
      her story, when known, will absolve her L307, L380
      telling her story to Mr. and Mrs. Smith, Mrs. Lovick, and Belford L349
      her whole story not yet known to Anna L359
      her tragical story to be published by Anna and Mrs. Howe L372, L459, L515
      her story best recorded in Lovelace's letters L379
      perhaps her story should be forgotten as soon as possible L379
      wishing to leave behind an account to clear up her conduct L387.1
      asking Belford for copies of Lovelace's correspondence to help tell her story L387.1, L391
      no time to write her own story L389
      Clarissa's story summarized by Belford in relation to examples of Restoration drama L413
      Anna collecting Clarissa's letters to tell her story L428
      Counsellor Derham and Mr. Ackland will hear Clarissa's story and begin a process L429
      family not inquiring into the particulars of Clarissa's story L430
      Mrs. Norton wanting to hear Clarissa's story L459
      when James knows her story L490
      her story known by the neighborhood L504
      a compilement to be made of all that relates to L507
      her story not to give Morden cause for vengeance L518

Harlowe Family
      knowing not what Clarissa has suffered L368
      sending the family's attorneys to take minutes of Clarissa's story L430
      not inquiring into the particulars of Clarissa's story L430

Harlowe Family, hires, Ackland, Mr.
      and Counsellor Derham to attend Clarissa, hear her story, and begin a process L429

Howe, Miss Anna
      to all who will know your story, you will be an excellent example of watchfulness L177
      not knowing all the details of Clarissa's affairs L346, L359, L373
      collecting Clarissa's letters and papers to tell Clarissa's story L428
      every man...is not a Lovelace...neither is every woman a Clarissa L456
      threatening to publish the case L515

Lovelace, Mr. Robert, friends, Belton, Mr. Thomas
      his story L190.1, L191, L192, L344

Moore, Mrs., neighbors, Rawlins, Miss
      Clarissa informing her of her story L318

Morden, Colonel William
      not yet acquainted with Clarissa's L448

Norton, Mrs. Judith
      Mrs. Norton's story L301
      Clarissa's story
          family not inquiring into through Mrs. Norton L430
          Clarissa sending Mrs. Norton a packet of letters L433
          Mrs. Norton wanting to hear L459

styptic

Lovelace, Mr. Robert
      Eaton's styptic, a balsamic medicine to cure effects of ipecacuanha L209, L211

suffering see also **angel**; **divine qualities**; **example**; **fall**; **light**; **sacrifice**; **trials**; **virgin**
Harlowe, Miss Clarissa
>   Clarissa's L1, L121, L187, L189, L297, L308
>   writing a history of her sufferings L57
>   her sufferings her glory L274
>   her family knowing not what she has suffered L368
>   choosing to be a sufferer rather than an aggressor L451
>   brightened and purified by her sufferings L459, L492.2
>   her sufferings compared to Lovelace's L463
>   angelic sufferer L467
>   suffering her injuries herself rather than offering them to others L471
>   the right use of her sufferings L490
>   her undeserved sufferings L514

Lovelace, Mr. Robert
>   comparing his to Clarissa's L335, L463
>   his noted L511

suicide
Harlowe, Miss Clarissa
>   wishing it were not a sin to put an end to her own life L276
>   her penknife held to her bosom threatening to take her own life L281
>   accused of starving herself, self-murder L333, L366
>   will not shorten her own life L371
>   the threat of suicide L395

Lovelace, Mr. Robert
>   his thoughts of L511

suitors to Harlowe, Miss Clarissa
Harlowe, Miss Clarissa
>   generally
>>   list remembered by Lovelace: Wyerly, Biron, Symmes, Solmes, and the laced-hat orator himself L294
>   Byron, as Biron L15, L294
>   Mullins, Mr., rejected by Clarissa, attending her funeral L4, L6, L504
>   Solmes, Mr. Roger, as suitor L6, L294 *see also* **address to Clarissa by Mr. Roger Solmes**
>>   animals, vile reptile L36
>>   character
>>>   confident and offensive, monster L16, L17
>>>   boasting he will marry Clarissa L22, L76
>>>   account of, by Anna L27
>>>   compared to Lovelace L32.3, L277
>>>   illiterate L32.4
>>>   his persistence L33.2, L79
>>>   his impudent preparations L76
>>>   siccofant L90.1
>>   costume
>>>   yellow, full-buckled peruke, broad-brimmed beaver L10
>>>   white peruke, fine laced shirt and ruffles, coat trimmed with silver, and a waistcoat L78
>>   estates
>>>   upstart man, not born to immense riches L13
>>>   his fortunes affected by marriage to Clarissa L13, L17, L19, L27
>>>   disinheriting his own family L16, L27
>>   funeral of Clarissa, attending L504
>>   gossip
>>>   sources of information about L27, L56, L57, L58
>>>   public talk of Clarissa's aversion to him L81

suitors to Harlowe, Miss Clarissa, *Harlowe, Miss Clarissa*, Solmes, Mr. Roger, gossip (cont.)
   wishing to pass on information to Clarissa about Lovelace L59.1, L78, L79
   would have told Clarissa of Miss Betterton L139
  kidnapping, planned by Lovelace L117, L119
  marriage, unmarried CONCLUSION
  names, Squire Solmes L139
  opinions, on wives and marriage L56
  physical appearance, his ugliness L16, L21
  relations
    Solmes, Sir Oliver, his father
     his yellow, full-buckled peruke, broad-brimmed beaver L10
     wretched creature with vast fortunes L17
     compared to Roger Solmes L32.4
     surly old misogynist, opinions on women L40
    his sister L32.4
  rescue of Clarissa, James's plot, mentioned L300
  servants, treatment of L95
  tenants, treatment of L27
  vengeance, meditating vengeance on Clarissa L57
  visits, to Harlowe Place L8, L16, L21, L53, L78, L86
 Symmes, Mr., as suitor L36, L294
  blaming Harlowes' treatment of Lovelace following the duel L1
  rejected by Clarissa L4, L6
  brother of Mr. Edward Symmes L4
 Wyerley, Mr. Alexander
  address to Clarissa
    rejected by Clarissa L3, L4, L6)
    mentioned L7, L36, L58
    knowing Clarissa's choice of the single life L26
    suggested as compromise to the Solmes plan L44, L70
    renewing his address to Clarissa L436, L437
    Clarissa cannot love Mr. Wyerley L436
    has always and still loves Clarissa L437
    wishing to marry Clarissa L437
  character
    jester upon sacred things L40
    prophaning and ridiculing scripture L78
  duel between James and Lovelace
    blaming Harlowes' treatment of Lovelace following L1
  meals, tea, tea with Anna and Mrs. Howe L1
  names
    included in a list of Clarissa's suitors as Wyerly L294
    signing his letter Alexander Wyerley L437
  funeral of Clarissa, attending L504

suitors to Howe, Miss Anna (other than Mr. Charles Hickman)
Howe, Miss Anna
 Colmar, Sir George
  I throbbed no more about him L37
  her first passion L151
  one of Lovelace's class, once endangered Anna L174.3
  Anna saved by Clarissa from marrying a fop and a libertine L182, L355
  Anna signed for Sir George Colmar L198
  obliged to quit the kingdom L198
  Anna would have followed him into exile but for Clarissa L198

suitors to Howe, Miss Anna, *Howe, Miss Anna*, Colmar, Sir George (cont.)
        mentioned L252
        her first choice of a husband L523
        causing her aversion to matrimony L523
    Harlowe, Mr. James, Jun., mentioned as L5

suitors to Howe, Mrs. Annabella
Howe, Mrs. Annabella
    Harlowe, Mr. Antony
        their mutual attraction L74
        Antony wishing to marry her L183, L196, L201
        his offer rejected L197

supper see **meals, supper**

surgeons
Belford, Mr. John
    Tomkins, his surgeon-friend L499
Harlowe, Mr. James, Jun.
    Mr. Diggs, attending James's arm L1
Lovelace, Mr. Robert
    Anderson and Tomkins, hired by Lovelace to embalm Clarissa L497
    suggested by De la Tour for the duel L536
    attending Lovelace after the duel, Morden giving a purse of gold to L537
Sinclair, Mrs.
    Garon, Mr. L499

swordsmanship
Lovelace, Mr. Robert
    a sport he loves L535

T

Tatler see **newspapers**

tea see **drink**; **meals, tea**

tenant-courtesy
Belford, Mr. John
    Lovelace leaving his progeny a worse tenure than L143
Lovelace, Mr. Robert
    a vile tenure L118

tenants
Harlowe, Mr. Antony
    treatment of L13
    generosity to L15
Harlowe, Miss Clarissa, suitors to Harlowe, Miss Clarissa, Solmes, Mr. Roger
    treatment of L27
Lovelace, Mr. Robert
    never rack-renting old tenants L13
    kindness to his tenants L13, L116, L183

theatre

Lovelace, Mr. Robert

    attending Otway's *Venice Preserved*, with Clarissa and Miss Horton L194, L194n1, L198, L200

title see also **peerage**

Harlowe, Mrs. Charlotte

    daughter of the old viscount L27

    born a lady L60.1

Harlowe, Mr. James, Jun.

    hopes for peerage, rank, and title L13

        based on anticipated inheritances L13

        foolish L36

    will never marry but to qualify for L79

Harlowe Family

    peerage, not allied to L79

    beneath Lovelace L109

Hickman, Mr. Charles

    may one day be a baronet L46

Lord M.

    importance of, and legitimate descendants L206

    title reversionary L265

    titles going with the bulk of his estate L327

Lord M., relations, half-sisters

    hoping to procure title for Lovelace L13

    daughters of an earl L36

    dowagers L36, L323

Lovelace, Mr. Robert

    entitled to wear swords L26

    Harlowe Family beneath him, their *acquired* fortune L79, L109, L421

    giving himself airs on account of his family L79

    esquire, respectable though overused L104

    captain, usual travelling addition L105

    pride of ancestry L143, L308

    not using his family name to further his designs L191

    noble descent L196, L327

    may come in for the title when Lord M. is dead and gone L206

    no title to Clarissa's lip or cheek L216

    continuing liberties with Clarissa, as he feels entitled L219

    earl, looking forward to being Right Honorable Robert, Earl Lovelace L254

    hoping on Lord M.'s death, his title reversionary L265

    title to eternal infamy and disgrace L285

    titles going with the bulk of Lord M.'s estate L327

Morden, Colonel William

    having no title to avenge Clarissa's wrongs L474

Townsend plot see **rescue of Clarissa**, *Howe, Miss Anna*

tragedy

Harlowe, Miss Clarissa

    too late, to remedy the apprehended evil L86

Sinclair, Mrs.

    preferring comedy to tragedy L194

transportation

Belford, Mr. John

    dismissing his coach and taking a chair back to Rowland's L334

    taking a chair to Smith's L340

    taking a coach to Smith's L445

    taking a chair home from Smith's after seeing Clarissa's coffin L450

Harlowe, Miss Clarissa

    abducted in a chariot and six L94

    to Mrs. Sorlings's in a chaise L98

    to London in a chaise L152

    to church in a chair, a coach L159, L320

    airing in a chariot with Lovelace L218

    inquiring about stages and their prices L228

    taking a coach to Hampstead to escape Mrs. Sinclair's L230, L232

    paying for vacant seats to Hampstead L232

    ordering Mabel to get her a coach L293

    her rings, her watch, her little money for a coach L314

    writ against her, she is taken away by the sheriff's officers in a chair L333

    taking a chair back to Smith's L336

    airing in a coach cancelled L399

    her habit of taking a sedan or chair to morning prayers L444

Harlowe Family

    not offering Mrs. Norton the family chariot to visit Clarissa L483

Hickman, Mr. Charles

    offering his chariot and four L252.1

    taking his own chariot to Dormer's L346

Howe, Miss Anna

    her chariot and four L47

    her chariot L87

    arriving at Harlowe Place in a chariot to view the body L502

Howe, Mrs. Annabella

    her chariot, her chaise L80

Lord M.

    his chariot and six used for Clarissa's abduction L76, L80

    his chaise taking Clarissa to London L149

    will set out in a litter to the wedding L207

    sending his chariot and six for Lovelace L278

    his chariot and six used by his nieces to visit Anna L327

    Lovelace taking Lord M.'s chariot to Colonel Ambrose's ball L350

    Lovelace taking his chariot and six to town L416

Lord M., relations, nieces, Montague, Miss Patty

    sharing Lovelace's phaeton L332

Lovelace, Mr. Robert

    using Lord M.'s chariot and six to take Clarissa from Harlowe Place L76, L80, L85, L98

    chaise and pair from Lord M.'s Hertfordshire seat L98

    chariot and six with horsemen L144

    taking a chair to the Park L209, L212

    sending for a Blunt's chariot L231, L231n1, L255

    his chariot L232, L233

    Lady Betty's arms and crest upon a coach, hers in for repairs L255

    a set will be ready to carry Lovelace L284

    flying coaches and flying horses at a county fair L294

    his phaeton ready to drive, Miss Patsey Montague sharing L322, L332

    attending a ball at Colonel Ambrose's in Lord M.'s chariot L350

    taking Lord M.'s chariot and six to London to visit Clarissa L416

transportation, *Lovelace, Mr. Robert* (cont.)
>taking a chair to Smith's L416
Norton, Mrs. Judith
>taking a chariot to Harlowe Place L459
>not offered the Harlowe Family chariot to visit Clarissa L483
>visiting Clarissa in a chaise and pair L483

transportation (sentence) see **exile**

travel
Belford, Mr. John
>out of town till Monday L391
>to visit Lovelace in Paris L514
Harlowe, Miss Clarissa
>going abroad rather than returning to Harlowe Place L248
>Morden wishing to take Clarissa on a tour of France and Italy L459
Harlowe, Mr. James, Jun.
>Scotland, whereabouts at the time of Lovelace's address to Arabella L2, L3
>not intending a journey with Singleton and Solmes L301, L307
>once thought of setting out for his northern estates L301
>sent to Edinburgh by Papa to avoid trouble with Lovelace L378
>in Edinburgh L382, L406
>coming soon from Edinburgh L443
>returned home L455
Hickman, Mr. Charles
>escorting Mrs. Howe and Anna to Mrs. Larkin's L65
>to accompany Anna and Mrs. Howe to the Isle of Wight L342
Howe, Miss Anna
>offering to go to London with Clarissa L81
>to Aunt Harman in the Isle of Wight, planned L252, L342
>>to set out soon L357, L358, L359, L365, L366, L372
>>returned home L455
>would accompany Clarissa abroad L252.1
>abroad when Clarissa escapes Mrs. Sinclair's and writes Letter 295 L296, L297
Howe, Mrs. Annabella
>to the Isle of Wight to visit Aunt Harman L342, L357, L366
Lord M., relations, nieces
>unlikely to accompany Clarissa abroad to find Morden L124
Lovelace, Mr. Robert
>abroad after his affair with Miss Betterton L139
>to France and Italy to forget about Clarissa, if she reject him L341
>preparing to go abroad L394
>will go abroad L480
>Belford asking Lord M. to urge Lovelace to go abroad L509
>preparing for a foreign tour L510
>planning to leave the kingdom L511, L513, L516
>departed from England L524
>to London, then Dover to embark L525, L526
>De la Tour, travelling valet engaged by Lovelace L530
>returning to England in March L534
>travelling to Munich with French valet and English footman L535.2
Lovelace, Mr. Robert, friends, Mowbray, Mr. Richard
>joining Lovelace abroad, setting out with L513, L514, L516, L525, L526
Lovelace, Mr. Robert, friends, Tourville, Mr. James
>out of town L290

travel, *Lovelace, Mr. Robert*, friends, Tourville, Mr. James (cont.)
    joining Lovelace abroad, setting out with L513, L514, L516, L525, L526
Morden, Colonel William
    wishing to take Clarissa on a tour of France and Italy L459
    setting out for Italy, will settle his affairs in Florence L526

trial
Lovelace, Mr. Robert
    confrontation with his family over Clarissa's to Lady Betty L323–L325, L339

trials see also **angel**; **divine qualities**; **example**; **fall**; **light**; **sacrifice**; **suffering**; **virgin**
Harlowe, Miss Clarissa
    before her family L98, L100, L144, L151
    if she stand her trial, Lovelace will marry her L110, L202
    Belford cautioning Lovelace against further trials of Clarissa L143, L222
    trials which will prove her woman or angel L157.1
    at the height of her trial L244
    should she fail in the trial L253
    the hour of her trial L256
    insensible in her moment of trial, her glory and her pride L279
    another trial, her last L280
    her trials over if she marry him L287
    her trials make her shine brighter L301
    her talents proportionate to her trials L308
    her trials withstood L319
    her trials, her sufferings L324, L346
    superior to all trials L395
    Lovelace's cruelty, her trial L440
Lovelace, Mr. Robert
    if I doubt her love, I can put her to trials as mortifying to her niceness, as glorious to my pride L97
    not yet found virtue to withstand his test L110
    will marry Clarissa if she stand her trial L110, L152, L191
    inclined to spare her all further trial L138
    bringing virtue to a trial L191
    resolved to continue Clarissa's trials, then marry her L202
    trials his pretense L222
    her trials continue L223
    she resists his trial of the fire L225
    would put an end to her trials L227
    mentioned L244, L253
    the hour of her trial...so long premeditated L256
    another trial for Clarissa, if she refuse to forgive him L280

trustees see also **estates**; **inheritances**
Harlowe, Mr. John
    of Clarissa's estate L27, L55, L406
    co-trustee with Morden L214
Morden, Colonel William
    of Grandfather Harlowe's will L27, L32.3, L87, L173
    co-trustee with John Harlowe L214
    of Clarissa's estate L248, L253, L455

U

undertaker
Harlowe, Miss Clarissa
> ordering her coffin at the undertaker's in Fleet Street L440
> paid by Clarissa L451

V

Valentine's Day
Lovelace, Mr. Robert
> birds changing mates every Valentine's Day L254

valets
Lovelace, Mr. Robert
> De la Tour, F. J., travelling valet L530
>> not speaking English L535
>> will write to Belford if anything happen to Lovelace L535
>> suggesting a surgeon for the duel L536
>> dispatching a packet of Lovelace's papers after the duel L537
Morden, Colonel William
> his valet, attending the duel L536

vanity
Lovelace, Mr. Robert
> vanity, and Clarissa curing him of L117, L161, L236, L322
> so light, so vain, so various L125

vault see **burial of Clarissa**

vengeance
Harlowe, Miss Clarissa, suitors to Harlowe, Miss Clarissa, Solmes, Mr. Roger
> meditating vengeance on Clarissa L57
Harlowe, Mr. James, Jun.
> his causeless vengeance L276
Hervey, Mrs. Dorothy
> cautioning Clarissa about Lovelace's vengefulness L44
Hickman, Mr. Charles
> Lovelace wishing for vengeance on L326
Lovelace, Mr. Robert
> vengeful nature, vengeance uppermost L44, L216
> vengeance on the Harlowe Family L169
> Lovelace an instrument, implement of James's vengeance L191, L276
> vengeance justified L252
> defying Clarissa's right to vengeance through the law or Morden L274
> his punishment, justice of his country and vengeance of her friends L336

victims of Belford
Belford, Mr. John
> Bab Wallis, or Barbara, has lain with L255
> Farley, restitution L514

victims of Belford, *Belford, Mr. John* (cont.)
    John Loftus, young mistress of, restitution L514

victims of Belton
Lovelace, Mr. Robert, friends, Belton, Mr. Thomas
    sister of Tom Metcalf, who died protecting her from Belton L419, L422

victims of Lovelace (other than Clarissa)
Lovelace, Mr. Robert
    generally, Lovelace making them laugh and cry at once L370
    Miss Betterton
        of Nottingham L127
        her family's resentment L127
        dying in childbirth, eighteen months ago L139, L140
        child surviving L139
        rape victim of Lovelace L139
        loving Lovelace L140
        mentioned L177, L198
    Polly Horton L157.1, L198, L226, L277
    Sally Martin L157.1, L198, L209, L226, L227
    D—r's wife L157.1
    Miss Lockyer L177, L198
    the French marquis's wife L209
    his attempt on a bride L219
    Lucy Villars L252
    the pretty gipsy L252

villains
Harlowe, Mr. James, Jun.
    James as L142
Lovelace, Mr. Robert
    his plotting villain of a heart L153
    mentioned as L154, L188, L207, L225, L227, L229, L229.1, L238, L252.1, L256, L260, L274, L276, L281, L314, L367, L402, L429, L470, L510.3
    called the V. L316
    blackest of L456
    execrable villain L497

violent behavior
Belford, Mr. John
    cutting the throat of Clarissa's destroyer L334, L387
Harlowe, Miss Clarissa
    taking sharp-pointed scissors against Lovelace L225
    Lovelace trying to raise her, Clarissa wildly slapping his hands L267
Howe, Miss Anna
    snapping her fan in Lovelace's face at the ball L367
Lovelace, Mr. Robert
    generally
        abusing the messenger who brought him news of Clarissa's arrest L333
        threatening to cut the throat of anyone happy while he is dejected L463
        threatening to kill his messenger bringing bad news L472
    toward Joseph Leman, threatening to cut off his ear L113
    toward Clarissa
        dragging Clarissa, sword in hand L94
        trying to seize Clarissa's letter L175, L176

violent behavior, *Lovelace, Mr. Robert*, toward Clarissa (cont.)
> nearly making a violent attempt upon Clarissa L187.1–L187.4
> seizing, grasping, snatching Clarissa's hands in anger L199, L281, L314
> very angry at Clarissa, ugly in his violent outburst L200
> wrapping his arms around her knees L201
> physically detaining her from going abroad L201
> continuing liberties with Clarissa, as he feels entitled L219
> his midnight attempt on Clarissa after the fire L227
> stopping her way as she tries to leave the room L243
> stopping her attempt to leave Mrs. Sinclair's, folding his arms about her L256
> clasping his arms about, stops her leaving Mrs. Sinclair's, carries her upstairs L264
> stopping her leaving, bruising her hands and arms L266
> stopping Clarissa escaping L267, L277
> wishing he had given Clarissa cause to hate him L395
> toward Belford
> > will cut Belford's throat to prevent telling tales L326
> > killing Belford L516
> toward Thomasine, offering to take Thomasine and hers on a boat trip and drown them L347
> toward Anna, refusing to let go Anna's hand L367
> toward Mrs. Howe, refusing to let go Mrs. Howe's hand L367
> toward Joseph, threatening to remove his teeth with Will's pruning knife L416
> toward Joel, may pistol him if he brings bad news L475

virgin see also **angel**; **divine qualities**; **example**; **fall**; **light**; **sacrifice**; **sufferings**; **trials**
Harlowe, Miss Clarissa
> virgin saint L224
> fearful virgin, Clarissa L261 Paper VI
> country funeral and coffin, a flower bed, mentioned by Lovelace referring to a virgin L313
> more pure than a vestal L346
> dressed in virgin white L474
Hickman, Mr. Charles
> male-virgin, virtuous and innocent L236

virtue
Harlowe, Miss Clarissa
> noted L1, L31, L187.1–L187.4, L222, L225, L248, L259, L266, L301, L316, L339, L427, L437, L447, L517
> loving virtue for its own sake L106
> tested by family and found wanting L110
> paragon of L110, L243
> female virtue founded on pride L110
> a cloak L201
> Clarissa, virtue itself L287
> unsullied L319
> baffling to Lovelace L349
> admired by Lovelace L358
> a vixen in her virtue L496
> Lovelace's principal intention to try her virtue L517
Howe, Miss Anna
> hers noted L435
Lovelace, Mr. Robert
> his principal intention to try Clarissa's virtue L517

visits
Belford, Mr. John
> to Clarissa
>> on behalf of Lovelace L284, L285
>> at Rowland's L334
>> at Smith's L339, L348, L365, L385, L413, L440, L441, L457
>>> disapproved by Harlowe Family L431, L459
>>> causing a scandal L433
>>> investigated by Mr. Alston L459
> to Dorrell L364, L365
> to Belton L364, L414, L419
> to Mrs. Sinclair on her death bed L499

Harlowe, Mr. Antony
> to Mrs. Howe L1, L10, L87, L100, L101
> from Lovelace L3

Harlowe, Miss Arabella
> from Lovelace L2

Harlowe, Mrs. Charlotte
> to Mrs. Norton, planned, to read Clarissa's letter L376

Harlowe, Miss Clarissa
> to the dairy house L2
> to Miss Anna Howe L6
>> where she first introduced Lovelace to Anna L252
> to Mrs. Knollys, where she had once been a guest L26
> to Sir Robert Biddulph, where she Clarissa met Patty Montague two years ago L233.3
> from Arabella L2
> from Lovelace
>> while at Anna's L7
>> Lovelace ambivalent about visiting Clarissa L341, L371, L391, L414
>> Clarissa fearing a visit from Lovelace L440, L446, L467
>> not wishing Lovelace to see her after her death L482
> from Uncle Harlowe L75
> from Dr. Lewin L75, L77, L82, L83
> from the ladies of Lovelace's family
>> expected L98, L157, L158, L178, L194, L203.1, L233, L242, L245
>> not expected L244
>> if she marry Lovelace L339
> from Belford
>> on behalf of Lovelace L284, L285
>> at Rowland's L334
>> at Smith's L339, L348, L365, L385, L413, L440, L441, L457
>>> disapproved by Harlowe Family L431, L459
>>> causing a scandal L433
>>> investigated by Mr. Alston L459
> from Hickman
>> planned L360
>> while at Smith's L365, L444
> from the parish minister L440, L454, L457, L467, L473
> from Morden L473, L518
> from Anna, planned L473.1

Harlowe, Miss Clarissa, suitors to Harlowe, Miss Clarissa, Solmes, Mr. Roger
> to Harlowe Place L8, L16, L21, L53, L78, L86

Harlowe, Miss Clarissa, suitors to Harlowe, Miss Clarissa, Wyerley, Mr. Alexander
> to Miss Howe, for tea L1

visits (cont.)

Harlowe, Mr. James, Jun., friends, Singleton, Captain
    to Harlowe Place L137

Harlowe, Mr. John
    to Clarissa, in her confinement L75
    from Clarissa, none for ten months L217

Harlowe Family, clergymen, Lewin, Dr. Arthur
    to Clarissa L75, L77, L82, L83
    to Harlowe Place, not visiting L408

Hervey, Mrs. Dorothy
    to Mrs. Norton L432

Hickman, Mr. Charles
    to Lovelace, interview with Lovelace L341, L346, L358, L510.1
    to Clarissa L358, L360, L365, L444
        planned, but being watched by Lovelace L319
    to a neighborhood coffee-house with Belford L366
    to Dr. H., to inquire about Clarissa L366

Howe, Miss Anna
    to Mrs. Larkin L47, L65
    to Clarissa, planned L456, L459, L473.1
        unable to attend Clarissa because of her mother's illness L455
    to Miss Lloyd L473.1
    from Mr. Diggs, Anna inquiring about the duel L1
    from Mr. Wyerley, for tea L1
    from Clarissa L7
    from Lovelace L7, L12, L49
        early social meeting with Lovelace mentioned L27
        Clarissa introducing Lovelace to Anna L252
    from Jenny Fynnett L46, L47
    from Miss Lloyd, inquiring about Clarissa L93
    from Miss Biddulph, inquiring about Clarissa L93
    from Captain Singleton L177
    from the Misses Montague L326, L327
    from Morden, with the ring and other bequests L455, L519, L520
    from Spilsworth and Herbert, her two cousins L456

Howe, Miss Anna, servants, Kitty
    to Hannah, requesting her to attend Clarissa L128

Howe, Mrs. Annabella
    to Mrs. Larkin L46, L65
    from Antony L10
        daily L87
        after Clarissa's flight L101
    from Sir Harry Downeton L56

Lord M.
    to Harlowe Place L3
    to Clarissa, planned L88, L194, L206, L231.3
    to Lovelace, at Uxbridge L496, L497
    from Lady Betty L233.2
    from Morden, to inquire about Lovelace's intentions L431, L442
    from Belford, invited to visit M. Hall L525, L527
    from Lovelace L275, L277, L278

Lord M., relations, Knollys, Mrs.
    from Clarissa, at whose home Clarissa had once been a guest L26

Lord M., relations, half-sisters
    to Clarissa, looking forward to L282

visits, *Lord M.*, relations, half-sisters (cont.)
  to Lord M. L323
Lord M., relations, nieces
  to Clarissa
    anticipated L125, L282
    Clarissa asking Lovelace for their company L231.3
    would attend Clarissa but for Lord M.'s illness L284
  to Anna, dining with Anna L327, L358
  to Lovelace, in his dangerous fever L410
Lord M., relations, nieces, Montague, Miss Charlotte
  to Clarissa
    planned L88, L98, L157, L233, L248
    Clarissa wondering whether she intends to visit L243
Lord M., relations, nieces, Montague, Miss Patty
  to Sir Robert Biddulph's, where she met Clarissa L233.3
Lovelace, Mr. Robert
  to Anna Howe
    mentioned L7, L12, L49
    early social meeting mentioned L27
    where Clarissa first introduced him to Anna L252
    wishing to visit L346
  to Lord M.
    who is very ill L275
    must go to M. Hall, to Berkshire L277
    Lord M. wishing to see Lovelace before Lord M. dies L278
  to Colonel Ambrose *see also* **ball, Colonel Ambrose's**
    breakfast and dinner with the Colonel and his nieces L322
  to Clarissa
    Belford assuring Clarissa that Lovelace will not visit her at Smith's L337
    agreeing not to visit Clarissa L341
    determined to visit Clarissa L370, L371
    will visit Clarissa in a few days with a parson to marry them L383
    Belford asking Lovelace not to visit Clarissa L391, L400, L413
    will try to visit Clarissa L395
    will visit Clarissa L410, L414
    still trying to visit Clarissa at Smith's L421
    expecting to visit Clarissa at Harlowe Place L439
    will not further molest Clarissa L449, L452
    may visit Clarissa L453
    Clarissa specifying in her will that she does not wish Lovelace to see her dead L482
  to Doleman, in Uxbridge L449
  to Hickman, interview at Dormer's, mentioned L346, L358, L510.1
  to Smith's, in search of Clarissa L416, L418
  to Belford, in London L525
  from Lord M. L497
  from the Montagues, while he is ill with a fever L410
  from Morden, at M. Hall L426, L442, L445, L446
Lovelace, Mr. Robert, friends, Belton, Mr. Thomas
  from Belford, going to Epsom to keep him company L364, L414
Lovelace, Mr. Robert, friends, Doleman, Mr. Tom
  from Lovelace in Uxbridge L449
Lovelace, Mr. Robert, friends, Mowbray, Mr. Richard
  to M. Hall with Lovelace L341, L421, L425, L511
Moore, Mrs., relations, Bevis, Mrs.
  to Lovelace L239, L242, L251

visits (cont.)

Morden, Colonel William

    to Lovelace L426, L433, L439, L440, L441

        interview with Lovelace L442, L445, L447

    to Lord M., planned, to inquire about Lovelace's intentions L431, L439, L440

    to Clarissa L441, L473, L474, L518

    to Miss Howe, with Clarissa's bequest L455, L519, L520

Norton, Mrs. Judith

    to Clarissa

        visits with Clarissa forbidden L8, L13

        urging her on family's behalf to wed Solmes L39, L90

        Clarissa asking her not to come L382

        wanting to visit Clarissa L459

        planned L483

        finding Clarissa dead L487

    to Harlowe Place, for family conference L459

    from Mamma, planned, to read Clarissa's letter L376

    from Aunt Hervey L432

Sinclair, Mrs.

    from Belford, on her death bed L499

Sinclair, Mrs., whores, Martin, Sarah (Sally)

    to Smith's, to find Belford and finding Clarissa dead L493

    to Belford, to bring him to Mrs. Sinclair L499

Smith, Mr. John

    from Belford L334

    from Lovelace L416

Smith, Mr. John, lodgers, Lovick, Mrs.

    Clarissa visiting Mrs. Lovick's friend L426

W

waking fantasies see also **dreams**; **reveries**

Lovelace, Mr. Robert

    guilty of murdering Clarissa L246

    as Clarissa's hour of trial nears L256

Waltham disguises

Lovelace, Mr. Robert

    mentioned L243

warning see also **story**

Harlowe, Miss Clarissa

    Clarissa, a warning to others L222, L428, L458

weapons

Belford, Mr. John

    sword, pistol, halter, or knife, ending his misery by L333

Harlowe, Miss Clarissa

    taking sharp-pointed scissors against Lovelace L225

    penknife, threatening to take her own life L281

    her penknife, to mend her pen L333

weapons (cont.)

Harlowe, Mr. James, Jun.

his sword, mentioned L4, L142

Harlowe, Mr. James, Jun., friends, Singleton, Captain

oaken plant in hand, couteau by his side L194

Lovelace, Mr. Robert

his sword L4

entitled to wear swords L26

offering Clarissa his unsheathed sword L94

swords, pistols, guns, blunderbusses L95

fire and faggot...private dagger L127

the pommel of his sword L233

his sword drawn, threatening Dorcas L281

the matrimonial sword hanging over his head by a thread L325

sword, pistol, halter, or knife, ending his misery by L333

snatching Will's pistol L443

his pistol, too ready a mischief L463, L466

may pistol Joel if he returns too slowly with Belford's letter L475

Will taking Lovelace's pistols away to prevent mischief L480

Lovelace, Mr. Robert, friends, Mowbray, Mr. Richard

during Lovelace's interview with Morden, offering his sword L442, L445

Lovelace, Mr. Robert, servants, Summers, Will

a gardener, carrying a pruning knife L416

his pistol snatched by Lovelace L443

taking Lovelace's pistols away to prevent mischief L480

Morden, Colonel William

skilful swordsman L533

a single rapier, weapon of choice for the duel with Lovelace L536

weddings see

address to Clarissa by Mr. Roger Solmes, *Harlowe, Miss Clarissa*, family's intimidations

contrivances of Lovelace, *Lovelace, Mr. Robert*, specifically, contrivance of Captain Tomlinson and Uncle Harlowe's birthday, Tomlinson, Captain Antony, contrivance

marriages, Clarissa's to Lovelace, *Harlowe, Miss Clarissa*, wedding

marriages, Clarissa's to Lovelace, *Lovelace, Mr. Robert*, wedding

weeping

Harlowe, Miss Clarissa

I wept L17, L20, L94

during an interview with Lovelace L201

for Lovelace when he is ill L211

for joy at the prospect of reconciliation L216

at Lovelace's behavior after the fire L227

crying as she escapes Mrs. Sinclair's L228

weeping at Mrs. Moore's L232, L233, L235

weeping as Tomlinson talks of her family and reconciliation L243

weeping after the rape L260

I have wept away all my brains. I can weep no more L261.1

weeping, shouting Murder! Help! out the window at Mrs. Sinclair's L264

eyes red and swollen with weeping L276

weeping, bitterly L333, L349, L426

Hickman, Mr. Charles

for Clarissa L366

white

Harlowe, Miss Clarissa

    wearing a white damask night-gown, white handkerchief in hand L263

    her snowy hand L263

    white to come, having seen nothing but black L295

    her white flowing robes L334

    her linen white L334

    dressed in white damask L334

    her hand, the lily not of so beautiful a white L340

    all in translucent white in Lovelace's dream L417

    white lily inscribed on Clarissa's coffin L451

    white satin lining Clarissa's coffin L451

    in a white satin nightgown L471

    dressed in virgin white L474

    her hands white as the lily L474

    returning in white paper her miniature of Anna to Hickman L476

Harlowe, Miss Clarissa, suitors to Harlowe, Miss Clarissa, Solmes, Mr. Roger

    his white peruke L78

Hickman, Mr. Charles

    his white hand and fine diamond ring L136

Howe, Miss Anna

    Rosebud, a plot...to wash a blackamoor white L72

    her mind all robed in spotless white L295

Lovelace, Mr. Robert

    the black angels and the white ones L152

    appearing white as an angel L235

    imagining an old spectacled parson with a white surplice thrown over a black habit performing the irrevocable ceremony L276

    his cause having a black and a white side L323

whores

Lovelace, Mr. Robert, contrivances of Lovelace, specifically, contrivance of the impersonators

    Wallis, Bab (or Barbara), a whore, as Lady Betty L255

Sinclair, Mrs.

    generally

        airing, with Clarissa and Lovelace L210

        animals, vipers, serpents L317, L330

        character

            readers L154

            brought up too high for their fortunes L157.1

            jealous, proud, vain L157.1

            compared L158

            young persons of good sense L159

            sensualists L169

            Hottentots L175

            seeking Clarissa's advice L194

            full of cruelty and enterprise L277

            sorceresses L416

            hellborn nymphs L511

        collation, attending L511

        contrivances of Lovelace

            contrivance of the promissory note

                their role L281

                ridiculing Lovelace for his failed contrivance L281

whores, *Sinclair, Mrs.*, generally (cont.)

    correspondence, Harlowe, Miss Clarissa with Anna
        helping Dorcas transcribe Clarissa's letters for Lovelace L174.3, L198
        confiscating any letters to or from Clarissa L279
    costume
        trying to steal some of Clarissa's clothes L336
        their dress and makeup the next morning L499
    escape of Clarissa
        stopping her attempt L264
        fearing Lovelace, blubbering L228, L292
    rape of Clarissa
        urging Lovelace to make a daytime attempt upon Clarissa L218
        advising Lovelace to try terror rather than love L264
        Mrs. Sinclair and her whores should be prosecuted for L317
    victims of Lovelace
        mentioned as L157.1, L198
        Polly and Sally ruined by Lovelace L277
  Carberry, Betty
    veteran, breaking the news to Lovelace that Clarissa is gone L228
  Horton, Mary (Polly)
    character
        taking a liking to Clarissa L158
        gentler temper and manners than Miss Martin L158
        well educated, has read L277
        her insolence to Clarissa L416
    death, by a violent cold CONCLUSION
    death of Sinclair, Mrs. L499
    duties, comforting Clarissa, attending to her L201, L293
    escape of Clarissa
        stopping Clarissa from leaving L276
        trying to cajole Clarissa back to Mrs. Sinclair's L333
    names, called Polly L154
    relations, niece of Mrs. Sinclair L155
    theatre, accompanying Clarissa and Lovelace L200
    victim of Lovelace L157.1, L198, L226, L277
  Martin, Sarah (Sally)
    angel L157.1
    animals, a toad L333, L416
    arrest of Clarissa, discovering Clarissa's whereabouts and having her arrested L330
    biblical references
        Prior, Matt, *Poems on Several Occasions*, on doubling down places of the Bible L333, L333n1
        Bible, *Book of Job*, *Ecclesiasticus*, Apocrypha, remarking over L333
    character
        thinking herself as well descended and educated as Clarissa L333
        her insolence to Clarissa L416
    contrivances of Lovelace
        contrivance of Mrs. Fretchville's house
            known to Mrs. Fretchville L194
    costume
        hoping Lovelace will give her Clarissa's clothes L333
        trying to steal Clarissa's fine Brussels lace head L336
        searching for the ruffles belonging to Clarissa's fine Brussels lace head L336
    death, died of a fever and surfeit CONCLUSION
    death of Harlowe, Miss Clarissa, visiting Smith's to find Belford and finding Clarissa.dead L493
    devils, a devil L157.1, L209, L333

whores, *Sinclair, Mrs.*, Martin, Sarah (Sally) (cont.)

education, well educated L277

escape of Clarissa

leaving after Clarissa's escape, escaping to her relations L293

locating Clarissa and having her arrested L330

trying to cajole Clarissa back to Mrs. Sinclair's L333

literary references

Shakespeare misquoted L157, L157n2

preferring comedy to tragedy L194

Prior, Matt, *Poems on Several Occasions*, on doubling down places of the Bible L333, L333n1

marriage

her humble servant a woollen-draper of great reputation L159

near marriage with a tradesman in the Strand L163

quarreling with her woollen draper L194

expecting Lovelace to marry her L333

medicine, taking salts L493

names, called Sally L154

opinions, on vows L157

reading, has read L227

relations, niece of Mrs. Sinclair L155, L333

sayings, Clarissa not to quarrel with her bread and butter L228

victim of Lovelace, Lovelace as Sally's first lover L209, L226, L277

visits

to Smith's, to find Belford and finding Clarissa dead L493

to Belford, to take him to visit Mrs. Sinclair L499

Partington, Priscilla

character

modest, genteel girl, specious, flippant L158.1, L169, L222

disliked by Clarissa L167

collation, attending L161

contrivances of Lovelace

contrivance of the bedfellows

wishing to be Clarissa's bedfellow L162

rejected by Clarissa L164, L169

sharing a press-bed with Dorcas L167

Lovelace attempting to fasten her upon Clarissa L229.1

marriage, spinster L158.1

names, called Priscilla, Miss Partington L158.1

relations, her guardian, Mrs. Sinclair L158

Wykes, Dorcas

accomplishments, her skill in the needle L155

animals, a toad L228, L261, L281

bribes, Clarissa offering her twenty pounds a year and a diamond ring to help her escape L269

character

honest, neat in person and dress...not vulgar L154

Clarissa's dislike of her L154

discrete, loyal, genteel, obliging, sly eye, well-bred, well-spoken L155

compassionate temper L269

contrivances of Lovelace

contrivance of the escape

assisting Lovelace L272

recognizing the lozenge on the widow lady's chariot L273

contrivance of the fire, crying Fire! Fire!, petticoats in hand L225

correspondence, Harlowe, Miss Clarissa with Anna

searching Clarissa's clothing for letters L174.3

whores, *Sinclair, Mrs.*, Wykes, Dorcas, correspondence, Harlowe, Miss Clarissa with Anna (cont.)

      helping Lovelace come by Clarissa's letters L175

      searching Clarissa's room while she is at the theatre with Lovelace L194

      searching Clarissa's chamber for letters L198

      transcribing Clarissa's letters for Lovelace L198, L202, L210

      noting that Clarissa has moved her letters L210

      trying to open the wainscot box to get Clarissa's letters L218

      transcribing Clarissa's fragments and letters for Lovelace to send Belford L261

   costume, dangling in her own garters from her bed's tester L292

   death, untimely CONCLUSION

   death of Sinclair, Mrs. L499

   duties

      attending Clarissa L154, L155, L175

      having a key to Clarissa's clothing chest L174.3

      using her key to search Clarissa's chamber for letters L198

      carrying messages between Clarissa and Lovelace L157, L184, L185, L186, L198, L200, L226

      preparing tea, offering Clarissa food and drink L201, L261.1

      the upper servant, greeting a footman who appears at Mrs. Sinclair's door L213

      watching Clarissa L262

   escape of Clarissa

      to be watchful of any attempt to escape L174.3

      her opinion that Clarissa should be allowed to go L267

      Clarissa offering her £20 a year and a diamond ring to help her escape L269

      trying to cajole Clarissa back to Mrs. Sinclair's L333

      first to discover Clarissa at Smith's L334

   fearing Lovelace, hiding from Lovelace's rage after Clarissa escapes Mrs. Sinclair's L228

   friendship with Clarissa

      Clarissa trying to befriend Dorcas L177, L268, L270, L271, L275

      sympathetic to Clarissa L264

      seeming to come into favor with Clarissa L267

   heraldry, recognizing the lozenge on the widow lady's chariot L273

   keys

      having keys to Clarissa's clothing chest L174.3

      using her key to search Clarissa's chamber for letters L198

   loyal to Lovelace L273

   name, as Dorcas Martindale L269, L270

   reading, illiterate wench, can neither write, nor read writing L154, L155

   relations, Mrs. Sinclair's niece L154, L273

   sleeping arrangements

      Lovelace hoping Clarissa will accept her as a bedfellow L154

      in a press-bed, with Miss Partington L162, L167

widow

Harlowe, Miss Clarissa

   Clarissa as Lovelace's widow L410

widow's weeds

Lovelace, Mr. Robert, friends, Belton, Mr. Thomas, family, Thomasine

   and widow's weeds L399

wife see also **contrivances of Lovelace**, *Lovelace, Mr. Robert*, specifically, contrivance of pretending marriage to
  Clarissa

Lovelace, Mr. Robert

   Clarissa's reference to a first wife and a second wife for Lovelace L187

   will advertise in the *Gazette* for his eloped wife L228

wills see also **bequests of...**; **executors**
Belford, Mr. John
    to make his will L528
Harlowe, Mr. Antony
    his favoring Clarissa L13
    carrying his great fortune into another family on Clarissa's account L182
Harlowe, Miss Clarissa
    bequeathing her estate, empowered by Grandfather L123, L400
    dated, second day of September, year not given L507, L507fn
    estate sale
        diamond necklace, solitaire, and buckles from Sir Josias Brookland, proceeds of sale, to estate L507
        her grandmother's jewels, proceeds of sale, to Poor's Fund, or estate, or Papa L507
    executed
        beginning to execute the will now that the funeral is over L503, L505
        Morden giving Belford proceeds of Grandfather's estate since his death L504
        to perform every article within two months time L507
        Morden assisting Belford in execution L507, L520
    executorship disputed
        James not accepting Belford as executor L494.1, L501, L506
        James will execute the will himself, where it is fit or reasonable L494.1
        Morden intending to enforce Belford's executorship L495
        Lovelace wanting to execute the will L497
        James wanting John and Antony to execute the will L506
    historical references, compared to Louis XIV, whose will flagrantly broken L508
    preamble, attached on black silk L507
    reading, Belford and Morden reading her will together L486
    text
        completed by Clarissa L454
        showing her will to Belford and giving him keys to the drawer L460
        Belford unlocking drawer holding her will and parcel of letters sealed with three black seals L486
        full text L507
        Belford giving Lovelace a copy of Clarissa's will L527
    witnesses, John Williams, Arthur Bedall, Elizabeth Swanton L507
Harlowe, Mr. James, Jun.
    Clarissa's
        not accepting Belford as Clarissa's executor L494.1
        wanting to execute Clarissa's will himself where it is fit or reasonable L494.1
        no need for an executor outside the family L501
        asking Belford to relinquish executorship of Clarissa's will L506
        wanting John and Antony to execute Clarissa's will L506
Harlowe, Mr. John
    his to favor Clarissa L13, L75
Harlowe Family, relations, Harlowe, Grandfather
    Aunt Harman requesting to see L1
    source for family genealogy L4
    flawed, deeds flawed L4, L20, L55
    partial text L4
    mentioning Lovell as James's benefactress L4
    family setting aside his will L7
    disappointing James L13
    trustees
        Morden L27, L32.2, L87, L173
        Uncle Harlowe L27, L55
    purpose of L27
    opinion of the Harlowe Family L27

wills, *Harlowe Family*, relations, Harlowe, Grandfather (cont.)
>> giving Clarissa power to bequeath her estate L123, L400
>> intending Clarissa to live upon her own estate L248
>> Clarissa knowing his will by heart L460
>> uncles not following his example with respect to Clarissa L472

Howe, Mrs. Annabella, relations, Larkin, Mrs.
>> her will L46, L65

Lord M.
>> Lovelace his heir presumptive L2, L13, L118
>> will leave Lovelace more than he could ever wish for L105
>> will settle all upon Clarissa if Lovelace is not a good husband L206, L233.4
>> first boy will take Lord M.'s surname by Act of Parliament L233.4
>> Pritchard altering Lord M.'s will to leave out Lovelace L323
>> bequeathing his grandson his Hertfordshire estate CONCLUSION

Lovelace, Mr. Robert
>> wanting to execute Clarissa's will L497
>> wanting to see a copy of Clarissa's will L526
>> receiving a copy of Clarissa's will from Belford L527

Lovelace, Mr. Robert, friends, Belton, Mr. Thomas
>> his heir, a nephew in Antigua L440

Morden, Colonel William
>> if he die unmarried and without children, leaving to Clarissa as her grandfather did L443
>> leaving his ample fortune to Clarissa L455
>> Clarissa his heir and executrix L459
>> James will not be his heir L508
>> Belford, along with Hickman, to be his executor L528
>> giving Belford his will, copy to Hickman, copy to his banker L528

wine see **drink**

women's language
Lovelace, Mr. Robert
>> women's words: figaries, tostications, marry come up L242
>> expressing himself in women's dialect L323
>> broken heart being women's language L341

writ
Harlowe, Miss Clarissa
>> writ against her, she is taken away in a chair by the sheriff's officers L333

writing see also **codes**; **narration**
Belford, Mr. John
>> dealing with Lovelace in writing, not in conversation L526
>> supposed author of the conclusion CONCLUSION
Harlowe, Miss Clarissa
>> her love of writing L3, L101, L107, L135, L296
>> its length L16
>> her knack of writing, her natural talent L32.4, L33.3, L101, L206, L392, L486, L529
>> writing a history of my sufferings L57
>> writing on the cover...with a pencil L57
>> her anonymous letter to Lady Drayton on severity in parents L58, L59
>> to be refused pen and ink when she goes to Antony's L63
>> beginning to hide her writing supplies L78
>> writing materials taken away L79
>> leaving harmless pieces of writing for the family to find L90, L91

writing, *Harlowe, Miss Clarissa* (cont.)

I know not how to forbear writing....I must write on L135

writing a little book upon the principal acting plays L200

writing continually at Mrs. Moore's L233

resuming her writing after the rape L260

delirious writings L261 Papers I–X

keeps forgetting what she is writing L261.1

asking for pen, ink, and paper when she goes to Bedlam L261.1

penknife, to mend her pen L333

writing materials, paper, pens, ink available at Rowland's L334

Mrs. Lovick writing for Clarissa L338

has been up writing since five L348

writing is all her diversion L365

tiring herself writing L372, L405, L457

book-learned and a scribbler L405

too ill to read or write L458, L467, L473.2

Harlowe, Mr. James, Jun.

his writing ability L53

Harlowe Family, clergymen, Brand, Mr. Elias

talent is letter-writing L444

Howe, Miss Anna

her talent for scribbling L111

using crow-quill pens L239.1

Lovelace, Mr. Robert

his knack of writing L3

love of writing L12

Lovelace and Clarissa, a pair of scribbling lovers L105

his poetry L116

writing a comedy, *The Quarrelsome Lovers* L175, L216

wrong to scribble so freely to Belford, but must write on L223

I love to write to the moment L224

crow-quills, ladies always writing with L239

writing in his vellum-leaved book L243

though this was written afterwards, yet...I write it as it was spoken, and happened; as if I had retired to put down every sentence as spoken. I know thou likest this lively *present-tense* manner, as it is one of my peculiars L256

I must write on. Nothing else can divert me L264

familiar writing is but talking L268

writing a book about dreams, *Lovelace's Reveries* L272, L273

compelled to write L281

A

abroad

where Lovelace has recently come from as the book begins L31

where Lovelace will put out that Clarissa has gone after her escape L85

where Lovelace went after his affair with Miss Betterton L139

where, and in England, Lovelace has made good use of his observations on what women read L154

where Lovelace lives expensively L186

where Clarissa would go rather than return to Harlowe Place L248

where Clarissa wishes to go L252.1

where Anna is when Clarissa first writes after her escape from Mrs. Sinclair's L296

where Clarissa once thought of going L318

where Lovelace will go if Clarissa rejects him L367, L383

where Clarissa may go with Morden for a year or two L459

where Lovelace may go for fear that Clarissa may die L472

where Morden will go again L476

where Belford advises Lovelace to go L498

where Belford asks Lord M. to urge Lovelace to go L509

where Morden's father chiefly resides L529

where Lovelace is miserable L535

Acton Road

where Lovelace rode hoping to meet Will with a letter from Belford L463

Albemarle Street

as Albermarle, where Lady Betty would like to see Lovelace Sunday night at her cousin Leeson's L233.2

Clarissa asks whether Lady Betty attended her cousin Leeson there L302

Ambrose, Colonel, his house

where Lovelace is invited to breakfast and dine with the Colonel and his nieces L322

the scene of a ball L350, L358, L366, L367, L368

Antigua

where Belton's nephew and heir lives L440

B

Barn Elms

where an Earl of Shrewsbury met with his death in an act of vengeance L518

Barnet

where Mrs. Sorlings's daughter parts company with Clarissa and Lovelace on their way to London L154

where Miss Sorlings had an uncle L155

where Miss Partington's guardian lives L167

where Mrs. Howe's messenger will deliver hers to Clarissa, as he has business there L296

Bath

where Lovelace will put out that Clarissa has gone after her escape L85

Bavaria
where Lovelace will visit the Electoral court L513, L530, L530n4

Bedford Head
where Morden lodges after leaving Antony's L474
in Covent Garden, where Morden invites Belford to spend the evening L526

Bedford Street
in Covent Garden, where Doleman has located lodgings for Clarissa L130.1
Covent Garden church having a door fronting L333

Bedlam
where Anna's messenger will visit while in London L251
where Clarissa wishes to go after being raped, or to a private madhouse L261.1
the whole world is but one great Bedlam L497

Belle Savage
on Ludgate Hill L302, L318
where Lady Betty should send hers for Clarissa L302
as Bell Savage Inn, where Miss Rawlins should leave hers for Clarissa L318

Berkshire see also **M. Hall**
where Lord M. has a seat L98
where Lovelace wants Clarissa to go L107
where Lord M. is at present L116
where Lovelace will go to bring Charlotte to London to visit Clarissa L157, L158
where Lovelace will take Clarissa after he can call her lawfully his L266
where Lovelace wants Clarissa to accompany him L276
where Lovelace will go to attend Lord M. L277
where Simon Parsons is Lord M.'s bailiff L278
where Captain Tomlinson comes from L304
where Lovelace puts out that he is married to Clarissa L308
where Lovelace set out for after his second attempt on Clarissa L386
where Lovelace is setting out for to show his family the letter from Clarissa L421, L424
Lord M.'s seat here bequeathed Patty Montague CONCLUSION

Berlin
where Lovelace will visit the Electoral court L530, L530n4

Bishopsgate Street
location of the Four Swans Inn L304

Blackwell Hall
exhausted of its sables in anticipation of the death of Charles II L294

Blenheim
where Lovelace is to gallant his two aunts L326

Bloomsbury
location of a church near Mrs. Sinclair's L157
where Mrs. Carter keeps a bagnio L499

Blue Boar Inn
and Leman, to be Leman's, from Lovelace L139, L140

Blue Boar Inn, horsepond
mentioned L139

Bohemia Head
where Mowbray found Lovelace L480, L480n1

bowling-green see also **Hampstead, bowling-green**
where John Harlowe and Captain Tomlinson met L214

Bowling Green House
in Highgate, where Clarissa breakfasted L426

Brentford Ait
location of the Swan L426

Bristol
where Lovelace will put out that Clarissa has gone after her escape L85

Brixen
where De la Tour finds a surgeon for the duel L536

Brown's, Mr.
Westminster, where Patrick M'Donald has lodgings L289

Bull and Gate
in Holborn, where Mr. Brand puts up L444

C

Calais
where Lovelace loitered for two days after crossing from Dover L530

Canterbury
where Morden attends to his concerns, having arrived in England L408

cascade see **Harlowe Place, cascade at the bottom of the garden**

Castle Inn on Hampstead Heath
Clarissa passing by the sign of the Castle on the Heath, on the way to Hedon L232
where Anna's messenger stopped on his way to Mrs. Moore's L251, L251n1

Cecil Street
where the widow lives, with whom Clarissa considers lodging after leaving Mrs. Sorlings's L130
where Mrs. Doleman has seen lodgings for Clarissa L130.1

cedar summer-house see **Harlowe Place, cedar summer-house**

Chandos Street
location of Lebeck's Head L366

chapels see
> **Harlowe Place, chapel ruins**
> **Harlowe, Mr. Antony, his chapel**
> **Lincoln's Inn Chapel**
> **Lord M., his chapel**
> **Royal Chapel**
> **St. Stephen's Chapel**

Chatham
where Charlotte may pick up someone the likes of Belford L516

Chelsea
where Clarissa was rowed to and breakfasted to escape Lovelace's visit L426

Cheshunt
where Malory's friend, the proctor, suddenly had to go to make an old lady's will L220

Chick Lane
in West Smithfield, where Mabel's mother lives L291

church
where Lovelace looks challenge at the Harlowe Family L30, L31, L36, L40, L106
as parish church
> where the funeral bell tolls for Clarissa as the hearse passes, returning her to Harlowe Place L500
> where Clarissa's funeral takes place, half a mile from Harlowe Place L504

churchyard
where Clarissa dreams she is murdered by Lovelace L84

Cocoa Tree
in Pall Mall, where Lovelace meets his friends in London L48, L48n1
where Lovelace may amuse himself L209
where Lovelace wrote Letter 211 L211, L211n1
where Lovelace might be L228

coffee-house
neighboring coffee-house, near Smith's L340, L366
where Belford relates Clarissa's story to Dr. H. and Mr. Goddard L340
where Belford goes with Hickman after breakfast with Clarissa L366

College of Doctors of Civil Law in St. Paul's Churchyard
as Doctors' Commons, where Lovelace went to get a marriage license L219, L219n1, L220, L227.5, L228
as Doctors' Commons, near which is a tavern, where Clarissa sent Will with a letter for Lovelace L230

colonies
English colonies, to any one of which Clarissa would like to go, to escape Lovelace L230
American colonies, where Clarissa would like to go to escape Lovelace L230, L248
where her family want Clarissa to go L443
foreign colonies, where her family would like Clarissa to go L444

coppice, Harlowe Place see **Harlowe Place, coppice**

courts see also **Lincoln's Inn**; **Old Bailey**; **Westminster Hall**
where Clarissa could not bear to appear to prosecute Lovelace L315
where Lord M. could never appear as the principal man L321

courts (cont.)
where Dr. Lewen urges Clarissa to confront Lovelace L427
Clarissa's story better told in letters than in open court L428
where Clarissa must appear to prosecute Lovelace, as a prerequisite to reconciliation L456

Covent Garden
where Mr. Brand went to inquire about Clarissa L444
in St. Paul's parish L507
location of the Bedford Head L526

Covent Garden church see also **St. Paul's church**
the neighboring church in Covent Garden L320
where Clarissa attends morning prayers, church, prayers L320, L329, L330, L368, L440
Covent Garden church L329, L368
having a door fronting Bedford Street L333
where Clarissa was too ill to go L426

Cowcross
where Mabel's uncle keeps an alehouse L291

Croydon, the inn
where Belton skulked while Belford, Mowbray, and Tourville put Belton's sister into possession of his house L399

D

dairy-house see also **Grove; Harlowe, Grandfather, his late house**
built for and bequeathed Clarissa by her grandfather L2
later name of the Grove L2
where Clarissa wishes to visit, but fears to show independence L6
where Clarissa asks to be allowed to go L116
Clarissa's once beloved L465
where Clarissa wishes Mrs. Norton to spend the rest of her days L503.1
bequeathed Papa with the request that Mrs. Norton be allowed to live out her days there L507
the house late my grandfather's, called *The Grove*, and by him in honour of me and of some of my voluntary
  employments, my dairy-house L507
where Mrs. Norton lived the rest of her days CONCLUSION

dairy works see **Sorlings, Mrs., her farm**

Deptford
Mrs. Townsend's place of residence and location of her principal warehouse L196
where Mrs. Townsend, her brothers, and their crews would take Clarissa to safety L252.1

Deptford road
the direction to hear of a passage for Clarissa to escape Lovelace L230

Doctors' Commons
where Lovelace went to get a marriage license L219, L219n1, L220, L227.5, L228
near which is a tavern, where Clarissa sent Will with a letter for Lovelace L230

Dorking
where Thomasine's father is an innkeeper L192

Dormer, Mr., his house
where Mr. Hickman has an interview with Lovelace L341, L346

Dorrell's, Mr.
where Belford visited L364

Dover
where Lovelace will embark for France L416, L516, L525

Dover Street
address of a certain widow with accommodations for Clarissa L130.1
wrong address for the widow Sinclair, which Lovelace contrives for Clarissa to give Anna L131

Dresden
where Lovelace will visit the Electoral court L530, L530n4

Dublin University
Patrick McDonald was expelled from L217

E

Eagle
in Suffolk Street, where Belford will meet Lovelace L526

Edgware
where Belford was when Lovelace and Clarissa arrived in London L154
where Lovelace may join Belford tomorrow L155
where Lovelace went after taking Clarissa to London L158
where Belford lodges L167
where Lovelace's messenger will look for Belford on a Sunday L330, L333
where Belford is setting out for with Belton L340
where Belford visits for a day, Clarissa's health permitting L454, L457
Mr. Belford, of Edgworth [Edgware?] in the county of Middlesex L507
where Belford hires Mrs. Lovick to be his housekeeper L514

Edinburgh
where Papa has sent James to avoid trouble with Lovelace L378
where James is L382, L406
James will soon return from L443
where James threatens to go never to return if Clarissa returns to Harlowe Place L459

Elden
where Lovelace, in his dream, dropped into a hole L417

Electoral courts
where Lovelace will spend time in Berlin, Bavaria, and Dresden L530, L530n4

Enfield
heading of Letter 304 L304

England
where, and abroad, Lovelace has made good use of his observations about what women read L154·

England (cont.)
Lovelace threatens to leave this plaguy island and live abroad L233
where Morden will return to avenge Clarissa L274
Lovelace one of the handsomest men in L346
death having an estate in every county in...and out of L346
where any gentleman would have an interest in being faithful to his vows to Clarissa L349
where Lovelace will never return if Clarissa reject him L383
where Morden has arrived, at Canterbury L408
dignity of trade in this mercantile nation L416
where Morden has not been for seven years L442
where Morden wishes he had returned sooner L443, L447
where Morden will not leave until justice has been done Clarissa L455
where James will never return if Clarissa is allowed to return to Harlowe Place L459
this hated island, which Lovelace will leave, should the worst happen L463
where Morden wishes he had never come at all L476
Lovelace preparing to leave the kingdom L511, L513
Lovelace has departed from L524, L525
if Lovelace lives to return to L527
Lovelace leaving before he knew of Morden's threat L532
where Morden will return to settle L533
where Lovelace will return in March L534
where Lovelace will soon return if he is miserable abroad L534

Epsom
where Belford will go to keep Belton company and attend to his affairs L364, L399, L414, L426, L440
where Belford will put Belton's sister into possession of Belton's house L385

Erebus
some of our brethern now wandering in L370

F

farm see **Sorlings, Mrs., her farm**

farmhouse
neighboring farmhouse, where Anna has apartments ready for Clarissa L366

Favorita
in Vienna, where Baron Windisgratz resides, and where Morden can direct mail for Lovelace L534.1

Fetter Lane
where the son of Anna's tenant will visit his cousin L251

filbert walk see **Harlowe Place, filbert walk**

Finch Lane
where Filmer, a husbandman, lives near Howe residence L100

Flask
mentioned L210n1, L233

Flask, Lower Flask
where Will found Grimes and stole Anna's to Clarissa L238

Flask, Upper Flask
a tavern in Hampstead where Clarissa and Lovelace stop on an airing L210, L210n1
as Upper Flax—called by Will L231.1
where the coach set Clarissa down after she fled Mrs. Sinclair's L232

Fleet Street
location of St. Dunstan's L320, L368
where the Reading stage-coach inns L327
location of the undertaker's, where Clarissa ordered her coffin L440

Florence
where cousin Morden is when first mentioned L25
where Clarissa offers to go rather than marry Solmes L42, L45
where Lovelace offers to take Clarissa to Morden L124
where Morden resides L173.1
where Anna will put out that Clarissa has gone to claim protection of Morden L252.1
where Morden was when he wrote Letter 173.1, warning Clarissa of Lovelace L447
where Morden may resettle L476
where Lovelace will go L513
where Morden will go L526, L533
where Belford wishes Lovelace to avoid travel L533
where Morden is when Lovelace writes a letter of challenge L534
where Morden was when he received Lovelace's offer to accept a challenge L535.1
where Morden finally settled CONCLUSION

Four Swans Inn
in Bishopsgate Street, where Mrs. Hodges directs hers for Clarissa L304

France
where the Montagues would like to accompany Clarissa on her way to Morden L124
where Lovelace may go live to leave this plaguy island L233
where Lovelace will travel to forget about Clarissa, if she rejects him L341
where Hickman has not travelled L346
where Lovelace will go if Clarissa rejects him L416
tour of France and Italy, where Morden will take Clarissa L459
where Lovelace will go L513, L526
where Lovelace travels L532
Lovelace will return from L533

French Court
where Lovelace learned to corrupt servants of other families L62

G

Gad's Hill
near Rochester, where Belford accompanied Lovelace leaving the kingdom L527

gardens see
> Harlowe Place, garden
> Moore, Mrs., her garden
> Sinclair, Mrs., her garden
> Sorlings, Mrs., her garden

George
one of his cousins Montague to be...at the George in the neighboring village L76

Germany
German courts, where Lovelace will go L513
where Lovelace will go L514, L531

Glenham Hall
where Lady Betty wants Clarissa to accompany her for a month L303
where the pretend Lady Betty wants Clarissa to accompany her L313
where Clarissa is perched under Lady Betty's window L325

Golden Square
where lodgings may be found for Clarissa L130.1

Gore (Kensington Gore)
where Lovelace rode hoping to meet Will with a letter from Belford L463

grand tour see also **tour**
Uncle Hervey will send a young man L3
Clarissa will write down Lovelace's advice to the young man L3
Hickman must have made the grand tour L198

gravel pits, Kensington
site of rencounter among Lovelace's friends, possibly about a lady L161

green lane see **Harlowe Place, green lane**

grocer's shop
where the matronly lady will be conveniently waiting to assist Clarissa's escape L272

Grosvenor Square
where, in some of the new streets, lodgings may be found for Clarissa L130n1, L130.1

Grove see also **dairy-house**; **Harlowe, Grandfather, his late house**
earlier name of the dairy-house L2n
where Clarissa may want to live independent L44
where James threatens to establish domicile L55
where Clarissa requests permission to go after her flight L102
the house late my grandfather's, called the Grove L507
where Mrs. Norton will be housekeeper L524

H

Hackney
where Tony Jenyns took lodgings for his fencing-master's daughter, with whom he had an affair L192

Hammersmith Road
where Lovelace rode hoping to meet Will with a letter from Belford L463

Hampstead
where Clarissa and Lovelace go for an airing L210, L228
where Mrs. Moore resides L230
where Clarissa went by coach to escape Lovelace L230
where Clarissa and Lovelace had been together more than once L230
where Lovelace found Clarissa after her escape from Mrs. Sinclair's L231
where Lovelace claims Colonel Sinclair had lodgings L233
where Lovelace wants to walk with Clarissa, she refusing L247, L248
where Lovelace returns to Mrs. Moore's to say that he and Clarissa are now happy L259
where Will goes on an errand L261
where Lovelace brought the impersonators of Lady Betty and Charlotte to meet Clarissa L266
where Clarissa would like to return to Mrs. Moore's L277, L281
where Lovelace hinders Clarissa from going L282
where Clarissa would hardly have gone a second time to escape Lovelace L294
Clarissa asks whether Lady Betty and Miss Montague went to Hampstead L302
where Lady Betty says she has not been for several years L303
Clarissa's escape to, related to Lady Betty L306
Clarissa's departure from, related L310–L312
where Clarissa expected to return with the impersonators L314
where Anna sent Rogers with hers for Clarissa L319
where Miss Rawlins lives L319
where Clarissa went on her day out to escape Lovelace's visit L426

Hampstead, bowling-green see also **bowling-green**
where Lovelace, in disguise, practiced his limp L232

Hampstead, Castle Inn on Hampstead Heath
Clarissa passing by the sign of the Castle on the Heath, on the way to Hedon L232
where Anna's messenger stopped on his way to Mrs. Moore's L251, L251n1

Hampstead, heath
where Clarissa and Lovelace walked L210

Hampstead Hill
at the foot of which a robbery was committed two days ago L313

Hampstead, post-house
where Will's sweetheart carried Clarissa's for Anna L240
post, general and penny L241, L241n1

Hampstead, taphouse
where the footman who watched Clarissa drank with Kit the hostler L232

Hannah's
the windmill near Slough, where Lovelace's and Belford's servants met L445, L445fn

Hanover Square
mentioned L130, L130n1
where lodgings may be found in London for Clarissa L130.1

Harlowe, Grandfather, his late house see also **dairy-house**; **Grove**
Grandfather's late house, the dairy-house L53.1

Harlowe, Grandfather, his late house (cont.)
where Clarissa would like to seek refuge L53.1
where Harlowe Family expect Clarissa will want to live L459

Harlowe, Mr. Antony, his chapel
where Clarissa will wed Solmes L41.2, L50.1, L52.1
mentioned L62, L75

Harlowe, Mr. Antony, his house
his moated house L50, L50.1, L51.2, L52.1, L53.1, L62, L75
where the Harlowe Family wish to send Clarissa to receive Solmes L51.1, L51.2, L53.1, L62, L73, L75
where Anna tells Clarissa she must not go L81
where Clarissa is no longer asked to go to meet Solmes L83
where Clarissa addresses her letter to Morden L447
where Morden lodges while in England L459

Harlowe, Mr. James, Jun., his estates see **northern estates**; **Scotland**; **Yorkshire**

Harlowe, Mr. James, Jun., his house
near port of Leith L137

Harlowe, Mr. John, his house
where Clarissa would like to visit till the Solmes affair blows over L32.1
where Clarissa would like to seek refuge L53.1

Harlowe Place
described by Lovelace L34
White Hart Inn, inn, little alehouse, in a village five miles from Harlowe Place, where Lovelace stays L34
like Versailles, sprung up from a dunghill within every elderly person's memory L34
description of the grounds L86
where Clarissa would rather return to than marry Lovelace L191
where Lovelace threatens to visit if Clarissa is found missing L200
its purlieus, where Lovelace lurked L223
where Clarissa cannot think of returning L248
where Mrs. Norton seldom goes L301
Morden wishing he had returned to England before Clarissa left Harlowe Place L443
where Mrs. Norton is invited to breakfast and the Harlowe Family meeting L459
where the family assembled on hearing of Clarissa's dangerous way L494
where Clarissa is to return in a coffin L494.1
Morden accompanying the hearse to L500
this hated house L502
half a mile from the church where Clarissa's funeral takes place L504
where Morden declares that he will avenge Clarissa L517

Harlowe Place, back stairs
where Harlowe Family go, at their inconvenience, to avoid passing Clarissa's apartment L519

Harlowe Place, bank
divides green lane from poultry-yard L74
separates wood-yard from green lane L82
Clarissa must slide down the bank to escape Harlowe Place L82
high bank that bounds poultry-yard L86

Harlowe Place, cascade at the bottom of the garden
great cascade, where Lovelace would like to meet Clarissa L62

Harlowe Place, cascade at the bottom of the garden (cont.)
where Clarissa walks L69
great cascade, lately mended L91, L94
where Clarissa hints she may be, if not in the ivy summer-house L94
where Aunt Hervey did not find Clarissa L100
where Clarissa was thought to be the night she fled L144

Harlowe Place, cedar summer-house
mentioned L91

Harlowe Place, chapel ruins
in the middle of the coppice L86

Harlowe Place, coppice
haunted coppice, where a man was found hanging, about twenty years ago L35, L86
part of garden L61
where Lovelace waited for Clarissa L62, L223
lonely coppice L76
adjoining paddock L76, L80
bleak coppice L223

Harlowe Place, courtyard
where Morden ordered his horse upon leaving Harlowe Place L459

Harlowe Place, doors, back door
seldom opened, leading to a place pathless and lonesome L86, L86n

Harlowe Place, doors, garden door
leading to the haunted coppice L35
to which Lovelace has key L61
Clarissa will unbolt it for Lovelace L86, L94
where the key lay when Lovelace picked it up, offering it to Clarissa if she would return to the house L94
garden back door, from which Clarissa sought flight L144

Harlowe Place, filbert walk
in the garden L80

Harlowe Place, garden
my father's garden
      where Lovelace wishes to meet Clarissa L22, L35
      where Lovelace lurked about L99
      where Clarissa was led out of L201
where Clarissa takes her liberty, her poultry visits L25, L62
where Clarissa gives letters to a servant for her uncles, requesting relief from Solmes L29
where Clarissa walks L35
rambling, Dutch-taste L35
where James, Arabella, and Solmes walked L53
where Clarissa retires after meeting with Solmes L78
where Clarissa sees Papa for the last time L80
where Clarissa is now prohibited to walk L80
where Aunt Hervey walks with Betty L84
where Papa walks L84

Harlowe Place, garden wall
where Lovelace deposited a letter for Clarissa requesting to make a proposal L22

Harlowe Place, garden wall (cont.)
where Lovelace is forced to creep around to glimpse Clarissa L31, L34
garden and park wall
      where Lovelace waited in disguise for Clarissa L62
      where Lovelace skulked about as a thief L94
      her father's garden wall, where Lovelace lurked about L99

Harlowe Place, green lane
where Clarissa keeps bantams, pheasants, and pea-hens which belonged to her grandfather L9
site of exchange of secret correspondence with Anna L9
divided from poultry-yard by a bank L74
separated from wood-yard by a bank L82

Harlowe Place, hall
where Clarissa's coffin is set L500

Harlowe Place, ivy-bower see **Harlowe Place, ivy summer-house**

Harlowe Place, ivy-cavern in the coppice
where Lovelace waits for Clarissa, and, disappointed, writes her another letter L64.1

Harlowe Place, ivy summer-house
where Lovelace would like to meet Clarissa L62
where Clarissa will request to dine Monday before her escape L83, L86
where Clarissa visits L85
history of the place L86
or ivy-bower as it is sometimes called L86fn
where Clarissa has hidden writing supplies L90
where Clarissa dined L90, L91, L103, L144
where Aunt Hervey visits Clarissa L91
where Aunt Hervey did not find Clarissa L100
where Anna once read poetry to Clarissa L458
shunned by the Harlowe Family since Clarissa's death L519

Harlowe Place, paddock
adjoins coppice L76, L80
mentioned L223

Harlowe Place, parlour, Arabella's
mentioned L21, L78

Harlowe Place, parlour, Clarissa's
mentioned L4, L21, L79
having two doors L78
where Clarissa interviews Solmes L78
where the whole length picture of Clarissa in the Vandyke taste is kept L147
her parlour, where the coffin is put L500
locked up since Clarissa's death L519

Harlowe Place, parlour, Papa's
mentioned 78

Harlowe Place, plashy lane
by which Anna's servant reaches the wood-house L86
accessible by descending a high bank that bounds the poultry-yard L86

Harlowe Place, poultry-yard
where Clarissa walks L53
where Leman warns Robert away L74
divided from green lane by a bank L74
where Clarissa checks for Lovelace's answer L84
poultry visits not carefully watched by the family, as they depend on Leman L86
bounded by high bank L86
mentioned L91

Harlowe Place, stile
where Anna's tenant's son once met Clarissa and Anna L251

Harlowe Place, stile leading to the coppice
where Lovelace would like Clarissa to meet his chariot and six L76, L80
where Anna will meet Clarissa, if she chooses, and escape to London L81

Harlowe Place, wood-house
where Clarissa visits her poultry every morning and evening L35
where Lovelace surprised Clarissa L36, L86
where Clarissa walks L41
mentioned L54
where Clarissa asks Lovelace not to meet her L62
where Clarissa asks Anna to hide a disguise in which she could escape L82
accessible by plashy lane L86
its convenience as an escape route L86
where Lovelace had once planned to carry Clarissa off by surprise L103
remote from the dwelling house L103

Harlowe Place, wood-yard
a bank separates wood-yard from green lane L82

Harlowe Place, yew hedge
divides the yard from the garden L53
where Clarissa is obliged to conceal herself from her family L80
behind which Clarissa saw Papa, Antony, and her siblings for the last time L377

Harman, Aunt, her house
where Clarissa will direct hers for Anna L379
where Anna may celebrate her nuptials L379

Hart see **White Hart Inn**

heath, Hampstead
where Clarissa and Lovelace walked L210

Hedon
village a little distant from Hampstead L230
Clarissa pretends to be on her way to Hedon L230
where Clarissa will proceed after Hampstead L232
Clarissa going towards Hedon, passing by the sign of the Castle on the Heath L232
Clarissa inquires about a coach from Hampstead to Hedon L235

Henrietta Street
passage to, from Covent Garden church L333

Hertford
where Lovelace tells Mrs. Sinclair he and Clarissa were privately married L155

Hertford, post-house
where Belford is to address his for Lovelace to Mr. Robert Huntingford L105

Hertfordshire see also **The Lawn**
where Lord M. has a seat L88, L98, L149
where Lovelace offers to take Clarissa L98
their destination when Clarissa and Lovelace leave the inn L98
where the chaise will return after taking Clarissa to London L149
location of the Lawn L186, L206

High Holborn
location of Mr. Rowland's house, where Clarissa was taken after her arrest L333
where Mrs. Smith was preparing to attend Clarissa, at Rowland's L336

Highgate
where Clarissa and Lovelace go for an airing L210, L228
town near Hampstead L235
where Clarissa may meet Uncle Harlowe and throw herself on his protection L273
where Clarissa attended divine service L399
location of Bowling Green House L426

Holborn
location of the Bull and Gate L444

Holborn Bars
where Clarissa directed the coach to take her after leaving Mrs. Sinclair's L228

Holborn Hill
going up Holborn Hill L419, L419n3

Holland
where Hickman has travelled L346

Horn Tavern
where Lovelace was, and where Clarissa directs Will to take hers for Lovelace L228

horsepond, Blue Boar Inn
mentioned L139

Hull
where James will take Clarissa after he rescues her from Lovelace L132

Hungary
where Lovelace intends to travel L535
suspends his travel to L535.2

I

Inn of Court see also **courts**
Anna's mother of no Inn of Court L196

Isle of Man
where a rape victim chooses the sentence: rope, sword, or ring L317

Isle of Sheppey
where Lovelace offers to take Thomasine and hers on a boat trip and drown them L347

Isle of Wight
called the little island L10, L342, L367, L379, L435
where Anna's cousin lives, to whom Anna sends parts of Clarissa's letters L10
where Anna, Mrs. Howe, and Hickman set out for, to visit Anna's rich aunt L207.1
when Miss Howe sets out for the Isle of Wight, Lovelace will take his revenge L208, L252
where Anna, Mrs. Howe, and Hickman plan to visit Anna's Aunt Harman L342
where Mrs. Howe and Anna will set out for soon L357
where Mrs. Howe and Anna will set out for Monday next and stay a fortnight L366
where Anna will visit and may even celebrate her nuptials L379
where Anna and hers are visiting relations L435

Isle of Wight, Yarmouth
where Anna is visiting her Aunt Harman L404

Islington Church
where Clarissa was in the afternoon L399

Italy
where the Montagues would like to accompany Clarissa L124
where the Bishop of Salisbury was when he wrote a letter quoted by Lovelace L157.1
where Lovelace may go to leave this plaguy island L233
where Lovelace will travel to forget about Clarissa, if she rejects him L341
where Hickman has not travelled L346
Morden's knowledge of Lovelace in Italy L442
tour of France and Italy, where Morden will take Clarissa L459
where Lovelace will visit Turin, Tyrol L513, L530
where Lovelace will go L514, L526, L530
where Morden will set out for L526
where Morden's father wanted to show Clarissa's needlework L529
where Lovelace travels L532
Trent in confines of L535.2

ivy-bower see **Harlowe Place, ivy-cavern in the coppice**

ivy-cavern in the coppice see **Harlowe Place, ivy-cavern in the coppice**

ivy summer-house see **Harlowe Place, ivy summer-house**

J

Jericho
the measure of how far Anna's messenger would travel for her L251

K

Kensington
where Lovelace rode hoping to meet Will with a letter from Belford L463
and Piccadilly, where Mowbray will find Lovelace L477

Kensington Gore
from the Palace to the Gore, where Lovelace rode hoping to meet Will with a letter from Belford L463

Kensington, gravel pits
site of rencounter among Lovelace's friends, possibly about a lady L161

Kensington Palace
from the Palace to the Gore, where Lovelace rode hoping to meet Will with a letter from Belford L463

Kent
where Belton has a paternal estate L192
where Morden will return to reside upon his paternal estate L526

Kentish Town
through which Clarissa and Lovelace pass on an airing L210, L228
where Lovelace, in his contrivance, will have Uncle Harlowe's birthday and his own marriage to Clarissa L271, L272.1, L273, L281

King Street
where Mr. Smith has a glove shop L295, L298, L351, L363
where Clarissa stays after her escape from Mrs. Sinclair's L295
passage to, from Covent Garden church L333

King's Arms
where Lovelace will tell Clarissa he can meet Pritchard to receive Lord M.'s response L218
where Lovelace might be L228

Knightsbridge
where Lovelace will meet his messenger with Belford's letter L466, L475
location of the Rose, where Lovelace visited L478

L

Lancashire see also **Sandoun Hall**
where Lord M. has a seat L88
Lancaster County, location of Sandoun Hall L158.1
where Lovelace has part of his estate L186
Lord M.'s seat here may be a wedding present to Clarissa L206

Larkin, Mrs., her house
seventeen miles off from Anna and Mrs. Howe L46

The Lawn see also **Hertfordshire**
Lord M.'s seat in this county L98
where Clarissa refuses to go after her flight L104
where Lovelace's attendant returned after Clarissa and Lovelace arrived in London L155
Lord M.'s estate in Hertfordshire, which he will give Lovelace upon his nuptials L186
where Lovelace would like them to spend two or three of the summer months when married L203
where Lovelace and Clarissa may go after they are married L204, L207, L220, L233.4
may be a wedding present to Clarissa L206
in Hertfordshire L206
Hertfordshire estate, Lord M.'s bequest to his grandson CONCLUSION

Lawrance, Lady Betty, her house
Clarissa wishes to lodge near her after escaping from Harlowe Place L86
where Lovelace offers to take Clarissa L98
where Anna encourages Clarissa to go L100
where the Harlowe Family expect Clarissa to go L100

Lebeck's Head
in Chandos Street, where Belford dined with Hickman L366, L366n1

Leghorn
where Clarissa may go on her way to her cousin Morden L54, L124
where Morden may resettle L476
where Belford wishes Lovelace to avoid travel L533

Leith
where James will take Clarissa after rescuing her from Lovelace L132, L140
a port where Singleton lives L137
where both James and Singleton have houses L140

Lepanto
where in 1571 Don John of Austria defeated the Turks L171

Libyan wilds and deserts
where Belford will hunt Lovelace and his fellow savages L333

Lincoln's Inn
where Hickman once had chambers L196

Lincoln's Inn Chapel
where Clarissa attended morning prayers L320, L368
where Clarissa took a chair L399
where Lovelace hunts Clarissa L418

Lincoln's Inn Fields
where the matronly lady lived in Lovelace's dream L271

Lions in the Tower
where Anna's messenger will visit while in London L251

Lithuania
where cuckholdom is the fashion L371

little island see **Isle of Wight**

London
where Lovelace went after Arabella rejected him L3
Antony met Lovelace in town L3
where Lovelace chiefly resides L4
where Hickman is sent to inquire about Lovelace's life in town L27
where Lovelace is invited by his friends L31
where Clarissa may escape L61
where Lovelace has business L62
where Lovelace offers to take Clarissa for refuge L76, L98
where Anna advises Clarissa to hide till Morden arrives L81
where Anna offers to go with Clarissa L81
the best hiding-place in the world L81
where Lovelace will procure lodgings for Clarissa L85, L98
where Clarissa asks Lovelace to go, after he takes her from Harlowe Place L86, L98, L116
where Clarissa's family should think she has gone L98
where Lovelace wants to take Clarissa L103, L107, L110, L116, L117, L125
where Lovelace has an acquaintance to whom he wished to take Clarissa L104
Clarissa a stranger to L123, L189
the privatest place to be L125, L317
where Clarissa begins to consider going L125
where Anna does not object to Clarissa removing L128
residence of Mr. Doleman, and where he has found lodgings for Clarissa L130
where Clarissa will remove on Monday L135
where Belford advises Lovelace against bringing Clarissa L143
where Anna offers to find Clarissa lodging if she does not like Lovelace's L148
where Clarissa is just setting out for in Lord M.'s chaise L149
where Clarissa will set out for on Wednesday L152
where Clarissa and Lovelace have finally arrived L154
Clarissa knowing nothing of the town's diversities L154
where Simon Collins goes on Mondays, Wednesdays, and Fridays L156
where Anna may fly to Clarissa if Clarissa ceases to write L164
in which direction Clarissa turned her gaze while proceeding to Hedon L232
where Lady Betty and Miss Montague will visit Clarissa in a day or two, thinking her married L233
this wicked town, great wicked town L270, L368
where Lady Betty says she has not been for six months L303
a pestilent place, the smoky town L305, L313
where Anna would have run away to, to attend Clarissa L357
where Sir Robert Beachcroft's servant rides on his master's business, delivering Mrs. Norton's for Clarissa L361
where Anna will visit Clarissa after she returns from the Isle of Wight L372
streets of London, where Clarissa was arrested L374
where Mr. Brand has business and will inquire about Clarissa L381
where Lovelace will go in a few days to visit Clarissa L383, L410
where Lovelace arrived intending to visit Clarissa L416
where frequently morning prayers is a pretence for private assignations L444
where Mr. Brand has just arrived L444
where Anna will buy clothes for her approaching nuptials L459
where Lovelace will see Belford before leaving the country L516, L525

Lord M., his chapel
proposed by Lovelace for the wedding celebration L207
Clarissa not wishing to be married in so public a ceremony L207

Lower Flask see **Flask, Lower Flask**

Ludgate Hill
location of the Belle Savage L302, L318

M

M. Hall see also **Berkshire**
where Lord M. lives L31
where Lovelace visits Lord M. L34
where Montagues and the rest look forward to seeing Clarissa after her speedy nuptials L121
where Lord M. pressed Belford to use his influence with Lovelace to enter the pale L143
where Lord M. looks forward to seeing Belford after Lovelace marries Clarissa L190
where Lady Betty will visit her brother Lord M. L233.2
where Lovelace will go to visit the dangerously ill Lord M. L275
where Lovelace must go, to Berkshire, to M. Hall, to attend Lord M. L277, L280
Lovelace will detain Clarissa at Mrs. Sinclair's until he returns from L279
where Lovelace is going to visit the dying Lord M. L281
where Lovelace will take Clarissa after they are married, to visit the dying Lord M. L284
Clarissa's captors' messenger has not yet returned from L333
where Lovelace and his friends merrily pass time waiting for Lord M. to die L344
where everyone is Lovelace's prisoner L399
Lovelace returning to M. Hall L421
where Belford may travel thirty or forty miles to visit L525
where Belford will visit Lord M. L527

Madrid
where the French marquis was when Lovelace seduced his wife in Paris L209
where the honest corregidor said: Good actions are remembered but for a day: bad ones for many years after the
    life of the guilty L252
where Belford wishes Lovelace to travel, to avoid Morden L526, L532
where Lovelace will not go to avoid Morden L534

Maidstone Gaol
where Tomlinson is dying L514

Mall see **Pall Mall**

Medway
where Lovelace offers to take Thomasine and hers on a boat trip and drown them L347

Middlesex
location of St. Giles's in the Fields and St. Martin in the Fields (or St. Martin's in the Fields) L254
county where the marriage license authorizes Lovelace to marry Clarissa L254
Mr. Belford of Edgworth [Edgware?] in the county of Middlesex L507

Mill Hill
where Mrs. Moore has a friend who may help Clarissa L235

moated house see **Harlowe, Mr. Antony, his house**

Monmouth Street
where M'Donald can get clothes for Thursday L289, L289n1

Moore, Mrs., her garden
where Clarissa walks with Lovelace L248, L253

Moore, Mrs., her house
where Clarissa was put down in Hampstead after she escaped from Mrs. Sinclair's L230

Mortlake
where Clarissa went on her day out to escape Lovelace's visit L426

Mother *Damnable*'s park see **Sinclair, Mrs., her house**

Mount Cenis
where Lovelace will go on the way to France L513

Munich
where Lovelace will meet Morden L535.2

Muswell Hill
where Clarissa and Lovelace go for an airing L210, L228
where Clarissa went to escape Lovelace's visit, stopping at a public house L426

N

Neale
poor village where Lovelace puts up L63
mentioned L223

Norfolk Street
where Clarissa considers lodgings after leaving Mrs. Sorlings's L130
where Mrs. Doleman has seen lodgings for Clarissa L130.1

North End
little village on the side of the heath, where Miss Rawlins's kinswoman may help Clarissa L235

Northamptonshire
Captain Tomlinson recently removed from L214, L304

northern estates see also **Scotland**; **Yorkshire**
where James thought of setting out for L301

Northhampton
where Tomlinson has a little farm-house L243

Norwood
where Lovelace met the pretty gipsy L252

Nottingham
where Miss Betterton resided L127

Nottinghamshire
where Tourville retired CONCLUSION

Novogrod
in Russia, a city of the ancient Sarmatia L344, L344n1

O

Old Bailey
and this flight...was in the true Old Bailey construction L293
an Old Bailey forecast by Rowland, if Clarissa dies at his house L333

Osgood, Mr., his residence
near Soho Square, where Clarissa should direct her things sent L98

Oxford
near where Lady Betty lives L116
location of St. Mary's church L237
where Lord M.'s chaplin has gone L410

Oxfordshire
where Lady Betty would like Clarissa to accompany her L233.2, L243, L253, L256
where Tomlinson's wife comes from L304

P

paddock see **Harlowe Place, paddock**

Palace (Kensington Palace)
from the Palace to the Gore, where Lovelace rode hoping to meet Will with a letter from Belford L463

Pall Mall
location of the Cocoa Tree, where Lovelace meets his friends in London L48, L48n1
address of Mr. Wilson, to whom Anna's for Clarissa should be sent L155
as the Mall, where Lovelace will walk L209

Paris
where Morden has resided L173.1
where Lovelace had an affair with the French marquis's wife L209
where Belford will advise Lovelace to go should Clarissa die L449
where Belford advises Lovelace to go, now that Clarissa is dead L479
where Lovelace will go L513, L531
where Lovelace has lodgings in Rue St Antoine L530
where Lovelace hopes to meet Mowbray, Tourville, and Belford L530
where Morden may find Lovelace L532

Park
where Lovelace will take a chair and walk half the length of the Mall L209
where Lovelace rode hoping to meet Will with a letter from Belford L463

Pennsylvania
where the Harlowe Family believe Clarissa should go for a few years till all blows over L429
where Clarissa agrees to go after one month if she is able L430

Piccadilly
where Lovelace hopes to meet his messenger L466
and Kensington, where Mowbray will find Lovelace L477

plantations
Harlowe Family wanting Clarissa to go to one of the plantations L408

plashy lane see **Harlowe Place, plashy lane**

Portsmouth
where Charlotte may pick up someone the likes of Belford L516

post
how Clarissa and Anna must continue to correspond L316
post-office, mail conveyance for Anna to Clarissa L328, L329
post-office bullet L341, L341n1
post-day L474, L474n1

post-house, Hampstead
where Will's sweetheart carried Clarissa's for Anna L240
post, general and penny L241, L241n1

post-house, Hertford
where Belford is to address his for Lovelace to Mr. Robert Huntingford L105

post-house, Vienna
where Morden can direct mail to Lovelace L534.1

poultry-yard see **Harlowe Place, poultry-yard**

Pressburg
where Lovelace travelled L535

prison
where Clarissa will be sent if she does not pay Mrs. Sinclair L333

Pultowa
where Charles XII was routed by Peter the Great L416, L416n3

Pyreneans
where Belford wishes Lovelace to visit L531

R

Reading
where Lady Betty asked Charlotte to meet her L233.2, L233.3
Clarissa asks whether Lady Betty met Miss Montague there L302
where Lady Betty says she did not meet Miss Montague L303
Clarissa to take the Reading stage-coach, which inns somewhere in Fleet Street L327
where Miss Montague and Lady Betty will receive Clarissa L327

Richmond
where Clarissa went on her day out to escape Lovelace L426

Rochester
location of Gad's Hill L527

Rome
where Morden has resided L173.1

Rose
located at Knightsbridge L478
where Lovelace left to go to the Bohemia Head L478, L480

Rotherhithe
where Singleton's vessel lies L155, L213
where Charlotte may pick up someone the likes of Belford L516

Rowland, Mr., his house
filthy bedroom at Mr. Rowland's where Clarissa is held after her arrest, her prison L333, L339
in a wretched court L333
where Clarissa wishes to die L334

Royal Chapel
where Lovelace attends church when in town L157
where the royal family attend church L157

Rue St Antoine
where Lovelace has lodgings in Paris L530

S

St. Albans
where Hannah's mother lives L298
where Hannah is with her mother L301
Morden will go home by way of, from M. Hall L442
where Morden leaves Mrs. Norton who is too ill to continue in company with the hearse L500

St. Albans, inn
where the Montagues failed to attend Clarissa L88, L121
where a gentlewoman and her niece attend Clarissa after her departure from Harlowe Place L98

St. Anna's (Santa Anna's)
a church to be appropriated for women L106

St. Anne's church
named by Mrs. Sinclair as a nearby church L157

St Antoine, Rue
where Lovelace has lodgings in Paris L530

St. Dunstan's
in Fleet Street L320, L368
where Clarissa attended morning prayers, took a chair to prayers L320, L368, L426, L440

St. George's
a church to be appropriated for men L106

St. Giles's in the Fields
parish church in the county of Middlesex L254
where, or possibly at St. Martin's, Lovelace wishes to marry Clarissa on Thursday L283

St. James's church
named by Mrs. Sinclair as a nearby church L157
where Mrs. Sinclair and her nieces attend church L157
where Clarissa attends church alone L198, L198n2
where Clarissa took a chair without Lovelace L200
where Clarissa was seen alone by Miss Lardner L229.1
where Belford, looking to his reform, will go to hear the celebrated preacher L499

St. Katharina's (Santa Katharina's)
a church to be appropriated for women L106

St. Margaretta's (Santa Margaretta's)
a church to be appropriated for women L106

St. Maria's (Santa Maria's)
a church to be appropriated for women L106

St. Martin in the Fields
Robert Lovelace...of the parish of St. Martin's in the Fields L254
in the parish church of St. Martin in the Fields...in the county of Middlesex L254
in the home parish of Lovelace and Clarissa L254
as St. Martin's church, where, or at St. Giles's, Lovelace wishes to marry Clarissa on Thursday L283

St. Martin's Lane
Westminster, where Patrick M'Donald has lodgings at Mr. Brown's L289

St. Mary's church
Oxford, where Lovelace saw Mrs. Fetherstone, among other grotesque figures L237

St. Paul's church see also **Covent Garden, church**
where Lovelace accompanies Clarissa to church L159
where Clarissa wishes to attend church without Lovelace L178

St. Paul's Churchyard, College of Doctors of Civil Law in see **Doctors' Commons**

St. Paul's parish
location of Smith's, Covent Garden, where Clarissa dies L507

St. Stephen's
a church to be appropriated for men L106

St. Stephen's Chapel
where Lord M. advises Lovelace to attend House of Commons meetings L206, L206n1

St. Swithin's
a church to be appropriated for men L106

St. Thomas's
a church to be appropriated for men L106

Salt Hill
where Lovelace awaited Clarissa's answer to his offer of marriage L325

Sandoun Hall see also **Lancashire**
Robert Lovelace of Sandoun Hall, in the County of Lancaster L158.1

Saracen's Head
on Snow Hill L316
where Collins will leave Anna's for Clarissa L316, L328
as Saracen's Head inn L328

Sarmatia
location of Novogrod L344, L344n1

Scotland see also **northern estates**; **Yorkshire**
where James inherited an estate from his godmother, Lovell L2
where James is when Lovelace first addresses Arabella L3
where James wishes Clarissa to care for his home L6
where Clarissa offers to go rather than marry Solmes L42, L45
where James will take some of Clarissa's poultry L75
Mrs. Sinclair of highland extraction L131
Colonel Sinclair, related to the best families of Scotland L233
James refuses to set out for, until the family has promised not to reconcile with Clarissa in his absence L432

Sinclair, Mrs., her garden
back house looking to a garden L137
Mrs. Sinclair must let Clarissa out or murder her and bury her in the garden L293
Clarissa walking in Mrs. Sinclair's little garden L293

Sinclair, Mrs., her house
where Clarissa arrives after leaving Mrs. Sorlings's L154
called Mother *Damnable*'s park L228
Clarissa escaping from, to Hampstead L228, L230
Clarissa returns to, from Hampstead, as recounted by Clarissa L256, L310
where Clarissa is raped L257
Clarissa finally escaping from, disguised as Mabel L291
where Belford first sought Clarissa L333
Sally and Polly trying to take Clarissa back to L333
Lovelace's marriage would ruin L336
where Lovelace has returned to from M. Hall, after his illness L416

Slough
where Lovelace will meet Tomlinson's messenger with Clarissa's answer to the Thursday wedding plan L288, L289
where Mr. Hickman will attend Clarissa L327
where Belford's and Lovelace's messengers meet to exchange correspondence L441
location of the windmill near Hannah's L445, L445fn
where fellows of Lovelace and Belford met L449

Snow Hill
location of the Saracen's Head L316

Soho Square
where Mr. Osgood resides, where Clarissa's family should send her things L98, L102
where Belford lodges with a relation L125, L493
where lodgings may be found in London for Clarissa L130.1
where Arabella sent Letter 147 to Clarissa L147
where Sally Martin found Belford not L493

Sorlings, Mrs., her farm
eight miles off from the inn at St. Albans L98
where Mrs. Greme accompanies Clarissa from St. Albans L98
her dairy works, country dairy, her farm L105, L117, L118, L130

Sorlings, Mrs., her garden
where Clarissa and Lovelace meet early in the morning to discuss lodgings in London L126

Southwark
where Mrs. Townsend rents a chamber in an inn L196

Spain
where it is the custom to wear spectacles L346
where Hickman has not travelled L346
where Belford wishes Lovelace to travel to avoid Morden L533

stile see **Harlowe Place, stile**

Strand
where a tradesman lives whom Miss Martin is near to marrying L163

Suffolk Street
location of the Eagle L526

Surrey hills
mentioned L130.1

Swan
at Brentford Ait, where Clarissa dined L426

Symmes, Mr. Edward, his home
scene of the duel between James and Lovelace L4

T

taphouse see **Hampstead, taphouse**

Temple
where Clarissa went to take a boat to Chelsea L426
where Clarissa returned to, coming back from Mortlake L426

Thames
mentioned L130.1

Tilbury
where Lovelace offers to take Thomasine and hers on a boat trip and drown them L347

Tipperary
where Hickman must have come home by way of, from the grand tour L198

Tombs
in Westminster Abbey, where Anna's messenger will visit while in London L251, L251n2

tour see also **grand tour**
of France and Italy, where Morden will take Clarissa L459
foreign tour, where Lovelace is preparing to go L510

Tower, Lions in the see **Lions in the Tower**

Trent
where Lovelace goes to meet Morden L535
where Lovelace will go if he finds Morden not in Munich L535.2

Turin
where Lovelace will go L513, L530

Tuscany
where Morden conveniently returns L535.2

Tyrol
where Lovelace will go L513, L530

U

undertaker's
in Fleet Street, where Clarissa went, after prayers at St. Dunstan's, to order her coffin L440

Upper Flask see **Flask, Upper Flask**

Uxbridge
where Lovelace will visit Tom Doleman L449
where Lovelace is visiting L463
Mr. Doleman, of Uxbridge L526

V

Venetian territories
where the survivor of the duel is to be carried off L536
where Morden rides after the duel L537

Venice
where Lovelace will go, and keep the carnival L513

Versailles
Harlowe Place, like Versailles, sprung up from a dunghill within every elderly person's memory L34

Vienna
where Lovelace will go L513, L530
where Lovelace is setting out for L534, L534.1
location of the Favorita L534.1

Vienna, post-house
where Morden can direct mail to Lovelace L534.1

W

Wales
where Dorcas has near relations L270

Wapping
where Charlotte may pick up someone the likes of Belford L516

waterside
where Clarissa went to avoid Lovelace L418

Watford
where Belford is attending his dying uncle L190.1
where Belford has affairs L383
where Belford has let the house L514

West Smithfield
where Mabel's mother lives, in Chick Lane L291

Westminster
where Lovelace prefers the air to Hampstead's L253
where Patrick M'Donald lives, at Mr. Brown's, in St. Martin's Lane L289

Westminster Abbey
location of monument to Dame Elizabeth Carteret, Belford compared L449, L449n1

Westminster Abbey, Tombs
in Westminster Abbey, where Anna's messenger will visit while in London L251, L251n2

Westminster Hall
where there are, every day, defenses as confident as Lovelace's L323

Westphalia
where Lovelace journeyed L31

White Hart Inn
where Lovelace suffers vile accommodations, awaiting an opportunity to address Clarissa L31
inn, little alehouse, in a village five miles from Harlowe Place, where Lovelace stays L34

White Hart Inn (cont.)
where Rosebud lives with her grandmother and her father, the proprietor L34
five miles from Harlowe Place L62
at the inn Lovelace puts up at in the poor village of Neale, as he calls it L63
which Lovelace calls an inn L70
where Lovelace stays with his brother rakes L70
where Belford attended Lovelace L99
the Hart, where Lovelace discussed with Belford the Harlowes' plan to carry Clarissa off to Antony's L103
mentioned L223

White's
an establishment where Lovelace may amuse himself L209
where Lovelace went after visiting Smith's L416, L416n2

Wilson, Mr., his house
in Pall Mall, where Anna should direct hers to Clarissa L155
where Simon Collins will deliver and pick up Clarissa's to and from Anna L156
where Clarissa's letter is brought from L201

Windsor
where Lovelace wants to take Clarissa, on the way to Berkshire, Oxford, and London L116
where Lovelace has hunted in the forest L116
where Clarissa would like to lodge, near the castle L116
where Clarissa may go with Hannah L116
where Lovelace has gone L116
where Lovelace may find appropriate lodgings for Clarissa L117
where the canon's house may provide lodging for Clarissa L119, L125
where Anna advises Clarissa to go and marry Lovelace L119
where Lovelace advises Clarissa against lodging L121

wood-house see **Harlowe Place, wood-house**

wood-yard see **Harlowe Place, wood-yard**

Y

Yarmouth, Isle of Wight
where Anna is visiting her Aunt Harman L404

yew hedge see **Harlowe Place, yew hedge**

Yorkshire see also **northern estates**; **Scotland**
where James has a large estate inherited from Lovell L2
where Aunt Hervey wants to send James, till all blows over L6
where Colonel Ambrose's nieces live L322
where Mowbray retired CONCLUSION

SUMMARIES OF LETTERS

The three letter numbers to the left of each letter summary correspond to the following editions:
Penguin Classics printing (1985) of the first edition, in one volume
>Letters are numbered continuously 1–537, skipping numbers 43, 66, 67, 122, 208, 468, and 469. These numbers represent letters added in the third edition. Letters included in other letters have been supplied with numbers; for example, Letter 32 includes Letter 32.1.

Samuel Richardson's printing of the first edition (1747–1748), in seven volumes
>Letters are numbered within each volume. Richardson does not separately number letters included in other letters. The copy used for this project is held by the Berg Collection of The New York Public Library, of which copy the first two volumes carry an imprint date of 1748.

Samuel Richardson's printing of the third edition (1751), in eight volumes
>Letters are numbered within each volume. The seven letters added in the third edition are summarized below. The edition used is the facsimile published by AMS Press in 1990.

Letter 1 Vol.1, Letter I Vol.1, Letter I	Miss Anna Howe To Miss Clarissa Harlowe	[Howe residence] [Harlowe Place]	Jan. 10
	Anna inquires about the recent duel between James and Lovelace and about Grandfather Harlowe's will.		

Letter 2 Vol.1, Letter II Vol.1, Letter II	Miss Clarissa Harlowe To Miss Howe	Harlowe Place [Howe residence]	Jan. 13
	Her inheritance from her Grandfather and her brother's duel have created conflict between Clarissa and her family. She recounts Lovelace's attentions to Arabella before the duel.		

Letter 3 Vol.1, Letter III Vol.1, Letter III	Miss Clarissa Harlowe To Miss Howe	[Harlowe Place] [Howe residence]	Jan. 13, 14
	Lovelace turns his attention from Arabella to Clarissa, and their correspondence begins.		

Letter 4 Vol.1, Letter IV Vol.1, Letter IV	Miss Clarissa Harlowe To Miss Howe	[Harlowe Place] [Howe residence]	Jan. 15
	Report of the duel mentioned in Letter 1. James returns from Scotland and is wounded in a duel with Lovelace, which precedes Letter 1. Clarissa continues correspondence with Lovelace, fearing consequences of Harlowes' ill treatment of Lovelace following the duel. Enclosure: Preamble of Grandfather Harlowe's will.		

Letter 5 Vol.1, Letter V Vol.1, Letter V	Miss Clarissa Harlowe To Miss Howe	[Harlowe Place] [Howe residence]	Jan. 20
	Mamma and Papa are plagued with illnesses, fearing repercussions from the Harlowes' ill treatment of Lovelace.		

Letter 6 Vol.1, Letter VI Vol.1, Letter VI	Miss Clarissa Harlowe To Miss Howe	Harlowe Place [Howe residence]	Jan. 20
	To thwart Lovelace, James arranges an offer of marriage to Clarissa from Solmes. Clarissa visits Anna but is forbidden to receive visits from Lovelace.		

Letter 7   Miss Clarissa Harlowe   Harlowe Place   Feb. 20
Vol.1, Letter VII   To Miss Howe   [Howe residence]
Vol.1, Letter VII   Clarissa returns home from Anna's after an absence of three weeks to find that the family have arranged for her to marry Solmes. She is accused of receiving visits from Lovelace while at Anna's.

Letter 8   Miss Clarissa Harlowe   [Harlowe Place]   Feb. 24
Vol.1, Letter VIII   To Miss Howe   [Howe residence]   February 25
Vol.1, Letter VIII   The family try to intimidate Clarissa into accepting Solmes. She is expected to marry Solmes to protect the family honor, damaged by Lovelace in the duel with James.   Feb. 25 in the evening

Letter 9   Miss Clarissa Harlowe   Harlowe Place   Feb. 26,
Vol.1, Letter IX   To Miss Howe   [Howe residence]   in the
Vol.1, Letter IX   Aunt Hervey advises Clarissa to accept Solmes. Clarissa's correspondence with Anna becomes secret.   morning

Letter 10   Miss Howe   [Howe residence]   Feb. 27
Vol.1, Letter X   To Miss Clarissa Harlowe   [Harlowe Place]
Vol.1, Letter X   Harlowe Family motivations. Lovelace has managed to establish a clandestine relationship with Clarissa. Her feelings for Lovelace.

Letter 11   Miss Clarissa Harlowe   [Harlowe Place]   Wednesday,
Vol.1, Letter XI   To Miss Howe   [Howe residence]   March 1
Vol.1, Letter XI   Thanks her for her observations on Clarissa's feelings for Lovelace.

Letter 12   Miss Howe   [Howe residence]   Thurs.
Vol.1, Letter XII   To Miss Clarissa Harlowe   [Harlowe Place]   morn.
Vol.1, Letter XII   Information from Mrs. Fortescue on Lovelace's reputation. His visit to Anna. His threats to the Harlowe Family.   March 2

Letter 13   Miss Clarissa Harlowe   [Harlowe Place]   Wed.
Vol.1, Letter XIII   To Miss Howe   [Howe residence]   March 1
Vol.1, Letter XIII   Family background and incidents preceding Letter 1. Motives clarified: family aggrandizement and paternal authority.

Letter 14   Miss Clarissa Harlowe   [Harlowe Place]   Thursday
Vol.1, Letter XIV   To Miss Howe   [Howe residence]   evening
Vol.1, Letter XIV   James pushes to set a wedding date for Clarissa and Solmes.   March 2

Letter 15   Miss Howe   [Howe residence]   Friday,
Vol.1, Letter XV   To Miss Clarissa Harlowe   [Harlowe Place]   March 3
Vol.1, Letter XV   Arabella loves Lovelace. Jealousy and rivalry in the Harlowe Family.

Letter 16   Miss Clarissa Harlowe   [Harlowe Place]   Friday,
Vol.1, Letter XVI   To Miss Howe   [Howe residence]   March 3
Vol.1, Letter XVI   Solmes attempts to address Clarissa and is rebuffed. Mamma insists that Clarissa accept Solmes.

Letter 17   Miss Clarissa Harlowe   [Harlowe Place]   ---
Vol.1, Letter XVII   To Miss Howe   [Howe residence]
Vol.1, Letter XVII   Mamma urges Clarissa to accept but will speak to Papa.

412

Letter 18 Vol.1, Letter XVIII Vol.1, Letter XVIII	Miss Clarissa Harlowe To Miss Howe Clarissa continues to plead with Mamma.	[Harlowe Place] [Howe residence]	Sat. Mar. 4
Letter 19 Vol.1, Letter XIX Vol.1, Letter XIX	Miss Clarissa Harlowe To Miss Howe She refuses to marry Solmes. Mamma is conflicted.	[Harlowe Place] [Howe residence]	Sat. March 4, 12 o'clock
Letter 20 Vol.1, Letter XX Vol.1, Letter XX	Miss Clarissa Harlowe To Miss Howe Mamma alternately begs and threatens.	[Harlowe Place] [Howe residence]	Sat. p.m.

Letter 21
Vol.1, Letter XXI
Vol.1, Letter XXI
	Miss Clarissa Harlowe
	To Miss Howe
	  Clarissa continues to refuse Solmes. She is threatened with
	  confinement.
		[Harlowe Place]
		[Howe residence]
			Sat.
			night

Letter 22
Vol.1, Letter XXII
Vol.1, Letter XXII
	Miss Clarissa Harlowe
	To Miss Howe
	  Clarissa has received a letter from Lovelace wishing to make
	  a proposal.
		[Harlowe Place]
		[Howe residence]
			Sunday
			morning,
			March 5

Letter 22.1	Clarissa Harlowe To James Harlowe, Jun. Clarissa requests permission to attend church.	[Harlowe Place] [Harlowe Place]	---
Letter 22.2	James Harlowe, Jun. To Miss Clarissa Harlowe James's angry response.	[Harlowe Place] [Harlowe Place]	---

Letter 23
Vol.1, Letter XXIII
Vol.1, Letter XXIII
	Miss Clarissa Harlowe
	To Miss Howe
	  Hannah dismissed, suspected of assisting Clarissa in her
	  secret correspondence.
		[Harlowe Place]
		[Howe residence]
			Mon.
			morning
			Mar. 6

Letter 24
Vol.1, Letter XXIV
Vol.1, Letter XXIV
	Miss Clarissa Harlowe
	To Miss Howe
	  Includes James's letter to Clarissa and a copy of her answer.
	  Clarissa is confined.
		[Harlowe Place]
		[Howe residence]
			Mon.
			near
			12 o'clock

Letter 24.1	James Harlowe, Jun.
	To Clarissa Harlowe
	  Advises Clarissa not to appear before her parents, not to go into
	  the garden, and to correspond neither with Anna nor with Lovelace.
		[Harlowe Place]
		[Harlowe Place]
			Mon.
			March 6

Letter 24.2	Clarissa Harlowe To James Harlowe, Jun. Clarissa begs James to cease.	[Harlowe Place] [Harlowe Place]	---
Letter 25 Vol.1, Letter XXV Vol.1, Letter XXV	Miss Clarissa Harlowe To Miss Howe Clarissa awaits Morden's arrival.	[Harlowe Place] [Howe residence]	Tues. March 7 & Tuesday night

413

Letter 25.1   Clarissa   [Harlowe Place]   ---
To Mrs. Harlowe   [Harlowe Place]
     Clarissa tells Mamma of another letter from Lovelace requesting
     to wait on Papa. Her fear of not answering Lovelace. She asks
     Mamma how to respond.

Letter 25.2   Mrs. Harlowe   [Harlowe Place]   ---
To Clarissa   [Harlowe Place]
     She has kept secret her knowledge of Clarissa's correspondence
     with Lovelace. She advises Clarissa to end it and burn this letter.

Letter 25.3   Clarissa Harlowe   [Harlowe Place]   ---
To James Harlowe   [Harlowe Place]
     She begs not to be sacrificed to James's projects.

Letter 25.4   James Harlowe   [Harlowe Place]   Wednesday
To Clarissa Harlowe   [Harlowe Place]
     Papa banishes Clarissa from his presence.

Letter 26   Miss Clarissa Harlowe   [Harlowe Place]   Thursd.
Vol.1, Letter XXVI   To Miss Howe   [Howe residence]   morn.
Vol.1, Letter XXVI   She explains her attempt to end her clandestine correspondence   Mar. 9
     with Lovelace.

Letter 27   Miss Howe   [Howe residence]   Thursday
Vol.1, Letter XXVII   To Miss Clarissa Harlowe   [Harlowe Place]   night,
Vol.1, Letter XXVII   She encourages Clarissa to assert the independence conferred   March 9
     upon her by her estate and to resume control of it. She tells
     what she knows of Solmes's character.

Letter 28   Miss Clarissa Harlowe   [Harlowe Place]   Friday,
Vol.1, Letter XXVIII   To Miss Howe   [Howe residence]   Mar. 10
Vol.1, Letter XXVIII   She defends her family to Anna but will not resume her estate
     as it may encourage Lovelace.

Letter 29   Miss Clarissa Harlowe   [Harlowe Place]   Saturday,
Vol.1, Letter XXIX   To Miss Howe   [Howe residence]   March 11
Vol.1, Letter XXIX   She changes her tactics to show a preference for Lovelace.

Letter 29.1   [Clarissa Harlowe]   [Harlowe Place]   ---
To [James Harlowe, Jun.]   [Harlowe Place]
     Trying to bring James to reason, she says she deserves her
     choice of suitors.

Letter 29.2   [James Harlowe, Jun.]   [Harlowe Place]   ---
To Miss Clarissa Harlowe   [Harlowe Place]
     He accuses her of preferring Lovelace.

Letter 29.3   [Clarissa Harlowe]   [Harlowe Place]   ---
To [Arabella Harlowe]   [Harlowe Place]
     She pleads with Arabella to cease as her siblings' behavior
     inspires her to prefer Lovelace.

Letter 29.4	[Arabella Harlowe]	[Harlowe Place]	---
	To Miss Clary Harlowe	[Harlowe Place]	
	Angry letter accusing Clarissa of failing to do her duty.		

Letter 30	Miss Clarissa Harlowe	[Harlowe Place]	Sunday
Vol.1, Letter XXX	To Miss Howe	[Howe residence]	night
Vol.1, Letter XXX	Lovelace looks challenge and defiance at the Harlowes at church.		March 12

Letter 31	Mr. Lovelace	[White Hart Inn]	Monday,
Vol.1, Letter XXXI	To John Belford, Esq.	[London]	March 13
Vol.1, Letter XXXI	Reveals his plan to deal with the Harlowes and win Clarissa.		

Letter 32	Miss Clarissa Harlowe	[Harlowe Place]	Tuesday,
Vol.1, Letter XXXII	To Miss Howe	[Howe residence]	March 14
Vol.1, Letter XXXII	Clarissa sends Anna copies of her letters to her uncles.		

Letter 32.1	[Clarissa Harlowe]	[Harlowe Place]	Sat.
	To John Harlowe, Esq.	---	March 11
	She asks him to influence Papa in her favor and requests refuge at his house until all blows over.		

Letter 32.2	[John Harlowe]	---	Sunday
	To [Clarissa Harlowe]		night
	He refuses her request for refuge and accuses her of corresponding with Lovelace.		

Letter 32.3	[Clarissa Harlowe]	[Harlowe Place]	Saturday,
	To Antony Harlowe, Esq.	---	March 11
	She argues her case and begs him to intercede. She prefers Lovelace to Solmes.		

Letter 32.4	Mr. Antony Harlowe	---	---
	To Miss Clarissa Harlowe	[Harlowe Place]	
	He tells Clarissa not to write and rails at her to obey the family and accept Solmes.		

Letter 33	Miss Clarissa Harlowe	[Harlowe Place]	Thursday,
Vol.1, Letter XXXIII	To Miss Howe	[Howe residence]	March 16
Vol.1, Letter XXXIII	She encloses a copy of her letter to Solmes and his reply.		

Letter 33.1	[Clarissa Harlowe]	[Harlowe Place]	Wednesday,
	To Roger Solmes, Esq.	---	Mar. 15
	She begs him not to continue his address.		

Letter 33.2	[Roger Solmes]	---	Thursday,
	To Miss Clarissa Harlowe	[Harlowe Place]	March 16
	He expects to overcome the difficulty of her rejection.		

Letter 33.3	[James Harlowe, Jun.]	[Harlowe Place]	Thursday,
	To Miss Clarissa Harlowe	[Harlowe Place]	March 16
	He is angry at Clarissa for writing to Solmes.		

Letter 34	Mr. Lovelace	White Hart Inn	Friday,
Vol.1, Letter XXXIV	To John Belford, Esq.	---	March 17
Vol.1, Letter XXXIV	He asks Belford to spare Rosebud.		

Letter 35	Mr. Lovelace	[White Hart Inn]	---
Vol.1, Letter XXXV	To John Belford, Esq.	---	
Vol.1, Letter XXXV	His plan to meet Clarissa in the garden.		

Letter 36	Miss Clarissa Harlowe	[Harlowe Place]	Sat.
Vol.1, Letter XXXVI	To Miss Howe	[Howe residence]	night
Vol.1, Letter XXXVI	Lovelace surprises Clarissa in the garden with false offers of protection. An offer from Lady Betty.		Mar. 18

Letter 37	Miss Howe	[Howe residence]	Sunday,
Vol.1, Letter XXXVII	To Miss Clarissa Harlowe	[Harlowe Place]	March 19
Vol.1, Letter XXXVII	Clarissa must be either Solmes's or Lovelace's. Has Clarissa a liking for Lovelace? Her friends are curious.		

Letter 38	Miss Clarissa Harlowe	[Harlowe Place]	Monday,
Vol.1, Letter XXXVIII	To Miss Howe	[Howe residence]	March 20
Vol.1, Letter XXXVIII	Her feelings for Lovelace.		

Letter 39	Miss Clarissa Harlowe	[Harlowe Place]	Monday,
Vol.1, Letter XXXIX	To Miss Howe	[Howe residence]	March 20
Vol.1, Letter XXXIX	The family have called upon Mrs. Norton to persuade Clarissa to accept Solmes.		

Letter 40	Miss Clarissa Harlowe	[Harlowe Place]	---
Vol.1, Letter XL	To Miss Howe	[Howe residence]	
Vol.1, Letter XL	Her opinions on love and marriage, and figure in men and women.		

Letter 41	Miss Clarissa Harlowe	[Harlowe Place]	Tuesday,
Vol.1, Letter XLI	To Miss Howe	[Howe residence]	March 21
Vol.1, Letter XLI	Includes letters from Mamma and Papa, their efforts on Solmes's behalf redoubled.		and Tuesday evening

Letter 41.1	Mrs. Harlowe	[Harlowe Place]	---
	To Clarissa Harlowe	[Harlowe Place]	
	Clothes, jewels, forgiveness, all for Clarissa if she will comply with the wishes of the family. Otherwise, she will lose her family.		

Letter 41.2	James Harlowe	[Harlowe Place]	---
	To Clarissa Harlowe	[Harlowe Place]	
	An angry letter. Clarissa's wedding will take place next week at Uncle Antony's chapel.		

Letter 42	Miss Clarissa Harlowe	[Harlowe Place]	---
Vol.1, Letter XLII	To Miss Howe	[Howe residence]	
Vol.1, Letter XLII	Confrontation between Clarissa and Arabella. Clarissa offers to leave for Scotland or Florence.		

Letter 42.1	James Harlowe, Jun.	[Harlowe Place]	---
	To Clarissa Harlowe	[Harlowe Place]	
	James threatens to return permanently to Scotland.		

[43 skipped in Penguin] [not in the first edition] Vol.1, Letter XLIII	Miss Clarissa Harlowe To Miss Howe	[Harlowe Place] [Howe residence]	Tuesday, March 21
	Arabella visits Clarissa to insist that she appear downstairs, humble herself before her family, and agree to marry Solmes. Lovelace presses her to escape.		Tuesday noon, March 21
Letter 44 Vol.1, Letter XLIII Vol.1, Letter XLIV	Miss Clarissa Harlowe To Miss Howe	[Harlowe Place] [Howe residence]	Wednesday morning, 9 o'clock
	Aunt Hervey and Arabella try to persuade Clarissa to comply.		
Letter 45 Vol.1, Letter XLIV Vol.1, Letter XLV	Miss Clarissa Harlowe To Miss Howe	[Harlowe Place] [Howe residence]	---
	Clarissa is not permitted to see Mamma. Aunt Hervey and Arabella return to plead and threaten. James threatens to leave Harlowe Place.		
Letter 46 Vol.2, Letter I Vol.2, Letter I	Miss Howe To Miss Harlowe	[Howe residence] [Harlowe Place]	Wednesday night, March 22
	Amusing comparison of Hickman to Solmes and Lovelace.		
Letter 47 Vol.2, Letter II Vol.2, Letter II	Miss Howe To Miss Clarissa Harlowe	[Howe residence] [Harlowe Place]	Thursday, morn. 7 o'clock
	She cautions Clarissa to resume control of her estate and declaims on the position of women.		
Letter 48 Vol.2, Letter III Vol.2, Letter III	Miss Howe To Miss Clarissa Harlowe	[Howe residence] [Harlowe Place]	Thursday morn. 10 o'clock (Mar. 23)
	The results of Hickman's investigations into Lovelace's life in London and the company he keeps.		
Letter 49 Vol.2, Letter IV Vol.2, Letter IV	Miss Howe To Miss Clarissa Harlowe	[Howe residence] [Harlowe Place]	Thursday afternoon, March 23
	Lovelace visits Anna, knowing she will tell Clarissa all he says. They agree that Clarissa should resume her estate.		
Letter 50 Vol.2, Letter V Vol.2, Letter V	Miss Clarissa Harlowe To Miss Howe	[Harlowe Place] [Howe residence]	Wed. night, March 22
	Family unanimous against Clarissa.		
Letter 50.1	James Harlowe, Jun. To Clarissa Harlowe	[Harlowe Place] [Harlowe Place]	---
	Clarissa will be sent to Uncle Antony's for a fortnight where she must receive Solmes.		
Letter 50.2	Clarissa Harlowe To James Harlowe, Jun.	[Harlowe Place] [Harlowe Place]	---
	Clarissa refuses to go anywhere to receive Solmes.		
Letter 51 Vol.2, Letter VI Vol.2, Letter VI	Miss Clarissa Harlowe To Miss Howe	[Harlowe Place] [Howe residence]	Thursday morning, Mar. 23
	Family in tumult over her last.		

Letter 51.1	James Harlowe, Jun.	[Harlowe Place]	Thursday
	To Miss Clarissa Harlowe	[Harlowe Place]	morning
	He requests in more moderate language that Clarissa go to Antony's for a fortnight to receive Solmes.		

Letter 51.2	Clarissa Harlowe	[Harlowe Place]	Thursday,
	To James Harlowe, Jun.	[Harlowe Place]	March 23
	Knowing James will read this letter aloud to the family, she uses the occasion to address Mamma and Papa directly.		

Letter 52	Miss Clarissa Harlowe	[Harlowe Place]	Thursday
Vol.2, Letter VII	To Miss Howe	[Howe residence]	night,
Vol.2, Letter VII	Clarissa has no friend and no refuge.		Mar. 23

Letter 52.1	James Harlowe, Jun.	[Harlowe Place]	---
	To Miss Clarissa Harlowe	[Harlowe Place]	
	Continuing intimidation of Clarissa.		

Letter 53	Miss Clarissa Harlowe	[Harlowe Place]	Friday
Vol.2, Letter VIII	To Miss Howe	[Howe residence]	morning,
Vol.2, Letter VIII	Clarissa visits her poultry and overhears her siblings laughing with Solmes.		six o'clock, and Friday, ten o'clock

Letter 53.1	Clarissa Harlowe	[Harlowe Place]	Friday
	To Mr. James Harlowe, Jun.	[Harlowe Place]	morning
	Clarissa proposes solutions and offers to seek refuge elsewhere.		

Letter 54	Miss Clarissa Harlowe	[Harlowe Place]	Friday
Vol.2, Letter IX	To Miss Howe	[Howe residence]	night
Vol.2, Letter IX	Clarissa asks Anna's advice.		March 24, and eleven o'clock at night

Letter 54.1	Arabella Harlowe	[Harlowe Place]	---
	To Miss Clarissa Harlowe	[Harlowe Place]	
	Arabella answers Clarissa's proposals and insists that Clarissa will go to Antony's soon. Includes music.		

Letter 55	Miss Clarissa Harlowe	[Harlowe Place]	Friday
Vol.2, Letter X	To Miss Howe	[Howe residence]	night
Vol.2, Letter X	Clarissa appreciates Hickman, sees Lovelace's artful intimidation, and fears going to Antony's.		

Letter 56	Miss Howe	[Howe residence]	Sat.
Vol.2, Letter XI	To Miss Clarissa Harlowe	[Harlowe Place]	March 25
Vol.2, Letter XI	She cautions Clarissa against going to Antony's.		

Letter 57	Miss Clarissa Harlowe	[Harlowe Place]	Sunday
Vol.2, Letter XII	To Miss Howe	[Howe residence]	morning,
Vol.2, Letter XII	Clarissa continues to correspond with Lovelace. Leaving home would be an extreme.		Mar. 26

Letter 58 Vol.2, Letter XIII Vol.2, Letter XIII	Miss Howe To Miss Clarissa Harlowe	[Howe residence] [Harlowe Place]	Sat. Mar. 25

Anna and Mrs. Howe discuss Clarissa's case, marriage in general, and Lovelace.
Enclosure: Clarissa's anonymous letter to Lady Drayton on the consequences of severity in parents.

Letter 59 Vol.2, Letter XIV Vol.2, Letter XIV	Miss Clarissa Harlowe To Miss Howe	[Harlowe Place] [Howe residence]	Sunday afternoon

Mamma and Papa return her letters unopened.

Letter 59.1	Roger Solmes To Miss Clarissa Harlowe	--- [Harlowe Place]	Sunday, Mar. 26

He wants to pass on to Clarissa some information about Lovelace.
Mr. Solmes is a poor speller.

Letter 59.2	Miss Clarissa Harlowe To Roger Solmes, Esq.	[Harlowe Place]	---

If the Harlowe Family will rid Clarissa of Solmes, she will rid them of Lovelace.

Letter 59.3	Miss Dorothy Hervey To Miss Clarissa Harlowe	--- [Harlowe Place]	---

Clarissa must leave for Antony's at once.

Letter 59.4	Miss Clarissa Harlowe To John Harlowe, Esq.	[Harlowe Place] ---	---

Clarissa fears going to Antony's.
Enclosure: Her letters to her parents are returned unopened.

Letter 60 Vol.2, Letter XV Vol.2, Letter XV	Miss Clarissa Harlowe To Miss Howe	[Harlowe Place] [Howe residence]	Monday morning, March 27

Clarissa offers to give up her estate to rid herself of both Solmes and Lovelace.

Letter 60.1	John Harlowe To Clarissa Harlowe	--- [Harlowe Place]	Sunday night, or rather Monday morning

His affection for Clarissa, his disappointment.

Letter 60.2	Clarissa Harlowe To John Harlowe	[Harlowe Place] ---	---

She offers Solmes to Arabella. Clarissa will resign her estate and never marry.

Letter 61 Vol.2, Letter XVI Vol.2, Letter XVI	Miss Clarissa Harlowe To Miss Howe	[Harlowe Place] [Howe residence]	Monday afternoon, March 27 Monday evening

Family assembled in close debate over Clarissa's proposals.
Refused, she opens Lovelace's letter. He requests an interview with her in the garden at night.

Letter 61.1	James Harlowe, Jun. To Clarissa Harlowe	[Harlowe Place] [Harlowe Place]	Monday, 5 o'clock

Angry at Clarissa's proposals, he shames Uncle Harlowe into refusing her.

Letter 61.2	Clarissa Harlowe	[Harlowe Place]	Monday
	To John Harlowe, Esq.	---	night
	Begs an answer to her proposals from Uncle Harlowe himself, rather than from James.		
Letter 62	Miss Clarissa Harlowe	[Harlowe Place]	Tuesday
Vol.2, Letter XVII	To Miss Howe	[Howe residence]	morning,
Vol.2, Letter XVII	Thursday Clarissa must go to Antony's. Lovelace proposes a meeting with Clarissa.		7 o'clock Tuesday morning eight o'clock Tuesday, eleven o'clock
Letter 62.1	John Harlowe	---	Monday
	To Clarissa Harlowe	[Harlowe Place]	night
	His angry refusal of Clarissa's proposals. She must go to Antony's on Thursday.		
Letter 63	Miss Clarissa Harlowe	[Harlowe Place]	Tuesday,
Vol.2, Letter XVIII	To Miss Howe	[Howe residence]	three
Vol.2, Letter XVIII	Long conversation with Betty draws her out on the family's plans. Clarissa asks Anna to inquire in the village about Lovelace.		o'clock March 28
Letter 63.1	Clarissa Harlowe	[Harlowe Place]	Tuesday
	To John Harlowe	---	afternoon
	She requests a fortnight's respite before going to Antony's.		
Letter 63.2	John Harlowe	---	---
	To Clarissa Harlowe	[Harlowe Place]	
	Request for delay granted, if she will agree to see Solmes for one hour.		
Letter 63.3	Clarissa Harlowe	[Harlowe Place]	---
	To John Harlowe	---	
	She agrees to see Solmes.		
Letter 63.4	John Harlowe	---	---
	To Clarissa Harlowe	[Harlowe Place]	
	A reasonable reply.		
Letter 64	Miss Clarissa Harlowe	[Harlowe Place]	Wednesday
Vol.2, Letter XIX	To Miss Howe	[Howe residence]	morning,
Vol.2, Letter XIX	Lovelace has waited in the coppice and been disappointed. He writes to press her.		nine o'clock Wednesday noon March 29
Letter 64.1	Robert Lovelace	Ivy-Cavern in the Coppice	day
	To Miss Clarissa Harlowe	[Harlowe Place]	but just
	He chides Clarissa for not meeting him.		breaking

Letter 65 Vol.2, Letter XX Vol.2, Letter XX	Miss Howe To Miss Clarissa Harlowe Her visit to Larkin's with Mrs. Howe and Hickman. Larkin's death.	[Howe residence] [Harlowe Place]	Thursday morning, daybreak, March 30
[66 skipped in Penguin] [not in the first edition] Vol.2, Letter XXI	Mr. Hickman To Mrs. Howe He complains of Miss Howe's poor treatment of him and wonders whether he should discontinue his address.	--- [Howe residence]	Wednesday, March 29
[67 skipped in Penguin] [not in the first edition] Vol.2, Letter XXII	Mrs. Howe To Charles Hickman, Esq. She encourages him not to give up.	[Howe residence] ---	Thursday, March 30
Letter 68 Vol.2, Letter XXI Vol.2, Letter XXIII	Miss Howe To Miss Clarissa Harlowe She discusses Lovelace, calls him a devil, and opines that Clarissa should prefer Solmes. She offers Clarissa refuge.	[Howe residence] [Harlowe Place]	Thursday morning
Letter 69 Vol.2, Letter XXII Vol.2, Letter XXIV	Miss Clarissa Harlowe To Miss Howe Anticipating refuge with Anna, she sends her a parcel of linen and letters.	[Harlowe Place] [Howe residence]	Friday, March 31 Friday morning, eleven o'clock
Letter 70 Vol.2, Letter XXIII Vol.2, Letter XXV	Miss Howe To Miss Clarissa Harlowe An account of Lovelace and his fellow rakes at the inn. She fears Rosebud is undone.	[Howe residence] [Harlowe Place]	Thursday night, March 30
Letter 71 Vol.2, Letter XXIV Vol.2, Letter XXVI	Miss Clarissa Harlowe To Miss Howe Fears for Rosebud.	[Harlowe Place] [Howe residence]	Friday, three o'clock
Letter 72 Vol.2, Letter XXV Vol.2, Letter XXVII	Miss Howe To Miss Clarissa Harlowe Rosebud is spared.	[Howe residence] [Harlowe Place]	Friday noon, March 31
Letter 73 Vol.2, Letter XXVI Vol.2, Letter XXVIII	Miss Clarissa Harlowe To Miss Howe Pleased that Rosebud has not come to harm. How to avoid being sent to Antony's. She has written to Lovelace a long, severe letter on her reasons for granting an interview with Solmes.	[Harlowe Place] [Howe residence]	Saturday, April 1
Letter 74 Vol.2, Letter XXVII Vol.2, Letter XXIX	Miss Howe To Miss Clarissa Harlowe Clarissa's parcels have arrived at Anna's. She will ask Mrs. Howe to offer refuge for Clarissa.	[Howe residence] [Harlowe Place]	Sunday, April 2
Letter 75 Vol.2, Letter XXVIII Vol.2, Letter XXX	Miss Clarissa Harlowe To Miss Howe Meets up with James and Arabella on her poultry visit. John visits her in her apartment. Lovelace responds to her severe letter. She may flee to Anna's.	[Harlowe Place] [Howe residence]	Sunday night, April 2

Letter 76 Vol.2, Letter XXIX Vol.2, Letter XXXI	Miss Clarissa Harlowe To Miss Howe	[Harlowe Place] [Howe residence]	Monday, April 3
	Tomorrow she must grant Solmes an interview. Lovelace presses her to flee.		
Letter 77 Vol.2, Letter XXX Vol.2, Letter XXXII	Miss Clarissa Harlowe To Miss Howe	[Harlowe Place] [Howe residence]	Tuesday morning, six o'clock
	She recites her revulsion toward Solmes to Aunt Hervey.		Tuesday, eleven o'clock
Letter 78 Vol.2, Letter XXXI Vol.2, Letter XXXIII	Miss Clarissa Harlowe To Miss Howe	[Harlowe Place] [Howe residence]	Tuesday evening, and continued through the night
	Her *long letter.* Clarissa grants Solmes an interview and states her objections to his address. Family uproar. Clarissa is roughly handled and ordered to Antony's. The family search her room for writing supplies, but she has kept some hidden.		Three o'clock Wednesday morning
Letter 79 Vol.2, Letter XXXII Vol.2, Letter XXXIV	Miss Clarissa Harlowe To Miss Howe	[Harlowe Place] [Howe residence]	Wednesday, eleven o'clock, April 5
	Aunt Hervey tries to persuade Clarissa. She is tricked into seeing Solmes again. James uses force. Uproar. Clarissa must go to Anthony's. Her pen and ink are seized.		
Letter 80 Vol.2, Letter XXXIII Vol.2, Letter XXXV	Miss Clarissa Harlowe To Miss Howe	[Harlowe Place] [Howe residence]	Wednesday, four o'clock in the afternoon
	Her *long letter* still not picked up. She asks Anna for refuge, and Lovelace presses her to flee. Garden walks and poultry visits to be forbidden. Clarissa must make a decision.		
Letter 81 Vol.2, Letter XXXIV Vol.2, Letter XXXVI	Miss Howe To Miss Clarissa Harlowe	[Howe residence] [Harlowe Place]	Thursday morning, April 6
	Anna responds to Clarissa's interview with Solmes. Mrs. Howe refuses Clarissa refuge. Clarissa has three choices: go to London with Anna, seek protection of Lovelace's family, or marry Lovelace directly.		
Letter 82 Vol.2, Letter XXXV Vol.2, Letter XXXVII	Miss Clarissa Harlowe To Miss Howe	[Harlowe Place] [Howe residence]	Thursday, April 6
	She responds to the three choices.		
Letter 83 Vol.2, Letter XXXVI Vol.2, Letter XXXVIII	Miss Clarissa Harlowe To Miss Howe	[Harlowe Place] [Howe residence]	Thursday night
	Lovelace's intimidations have stopped her being carried off to Antony's. Preparations for a wedding at Harlowe Place. She refuses to sign the parchments and panics as she overhears her siblings plotting. She writes to Lovelace asking for protection of his aunts.		

Letter 84 Vol.2, Letter XXXVII Vol.2, Letter XXXIX	Miss Clarissa Harlowe To Miss Howe Dreams she is murdered by Lovelace. Another visit from Aunt Hervey.	[Harlowe Place] [Howe residence]	Friday morning, seven o'clock April 7 Eight o'clock Friday, eleven o'clock
Letter 85 Vol.2, Letter XXXVIII Vol.2, Letter XL	Miss Clarissa Harlowe To Miss Howe Lovelace promises protection of his aunts, or other options. Clarissa still hopes her family will give up. Aunt Hervey assures her they will not.	[Harlowe Place] [Howe residence]	Friday, one o'clock Friday, four o'clock Friday, six o'clock Friday, nine o'clock
Letter 86 Vol.2, Letter XXXIX Vol.2, Letter XLI	Miss Clarissa Harlowe To Miss Howe Letter sent to Lovelace confirming her plan to flee.	[Harlowe Place] [Howe residence]	Sat. morn., 8 o'clock, April 8 Saturday, ten o'clock
Letter 87 Vol.2, Letter XL Vol.2, Letter XLII	Miss Howe To Miss Clarissa Harlowe Her desire to provide transportation and to accompany Clarissa. She cautions Clarissa to marry Lovelace at the first opportunity, if she chooses to escape with his help rather than Anna's.	[Howe residence] [Harlowe Place]	Sat. afternoon
Letter 88 Vol.2, Letter XLI Vol.2, Letter XLIII	Miss Clarissa Harlowe To Miss Howe Lovelace's ecstatic answer to Clarissa's request for his assistance. His promises.	[Harlowe Place] [Howe residence]	Saturday afternoon
Letter 89 Vol.2, Letter XLII Vol.2, Letter XLIV	Miss Clarissa Harlowe To Miss Howe Her friendship with Anna. She reconsiders and decides not to go off with Lovelace.	[Harlowe Place] [Howe residence]	Sunday morning, April 9
Letter 90 Vol.2, Letter XLIII Vol.2, Letter XLV	Miss Clarissa Harlowe To Miss Howe Letter from Dolly keeps Clarissa informed of the family's plans. She is still resolved not to go off with Lovelace.	[Harlowe Place] [Howe residence]	Sunday morning, April 9 Sunday, four o'clock p.m. Sunday evening, seven o'clock Sunday night, nine o'clock Mon. morn. April 10, seven o'clock

Letter 90.1   Dorothy Hervey   [Harlowe Place]   ---
     To Clarissa Harlowe   [Harlowe Place]
         She informs Clarissa of the family's plans for the wedding.

Letter 91   Miss Clarissa Harlowe   Ivy summer-house   eleven
Vol.2, Letter XLIV   To Miss Howe   [Howe residence]   o'clock
Vol.2, Letter XLVI   Clarissa's last letter from Harlowe Place. She dines in the ivy
         summer-house awaiting Lovelace, still resolved *not* to go away
         with him, even though she may become the miserable property
         of that Solmes.

Letter 92   Miss Clarissa Harlowe   St. Albans   Tuesday
Vol.2, Letter XLV   To Miss Howe   [Howe residence]   morn.
Vol.2, Letter XLVII   "Your Clarissa Harlowe is gone off with a man!"   past one

Letter 93   Miss Howe   [Howe residence]   Tuesday,
Vol.2, Letter XLVI   To Miss Clarissa Harlowe   ---   nine o'clock
Vol.2, Letter XLVIII   Misses Howe, Lloyd, and Biddulph want to know the details.
         Anna advises her to marry Lovelace, and quickly.

Letter 94   Miss Clarissa Harlowe   ---   Tuesday
Vol.3, Letter I   To Miss Howe   [Howe residence]   night
Vol.2, Letter XLIX   She recounts the circumstances of her departure.

Letter 95   Mr. Lovelace   ---   Sat.
Vol.3, Letter II   To Joseph Leman   ---   April 8
Vol.2, Letter L   His instructions to Leman, the escape plan.

Letter 96   Joseph Leman   ---   Sunday
Vol.3, Letter III   To Mr. Robert Lovelace   ---   morning,
Vol.2, Letter LI   Unsure of his scruples. Thoughts on marrying Betty. He would   April 9
         like Lovelace's receipt to cure a shrewish wife.

Letter 97   Mr. Lovelace   St. Albans   Monday
Vol.3, Letter IV   To John Belford, Esq.   ---   night
Vol.3, Letter I   Woe to Clarissa, should he doubt her love.   Tuesday,
         day-dawn

Letter 98   Miss Clarissa Harlowe   [Mrs Sorlings's]   Wednesday,
Vol.3, Letter V   To Miss Howe   [Howe residence]   April 12
Vol.3, Letter II   Continues the story of her escape. She is grief stricken and
         argues with Lovelace. On the way to Mrs. Sorlings's dairy farm
         Mrs. Greme tells Clarissa about Lovelace

Letter 99   Mr. Lovelace   ---   Tuesday,
Vol.3, Letter VI   To John Belford, Esq.   ---   Wed.
Vol.3, Letter III   Ecstasy, triumph, resentment, revenge.   Apr. 11,12

Letter 100   Miss Howe   [Howe residence]   Wednesday
Vol.3, Letter VII   To Miss Clarissa Harlowe   ---   night,
Vol.3, Letter IV   Antony, all ablow, visits Mrs. Howe and reports the family's   April 12
         reaction to Clarissa's escape. Advice and assistance from Anna.   Thursday,
         April 13

Letter 101 Vol.3, Letter VIII Vol.3, Letter V	Miss Clarissa Harlowe To Miss Howe	[Mrs. Sorlings's] [Howe residence]	Thursday, p.m. April 13
	Lacking confidence in Lovelace, Clarissa hopes for reconciliation with her family. She fears to say she was carried off against her will. Enclosure: copy of Letter 102 to Arabella		
Letter 102 Vol.3, Letter IX Vol.3, Letter VI	Miss Clarissa Harlowe To Miss Arabella Harlowe	St. Albans [Harlowe Place]	Tuesday, Apr. 11
	She asks to be allowed to go to the Grove, if not to return home, and to call all a temporary misunderstanding. She asks for her clothes, money, books, and jewels to be sent to Mr. Osgood's.		
Letter 103 Vol.3, Letter X Vol.3, Letter VII	Mr. Lovelace To John Belford, Esq.	--- ---	---
	(in continuation of Letter 99) He relates their stay at the inn, his ambivalence toward Clarissa, and his triumph over the abduction.		
Letter 104 Vol.3, Letter XI Vol.3, Letter VIII	Mr. Lovelace To John Belford, Esq.	--- ---	---
	(in continuation) His goal, to get Clarissa to his acquaintance in London. He regrets he cannot also have Anna.		
Letter 105 Vol.3, Letter XII Vol.3, Letter IX	Mr. Lovelace To John Belford, Esq.	--- ---	---
	(in continuation) He controls Anna by using Antony to influence Mrs. Howe, and Leman to influence Antony. At Mrs. Sorlings's he flirts with her two daughters.		
Letter 106 Vol.3, Letter XIII Vol.3, Letter X	Mr. Lovelace To John Belford, Esq.	--- ---	---
	(in continuation) His spider and fly analogy. Recounts the church scene with the Harlowe Family in Letter 30. His love of seduction.		
Letter 107 Vol.3, Letter XIV Vol.3, Letter XI	Miss Clarissa Harlowe To Miss Howe	[Mrs Sorlings's] [Howe residence]	Thursday night, April 13
	Her angry discussion with Lovelace. She wants him to leave her. He proposes a speedy solemnization, but she is unconvinced and indignant.		
Letter 108 Vol.3, Letter XV Vol.3, Letter XII	Mr. Lovelace To John Belford, Esq.	--- ---	---
	Disappointed and humiliated at Clarissa's grief over being abducted, he hints at revenge.		
Letter 109 Vol.3, Letter XVI Vol.3, Letter XIII	Mr. Lovelace To John Belford, Esq.	--- ---	---
	(in continuation) Clarissa is unreceptive on the subject of matrimony. Lovelace does not bear the Harlowe Family's insults well.		
Letter 110 Vol.3, Letter XVII Vol.3, Letter XIV	Mr. Lovelace To John Belford, Esq.	--- ---	---
	(in continuation) Realizing Clarissa's chief motivation has been to prevent mischief between him and the Harlowe Family, he contrives to test her virtue. If she stands her trial, he will marry her. If he reforms, she will marry him.		

Letter 111   Miss Howe   [Howe residence]   ---
Vol.3, Letter XVIII   To Miss Clarissa Harlowe   [Mrs. Sorlings's]
Vol.3, Letter XV

> (in answer to Letters 101 and 107) Her continued correspondence with Clarissa forbidden. Harlowe Family will not send Clarissa her things. She cautions Clarissa not to make Lovelace resentful.

Letter 112   Miss Clarissa Harlowe   [Mrs. Sorlings's]   ---
Vol.3, Letter XIX   To Miss Howe   [Howe residence]
Vol.3, Letter XVI

> She recounts events leading to the present situation, still hoping that her family will send her her things and that Lovelace will not be resentful. She considers herself an example of failure to do one's duty.

Letter 113   Miss Clarissa Harlowe   [Mrs. Sorlings's]   ---
Vol.3, Letter XX   To Miss Howe   [Howe residence]
Vol.3, Letter XVII

> Lovelace has explained his use of Leman in Clarissa's abduction. Clarissa is very disapproving.

Letter 114   Miss Clarissa Harlowe   [Mrs. Sorlings's]   ---
Vol.3, Letter XXI   To Miss Howe   [Howe residence]
Vol.3, Letter XVIII

> Her concerns about Lovelace's character, his threats to James and Solmes, and his carelessness of his own reputation.

Letter 115   Mr. Lovelace   ---   Friday,
Vol.3, Letter XXII   To John Belford, Esq.   ---   April 14
Vol.3, Letter XIX

> He rails against the Harlowes, their motives, their stupidity. His opinions on women and modesty, and rakes.

Letter 116   Miss Clarissa Harlowe   [Mrs. Sorlings's]   Friday,
Vol.3, Letter XXIII   To Miss Howe   [Howe residence]   April 14
Vol.3, Letter XX

> Lovelace suggests Clarissa secure lodgings at Windsor, Berkshire, Oxford, or London. She hopes for Lovelace's reform and writes to Aunt Hervey for clothes, books, and money. She asks for permission to go to her dairy house and for reconciliation.

Letter 117   Mr. Lovelace   ---   Friday,
Vol.3, Letter XXIV   To John Belford, Esq.   April 14
Vol.3, Letter XXI

> Schemes and revenge.

Letter 118   Mr. Lovelace   ---   ---
Vol.3, Letter XXV   To John Belford, Esq.   ---
Vol.3, Letter XXII

> (in continuation) Plans to manipulate Clarissa, Hannah, Mrs. Sorlings's daughters, Will, and Lord M.'s chaplain. Clarissa may fall.

Letter 119   Miss Howe   [Howe residence]   Sat.
Vol.3, Letter XXVI   To Miss Clarissa Harlowe   [Mrs. Sorlings's]   April 15
Vol.3, Letter XXIII

> Her suspicions of Lovelace. Her offer to send Clarissa money.

Letter 120   Miss Clarissa Harlowe   [Mrs. Sorlings's]   Sat.
Vol.3, Letter XXVII   To Miss Howe   [Howe residence]   afternoon
Vol.3, Letter XXIV

> Mrs. Greme hopes Clarissa will marry Lovelace. Why has Lovelace passed up opportunities to declare himself?

Letter 121 Vol.3, Letter XXVIII Vol.3, Letter XXV	Miss Clarissa Harlowe To Miss Howe	[Mrs. Sorlings's] [Howe residence]	Saturday evening Sunday morning
	Lovelace has received letters from Lady Betty and Miss Montague, both hoping for speedy nuptials and looking forward to seeing Clarissa afterwards. They do not offer to see her before the speedy nuptials.		
[122 skipped in Penguin] [not in the first edition] Vol.3, Letter XXVI	Miss Clarissa Harlowe To Miss Howe	[Mrs. Sorlings's] [Howe residence]	Sunday night (April 16)
	She is puzzled that Lovelace now seems to favor reconciliation with her family. He shows her letters from Lady Betty and Miss Montague.		
Letter 123 Vol.3, Letter XXIX Vol.3, Letter XXVII	Miss Clarissa Harlowe To Miss Howe	[Mrs. Sorlings's] [Howe residence]	---
	(in continuation) Clarissa wishes Lovelace to leave her at Mrs. Sorlings's. Her power to bequeath her estate still gives her some independence. She still hopes for reconciliation.		
Letter 124 Vol.3, Letter XXX Vol.3, Letter XXVIII	Miss Clarissa Harlowe To Miss Howe	[Mrs. Sorlings's] [Howe residence]	---
	(in continuation) Clarissa takes Lovelace severely to task. He is offended. He offers to take her to Anna's or to Morden in Florence. She still hopes for an answer from Aunt Hervey or Arabella.		
Letter 125 Vol.3, Letter XXXI Vol.3, Letter XXIX	Miss Clarissa Harlowe To Miss Howe	[Mrs. Sorlings's] [Howe residence]	---
	(in continuation) Clarissa needs a servant, lodgings, and clothes. She begins to consider removing to London.		
Letter 126 Vol.3, Letter XXXII Vol.3, Letter XXX	Miss Clarissa Harlowe To Miss Howe	[Mrs. Sorlings's] [Howe residence]	Monday morning, April 17
	In Mrs. Sorlings's garden Clarissa and Lovelace discuss accommodations for her in London.		
Letter 127 Vol.3, Letter XXXIII Vol.3, Letter XXXI	Mr. Lovelace To John Belford, Esq.	--- ---	Sat., Sunday, Monday Monday, April 17
	He manipulates Clarissa into removing to London.		
Letter 128 Vol.3, Letter XXXIV Vol.3, Letter XXXII	Miss Howe To Miss Clarissa Harlowe	[Howe residence] [Mrs. Sorlings's]	Tuesday, April 18
	(in answer to Letters 120-126) She compares the courtship styles of Hickman and Lovelace. Her contempt for Hickman. She has sounded Lovelace's relations, and they favor alliance with Clarissa. She does not object to London, nor should Clarissa delay marriage.		
Letter 129 Vol.3, Letter XXXV Vol.3, Letter XXXIII	Miss Clarissa Harlowe To Miss Howe	[Mrs. Sorlings's] [Howe residence]	Wedn. morn. April 19
	She mentions removal to London and asks Anna for two guineas.		

Letter 130   Miss Clarissa Harlowe   [Mrs. Sorlings's]   Thursday,
Vol.3, Letter XXXVI   To Miss Howe   [Howe residence]   April 20
Vol.3, Letter XXXIV   Forwards to Anna, Doleman's answer to Lovelace in response to the latter's inquiry about lodgings for Clarissa in London. Her optimism at Lovelace's consideration.

Letter 130.1   Thomas Doleman   [London]   Tuesday
     To Robert Lovelace, Esq.   ---   night,
     Appearing to believe Clarissa and Lovelace married, he suggests several appropriate locations for them in London.   April 18

Letter 131   Mr. Lovelace   ---   Thursday,
Vol.3, Letter XXXVII   To John Belford, Esq.   ---   April 20
Vol.3, Letter XXXV   He manipulates Clarissa into going to Mrs. Sinclair's and contrives to pass along the wrong address to Anna.

Letter 132   Miss Howe   [Howe residence]   Wednesday,
Vol.3, Letter XXXVIII   To Miss Clarissa Harlowe   [Mrs. Sorlings's]   April 19
Vol.3, Letter XXXVI   James has a rescue plan. Details of Mrs. Howe's marriage and her own opinions on the topic. Miss Howe is warming up to Hickman.

Letter 133   Miss Clarissa Harlowe   [Mrs. Sorlings's]   Thursday,
Vol.3, Letter XXXIX   To Miss Howe   [Howe residence]   April 20
Vol.3, Letter XXXVII   She reproves Anna for disobeying Mrs. Howe's instruction to cease their correspondence.

Letter 134   Miss Clarissa Harlowe   [Mrs. Sorlings's]   ---
Vol.3, Letter XL   To Miss Howe   [Howe residence]
Vol.3, Letter XXXVIII   (in continuation) She reproves Anna for her treatment of Hickman.

Letter 135   Miss Clarissa Harlowe   [Mrs. Sorlings's]   ---
Vol.3, Letter XLI   To Miss Howe   [Howe residence]
Vol.3, Letter XXXIX   Conditions of their continued correspondence.

Letter 136   Miss Howe   [Howe residence]   Friday
Vol.3, Letter XLII   To Miss Clarissa Harlowe   [Mrs. Sorlings's]   morn.
Vol.3, Letter XL   Her relationship with Mrs. Howe and with Mr. Hickman.   April 21

Letter 137   Miss Clarissa Harlowe   [Mrs. Sorlings's]   Friday,
Vol.3, Letter XLIII   To Miss Howe   [Howe residence]   April 21
Vol.3, Letter XLI   Lovelace asks her hand, but in a reproachful tone. He surprises her with a half proposal. Lovelace uses James's rescue plan as an excuse to refuse leaving Clarissa alone in London.

Letter 138   Mr. Lovelace   ---   Friday,
Vol.3, Letter XLIV   To John Belford, Esq.   ---   April 21
Vol.3, Letter XLII   His unintended proposal. James's plan to rescue Clarissa gives Lovelace an excuse to hide Clarissa in London and stay near her.

Letter 139   Joseph Leman   [Harlowe Place]   April 15
Vol.3, Letter XLV   To Robert Lovelace, Esq.   ---   and 16
Vol.3, Letter XLIII   He passes information to Lovelace about James's desire for revenge, and to the Harlowes about Lovelace.

SUMMARIES OF LETTERS

Letter 140 Vol.3, Letter XLVI Vol.3, Letter XLIV	Mr. Lovelace To Joseph Leman	--- [Harlowe Place]	April 17

Bribes Leman into passing on information to the Harlowes about Clarissa's situation and whereabouts. He wants Joseph to offer to assist in James's rescue plan so Leman can pass on the details to Lovelace.

Letter 141 Vol.3, Letter XLVII Vol.3, Letter XLV	Miss Clarissa Harlowe To Mrs. Hervey	[Mrs. Sorlings's] ---	Thursday, April 20

(enclosed in her last to Miss Howe) A second attempt to elicit help from Aunt Hervey, enclosing a copy of her earlier attempt. She requests clothing, money, and other things.

Letter 142 Vol.3, Letter XLVIII Vol.3, Letter XLVI	Miss Howe To Miss Clarissa Harlowe	[Howe residence] [Mrs. Sorlings's]	Sat. April 22

With a sense of urgency about Clarissa's situation, she retrospects Lovelace's character and conduct, advising Clarissa to put herself into the protection of the ladies of Lovelace's family and marry Lovelace soon, as his doubts about her love serve to endanger her.

Letter 143 Vol.3, Letter XLIX Vol.3, Letter XLVII	Mr. Belford To Robert Lovelace, Esq.	--- ---	Friday, April 21

He cautions Lovelace against further trials and against bringing Clarissa to town.

Letter 144 Vol.3, Letter L Vol.3, Letter XLVIII	Mrs. Hervey To Miss Clarissa Harlowe	--- [Mrs. Sorlings's]	---

(in answer to Letter 141) Breaking her word not to write, she answers Clarissa's. She believes Clarissa planned her escape. Harlowe Family would have given in had Clarissa not escaped. Clarissa is to expect no help from home.

Letter 145 Vol.3, Letter LI Vol.3, Letter XLIX	Miss Clarissa Harlowe To Miss Howe	[Mrs. Sorlings's] [Howe residence]	Sat. morn. April 22

She regrets her flight. Prayer foreshadows future trials.

Letter 146 Vol.3, Letter LII Vol.3, Letter L	Miss Clarissa Harlowe To Miss Howe	[Mrs. Sorlings's] [Howe residence]	Saturday, p.m. April 23

She has received a cruel letter from Arabella saying her family rejects her and her father has cursed her.
Enclosure: Letter from Arabella, the original.

Letter 147 Vol.3, Letter LIII Vol.3, Letter LI	Miss Arabella Harlowe To Miss Clarissa Harlowe	[Harlowe Place] [Mrs. Sorlings's]	Friday, April 23

(to be left at Mr. Osgood's, near Soho Square) The family will not answer any more letters from Clarissa. No attempt will be made to rescue her. Mamma will send her her clothes.

	[Miss Arabella Harlowe] To [Miss Clarissa Harlowe]	Harlowe Place ---	Sat. April 15

(previously written and enclosed in Letter 147) Clarissa has disgraced her family and is cursed. James will avenge the family honor but not Clarissa.

Letter 148 Vol.3, Letter LIV Vol.3, Letter LII	Miss Howe To Miss Clarissa Harlowe	[Howe residence] [Mrs. Sorlings's]	Tuesday, April 25

She advises Clarissa to marry Lovelace soon. Trying to comfort and reassure her, she sends fifty guineas. She will inquire about Aunt Hervey's pretense that the family would have changed their plan had Clarissa held firm.

Letter 149 Vol.3, Letter LV Vol.3, Letter LIII	Miss Clarissa Harlowe To Miss Howe	[Mrs. Sorlings's] [Howe residence]	Wednesday morning, April 26

Clarissa sets out for London, having been ill after reading Arabella's letter. Fears she has written too freely about Lovelace. Lovelace proposed, but she objected as she was ill, despairing, and unprepared.

Letter 150 Vol.3, Letter LVI Vol.3, Letter LIV	Miss Howe To Miss Clarissa Harlowe	[Howe residence] [Mrs. Sorlings's]	Thursday, April 27

She urges Clarissa to marry Lovelace. She does not know where to direct this letter.

Letter 151 Vol.3, Letter LVII Vol.3, Letter LV	Miss Howe To Miss Clarissa Harlowe	[Howe residence] ---	Thursday, April 27

(enclosed in Letter 150) Her information on whether the family had any intention of a change of measures.
Includes: Fragments of Clarissa's answers to Letters 150 and 151. Her observations on Anna's lack of passion for Hickman, and her own reasons for not accepting Lovelace's proposal in Letter 149. Defends her mother's somewhat slow response in coming to her defense.

Letter 152 Vol.3, Letter LVIII Vol.3, Letter LVI	Mr. Lovelace To John Belford, Esq.	--- ---	Monday, April 24

Sums up his efforts to get Clarissa in his power.

Letter 153 Vol.3, Letter LIX Vol.3, Letter LVII	Mr. Lovelace To John Belford, Esq.	--- ---	Tuesday, April 25 Tuesday afternoon

His ambivalent attitude toward marrying Clarissa. His thrill at setting out for London with Clarissa.

Letter 154 Vol.3, Letter LX Vol.3, Letter LVIII	Mr. Lovelace To John Belford, Esq.	--- ---	Wed. Apr. 26

Residents at Mrs. Sinclair's believe that Lovelace and Clarissa are already married, but the marriage not yet consummated.

Letter 155 Vol.3, Letter LXI Vol.3, Letter LIX	Miss Clarissa Harlowe To Miss Howe	[Mrs. Sinclair's] [Howe residence]	Wed. p.m. Apr. 26

Clarissa arrives in London and settles in at Mrs. Sinclair's. She dislikes Mrs. Sinclair and Dorcas.

Letter 156 Vol.3, Letter LXII Vol.3, Letter LX	Miss Howe To Miss Clarissa Harlowe	[Howe residence] [Mrs. Sinclair's]	Thursday night, April 27

(with her last two Letters 150-151 enclosed) She has heard from Clarissa in London. She advises Clarissa to marry Lovelace.

Letter 157 Vol.3, Letter LXIII Vol.3, Letter LXI	Miss Clarissa Harlowe To Miss Howe	[Mrs. Sinclair's] [Howe residence]	Thursday morning, eight o'clock ten o'clock

Clarissa has breakfast with Mrs Sinclair, Miss Martin, and Miss Horton. Lovelace will leave for Berks to bring Charlotte Montague to visit Clarissa.

Letter 157.1	Mr. Lovelace To John Belford, Esq.	[Mrs. Sinclair's] ---	--- ---

Lovelace's opinion of Sally, Polly, and fallen women in general. His contempt for Mrs. Sinclair's house and regret at bringing Clarissa here.

Letter 158 Vol.3, Letter LXIV Vol.3, Letter LXII	Miss Clarissa Harlowe To Miss Howe	[Mrs. Sinclair's] [Howe residence]	Friday, April 28 Friday evening Saturday morning

Lovelace makes reference to their wedding and goes in search of a house. A collation is planned for Clarissa to be introduced to Lovelace's friends.

Letter 158.1	Mr. Lovelace To John Belford, Esq.	--- ---	--- Saturday night

A collation is arranged for Clarissa on Monday to meet Tourville, Belton, and Mowbray. Clarissa will be introduced as Mrs. Lovelace and congratulated on her nuptials.

Letter 159 Vol.3, Letter LXV Vol.3, Letter LXIII	Mr. Lovelace To John Belford, Esq.	--- ---	Sunday

He accompanies Clarissa to church at St. Paul's. Clarissa getting on with Mrs. Sinclair and the others in the house and anticipating tomorrow's collation.

Letter 160 [not numbered in first ed] Vol.3, Letter LXIV	Miss Clarissa Harlowe To Miss Howe	[Mrs. Sinclair's] [Howe residence]	[Monday morning]

Clarissa is pleased with Lovelace at church but displeased at being introduced to Miss Partington and at being obliged to appear at the collation.

Letter 161 Vol.3, Letter LXVI Vol.3, Letter LXV	Miss Clarissa Harlowe To Miss Howe	[Mrs. Sinclair's] [Howe residence]	Monday night, May 1

She relates the collation, describing each guest and her displeasure with Lovelace's friends.

Letter 162 Vol.3, Letter LXVII Vol.3, Letter LXVI	Miss Clarissa Harlowe To Miss Howe	[Mrs. Sinclair's] [Howe residence]	Monday midnight

Mrs. Sinclair requests that Clarissa take Miss Partington as a bedfellow. Clarissa wonders at the odd request.

Letter 163 Vol.3, Letter LXVIII Vol.3, Letter LXVII	Miss Clarissa Harlowe To Miss Howe	[Mrs. Sinclair's] [Howe residence]	Tuesday, May 2

Mrs. Howe has sent a letter to Clarissa forbidding any further correspondence between Clarissa and Anna. Clarissa dislikes Lovelace's friends.

Letter 164 — Miss Howe — [Howe residence] — Wed.
Vol.3, Letter LXIX — To Miss Clarissa Harlowe — [Mrs. Sinclair's] — May 3
Vol.3, Letter LXVIII — Anna will fly to Clarissa in London if Clarissa ceases to correspond.

Letter 165 — Miss Clarissa Harlowe — [Mrs. Sinclair's] — Thursday,
Vol.3, Letter LXX — To Miss Howe — [Howe residence] — May 4
Vol.3, Letter LXIX — Clarissa advises Anna to let Hickman write for her. Clarissa's clothes have arrived.

Letter 166 — Mr. Hickman — --- — Friday,
Vol.3, Letter LXXI — To Miss Clarissa Harlowe — [Mrs. Sinclair's] — May 5
Vol.3, Letter LXX — His concern for Clarissa.

Letter 167 — Mr. Lovelace — --- — Tuesday
Vol.3, Letter LXXII — To John Belford, Esq. — --- — May 2
Vol.4, Letter I — Clarissa's dislike for Lovelace's friends and for Miss Partington. Lovelace will send Hannah, who is better, a physician with medicines that may weaken her.

Letter 168 — Mr. Lovelace — --- — Tuesday,
Vol.3, Letter LXXIII — To John Belford, Esq. — --- — May 2
Vol.4, Letter II — He guesses that Mrs. Howe has written to Clarissa forbidding further correspondence with Anna.

Letter 169 — Mr. Belford — Edgware — Tuesday
Vol.3, Letter LXXIV — To Robert Lovelace, Esq. — --- — night,
Vol.4, Letter III — All Lovelace's friends admire Clarissa, her ill opinion of them notwithstanding. Belford advises Lovelace to marry her. The letter is signed by all four, Belford, Belton, Mowbray, and Tourville. — May 2

Letter 170 — Mr. Lovelace — --- — Wednesday,
Vol.3, Letter LXXV — To John Belford, Esq. — --- — May 3
Vol.4, Letter IV — Defends his pursuit of Clarissa, he the hunter and she the quarry.

Letter 171 — Mr. Lovelace — --- — ---
Vol.3, Letter LXXVI — To John Belford, Esq. — ---
Vol.4, Letter V — (in continuation) Further defends himself and his pursuit. Women as quarry.

Letter 172 — Mr. Belford — Edgware — Thursday,
Vol.3, Letter LXXVII — To Robert Lovelace, Esq. — --- — May 4
Vol.4, Letter VI — Belford would be less displeased if Clarissa were to be fairly seduced rather than tricked. Belford must attend his dying uncle. He is his uncle's heir.

Letter 173 — Miss Clarissa Harlowe — [Mrs. Sinclair's] — ---
Vol.3, Letter LXXVIII — To Miss Howe — [Howe residence]
Vol.4, Letter VII — Lovelace continues to encroach and Clarissa thinks the worse of him. Her family has sent her her clothes, some books, and a letter from Morden.
Enclosed: Letter 173.1 from Morden

Letter 173.1 Vol.3, Letter LXXIX [not numbered in third ed]	Colonel Morden To Miss Clarissa Harlowe	Florence [Mrs. Sinclair's]	April 13
	His observations on the Harlowe Family situation, on Lovelace, on Solmes. His low opinion of Lovelace. He encourages Clarissa to comply with her parents' wishes.		
Letter 174 Vol.4, Letter I Vol.4, Letter VIII	Miss Clarissa Harlowe To Miss Howe	[Mrs. Sinclair's] [Howe residence]	Sunday night, May 7
	Clarissa requests that Hickman plead her case with Uncle Harlowe.		
Letter 174.1	Miss Clarissa Harlowe To Miss Howe	[Mrs. Sinclair's] [Howe residence]	Monday
	(continues Letter 174) Lovelace introduces Mr. Mennell, a kinsman of Mrs. Fretchville, to Clarissa. Mrs. Fretchville is fictitious, and Mr. Mennell an imposter. Lovelace makes false plans to buy a house for Clarissa. Clarissa waits to hear what success Hickman has had with Uncle Harlowe.		
Letter 174.2	[Mr. Lovelace] To [John Belford, Esq.]	--- ---	---
	He has persuaded Doleman's nephew, Newcomb, to pose as Mr. Mennell and offers to show Clarissa Mrs. Fretchville's house.		
Letter 174.3	[Mr. Lovelace] To [John Belford, Esq.]	--- ---	Monday night
	Lovelace suspects that Miss Howe and Clarissa have a plan afoot. He will contrive to steal Clarissa's letters.		
Letter 175 Vol.4, Letter II Vol.4, Letter IX	Mr. Lovelace To John Belford, Esq.	--- ---	Tuesday, May 9 Wednesday morning
	Lovelace attempts to seize a letter from Clarissa. She has shut herself up from him. Lovelace is through with Leman and Betty Barnes and has decided to punish them.		
Letter 176 Vol.4, Letter III Vol.4, Letter X	Miss Clarissa Harlowe To Miss Howe	[Mrs. Sinclair's] [Howe residence]	Tuesday, May 9
	She hopes Uncle Harlowe can be persuaded to take her part.		
Letter 177 Vol.4, Letter IV Vol.4, Letter XI	Miss Howe To Miss Clarissa Harlowe	[Howe residence] [Mrs. Sinclair's]	Wednesday, May 10
	Cautions Clarissa about Lovelace and advises her to leave him. Kind words for Clarissa and encouragement to withstand her trials.		
Letter 178 Vol.4, Letter V Vol.4, Letter XII	Miss Clarissa Harlowe To Miss Howe	[Mrs. Sinclair's] [Howe residence]	Friday, May 12 Sunday, May 14
	Keeping Lovelace at a distance, Clarissa wishes to attend church. Lovelace will not allow her to go unattended. Is she a prisoner?		
Letter 179 Vol.4, Letter VI Vol.4, letter XIII	Miss Howe To Mrs. Judith Norton	[Howe residence] ---	Thursday, May 11
	She asks her to press Mrs. Harlowe for reconciliation, while Hickman will try to engage Uncle Harlowe in Clarissa's favor. Clarissa prefers reconciliation to wedding Lovelace and will defer to Papa on the disposition of her estate.		

Letter 180 Vol.4, Letter VII Vol.4, Letter XIV	Mrs. Norton To Miss Howe No success can be expected from her applications for reconciliation.	--- [Howe residence]	Saturday, May 13

Letter 181
Vol.4, Letter VIII
Vol.4, Letter XV

Miss Howe   [Howe residence]
To Mrs. Judith Norton   ---
     Anna's hatred of tyrants.

Saturday
evening,
May 13

Letter 182
Vol.4, Letter IX
Vol.4, Letter XVI

Mrs. Harlowe   [Harlowe Place]
To Mrs. Judith Norton   ---
     She asks this correspondence be kept secret. Clarissa was the pride
     and joy of the Harlowe Family. Now she is the disgrace. Mamma
     cannot move for Clarissa as the family is too much against her.
     Hickman's application to Uncle Harlowe was rejected.

Saturday,
May 13

Letter 183
Vol.4, Letter X
Vol.4, Letter XVII

Miss Howe   [Howe residence]
To Miss Clarissa Harlowe   [Mrs. Sinclair's]
     Nothing stirring in the Harlowe Family. Clarissa must take Lovelace
     and try to save the wretch. Anna thinks he may not be so bad.
     Antony is disposed to marry Mrs. Howe.

Sunday,
May 14

Letter 184
Vol.4, Letter XI
Vol.4, Letter XVIII

Miss Clarissa Harlowe   [Mrs. Sinclair's]
To Miss Howe   [Howe residence]
     Lovelace enjoys having Clarissa in his power. Clarissa has not the
     strength to see him.

Monday,
p.m.
May 15

Letter 185
Vol.4, Letter XII
Vol.4, Letter XIX

Miss Clarissa Harlowe   [Mrs. Sinclair's]
To Miss Howe   [Howe residence]
     A long stormy conversation between Lovelace and Clarissa. His
     displeasure at her keeping her distance. Her hesitation to discuss
     settlements with Lovelace. His failure to declare his intentions.
     Her preference for a single life and her belief that she and Lovelace
     are unsuited for each other.

Tuesday,
May 16

Letter 186
Vol.4, Letter XIII
Vol.4, Letter XX

Miss Clarissa Harlowe   [Mrs. Sinclair's]
To Miss Howe   [Howe residence]
     Lovelace sends Clarissa his proposals. She will have her own estate,
     part of his in Lancashire, and £1000 *per annum* from Lord M. Yet
     his generosity is not followed by a suggestion to set a date. All seems
     to depend upon Clarissa.

Tuesday
night,
May 16

Letter 187
Vol.4, Letter XIV
Vol.4, Letter XXI

Miss Clarissa Harlowe   [Mrs. Sinclair's]
To Miss Howe   [Howe residence]
     Lovelace again accuses Clarissa of indifference and insists on an
     answer to his proposed terms. Lovelace wishes to ask Lord M. to be
     Clarissa's nuptial father and suggests tomorrow, or the next day, or the
     day after. He tries to kiss Clarissa and becomes angry at her rejection.

Wednesday
morning,
May 17

Letter 187.1-187.4

Mr. Lovelace   [Mrs. Sinclair's]
To John Belford   ---
     Lovelace resents Clarissa's wish to reconcile with her family. He
     doubts her love and threatens revenge. He enjoys Clarissa's confusion.
     He will marry her after gratifying his pride, ambition, and revenge.

Letter 188 Vol.4, Letter XV Vol.4, Letter XXII	Miss Howe To Miss Clarissa Harlowe	[Howe residence] [Mrs. Sinclair's]	Thursday, May 18
	Lovelace delays and accuses Clarissa of delaying. Anna advises Clarissa to take the fool as punishment since she cannot take him as reward.		
Letter 189 Vol.4, Letter XVI Vol.4, Letter XXIII	Mr. Belford To Robert Lovelace, Esq.	--- [Mrs. Sinclair's]	Wednesday, May 17
	He advises Lovelace to be just to Clarissa, a moving plea. Enclosure: Letter 190 from Lord M. to Belford		
Letter 190 Vol.4, Letter XVII Vol.4, Letter XXIV	Lord M. To John Belford, Esq.	M. Hall ---	Monday, May 15
	He asks Belford to persuade Lovelace to marry Clarissa.		
Letter 190.1	Mr. Belford To Robert Lovelace, Esq.	[Watford] [Mrs. Sinclair's]	---
	Attending his dying uncle, he is eager for correspondence from Lovelace. He hopes he has not offended Lovelace. Tells him of some wickedness of others of their companions.		
Letter 191 Vol.4, Letter XVIII Vol.4, Letter XXV	Mr. Lovelace To John Belford, Esq.	[Mrs. Sinclair's] [Watford]	Friday night, May 19
	He will test Clarissa's virtue and reward her with marriage. He defends his position. He does not want to use his family name to further his designs on Clarissa. His enthusiasm for euthanasia in regard to Belford's dying uncle.		
Letter 192 Vol.4, Letter XIX Vol.4, Letter XXVI	Mr. Belford To Robert Lovelace, Esq.	[Watford] [Mrs. Sinclair's]	Saturday, May 20
	The advantages of marriage. He relates the story of Belton's unhappy relationship with Thomasine and his own cousin Tony Jenyns's equally sad story.		
Letter 193 Vol.4, Letter XX Vol.4, Letter XXVII	Mr. Lovelace To John Belford, Esq.	[Mrs. Sinclair's] [Watford]	Saturday, May 20
	He thanks Belford for his advice but would never take up with a low-bred girl, as Belton and Tony Jenyns did.		
Letter 194 Vol.4, Letter XXI Vol.4, Letter XXVIII	Mr. Lovelace To John Belford, Esq.	[Mrs. Sinclair's] [Watford]	Saturday, May 20
	His progress with his plans for Clarissa. He invites her to attend a play. Dorcas will search Clarissa's room while she is out.		
Letter 195 [not numbered in first ed] Vol.4, Letter XXIX	Miss Clarissa Harlowe To Miss Howe	[Mrs. Sinclair's] [Howe residence]	Friday, May 19
	Pleased with Lovelace's recent behavior, she will attend the play. She must be watchful but is mistress of her comings and goings, though this has not often been put to the test.		
Letter 196 Vol.4, Letter XXII Vol.4, Letter XXX	Miss Howe To Miss Clarissa Harlowe	[Howe residence] [Mrs. Sinclair's]	Saturday, May 20
	Her scheme to arrange protection for Clarissa with Mrs. Townsend. Anna shows Hickman Lovelace's proposals to Clarissa. Singleton tries to corrupt Kitty. Antony's formal proposal to Mrs. Howe.		

Letter 197	Miss Howe	[Howe residence]	Sat.,
Vol.4, Letter XXIII	To Miss Clarissa Harlowe	[Mrs. Sinclair's]	Sunday,
Vol.4, Letter XXXI	Enclosed is Antony's proposal to Mrs. Howe and her answer.		May 20, 21
	Anna and Mrs. Howe discuss the proposal.		

Letter 197.1	Antony Harlowe	---	Monday,
	To Mrs. Annabella Howe	[Howe residence]	May 15
	He will leave Mrs. Howe ten thousand pounds richer if they marry,		
	but Anna may not live with them. She must marry Hickman.		

Letter 197.2	Mrs. Annabella Howe	[Howe residence]	Friday,
	To Antony Harlowe, Esq.	---	May 19
	Neither Anna nor Mrs. Howe favors the proposal.		

Letter 198	Mr. Lovelace	[Mrs. Sinclair's]	Sunday,
Vol.4, Letter XXIV	To John Belford, Esq.	[Watford]	May 21
Vol.4, Letter XXXII	Clarissa has slipped out to church alone. Lovelace is enraged after		
	reading extracts from her letters.		

Letter 199	Mr. Lovelace	[Mrs. Sinclair's]	---
Vol.4, Letter XXV	To John Belford, Esq.	[Watford]	
Vol.4, Letter XXXIII	He continues to rage.		

Letter 200	Miss Clarissa Harlowe	[Mrs. Sinclair's]	Sunday
Vol.4, Letter XXVI	To Miss Howe	[Howe residence]	morning,
Vol.4, Letter XXXIV	She attends a play with Lovelace and Miss Norton. She attends		7 [a.m.],
	church alone, without Lovelace. Lovelace still rages.		May 21
			Near nine
			o'clock

Letter 201	Mr. Lovelace	[Mrs. Sinclair's]	Monday
Vol.4, Letter XXVII	To John Belford, Esq.	[Watford]	morn.
Vol.4, Letter XXXV	Lovelace prevents Clarissa from going out. She is not well and		May 22
	is frightened by his behavior. After a long, heated dialogue she		Monday
	asks to be free of all obligations to Lovelace and will not marry		two o'clock
	him. She hates him.		Monday
			evening

Letter 202	Mr. Lovelace	[Mrs. Sinclair's]	Tuesday
Vol.4, Letter XXVIII	To John Belford, Esq.	[Watford]	morning,
Vol.4, Letter XXXVI	Resolves to marry Clarissa if she withstands her trials. Includes		May 23
	a copy of a letter written by Clarissa but torn and discarded, then		
	found and transcribed by Dorcas, in which she seems to assume		
	they will marry, telling Lovelace that a reconciliation with her		
	family would be necessary, and describing her responsibilities and		
	expectations as his wife. Lovelace is troubled by his conscience.		

Letter 203	Mr. Lovelace	[Mrs. Sinclair's]	Tuesday,
Vol.4, Letter XXIX	To John Belford, Esq.	[Watford]	May 23
Vol.4, Letter XXXVII	He has done with the affair of Mrs. Fretchville's house. Newcomb		
	refuses to continue deceiving Clarissa. Still no answer from Lord M.		
	Charlotte is ill with a stomach disorder.		

Letter 203.1	Lady Charlotte Montague To Robert Lovelace, Esq.	M. Hall [Mrs. Sinclair's]	May 22

She has been ill and Lady Betty has been busy, but they will visit Clarissa in her new habitation, Mrs. Fretchville's house. She and Lord M. await the announcement of Lovelace's nuptials.

Letter 203.2	Miss Clarissa Harlowe To Miss Howe	[Mrs. Sinclair's] [Howe residence]	---

After receiving Mr. Mennell's letter, she resolves to leave Lovelace and asks Anna to perfect her smuggling scheme. Then, after reading Charlotte's letter, she asks Anna to suspend her scheme for the moment. She had begun to suspect both Mrs. Fretchville and Mr. Mennell, but Charlotte's letter allayed her suspicions.

Letter 204 Vol.4, Letter XXX Vol.4, Letter XXXVIII	Mr. Lovelace To John Belford, Esq.	[Mrs. Sinclair's] [Watford]	Wed. May 24

To discourage Clarissa, he emphasizes the danger of small-pox at Mrs. Fretchville's. A man has been in the neighborhood inquiring of Dorcas whether he and Clarissa were married.

Letter 205 Vol.4, Letter XXXI Vol.4, Letter XXXIX	Mr. Lovelace To John Belford, Esq.	[Mrs. Sinclair's] [Watford]	May 24

He has received a letter from Lord M., shown it to Clarissa, and forwarded it to Belford.

Letter 206 Vol.4, Letter XXXII Vol.4, Letter XL	Lord M. To Robert Lovelace, Esq.	[M. Hall] [Mrs. Sinclair's]	Tuesday, May 23

With many proverbs he gives Lovelace fatherly advice on public and private life. He specifically names wedding gifts for Clarissa. He threatens to disown Lovelace if he disappoint him. He, his sisters, and his cousins Montague all look forward to the wedding.

Letter 207 Vol.4, Letter XXXIII Vol.4, Letter XLI	Mr. Lovelace To John Belford, Esq.	[Mrs. Sinclair's] [Watford]	Thursday, May 25

Clarissa is quiet as Lovelace talks about the wedding, her clothes and jewels, and the settlements. Privately he regrets that Lord M., in his displeasure with Lovelace, may make Clarissa an independent wife with his generosity. Lovelace's desire to be adored by women. Clarissa does not want a public wedding, as it would embarrass her family. She declines Lord M.'s chapel.

Letter 207.1	Miss Clarissa Harlowe To Miss Howe	[Mrs. Sinclair's] [Howe residence]	---

It seems that, however unhappily, she will be married to Lovelace.

[208 skipped in Penguin] [not in the first edition] Vol.4, Letter XLII	Omitted in the first edition, as Mr. Lovelace abandons his scheme to have his revenge on Miss Howe.		
	Mr. Lovelace To John Belford, Esq.	[Mrs. Sinclair's] [Watford]	---

He and his accomplices will commandeer the boat taking Miss Howe and hers to the Isle of Wight. They will draw lots for the women, then set them ashore on the French coast. He is certain that no jury would ever convict them.

Letter 209
Vol.4, Letter XXXIV
Vol.4, Letter XLIII

Mr. Lovelace
To John Belford, Esq.

[Mrs. Sinclair's]
[Watford]

He will feign illness to worry Clarissa and test her love. He tells
the story of an affair he had in Paris with a French marquis's wife,
who later died in childbirth.

Letter 210
Vol.4, Letter XXXV
Vol.4, Letter XLIV

Mr. Lovelace
To John Belford, Esq.

[Mrs. Sinclair's]
[Watford]

Friday
evening

He takes an airing with Clarissa and the nymphs. Clarissa has
moved her letters to a wainscot box to which Lovelace has no key.
Tomorrow he will feign a stomach disorder to gain her sympathy.

Letter 211
Vol.4, Letter XXXVI
Vol.4, Letter XLV

Mr. Lovelace
To John Belford, Esq.

Cocoa Tree
[Watford]

May 27

Vomiting up blood, Lovelace feigns illness, brought on by ingesting
ipecacuanha. He appears to have burst a vessel. Clarissa is moved.

Letter 212
Vol.4, Letter XXXVII
Vol.4, Letter XLVI

Miss Clarissa Harlowe
To Miss Howe

[Mrs. Sinclair's]
[Howe residence]

Saturday,
May 27

She feels guilty for Lovelace's illness but fears she has exposed
herself by her concern.

Letter 213
Vol.4, Letter XXXVIII
Vol.4, Letter XLVII

Mr. Lovelace
To John Belford, Esq.

[Mrs. Sinclair's]
[Watford]

Sat.
evening

While Lovelace is out for an airing, a footman calls at Mrs. Sinclair's
inquiring after Mr. and Mrs. Lovelace.

Letter 214
Vol.4, Letter XXXIX
Vol.4, Letter XLVIII

Mr. Lovelace
To John Belford, Esq.

[Mrs. Sinclair's]
[Watford]

Sunday,
May 28

Reported with stage directions. Captain Tomlinson, supposedly on
behalf of John Harlowe, inquires whether Lovelace and Clarissa are
married. If so, would Lovelace consider a reconciliation.

Letter 215
Vol.4, Letter XL
Vol.4, Letter XLIX

Mr. Lovelace
To John Belford, Esq.

[Mrs. Sinclair's]
[Watford]

Sunday
night

Clarissa objects to lying to Tomlinson about their marriage. She
would not want him to report a lie to Uncle Harlowe. She will
tell him the truth tomorrow.

Letter 216
Vol.4, Letter XLI
Vol.4, Letter L

Mr. Lovelace
To John Belford, Esq.

[Mrs. Sinclair's]
[Watford]

Monday,
May 19

Captain Tomlinson is told the truth about Clarissa's unwedded state
and given Lovelace's proposals of settlement to show Uncle Harlowe,
with words of reconciliation from Lovelace. Clarissa is transported.

Letter 217
Vol.4, Letter XLII
Vol.4, Letter LI

Mr. Lovelace
To John Belford, Esq.

[Mrs. Sinclair's]
[Watford]

Captain Tomlinson is an imposter. Lovelace will withhold Anna's
to Clarissa for a week, so the results of Anna's inquiries about
Tomlinson will not become known to Clarissa. Now that Clarissa is
happy about the possibility of reconciliation, Lovelace will contrive
to make her equally unhappy.

| Letter 217.1 | Miss Clarissa Harlowe | [Mrs. Sinclair's] | --- |
| | To Miss Howe | [Howe residence] | |

Her happiness that Uncle Harlowe has apparently reconsidered Hickman's application for reconciliation.

| Letter 217.2 | Miss Clarissa Harlowe | [Mrs. Sinclair's] | --- |
| | To Miss Howe | [Howe residence] | |

Clarissa puzzles over the good and bad in Lovelace's character. He seems to do good to atone for bad. Revenge is his predominant quality. At least he is not an infidel.

| Letter 217.3 | Miss Clarissa Harlowe | [Mrs. Sinclair's] | --- |
| | To Miss Howe | [Howe residence] | |

Why do men try to conceal their emotions?

Letter 218	Mr. Lovelace	[Mrs. Sinclair's]	Tuesday,
Vol.4, Letter XLIII	To John Belford, Esq.	[Watford]	May 30
Vol.4, Letter LII			Wednesday, May 31

He has received an answer from Lord M. agreeing to the proposed settlements but will not show it to Clarissa. They take an airing and talk about reconciliation. He feels remorse. He curses Miss Howe's letters. Mrs. Sinclair and her nymphs urge him to make a day time attempt on Clarissa.

Letter 219	Mr. Lovelace	[Mrs. Sinclair's]	Friday,
Vol.4, Letter XLIV	To John Belford, Esq.	[Watford]	June 2
Vol.4, Letter LIII			

He continues his attempts to take liberties with Clarissa as he feels entitled. If she breaks with Lovelace now, she will lose the chance for reconciliation with her family. Women have no souls. To whom is Lovelace accountable for what he does to women?

Letter 220	Mr. Lovelace	[Mrs. Sinclair's]	Monday,
Vol.4, Letter XLV	To John Belford, Esq.	[Watford]	June 5
Vol.4, Letter LIV			

Lovelace is taking bolder freedoms with Clarissa.

Letter 221	Mr. Lovelace	[Mrs. Sinclair's]	Monday,
Vol.4, Letter XLVI	To John Belford, Esq.	[Watford]	p.m.
Vol.4, Letter LV			

Lovelace reports to Clarissa that Uncle Harlowe, through Tomlinson, advises them to marry privately and afterwards proceed with reconciliation. This contrivance with Tomlinson should provide against Miss Howe's smuggling scheme.

Letter 222	Mr. Belford	[Watford]	Tuesday,
Vol.4, Letter XLVII	To Robert Lovelace, Esq.	[Mrs. Sinclair's]	June 6
Vol.4, Letter LVI			

Reports more details of the collation with Clarissa and how it changed him. He tries to persuade Lovelace to cease his trials and remove Clarissa from Mrs. Sinclair's. He is also affected by his dying uncle.

Letter 223	Mr. Lovelace	[Mrs. Sinclair's]	Tuesday
Vol.4, Letter XLVIII	To John Belford, Esq.	[Watford]	p.m.,
Vol.4, Letter LVII			June 6

He thinks of revenge as he considers Anna's letters and remembers his night in the cold coppice waiting for Clarissa. He explains his strategy and his contrivances. His opinion on rape. He envisions life with Clarissa out of wedlock.

Letter 224 Vol.4, Letter XLIX Vol.4, Letter LVIII	Mr. Lovelace To John Belford, Esq. He has a plot in mind.	[Mrs. Sinclair's] [Watford]	Wednesday night, 11 o'clock
Letter 225 Vol.4, Letter L Vol.4, Letter LIX	Mr. Lovelace To John Belford, Esq. Fire! Fire! He contrives to frighten Clarissa out of her apartment late at night in her nightclothes, then refuses to leave her. He takes more liberties than usual. She threatens to use sharp scissors.	[Mrs. Sinclair's] [Watford]	Thursday morning, five o'clock (June 8)
Letter 226 Vol.4, Letter LI Vol.5, Letter I	Mr. Lovelace To John Belford, Esq. Clarissa refuses to see Lovelace. She sends a billet down saying she will not see Lovelace for one week.	[Mrs. Sinclair's] [Watford]	Thursday morning, eight o'clock Past ten o'clock Past eleven o'clock
Letter 227 Vol.4, Letter LII Vol.5, Letter II	Mr. Lovelace To John Belford, Esq. Clarissa and Lovelace exchange billets, his addressed to Mrs. Lovelace. His contradictory, ambivalent feelings about Clarissa and marriage. He believes that her refusal to see him for one week means that she and Anna need time to revive Anna's smuggling scheme.	King's Arms, Pall Mall [Watford]	Thursday, two o'clock
Letter 227.1	[Lovelace] To Mrs. Lovelace He regrets offending her and begs her presence in the dining room.	[Mrs. Sinclair's] [Mrs. Sinclair's]	---
Letter 227.2	[Clarissa Harlowe] To Mr. Lovelace She will not see him.	[Mrs. Sinclair's] [Mrs. Sinclair's]	---
Letter 227.3	[Lovelace] To Mrs. Lovelace He accuses her of over-niceness. He must consult her about the license.	[Mrs. Sinclair's] [Mrs. Sinclair's]	---
Letter 227.4	[Clarissa Harlowe] To Mr. Lovelace She does not ever wish to see Lovelace, her Judas protector.	[Mrs. Sinclair's] [Mrs. Sinclair's]	---
Letter 227.5	[Lovelace] To Mrs. Lovelace He will go to the Commons to get a license.	[Mrs. Sinclair's] [Mrs. Sinclair's]	---
Letter 228 Vol.4, Letter LIII Vol.5, Letter III	Mr. Lovelace To John Belford, Esq. The lady is gone off! He rages that Clarissa has been let to escape. The story of her escape. Lovelace vows revenge if he gets his hands on her again.	[Mrs. Sinclair's] [Watford]	Thursday evening, June 8

Letter 229 Vol.4, Letter LIV Vol.5, Letter IV	Mr. Lovelace To John Belford, Esq.	[Mrs. Sinclair's] [Watford]	---

Lovelace intercepts Anna's to Clarissa. Collins had taken the letter to Mr. Wilson's, then, as there was a hurry, he tried to deliver it directly to Clarissa at Mrs. Sinclair's. Finding Clarissa not in, he took the letter back to Wilson's. Lovelace is enraged at its contents.

Letter 229.1	[Anna Howe] To Miss Laetitia Beaumont	[Howe residence] [Mrs. Sinclair's]	Wednesday, June 7 Thurs. morn. 5 [a.m.] I have written all night.

Clarissa was seen alone in St. James's church by Miss Lardner, who told Miss Biddulph, who told Miss Lloyd. Miss Lardner's servant followed Clarissa back to Mrs. Sinclair's, so her whereabouts is now known. Anna has inquired about Tomlinson and found no such person, nor any such as a Mrs. Fretchville. Mrs. Townsend will accommodate Clarissa. Anna offers to come to her, but advises her to fly. Called by Lovelace her *double-dated* letter. [His forgery of this letter, Letter 239.1, mistakes the date as Thurs. the 5th.]

Letter 229.2	['Clarissa Harlowe'] To Miss Howe	--- [Howe residence]	---

Expresses shock at Anna's letter and asks her not to come to her. A forgery.

Letter 230 Vol.4, Letter LV Vol.5, Letter V	Miss Clarissa Harlowe To Miss Howe	[Mrs. Moore's at Hampstead] [Howe residence]	Thursday evening, June 8

She relates the particulars of her escape and of the fire at Sinclair's. She hopes to go abroad.

Letter 231 Vol.4, Letter LVI Vol.5, Letter VI	Mr. Lovelace To John Belford, Esq.	[Mrs. Sinclair's] [Watford]	Friday morning, past two o'clock

Clarissa has been found in Hampstead. Lovelace received two letters by Will, one a feint to Anna to send Will out of the way and another to Lovelace. Lovelace orders a Blunt chariot to go to Hampstead.

Letter 231.1	Will Summers To Mr. Lovelace	[Hampstead] [Mrs. Sinclair's]	---

Disguised, he keeps Clarissa under close observation at Mrs. Moore's.

Letter 231.2	Miss Clarissa Harlowe To Miss Howe	[Mrs. Sinclair's] [Howe residence]	Thursday, June 8

This letter is a feint to send Will out of the way.

Letter 231.3	Miss Clarissa Harlowe To Mr. Lovelace	[Mrs. Sinclair's] [a tavern near Doctors' Commons]	Thursday, June 8

Asks Lovelace to agree not to see her for one week. She asks for the company of the ladies of his family.

Letter 232 Vol.5, Letter I Vol.5, Letter VII	Mr. Lovelace To John Belford, Esq.	Upper Flask, Hampstead [Watford]	Friday (June 9) morn. 7 o'clock

Lovelace's account of how Clarissa escaped. Lovelace arrives at Hampstead and disguises himself with the help of Mrs. Moore.

Letter 233 Vol.5, Letter II Vol.5, Letter VIII	Mr. Lovelace To John Belford, Esq.	Hampstead [Watford]	Friday night, June 9

Disguised, Lovelace surprises Clarissa at Hampstead. She faints, then comes to in a state of high resentment. Lovelace tells his story to Mrs. Moore and Miss Rawlins to enlist their support. He shows them letters, forged, from his family supporting his claim that he is married to Clarissa.

Letter 233.1	['Captain Tomlinson'] To Robert Lovelace, Esq.	--- ---	Wed. June 7

Lady Betty has found out from her steward that Lovelace and Clarissa are married. Her Uncles Harlowe and Mr. Solmes are to set out to find the truth of the matter. Lovelace shows this letter to Mrs. Moore and Miss Rawlins. A forgery.

Letter 233.2	['Lady Elizabeth Lawrance'] To Robert Lovelace, Esq.	--- ---	Wed. morn. June 7

She is disappointed to find out about Lovelace's marriage from another source. Her compliments and invitation to Clarissa to accompany her to Oxfordshire. A forgery.

Letter 233.3	['Miss Charlotte Montague'] To Robert Lovelace, Esq.	--- ---	---

To meet Lady Betty at Reading and accompany her to town to Leeson's. The family all long to see Clarissa. A forgery.

Letter 233.4	['Lord M.'] To Robert Lovelace, Esq.	M. Hall ---	Wed. June 7

Wishing he had heard from Lovelace about the marriage. Lady Betty and Charlotte will soon be in town. He expects Lovelace and Clarissa to be at the Lawn soon. A forgery.

Letter 234 Vol.5, Letter III Vol.5, Letter IX	Mr. Lovelace To John Belford, Esq.	[Hampstead] [Watford]	---

Mrs. Moore and Miss Rawlins attend Clarissa. Lovelace's opinion on Clarissa's lack of experience and on parenting. His revenge is up.

Letter 235 Vol.5, Letter IV Vol.5, Letter X	Mr. Lovelace To John Belford, Esq.	[Hampstead] [Watford]	---

Lovelace relates a conversation overheard among Clarissa, Mrs. Moore, and Miss Rawlins. They question Clarissa about Lovelace's story. Lovelace has convinced them that he and Clarissa are married. He prevents Clarissa from leaving. She dines alone.

Letter 236 Vol.5, Letter V Vol.5, Letter XI	Mr. Lovelace To John Belford, Esq.	[Hampstead] [Watford]	---

(in continuation) Lovelace has dinner with the ladies. He lets them think Anna loves him and is jealous. Women, it seems, prefer rakes.

Letter 237 Vol.5, Letter VI Vol.5, Letter XII	Mr. Lovelace To John Belford, Esq.	[Hampstead] [Watford]	---

(in continuation) Captain Tomlinson arrives, reporting to Lovelace before Mrs. Moore, Miss Rawlins, and Mrs. Bevis, on his negotiations with Mr. John Harlowe. Tomlinson expresses John Harlowe's doubt about the marriage, but Lovelace puts all doubt to rest.

Letter 238 Vol.5, Letter VII Vol.5, Letter XIII	Mr. Lovelace	[Hampstead]	---
	To John Belford, Esq.	[Watford]	
	(in continuation) Clarissa refuses to see Tomlinson. Will finds Clarissa's messenger Grimes drunk at the Lower Flask, steals Anna's for Clarissa from him, and brings it to Lovelace. When Clarissa sends a messenger to Wilson's for the letter which Anna mentions leaving there, Lovelace has already replaced it with his rewrite, Letter 239.1		
Letter 238.1	[Anna Howe]	---	June 9
	To 'Mrs. Harriot Lucas'	---	
	Congratulations on her escape from Mrs. Sinclair's. Worries about the letter she sent to Wilson's by Collins, as Lovelace may have got hold of it. A forgery.		
Letter 239 Vol.5, Letter VIII Vol.5, Letter XIV	Mr. Lovelace	[Hampstead]	---
	To John Belford, Esq.	[Watford]	
	(in continuation) Clarissa strongly objects to Lovelace's lodging at Mrs. Moore's. Clarissa's messenger returns with Anna's to Miss Laetitia Beaumont. Lovelace has shortened it and made additions.		
Letter 239.1	['Anna Howe']	---	Thursday morn. 5th [Thursday was June 8th]
	To Clarissa	---	
	Lovelace's forged version of Anna's Letter 229.1 to Miss Laetitia Beaumont, which Lovelace has already read and returned to Wilson's rewritten and misdated, the time of day mistaken for the date.		
Letter 240 Vol.5, Letter IX Vol.5, Letter XV	Mr. Lovelace	[Hampstead]	Saturday, 6 o'clock, June 10
	To John Belford, Esq.	[Watford]	
	Lovelace steals Clarissa's to Anna and substitutes a forgery. A servant of Mowbray's delivers it to Hickman.		
Letter 240.1	['Clarissa Harlowe']	Hampstead	Tuesday evening
	To Anna Howe	[Howe residence]	
	A forgery, briefly thanking Anna for hers.		
Letter 241 Vol.5, Letter X Vol.5, Letter XVI	Mr. Lovelace	Mrs. Moore's	Eight o'clock, Sat. morn. June 10
	To John Belford, Esq.	[Watford]	
	Miss Rawlins is not entirely convinced by Lovelace. The Widow Bevis is Lovelace's. Mrs. Moore is held by interest, as Lovelace has engaged all her spare rooms for one month. Will sleeps at Mrs. Moore's. The post is watched. James and Singleton are warned against. Mowbray, Tourville, and Belton will take up quarters at Hampstead for one week. Tomlinson is expected.		
Letter 242 Vol.5, Letter XI Vol.5, Letter XVII	Mr. Lovelace	From my apartments at Mrs. Moore's	Saturday, one o'clock
	To John Belford, Esq.	[Watford]	
	Clarissa considers removing from Mrs. Moore's. Tomlinson arrives. Lovelace may carry Clarissa back to Mrs. Sinclair's or consummate his marriage at Mrs. Moore's.		

Letter 243   Mr. Lovelace   [Hampstead]   Sat.
Vol.5, Letter XII   To John Belford, Esq.   [Watford]   night,
Vol.5, Letter XVIII   Clarissa is unwilling to negotiate reconciliation with her family on   June 10
                        Lovelace's terms. Tomlinson has told her family of her marriage
                        to Lovelace. Lovelace's family has also heard. Lovelace offers
                        Clarissa the protection of Lady Betty.

Letter 244   Mr. Lovelace   [Hampstead]   ---
Vol.5, Letter XIII To John Belford, Esq.   [Watford]
Vol.5, Letter XIX   (in continuation) Continuing negotiations between Clarissa and
                        Tomlinson. Lovelace and Tomlinson urge that Lady Betty mediate
                        a reconciliation between Clarissa and Lovelace.

Letter 245   Mr. Lovelace   [Hampstead]   ---
Vol.5, Letter XIV   To John Belford, Esq.   [Watford]
Vol.5, Letter XX   Clarissa expects a letter from Anna and hopes for a visit from Lady
                        Betty. Lovelace urges Clarissa to reperuse letters from Lady Betty,
                        Charlotte, and Lord M. He reminds her that James, Solmes, and
                        Singleton still pose a threat. Lovelace has gone to get the license,
                        Lady Betty, and Charlotte.

Letter 246   Mr. Lovelace   [Hampstead]   Sat.
Vol.5, Letter XV   To John Belford, Esq.   [Watford]   midnight
Vol.5, Letter XXI   Tomlinson urges Lovelace to get off his contrivances and marry
                        Clarissa. Lovelace dreams of murdering Clarissa and bringing
                        about his own destruction.

Letter 247   Mr. Lovelace   [Hampstead]   Sunday
Vol.5, Letter XVI   To John Belford, Esq.   [Watford]   morn.
Vol.5, Letter XXII   Belford's uncle has died. Lovelace will either marry Clarissa or   (June 14)
                        rape her.   4 o'clock

Letter 248   Mr. Lovelace   [Hampstead]   Sunday
Vol.5, Letter XVII To John Belford, Esq.   [Watford]   morning
Vol.5, Letter XXIII   Clarissa and Lovelace walk in Mrs. Moore's garden. Clarissa tells
                        Lovelace of her preference to live either on her own estate or abroad.
                        She goes to church. Lovelace's hopes depend on a visit from Lady
                        Betty and Miss Montague and intercepting Anna's next.

[Letter 249]   Mr. Lovelace   [Hampstead]   ---
Vol.5, [Letter XVIII] To John Belford, Esq.   [Watford]
Vol.5, Letter XXIV   Clarissa has gone to church with Mrs. Moore and Mrs. Bevis.
                        Lovelace seems intent on revenge.

Letter 250   Mr. Lovelace   [Hampstead]   Sunday
Vol.5, Letter XIX   To John Belford, Esq.   [Watford]   afternoon
Vol.5, Letter XXV   He has intercepted the awaited letter from Anna.

Letter 251   Mr. Lovelace   [Hampstead]   ---
Vol.5, Letter XX   To John Belford, Esq.   [Watford]
Vol.5, Letter XXVI   (in continuation) Anna's letter arrives while Clarissa is at church.
                        Mrs. Bevis impersonates Clarissa to receive the letter, then gives
                        it to Lovelace who sets about to rewrite it.

Letter 252 Vol.5, Letter XXI Vol.5, Letter XXVII	Mr. Lovelace To John Belford, Esq.	[Hampstead] [Watford]	---

He intercepts Anna's for Mrs. Harriot Lucas and realizes his contrivances have been detected by Miss Howe. He considers seducing Miss Howe. His opinion on friendship and women. As Mrs. Townsend is expected in Hampstead by Wednesday, Lovelace will have to remove Clarissa soon.

Letter 252.1	Anna Howe To Mrs. Harriot Lucas	[Howe residence] Mrs. Moore's at Hampstead	---

She has heard new stories about Lovelace. She has arranged for Mrs. Townsend and her two brothers with their crews to come to Mrs. Moore's and take Clarissa to safety in Deptford. Anna realizes she has not received Clarissa's feint. Lovelace must have it.

Letter 253 Vol.5, Letter XXII Vol.5, Letter XXVIII	Mr. Lovelace To John Belford, Esq.	[Hampstead] [Watford]	Sunday night- Monday morning

Clarissa and Lovelace walk in Mrs. Moore's garden. She tells him to think no more of her. She still awaits Anna's letter and a visit from Lady Betty and Charlotte. Lovelace will fetch the license.

Letter 254 Vol.5, Letter XXIII Vol.5, Letter XXIX	Mr. Lovelace To John Belford, Esq.	[Hampstead] [Watford]	Monday, June 12

He quotes the license to Belford. His objections to being married for life. He favors changes in the law to allow annual marriages.

Letter 255 Vol.5, Letter XXIV Vol.5, Letter XXX	Mr. Lovelace To John Belford, Esq.	[Hampstead] [Watford]	---

Lovelace must act quickly to remove Clarissa, as Mrs. Townsend is expected next Wednesday. Ladies are found to impersonate Lady Betty and Charlotte and trick Clarissa back to Mrs. Sinclair's.

Letter 256 Vol.5, Letter XXV Vol.5, Letter XXXI	Mr. Lovelace To John Belford, Esq.	At Mrs. Sinclair's [Watford]	Monday afternoon

Clarissa has returned to Mrs. Sinclair's for her clothes, expecting to return to Hampstead the same night. Lovelace plans the hour of Clarissa's trial. She realizes Lady Betty and Charlotte are impersonators and begs to return to Hampstead, but no coach is to be found. Clarissa is wild with fear. Sinclair terrifies her further.

Letter 256.1	'Lady Elizabeth Lawrance' To Robert Lovelace, Esq.	--- [Mrs. Sinclair's]	Monday night

A forgery by Lovelace to say that Charlotte has been taken violently ill. They will return for Clarissa tomorrow instead of tonight.

Letter 257 Vol.5, Letter XXVI Vol.5, Letter XXXII	Mr. Lovelace To John Belford, Esq.	[Mrs. Sinclair's] [Watford]	Tuesday morn. June 13

"And now, Belford, I can go no farther. The affair is over. Clarissa lives. And I am your humble servant, R. Lovelace"

Letter 258 Vol.5, Letter XXVII Vol.5, Letter XXXIII	Mr. Belford To Robert Lovelace, Esq.	Watford [Mrs. Sinclair's]	Wed. June 14

"O thou savage-hearted monster!" He urges Lovelace to marry Clarissa. He severely condemns Lovelace. He would give his entire inheritance to Lovelace if he would marry Clarissa.

Letter 259 Vol.5, Letter XXVIII Vol.5, Letter XXXIV	Mr. Lovelace To John Belford, Esq.	[Mrs. Sinclair's] [Watford]	Thursday, June 15

He owns he has done wrong but is surprised at Clarissa's state of insensibility and stupefaction. Lovelace returns to Hampstead to discharge his obligations there and tell Mrs Moore that he and Clarissa are now happy.

Letter 260 Vol.5, Letter XXIX Vol.5, Letter XXXV	Mr. Lovelace To John Belford, Esq.	[Mrs. Sinclair's] [Watford]	---

Lovelace confesses to Belford that he allowed Mrs. Sinclair to administer something to Clarissa to make her insensible. Her insensibility robbed him of his pleasure.

Letter 261 Vol.5, Letter XXX Vol.5, Letter XXXVI	Mr. Lovelace To John Belford, Esq.	[Mrs. Sinclair's] [Watford]	Friday, June 16

Belford has fallen from his horse. Lovelace has still not succeeded in obtaining Clarissa's consent. Clarissa resumes writing, tearing and throwing the fragments. Lovelace fears Clarissa may not regain her intellect. He plans a visit to Clarissa from Mrs. Moore, Miss Rawlins, Mrs. Bevis, Belton, Mowbray, and Tourville. Clarissa is recovering. Clarissa's fragments transcribed by Dorcas:

PAPER I [to Miss Howe]	She hopes Anna is not ill as Lovelace says. Her confusion. "Whatever they have done to me, I cannot tell."
PAPER II [to Papa]	Confessing to Papa and begging forgiveness.
PAPER III	Parable of the lady and the lion.
PAPER IV	Her pride and vanity, now humbled.
PAPER V [to Bella]	Admitting to Bella her proud heart.
PAPER VI [to Lovelace]	No prospects of a happy life.
PAPER VII [to Lovelace]	"How great must be thy condemnation."
PAPER VIII [to Lovelace]	At first Clarissa was not displeased with Lovelace. She now knows him to be vice itself.
PAPER IX [to Lovelace]	Her misery with no one to comfort her.
PAPER X [to Miss Howe]	A poem, made up of fragments of various literary works. She expects to die.

Letter 261.1	[Clarissa Harlowe] To Mr. Lovelace	[Mrs. Sinclair's] [Mrs. Sinclair's]	---

Her mind wanders. Condemnation of Lovelace. She asks to be taken to Bedlam.

Letter 262 Vol.5, Letter XXXI Vol.5, Letter XXXVII	Mr. Lovelace [Mrs. Sinclair's] To John Belford, Esq. [Watford] Clarissa has tried to escape from Mrs. Sinclair's.	Sunday afternoon, 6 o'clock (June 18)

Letter 263
Vol.5, Letter XXXII
Vol.5, Letter XXXVIII
	Mr. Lovelace [Mrs. Sinclair's]
	To John Belford, Esq. [Watford]
	    Clarissa approaches Lovelace. He is shaken by her eloquence and
	    composure.
		Sunday
		night
		Monday
		morn.
		past 3

Letter 264
Vol.5, Letter XXXIII
Vol.5, Letter XXXIX
	Mr. Lovelace [Mrs. Sinclair's]
	To John Belford, Esq. [Watford]
	    Lovelace is sleepless. He peeks through the keyhole of Clarissa's
	    door. Clarissa tries to leave. Stopped, she shouts to passers-by for
	    help. The constable is brought. Stung by her rejection, Lovelace is
	    overmatched.
		Monday
		morn.
		5 o'clock
		(June 19)

Letter 265 Vol.5, Letter XXXIV Vol.5, Letter XL	Mr. Lovelace [Mrs. Sinclair's] To John Belford, Esq. [Watford] Lord M. is ill. Clarissa agrees to see Lovelace.	---

Letter 266
Vol.5, Letter XXXV
Vol.5, Letter XLI
	Mr. Lovelace [Mrs. Sinclair's]
	To John Belford, Esq. [Watford]
	    Clarissa asks Lovelace for her freedom. He will detain her until she
	    forgives him. She questions him on the true identity of Tomlinson
	    and the impersonators of Lady Betty and Charlotte. He is evasive.
	    She will never be his and believes they will both die.
		Monday
		afternoon,
		June 19

Letter 267
Vol.5, Letter XXXVI
Vol.5, Letter XLII
	Mr. Lovelace [Mrs. Sinclair's]
	To John Belford, Esq. [Watford]
	    Clarissa begs to be a free agent. Lovelace wishes to meet her at the
	    altar. Dorcas coming into favor with Clarissa.
		--- 	
		Monday
		night

Letter 268
Vol.5, Letter XXXVII
Vol.5, Letter XLIII
	Mr. Lovelace [Mrs. Sinclair's]
	To John Belford, Esq. [Watford]
	    Still ambivalent about marriage to Clarissa, he prefers cohabitation.
	    Lovelace believes her broken heart will be mended by marriage.
	    He hopes for a boy by Clarissa, as revenge on the Harlowes.
		--- 	

Letter 269
Vol.5, Letter XXXVIII
Vol.6, Letter I
	Mr. Lovelace [Mrs. Sinclair's]
	To John Belford, Esq. [Watford]
	    Resents Clarissa's continued refusal to allow him to make amends.
	    Includes: Clarissa's promissory note to Dorcas offering her money
	    and a diamond ring to help her escape.
		Tuesday
		morn.
		June 20

Letter 270 Vol.5, Letter XXXIX Vol.6, Letter II	Mr. Lovelace [Mrs. Sinclair's] To John Belford, Esq. [Watford] Clarissa is determined to remove. Dorcas seems sympathetic.	Tuesday morn. 10 o'clock

Letter 271
Vol.5, Letter XL
Vol.6, Letter III
	Mr. Lovelace [Mrs. Sinclair's]
	To John Belford, Esq. [Watford]
	    Lovelace dreams that Dorcas helps Clarissa escape. He plots
	    another contrivance that will allow Clarissa to escape into the
	    arms of his accomplice.
		--- 	

Letter 272   Mr. Lovelace   [Mrs. Sinclair's]   Tuesday
Vol.5, Letter XLI   To John Belford, Esq.   [Watford]   night,
Vol.6, Letter IV   Lovelace has arranged for Dorcas to assist Clarissa in an escape.   June 20
                 The matronly lady will be waiting at the grocer's shop at nine.
                 Lovelace has received a letter from Tomlinson, a forgery.

Letter 272.1   'Captain Tomlinson'   ---   Monday,
                 To Robert Lovelace, Esq.   ---   June 19
                 Uncle Harlowe looks forward to meeting both Lovelace and Clarissa
                 in Kentish Town. Lovelace has not yet given up his contrivance.

Letter 273   Mr. Lovelace   [Mrs. Sinclair's]   Wed.
Vol.5, Letter XLII To John Belford, Esq.   [Watford]   noon,
Vol.6, Letter V   Clarissa does not fall for Lovelace's escape plan. Because   June 21
                 Lovelace does not know why his plan fails, the explanation is
                 given by the compiler from Clarissa's Memoranda, accounts of
                 events which she keeps until such time as she will again be able to
                 correspond with Anna. The explanation is that she doubts Dorcas.

Letter 274   Mr. Lovelace   [Mrs. Sinclair's]   Wednesday
Vol.5, Letter XLIII To John Belford, Esq.   [Watford]   afternoon
Vol.6, Letter VI   Clarissa will not forgive Lovelace and will not be his. She may seek
                 vengeance by law or through Morden. Lovelace defies both.

Letter 275   Mr. Lovelace   [Mrs. Sinclair's]   Wednesday
Vol.5, Letter XLIV To John Belford, Esq.   [Watford]   night
Vol.6, Letter VII   Lord M. is very ill. Lovelace will go to M. Hall.

Letter 275.1   Miss Howe   [Howe residence]   Tuesday,
                 To Miss Clarissa Harlowe ---   June 20
                 This letter is intercepted by Lovelace. Anna wonders why Clarissa
                 has returned to Mrs. Sinclair's, why she has not heard from Clarissa,
                 and whether Clarissa is married. She has had confusing information
                 from her tenant's son and from Mrs. Townsend.

Letter 276   Mr. Lovelace   [Mrs. Sinclair's]   Thursday
Vol.5, Letter XLV   To John Belford, Esq.   [Watford]   noon,
Vol.6, Letter VIII   Clarissa asks to be allowed to leave Mrs. Sinclair's, but Lovelace June 22
                 cannot part with her. She again tries to leave and again shouts from
                 the window for help. Lovelace thinks of revenge for his slighted love.

Letter 277   Mr. Lovelace   [Mrs. Sinclair's]   Thursday
Vol.5, Letter XLVI To John Belford, Esq.   [Watford]   night
Vol.6, Letter IX   He is afraid to leave Clarissa alone while he visits Lord M.
                 Lovelace terrifies Clarissa.

Letter 278   Mr. Lovelace   [Mrs. Sinclair's]   June 23,
Vol.5, Letter XLVII To John Belford, Esq.   [Watford]   Friday
Vol.6, Letter X   Lovelace's family sends for him to attend the dying Lord M.   morning
                 Clarissa wishes to go to Hampstead. Lovelace agrees.

Letter 279 Vol.5, Letter XLVIII Vol.6, Letter XI	Mr. Lovelace To John Belford, Esq.	[Mrs. Sinclair's] [Watford]	---

Having agreed that Clarissa may return to Hampstead, Lovelace will find pretense to detain her further. He will make a show of being angry about Clarissa's promissory note to Dorcas.

Letter 280 Vol.5, Letter XLIX Vol.6, Letter XII	Mr. Lovelace To John Belford, Esq.	[Mrs. Sinclair's] [Watford]	---

Clarissa expects to be allowed to go to Hampstead after Lovelace leaves for Berkshire. If Clarissa will not forgive him, he will make a show of anger about the promissory note. This will be Clarissa's last trial, all her senses about her. Then he will end her suffering.

Letter 281 Vol.5, Letter L Vol.6, Letter XIII	Mr. Lovelace To John Belford, Esq.	[Mrs. Sinclair's] [Watford]	Fri. night, or rather Sat. morn. 1 o'clock

Lovelace's contrivance of the promissory note prevents Clarissa from returning to Hampstead. Clarissa foils Lovelace's attempt at a second rape by threatening to end her own life.

Letter 282 Vol.5, Letter LI Vol.6, Letter XIV	Mr. Lovelace To Miss Clarissa Harlowe	M. Hall [Mrs. Sinclair's]	Sat. night, June 24

(superscribed to Mrs. Lovelace) He is sorry for his poor contrivance of the promissory note. Clarissa may not leave Mrs. Sinclair's nor correspond with anyone until Lovelace returns. He wishes to meet her at the altar on Thursday. Tomlinson will be Uncle Harlowe's proxy. Lord M. is dying.

Letter 283 Vol.5, Letter LII Vol.6, Letter XV	Mr. Lovelace To Miss Clarissa Harlowe	M. Hall [Mrs. Sinclair's]	Sunday night, June 25

Lovelace asks Clarissa's forgiveness and asks her to choose the church for next Thursday.

Letter 284 Vol.5, Letter LIII Vol.6, Letter XVI	Mr. Lovelace To Miss Clarissa Harlowe	M. Hall [Mrs. Sinclair's]	Monday, June 26

(superscribed to Mrs. Lovelace) He wishes to marry Clarissa on Thursday. Tomlinson will be Uncle Harlowe's proxy. Lovelace intercepts and returns to Clarissa hers to Anna.

Letter 285 Vol.5, Letter LIV Vol.6, Letter XVII	Mr. Lovelace To John Belford, Esq.	[M. Hall] [Watford]	Monday, June 26

Hoping Clarissa will marry him on Thursday, and hopelessly entangled in his own devices, he asks Belford to attend Clarissa and have her answer about the ceremony on Thursday. Trouble anticipated with some of Lovelace's relations upon Lord M.'s death. Lovelace hopes Lord M. will die this bout.

Letter 286 Vol.5, Letter LV Vol.6, Letter XVIII	Mr. Belford To Robert Lovelace, Esq.	London [M. Hall]	June 27. Tuesday

He refuses to assist Lovelace in another contrivance.

Letter 287
Vol.5, Letter LVI
Vol.6, Letter XIX

Mr. Lovelace   M. Hall
To John Belford, Esq.   ---
    Wanting to marry Clarissa on Thursday, before all his contrivances
    are found out, and while he is still remorseful. He will not be
    responsible for what happens if she refuse.

June 27.
Tuesday
night,
near 12

Letter 288
Vol.5, Letter LVII
Vol.6, Letter XX

Mr. Lovelace   M. Hall
To Miss Clarissa Harlowe   [Mrs. Sinclair's]
    (Superscribed to Mrs. Lovelace) Tomlinson, instead of Belford, will
    attend Clarissa. Lovelace tries to tempt Clarissa with talk of
    reconciliation with her family.

Wed.
morn.
one o'clock,
June 28

Letter 289
Vol.5, Letter LVIII
Vol.6, Letter XXI

Mr. Lovelace   M. Hall
To Patrick M'Donald   at his lodgings at Mr. Brown's,
                               perukemaker, in St. Martin's Lane,
                               Westminster
    Lovelace instructs Patrick M'Donald to attend Clarissa. He gives
    details about how M'Donald should dress and how he should behave
    to gain Clarissa's confidence.

Wed.
morning,
two o'clock,
June 28

Letter 290
Vol.5, Letter LIX
Vol.6, Letter XXII

Mr. Lovelace   M. Hall
To Captain Antony Tomlinson   ---
    This spurious letter is for Tomlinson to show Clarissa to gain her
    confidence, the Tomlinson contrivance continuing. Lord M. is ill,
    and Lovelace wishes to gratify his desire to see Clarissa as his niece.
    Mention is made of reconciliation between Clarissa and her family.

Tuesday
morn.

Letter 291
Vol.5, Letter LX
Vol.6, Letter XXIII

Patrick M'Donald   ---
To Robert Lovelace, Esq.   ---
    "The lady is gone off," and Mabel as well.

Wed.
June 28
near
12 o'clock

Letter 292
Vol.5, Letter LXI
Vol.6, Letter XXIV

Mr. Mowbray   ---
To Robert Lovelace, Esq.   [M. Hall]
    "Miss Harlowe is gon off!—Quite gon." The ladies at Mrs. Sinclair's
    are blubbering. Will is near taking his own life. Belford is serenely
    taking notes.

Wednesday,
12 o'clock

Letter 293
Vol.5, Letter LXII
Vol.6, Letter XXV

Mr. Belford   ---
To Robert Lovelace, Esq.   [M. Hall]
    Clarissa has sent Mabel to the mantua-maker's for a journeywoman
    to alter her gown for Mabel's use. As Mabel tries on the gown,
    Clarissa slips on Mabel's gown and cloak in the next room and
    escapes from Mrs. Sinclair's, Will mistaking her for Mabel.

Thursday,
June 29

Letter 294
Vol.6, Letter I
Vol.6, Letter XXVI

Mr. Lovelace   [M. Hall]
To John Belford, Esq.   [Watford]
    Ruined! Lovelace blames Clarissa for trusting him, a known rake.
    He will marry her, hoping to avoid failure of the Tomlinson
    contrivance. Lovelace is disappointed at Lord M.'s improvement.

Friday,
June 30

Letter 295
Vol.6, Letter II
Vol.6, Letter XXVII

Miss Clarissa Harlowe   [Mr. Smith's]
To Miss Howe   [Howe residence]
    She has escaped! She writes briefly to Anna to inquire about her
    health and to give her her new address.

Wednesday
night,
June 28

Letter 296	Mrs. Howe	[Howe residence]	Friday,
Vol.6, Letter III	To Miss Clarissa Harlowe	[Mr. Smith's]	June 30
Vol.6, Letter XXVIII			

Mrs. Howe answers Clarissa's Letter 295. The letter was intercepted by Mrs. Howe, as Anna was abroad when it arrived. Mrs. Howe forbids Clarissa to correspond with Anna.

Letter 297	Miss Clarissa Harlowe	[Mr. Smith's]	Saturday,
Vol.6, Letter IV	To Mrs. Howe	[Howe residence]	July 1
Vol.6, Letter XXIX			

She thanks Mrs. Howe for her just reproofs. Clarissa wants to know whether it was true, as Lovelace had said, that Anna was ill.

Letter 298	Miss Clarissa Harlowe	[Mr. Smith's]	Thursday,
Vol.6, Letter V	To Hannah Burton	[St. Albans]	June 29
Vol.6, Letter XXX			

She asks Hannah to come to her.

Letter 299	Hannah Burton	[St. Albans]	Monday,
Vol.6, Letter VI	To Miss Clarissa Harlowe	[Mr. Smith's]	July 3
Vol.6, Letter XXXI			

Hannah cannot come. She is too ill to stir from her mother's.

Letter 300	Miss Clarissa Harlowe	[Mr. Smith's]	Thursday,
Vol.6, Letter VII	To Mrs. Judith Norton	---	June 29
Vol.6, Letter XXXII			

Clarissa asks Mrs. Norton whether what Lovelace said about the family celebrating Uncle Harlowe's birthday was true, and whether it was also true that Mr. Singleton, James, and Mr. Solmes planned to take a journey together. Clarissa is concerned about her poor.

Letter 301	Mrs. Norton	---	Saturday,
Vol.6, Letter VIII	To Miss Clarissa Harlowe	[Mr. Smith's]	July 1
Vol.6, Letter XXXIII			

She reports the situation at Harlowe Place and tells her own story. Her son is ill, but she wishes to attend Clarissa and offers her money.

Letter 302	Miss Clarissa Harlowe	[Mr. Smith's]	Thursday,
Vol.6, Letter IX	To Lady Betty Lawrance	---	June 29
Vol.6, Letter XXXIV			

Clarissa queries her on Lovelace's contrivance of the impersonators. Did Lady Betty come to Hampstead?

Letter 303	Lady Betty Lawrance	---	Saturday,
Vol.6, Letter X	To Miss Clarissa Harlowe	[Mr. Smith's]	July 1
Vol.6, Letter XXXV			

She hopes Clarissa can forgive Lovelace for whatever he has done and that they will marry. Her answers to Clarissa's questions confirm Clarissa's suspicions about Lovelace's contrivances.

Letter 304	Miss Clarissa Harlowe	Enfield	June 29
Vol.6, Letter XI	To Mrs. Hodges	[Uncle Harlowe's]	
Vol.6, Letter XXXVI			

Clarissa queries Mrs. Hodges about the details of Lovelace's Tomlinson contrivance.

Letter 305	Mrs. Hodges	---	Sat.
Vol.6, Letter XII	To Miss Clarissa Harlowe	[Mr. Smith's]	July 1
Vol.6, Letter XXXVII			

Uncle Harlowe has not kept his birthday and knows no Tomlinson.

Letter 306	Miss Clarissa Harlowe	[Mr. Smith's]	Monday,
Vol.6, Letter XIII	To Lady Betty Lawrance	---	July 3
Vol.6, Letter XXXVIII			

Clarissa relates the particulars of her story.

Letter 307   Miss Clarissa Harlowe   [Mr. Smith's]   Sunday
Vol.6, Letter XIV   To Mrs. Norton   ---   evening,
Vol.6, Letter XXXIX   Clarissa asks Mrs. Norton not to come, as Lovelace may discover   July 2
     her whereabouts. Her main concern now is her father's curse.

Letter 308   Mrs. Norton   ---   Monday
Vol.6, Letter XV   To Miss Clarissa Harlowe   [Mr. Smith's]   night,
Vol.6, Letter XL   Miss Howe has been railing against the Harlowe Family. She   July 3
     comforts Clarissa. Her son, Tommy, has a violent fever.

Letter 309   Miss Clarissa Harlowe   [Mr. Smith's]   Thursday,
Vol.6, Letter XVI   To Mrs. Judith Norton   ---   July 6
Vol.6, Letter XLI   Clarissa has received a severe letter from Anna. Clarissa's goal is
     reconciliation with her family, but she has little hope. She will
     apply to Arabella.

Letter 310   Miss Howe   [Howe residence]   Wednesday,
Vol.6, Letter XVII   To Miss Clarissa Harlowe   [Mr. Smith's]   July 5
Vol.6, Letter XLII   Mrs. Howe confiscated Clarissa's letter but allows Anna to answer it.
     Anna tells Clarissa that she wrote three letters and wonders whether
     they were received.

Letter 311   Miss Clarissa Harlowe   [Mr. Smith's]   Thursday,
Vol.6, Letter XVIII   To Miss Howe   [Howe residence]   July 6
Vol.6, Letter XLIII   Clarissa will write in more detail in her next. She encloses, for Anna
     to see, Letter 239.1 (Anna's Letter 229.1 as rewritten by Lovelace).
     She does not remember receiving the other letters mentioned by Anna.

Letter 312   Miss Clarissa Harlowe   [Mr. Smith's]   Thursday
Vol.6, Letter XIX   To Miss Howe   [Howe residence]   night
Vol.6, Letter XLIV   Clarissa does not understand how Lovelace found her at Hampstead.
     She relates how the impersonators of Lady Betty and Charlotte
     Montague persuaded her to return to Mrs. Sinclair's.

Letter 313   Miss Clarissa Harlowe   [Mr. Smith's]   ---
Vol.6, Letter XX   To Miss Howe   [Howe residence]
Vol.6, Letter XLV   Clarissa recounts how she was tricked into returning to London.

Letter 314   Miss Clarissa Harlowe   [Mr. Smith's]   ---
Vol.6, Letter XXI   To Miss Howe   [Howe residence]
Vol.6, Letter XLVI   Continues the story of the impersonators and her return to London.

Letter 315   Miss Clarissa Harlowe   [Mr. Smith's]   Saturday,
Vol.6, Letter XXII   To Miss Howe   [Howe residence]   July 8
Vol.6, Letter XLVII   (in continuation) Continuing her story, she requests that Anna and
     Mrs. Howe keep secret all that she tells them as she could not bear
     to appear in court to prosecute Lovelace.

Letter 316   Miss Howe   [Howe residence]   Sunday,
Vol.6, Letter XXIII   To Miss Clarissa Harlowe   [Mr. Smith's]   July 9
Vol.6, Letter XLVIII   She confirms that Letter 239.1 of June 7th was a forgery. She rails
     against Lovelace and the Harlowes.

Letter 317 Vol.6, Letter XXIV Vol.6, Letter XLIX	Miss Howe To Miss Clarissa Harlowe	[Howe residence] [Mr. Smith's]	Monday, July 10
	Mrs. Howe wants Clarissa to prosecute Lovelace, even making it a precondition for her reconciling Clarissa with her family and allowing Anna to correspond with Clarissa.		
Letter 318 Vol.6, Letter XXV Vol.6, Letter L	Miss Clarissa Harlowe To Miss Howe	[Mr. Smith's] [Howe residence]	Tuesday, July 11
	Her health is declining. She has written to Miss Rawlins to inform her and to settle her account with Mrs. Moore.		
Letter 319 Vol.6, Letter XXVI Vol.6, Letter LI	Miss Howe To Miss Clarissa Harlowe	[Howe residence] [Mr. Smith's]	Wedn. night, July 12
	Encourages Clarissa not to be dejected. Morden will soon arrive. Hickman could attend Clarissa, but he is probably watched by Lovelace, as is Anna.		
Letter 320 Vol.6, Letter XXVII Vol.6, Letter LII	Miss Clarissa Harlowe To Miss Howe	[Mr. Smith's] [Howe residence]	Thursday, July 13
	Clarissa will prosecute Lovelace if he harms Anna or Hickman. She tells Anna about her lodgings at Smith's.		
Letter 321 Vol.6, Letter XXVIII Vol.6, Letter LIII	Mr. Lovelace To John Belford, Esq.	[M. Hall] ---	Friday, July 7
	Grieving over the loss of Clarissa, Lovelace has his emissaries searching for her. He continues to attend the failing Lord M.		
Letter 322 Vol.6, Letter XXIX Vol.6, Letter LIV	Mr. Lovelace To John Belford, Esq.	[M. Hall] ---	Six Sat. morning, July 8
	He still attends Lord M. He visits Colonel Ambrose and his nieces. He considers seducing the Colonel's nieces as well as his own cousins.		
Letter 323 Vol.6, Letter XXX Vol.6, Letter LV	Mr. Lovelace To John Belford, Esq.	[M. Hall] ---	Sunday night, July 9
	Lovelace's trial. He is questioned by Lady Betty, Lady Sarah, his cousins, and Lord M., on account of Clarissa's letter to Lady Betty.		
Letter 324 Vol.6, Letter XXXI Vol.6, Letter LVI	Mr. Lovelace To John Belford, Esq.	[M. Hall] ---	---
	(in continuation) His trial continues. Is he willing to marry Clarissa?		
Letter 325 Vol.6, Letter XXXII Vol.6, Letter LVII	Mr. Lovelace To John Belford, Esq.	[M. Hall] ---	---
	Charlotte Montague will visit Miss Howe and try, with her cooperation, to arrange a reconciliation between Clarissa and Lovelace. Rich gifts from Lovelace's family for Clarissa's wedding. The trial ends on a happy note. Lovelace's word is comedy.		
Letter 326 Vol.6, Letter XXXIII Vol.6, Letter LVIII	Mr. Lovelace To John Belford, Esq.	[M. Hall] ---	Wed. July 12
	Miss Howe and Hickman should fear vengeance from Lovelace. Lovelace asks Belford to return his, Lovelace's, letters. His cousins Montague will visit Miss Howe tomorrow.		

Letter 327 Vol.6, Letter XXXIV Vol.6, Letter LIX	Miss Howe To Miss Clarissa Harlowe	[Howe residence] [Mr. Smith's]	Thursday night, July 13
	Misses Montague visit Anna saying Lovelace is reformed and prepared to marry Clarissa. Anna advises Clarissa to put herself into Lady Betty's protection and say no more about what is past.		
Letter 328 Vol.6, Letter XXXV Vol.6, Letter LX	Miss Howe To Miss Clarissa Harlowe	[Howe residence] [Mr. Smith's]	Sunday night, July 16
	She worries that she has not heard from Clarissa. Anna is eager for Clarissa to put herself into the protection of Lady Betty and marry Lovelace.		
Letter 329 Vol.6, Letter XXXVI Vol.6, Letter LXI	Miss Howe To Miss Charlotte Montague	[Howe residence] [M. Hall]	Tuesday morning, July 18
	Clarissa is missing from her lodgings at Smith's.		
Letter 330 Vol.6, Letter XXXVII Vol.6, Letter LXII	Mr. Lovelace To John Belford, Esq.	[M. Hall] [Edgware]	Sat. night, July 15
	Clarissa was found out by Sally Martin, who had her arrested on the pretense that she bilked her lodgings at Mrs. Sinclair's. Lovelace sends Belford to set Clarissa free.		
Letter 331 Vol.6, Letter XXXVIII Vol.6, Letter LXIII	Miss Charlotte Montague To Miss Howe	M. Hall [Howe residence]	Tuesday afternoon
	She believes Clarissa's arrest was a mistake.		
Letter 332 Vol.6, Letter XXXIX Vol.6, Letter LXIV	Miss Montague To Miss Howe	M. Hall [Howe residence]	July 18
	They have received news of Clarissa's arrest and heard the story reported by Lovelace. Details from Belford soon forthcoming.		
Letter 332.1	Lady Sarah Sadleir To Anna Howe	[M. Hall] [Howe residence]	---
	She believes Clarissa's arrest was an accident.		
Letter 332.2	Lovelace To Anna Howe	[M. Hall] [Howe residence]	Tuesday, July 18
	His fate, church or gallows, he leaves up to Clarissa.		
Letter 333 Vol.6, Letter XL Vol.6, Letter LXV	Mr. Belford To Robert Lovelace, Esq.	--- M. Hall	Sunday night, July 16
	His report to Lovelace of Clarissa's arrest, as he has heard it from Mrs. Sinclair and her whores.		
Letter 334 Vol.6, Letter XLI Vol.6, Letter LXVI	Mr. Belford To Robert Lovelace, Esq.	--- [M. Hall]	Monday, July 17
	Belford visits Clarissa in her prison-room at Rowland's. She asks him to sell her valuables and pay her debts. She prefers to stay at Rowland's and die there.		
Letter 335 Vol.6, Letter XLII Vol.6, Letter LXVII	Mr. Lovelace To John Belford, Esq.	[M. Hall] ---	Monday, July 17, eleven at night
	His anguish at not being told the outcome of Clarissa's arrest. Belford ends the letter leaving Lovelace in tortured suspense.		

Letter 336 Vol.6, Letter XLIII Vol.6, Letter LXVIII	Mr. Belford --- To Robert Lovelace, Esq. [M. Hall] He persuades Clarissa to return to Smith's.	Monday night, July 17
Letter 337 Vol.6, Letter XLIV Vol.6, Letter LXIX	Mr. Belford --- To Robert Lovelace, Esq. [M. Hall] He assures Clarissa that Lovelace will not visit her.	Tuesday morn. (July 18) 6 o'clock
Letter 338 Vol.6, Letter XLV Vol.6, Letter LXX	Mr. Belford --- To Robert Lovelace, Esq. [M. Hall] Clarissa's weak condition. Belford cautions Lovelace not to visit.	Tuesday, July 18, afternoon
Letter 339 Vol.6, Letter XLVI Vol.6, Letter LXXI	Mr. Belford --- To Robert Lovelace, Esq. [M. Hall] Belford relates his visit to Clarissa and her chastisement of him.	Tuesday night, July 18

Letter 340
Vol.6, Letter XLVII
Vol.6, Letter LXXII
	Mr. Belford ---
	To Robert Lovelace, Esq. [M. Hall]
	    Dr. H. is called to visit Clarissa and pronounces her a love case.
	    Clarissa asks Mrs. Smith to sell her clothes.
		Wednesday,
		July 19

Letter 341 Vol.6, Letter XLVIII Vol.6, Letter LXXIII	Mr. Lovelace [M. Hall] To John Belford, Esq. --- Hickman asks to meet with Lovelace. Lovelace hopes Lord M. will not live much longer. He asks about Belton and feels occasional qualms about Clarissa—but will make amends.	Wed. night, July 19
Letter 342 Vol.6, Letter XLIX Vol.6, Letter LXXIV	Miss Howe [Howe residence] To Miss Clarissa Harlowe [Mr. Smith's] Encouraging Clarissa not to despond but to marry Lovelace. She must soon visit her Aunt Harman in the Isle of Wight.	Thursday morn. July 20
Letter 343 Vol.6, Letter L Vol.6, Letter LXXV	Miss Clarissa Harlowe [Mr. Smith's] To Miss Howe [Howe residence] She will not marry Lovelace. She describes herself as being on a long journey.	Thursday afternoon
Letter 344 Vol.6, Letter LI Vol.6, Letter LXXVI	Mr. Belford --- To Robert Lovelace, Esq. [M. Hall] Belton's story. Belford wishes to marry and desert Lovelace and his friends for a better life.	Thursday, July 20
Letter 345 Vol.6, Letter LII Vol.6, Letter LXXVII	Mr. Belford --- To Robert Lovelace, Esq. [M. Hall] Mrs. Lovick has sold some of Clarissa's lace to pay her doctor's fee.	Thursday night
Letter 346 Vol.6, Letter LIII Vol.6, Letter LXXVIII	Mr. Lovelace M. Hall To John Belford, Esq. --- Hickman interviews Lovelace to determine whether he intends to marry Clarissa. He would marry her but fears she is now courting Death.	Friday, July 21

Letter 347	Mr. Lovelace	[M. Hall]	Friday
Vol.6, Letter LIV	To John Belford, Esq.	---	night,
Vol.6, Letter LXXIX	Concerned that Clarissa has sold her clothes. As to Belton's declining state, he is still welcome to visit Lovelace. Lovelace offers to take Thomasine and hers on a boat trip and drown them.		July 21

Letter 348	Mr. Belford	---	Friday
Vol.6, Letter LV	To Robert Lovelace, Esq.	[M. Hall]	noon,
Vol.6, Letter LXXX	Clarissa writes to Arabella asking Papa to revoke his curse. If Papa can forgive her, she can learn to forgive Lovelace.		July 21

Letter 349	Mr. Belford	---	---
Vol.6, Letter LVI	To Robert Lovelace, Esq.	[M. Hall]	
Vol.6, Letter LXXXI	He offers to be Clarissa's banker. Clarissa tells her story to the Smiths and Mrs. Lovick with Belford present. She welcomes death.		

Letter 350	Mr. Lovelace	[M. Hall]	Sat.
Vol.6, Letter LVII	To John Belford, Esq.	---	July 22
Vol.6, Letter LXXXII	Lovelace will attend a ball at Colonel Ambrose's. Mrs. Howe, Miss Howe, and Hickman will also attend. Lovelace's cousins Montague refuse to accompany him.		

Letter 351	Miss Howe	[Howe residence]	Thursday,
Vol.6, Letter LVIII	To Miss Arabella Harlowe	[Harlowe Place]	July 20
Vol.6, Letter LXXXIII	Advising her that Clarissa is very ill, that she has lodgings at Smith's, and that her father's imprecation is affecting her badly in her already weakened state.		

Letter 352	Miss Arabella Harlowe	[Harlowe Place]	Thursday,
Vol.6, Letter LIX	To Miss Anna Howe	[Howe residence]	July 20
Vol.6, Letter LXXXIV	Her indifference to Clarissa's state. Let Lovelace be her comfort. The family do not believe Lovelace will marry Clarissa.		

Letter 353	Miss Howe	[Howe residence]	Friday,
Vol.6, Letter LX	To Miss Arabella Harlowe	[Harlowe Place]	July 21
Vol.6, Letter LXXXV	She answers in a pert tone that Arabella has less sense than ill-nature and that her own kind intentions have been misunderstood.		

Letter 354	Miss Arabella Harlowe	[Harlowe Place]	Friday,
Vol.6, Letter LXI	To Miss Howe	[Howe residence]	July 21
Vol.6, Letter LXXXVI	She accuses Anna of influencing Clarissa to run away.		

Letter 355	Miss Howe	[Howe residence]	Sat.
Vol.6, Letter LXII	To Miss Arabella Harlowe	[Harlowe Place]	July 22
Vol.6, Letter LXXXVII	She blames James and Arabella for the family's loss of Clarissa.		

Letter 356	Mrs. Harlowe	[Harlowe Place]	Sat.
Vol.6, Letter LXIII	To Mrs. Howe	[Howe residence]	July 22
Vol.6, Letter LXXXVIII	Complaining of Anna's letters to Arabella.		

Letter 357 Vol.6, Letter LXIV Vol.6, Letter LXXXIX	Mrs. Howe To Mrs. Harlowe	[Howe residence] [Harlowe Place]	Sat. July 22

She apologizes for Anna's letters, noting also that Clarissa is very ill. But parental forgiveness is, of course, the Harlowes' decision. Mrs. Howe and Anna will set out soon for the Isle of Wight, partly to take Anna's mind off Clarissa's sufferings.

Letter 358 Vol.6, Letter LXV Vol.6, Letter XC	Miss Howe To Miss Clarissa Harlowe	[Howe residence] [Mr. Smith's]	Sat. July 22

Her concern for Clarissa's health. She must attend Colonel Ambrose's ball, set for his wife's, and, coincidentally, Clarissa's, birthday. Both Mrs. Howe and Anna hope that Clarissa will marry Lovelace.

Letter 359 Vol.6, Letter LXVI Vol.6, Letter XCI	Miss Clarissa Harlowe To Miss Howe	[Mr. Smith's] [Howe residence]	Sunday, July 23

Her detailed explanation for not marrying Lovelace, the main point being his faulty morals. Her expectation that she will not live long.

Letter 360 Vol.6, Letter LXVII Vol.6, Letter XCII	Miss Clarissa Harlowe To Miss Howe	[Mr. Smith's] [Howe residence]	Sunday, July 23

She asks Anna not to take liberties with her family and hopes Mrs. Howe will allow their correspondence to continue for at least one more month. She hopes for a visit from Hickman.

Letter 361 Vol.6, Letter LXVIII Vol.6, Letter XCIII	Mrs. Norton To Miss Clarissa Harlowe	--- [Mr. Smith's]	Monday, July 24

Anna's angry letters have incensed the Harlowe Family. Mrs. Norton cannot attend Clarissa because both she and her son are in very bad health. She wishes Clarissa no more unhappy birthdays.

Letter 362 Vol.6, Letter LXIX Vol.6, Letter XCIV	Miss Clarissa Harlowe To Mrs. Norton	[Mr. Smith's] ---	Monday night, July 24

She tells Mrs. Norton about her arrest, which prevented her from writing sooner. She is now in comfortable enough circumstances. She has asked Anna not to take such liberties with her family.

Letter 363 Vol.6, Letter LXX Vol.6, Letter XCV	Miss Clarissa Harlowe To Miss Arabella Harlowe	[Mr. Smith's] [Harlowe Place]	Friday, July 21

She asks Arabella to intercede for her and ask Papa to revoke the part of his curse which relates to the hereafter as she has already been punished the here.

Letter 364 Vol.6, Letter LXXI Vol.6, Letter XCVI	Mr. Belford To Robert Lovelace, Esq.	Edgware [M. Hall]	Monday, July 24

He is keeping poor Belton company. He encloses Clarissa's meditation and expounds on the nature of man and his own admiration for the Bible.

Letter 365 Vol.6, Letter LXXII Vol.6, Letter XCVII	Mr. Belford To Robert Lovelace, Esq.	--- [M. Hall]	Wednesday, July 26

He relates his visit to Clarissa. She asks him to return to Lovelace all their correspondence, his to her and hers to him. Hickman visits Clarissa and is affected by her changed appearance.

Letter 366
Vol.6, Letter LXXIII
Vol.6, Letter XCVIII

Mr. Belford   ---   Thursday,
To Robert Lovelace, Esq.   [M. Hall]   July 27
    Clarissa breakfasts with Hickman and Belford. She gives her
    blessing to Anna and Hickman. Hickman fears he will never see
    Clarissa again.

Letter 367
Vol.6, Letter LXXIV
Vol.6, Letter XCIX

Miss Howe   [Howe residence]   Tuesday,
To Miss Clarissa Harlowe   [Mr. Smith's]   July 25
    She gives an account of Colonel Ambrose's ball and her interview
    with Lovelace.

Letter 368
Vol.6, Letter LXXV
Vol.6, Letter C

Miss Clarissa Harlowe   [Mr. Smith's]   Thursday,
To Miss Howe   [Howe residence]   July 27
    She thanks her for sending Hickman and asks Anna to send her
    refusal of Lovelace to the ladies of his family.

Letter 369
Vol.6, Letter LXXVI
Vol.6, Letter CI

Miss Clarissa Harlowe   [Mr. Smith's]   Thursday,
To Miss Howe   [Howe residence]   July 27
    She will not marry Lovelace but will forgive him if he promises
    not to molest her further.

Letter 370
Vol.6, Letter LXXVII
Vol.7, Letter I

Mr. Lovelace   [M. Hall]   Friday,
To John Belford, Esq.   ---   July 28
    If Belford cannot influence Clarissa in his favor, Lovelace will
    disguise himself and contrive to see her himself. "All my vice is
    women, and the love of plots and intrigues."

Letter 371
Vol.6, Letter LXXVIII
Vol.7, Letter II

Mr. Lovelace   [M. Hall]   ---
To John Belford, Esq.   ---
    Tired of his family and friends at M. Hall, he will go to town for
    an interview with Clarissa.

Letter 372
Vol.6, Letter LXXIX
Vol.7, Letter III

Miss Howe   [Howe residence]   Friday
To Miss Clarissa Harlowe   [Mr. Smith's]   night,
    Her thoughts on years and wisdom, husbands and their prerogatives.   July 28
    She hopes to visit Clarissa after her return from the Isle of Wight.
    Anna and Mrs Howe favor publishing Clarissa's tragical story.

Letter 373
Vol.6, Letter LXXX
Vol.7, Letter IV

Miss Howe   [Howe residence]   Sat.
To The Two Misses Montague   ---   July 29
    She forwards to them Clarissa's refusal of Lovelace.

Letter 374
Vol.6, Letter LXXXI
Vol.7, Letter V

Mrs. Norton   ---   Friday,
To Miss Clarissa Harlowe   [Mr. Smith's]   July 28
    Mrs. Norton and Tommy are both recovering. Betty Barnes has told
    Mrs. Norton that Clarissa's letter to Arabella was not well received.

Letter 375
Vol.6, Letter LXXXII
Vol.7, Letter VI

Mrs. Norton   ---   Friday,
To Mrs. Harlowe   [Harlowe Place]   July 28
    She tells Mrs. Harlowe that Clarissa has refused Lovelace though
    his family favored the marriage. She also says, in an effort to bring
    about reconciliation, that Clarissa believes she will not live long
    and would not give a husband the right to interfere with her estate.

Letter 376 Vol.6, Letter LXXXIII Vol.7, Letter VII	Mrs. Harlowe To Mrs. Norton	[Harlowe Place] ---	Sunday, July 30
	She fears that Clarissa may be pregnant. She is unable to oppose the rest of the family but may visit Mrs. Norton where she can read Clarissa's letter.		
Letter 377 Vol.6, Letter LXXXIV Vol.7, Letter VIII	Miss Clarissa Harlowe To Mrs. Judith Norton	[Mr. Smith's] ---	Sat. July 29
	Papa's malediction has been withdrawn. She asks Mrs. Norton not to intercede on her behalf with her family. She awaits Morden.		
Letter 378 Vol.6, Letter LXXXV Vol.7, Letter IX	Miss Arabella Harlowe To Miss Clarissa Harlowe	[Harlowe Place] [Mr. Smith's]	Thursday, July 27
	In a very severe letter, she says that Papa's curse is withdrawn. Why has Lovelace abandoned Clarissa? Morden is expected daily.		
Letter 379 Vol.6, Letter LXXXVI Vol.7, Letter X	Miss Clarissa Harlowe To Miss Howe	[Mr. Smith's] [Howe residence]	Sunday, July 30
	Clarissa will ask Belford to be her executor. He will be in no danger from Lovelace, nor will he be intimidated by Lovelace nor the Harlowes. Clarissa may then come by Lovelace's correspondence and find out how he planned her ruin.		
Letter 380 Vol.6, Letter LXXXVII Vol.7, Letter XI	Miss Clarissa Harlowe To Miss Harlowe	[Mr. Smith's] [Harlowe Place]	Saturday, July 29
	She asks her parents' last blessing.		
Letter 381 Vol.6, Letter LXXXVIII Vol.7, Letter XII	Mrs. Norton To Miss Clarissa Harlowe	--- [Mr. Smith's]	Monday, July 31
	Mrs. Norton will not interfere with any efforts at reconciliation between Clarissa and her family. Uncle Harlowe is sending Mr. Brand to inquire about Clarissa. Mrs. Norton does not like Mr. Brand. She sends Clarissa money.		
Letter 382 Vol.6, Letter LXXXIX Vol.7, Letter XIII	Miss Clarissa Harlowe To Mrs. Norton	[Mr. Smith's] ---	Wednesday, Aug. 2
	Clarissa wants her family's blessing before she dies. She asks Mrs. Norton not to visit her as it would distress the family. Clarissa expects Mr. Brand to report nothing to the family that they do not wish to hear.		
Letter 383 Vol.6, Letter XC Vol.7, Letter XIV	Mr. Lovelace To John Belford, Esq.	[M. Hall] ---	Tuesday, Aug. 1
	Though he has received his final rejection from Clarissa, he plans to visit her and bring with him a parson to marry them.		
Letter 384 Vol.6, Letter XCI Vol.7, Letter XV	Miss Montague To Miss Clarissa Harlowe	[M. Hall] [Mr. Smith's]	Tuesday, Aug. 1
	She asks Clarissa to marry Lovelace and make his family happy. They would make reparations for Clarissa's injuries.		

Letter 385   Mr. Belford   ---   Thursday

Vol.6, Letter XCII   To Robert Lovelace, Esq.   [M. Hall]   morning,

Vol.7, Letter XVI   His own affairs now in order, he will go to Epsom to take care of   Aug. 3,

Belton's. Then he can turn his attention to Lovelace and Clarissa.   six o'clock

He asks Lovelace not to molest Clarissa further.

Letter 386   Miss Clarissa Harlowe   [Mr. Smith's]   Thursday,

Vol.6, Letter XCIII   To Miss Montague   [M. Hall]   Aug. 3

Vol.7, Letter XVII   She asks Lovelace's family to prevail on him not to molest her.

She wishes to die in peace, wishing him also a peaceable and

happy end.

Letter 387   Mr. Belford   ---   Thursday

Vol.6, Letter XCIV   To Robert Lovelace, Esq.   [M. Hall]   afternoon,

Vol.7, Letter XVIII   Clarissa's absolute rejection of Lovelace.   Aug. 3

Letter 387.1   Miss Clarissa Harlowe   [Mr. Smith's]   Aug. 3

To John Belford, Esq.   ---

She asks Belford for two favors: first, that he give her copies

of Lovelace's correspondence, especially in regard to the fire at

Mrs. Sinclair's, and second, that he agree to be her executor.

Letter 388   Mr. Belford   ---   Aug. 3, 4

Vol.6, Letter XCV   To Miss Clarissa Harlowe   [Mr. Smith's]

Vol.7, Letter XIX   Belford sends Clarissa extracts from Lovelace's letters from about

the time she was at Hampstead.

Letter 389   Miss Clarissa Harlowe   [Mr. Smith's]   Friday,

Vol.6, Letter XCVI   To John Belford, Esq.   ---   Aug. 4

Vol.7, Letter XX   She thanks Belford for the extracts and asks him to be her executor.

Letter 390   Mr. Belford   ---   Friday,

Vol.6, Letter XCVII   To Miss Clarissa Harlowe   [Mr. Smith's]   Aug. 4

Vol.7, Letter XXI   He accepts the executorship.

Letter 391   Mr. Belford   ---   Friday

Vol.6, Letter XCVIII To Robert Lovelace, Esq.   [M. Hall]   night,

Vol.7, Letter XXII   He tells Lovelace that Clarissa will use extracts from his letters   Aug. 4

to tell her story, and that Belford will be her executor.   Saturday

morning,

Aug. 5

Letter 392   Miss Arabella Harlowe   [Harlowe Place]   Thursday

Vol.6, Letter XCIX   To Miss Clarissa Harlowe   [Mr. Smith's]   morn.

Vol.7, Letter XXIII   She asks Clarissa not to write any more letters. The family is   Aug. 3

disgraced and unwilling to forgive Clarissa.

Letter 393   Miss Clarissa Harlowe   [Mr. Smith's]   Sat.

Vol.6, Letter C   To Her Mother   [Harlowe Place]   Aug. 5

Vol.7, Letter XXIV   She tells Mamma that she had determined not to go off with

Lovelace. She asks her blessing and forgiveness.

Letter 394 Vol.6, Letter CI Vol.7, Letter XXV	Miss Montague To Miss Clarissa Harlowe	[M. Hall] [Mr. Smith's]	Monday, Aug. 7

Lord M has banished Lovelace. His family offers Clarissa one hundred guineas *per* quarter for life. Lovelace is preparing to go abroad. The letter is signed by Lady Sarah, Lady Betty, and the Montagues.

Letter 395 Vol.6, Letter CII Vol.7, Letter XXVI	Mr. Lovelace To John Belford, Esq.	[M. Hall] ---	Sat. Aug. 5

Lovelace is anathematized and shunned by his family. Clarissa has power over him by her rejection. Lovelace will see Clarissa or avenge himself on Miss Howe then quit the kingdom forever.

Letter 396 Vol.6, Letter CIII Vol.7, Letter XXVII	Mr. Lovelace To John Belford, Esq.	[M. Hall] ---	Monday, Aug. 7

Belford has broken a confidence in giving the extracts to Clarissa. With increasingly violent expression Lovelace demands that Belford not be Clarissa's executor. If Clarissa reject him, he will set fire to that den of serpents, Mrs. Sinclair's.

Letter 397 Vol.6, Letter CIV Vol.7, Letter XXVIII	Mr. Lovelace To Miss Clarissa Harlowe	[M. Hall] [Mr. Smith's]	Monday, Aug. 7

He talks of forgiveness and reformation and marriage. He cautions Clarissa that her refusal will make him desperate. He will not forgive his family for presuming to control him.

Letter 398 Vol.6, Letter CV Vol.7, Letter XXIX	Miss Clarissa Harlowe To Lord M. and the Ladies of His House	[Mr. Smith's] [M. Hall]	Tuesday, Aug. 8

Clarissa fears that banishment by his family him will put him under less restraint. She asks his family to forgive him and share her hopes for his reformation.

Letter 399 Vol.6, Letter CVI Vol.7, Letter XXX	Mr. Belford To Robert Lovelace, Esq.	--- [M. Hall]	Thursday night, Aug. 10

Belford has put Thomasine and hers out of Belton's house. Clarissa's Meditation. Mr. Brand visits Mrs. Smith but does not see Clarissa. His indifference to Clarissa's health.

Letter 400 Vol.6, Letter CVII Vol.7, Letter XXXI	Mr. Belford To Robert Lovelace, Esq.	--- [M. Hall]	Friday, Aug. 11

The compiler summarizes most of this letter and quotes part. Clarissa at eighteen years was enabled by her grandfather to make her will. She resolves to do so.

Letter 401 Vol.6, Letter CVIII Vol.7, Letter XXXII	Miss Clarissa Harlowe To Robert Lovelace, Esq.	[Mr. Smith's] [M. Hall]	Friday, Aug. 11

She writes, briefly, as she must choose between writing and being visited by Lovelace. She forgives him but will not see him.

Letter 402 Vol.6, Letter CIX Vol.7, Letter XXXIII	Mr. John Harlowe To Miss Clarissa Harlowe	--- [Mr. Smith's]	Monday, Aug. 7

He upbraids Clarissa and asks whether she is with child. Her Meditation is stitched to the bottom of this letter in black silk.

461

Letter 403   Miss Clarissa Harlowe   [Mr. Smith's]   Thursday,
Vol.6, Letter CX   To John Harlowe, Esq.   ---   Aug. 10
Vol.7, Letter XXXIV   She asks a last blessing, as much for her parents sake as for her
own, that she may die in peace.

Letter 404   Miss Anna Howe   Yarmouth, Isle of Wight   Monday,
Vol.6, Letter CXI   To Miss Clarissa Harlowe   [Mr. Smith's]   Aug. 7
Vol.7, Letter XXXV   She hopes to read some of Clarissa's letters and wishes to hear of
Clarissa's improved health.

Letter 405   Miss Clarissa Harlowe   [Mr. Smith's]   Friday,
Vol.6, Letter CXII   To Miss Howe   [Yarmouth, Isle of Wight]   Aug. 11
Vol.7, Letter XXXVI   She sends Anna a large packet of letters to read along with a list of
the specific letters enclosed.

Letter 406   Mr. Antony Harlowe   ---   Aug. 12
Vol.6, Letter CXIII   To Miss Clarissa Harlowe   [Mr. Smith's]
Vol.7, Letter XXXVII   He accuses Clarissa of free living with Lovelace and asks whether
she is with child. She may be allowed to have some part of her estate.

Letter 407   Miss Clarissa Harlowe   [Mr. Smith's]   Sunday,
Vol.6, Letter CXIV   To Antony Harlowe, Esq.   ---   Aug. 13
Vol.7, Letter XXXVIII   Impatient in tone she reiterates that all she asks for is a last blessing.
She prays for protection for James from himself and from Lovelace
as well as for the happiness of her uncles.

Letter 408   Mrs. Norton   ---   Monday,
Vol.6, Letter CXV   To Miss Clarissa Harlowe   [Mr. Smith's]   Aug. 14
Vol.7, Letter XXXIX   The Harlowe Family prohibit Mrs Norton from attending Clarissa.
James has offended Dr. Lewen, who expressed disapproval of the
family's treatment of Clarissa. Morden has arrived in England.

Letter 409   Miss Clarissa Harlowe   [Mr. Smith's]   Thursday,
Vol.6, Letter CXVI   To Mrs. Norton   ---   Aug. 17
Vol.7, Letter XL   Clarissa will send Mrs. Norton a packet of letters that she dare not
show Anna. The letters will help tell her story. Clarissa fears that
Morden will avenge her.

Letter 410   Mr. Lovelace   [M. Hall]   Sunday,
Vol.6, Letter CXVII   To John Belford, Esq.   ---   Aug. 13
Vol.7, Letter XLI   Lovelace has been quite ill but will visit Clarissa when he recovers.

Letter 411   Mr. Belford   ---   Monday,
Vol.6, Letter CXVIII   To Robert Lovelace, Esq.   [M. Hall]   Aug. 14
Vol.7, Letter XLII   Sorry that Lovelace is ill, he nevertheless opines that if Lovelace is
to die, better he had died last April.

Letter 412   Mr. Lovelace   [M. Hall]   Tuesday,
Vol.6, Letter CXIX   To John Belford, Esq.   ---   Aug. 15
Vol.7, Letter XLIII   Almost recovered, he is determined not to lose Clarissa.

Letter 413 Vol.6, Letter CXX Vol.7, Letter XLIV	Mr. Belford --- To Robert Lovelace, Esq. [M. Hall] Treatment of virtue, vice, pride, and penitence in Restoration drama, summing up the case of Clarissa by way of illustration. Belford again asks Lovelace not to visit Clarissa. Belford must go to Belton who is at death's door.	Thursday, Aug. 17
Letter 414 Vol.6, Letter CXXI Vol.7, Letter XLV	Mr. Belford --- To Miss Clarissa Harlowe [Mr. Smith's] He warns Clarissa that Lovelace, recently recovered from a dangerous fever, may try to visit her.	Sat. morn. Aug. 19
Letter 415 Vol.6, Letter CXXII Vol.7, Letter XLVI	Mr. Lovelace [M. Hall] To John Belford, Esq. --- Lovelace intends to visit Clarissa as soon as he is well enough. He believes Morden is also a rake. He believes that neither Belton nor Clarissa is near death. He reminds Belford of his disloyalty in giving extracts of his letters to Clarissa.	Sunday, Aug. 20
Letter 416 Vol.6, Letter CXXIII Vol.7, Letter XLVII	Mr. Lovelace London To John Belford, Esq. --- Lovelace visits Smith's, where he exercises his privilege as a gentleman and abuses the shop owners, servants, and customers. He returns to Mrs. Sinclair's where he alarms the household.	Aug. 21 Monday
Letter 417 Vol.6, Letter CXXIV Vol.7, Letter XLVIII	Mr. Lovelace [Mrs. Sinclair's] To John Belford, Esq. --- Lovelace dreams that his family has interceded and Clarissa has forgiven him. Morden threatens him. Clarissa then ascends into Heaven and Lovelace drops into a hole.	Thursday, Aug. 22
Letter 418 Vol.6, Letter CXX[V] Vol.7, Letter XLIX	Mr. Lovelace [Mrs. Sinclair's] To John Belford, Esq. --- Lovelace returns to Smith's, believing that Clarissa has returned. Not finding her, he continues to hunt her at Lincoln's Inn chapel.	--- Monday, Aug. 21
Letter 419 Vol.7, Letter I Vol.7, Letter L	Mr. Belford --- To Robert Lovelace, Esq. [Mrs. Sinclair's] Belford comforts the dying Belton. Mowbray is unsympathetic. Belford fears Lovelace will try to visit Clarissa.	Tuesday, Aug. 22
Letter 420 Vol.7, Letter II Vol.7, Letter LI	Mr. Belford --- To Robert Lovelace, Esq. [Mrs. Sinclair's] Belford's and Mowbray's treatment of drunken and forgetful servants. Belford asks Lovelace to visit the dying Belton.	Wednesday morn. 11 o'clock
Letter 421 Vol.7, Letter III Vol.7, Letter LII	Mr. Lovelace [Mrs. Sinclair's] To John Belford, Esq. --- He has received a letter from Clarissa saying that she is returning to her father's house and may see him there. A forgery?	Wednesday morn. Aug. 23
Letter 421.1	[Clarissa Harlowe] [Mr. Smith's] To Robert Lovelace, Esq. [Mrs. Sinclair's] Clarissa "setting out with all diligence for my father's house." A forgery by Lovelace?	Tuesday night, 11 o'clock (Aug. 22)

Letter 422 Mr. Lovelace [Mrs. Sinclair's] Wed.
Vol.7, Letter IV To John Belford, Esq. --- evening
Vol.7, Letter LIII The story of Belton and Metcalfe's death in defending his sister.
Lovelace looks forward to seeing Clarissa.

Letter 423 Mr. Lovelace [Mrs. Sinclair's] ---
Vol.7, Letter V To John Belford, Esq. ---
Vol.7, Letter LIV The art of governing servants. Lovelace believes Clarissa is pregnant.

Letter 424 Mr. Belford --- Wed. three
Vol.7, Letter VI To Robert Lovelace, Esq. [Mrs. Sinclair's] o'clock,
Vol.7, Letter LV Belton's death watch. Belton's and Belford's opinions on physicians. Wednesday,
Belton's agonizing reflections upon his past. His death. 9 o'clock
at night
Eleven
o'clock
One o'clock
in the
morning
Thursday,
three in the
morning
Four o'clock
Seven
o'clock
Thursday
morning

Letter 425 Mr. Lovelace [Mrs. Sinclair's] Aug. 24.
Vol.7, Letter VII To John Belford, Esq. --- Thursday
Vol.7, Letter LVI Unmoved by Belton's death, neither Lovelace nor Mowbray attends morn
the funeral. They will go to Lord M.'s.

Letter 426 Mr. Belford --- Sat.
Vol.7, Letter VIII To Robert Lovelace, Esq. --- Aug. 26
Vol.7, Letter LVII Belton's will was read, Belford his executor. Clarissa's day out in
a coach to escape Lovelace's visit. She is greatly weakened by
Lovelace's harassment. The doctor gives her three or four weeks
to live. Morden plans to visit Lovelace.

Letter 427 The Rev. Dr. Lewen --- Friday,
Vol.7, Letter IX To Miss Clarissa Harlowe [Mr. Smith's] Aug. 18
Vol.7, Letter LVIII He urges Clarissa to marry Lovelace or prosecute him, as much to
save the honor of her family as to protect both her brother and
Morden from mischief, should one of them attempt to avenge her.

Letter 428 Miss Clarissa Harlowe [Mr. Smith's] Sat.
Vol.7, Letter X To The Rev. Dr. Lewen --- Aug. 19
Vol.7, Letter LIX Her reasons for not prosecuting Lovelace. She is at a disadvantage
in that Lovelace offers to marry her, even avowing his penitence.
His family has been kind. Her story is better told in her letters than
in open court.

Letter 429 Vol.7, Letter XI Vol.7, Letter LX	Miss Arabella Harlowe To Miss Clarissa Harlowe	[Harlowe Place] [Mr. Smith's]	Monday, Aug. 21
	Wanting revenge on Lovelace and wanting Clarissa to prosecute Lovelace. The family want to send Clarissa to Pennsylvania until she is twenty-one.		
Letter 430 Vol.7, Letter XII Vol.7, Letter LXI	Miss Clarissa Harlowe To Miss Arabella Harlowe	[Mr. Smith's] [Harlowe Place]	Tuesday, Aug. 22
	Clarissa refuses to see the attorney to tell her story. She wonders why the family have not themselves inquired into the particulars of her story. She agrees to go to Pennsylvania after one month, if she is able.		
Letter 431 Vol.7, Letter XIII Vol.7, Letter LXII	Mrs. Judith Norton To Miss Clarissa Harlowe	--- [Mr. Smith's]	Tuesday, Aug. 22
	Mr. Brand's report to the family has made them suspicious of Belford's visits to Clarissa. Morden will visit Lord M. to inquire about Lovelace's intentions. A coldness has grown up between Morden and the Harlowe Family.		
Letter 432 Vol.7, Letter XIV Vol.7, Letter LXIII	Mrs. Judith Norton To Miss Clarissa Harlowe	--- [Mr. Smith's]	Tuesday, Aug. 22
	She tells Clarissa of her visit from Aunt Hervey, who hints that some of the family would have sympathized with Clarissa. No one has been permitted to visit Clarissa.		
Letter 433 Vol.7, Letter XV Vol.7, Letter LXIV	Miss Clarissa Harlowe To Mrs. Judith Norton	[Mr. Smith's] ---	Thursday, Aug. 24
	Clarissa's brother usurping Papa's authority. Mamma and Aunt Hervey intimidated into silence. Clarissa fearing Morden's visit to Lovelace. Her forgiveness of Mr. Brand and Arabella.		
Letter 434 Vol.7, Letter XVI Vol.7, Letter LXV	Miss Howe To Miss Clarissa Harlowe	Yarmouth, Isle of Wight [Mr. Smith's]	Aug. 23
	Anna's family is quite taken with Hickman.		
Letter 435 Vol.7, Letter XVII Vol.7, Letter LXVI	Miss Clarissa Harlowe To Miss Howe	[Mr Smith's] [Yarmouth]	Friday, Aug. 25
	Clarissa chastises Anna for her indifferent treatment of Hickman. Her opinion on a wife's duty to her husband.		
Letter 436 Vol.7, Letter XVII[I] Vol.7, Letter LXVII	Miss Clarissa Harlowe To Miss Howe	[Mr. Smith's] [Yarmouth]	Three o'clock, Friday Seven o'clock
	Keeping Anna up-to-date on correspondence between herself and her family. She has recently received a letter from Mr. Wyerley.		
Letter 437 Vol.7, Letter XVIII Vol.7, Letter LXVIII	Mr. Wyerley To Miss Clarissa Harlowe	--- [Mr. Smith's]	Wednesday, Aug. 23
	He loves and admires Clarissa and renews his offer of marriage.		
Letter 438 Vol.7, Letter XIX Vol.7, Letter LXIX	Miss Clarissa Harlowe To Alexander Wyerley, Esq.	[Mr. Smith's] ---	Sat. Aug. 26
	She thanks him for so distinguishing her, but her choice was always the single life.		

Letter 439   Mr. Lovelace   [M. Hall]   Monday
Vol.7, Letter XX   To John Belford, Esq.   ---   noon,
Vol.7, Letter LXX   Only Charlotte is suspicious of Clarissa's reference to her father's   Aug. 28
house. Lovelace awaits a visit from Morden.

Letter 440   Mr. Belford   ---   Monday
Vol.7, Letter XXI   To Robert Lovelace, Esq.   [M. Hall]   night,
Vol.7, Letter LXXI   He is settling Belton's affairs. Belton's last office. He visits Clarissa   Aug. 28
who now fears that she no longer has the strength to flee Lovelace.

Letter 441   Mr. Belford   ---   Wednesday,
Vol.7, Letter XXII   To Robert Lovelace, Esq.   [M. Hall]   Aug. 30
Vol.7, Letter LXXII   Clarissa's preparation for death.

Letter 442   Mr. Lovelace   [M. Hall]   Tuesday
Vol.7, Letter XXIII   To John Belford, Esq.   ---   morn.
Vol.7, Letter LXXIII   Lovelace's report of his interview with Morden. He persuades   Aug. 29
Morden of his sincere desire to marry Clarissa.

Letter 443   Mr. Lovelace   [M. Hall]   Tuesday
Vol.7, Letter XXIV   To John Belford, Esq.   ---   afternoon,
Vol.7, Letter LXXIV   (in continuation) Continues the report of his interview with Morden.   Aug. 29
He misleads Morden, who is now confused by Clarissa's refusal to
see Lovelace. Morden, Lovelace, and Lord M. part in good spirits.

Letter 444   Mr. Brand   ---   ---
Vol.7, Letter XXV   To John Harlowe, Esq.   ---
Vol.7, Letter LXXV   His report on Clarissa's circumstances. His suspicions of Belford's
frequent visits to Clarissa.

Letter 445   Mr. Belford   ---   Wednesday
Vol.7, Letter XXVI   To Robert Lovelace, Esq.   [M. Hall]   night,
Vol.7, Letter LXXVI   He discovers and confronts Mr. Brand's informants, Mr. Walton, the   Aug. 30
milliner, and his wife, whose shop is over-against Smith's.

Letter 446   Mr. Belford   ---   Thursday,
Vol.7, Letter XXVII   To Robert Lovelace, Esq.   [M. Hall]   11 o'clock,
Vol.7, Letter LXXVII   Clarissa's forgiveness for her family and for Mr. Brand.   Aug. 31

Letter 447   Colonel Morden   [Antony's]   Tuesday,
Vol.7, Letter XXVIII   To Miss Clarissa Harlowe   [Mr. Smith's]   Aug. 29
Vol.7, Letter LXXVIII   He believes Lovelace wishes to marry Clarissa. Her forgiveness
for Lovelace will bring about general reconciliation.

Letter 448   Miss Clarissa Harlowe   [Mr. Smith's]   Thursday,
Vol.7, Letter XXIX   To Wm. Morden, Esq.   [Antony's]   Aug. 31
Vol.7, Letter LXXIX   Her reasons for refusing Lovelace, Morden not yet being fully
acquainted with her story.

Letter 449   Mr. Lovelace   [M. Hall]   Thursday,
Vol.7, Letter XXX   To John Belford, Esq.   ---   Aug. 31
Vol.7, Letter LXXX   Clarissa's deceit in writing to him about returning to her father's
house. He will visit Tom Doleman at Uxbridge. His generosity to
Belton's sister.

Letter 450 Vol.7, Letter XXXI Vol.7, Letter LXXXI	Mr. Belford To Robert Lovelace, Esq.	--- [M. Hall]	Thursday night, Aug. 31
	Clarissa's coffin is delivered during a visit from Belford.		
Letter 451 Vol.7, Letter XXXII Vol.7, Letter LXXXII	Mr. Belford To Robert Lovelace, Esq.	--- [M. Hall]	Friday morn. Sept. 1
	Description of Clarissa's coffin.		
Letter 452 Vol.7, Letter XXXIII Vol.7, Letter LXXXIII	Mr. Belford To Robert Lovelace, Esq.	[Mr. Smith's] [M. Hall]	Friday, Sept. 1 Friday, Sept. 1, two o'clock
	Clarissa has had two severe fits. The doctor has called for Belford as her executor. She may not survive a third fit.		
Letter 453 Vol.7, Letter XXXIV Vol.7, Letter LXXXIV	Mr. Lovelace To John Belford, Esq.	Uxbridge ---	Sept. 1, twelve o'clock at night
	Lovelace makes jest of all that has passed between him and Clarissa and of her nearness to death.		
Letter 454 Vol.7, Letter XXXV Vol.7, Letter LXXXV	Mr. Belford To Robert Lovelace, Esq.	--- ---	Sat. morning, Sept. 2 Saturday, six in the afternoon
	Confined to her room, visited by the parish minister, Clarissa has finished her will. Morden is trying to effect a reconciliation.		
Letter 455 Vol.7, Letter XXXVI Vol.7, Letter LXXXVI	Miss Howe To Miss Clarissa Harlowe	[Howe residence] [Mr. Smith's]	Tuesday, Aug. 29
	Mrs. Howe has been very ill but is recovering. Reconciliation depends on an acceptable will from Clarissa.		
Letter 456 Vol.7, Letter XXXVII Vol.7, Letter LXXXVII	Miss Howe To Miss Clarissa Harlowe	[Howe residence] [Mr. Smith's]	Thursday, Aug. 31
	Her interview with Morden reported. Anna cannot visit Clarissa because her own relations are visiting and Mrs. Howe has been ill.		
Letter 457 Vol.7, Letter XXXVIII Vol.7, Letter LXXXVIII	Mr. Belford To Robert Lovelace, Esq.	--- ---	Sunday evening, Sept. 3
	Clarissa's coffin is a comfort to her but not to others.		
Letter 458 Vol.7, Letter XXXIX Vol.7, Letter LXXXIX	Miss Clarissa Harlowe To Miss Howe	[Mr. Smith's] [Howe residence]	Saturday, Sept. 2
	She hopes the disposition of her estate will please everyone. Opinions on men, unpardonable crimes, women, and virtue. Hickman's patience with Anna.		
Letter 459 Vol.7, Letter XL Vol.7, Letter XC	Mrs. Norton To Miss Clarissa Harlowe	--- [Mr. Smith's]	Thursday, Aug. 31
	The family conference at Harlowe Place. Should anyone visit Clarissa? Should there be reconciliation? The family lean toward reconciliation, but James prevails, even threatening to go to Edinburgh never to return if Clarissa is allowed to return home. Morden is outraged. Anna will visit Clarissa next week. Mrs. Norton awaits Clarissa's invitation.		

Letter 460　　　　　　Mr. Belford　　　　　　　　---　　　　　　　　　Monday,
Vol.7, Letter XLI　　To Robert Lovelace, Esq.　[Uxbridge]　　　　Sept. 4
Vol.7, Letter XCI　　　　　Clarissa shows Belford where he can find her correspondence and
　　　　　　　　　　　　will after her death. Her sight is failing. Morden continues his
　　　　　　　　　　　　efforts to reconcile the family and Clarissa. Dr. H. has written to
　　　　　　　　　　　　Papa, and Belford has written to Morden.

Letter 461　　　　　　Dr. H.　　　　　　　　　　London　　　　　　　Sept. 4
Vol.7, Letter XLII　　To James Harlowe, Senior, Esq.　[Harlowe Place]
Vol.7, Letter XCII　　　　Clarissa will not live a week.

Letter 462　　　　　　Mr. Belford　　　　　　　　London　　　　　　　Sept. 4
Vol.7, Letter XLIII　　To William Morden, Esq.　　---
Vol.7, Letter XCIII　　　　Clarissa will not live three days.

Letter 463　　　　　　Mr. Lovelace　　　　　　　Uxbridge　　　　　　Tuesday
Vol.7, Letter XLIV　　To John Belford, Esq.　　　---　　　　　　　　morn.
Vol.7, Letter XCIV　　　　He anxiously awaits an answer to his letter to Belford inquiring　between
　　　　　　　　　　　　about Clarissa's health. He is not convinced she is seriously ill.　4 and 5

Letter 464　　　　　　Mr. Belford　　　　　　　　Mr. Smith's　　　　Tuesday,
Vol.7, Letter XLV　　To Robert Lovelace, Esq.　[Uxbridge]　　　　5 Sept.
Vol.7, Letter XCV　　　　Belford has taken a room at Smith's to be near Clarissa. She　9 in the
　　　　　　　　　　　　describes her progressive weakness.　　　　　　　　　　morning

Letter 465　　　　　　Miss Clarissa Harlowe　　　[Mr. Smith's]　　　---
Vol.7, Letter XLVI　　To Mrs. Norton　　　　　　---
Vol.7, Letter XCVI　　　　Forebodings of happiness. She no longer wants to see anyone who
　　　　　　　　　　　　may bring her back again into sense. She is prepared for death.

Letter 466　　　　　　Mr. Lovelace　　　　　　　[Uxbridge]　　　　Wed.
Vol.7, Letter XLVII　　To John Belford, Esq.　　　---　　　　　　　　morn.
Vol.7, Letter XCVII　　　Anxiously expecting news from Belford about Clarissa's health.　Sept. 6,
　　　　　　　　　　　　　　　　　　　　　　　　　　　　　　　　half an hour
　　　　　　　　　　　　　　　　　　　　　　　　　　　　　　　　after three

Letter 467　　　　　　Mr. Belford　　　　　　　　[Mr. Smith's]　　Tuesday,
Vol.7, Letter XLVIII　　To Robert Lovelace, Esq.　[Uxbridge]　　　Sept. 5,
Vol.7, Letter XCVIII　　　Clarissa has but a day or two to live. She forgives Lovelace but　six o'clock
　　　　　　　　　　　　again refuses to see him.　　　　　　　　　　　　　eight o'clock

[468 skipped in Penguin]　Mr. Brand　　　　　　　　---　　　　　　　Sat.
[not in the first edition]　To Mr. John Walton　　　---　　　　　　　night,
Vol.7, Letter XCIX　　　　Recanting his earlier information about Clarissa. He is sorry for　Sept. 2
　　　　　　　　　　　　the harm he has done Miss Harlowe but insists that Mr. Belford is
　　　　　　　　　　　　a libertine.

[469 skipped in Penguin]　Mr. Brand　　　　　　　　---　　　　　　　Sat.
[not in the first edition]　To John Harlowe, Esq.　　---　　　　　　　night,
Vol.7, Letter C　　　　　Recanting his earlier information about Clarissa.　　　Sept. 2

Letter 470　　　　　　Mr. Lovelace　　　　　　　[Uxbridge]　　　　Wed.
Vol.7, Letter XLIX　　To John Belford, Esq.　　　[Mr. Smith's]　　morn,
Vol.7, Letter CI　　　　　Repentant, wishing to marry Clarissa if she recovers.　　Sept. 6

Letter 471 Vol.7, Letter L Vol.7, Letter CII	Mr. Belford To Robert Lovelace, Esq. Clarissa is at death's door.	[Mr. Smith's] [Uxbridge]	Wed. morn, eight o'clock (6 Sept.)
Letter 472 Vol.7, Letter LI Vol.7, Letter CIII	Mr. Lovelace To John Belford, Esq. Repenting and praying for Clarissa. He believes Clarissa's forgiveness and death are her revenge.	Kensington [Mr. Smith's]	Wednesday noon
Letter 473 Vol.7, Letter LII Vol.7, Letter CIV	Mr .Belford To Robert Lovelace, Esq. Clarissa will not see tomorrow night. She has written her last to Anna. Morden arrives.	[Mr. Smith's] ---	Wednesday, 11 o'clock
Letter 473.1	Miss Howe To Miss Clarissa Harlowe Realizing how ill Clarissa is, she sets out to visit.	[Howe residence] [Mr. Smith's]	Tuesday, Sept. 5
Letter 473.2	Miss Clarissa Harlowe To Miss Howe Mrs. Lovick writes for Clarissa who is too weak, until Clarissa drops to her knees to write, as best she can, a last blessing for Anna.	[Mr. Smith's] [Howe residence]	Wed. near 3 o'clock
Letter 474 Vol.7, Letter LIII Vol.7, Letter CV	Mr. Belford To Robert Lovelace, Esq. Morden visits Clarissa. He is alarmed at her state and at her coffin. He has not seen her since she was twelve years old.	[Mr. Smith's] ---	Eight in the evening Ten o'clock
Letter 475 Vol.7, Letter LIV Vol.7, Letter CVI	Mr. Belford To Robert Lovelace, Esq. (in continuation) Clarissa is now weaker and in bed. Morden and Belford visit.	Soho, Mr. Smith's ---	Six o'clock, Sept. Eight o'clock in the morning Ten o'clock Eleven o'clock
Letter 476 Vol.7, Letter LV Vol.7, Letter CVII	Mr. Belford To Robert Lovelace, Esq. Morden will resettle abroad. Clarissa sends her miniature of Anna to Hickman.	[Mr. Smith's] ---	Thursday afternoon 4 o'clock
Letter 477 Vol.7, Letter LVI Vol.7, Letter CVIII	Mr. Belford To Richard Mowbray, Esq. He asks Mowbray to go to Lovelace to keep him from harming himself or his servant when he receives news of Clarissa's death.	[Mr. Smith's] ---	Thursday afternoon
Letter 478 Vol.7, Letter LVII Vol.7, Letter CIX	Mr. Lovelace To John Belford, Esq. He does not yet know that Clarissa is dead.	Knightsbridge [Mr. Smith's]	5 o'clock
Letter 479 Vol.7, Letter LVIII Vol.7, Letter CX	Mr. Belford To Robert Lovelace, Esq. "I have only to say at present—thou wilt do well to take a tour to Paris; or wherever else thy destiny shall lead thee!!!—"	[Mr. Smith's] ---	Seven o'clock Thursday even.Sept.7

Letter 480   Mr. Mowbray   Uxbridge   Sept. 7,
Vol.7, Letter LIX   To John Belford, Esq.   [Mr. Smith's]   between
Vol.7, Letter CXI   Lovelace is distraught at news of Clarissa's death. Mowbray does   11 and 12
not appreciate the gravity of the situation.   at night

Letter 481   Mr. Belford   [Mr. Smith's]   Thursday
Vol.7, Letter LX   To Robert Lovelace, Esq.   ---   night
Vol.8, Letter I   And thus died Miss Clarissa Harlowe in the blossom of her youth.   One o'clock,
Friday
morning

Letter 482   Mr. Belford   [Mr. Smith's]   Nine,
Vol.7, Letter LXI   To Robert Lovelace, Esq.   [Uxbridge]   Friday
Vol.8, Letter II   Clarissa does not wish Lovelace to see her after her death.   morn.

Letter 483   Mrs. Norton   ---   Wednesday,
Vol.7, Letter LXII   To Miss Clarissa Harlowe [received after her death]   Sept. 6
Vol.8, Letter III   All Clarissa's relations favor reconciliation. Mrs. Norton to visit.

Letter 484   Miss Arabella Harlowe   [Harlowe Place]   Wed.
Vol.7, Letter LXIII   To Miss Clarissa Harlowe [received after her death]   morn.
Vol.8, Letter IV   Expressing her love and the family's desire for reconciliation.   Sept. 6
Mamma plans to visit.

Letter 485   John Harlowe   ---   Wed.
Vol.7, Letter LXIV   To His Dear Niece Miss Clarissa Harlowe [received after her death]   Sept. 6
Vol.8, Letter V   All forgiveness, love, and reconciliation. Visits to Clarissa planned.

Letter 486   Mr. Belford   [Mr. Smith's]   Friday
Vol.7, Letter LXV   To Robert Lovelace, Esq.   [Uxbridge]   night,
Vol.8, Letter VI   Belford, Morden, Mrs. Smith, and Mrs. Lovick enter Clarissa's   Sept. 8,
chamber together. Belford unlocks the drawer holding her will and   past ten
the parcel. Belford opens the parcel sealed with three black seals. It
contains eleven letters to Belford, Morden, and the Harlowe Family.

Letter 486.1   Clarissa Harlowe [sent after her death]   Sunday
To John Belford, Esq.   [Mr. Smith's]   evening,
Her final communication with Belford. She asks him to execute her   Sept. 3
will, reconcile all parties, and look to his own reform.

Letter 486.2   Colonel Morden   ---   Friday
To James Harlowe, Jun., Esq.   [Harlowe Place]   morn.
Advising him of Clarissa's death, time of death, and her wishes   Sept. 8
as to burial. Belford will send a copy of her will.

Letter 487   Mr. Belford   [Mr. Smith's]   Sat.
Vol.7, Letter LXVI   To Robert Lovelace, Esq.   [Uxbridge]   ten
Vol.8, Letter VII   Mrs. Norton arrives at Smith's to find that Clarissa has died.   o'clock

Letter 488   Miss Clarissa Harlowe [sent after her death]   ---
Vol.7, Letter LXVII   To The Ever-Honoured James Harlowe, Sen., Esq. [Harlowe Place]
Vol.8, Letter VIII   Farewell and blessing and begging his pardon.

Letter 489
Vol.7, Letter LXVIII
Vol.8, Letter IX

Miss Clarissa Harlowe [sent after her death]
To The Ever-Honoured Mrs. Harlowe [Harlowe Place]
    Farewell and begging her pardon.

Letter 490
Vol.7, Letter LXIX
Vol.8, Letter X

Miss Clarissa Harlowe [sent after her death]
To James Harlowe, Jun., Esq.   [Harlowe Place]
    Farewell to James asking his forgiveness and that he not seek
    vengeance on Lovelace.

Letter 491
Vol.7, Letter LXX
Vol.8, Letter XI

Miss Clarissa Harlowe [sent after her death]
To Miss Harlowe   [Harlowe Place]
    Farewell to her sister, Arabella.

Letter 492
Vol.7, Letter LXXI
Vol.8, Letter XII

Miss Clarissa Harlowe [sent after her death]
To John and Antony Harlowe, Esqrs. ---
    Farewell to her uncles.

Letter 492.1

Miss Clarissa Harlowe [sent after her death]
To Mrs. Hervey   ---
    Farewell to Aunt Hervey.

Letter 492.2

Miss Clarissa Harlowe [sent after her death]
To Miss Howe   [Howe residence]
    Farewell to Miss Howe.

Letter 493
Vol.7, Letter LXXII
Vol.8, Letter XIII

Mr. Belford   [Mr. Smith's]
To Robert Lovelace, Esq.   [Uxbridge]
    Mrs. Sinclair took a fall and broke her leg. Sally Martin calls
    on Belford at Smith's and finds that Clarissa has died.

Sat.
afternoon,
Sept. 9

Letter 494
Vol.7, Letter LXXIII
Vol.8, Letter XIV

Mr. Belford   [Mr. Smith's]
To Robert Lovelace, Esq.   [Uxbridge]
    Harry delivers Clarissa's posthumous letters to the Harlowe Family,
    to Mrs. Norton, and to Anna.

Sat.
night

Letter 494.1

James Harlowe, Jun.   [Harlowe Place]
To William Morden, Esq.   ---
    His grief, shouldering the blame. Lovelace deserving vengeance.
    He will execute the will himself, where it is fit and reasonable.

Saturday,
Sept. 9

Letter 495
Vol.7, Letter LXXIV
Vol.8, Letter XV

Mr. Belford   [Mr. Smith's]
To Robert Lovelace, Esq.   [Uxbridge]
    Belford sees the hearse out of sight on its way to Harlowe Place
    accompanied by Morden and his servants, then locks up her chamber.

Sunday
morn.
8 o'clock,
Sept. 10

Letter 496
Vol.7, Letter LXXV
Vol.8, Letter XVI

Mr. Mowbray   Uxbridge
To John Belford, Esq.   ---
    Lovelace is distraught and Mowbray lacks understanding. His
    boredom first with Belton and now with Lovelace has reduced
    him to reading for diversion.

Sunday
morn.
9 o'clock

Letter 497
Vol.7, Letter LXXVI
Vol.8, Letter XVII

Mr. Lovelace   Uxbridge
To John Belford, Esq.   ---
    He wants to embalm Clarissa and bury her in his family vault, as
    well as execute her will and perform the duties of a husband.

Sat.
Sept. 9

Letter 498
Vol.7, Letter LXXVII
Vol.8, Letter XVIII

Mr. Belford   ---
To Richard Mowbray, Esq.   [Uxbridge]
      Mowbray should encourage Lovelace to recover and travel abroad.
Morden is considering vengeance. As for himself, Belford will look
to his own reform and advise Mowbray and Tourville to do the same.

Sunday,
Sept. 10,
4 in the
afternoon

Letter 499
Vol.7, Letter LXXVIII
Vol.8, Letter XIX

Mr. Belford   ---
To Robert Lovelace, Esq.   [Uxbridge]
      His visit to Mrs. Sinclair, who is howling at the prospect of dying
of a mortified leg. She feels some guilt at Clarissa's death. She
herself dies September 21.

Letter 500
Vol.7, Letter LXXIX
Vol.8, Letter XX

Colonel Morden   ---
To John Belford, Esq.   ---
      The funeral bell tolls as the hearse passes the parish church and
arrives at Harlowe Place.

Sunday
night,
Sept. 10
One in the
morning

Letter 501
Vol.7, Letter LXXX
Vol.8, Letter XXI

Colonel Morden   ---
To John Belford, Esq.   ---
      (in continuation) Mr. Melvill is chosen to deliver the funeral
discourse. James objects to Belford as executor.

Letter 502
Vol.7, Letter LXXXI
Vol.8, Letter XXII

Colonel Morden   ---
To John Belford, Esq.   ---
      Anna arrives to view the body but does not visit the family.

Monday
afternoon,
Sept. 11

Letter 503
Vol.7, Letter LXXXII
Vol.8, Letter XXIII

Colonel Morden   ---
To John Belford, Esq.   ---
      Mrs. Norton arrives at Harlowe Place, somewhat recovered.
Mamma and Papa are unable to view the body.

Tuesday
morning,
Sept. 12

Letter 503.1

Miss Clarissa Harlowe [sent after her death]
To Mrs. Norton   ---
      Farewell to Mrs. Norton. Wanting Mrs. Norton to spend the
rest of her days at the dairy-house.

Letter 504
Vol.7, Letter LXXXIII
Vol.8, Letter XXIV

Colonel Morden   ---
To John Belford, Esq.   ---
      (in continuation) The funeral. The coffin. The vault.

Thursday
night,
Sept. 14

Letter 505
Vol.7, Letter LXXXIV
Vol.8, Letter XXV

Mr. Belford   ---
To William Morden, Esq.   ---
      He reflects on Morden's description of the funeral. He will begin
to examine the will.

Saturday,
Sept. 16

Letter 506
Vol.7, Letter LXXXV
Vol.8, Letter XXVI

Mr. James Harlowe   Harlowe Place
To John Belford, Esq.   ---
      He asks Belford to relinquish his executorship and allow John and
Antony to execute the will.

Friday
night,
Sept. 15

Letter 507
Vol.7, Letter LXXXVI
Vol.8, Letter XXVII

Mr. Belford   ---
To James Harlowe, Jun., Esq.   [Harlowe Place]
      The text of the will and Belford's intention to execute it.

Saturday,
Sept. 16

Letter 508
Vol.7, Letter LXXXVII
Vol.8, Letter XXVIII

Colonel Morden   [Harlowe Place]
To John Belford, Esq.   ---
    Morden reads the will to the family. Mamma and Papa are unable to listen. James and Arabella dispute and begrudge. John and Antony are very much affected. The reading took six hours.

Sat.
Sept. 16

Letter 509
Vol.7, Letter LXXXV[III]
Vol.8, Letter XXIX

Mr. Belford   London
To The Right Honourable Lord M. [M. Hall]
    He asks Lord M. to urge Lovelace to go abroad as bad consequences may attend his remaining in England.

Sept. 14

Letter 510
Vol.7, Letter LXXXVI
Vol.8, Letter XXX

Miss Montague   M. Hall
To John Belford, Esq.   [London]
    Lovelace's family very much affected by Clarissa's death. Lovelace is preparing for a foreign tour.

Friday,
Sept. 15

Letter 510.1

Mr. Belford   [London]
To Charles Hickman, Esq.   ---
    He tries to excuse Lovelace's behaviour at his interview with Hickman as Miss Howe will read about it in certain correspondence.

Letter 510.2

Mr. Hickman   ---
To John Belford, Esq.   [London]
    His reflections on that interview and thanks to Belford for his consideration.

Letter 510.3

Miss Howe   [Howe residence]
To John Belford, Esq.   [London]
    No pity for the Harlowe Family and none for Lovelace. She wishes to purchase Clarissa's jewels.

Letter 510.4

Miss Clarissa Harlowe [sent after her death]
To Mr. Lovelace   [M. Hall]
    She cautions him, at length, to reform.

Thursday,
Aug. 24

Letter 511
Vol.7, Letter LXXXVII
Vol.8, Letter XXXI

Mr. Lovelace   M. Hall
To John Belford, Esq.   [London]
    His grief. Wanting to avenge Clarissa and himself upon her family. He plans to leave the kingdom.

Thursday,
Sept. 14
Friday,
Sept. 15
Monday,
Sept. 18

Letter 512
Vol.7, Letter LXXXVIII
Vol.8, Letter XXXII

Mr. Lovelace   [M. Hall]
To John Belford, Esq.   [London]
    Ashamed of his earlier letter to Belford, he wants it returned. Recovering from his grief, he hopes that he will soon be what he was.

Wed.
Sept. 20

Letter 513
Vol.7, Letter LXXXIX
Vol.8, Letter XXXIII

Mr. Lovelace   [M. Hall]
To John Belford, Esq.   [London]
    He prepares to leave the kingdom and resume the life of a rake.

Letter 514   Mr. Belford   [London]   Friday,
Vol.7, Letter XC   To Robert Lovelace, Esq.   [M. Hall]   Sept. 22
Vol.8, Letter XXXIV
     Disappointed at Lovelace's lack of serious consideration of Clarissa's
     death, he describes the death of Mrs. Sinclair, and then the death of
     Tomlinson. He plans to live a reformed life and suggests that Lovelace
     do the same.

Letter 515   Mr. Lovelace   [M. Hall]   Tuesday,
Vol.7, Letter XCI   To John Belford, Esq.   [London]   Sept. 26
Vol.8, Letter XXXV
     Belford's uncle, Belton, Clarissa, Sinclair, and Tomlinson, all dead.
     Lovelace does not understand why he is condemned for his crime,
     only a common theft. He argues his case before Lord M. and his
     cousins Montague.

Letter 516   Mr. Lovelace   [M. Hall]   ---
Vol.7, Letter XCII   To John Belford, Esq.   [London]
Vol.8, Letter XXXVI
     Railing at Belford's intention to reform, he asks him why he did not
     save Clarissa. He suggests Charlotte as a wife for Belford, but then,
     taunting Belford, he says perhaps Mrs. Lovick would be better.

Letter 517   Mr. Belford   [London]   Thursday,
Vol.7, Letter XCIII   To Colonel Morden   [Harlowe Place]   Sept. 21
Vol.8, Letter XXXVII
     As executor enforcing Clarissa's personal injunctions as well as
     written will, he asks Morden to forego vengeance.

Letter 518   Miss Clarissa Harlowe [delivered after her death]   ---
Vol.7, Letter XCIV   To My Beloved Cousin, William Morden, Esq. ---
Vol.8, Letter XXXVIII
     She asks Morden not to avenge her.

Letter 519   Colonel Morden   [Harlowe Place]   Sat.
Vol.7, Letter XCV   To John Belford, Esq.   [London]   Sept. 23
Vol.8, Letter XXXIX
     "I am not exempt from violent passions, sir, any more than your
     friend." Imperfect as he is, he may indeed pursue vengeance.

Letter 519.1   Mr. Belford   [London]   ---
     To Colonel Morden   [Harlowe Place]
     Mr. Belford discourages any vindictive resolutions by Morden.

Letter 520   Colonel Morden   [Harlowe Place]   Tuesday,
Vol.7, Letter XCVI   To John Belford, Esq.   [London]   Sept. 26
Vol.8, Letter XL
     He has distributed some bequests. He writes of the friendship
     between Miss Howe and Clarissa and of Miss Howe's treatment
     of Hickman.

Letter 521   Mr. Belford   [London]   Thursday,
Vol.7, Letter XCVII   To Miss Howe   [Howe residence]   Sept. 28
Vol.8, Letter XLI
     He sends her Clarissa's correspondence and tells her of the deaths of
     Sinclair and Tomlinson. He reminds her that Clarissa in her will asks
     that Miss Howe set a date for her wedding.

Letter 522   Miss Howe   [Howe residence]   Sat.
Vol.7, Letter XCVIII   To John Belford, Esq.   [London]   Sept. 30
Vol.8, Letter XLII
     She thanks Belford for his execution of Clarissa's will. Her brief
     opinion of men as encroachers.

Letter 523 Vol.7, Letter XCIX Vol.8, Letter XLIII	Miss Howe To John Belford, Esq.	[Howe residence] [London]	Monday, Oct. 2

Her lengthier opinion of the male and female sexes and of matrimony. Her courtship and address from Hickman and the reason she will not soon fulfill her part of Clarissa's will.

Letter 524 Vol.7, Letter C Vol.8, Letter XLIV	Mr. Belford To Miss Howe	[London] [Howe residence]	Thursday night, Oct. 5

Thanking her for her letter on matrimony, he sends her subsequent correspondence acquainting her with Lovelace's departure from England.

Letter 525 Vol.7, Letter CI Vol.8, Letter XLV	Lord M. To John Belford, Esq.	M. Hall [London]	Friday, Sept. 29

Lovelace, on his way to Dover to embark, sets out for London to see Belford. Lord M. asks Belford to keep Morden and Lovelace apart and to visit M. Hall.

Letter 526 Vol.7, Letter CII Vol.8, Letter XLVI	Mr. Belford To Lord M.	London [M. Hall]	Tuesday night, Oct. 3

Lovelace is in London with Mowbray and Tourville visiting Belford. Morden is also in London preparing to go abroad.

Letter 527 Vol.7, Letter CIII Vol.8, Letter XLVII	Mr. Belford To Lord M.	[London] [M. Hall]	Wed. night, Oct. 4

He tells of Lovelace's departure and looks forward to visiting M. Hall. Morden has also departed for Italy but will return to live on his paternal estate in Kent.

Letter 528 Vol.7, Letter CIV Vol.8, Letter XLVIII	Mr. Belford To Lord M.	[London] [M. Hall]	Thursday morning, Oct. 5

Morden asks Belford to be his executor along with Mr. Hickman. In return, Belford asks Morden to be his executor.

Letter 529 Vol.7, Letter CV Vol.8, Letter XLIX	Miss Howe To John Belford, Esq.	[Howe residence] [London]	Thursday, October 12

A final eulogy, Miss Howe answers Belford's request for a character of Clarissa and his question as to how Clarissa disposed of her time.

Letter 530 Vol.7, Letter CVI Vol.8, Letter L	Mr. Lovelace To John Belford, Esq.	Paris [London]	Octob. 14-25

He plans to visit Germany then Italy. He will meet his friends in Paris.

Letter 531 Vol.7, Letter CVII Vol.8, Letter LI	Mr. Belford To Robert Lovelace, Esq.	London [Paris]	Oct. 25

His reformation, his desire to marry. Doleman's malady.

Letter 532 Vol.7, Letter CVIII Vol.8, Letter LII	Mr. Lovelace To John Belford, Esq.	Paris [London]	Oct. 16-27

Joseph Leman reports Morden's threats to Lovelace.

Letter 533 Vol.7, Letter CIX Vol.8, Letter LIII	Mr. Belford To Robert Lovelace, Esq.	London [Paris]	October 26

He assures Lovelace that Morden has made no threats. He asks Lovelace to repent and not to seek new violence.

Letter 534
Vol.7, Letter CX
Vol.8, Letter LIV

Mr. Lovelace
To John Belford, Esq.

Munich
[London]

Nov. 11-22

A perhaps too hasty letter to Morden offering to accept a challenge.

Letter 534.1

Mr. Lovelace
To William Morden, Esq.

Munich
[Florence]

Nov. 10-21

Taking notice of any challenge Morden may have made.

Letter 535
Vol.7, Letter CXI
Vol.8, Letter LV

Mr. Lovelace
To John Belford, Esq.

Linz
[London]

Nov. 21
Dec. 9

Setting out for Trent to meet Morden. His confession. He will not kill Morden unless he has to. He asks Belford to be his executor.

Letter 535.1

Colonel Morden
To Robert Lovelace, Esq.

Munich

Nov. 21
Dec. 2

"I cannot hesitate a moment upon the option...I will attend your appointment."

Letter 535.2

Mr. Lovelace
To Colonel Morden

Vienna

Nov. 25
Dec. 6

Setting out instantly for Munich to meet Morden.

Letter 536
Vol.7, Letter CXII
Vol.8, Letter LVI

Mr. Lovelace
To John Belford, Esq.

Trent
[London]

Dec. 3-14

Lovelace and Morden prepare for a duel. A single rapier, the weapon.

Letter 537
Vol.7, Letter CXIII
Vol.8, Letter LVII

F. J. De la Tour
To John Belford, Esq.

Trent
near Soho Square, London

December
18, N.S.

(translation) The duel. Lovelace falls. Morden rides off into the Venetian territories. Next day Lovelace, refusing the Sacraments in the Catholic way, dies, saying "LET THIS EXPIATE!"

CONCLUSION

"Supposed to be written by Mr. Belford" relates the fortunes of principals in the story, other than Mr. Lovelace, and how they fared after Clarissa's death.